W9-BKN-418

# THE GODS OF THE EGYPTIANS

## OR STUDIES IN EGYPTIAN MYTHOLOGY


BY

E. A. WALLIS BUDGE

Late Keeper of the Egyptian and Assyrian
Antiquities in the British Museum


IN TWO VOLUMES

Volume I


DOVER PUBLICATIONS, INC.

NEW YORK

This Dover edition, first published in 1969, is an unabridged republication of the work originally published by The Open Court Publishing Company, Chicago, and Methuen & Company, London, in 1904.

In addition to the 131 text illustrations from the standard edition, this reprint includes black-and-white halftone reproductions of the 98 color plates from the limited edition. Six of these plates are also reproduced in full color on an insert attached to the inside back cover of Volume II of this edition.

*Standard Book Number: 486-22055-9*
*Library of Congress Catalog Card Number: 72-91925*

Manufactured in the United States of America
Dover Publications, Inc.
180 Varick Street
New York, N.Y. 10014

I

DEDICATE THIS BOOK

ON

THE GODS AND MYTHOLOGY OF EGYPT

BY PERMISSION

TO THE RIGHT HONOURABLE

**THE EARL OF CROMER**

PRIVY COUNCILLOR, G.C.B., G.C.M.G., K.C.S.I., C.I.E.

THE REGENERATOR OF EGYPT

WITH

SINCERE GRATITUDE AND RESPECT

# PREFACE

AMONG the various branches of Egyptology which have been closely studied during the last twenty-five years, there are none which are more interesting to inquire into, or more difficult to understand fully, than the religion and mythology of the inhabitants of the Valley of the Nile. When we consider the number of works on these subjects which have been written and published, both by expert Egyptologists and by competent exponents of the science of religion during that period, such a statement may appear at first sight to be paradoxical, and many may think when reading it that some excuse must certainly be made for the philosopher who asked an eminent professor of Egyptology the somewhat caustic question, "Is it true that the more the subjects of Egyptian religion and mythology are studied the less is known about them?" The question is, however, thoroughly justified, and every honest worker will admit that there are at the present time scores of passages, even in such a comparatively well-known religious compilation as the *Book of the Dead*, which are inexplicable, and scores of allusions of a fundamentally important mythological character of which the meanings are still unknown. The reasons for this state of things are many, and the chief of them may be briefly recalled here.

The custom of relying absolutely upon the information about the ancient Egyptian religion and mythology, which is reported by Greek historians, was abandoned by Egyptologists long ago, for as soon as the native Egyptian religious texts could be read, it became evident that no Greek or Latin writer had any exact first-hand knowledge of these subjects, and that none of them succeeded wholly in reproducing accurately in their works the facts concerning them which they derived from Egyptian books or from Egyptian priests. This is hardly to be wondered at, for the cultured Greek writers must have, and did, as we know, look with mingled pity, and contempt, and ridicule, upon the animal cults of the Egyptians, and they had no sympathy with the materialistic beliefs and with the still more materialistic funeral customs and ceremonies, which have been, from time immemorial, so dear to certain Hamitic peoples, and so greatly prized by them. The only beliefs of the Egyptian religion which the educated Greek or Roman truly understood were those which characterized the various forms of Aryan religion, namely, the polytheistic and the solar; for the forms of the cults of the dead, and for all the religious ceremonies and observances, which presupposed a belief in the resurrection of the dead and in everlasting life, and which had been in existence among the indigenous inhabitants of north-east Africa from predynastic times, he had no regard whatsoever. The evidence on the subject now available indicates that he was *racially* incapable of appreciating the importance of such beliefs to those who held them, and that although, as in the case of the Ptolemies, he was ready to tolerate, and even, for state purposes, to adopt them, it was impossible for him to absorb them into his life. It is important to remember this fact when dealing with the evidence of Greek and Roman writers on the Egyptian religion and mythology, for it shows the futility of trying to prove an absolute identity in the indigenous religions of the Aryans and Egyptians.

Now, although a true decipherment of the ancient Egyptian hieratic and hieroglyphic texts has enabled us to draw our information on the religion and mythology of Egypt from native sources, we have still to contend against the ignorance of Egyptian scribes and the mistakes of careless copyists, and it must never be forgotten that the theologians at the court of the Pharaohs under the XVIIIth and XIXth Dynasties were just as ignorant of many facts connected with their religion and mythology as we ourselves are. In proof of this it is sufficient to refer to the different explanations of certain passages which are given along with the text in the xvii th Chapter of the *Book of the Dead*, and to the childish punning etymologies of the names of gods and of many mythological explanations which are set down in the texts inscribed on the walls of some chambers in the tomb of Seti I. at Thebes, and on the walls of the temple of Horus of Beḥuṭet at Edfû. It is satisfactory to be able to say that many of the absurd etymologies and trivial explanations which are products of the scribes of old can now be corrected. Recent researches have shown that the royal scribes under the New Empire (B.C. 1700-700) were unable to read correctly the hieratic characters which formed the names of some of the kings of the early Archaic Period, and this being so, little surprise need be felt at the difficulties in religious texts which are due to their ignorance or blunders. Apart from such considerations, however, the subjects of Egyptian religion and mythology themselves are full of inherent difficulties, which have, unfortunately, not been lessened by the manner in which some Egyptologists have treated them.

The number of the gods, even under the IVth Dynasty, about B.C. 3600, was very great, and as time went on it multiplied greatly. The Pyramid Texts, which were written under the IVth, Vth and VIth Dynasties, supply the names of about two hundred gods and mythological beings, but in the *Book of the Dead* according to the Theban Recension (B.C. 1700-1200) over five hundred gods are mentioned. If to these be added the names of all the mythological beings which occur in the various Books of the Underworld, we shall find that the number of the gods who were recognized by the theologians of the XIXth Dynasty at Thebes was about twelve hundred. If all the religious texts of this period from all the religious centres of Egypt were available for study, we should certainly find that the names of hundreds of additional local gods, goddesses, and mythological beings could be collected from them. With such a number of gods to consider, it was impossible for confusion not to arise in the mind of the Egyptian when dealing with them, and the texts prove that he found the gods as difficult to group and classify as the modern investigator. The attributes of hundreds of them were vague and shadowy, and the greater number of them were merely provincial gods, to whom circumstances had given some transient importance, which resulted in their names being recorded in writing. In fact, the theologian of ancient Egypt found it impossible to form a system of gods which should be consistent in all its parts, and should assign to earth gods, water gods, air gods, village gods, city gods, nome gods, national gods, and foreign gods, the exact position and attributes which were their due in it. From one point of view the modern investigator is more fortunate than the Egyptian theologian, for he has more materials upon which to work, and, as a rule, he is better equipped for his inquiry. The Egyptian knew nothing about the study of comparative religion, and he was sadly hampered by his own methods.

Modern scientific study of the Egyptian religion and mythology may be said to have begun with the publication in full of the texts, both hieratic and hieroglyphic, of the Heliopolitan, Theban, and Saïte Recensions of the *Book of the Dead* (PER-EM-HRU), and of the cognate funeral texts, such as "The Book of what is in the

Underworld," "The Book of Breathings," "The Book of Transformations," the "Lamentations," and the "Festival Songs of Isis and Nephthys," &c. The first to attempt to build up on a large scale a system of Egyptian theology and mythology from ancient native works was the late DR. HEINRICH BRUGSCH, who collected and published in his *Religion und Mythologie der alten Ægypter*, Leipzig, 1885-1888, a mass of facts of the greatest importance, and a summary of the conclusions which he deduced from them. In the same year in which the first section of Dr. Brugsch's work appeared, M. MASPERO published in the *Revue des Religions* (tom. xii., p. 123 f.) a masterly article, entitled *La Religion Égyptienne d'après les pyramides de la Ve et de la VIe dynastie*, in which he gave to the world some of the results of his study of the "Pyramid Texts," which contain the oldest known Recension, i.e., the Heliopolitan, of the *Book of the Dead*. In 1887, SIGNOR LANZONE published the last part of his *Dizionario di Mitologia Egizia*, which is one of the most valuable contributions to the study of Egyptian mythology ever made, and which contains the names of a large number of gods, demons, spirits, etc., arranged alphabetically, and a series of drawings of many of them printed in outline in red ink. In 1888 and 1889, M. Maspero, in two admirable articles in the *Revue des Religions* (*La Mythologie Égyptienne*, tom. xviii., p. 253 f., and tom. xix., p. 1 f.), discussed and criticized both the works of BRUGSCH and LANZONE, and shed a great deal of new light upon the facts collected in both.

To M. Maspero belongs the credit of being the first to consider the Egyptian religion and mythology from the anthropological point of view, and all the evidence on these subjects which has since become available goes to prove the general correctness of the opinion which he stated some fifteen or sixteen years ago. BRUGSCH, it must be admitted, regarded the origin of Egyptian religion from too lofty a metaphysical and philosophical standpoint, and appealed for proofs of his contentions to Egyptian texts belonging to too late a period to be entirely free from the influence of Greek culture and thought; in fact, he read into certain Egyptian texts, ideas, doctrines, and beliefs which the primitive and indigenous Egyptians could never have possessed. On the other hand, it seems to me that M. MASPERO has somewhat underrated the character of the spiritual conceptions of the dynastic Egyptians, and that he has done so because, when he wrote his great article, *La Mythologie Égyptienne*, Egyptologists had not thoroughly realized the distinction which exists between the primitive or predynastic element in the Egyptian religion and the Asiatic element. This element was of a solar character undoubtedly, and was introduced into Egypt by the "Followers of Horus," or the "Blacksmiths," who invaded the country, and conquered the natives, and settling down there, built up the great dynastic civilization which we call Egyptian. This seems to be the correct explanation of the diversity of view of two such eminent experts, and the opposite character of their conclusions appears to be due chiefly to the difference of the standpoints from which they viewed the subject.

A prolonged study of the religious and mythological texts of ancient Egypt has convinced me of the futility of attempting to reconcile the conflicting beliefs and to harmonize the contradictory statements which are found in them, so long as we regard the Egyptian religion as "one in its extension and principle." It must first of all be resolved into its constituent elements, and when this has been done, it will probably be possible to classify, and arrange, and assign to their proper sources the various material and spiritual conceptions and beliefs which the Egyptians heaped up in their minds and flung together in their religious writings.

It must, moreover, be studied by the light which the science of comparative religion has given us, and due regard must be paid to the important evidence on the subject that may be deduced from the remains and monuments of the Predynastic and Archaic Periods which have been unearthed during the last few years.

The primitive dwellers in Egypt undoubtedly belonged to a large and important section of the inhabitants of North-East Africa, and possessed physical and mental characteristics which were peculiar to themselves. In the earliest times they were savages, and lived and died like savages in other parts of the world; religious belief of any kind, in the modern sense of the term, they had none, and they probably regarded the animate and inanimate objects which they saw about them as akin to themselves. At a much later period they peopled the earth, air, sky, and water with beings of various kinds, and they paid a sort of homage or worship to certain stones, trees, and living creatures, in which they assumed that they lived. Some beings were held to be friendly and others unfriendly; and it was thought that gifts or offerings would secure the continuance of the friendship of the former and avert the hostility of the latter. Friendly beings gradually became gods, and unfriendly ones were classed as devils, and in the ceremonies which the Egyptian savage performed in their honour, and in the incantations which he recited, the magic of Egypt, the forerunner of her religion, had its origin. The chief object of the savage Egyptian was self-preservation, and self-interest was the mainspring of his actions, all of which were undertaken with a view to material benefits. When he first becomes known to us in the late Neolithic Period we find that he possessed a belief in an existence beyond the grave, and that it was of a material character is proved by the fact that he placed offerings of food in the graves of the dead. To prevent their return to this world, and their consequent claim for food and other material things, the heads of the dead were often severed from their bodies, and their feet cut off; thus the living made themselves secure in the possession of their homes, and wives, and goods. Nothing is known of the Egyptian religion and its ceremonies at this period, but whatever they were, it is pretty certain that the object of them all was to secure for themselves after death a renewal of life which should be full of carnal delights and pleasures, and there is no doubt that the ideas of a resurrection from the dead and immortality on these lines were firmly implanted in the native mind long before the Dynasty Period began.

The cult of Osiris, the dead man deified, and the earliest forms of his worship, were, no doubt, wholly of African origin; these are certainly the oldest elements in the religion of the Dynastic Period, and the most persistent, for Osiris maintained his position as the god and judge of the dead from the Predynastic to the Ptolemaïc Period. The Followers of Horus, who brought a solar religion with them into Egypt from the East, never succeeded in dislodging Osiris from his exalted position, and his cult survived undiminished notwithstanding the powerful influence which the priests of Rā, and the worshippers of Ȧmen, and the votaries of Ȧten respectively exercised throughout the country. The heaven of Osiris was believed to exist in a place where the fields were fertile and well stocked with cattle, and where meat and drink were abundant; the abodes of the blessed were thought to be constructed after the model of the comfortable Egyptian homesteads in which they had lived during life, and the ordinary Egyptian hoped to live in one of these with his wives and parents. On the other hand, the followers of Rā, the sun-god, believed in a heaven of a more spiritual character, and their great hope was to occupy a seat in the boat of the god, and, arrayed in light, to travel whithersoever he went. They wished to become bright and shining spirits, and to live upon the celestial meat and drink upon which he lived; as he was so they hoped to be in every respect. The materialistic heaven of Osiris appealed to the masses in Egypt, and the heaven where Rā lived to the priests of Rā and other solar gods, and to royal and aristocratic families, and to the members of the foreign section of the community who were of Eastern origin.

The various waves of religious thought and feeling, which swept over Egypt during the five thousand years of her history which are known to us, did not seriously disturb the cult of Osiris, for it held out to the people hopes of resurrection and immortality of a character which no other form of religion could give. Secure in these hopes the people regarded the various changes and developments of religious ideas in their country with equanimity, and modifications in the public worship of the gods, provided that the religious feasts and processions were not interrupted, moved them but little. Kings and priests from time to time made attempts to absorb the cult of Osiris into religious systems of a solar character, but they failed, and Osiris, the man-god, always triumphed, and at the last, when his cult disappeared before the religion of the Man CHRIST, the Egyptians who embraced Christianity found that the moral system of the old cult and that of the new religion were so similar, and the promises of resurrection and immortality in each so much alike, that they transferred their allegiance from Osiris to JESUS of Nazareth without difficulty. Moreover, Isis and the child Horus were straightway identified with MARY THE VIRGIN and her SON, and in the apocryphal literature of the first few centuries which followed the evangelization of Egypt, several of the legends about Isis and her sorrowful wanderings were made to centre round the Mother of Christ. Certain of the attributes of the sister goddesses of Isís were also ascribed to her, and, like the goddess Neith of Saïs, she was declared to possess perpetual virginity. Certain of the Egyptian Christian Fathers gave to the Virgin the title "Theotokos," or "Mother of God," forgetting, apparently, that it was an exact translation of *neter mut*, , a very old and common title of Isis. Interesting, however, as such an investigation would be, no attempt has been made in this work to trace out the influence of ancient Egyptian religious beliefs and mythology on Christianity, for such an undertaking would fill a comparatively large volume.

From what has been said in the preceding pages the plan followed in the preparation of the present volumes will be evident. In the opening chapter an attempt has been made to describe the religious beliefs of the primitive Egyptians, and to explain how their later ideas about the "gods" and God grew up, and how they influenced the religious writings and paintings of the Dynastic Period. The region which is commonly called Heaven, or the "Underworld," and its denizens are next considered at some length, and this section is followed by chapters on the ancient myths of Rā, the legend of Rā and Isis, and the legend of the destruction of mankind. The hieroglyphic texts of the myths and legends are given with interlinear transliteration and translation, so that the student may verify my statements for himself. Of the minor gods and demons, of which nothing but the names are known, lists only are printed. The great gods of Egypt have been grouped as far as possible, and they are discussed in connection with the various religious centres to which they belong, e.g., Ptaḥ, Sekhet, and I-em-ḥetep with Memphis, Åmen, Mut, and Khensu with Thebes, and the "Great Company" of the gods with Heliopolis. Speaking generally, the first volume of this work treats of the oldest and greatest gods and triads of gods of Egypt, and the second, of the gods of Heliopolis, among whom are included Osiris and the deities of his funeral cycle. The hymns to the gods have been freely quoted, because they illustrate so clearly the views which the Egyptians held concerning them, and the manner in which they sought to praise them. In a chapter entitled "Miscellaneous Gods" will be found several lists of gods of the hours, days, months, winds, Dekans, etc., which I have collected from Dr. Brugsch's *Thesaurus* of astronomical and other texts; for the main facts given in these volumes the authorities, both ancient and modern, will be found at the foot of the pages wherein they are first mentioned.

Most of the portraits of the gods which appear in the coloured plates have been reproduced from papyri, coffins, etc., but for the outlines of a few I am indebted to Signor Lanzone's *Dizionario Mitologia Egizia*, the value of which has been already mentioned. It has been thought advisable to print the portraits of the gods which are not taken from papyri upon a papyrus-coloured ground, and to enclose each within a coloured border, for the effect is better, and the plan is consistent with that followed by the ancient Egyptian artists at all periods.

My thanks are due to Reginald Lake, Esq., of Messrs. Gilbert & Rivington, and to Mr. G. E. Hay and Mr. F. Rainer, of his staff, for the care and attention which they have taken in printing this work.

E. A. WALLIS BUDGE.

LONDON, *September 5th*, 1903.

# CONTENTS

# LIST OF PLATES

# LIST OF ILLUSTRATIONS

# THE GODS OF THE EGYPTIANS

## CHAPTER I

## THE GODS OF EGYPT

THE Greek historian Herodotus affirms[1] that the Egyptians were "beyond measure scrupulous in all matters apper-"taining to religion," and he made this statement after personal observation of the care which they displayed in the performance of religious ceremonies, the aim and object of which was to do honour to the gods, and of the obedience which they showed to the behests of the priests who transmitted to them commands which they declared to be, and which were accepted as, authentic revelations of the will of the gods. From the manner in which this writer speaks it is clear that he had no doubt about what he was saying, and that he was recording a conviction which had become settled in his mind. He was fully conscious that the Egyptians worshipped a large number of animals, and birds, and reptiles, with a seriousness and earnestness which must have filled the cultured Greek with astonishment, yet he was not moved to give expression to words of scorn as was Juvenal,[2] for Herodotus perceived that beneath the acts of apparently

[1] ii. 64.

[2] "Quis nescit, Volusi Bithynice, qualia demens
"Aegyptus portenta colat? crocodilon adorat
"Pars haec, illa pavet saturam serpentibus ibin.
"Effigies sacri nitet aurea cercopitheci,
"Dimidio magicae resonant ubi Memnone chordae
"Atque vetus Thebe centum jacet obruta portis.
"Illic aeluros, hic piscem fluminis, illic

foolish and infatuated worship there existed a sincerity which betokened a firm and implicit belief which merited the respect of thinking men. It would be wrong to imagine that the Egyptians were the only people of antiquity who were scrupulous beyond measure in religious matters, for we know that the Babylonians, both Sumerian and Semitic, were devoted worshippers of their gods, and that they possessed a very old and complicated system of religion; but there is good reason for thinking that the Egyptians were more scrupulous than their neighbours in religious matters, and that they always bore the character of being an extremely religious nation. The evidence of the monuments of the Egyptians proves that from the earliest to the latest period of their history the observance of religious festivals and the performance of religious duties in connexion with the worship of the gods absorbed a very large part of the time and energies of the nation, and if we take into consideration the funeral ceremonies and services commemorative of the dead which were performed by them at the tombs, a casual visitor to Egypt who did not know how to look below the surface might be pardoned for declaring that the

---

"Oppida tota canem venerantur, nemo Dianam.
"Porrum et caepe nefas violare et frangere morsu:
"O sanctas gentes, quibus haec nascuntur in hortis
"Numina! Lanatis animalibus abstinet omnis
"Mensa, nefas illic fetum ingulare capellae:
"Carnibus humanis vesci licet."—*Satire,* xv. 1—13.

That the crocodile, ibis, dog-headed ape, and fish of various kinds were venerated in Egypt is true enough; they were not, however, venerated in dynastic times as *animals*, but as the *abodes of gods.* In certain localities peculiar sanctity was attributed to the leek and onion, as Juvenal suggests, but neither vegetable was an object of worship in the country generally; and there is no monumental evidence to show that the eating of human flesh was practised, for it is now known that even the predynastic Egyptians did not eat the flesh of the dead and gnaw their bones, as was once rashly asserted. Juvenal's statements are only partly true, and some of them are on a par with that of a learned Indian who visited England, and wrote a book on this country after his return to Bombay. Speaking of the religion of the English he declared that they were all idolators, and to prove this assertion he gave a list of churches in which he had seen a figure of a LAMB in the sculpture work over and about the altar, and in prominent places elsewhere in the churches. The Indian, like Juvenal, and Cicero also, seems not to have understood that many nations have regarded animals as symbols of gods and divine powers, and still do so.

Egyptians were a nation of men who were wholly given up to the worship of beasts and the cult of the dead.

The Egyptians, however, acted in a perfectly logical manner, for they believed that they were a divine nation, and that they were ruled by kings who were themselves gods incarnate; their earliest kings, they asserted, were actually gods, who did not disdain to live upon earth, and to go about and up and down through it, and to mingle with men. Other ancient nations were content to believe that they had been brought into being by the power of their gods operating upon matter, but the Egyptians believed that they were the issue of the great God who created the universe, and that they were of directly divine origin. When the gods ceased to reign in their proper persons upon earth, they were succeeded by a series of demi-gods, who were in turn succeeded by the Manes, and these were duly followed by kings in whom was enshrined a divine nature with characteristic attributes. When the physical or natural body of a king died, the divine portion of his being, i.e., the spiritual body, returned to its original abode with the gods, and it was duly worshipped by men upon earth as a god and with the gods. This happy result was partly brought about by the performance of certain ceremonies, which were at first wholly magical, but later partly magical and partly religious, and by the recital of appropriate words uttered in the duly prescribed tone and manner, and by the keeping of festivals at the tombs at stated seasons when the appointed offerings were made, and the prayers for the welfare of the dead were said. From the earliest times the worship of the gods went hand in hand with the deification of dead kings and other royal personages, and the worship of departed monarchs from some aspects may be regarded as meritorious as the worship of the gods. From one point of view Egypt was as much a land of gods as of men, and the inhabitants of the country wherein the gods lived and moved naturally devoted a considerable portion of their time upon earth to the worship of divine beings and of their ancestors who had departed to the land of the gods. In the matter of religion, and all that appertains thereto, the Egyptians were a "peculiar people," and in all ages they have exhibited a tenacity of belief and a conservatism which distinguish them from all the other great nations of antiquity.

But the Egyptians were not only renowned for their devotion to religious observances, they were famous as much for the variety as for the number of their gods. Animals, birds, fishes, and reptiles were worshipped by them in all ages, but in addition to these they adored the great powers of nature as well as a large number of beings with which they peopled the heavens, the air, the earth, the sky, the sun, the moon, the stars, and the water. In the earliest times the predynastic Egyptians, in common with every half-savage people, believed that all the various operations of nature were the result of the actions of beings which were for the most part unfriendly to man. The inundation which rose too high and flooded the primitive village, and drowned their cattle, and destroyed their stock of grain, was regarded as the result of the working of an unfriendly and unseen power; and when the river rose just high enough to irrigate the land which had been prepared, they either thought that a friendly power, which was stronger than that which caused the destroying flood, had kept the hostile power in check, or that the spirit of the river was on that occasion pleased with them. They believed in the existence of spirits of the air, and in spirits of mountain, and stream, and tree, and all these had to be propitiated with gifts, or cajoled and wheedled into bestowing their favour and protection upon their suppliants.

It is very unfortunate that the animals, and the spirits of natural objects, as well as the powers of nature, were all grouped together by the Egyptians and were described by the word NETERU; which, with considerable inexactness, we are obliged to translate by "gods." There is no doubt that at a very early period in their predynastic history the Egyptians distinguished between great gods and little gods, just as they did between friendly gods and hostile gods, but either their poverty of expression, or the inflexibility of their language, prevented them from making a distinction apparent in writing, and thus it happens that in dynastic times, when a lofty conception of monotheism prevailed among the priesthood, the scribe found himself obliged to call both God and the lowest of the beings that were supposed to possess some attribute of divinity by one and the same name, i.e., NETER. Other nations of antiquity found a way out of the difficulty of grouping all classes of divine beings by one name by inventing series of orders of angels, to each of which they gave names and assigned various duties in connexion with the service of the Deity. Thus in the Ḳur'ân (*Sura* xxxv.) it is said that God maketh the angels His messengers and that they are furnished with two, or three, or four pairs of wings, according to their rank and importance; the archangel Gabriel is said to have been seen by Muḥammad the Prophet with six hundred pairs of wings! The duties of the angels, according to the Muḥammadans, were of various kinds. Thus nineteen angels are appointed to take charge of hell fire (*Sura* lxxiv.); eight are set apart to support God's throne on the Day of Judgment (*Sura* lxix.); several tear the souls of the wicked from their bodies with violence, and several take the souls of the righteous from their bodies with gentleness and kindness (*Sura* lxxix.); two angels are ordered to accompany every man on earth, the one to write down his good actions and the other his evil deeds, and these will appear with him at the Day of Judgment, the one to lead him before the Judge, and the other to bear witness either for or against him (*Sura* l.). Muḥammadan theologians declare that the angels are created of a simple substance of light, and that they are endowed with life, and speech, and reason; they are incapable of sin, they have no carnal desire, they do not propagate their species, and they are not moved by the passions of wrath and anger; their obedience is absolute. Their meat is the celebrating of the glory of God, their drink is the proclaiming of His holiness, their conversation is the commemorating of God, and their pleasure is His worship. Curiously enough, some are said to have the form of animals. Four of the angels are Archangels, viz. Michael, Gabriel, Azrael, and Israfel, and they possess special powers, and special duties are assigned to them. These four are superior to all the human race, with the exception of the Prophets and Apostles, but the angelic nature is held to be inferior to human nature because all the angels were commanded to worship

Adam (*Sura* ii.). The above and many other characteristics might be cited in proof that the angels of the Muḥammadans possess much in common with the inferior gods of the Egyptians, and though many of the conceptions of the Arabs on this point were undoubtedly borrowed from the Hebrews and their writings, a great many must have descended to them from their own early ancestors.

Closely connected with these Muḥammadan theories, though much older, is the system of angels which was invented by the Syrians. In this we find the angels divided into nine classes and three orders, upper, middle, and lower. The upper order is composed of Cherubim, Seraphim, and Thrones; the middle order of Lords, Powers, and Rulers; and the lower order of Principalities, Archangels, and Angels. The middle order receives revelations from those above them, and the lower order are the ministers who wait upon created things. The highest and foremost among the angels is Gabriel, who is the mediator between God and His creation. The Archangels in this system are described as a "swift operative motion," which has dominion over every living thing except man; and the Angels are a motion which has spiritual knowledge of everything that is on earth and in heaven.[1] The Syrians, like the Muḥammadans, borrowed largely from the writings of the Hebrews, in whose theological system angels played a very prominent part. In the Syrian system also the angels possess much in common with the inferior gods of the Egyptians.

The inferior gods of the Egyptians were supposed to suffer from many of the defects of mortal beings, and they were even thought to grow old and to die, and the same ideas about the angels were held by Muḥammadans and Hebrews. According to the former, the angels will perish when heaven, their abode, is made to pass away at the Day of Judgment. According to the latter, one of the two great classes of angels, i.e., those which were created on the fifth day of creation, is mortal; on the other hand, the angels which were created on the second day of creation

[1] See my edition of the *Book of the Bee*, by Solomon of Al-Baṣra. Oxford, 1886, pp. 9–11.

endure for ever, and these may be fitly compared with the unfailing and unvarying powers of nature which were personified and worshipped by the Egyptians; of the angels which perish, some spring from fire, some from water, and some from wind. The angels are grouped into ten classes, i.e., the Erêlîm, the Îshîm, the Bĕnê Elôhîm, the Malachîm, the Ḥashmalîm, the Tarshîshîm, the Shishanîm, the Cherûbîm, the Ophannîm, and the Serâphîm; among these were divided all the duties connected with the ordering of the heavens and the earth, and they, according to their position and importance, became the interpreters of the Will of the Deity. A comparison of the passages in Rabbinic literature which describe these and similar matters connected with the angels, spirits, etc., of ancient Hebrew mythology with Egyptian texts shows that both the Egyptians and Jews possessed many ideas in common, and all the evidence goes to prove that the latter borrowed from the former in the earliest period.

In comparatively late historical times the Egyptians introduced into their company of gods a few deities from Western Asia, but these had no effect in modifying the general character either of their religion or of their worship. The subject of comparative Egyptian and Semitic mythology is one which has yet to be worked thoroughly, not because it would supply us with the original forms of Egyptian myths and legends, but because it would show what modifications such things underwent when adopted by Semitic peoples, or at least by peoples who had Semitic blood in their veins. Some would compare Egyptian and Semitic mythologies on the ground that the Egyptians and Semites were kinsfolk, but it must be quite clearly understood that this is pure assumption, and is only based on the statements of those who declare that the Egyptian and Semitic languages are akin. Others again have sought to explain the mythology of the Egyptians by appeals to Aryan mythology, and to illustrate the meanings of important Egyptian words in religious texts by means of Aryan etymologies, but the results are wholly unsatisfactory, and they only serve to show the futility

[1] See the chapter "Was die Juden von den guten Engeln lehren" in Eisenmenger, *Entdeckten Judenthums*, vol. ii. p. 370 ff.

of comparing the mythologies of two peoples of different race occupying quite different grades in the ladder of civilization. It cannot be too strongly insisted on that all the oldest gods of Egypt are of Egyptian origin, and that the fundamental religious beliefs of the Egyptians also are of Egyptian origin, and that both the gods and the beliefs date from predynastic times, and have nothing whatever to do with the Semites or Aryans of history.

Of the origin of the Egyptian of the Palaeolithic and early Neolithic Periods, we, of course, know nothing, but it is tolerably certain that the Egyptian of the latter part of the Neolithic Period was indigenous to North-East Africa, and that a very large number of the great gods worshipped by the dynastic Egyptian were worshipped also by his predecessor in predynastic times. The conquerors of the Egyptians of the Neolithic Period who, with good reason, have been assumed to come from the East and to have been more or less akin to the Proto-Semites, no doubt brought about certain modifications in the worship of those whom they had vanquished, but they could not have succeeded in abolishing the various gods in animal and other forms which were worshipped throughout the length and breadth of the country, for these continued to be venerated until the time of the Ptolemies.

We have at present no means of knowing how far the religious beliefs of the conquerors influenced the conquered peoples of Egypt, but viewed in the light of well-ascertained facts it seems tolerably certain that no great change took place in the views which the indigenous peoples held concerning their gods as the result of the invasion of foreigners, and that if any foreign gods were introduced into the company of indigenous, predynastic gods, they were either quickly assimilated to or wholly absorbed by them. Speaking generally, the gods of the Egyptians remained unchanged throughout all the various periods of the history of Egypt, and the minds of the people seem always to have had a tendency towards the maintenance of old forms of worship, and to the preservation of the ancient texts in which such forms were prescribed and old beliefs were enshrined. The Egyptians never forgot the ancient gods of the country, and it is typical of the spirit of conservatism which they displayed in most things that even in the Roman

Period pious folk among them were buried with the same prayers and with the same ceremonies that had been employed at the burial of Egyptians nearly five thousand years before. The Egyptian of the Roman Period, like the Egyptian of the Early Empire, was content to think that his body would be received in the tomb by the jackal-headed Anubis; that the organs of his corruptible body would be presided over and guarded by animal-headed gods; that the reading of the pointer of the Great Scales, wherein his heart was weighed, would be made known by an ape to the ibis-headed scribe of the gods, whom we know by the name of Thoth; and that the beatified dead would be introduced to the god Osiris by a hawk-headed god called Horus, son of Isis, who in many respects was the counterpart of the god Ḥeru-ur, the oldest of all the gods of Egypt, whose type and symbol was the hawk. From first to last the indigenous Egyptian paid little heed to the events which happened outside his own country, and neither conquest nor invasion by foreign nations had any effect upon his personal belief. He continued to cultivate his land diligently, he worshipped the gods of his ancestors blindly, like them he spared no pains in making preparations for the preservation of his mummified body, and the heaven which he hoped to attain was fashioned according to old ideas of a fertile homestead, well stocked with cattle, where he would enjoy the company of his parents, and be able to worship the local gods whom he had adored upon earth. The priestly and upper classes certainly held views on these subjects which differed from those of the husbandman, but it is a significant fact that it was not the religion and mythology of the dynastic Egyptian, but that of the indigenous, predynastic Egyptian, with his animal gods and fantastic and half-savage beliefs, which strongly coloured the religion of the country in all periods of her history, and gave to her the characteristics which were regarded with astonishment and wonder by all the peoples who came in contact with the Egyptians.

The predynastic Egyptians in the earliest stages of their existence, like most savage and semi-savage peoples, believed that the sea, the earth, the air, and the sky were filled to overflowing with spirits, some of whom were engaged in carrying on the works of nature, and others in aiding or obstructing man in the course of his existence upon earth. Whatsoever happened in nature was attributed by them to the operations of a large number of spiritual beings, the life of whom was identical with the life of the great natural elements, and the existence of whom terminated with the destruction of the objects which they were supposed to animate. Such spirits, although invisible to mental eyes, were very real creatures in their minds, and to them they attributed all the passions which belong to man, and all his faculties and powers also. Everything in nature was inhabited by a spirit, and it was thought possible to endow a representation, or model, or figure of any object with a spirit or soul, provided a name was given to it; this spirit or soul lived in the drawing or figure until the object which it animated was broken or destroyed. The objects, both natural and artificial, which we consider to be inanimate were regarded by the predynastic Egyptians as animate, and in many respects they were thought to resemble man himself. The spirits who infested every part of the visible world were countless in forms, and they differed from each other in respect of power; the spirit that caused the Inundation of the Nile was greater than the one that lived in a canal, the spirit that made the sun to shine was more powerful than the one that governed the moon, and the spirit of a great tree was mightier than the one that animated an ear of corn or a blade of grass. The difference between the supposed powers of such spirits must have been distinguished at a very early period, and the half-savage inhabitants of Egypt must at the same time have made a sharp distinction between those whose operations were beneficial to them, and those whose actions brought upon them injury, loss, or death. It is easy to see how they might imagine that certain great natural objects were under the dominion of spirits who were capable of feeling wrath, or displeasure, and of making it manifest to man. Thus the spirit of the Nile would be regarded as beneficent and friendly when the waters of the river rose sufficiently during the period of the Inundation to ensure an abundant crop throughout the land; but when their rise was excessive, and they drowned the cattle and washed away the houses of the people, whether made of wattles or mud, or when they rose insufficiently and caused want and famine, the spirit of the Nile would be considered unfriendly and evil to man. An ample and sufficient Inundation was regarded as a sign that the spirit of the Nile was not displeased with man, but a destructive flood was a sure token of displeasure. The same feeling exists to this day in Egypt among the peasant-farmers, for several natives told me in 1899, the year of the lowest rise of the Nile of the XIXth century,[1] that "Allah was angry with them, and would not let the water come"; and one man added that in all his life he had never before known Allah to be so angry with them.

The spirits which were always hostile or unfriendly towards man, and were regarded by the Egyptians as evil spirits, were identified with certain animals and reptiles, and traditions of some of these seem to have been preserved until the latest period of dynastic history. Āpep, the serpent-devil of mist, darkness, storm, and night, of whom more will be said later on, and his fiends, the "children of rebellion," were not the result of the imagination of the Egyptians in historic times, but their existence dates from the period when Egypt was overrun by mighty beasts, huge serpents, and noxious reptiles of all kinds. The great serpent of Egyptian mythology, which was indeed a formidable opponent of the Sun-god, had its prototype in some monster serpent on earth, of which tradition had preserved a record; and that this is no mere theory is proved by the fact that the remains of a serpent, which must have been of enormous size, have recently been found in the Fayyûm. The vertebræ are said to indicate that the creature to which they belonged was longer than the largest python known.[2] The allies of the great serpent-devil Āpep were as hostile to man as was their master to the Sun-god, and they were regarded with terror by the minds of those who had evolved them. On the other hand, there were numbers of spirits whose actions were friendly

[1] In October, 1899, the level of the water of Lake Victoria was 2 ft. below the normal, and in December the level at Aswân was 5 ft. 8 ins. below the average of previous years.

[2] "If the proportions of this snake were the same as in the existing *Python* "*seboe* it probably reached a length of thirty feet." C. W. Andrews, D.Sc., in *Geological Mag.*, vol. viii., 1901, p. 438.

and beneficial to man, and some of these were supposed to do battle on his behalf against the evil spirits.

Thus at a very early period the predynastic Egyptian must have conceived the existence of a great company of spirits whose goodwill, or at all events whose inaction, could only be obtained by bribes, i.e., offerings, and cajolery and flattery; and of a second large company whose beneficent deeds to man he was wont to acknowledge and whose powerful help he was anxious to draw towards himself; and of a third company who were supposed to be occupied solely with making the sun, moon, and stars to shine, and the rivers and streams to flow, and the clouds to form and the rain to fall, and who, in fact, were always engaged in carrying out diligently the workings and evolutions of all natural things, both small and great. The spirits to whom in predynastic times the Egyptians ascribed a nature malicious or unfriendly towards man, and who were regarded much as modern nations have regarded goblins, hobgoblins, gnomes, trolls, elves, etc., developed in dynastic times into a corporate society, with aims, and intentions, and acts wholly evil, and with a government which was devised by the greatest and most evil of their number. To these, in process of time, were joined the spirits of evil men and women, and the prototype of hell was formed by assuming the existence of a place where evil spirits and their still more evil chiefs lived together. By the same process of imagination beneficent and friendly spirits were grouped together in one abode under the direction of rulers who were well disposed towards man, and this idea became the nucleus of the later conception of the heaven to which the souls of good men and women were supposed by the Egyptian to depart, after he had developed sufficiently to conceive the doctrine of immortality. The chiefs of the company of evil spirits subsequently became the powerful devils of historic times, and the rulers of the company of beneficent and good spirits became the gods; the spirits of the third company, i.e., the spirits of the powers of Nature, became the great cosmic gods of the dynastic Egyptians. The cult of this last class of spirits, or gods, differed in many ways from that of the spirits or gods who were supposed to be concerned entirely with the welfare of man, and in dynastic times there are abundant proofs of this in religious texts and compositions. In the hymns to the Sun-god, under whatsoever name he is worshipped, we find that the greatest wonder is expressed at his majesty and glory, and that he is apostrophised in terms which show forth the awe and fear of his devout adorer. His triumphant passage across the sky is described, the unfailing regularity of his rising and setting is mentioned, reference is made to the vast distance over which he passes in a moment of time, glory is duly ascribed to him for the great works which he performs in nature, and full recognition is given to him as the creator of men and animals, of birds and fish, of trees and plants, of reptiles, and of all created things; the praise of the god is full and sufficient, yet it is always that of a finite being who appears to be overwhelmed at the thought of the power and might of an apparently infinite being. The petitions lack the personal appeal which we find in the Egyptian's prayers to the man-god Osiris, and show that he regarded the two gods from entirely different points of view. It is impossible to say how early this distinction between the functions of the two gods was made, but it is certain that it is coeval with the beginnings of dynastic history, and that it was observed until very late times.

The element of magic, which is the oldest and most persistent characteristic of the worship of the gods and of the Egyptian religion, generally belongs to the period before this distinction was arrived at, and it is clear that it dates from the time when man thought that the good and evil spirits were beings who were not greatly different from himself, and who could be propitiated with gifts, and controlled by means of words of power and by the performance of ceremonies, and moved to action by hymns and addresses. This belief was present in the minds of the Egyptians in all ages of their history, and it exists in a modified form among the Muḥammadan Egyptians and Sûdânî men to this day. It is true that they proclaim vehemently that there is no god but God, and that Muḥammad is His Prophet, and that God's power is infinite and absolute, but they take care to guard the persons of themselves and their children from the Evil Eye and from the assaults of malicious and evil spirits, by means of amulets of all kinds as zealously now as their ancestors did in the days before the existence of God Who is One was conceived. The caravan men protect their camels from the Evil Eye of the spirits of the desert by fastening bright-coloured beads between the eyes of their beasts, and by means of long fringes which hang from their *mahlûfas*, or saddles, and in spite of their firm belief in the infinite power of God, they select an auspicious day on which to set out on a journey, and they never attempt to pass certain isolated caves, or ravines, or mountains, in the night time. All the members of the great family of the Jinn are to them as real to-day as their equivalents were to the ancient Egyptians, and, from the descriptions of desert spirits which are given by those who have been fortunate enough to see them, it is clear that traditions of the form and appearance of ancient Egyptian fiends and evil spirits have been unconsciously preserved until the present day. The modern Egyptians call them by Arabic names, but the descriptions of them agree well with those which might be made of certain genii that appear in ancient Egyptian mythological works treating of the Underworld and its inhabitants.

The peoples of the Eastern Sûdân, who are also Muḥammadans, have inherited many ideas and beliefs from the ancient Egyptians, and this is not to be wondered at when we remember that the civilization of Nubia from the beginning of the XVIIIth Dynasty to the end of the XXVIth, i.e., from about B.C. 1550 to about B.C. 550, was nothing but a slavish copy of that of Egypt. A stay of some months in the village at the foot of Jebel Barkal, which marks the site of a part of the old Nubian city of Napata, convinced me of this fact, and visits to other places in the Eastern Sûdân proved that these ideas and beliefs were widespread. The hills and deserts are, according to native belief, peopled with spirits, which are chiefly of a disposition unfriendly to man, and they are supposed to have the power of entering both human beings and animals almost at pleasure. Palm-trees die or become unfruitful, and cattle fall sick through the operations of evil spirits, and any misfortune which comes upon the community or upon the individual is referred to the same cause. The pyramids, which they call *tarabîl*, on the hill, are viewed with almost childish fear by the natives who, curiously enough, speak of the royal personages buried therein as *illâhât*, or "gods," and none of them, if it can possibly be avoided, will go up after sundown into "the mountain," as they call the sandstone ridge on which they are built. Tombs and cemeteries are carefully avoided at night as a matter of course, but to approach the pyramids at night is regarded as a wilful act which is sure to bring down upon the visitor the wrath of the spirits of the kings, who have by some means acquired a divine character in the eyes of the natives. When I was opening one of the pyramids at Jebel Barkal in 1897, Muḥammad wad Ibrahîm, the shêkh of the village, tried to keep the workmen at work as long as daylight lasted, but after this had been done for two or three evenings, several of the wives of the men appeared and carried off their husbands, fearing they should either be bewitched, or suffer some penalty for intrusion in that place at the time when, in popular opinion, the spirits of the dead came forth to enjoy the cool of the evening. The same idea prevailed further south among the people who lived on the river near the pyramids of Baḳrawîyeh, which mark the site of the royal necropolis of the ancient city of Berua, or Marua, i.e., Meroë. The local shêkh was appointed to go with me and to help in taking measurements of some of the pyramids at this place, but when we were about half a mile from them he dismounted, and said he could go no further because he was afraid of the spirits of the gods, *illâhât*, who were buried there. After much persuasion he consented to accompany me, but nothing would induce him to let the donkeys go to the pyramids; having hobbled them and tied them to a large stone he came on, but seated himself on the ground at the northern end of the main group of pyramids, and nothing would persuade him to move about among the ruins. The natives of Jebel Barkal viewed the work of excavation with great disfavour from the very first, and their hostile opinion was confirmed by the appearance at the pyramids of great numbers of wasps, which, they declared, were larger than any which they had seen before; they were convinced that they were evil spirits who had taken the form of wasps, and that evil was coming upon their village. It was useless to explain to them that the wasps only came there to drink from the water-skins, which were kept full and hung there on pegs driven into the masonry for the use of the workmen; and when a harmless snake, about eight feet long, which had also crawled there to drink, was killed one morning by the men, their fears of impending evil were confirmed, for they were certain that the spirit of a king had been killed, and they expected that vengeance would be taken upon them by the divine spirits of his companions.

About halfway up Jebel Barkal there lived four large hawks which always seemed to be following any person who ascended the mountain, but yet never came very near; these were always regarded by the natives as the embodied spirits of the gods whose figures still remain sculptured and painted on the walls of the rock-hewn sanctuary at the foot of the hill, and I never heard of any attempt being made to shoot or snare them by the people of the villages of Barkal, Shibba, or Marâwi. The inhabitants could not know that the hawk was probably the first living creature which was worshipped in the Nile Valley, and therefore the respect which they paid to the hawks must have been due to a tradition which had been handed down to them through countless generations from a past age. Their connecting the hawks with the figures of the gods sculptured in the sanctuary of Ȧmen-Râ is worthy of note, for it seems to show that on such matters they thought along the same lines as their ancestors.

Concerning amulets, the Sûdânî man is as superstitious as were his ancestors thousands of years ago, and he still believes that stones of certain colours possess magical properties, especially when inscribed with certain symbols, of the meaning of which, however, he has no knowledge, but which are due, he says, to the presence of spirits in them. Women and children, especially female children, protect many parts of their bodies with strings of beads made of magical stones, and sometimes with plaques of metal or stone, which are cut into various shapes and ornamented with signs of magical power; the positions of such plaques on the body are frequently identical with those whereon the dynastic Egyptians laid amulets on the dead, and, if we could learn from the Sûdânî folk the reasons which prompt them to make use of such things, we should probably find that the beliefs which underlie the customs are also identical. The above facts concerning the Sûdânî belief in spirits might be greatly multiplied, and they are not so remotely connected with the beliefs of the dynastic, and even predynastic, Egyptians, as may appear to be the case at first sight, and the writer believes that a large amount of information of a similar kind awaits the investigator, who will devote the necessary time to living in some of the out-of-the-way villages of the black (not negro) peoples who dwell on the eastern bank of the Nile and of the Blue Nile.

In many isolated places in Southern Nubia and the Eastern Sûdân are trees which men regard with reverence, but this may be the result of contact with the natives of Central Africa, where people pray to trees on certain occasions,[1] believing that the spirits which are supposed to dwell in them can bestow gifts upon those whom they regard with favour, and ensure safety both to themselves and their animals when travelling. Still further to the south certain animals, e.g., the cynocephalus ape, which plays such a prominent part in dynastic Egyptian mythology, are supposed to be inhabited by divine spirits and to possess extraordinary powers of intelligence in consequence, and the various kinds of scarabaei, or beetles, are thought to be animated by spirits, which the natives connect with the sun. The dead bodies of these insects were, in former days, often eaten by women who wished to become mothers of large families, and to this day parts of them are cooked, and treated with oil, and made into medicines[2] for the cure of sore eyes, etc. The dynastic Egyptians believed that the scarab was connected

[1] "Under the wide-spreading branches of an enormous heglik-tree, and on a "spot beautifully clean and sprinkled with fine sand, the Bedeyat beseech an "unknown god to direct them in their undertakings and to protect them from "danger." Slatin Pâsha, *Fire and Sword in the Sudan*, London, 1896, p. 114.

[2] Ibrahîm Rûshdî, Clerk of Telegraphs at Benha, in Lower Egypt, told me in January, 1895, that in many districts the beetles were boiled, and the grease extracted from them; as they are being boiled the shells come off. The bodies are next roasted in olive oil, and then steeped in myrrh, and after this they are macerated in that liquid, and strained through muslin; the liquid which runs through is believed to cure the itching which is caused by a certain internal ailment. Some men drink a few drops of it in each cup of coffee, and women drink it to make them fat. The old women have a prescription for sore eyes, which is as follows:—Stick a splinter of wood through a series of beetles for twelve hours when a child is about to be born; when the child is born, pull the splinter out of the last beetle, and dip it in *kohl*, and rub the eyes of the child with it. If this be done in the proper way the child will never suffer from sore eyes.

with the Sun-god Rā, and in religious texts of all periods it is said that the beetle occupied a place in the boat of this god.

We have already seen that the dynastic Egyptians, and their predecessors, conceived the existence of spirits hostile towards man, of spirits beneficent towards man, and of spirits which were wholly occupied with carrying out the various operations of Nature, and we must now consider the manner and forms in which they became visible to man. The commonest form in which a spirit was believed to make itself visible to man was that of some beast, or bird, or fish, or reptile, and at a very early period adoration, in one form or another, of the so-called inferior animals was well-nigh universal in Egypt. At the time when this worship began animals, as well as inanimate objects, were not considered by the inhabitants of the Nile Valley to be greatly removed from themselves in intelligence. Primitive man saw nothing ridiculous in attributing speech to inanimate objects and animals, which were supposed to think, and reason, and act like human beings; and the religious literature of many of the most ancient nations contains numerous proofs of this fact. Among the baked clay tablets found in the ruins of the Royal Library of Nineveh, which contained copies of hundreds of documents preserved in the temples of the most ancient cities of Babylonia, were fragments of a dialogue between a horse and an ox, which is now known as the "Fable of the Horse and the Ox,"[1] and it is tolerably certain that this dialogue did not originate in the reign of Ashur-bani-pal (B.C. 668–626), although the tablet on which it was written is not older than his time. Again, in the Creation Legend the dragon-monster Tiamat, the representative of the powers of evil and darkness, is made to conspire against the gods, and to create a serpent brood[2] in order to do effective battle with them; and other instances might be quoted to show that the Babylonians and Assyrians attributed to the animals reason, passions, and language.

[1] See *Guide to the Babylonian and Assyrian Antiquities*, London, 1900, p. 48; the fragments are exhibited in the British Museum, Nineveh Gallery, Table-case C.

[2] *Ibid*, p. 36. For the cuneiform tablets in the British Museum see Nineveh Galler , Table-case A. See also L. W. King, *Seven Tablets of Creation*, vol. i., p. 1 ff.

From the Bible we learn that the Hebrews held the same views as their kinsmen on this matter, and we are told that the serpent beguiled and seduced Eve by his speech, and made her break the command of the Lord (Genesis iii. 1 ff.), and that the she-ass of Balaam remonstrated with her master and asked him why he had smitten her three times (Numbers xxii. 28). We may note in passing that this animal is said to have been able to see the Angel of the Lord standing in the way, whilst her master could not, and we are forcibly reminded of the belief which was current among Jews and Muḥammadans to the effect that dogs howled before a death because they were able to see the Angel of Death going about on his mission, to say nothing of our own superstition to the same effect, which, however, we seem to have derived not from the East, but from cognate northern European nations. We see also from the Book of Judges (ix. 8 ff.) that speech and reason were sometimes attributed to objects which we regard as inanimate, for we read that the trees "went forth on a time to anoint a king "over them; and they said unto the olive tree, Reign thou over us." When the olive tree refused, they went to the fig tree with the same request, and when the fig tree refused, they went to the vine, which refused to leave its wine "which cheereth God and man"; on this they applied to the bramble, which placed before them the choice of coming and putting their trust in its shadow, or of being burnt by the fire which should come forth from out of itself. In connexion with this idea may, perhaps, be mentioned the incident recorded in Numbers xxi. 17, wherein we are told that the princes and nobles digged a well "with their staves" by the direction of the lawgiver, and that the Children of Israel sang this song, "Spring up, O well; sing ye unto it." Many other examples might be quoted from Hebrew literature to show that animals and inanimate objects were on certain occasions regarded as beings which possessed thinking and reasoning powers similar to those of men.

Among the Egyptians animals thought, and reasoned, and spoke as a matter of course, and their literature is full of indications that they believed them to be moved by motives and passions similar to those of human beings. As a typical example may be quoted the instance of the cow, in the *Tale of the Two Brothers*, who tells her herd that his elder brother is standing behind the door of the byre with his dagger in his hand waiting to slay him; the young man having seen the feet of his brother under the door took to flight, and so saved his life. Here we have another proof that animals were sometimes credited with superhuman intelligence and discernment, since but for the warning of the cow, who had perceived what her master had failed to notice, the herd would have been slain as soon as he entered the byre. Here, too, must be noted the very important part which is played in the Judgment Scene in the *Book of the Dead* by animals. In the *Story of the Shipwreck* also we are told concerning a huge serpent thirty cubits long, with a beard two cubits long, which made a long speech to the unfortunate man who was wrecked on the island wherein it lived.

In the papyri of the XVIIIth Dynasty we have representations of the weighing of the heart of the deceased in the Great Balance, which takes place in the presence of the Great Company of the gods, who act as judges, and who pass the sentence of doom, that must be ratified by Osiris, according to the report of the god Thoth, who acts as scribe and secretary to the gods. The Egyptian hoped that his heart would exactly counterbalance the feather, symbolic of Maāt or the Law, and neither wished nor expected it to outweigh it, for he detested performing works of supererogation. The act of weighing was carefully watched by Anubis the god of the dead, whose duty was to cast to the Eater of the Dead the hearts which failed to balance the feather exactly; and by the guardian angel of the deceased, on behalf of the deceased; and by a dog-headed ape, who was seated on the top of the pillar, and who supported himself upon the bracket on which was balanced the beam of the Great Scales. This ape was the associate and companion of the god Thoth, and he was supposed to be skilled in the art of computation, and in the science of numbers, and in the measurement of time; his duty at the weighing of the heart was to scrutinize the pointer of the scales, and, having made sure that the beam of the scales was exactly level, i.e., that the heart and the feather exactly counterbalanced each other, to report the fact to Thoth, so that he in turn might make his report to the gods on the case under consideration. The ape seated on the pillar of the Scales belongs to a species which is now only found in the Sûdân, but which in late predynastic or in early dynastic times might have been found all over Egypt. The dog-headed ape is very clever, and even in modern times is regarded with much respect by the natives, who believe that its intelligence is of the highest order, and that its cunning is far superior to that of man; the high esteem in which it was held by the ancient Egyptians is proved by the fact that the god Thoth was held to be incarnate in him, and by the important functions which he performed in their mythology.

It will also be remembered that in the vignette which represents the sunrise in the *Book of the Dead* a company of six or seven dog-headed apes is depicted in the act of adoring the god of day, as he rises on the eastern horizon of heaven; they stand on their hind legs and their forepaws are raised in adoration, and they are supposed to be singing hymns to the Sun-god. In a text which describes this scene these apes are said to be the spirits of the dawn who sing hymns of praise to the Sun-god whilst he is rising, and who transform themselves into apes as soon as he has risen. It is a well known fact in natural history that the apes and the monkeys in the forests of Africa and other countries chatter noisily at dawn, and it is clear that it was the matutinal cries of these animals which suggested their connection with the spirits of the dawn. It is not stated in the text whether the spirits of the dawn were created afresh each day or not, or whether the monkeys transformed themselves into spirits daily, and so were able to greet the rising sun each morning. We may, however, connect the idea concerning them with that which is met with in an ancient Hebrew description[1] of the angels of Hebrew mythology, for one group of "angels of service" from the river of fire were supposed to be created daily in order to sing one hymn to God Almighty and then to come to an end.

Passing now to the consideration of the worship of animals by the Egyptians of the predynastic and dynastic periods, we have

[1] Compare Eisenmenger, *op. cit.*, vol. ii., p. 371. כל יומא ויומא נבראין מלאכי השרת מנהר דינור ואמרי שירה ובטלין

to endeavour to find the reasons which induced the early inhabitants of the Nile Valley to pay adoration to birds, beasts, fishes, and other creatures of the animal kingdom. A careful examination of the facts now available shows that in Egypt primitive man must have worshipped animals in the first instance because they possessed strength, and power, and cunning greater than his own, or because they were endowed with some quality which enabled them to do him bodily harm or to cause his death. The fundamental motive in man for worshipping animals was probably FEAR. When man first took up his abode in Egypt the physical conditions of the country must have resembled those of some parts of Central Africa at the present time, and the whole country was probably covered with forests and the ground obscured by dense undergrowth. In the forests great numbers of elephants and other large beasts must have lived, and the undergrowth formed a home for huge serpents of various species and for hosts of deadly reptiles of different kinds, and the river was filled with great crocodiles similar in length and bulk to those which have been seen in recent years in the Blue Nile and in the rivers further to the south. We have no means of knowing at what period the elephant was exterminated in Egypt, but it was probably long before dynastic times, because he finds no place in Egyptian mythology. The ivory objects which have been found in predynastic graves prove that this substance was prized by the primitive Egyptians, and that it was, comparatively, largely used by them for making personal ornaments and other small objects, but whether they imported elephants' tusks from the Sûdân, or obtained them from animals which they hunted and killed in some part of Egypt cannot be said. On the top of one of the standards[1] which are painted on predynastic vases we find the figure of an elephant, a fact which seems to show that this animal was the symbol of the family of the man for whom was made the vase on which it is found, or of his country, or of the tutelary deity, i.e., the god of his town or tribe. On the other hand, it is quite clear from several passages in the texts with which the walls of the chambers and corridors of the pyramid tombs of Unȧs and Tetȧ, and other kings of the Early

[1] See J. de Morgan, *Ethnographie Préhistorique*, p. 93.

Empire at Ṣaḳḳâra are inscribed that Egypt was infested with venomous snakes and noxious reptiles of various kinds when the original forms of those passages were written, and that they were sufficiently formidable and numerous to cause the living grave anxiety about the safety of the bodies of their dead. Thus in the text of Unȧs,[1] a king of the Vth Dynasty, we find a series of short magical formulae, many of which are directed against serpents and fierce animals, and all are couched in terms which prove that they must have been composed long before they were inscribed on the walls inside this king's pyramid, and M. Maspero is undoubtedly correct in thinking that they must have presented serious difficulties to the king's *literati*. In these formulae are mentioned the serpents Ufä, , Nāi, , Hekȧ, , Hekret, , Setcheḥ, , Ȧkeneh, , Ȧmen, 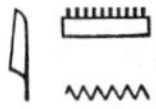, Ḥȧu, , Ȧnṭāf, , Tcheser-ṭep, 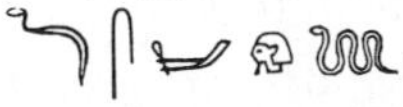, Thethu, , Hemth, , Senenahemthet, , and allusion is made to a most "terrible serpent," 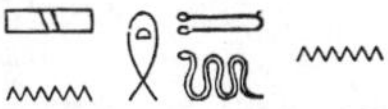 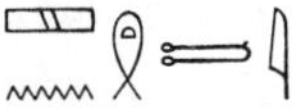. At the time when these formulae were composed each of these serpents was probably the type of a class of venomous snakes, and their names no doubt described their physical characteristics and their methods of attack. The abject fear of the Egyptians for the serpent seems to have been constant in all generations, and the texts of the latest as well as those of the earliest period contain numerous prayers intended to deliver the deceased from the "serpents which are in the Underworld, which live upon "the bodies of men and women, and consume their blood."[2] Long after Egypt was cleared of snakes and when the country was in the condition in which we now know it, the tradition remained that a

[1] Ed. Maspero, l. 533 ff.

[2] 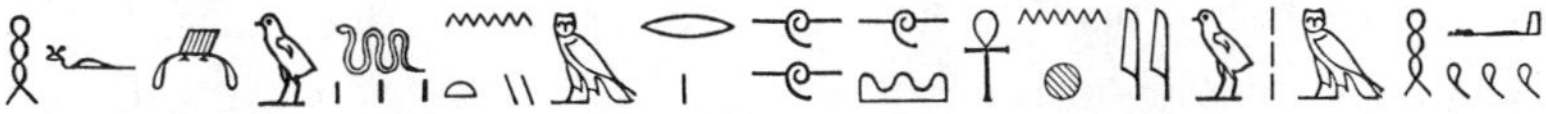
. *Book of the Dead*, Chapter ib., l. 4.

mighty serpent, some thirty cubits, i.e., about fifty feet long, lived on the top of Bakhau, , the Mountain of the Sunrise, and his name was Åmi-Hemf, i.e., "Dweller in his flame," .[1]

The worship of the serpent in Egypt is of great antiquity, and shrines to certain members of the species must have existed at a very early date. In predynastic times the uraeus was held in great veneration, and the great centre of its worship was in the Delta, at a place which the Egyptians in dynastic times called "Per-Uatchet," and the Greeks "Buto." At the period when the uraeus was being worshipped in Lower Egypt, the vulture was the chief object of adoration in Upper Egypt, its principal sanctuary being situated in the city which the Egyptians called "Nekhebet," and the Greeks "Eileithyiaspolis." The uraeus goddess was called "Uatchet," or "Uatchit," and the vulture goddess "Nekhebet," or "Nekhebit," and the cities which were the centres of their worship became so important, probably in consequence of this worship, that in the early dynastic period we find it customary for kings when they wished to proclaim their sovereignty over all Egypt to give themselves the title , which may be freely rendered by "Lord of the shrines of the Vulture and Uraeus." The equivalents of these signs are found on the now famous plaque inscribed with the name and titles of Āḥa, a king who is often, but without sufficient reason, assumed to be identical with Mena or Menes, and thus it is clear that the cities of Nekhebet and Per-Uatchet were important religious and administrative centres in predynastic times.

Other wild animals which were worshipped by the Egyptians about the same period were the lion, and the lynx, which they called *maftet*, , and the hippopotamus, and the quadruped which became the symbol of the god Set; among amphibious creatures the crocodile and the turtle were the most important. Among domestic animals the bull and the cow were the principal objects of worship, and proof is forthcoming that they were

[1] *Book of the Dead*, Chapter cviii., l. 5.

regarded as deities in predynastic times. The great strength of the bull, and his almost irresistible attack in fighting and headlong rush, excited the fear and admiration of primitive man, and his fecundating powers made him at a very early period the type of the generative principle in nature. For thousands of years the kings of Egypt delighted to call themselves "mighty bull," and the importance which they attached to this title is evinced by the fact that many of them inscribed it upon their *serekh*, or cognizance, which displayed their name as the descendant of Horus;

Usertsen II. receiving "life" from the god Sepṭ. Behind him is his *serekh* inscribed with his Horus name.

in fact, it formed their Horus name. The figure of a bull is found sculptured upon some of the green slate objects which date from the predynastic period, and which have been erroneously called palettes, and a flint model of the head and horns of the cow, which in later times became the animal symbolic of the goddess Hathor, was found in a predynastic grave; all these objects are in the British Museum (Nos. 20,790, 20,792, and 32,124). The warrior kings of the XVIIIth and XIXth Dynasties were pleased when the court scribes related in commemorative inscriptions how their lords raged and roared like lions as they mounted their chariots and set out to crush the foolish enemy who had the temerity to defy them, but they preferred to be likened to the "mighty bull," who trampled opposition beneath his hoofs, and gored and destroyed with his horns that which his hoofs had failed to annihilate. Out of the reverence which was paid to the bull in predynastic times grew the worship of two special bulls, Ḥāp and Mer-ur, which names the Greeks modified into Apis and Mnevis, the sacred animals of the ancient cities of Memphis and Heliopolis respectively. The worship of Apis is at least as old as the beginning of the dynastic period, and we know that the cult of this bull continued in Memphis until the close of the rule of the Ptolemies. In some way the beliefs concerning Apis were connected with those which the Egyptians held concerning Osiris, the god and judge of the dead, who is called in the *Book of the Dead*[1] the "Bull of Ȧmentet," i.e., the "Bull of the Underworld," ; and in the Ptolemaïc period the two gods were merged into one and formed the god Sarapis, to whom were ascribed the attributes of the Egyptian and Greek gods of the Underworld.

*Serekh* of Rameses II., on which is inscribed the Horus name of this king, i.e., KA-NEKHT-MERI-MAĀT. The canopy of the *serekh* is in the form of the sky, and from the standard on which it rests spring two human arms and hands. The right grasps a standard surmounted by the head of the king, which here represents the "royal ka", and the left the symbol of Maāt.

It now seems to be generally admitted by ethnologists that there are three main causes which have induced men to worship animals, i.e., they have worshipped them as animals, or as the dwelling-places of gods, or as representatives of tribal ancestors.

[1] Chapter i., l. 4.

There is no reason whatsoever for doubting that in neolithic times the primitive Egyptians worshipped animals as animals and as nothing more; the belief that animals were the abodes of spirits or deities grew up in their minds later, and it was this which induced them to mummify the dead bodies of birds, and beasts, and fishes, etc., in which they thought deities to have been incarnate. We have no means of knowing exactly when this belief arose, but it is certainly as old as the time when the Apis Bull began to be worshipped, and when the Egyptians began to keep the ram and other animals, and birds, and reptiles, and fishes in sanctuaries, and to worship them as deities incarnate. In connection with it we must notice that, in the case of the Apis Bull and the Ram of Mendes, the god Apis did not take up his abode in every bull, and that the soul of Osiris, which was supposed to dwell in the Ram of Mendes, did not make his habitation in every ram. The Apis Bull, like the Ram of Mendes, had to be sought for diligently, and no bull or ram was made the object of veneration in the sanctuaries of Memphis or Mendes unless he possessed the characteristic marks by which the priests recognized him. The ordinary bulls and rams of the species to which the Apis Bull and the Ram of Mendes belonged were not regarded in the same light as the animals which by the marks upon them proclaimed themselves to be the creatures to which worship should be offered, and they were, of course, sacrificed in the performance of funeral ceremonies and killed and eaten as food by the people, even though somewhat of the deity may have been incarnate in them. When the Apis Bull or the Ram of Mendes died the deity who had been incarnate in it transferred himself to another animal, and therefore did not leave the earth.

The question as to whether the Egyptians worshipped animals as representations of tribal ancestors, or "totems," is one which has given rise to much discussion, and this is not to be wondered at, for the subject is one of difficulty. We know that many of the standards which represent the nomes of Egypt are distinguished by figures of birds and animals, e.g., the hawk, the bull, the hare, etc., but it is not clear whether these are intended to represent "totems" or not. It is pretty certain that the nome-standard of dynastic times was derived from the standards which the predynastic

Egyptians set up in their boats, or caused to be carried in ceremonial processions, or during the performance of public functions, and there is no reason for doubting that, substantially, the same ideas and beliefs underlie the use of both classes of standards. The animal or bird standing on the top of a nome-perch or standard is not intended for a fetish or a representation of a tribal ancestor, but for a creature which was regarded as the deity under whose protection the people of a certain tract of territory were placed, and we may assume that within the limits of that territory it was unlawful to injure or kill such animal or bird. Thus in the Nome of the Black Bull a black bull of a certain kind would be regarded as a sacred animal, and it is certain that in predynastic times worship would be offered to it as a god; similarly in the Nome of the Hare the hare would be worshipped; and in the Nome of the Hawk the hawk would be worshipped. Outside these nomes, however, the bull and the hare and the hawk might be, and probably were, killed and eaten for food, and from this point of view the sacred creatures of the Egyptians may be thought to have something in common with the totems, or deified representatives of tribal ancestors, and with the fetishes of the tribes of nations which are on the lowest levels of civilization. In connexion with this matter it is customary to quote the statements of Greek and Roman writers, many of whom scoff at the religion of the Egyptians because it included the worship of animals, and charge the nation with fatuity because the animals, etc., which were worshipped and preserved with all care in some places were killed and eaten in others. The evidence of such writers cannot be regarded as wholly trustworthy, first, because they did not take the trouble to understand the views which the Egyptians held about sacred animals, and secondly, because they were not in a position to obtain trustworthy information. In the passage from one of Juvenal's *Satires* already quoted, he declares that the Egyptians ate human flesh, and it is possible that he believed what he wrote; still the fact remains that there is not a particle of evidence in the Egyptian inscriptions to show that they ever did so, and we have every reason for believing that they were not cannibals.

His other statements about the religion of the Egyptians are, probably, as untrustworthy. There is not enough ancient Egyptian religious literature extant to enable us to trace the history of religion in all periods of dynastic history, still less are we able to follow it back in the predynastic period, because of that time we have no literature at all; such monuments and texts as we have, however, serve to show that the Egyptians first worshipped animals as animals, and nothing more, and later as the habitations of divine spirits or gods, but there is no reason for thinking that the animal worship of the Egyptians was descended from a system of totems or fetishes, as Mr. J. F. M'Lennan believed.[1] It has been assumed by some ethnologists that many primitive peoples have been accustomed to name individuals after animals, and that such animal names have in certain cases become tribe names. These may have become family surnames, and at length the myths may have grown up about them in which it is declared that the families concerned were actually descended "from the animals in question as ancestors, "whence might arise many other legends of strange adventures "and heroic deeds of ancestors, to be attributed to the quasi-human "animals whose names they bore; at the same time, popular "mystification between the great ancestor and the creature whose "name he held and handed down to his race, might lead to veneration "for the creature itself, and thence to full animal-worship."[2] This theory may explain certain facts connected with the animal-worship of numbers of savage or half-savage tribes in some parts of the world, but it cannot, in the writer's opinion, be regarded as affording an explanation of the animal-worship of the Egyptians. In dynastic times kings were, it is true, worshipped as gods, and divine honours were paid to their statues, but the reason for this was that the king was believed to be of the seed of the god Horus, the oldest of all the gods of Egypt. There is reason for believing that to certain men who were famous for their knowledge or for some great works which they had accomplished divine honours were paid, but neither these nor the kings were held to be gods who were worshipped throughout the land as were the well-known or natural gods of the country. In short, the worship which

[1] See the *Fortnightly Review*, 1869–1870.

[2] See Tylor, *Primitive Culture*, vol. ii., p. 236.

was paid to kings after their death, or to ordinary men, who were sometimes deified, was quite different from that paid to the gods of the country, whether they were in animal or human form or whether they represented the spirits which concerned themselves with the welfare of men or those which occupied themselves with the direction of the operations of Nature.

We see, moreover, from the nome-standards that several objects besides animals were worshipped and regarded as gods, or that they, at all events, became the symbols of the deities which were worshipped in them. In predynastic times we know that some standards were surmounted by representations of two, three, four, or five hills,[1] , 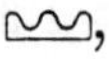, 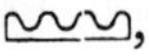, 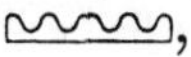, another by two arrows (?) , another by a fish, , another by two arrows and a shield, , etc. With the predynastic  is probably to be compared the dynastic sign , and with the predynastic 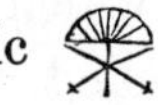 the dynastic sign . It is not easy at present to find a dynastic equivalent for the two arrows (?) , or to find the reason why the three hills  were connected with a god, but we shall probably be correct if we connect the two arrows (?) with some aboriginal god of war, and the three hills with the abode of some, at present, unknown god. The shield and the crossed arrows can, we think, be explained with more certainty. We know from the Nome-Lists that the fifth nome of Lower Egypt, , which was called Sȧpi by the Egyptians and Saïtes by the Greeks, had for its capital the city Saut or Saïs, and that the great deity of this city was the goddess Nit or Neith. The dynastic pictures of this goddess represent her in the form of a goddess who holds in her hands two arrows and a bow; she sometimes wears upon her head the crown of the north 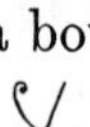, or , which is the sign for her name, or two crossed arrows ; in fact, such pictures prove beyond a doubt that Nit, the goddess of Saïs, was the goddess of the chase *par excellence*. That this goddess was worshipped in the earliest dynastic period is certain, for we find that her name forms part of

[1] See my "History of Egypt" (*Egypt in the Predynastic and Archaïc Periods*), vol. i., p. 78.

the name of Nit-ḥetep, who seems to have been the daughter of king Sma, and who was probably the wife of Āḥa, and also part of that of the early dynastic king Mer-Nit. That the dynastic sign  is the equivalent of the predynastic sign  there is no reason to doubt, and, as the former is known to represent the crossed arrows and shield of the hunting goddess of Saïs, we are justified in believing that its predynastic equivalent was intended to be a picture of the same objects, and to be symbolic of the same goddess.

We have already mentioned the predynastic standard surmounted by the figure of an elephant, which was, undoubtedly, intended to represent a god, and thus it is clear that both in predynastic and dynastic times the Egyptians symbolized gods both by means of animals and by objects connected with their worship or with their supposed occupations. In dynastic Nome-Lists we have for the name of Mȧtenu a knife , for the nome of Ten a pair of horns surmounted by a plumed disk , for the nome of Uas, or Us, a sceptre , for the nome of Sesheshet a sistrum , etc. The first, third, and fourth of this group of examples are clearly objects which were connected with the worship of the gods whom they symbolize, and the second is probably intended to be the headdress of the god of the nome which it symbolizes. At this period of the world's history it is impossible to fathom the reasons which led men to select such objects as the symbols of their gods, and we can only accept the view that they were the product of some indigenous, dominant people who succeeded in establishing their religious customs so strongly in Egypt that they survived all political commotions, and changes, and foreign invasions, and flourished in the country until the third century of our era at least.

The cult of Nit, or Neith, must have been very general in Egypt, although in dynastic times the chief seat thereof was at Saïs in the Delta, and we know that devotees of the goddess lived as far south as Naḳâda, a few miles to the north of Thebes, for several objects inscribed with the name of queen Nit-ḥetep have been found in a grave at that place. Of the early worship of the goddess nothing is known, but it is most probable that she was adored as a great hunting spirit as were adored spirits of like character by primitive peoples in other parts of the world. The crossed arrows and shield indicate that she was a hunting spirit in the earliest times, but a picture of the dynastic period represents her with two crocodiles[1] sucking one at each breast, and thus she appears in later times to have had ascribed to her power over the river.

It has already been said that the primitive Egyptians, though believing that their gods possessed powers superior to their own, regarded them as beings who were liable to grow old and die, and who were moved to love and to hate, and to take pleasure in meat and drink like man; they were even supposed to intermarry with human beings and to have the power of begetting offspring like the "sons of God," as recorded in the Book of Genesis (vi. 2, 4). These ideas were common in all periods of Egyptian history, and it is clear that the Egyptians never wholly freed themselves from them; there is, in fact, abundant proof that even in the times when monotheism had developed in a remarkable degree they clung to them with a tenacity which is surprising. The religious texts contain numerous references to them, and beliefs which were conceived by the Egyptians in their lowest states of civilization are mingled with those which reveal the existence of high spiritual conceptions. The great storehouse of religious thought is the *Book of the Dead*, and in one of the earliest Recensions of that remarkable work we may examine its various layers with good result. In these are preserved many passages which throw light upon the views which were held concerning the gods, and the powers which they possessed, and the place where they dwelt in company with the beatified dead.

One of the most instructive of these passages for our purpose forms one of the texts which are inscribed on the walls and corridors of the chambers in the pyramid tombs of Unas, a king of the Vth Dynasty, and of Tetȧ, a king of the VIth Dynasty.

[1] In the text of Unȧs (l. 627) the crocodile-god Sebek is called the son of Neith

The paragraphs in general of the great Heliopolitan Recension deal, as we should expect, with the offerings which were to be made at stated intervals in the little chapels attached to the pyramids, and many were devoted to the object of removing enemies of every kind from the paths of the king in the Underworld; others contain hymns, and short prayers for his welfare, and magical formulae, and incantations. A few describe the great power which the beatified king enjoys in the world beyond the grave, and, of course, declare that the king is as great a lord in heaven as he was upon earth. The passage in question from the pyramid of Unàs is of such interest and importance that it[1] is given in the Appendix to this Chapter, with interlinear translation and transliteration, and with the variant readings from the pyramid of Tetà, but the following general rendering of its contents may be useful. "The sky poureth down rain, the stars tremble, the bow-" bearers run about with hasty steps, the bones of Aker tremble, " and those who are ministrants unto them betake themselves to " flight when they see Unàs rising [in the heavens] like a god who " liveth upon his fathers and feedeth upon his mothers. Unàs is " the lord of wisdom whose name his mother knoweth not. The " noble estate of Unàs is in heaven, and his strength in the horizon " is like unto that of the god Tem his father, indeed, he is stronger " than his father who gave him birth. The doubles (*kau*) of Unàs " are behind him, and those whom he hath conquered are beneath " his feet. His gods are upon him, his uraei are upon his brow, " his serpent-guide is before him, and his soul looketh upon the " spirit of flame; the powers of Unàs protect him." From this paragraph we see that Unàs is declared to be the son of Tem, and has made himself stronger than his father, and that when the king, who lives upon his fathers and mothers, enters the sky as a god, all creation is smitten with terror. The sky dissolves in rain, the stars shake in their places, and even the bones of the great double lion-headed earth-god Aker, , quake, and all the lesser powers of heaven flee in fear. He is considered to have been a mighty conqueror upon earth, for those whom he has vanquished are

[1] The hieroglyphic texts are given by Maspero, *Les Inscriptions des Pyramides de Saqqarah*, Paris, 1894, p. 67, l. 496, and p. 134, l. 319.

beneath his feet; there is no reason why this statement should not be taken literally, and not as referring to the mere pictures of enemies which were sometimes painted on the cartonnage coverings of mummies under the feet, and upon the sandals of mummies, and upon the outside of the feet of coffins. An ordinary man possessed one *ka* or "double," but a king or a god was believed to possess many *kau* or "doubles." Thus in one text[1] the god Rā is said to possess seven souls (*bau*) and fourteen doubles (*kau*), and prayers were addressed to each soul and double of Rā as well as to the god himself; elsewhere[2] we are told that the fourteen *kau* of Rā, , were given to him by Thoth. Unås appears in heaven with his "gods" upon him, the serpents are on his brow, he is led by a serpent-guide, and is endowed with his powers. It is difficult to say what the "gods" here referred to really are, for it is unlikely that the allusion is to the small figures of gods which, in later times, were laid upon the bodies of the dead, and it seems that we are to understand that he, Unås, was accompanied by a number of divine beings who had laid their protecting strength upon him. The uraei on his brow and his serpent-guide were the emblems of similar beings whose help he had bespoken—in other words, they represented spirits of serpents which were made friendly towards man.

The passage in the text of Unås continues, "Unås is the Bull "of heaven which overcometh by his will, and which feedeth upon "that which cometh into being from every god, and he eateth "of the provender of those who fill themselves with words of "power and come from the Lake of Flame. Unås is provided "with power sufficient to resist his spirits (*khu*), and he riseth [in "heaven] like a mighty god who is the lord of the seat of the "hand (i.e., power) [of the gods]. He taketh his seat and his "back is towards Seb. Unås weigheth his speech with the god "whose name is hidden on the day of slaughtering the oldest "[gods]. Unås is the master of the offering and he tieth the "knot, and provideth meals for himself; he eateth men and he

[1] Dümichen, *Tempelinschriften*, vol. i., pl. 29.

[2] Lepsius, *Denkmäler*, iii., Bl. 194.

"liveth upon gods, he is the lord of offerings, and he keepeth "count of the lists of the same." The dead king is next likened to a young and vigorous bull which feeds upon what is produced by every god and upon those that come from the Fiery Lake to eat words of power. Here we have a survival of the old worship of the bull, which began in the earliest times in Egypt, and lasted until the Roman period. His food is that which is produced by every god, and when we remember that the Egyptians believed that every object, animate and inanimate, was the habitation of a spirit or god, it is easy to see that the allusion in these words is to the green herbage which the bull ordinarily eats, for from this point of view, every blade of grass was the abode of a god. In connexion with this may be quoted the words of Sankhôn-yâthân, the Sanchoniatho of the Greeks, as given by Eusebius, who says, "But these first men consecrated the productions of the "earth, and judged them gods, and worshipped those things, upon "which they themselves lived, and all their posterity, and all "before them; to these they made libations and sacrifices."[1]

Now the food of this bull Unȧs is also said to be those who came from the Lake of Fire, or the city of She-Sȧsȧ, and who are these? From Chapter cviii. of the *Book of the Dead* we learn that She-Sȧsȧ was situated in Sekhet-Sȧsȧ,[2] i.e., a district in heaven, and it is clear from the text of the Chapter that it was one of the abodes wherein the beatified dead obtained food. The deceased is made to say, "I have not lain down in death; I have stood over "thee,[3] and I have risen like a god. I have cackled like a goose, "and I have alighted like the hawk by the divine clouds and by "the great dew . . . . I have come from She-Sȧsȧ, which is in "Sekhet-Sȧsȧ, i.e., the Lake of Fire, which is in the Field of "Fire." Towards the end of the Chapter (line 10) mention is made of herbage or crops (), and it seems as if these

[1] Eusebius, *Praep. Evan.*, lib. i., c. 10 (in Cory, *Ancient Fragments*, London, 1832, p. 5).

[2] . See my *Chapters of Coming Forth by Day*, Text, p. 203.

[3] He speaks to the Thigh, , in heaven.

grew in the Field of Fire, or in the neighbourhood of it, and it is clear that it must be these which are referred to as the provender of those who come from the Lake of Fire. We are next told that Unȧs hath power sufficient to oppose or resist his spirits (*khu*), but it is not certain whether these are beings in the Underworld which are hostile to him, or spirits which belong to himself; in any case the meaning of the passage is not clear. Having risen in heaven Unȧs takes his seat with his back towards Seb, the great earth-god who was represented by the mythological goose which was supposed to have laid the great cosmic egg. In the latter part of the section of the text of Unȧs quoted above we have some remarkable ideas enunciated. It is asserted first of all that he "weigheth his speech with the god whose name is hidden," which indicates that Unȧs was supposed to be of equal rank and power with the god of judgment. From the Theban Recensions of the *Book of the Dead*[1] we know that the expression "weighing of words," 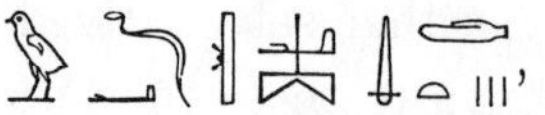, means also the "weighing of actions," and that it is applied to the examination of the deceased which is held on the day wherein his heart is weighed in the Great Scales. The examination was conducted by Thoth on behalf of Osiris, but the words in the text of Unȧs show that the dead king considers himself able to judge his own actions, and to award himself happiness. The god of the hidden name is probably Osiris. Finally it is said that Unȧs eats men and feeds upon the gods. We have already referred to the passage in Juvenal's *Fifteenth Satire* in which he declares that the Egyptians ate human flesh, and it has been already said that the dynastic inscriptions afford no proof whatsoever that the Egyptians were cannibals.

The statement here that Unȧs ate men is definite enough, and it is not easy to give any other than a literal meaning to the words; we can only assume then that this portion of the text has reference to some acts of cannibalism of which a tradition had come down from predynastic to dynastic times. We gather from other passages in the texts of Unȧs and Tetȧ what manner of treatment

[1] See my *Chapters of Coming Forth by Day*, Text, p. 18, l. 12; p. 19, l. 5; etc.

was meted out to the vanquished in battle by the victors, and it seems to find a parallel in the atrocious acts which were, and in some places still are, perpetrated by conquering tribes of Central Africa after a battle. In predynastic times all the property of those who were defeated in war was seized upon by the successful warriors, and all the women fell into their hands, and at times nameless abominations were committed upon the unfortunate male captives. The dead king in the texts of Unȧs and Tetȧ is, naturally, described as the lord of heaven and of all the beings and things which are therein; as such he is master of all the women, and it is said plainly of him that he is the "fecundator, and that "he carries off the women from their husbands to whatsoever place "he pleaseth whensoever he pleaseth."[1] Thus one of his attributes was that of the bull, which, because of his fecundity and strength, became the object of worship by the early Egyptians, and he exercised the rights of a victorious tribal chief. Upon the conquered men who were allowed to live terrible indignities were perpetrated, and in the text of Tetȧ the dead king is exhorted to rise up, "for Horus hath caused Thoth to bring unto thee thine "enemy, and he (i.e., Horus) hath put thee behind him in order "that he may not do thee an injury, and that thou mayest make "thy place upon him, so that when [thou] goest forth thou mayest "take thy place upon him, and he may not have union with "thee."[2] It is possible then that in predynastic times in addition to the wanton destruction which the Egyptians brought about after a victorious fight with their enemies, and the slaughter, and rapine, and nameless abominations which followed, they sometimes imitated the example of wild and savage beasts and ate the foes they had

1 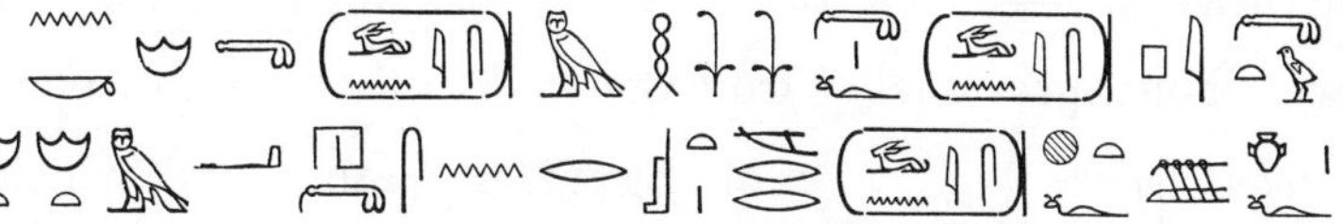 Unȧs, line 629.

2  Tetȧ, line 286.

conquered. The accounts of the battles of dynastic times show that the Egyptians looted and destroyed the cities and towns of the vanquished, and that they cut down orchards and gardens, and carried off all the flocks and herds which they could find; and there is abundant proof that they mutilated the bodies of their dead foes after a fight, but that they either ate them or behaved towards them in a manner contrary to nature there is absolutely no evidence to show.

We have now to consider the remaining paragraphs of the extract from the text of Unàs. The gods upon whose bodies Unàs fed were snared by Am-keḥuu, and they were examined as to their fitness and condition by Tcheser-ṭep-f, a divine being who was in later times one of the Forty-Two Judges in the Hall of Maāti, and is mentioned in the "Negative Confession" of the *Book of the Dead*. The gods were next bound by Ḥer-thertu, and the god Khensu cut their throats and took out their intestines; a being called Shesemu acted as butcher and cut them up and cooked the pieces thereof in his fiery cauldrons. Thereupon Unàs ate them, and in eating them he also ate their words of power and their spirits. The largest and finest of the gods he ate at daybreak, and the smaller sized ones for meals at sunset, and the smallest for his meals in the night; the old and worn-out gods he rejected entirely and used them up as fuel in his furnace. The cauldrons in which the bodies of the gods were cooked were heated by the "Great One in heaven," who shot flame under those which contained the thighs of the oldest of the gods; and the "Perer, who is in heaven," of Unàs cast also into cauldrons the thighs of their women. Unàs is then said to make a journey about every part of the double sky, or double heaven, , i.e., the night sky and the day sky, and also to travel about, presumably from one end to the other, through the two *àṭebu*, , of Egypt, i.e., the land which lies between the mountains and the Nile on each side of the river. As a result of eating of the bodies of the gods Unàs becomes the Great Sekhem, the Sekhem of the Sekhemu; he also becomes the Āshem of Āshem, the Great Āshem of the Āshemu. The power which protects Unàs and which he possesses is greater than that of all the *sāḥu* in the heavens, and he becomes the eldest of all the firstborn gods and he goes before thousands and makes offerings to hundreds [of them]; indeed, the power which has been given to him as the Great Sekhem makes him to become as the star Saḥu, i.e., Orion, with the gods. "Unȧs can repeat his rising in the sky, for he is "the Seben crown as lord of the heavens. He taketh count of the "knots (or, sinews) and of livers, and he hath taken possession of "the hearts of the gods. He hath eaten the Red Crown, he hath "eaten the White Crown, and he feedeth upon fat entrails; the "offerings made to him are those in whose hearts live words of "power. What the Red Crown emitteth that he hath eaten, and "he flourisheth; the words of power are in his belly, and his *sāḥu* "is not turned away from him. He hath eaten the knowledge of "every god, and his existence and the duration of his life are "eternal and everlasting in any *sāḥu* which he is pleased to "make. Whatsoever he hateth he shall never do within the limits, "or, inside the borders of heaven. Behold their soul, i.e., the "soul of the gods, is in Unȧs, and their spirits are with him; "his food is more abundant than that of the gods, in whose bones "is the flame of Unȧs. Behold their soul is with Unȧs, and their "Shadows are with their Forms, or Attributes. Unȧs is in, or "with, the doubly hidden Khā gods (?) [as] a Sekhem, and having "performed [all] the ordinances of the (ceremony of) ploughing "the seat of the heart of Unȧs shall be among the living upon this "earth for ever and ever."

The last portion of the extract is of peculiar interest because it affords some insight into the beliefs which the Egyptians held about the constituent parts of the economy of the gods. We have already seen that a *ba*, or soul, has been assigned to Unȧs, and *kau*, or "doubles," and *khu*, or spirits, and a *sāḥu*, and a *sekhem;* the last two words are difficult to translate, but they are rendered with approximate correctness by "spiritual body," and "power." The soul was intimately connected with the heart, and was supposed to be gratified by offerings, which it was able to consume; the "double" was an integral part of a man, and was connected with his shadow, and came into being when he was born, and lived in the tomb with the body after death; the spirit was the seat of the spiritual part of man, and gods and divine personages were credited with the possession of several spirits; the *sāḥu*, or spiritual body, was the ethereal, intangible, transparent and translucent body, which was supposed, in dynastic times at all events, to grow from the dead body, the form of which it preserved; the *sekhem* was the "power" which seems to have animated the *sāḥu* and to have made it irresistible. From the extract given above from the text of Unȧs we learn that the gods were composed of all these various parts, and that in fact their economy resembled that of man; in other words, the Egyptians made their gods in their own image, only they attributed to them superhuman powers. The gods, however, preserved their existence by means of a magical protection which they enjoyed, *meket*, , and also by *ḥekau*, , which is commonly translated "words of power"; the aim of every Egyptian was to obtain possession of both the magical protection and the words of power, for they thought that if they once were masters of these they would be able to live like the gods. In the earliest times in Egypt men thought that the only way to obtain the strength and immortality of the gods was to eat the gods themselves, and so we read that Unȧs, having eaten parts of the boiled bodies of the gods, "hath eaten "their words of power (*ḥeka*), and swallowed their spirits (*khu*)." As a result of this he becomes the "Great Power," the "Power of Powers," i.e., the greatest Power in heaven. He becomes also the Āshem of Ashem, the great Āshem of the Āshemu, that is to say, the very essence of Āshem, and the greatest powers of the Āshemu beings are enshrined within him because he has within him the spirits and the words of power of the gods.

But what is the meaning of Āshem? In the text of Tetȧ the word has for its determinative a hawk perched upon a standard, , which shows that it has some meaning connected with deity or divinity, but it cannot be the name of one divine being only, for we find it in the plural form Āshemu, . The determinative, however, does not help us very much, for it proves little more than that some attribute of the Hawk-god Ḥeru was ascribed to the Āshemu; the hawk was undoubtedly the first creature worshipped by the predynastic Egyptians, and  became in consequence the common determinative of all words implying the idea of deity or divinity, and of the proper names of the gods in a very large number of passages in the hieroglyphic texts inscribed on the walls of the chambers and corridors in the pyramids at Ṣaḳḳâra. The common name for "god," as we have already seen, is "neter," , or , with the plural "neteru," , or 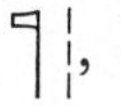, or , or , but we find that the male gods are sometimes called "hawks," , even when the female gods are called "netert," 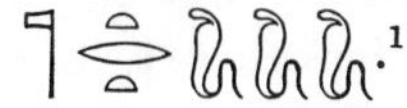.[1] In the *Book of the Dead*[2] the word Āshemu is written , which may be translated by "divine Āshemu," and as the first determinative is a squatting hawk, we may assume that the word āshemu means "hawks."[3] If this assumption be correct, "Āshem of Āshem, Great Āshem of the Āshemu," means "Hawk of Hawk, the Great Hawk of the Hawks," and since the hawk was not only a god to the predynastic Egyptians, but their oldest and greatest god, being in fact the spirit of that which is above, i.e., heaven, the passage "Āshem of Āshem, Great Āshem of the Āshemu," may very well be rendered "god of god, great god of the gods." Thus with the words of power and the spirits of the gods in him Unâs becomes the habitation of the power of God, and the firstborn of the gods. He is now able to go round about heaven at pleasure, and as the Great Sekhem, or Power, his visible emblem is Saḥ or Orion, and he is able to repeat his rising [daily] in heaven like this constellation. It is not improbable that the identification of Orion with kings who had eaten the gods filtered down in tradition to the Semitic people who lived in the Delta in dynastic times, and so became the base of the legends about Orion which are found among the Arabs and Hebrews.

[1] See the text of Unâs, line 209; in the text of Tetâ, line 197, the gods are described as "male and female," 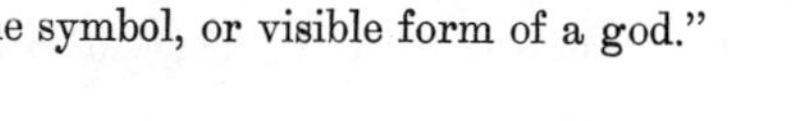.

[2] See my *Chapters of Coming Forth by Day*, Text, p. 128, l. 14.

[3] A variant form of the word is *ākhem* , and Brugsch (Wörterbuch, *Suppl.*, p. 279) renders it by "the symbol, or visible form of a god."

Modern travellers have put on record the fact that certain savage and semi-savage peoples were, even in recent times, in the habit of eating pieces of flesh of mighty wild animals or of strong men, and of drinking their blood with the view of absorbing their nature, and life, and strength into their own bodies.[1] This idea also existed among the Egyptians, both predynastic and dynastic, and we find an allusion to it in the extract from Unȧs under consideration, for he is said to take possession of the hearts of the gods, and to reckon up the *thesu* and *beqesu*, and to feed upon fat *smau*. The importance which the Egyptians attached to the possession of the physical heart, or of having power over it, is proved by many texts, and especially by several Chapters of the *Book of the Dead*, wherein we find many prayers which were specially written for the protection of the heart. Thus in Chapter xxvi. the deceased prays, "may my heart be to me in "the house of hearts, may my *ḥāti*[2] be to me in the house of "*ḥātu*"; Chapters xxvii., xxviii., and xxix. were written to prevent the heart being carried away by those who steal hearts and destroy them, 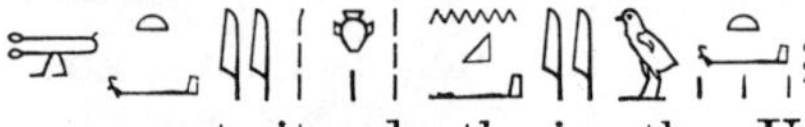; Chapter xxix.A was composed to prevent its death in the Underworld; and Chapters xxx.A and xxx.B were intended to prevent a man's heart from being driven away from him there, especially at the time of the Judgment, when it was weighed in the Great Scales. For the words *thesu*, *beqesu*, and *smau* it is not easy to find equivalents. From the connexion in which it occurs *thesu* must mean either the vertebra or some internal organ of the body which resembles a tied or knotted cord, whilst of *beqesu* the determinative proves that it also is an internal organ. In Chapter xxx.A the deceased says, "Homage to thee, O my "heart (*ȧb*)! Homage to thee, O my *ḥāti* (pericardium?)! "Homage to thee, O my *besek*," which is probably a variant form of *beqes*, but curiously enough the determinative of *besek*, 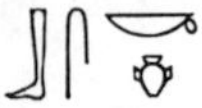, is a heart. In spite of this, however, it seems as if the

[1] See Robertson Smith, *The Religion of the Semites*, p. 295.

[2] , the pericardium (?). In the ancient texts the *ḥāt*, or *ḥāti* of a god was the seat of the words of power by means of which he maintained his life.

word actually means "liver." Mr. Frazer has quoted in his work[1] instances which prove that savage tribes look upon the liver as the seat of the soul or life of man, and that portions of it are eaten by them with the view of acquiring the qualities of the former possessor of the liver. The words of the text of Unȧs do not say definitely that the king ate the *thesu* and livers of the gods who had been killed for him, but it is evident from the context that they were supposed to form part of his food. On the other hand, it is said definitely that he did eat their *smau saau*, or "fat entrails," , and their hearts, , or those portions of them which were the seats of the *ḥekau*, , or words of magical power, which were the source of their life.

Now besides the spirits, and the words of power, and the internal organs of the gods, Unȧs, it is said, hath eaten the "knowledge,"  *sȧa*, of every god, and the period of his life and his existence are merged into eternity and everlastingness, which he may pass in any way that pleaseth his spiritual body (*sāḥ*), and during this existence he has no need whatsoever to do anything which is distasteful to him. Moreover, the soul[s] and spirits of the gods are in and with Unȧs, and their souls, and their shadows, and their divine forms are with him. Thus we see that Unȧs has absorbed within his spiritual body all the life and power of the gods, and his portion is everlasting life, and he can do anything and everything he pleases. Here we should naturally expect the section to come to an end, but the last sentence goes on to say that Unȧs is with the double Khā god, who is invisible, or unknown, and that being a Power (*sekhem*) who hath performed [the ceremony] of ploughing, "the seat of the heart[2] of Unȧs shall "be among those who live upon this earth for ever and for ever." In this sentence we have an illustration of the difficulty of understanding and explaining the Egyptian religion and the doctrine of the gods. In the early portion of the passage from the text of

[1] *The Golden Bough*, vol. ii., p. 357 (2nd edition).

[2] The word here used is *ȧb* .

Unȧs already translated and analyzed we are told how the dead king became the god of god, immortal and invisible, with supreme power in heaven, etc., but at the end of it we read that the seat of the heart of Unȧs shall be among those who live upon this earth for ever and ever, i.e., Unȧs shall enjoy after death a continuation of the life which he began in this world; in fact, shall have a double existence, the one heavenly and the other earthly.

## APPENDIX TO CHAPTER I

# UNÀS, THE SLAYER AND EATER OF THE GODS

496.  497.

*ḳep pet àḥi sebu nem*

Poureth down water heaven, tremble the stars, go about

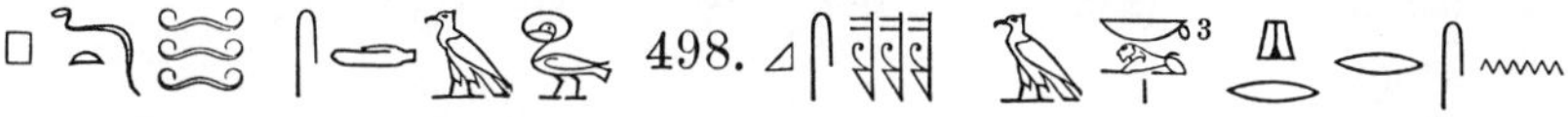 498.

*petchet seṭa qes Aker ḳer-er-sen*

the bow-bearers, quake the bones of Aker, those beneath them

 499.

*kenemu ma en sen Unàs khā ba*

take to flight [when] they see Unàs rising [as] a soul

*em neter ānkh em àt-f usheb*

like a god [who] liveth upon his fathers [and] feedeth

500. 

*em mut-f Unàs pà neb sabut*

upon his mothers. Unàs this [is] the lord of wisdom,

[1] The text here given is from the Pyramid of Unàs (Maspero, *Recueil*, tom. iv., p. 59); the variants are from the Pyramid of Tetà (*Recueil*, tom. v., p. 48, l. 319).

[2] 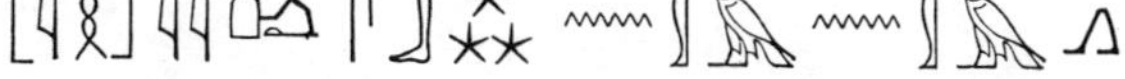

[3] [4] 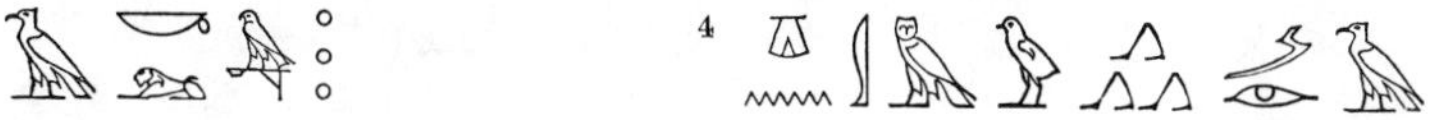

[5] [6] [7] 

*khem en* 501. *mut-f ren-f àu shepsu*[1]

knoweth not his mother his name. Is the noble rank

*Unȧs em pet àu user-f em khut*[2] 502. *mȧ Tem*

of Unȧs in heaven, is his strength in the horizon like Tem,

*ȧt-f*[3] *ȧu mes-nef su useru eref*

his father; he (i.e., Tem) begot him [and] he became stronger than he.

*ȧu kau*[4] 503. *Unȧs ḥa-f*[5] *ȧu ḥemu set-f* (?)

Are the doubles of Unȧs behind him, the conquered [are]

*kher reṭui-f*[6] *ȧu neteru-f ṭep-f*[7] *ȧu ȧārt-f*[8]

beneath his two feet. His gods are on him. His uraei are

504. *em ȧpt-f ȧu semtu Unȧs em ḥāt-f*

on his brow. The serpent guide of Unȧs is before him.

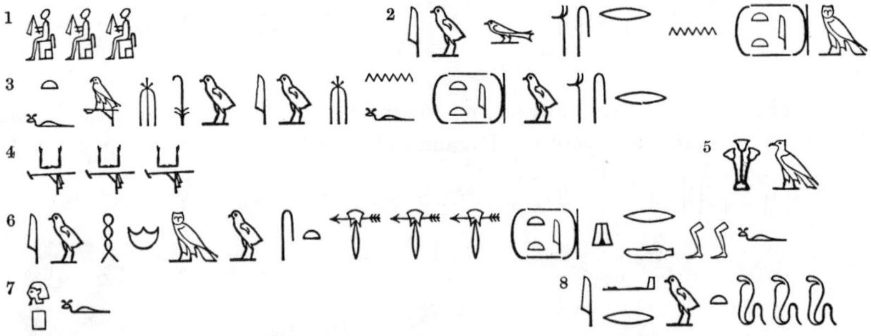

*petret ba* [1] *khut ent bes* 505. *àu useru Unàs*
Seeth soul [his] the spirit of flame. The powers of Unàs

*ḥer meket-f Unàs pà ka pet en heṭ*
protect him. Unàs this [is] the bull of heaven that thrusteth

*em àb-f ānkh* [2] *em kheper* 506. *en neter*
with his will, living upon what cometh into being of god

*neb ām* [3] *em semu-sen iu meḥ* [4]
every, and eating of their food who come to fill

*khat-sen em ḥekau* [5] *em She en Sàsà*
their belly with words of power from the lake of Flame.

*Unàs pà* [6] 507. *āper-ā er àāb* [7] *khu-f*
Unàs this [is] provided with power against his spirits.

*àu Unàs khā em ur* [8] *pu neb àmu àst-ā* [9]
Unàs riseth like a mighty one, the lord in the seat of the hand [of the gods].

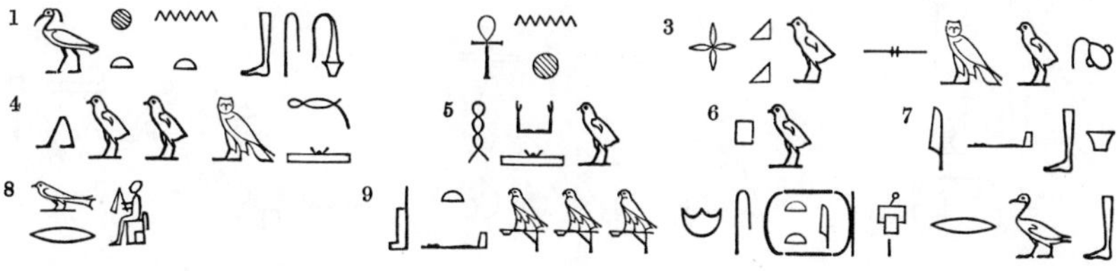

*ḥems-f* *sa-f* *ȧr* *Seb* 508. *Unȧs* *pȧ*

He is seated [with] his back to Seb. Unȧs this

*utchā*[1] *met-f* *ḥenā* *Ȧmen*[2] *ren-f* *hru*[3] *pu*

weigheth his word with Hidden of Name on day this

*en* *rekhes*[4] *semsu* *Unȧs* *p[u]* *neb*

of slaughtering the eldest [gods] Unȧs this [is] the lord

*ḥetep* *tes*[5] *āqa* *ȧri* *āut-f*[6]

of the offering, tying the knot, making his meals

*tchesef* 509. *Unȧs* *pȧ*[7] *ām* *remth*[8] *ānkh*

for himself. Unȧs this eateth men [and] liveth

*em* *neteru* *neb* *ȧnnu*[9] *khḥā* *ȧpt*

on the gods, the lord of the offerings, who examineth the lists of offerings.

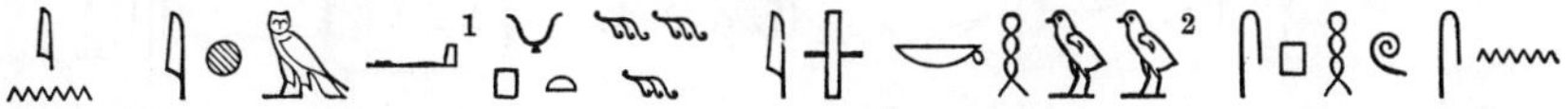

*àn* *àkhem* *àpt* *Àm-keḥuu* *sepeḥ - sen*

Behold, he who maketh to bow foreheads, Àm-keḥuu hath snared them

510.

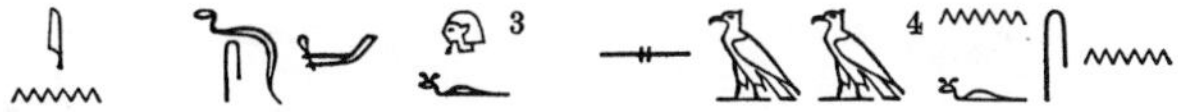

*en* *Unàs* *àn* *Tcheser-ṭep-f* *saa-nef-sen*

for Unàs. Behold, Tcheser-ṭep-f hath known them

*khesef - nef sen* *àn* *Ḥer - thertu* *qas - nef sen*

[and] he hath driven them [to him]. Behold, Ḥer-thertu hath bound them.

*àn* *Khensu* *meṭes* *nebu* *tchaṭ - f sen*

Behold, Khensu the slaughterer of lords hath cut the throats of them

511.

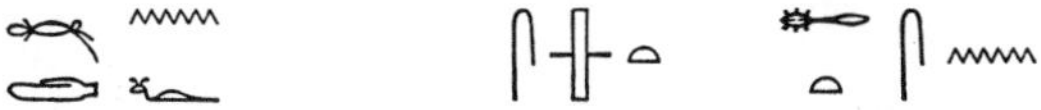

*en* *Unàs* *sheṭ-nef* *àmt* *khat - sen*

for Unàs, [and] he hath torn out what is in their belly,

*àpt* *pu* *habu - f* *er* *khesef*

[for] he is the messenger [whom] he sent to drive [them].

1  2 

3 . This creature is mentioned in the Negative Confession; see my *Chapters of Coming Forth by Day*, Text, p. 259, l. 41.

4  5 

6  7  8  wanting.

9  10 

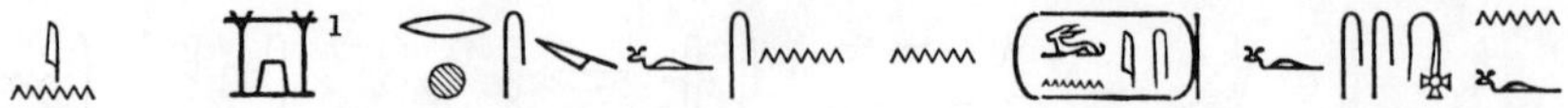

*ȧn Shesemu rekhes - f sen en Unȧs feses - nef*

Behold, Shesemu hath cut them up for Unȧs, he hath boiled

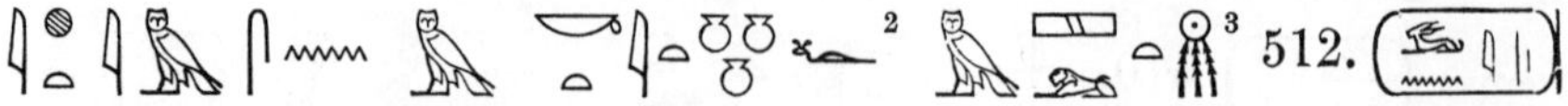

*ȧkhet ȧm - sen em ketȧt - f meshert Unȧs*

pieces of them in his cauldrons blazing. Unȧs

*pȧ ām ḥeka - sen ȧām khu - sen*

this hath eaten their words of power, [he] hath eaten their spirits.

*ȧu uru - sen en ȧshet-f ṭuat ȧu ḥer-ȧbu - sen*

Their great ones are for his meal of the morning, their middle ones are

*en meshert - f ȧu shereru - sen en ȧsht-f*

for his sunset meal, their little ones are for his meal

*ȧu ȧa - sen ȧatu - sen*

of the night, their old ones (male) their old ones (female) are

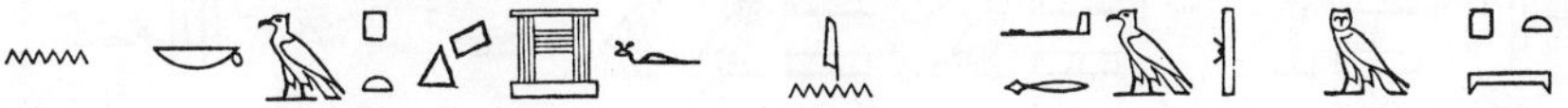

*en kapt - f ȧn āāa em pet*
for his furnace. Behold, the great one in heaven

*uṭu-nef setchet er uḥatu khert-sen*
hath shot flame against the cauldrons beneath them

*em khepeshu nu semsu - sen*[1] *ȧu Perer - ȧmu - pet*[2] 514.
with the thighs of the eldest ones. Perer-ȧmu-pet

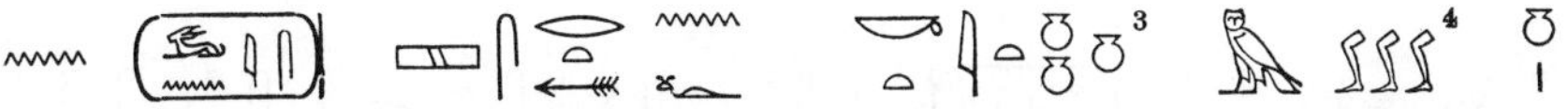

*en Unȧs shesert - nef ketȧt*[3] *em reṭu*[4] *nu*
of Unȧs hath thrown [into] the cauldrons the legs of

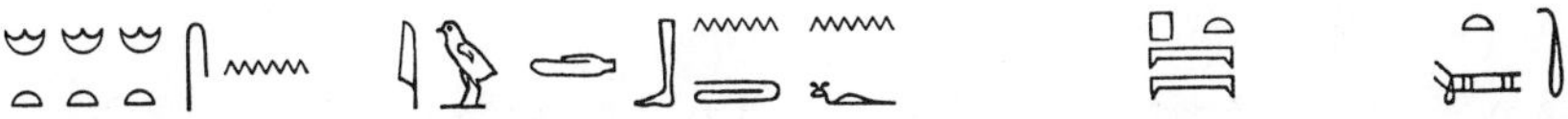

*ḥemt - sen ȧu ṭeben - nef pet tem-thȧ*
their women. He hath gone round about the double heaven, all of it,

*ȧu perer - nef ȧṭebu Unȧs pȧ*
he hath gone round about the two halves of Egypt. Unȧs this [is]

*sekhem ur*[5] *sekhem* 515. *em sekhemu*[6] *Unȧs*
the sekhem great, the sekhem of the sekhemu. Unȧs

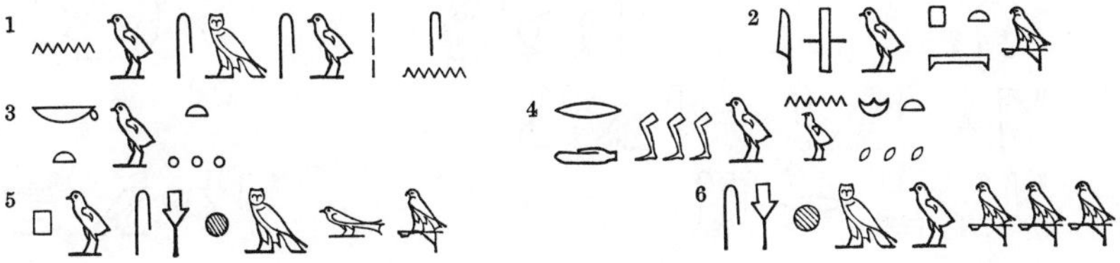

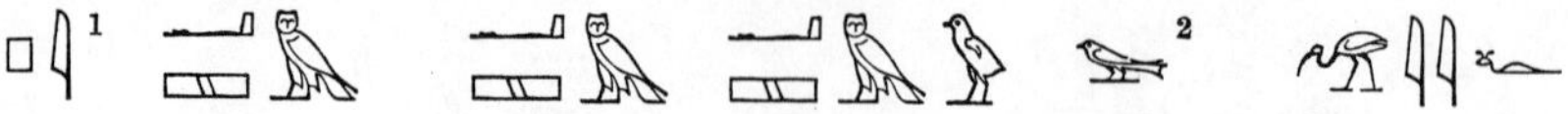

*pȧ āshem āshem āshemu ur qemi - f*

this [is] the āshem, the āshem of the āshemu great. [What] he findeth

*em uat - f ām - f nef su em umu*

on his way he eateth it greedily.

*ȧu meket Unȧs em ḥāt* 516. *sāḥu nebu*

The protection of Unȧs [is] before [that of] the sāḥu all

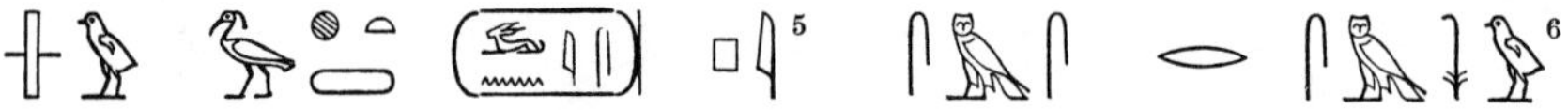

*ȧmu khut Unȧs pȧ semes er semsu*

in the horizon. Unȧs this is the eldest of the old ones.

*ȧu perer - nef khau ȧu uṭen - nef shāut*

He hath gone round thousands, he hath offered hundreds.

*ȧu erṭā - nef ā em sekhem ur ȧn*

Hath been given to him the hand as the sekhem great, behold

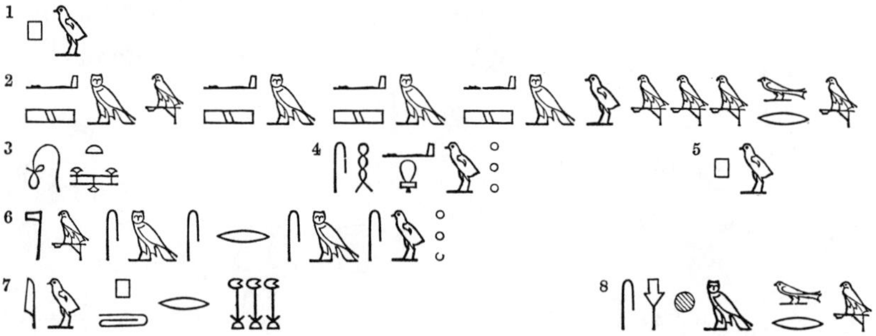

517.

*Saḥu* | *år* | *neteru* | *åu* | *nem* | *en* | *Unås* | *khātu*

Orion, with the gods. Hath repeated Unås [his] rising

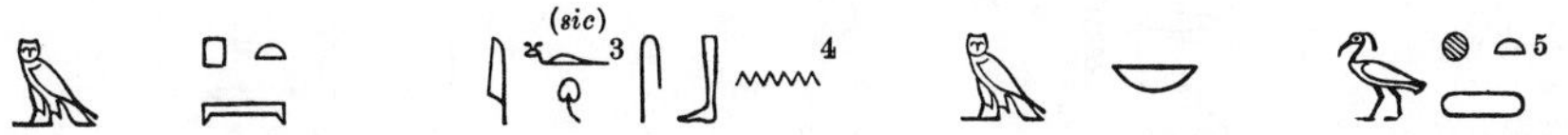

*em* | *pet* | .... | *seben* | *em* | *neb* | *khut*

in heaven. He is the *seben* crown as lord of the horizon.

*åu* | *ḥeseb - nef* | *ṭesu* | *beqesu* | *åu* | *thet - nef*

He hath counted up knots [and] livers. He hath taken possession of

518.

*ḥātu* | *neteru* | *åu* | *ām - nef* | *ṭeshert*

the hearts of the gods. He hath eaten the Red Crown,

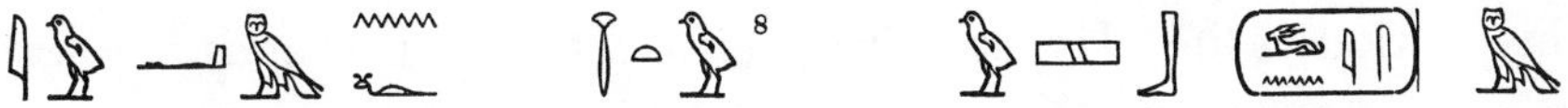

*åu* | *ām - nef* | *uatchetu* | *usheb* | *Unås* | *em*

he hath eaten the White Crown. Feedeth Unås upon

*smau* | *saau* | *ḥetep-f* | *em* | *ānkh* | *em* | *ḥātu*

entrails fat, his offering [is that] whereon live in [their] hearts

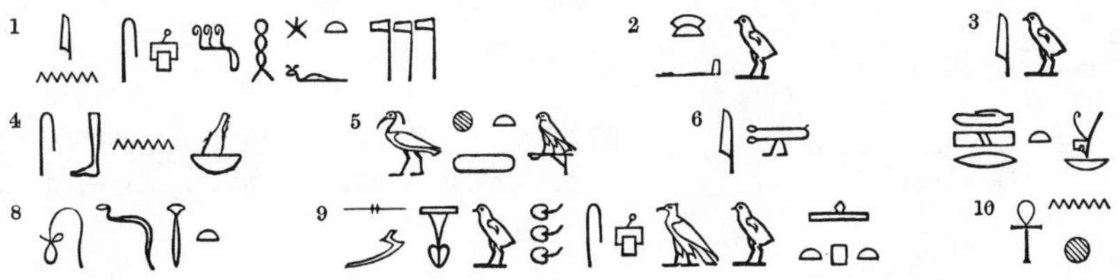

519. 

*ḥekau - sen* *àsth-f* *àu* *Unàs* *nesb - f* *sebeshu*

their words of power. Behold, Unȧs eateth what is cast out

*àmu* *ṭeshert* *àf* *uakhḥa - f* *àu* *ḥeka - sen*

[from] the Red Crown, he flourisheth, their words of power

 520. 

*em* *khat-f* *àn* *ḥem* *em* *sāḥu* *Unàs*

are in his belly, not is turned back the sāḥu of Unȧs

*mā-f* *àu* *ām - nej* *sàa* *en* *neter* *neb*

from him. He hath eaten the intelligence of god every,

 521. 

*āḥāu* *pà* *neḥeḥ* *tcher-f* *pà tchetta*

[his] period of life [is] eternity, his existence is everlastingness

*em* *sāḥ - f* *pen* *en* *merer - f* *àr - f*

in his sāḥ, this what he is pleased [to do] he doeth,

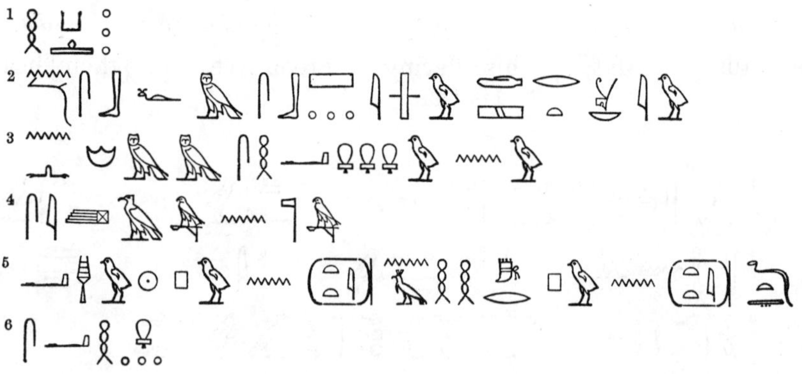

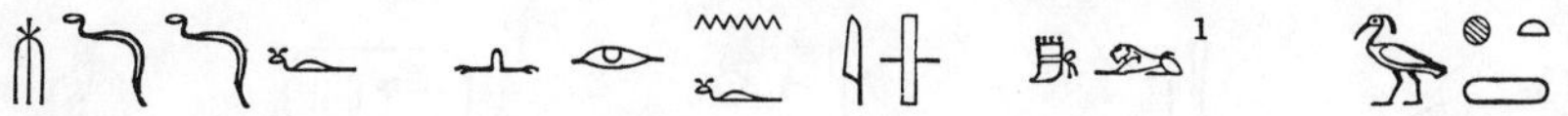

*mestchetch-f* *àn* *àr-nef* *àm* *tcher* *khut*

[what] he hateth not doeth he in the limits of the horizon

*tchetta er neḥeḥ* *sek* *ba - sen* 522. *àmt* *Unȧs*

for ever and ever. Behold, their soul [is] in Unȧs,

*khu - sen* *kher* *Unȧs* *em* *ḥa* *khet - f*

spirits their [are] with Unȧs, more abundant [is] his food

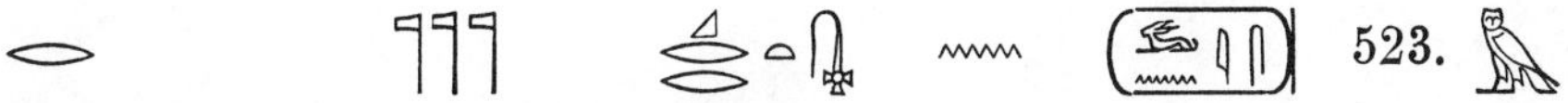

*er* *neteru* *qerert* *en* *Unȧs* 523. *em*

than [that of] the gods. The flame of Unȧs [is] in

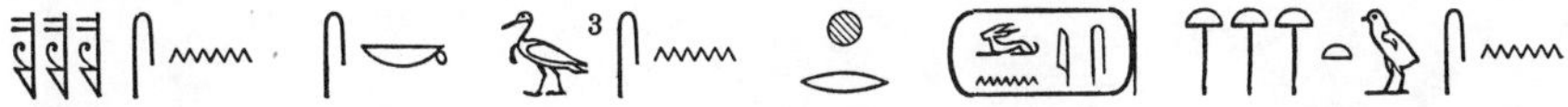

*qesu - sen* *sek* *ba-sen* *kher* *Unȧs* *khaibiṭu-sen*

their bones, behold, their soul is with Unȧs, their shadows

*mā* *àru - sen* 524. *àu* *Unȧs* *em* *enen* *khā* *khā*

are with their forms. Unȧs is with these, rising, rising,

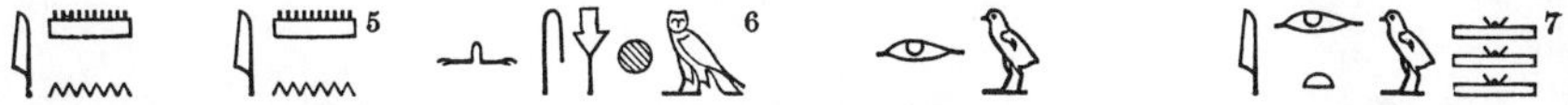

*àmen* *àmen* *sekhem* *àru* *àritu . . . .*

hidden, hidden, a sekhem having performed the ordinances

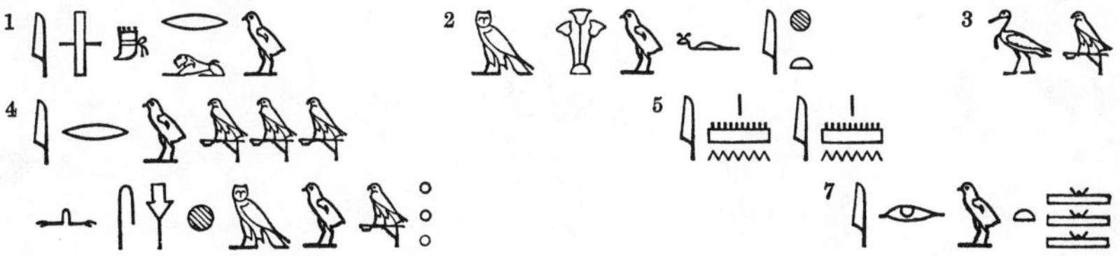

525. 

*em* *khebes*[1] *ȧst-ȧb* *Unȧs* *em*

of ploughing, the seat of the heart of Unȧs [is] among

*ānkhu*[2] *em* *ta* *pen* *tchetta* *er* *neḥeḥ*

the living on earth this for ever and for ever.

1 

2 

CHAPTER II

## CONCEPTION OF GOD AND THE "GODS"

THE texts in the pyramids of Unȧs and Tetȧ and their immediate successors prove that the religious literature of the Egyptians contains a multitude of beliefs and opinions which belong to all periods of their history, and represent different stages in the development of their civilization. Their ideas about the various parts which constitute their material, and mental, and spiritual existences cannot have been conceived all at once, but it is very hard to say in respect of some of them which came first. We need not trouble about the order of the development of their ideas about the constituent parts of the gods, for in the earliest times, at least, the Egyptians only ascribed to them the attributes which they had already ascribed to themselves; once having believed that they possessed doubles, shadows, souls, spirits, hearts, (i.e., the seats of the mental life), names, powers, and spiritual bodies, they assigned the like to the gods. But if the gods possessed doubles, and shadows, and hearts, none of which, in the case of man, can exist without bodies, they too must possess bodies, and thus the Egyptians conceived the existence of gods who could eat, and drink, and love, and hate, and fight, and make war, and grow old, and die, and perish as far as their bodies were concerned. And although the texts show that in very early times they began to conceive monotheistic ideas, and to develop beliefs of a highly spiritual character, the Egyptians never succeeded in abandoning the crude opinion about the gods which their indigenous ancestors had formed long before the dynastic period of their history. It is, of course, impossible to assume that educated classes of Egypt held such opinions, notwithstanding the fact that religious texts which were written for their benefit contain as great a mixture of views and beliefs of all periods as those which were written for humbler folk.

The *Book of the Dead* in all dynasties proves that the rich and the poor, and the educated and the uneducated alike prayed for funeral offerings in the very Chapters in which they proclaimed their sure belief in an existence in which material things were superfluities. In the texts of the Early Empire the deceased is declared to be a god, or God, and the son of god, or God, and the oldest god of all, Horus, gives him his eye, and he sits on a great throne by the side of God; yet in the same texts we read that he partakes of the figs and wine of the gods, that he drinks beer which lasts for ever, that he thirsts not like the gods Shu and Tefnut, and that the throne of God is made of iron, that its legs terminate in hoofs like those of bulls, and that its sides are ornamented with the faces of lions.[1] The great god Horus gives him his own "double" (*ka*), and yet there are in heaven enemies who dare to oppose the deceased; and although he is declared to be immortal, "all the gods give him of their food that he may not "die," and he sits down, clothed in white linen and wearing white sandals, with the gods by the lake in the Field of Peace, and partakes with them of the wood (or, tree) of life on which they themselves live that he also may live. Though he is the son of God he is also the child of Sothis, and the brother of the Moon, and the goddess Isis becomes his wife; though he is the son of God we are also told that his flesh and his bones have been gathered together, that his material body has been reconstructed; that his limbs perform all the functions of a healthy body; and as he lives as the gods live we see that from one point of view he and the gods are constituted alike. Instances of the mixture of spiritual with material ideas might be multiplied almost indefinitely, and numbers of passages containing the most contradictory statements might be adduced almost indefinitely to prove that the ideas of the Egyptians about the world beyond the grave, and about God and the gods were of a savage, childish, and inconsistent

[1] The passages from the Pyramid Texts are collected in my *Papyrus of Ani*, London, 1894, pp. lxxi. ff.

character. What, however, we have to remember in dealing with Egyptian religious texts is that the innate conservatism of the Egyptian in all ages never permitted him to relinquish any belief which had once found expression in writing, and that the written word was regarded by him as a sacred thing which, whether he believed it not, must be copied and preserved with great care, and if possible without any omission or addition whatsoever. Thus religious ideas and beliefs which had been entirely forgotten by the people of Egypt generally were preserved and handed down for thousands of years by the scribes in the temples. The matter would have been simple enough if they had done this and nothing more, but unfortunately they incorporated new texts into the collections of old ones, and the various attempts which the priests and scribes made to harmonize them resulted in the confusion of beliefs which we now have in Egyptian religious works.

The serpent-headed leopard SETCHA.

Before we pass to the consideration of the meaning of the old Egyptian name for god and God, i.e., "neter," mention must be made of a class of beings which were supposed to possess bodies partly animal and partly human, or were of a composite character. Among the latter class may be mentioned the creature which has the body of a leopard and the head and neck of a serpent, and was called "Setcha,"[1] ; and that which has the body of a lion, from which grow a pair of wings, and the head of an eagle, and is called "Sefer,"[2]; and that which has a body, the fore part being that of a lion, and the hind part that of a horse, and the head of a hawk, and an extended tail which terminates in a flower somewhat resembling the lotus. The name of this creature is Saḳ, , and she is represented with a collar round her

[1] See Champollion, *Monuments*, tom. iv., Paris, 1845, pl. 382.

[2] *Ibid.* See also Newberry, *Beni-Hasan*, ii., pl. iv.

neck, and with bars and stripes on her body, which has eight teats.[1] Among creatures, part animal part human, may be mentioned the leopard, with a human head and a pair of wings growing out of his back,[2] and the human-headed lion or sphinx. The winged human head which springs from the back of the leopard[3] strongly reminds one of the modern conventional representations of angels in religious pictures, but as the name of this fabulous creature is unknown, it is impossible even to guess at the reasons for which he was furnished with a winged man's head.

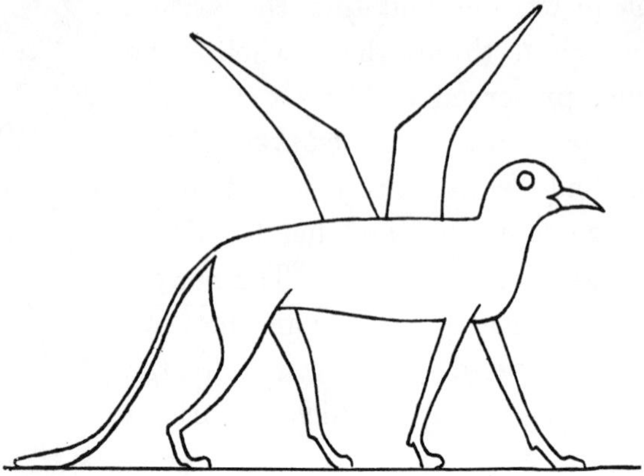

The eagle-headed lion SEFER.

In connexion with the composite animals enumerated above must be mentioned the "Devourer of Åmenti," called "Ām-mit, the Eater of the Dead," whose forequarters were those of a crocodile, and hindquarters those of a hippopotamus, and whose body was that of a lion,  . The tombs at Beni-hasan, in which the figures of the *Setcha*, the *Sefer*, and the *Saḳ* are depicted, date from the XIIth Dynasty, about B.C. 2500, and there is no reason for supposing that their existence was not conceived of long before that time. Side by side with these is also depicted an animal called *Sha*, , which has long square ears, and an extended tail resembling an arrow, and in its general appearance it much resembles the animal of the god Set.

The fabulous beast SAḲ.

[1] See Rosellini, *Monumenti Civili*, pl. xxiii., No. 4.
[2] *Ibid.*, pl. xxiii., No. 6.
[3] See Lepsius, *Denkmäler*, iii., pl. 131.

Two explanations of the existence of such composite creatures may be given. They may be due either to the imagination of the Egyptians, which conceived of the existence of quadrupeds wherein were united the strength of one animal and the wisdom or cunning of another, e.g., the Setcha which united within itself the strength of the leopard with the cunning of the serpent, and the nameless leopard with a man's winged head, or to the ignorance of the ancients of natural history.

A fabulous leopard.

The human head on an animal represented the intelligence of a man, and the wings the swift flight of the bird, and the body of the leopard the strength and the lithe motions of that animal. In conceiving the existence of such creatures the imagination may have been assisted in its fabrication of fabulous monsters by legends or stories of predynastic animals which were current in certain parts of Egypt during the dynastic period. Thus, as we have said before, the monster serpents of Egyptian mythology have their prototypes in the huge serpents which lived in the country in primeval times, and there is no doubt that Āpep was, originally, nothing more than a huge serpent which lived in some mountain on the western bank of the Nile.

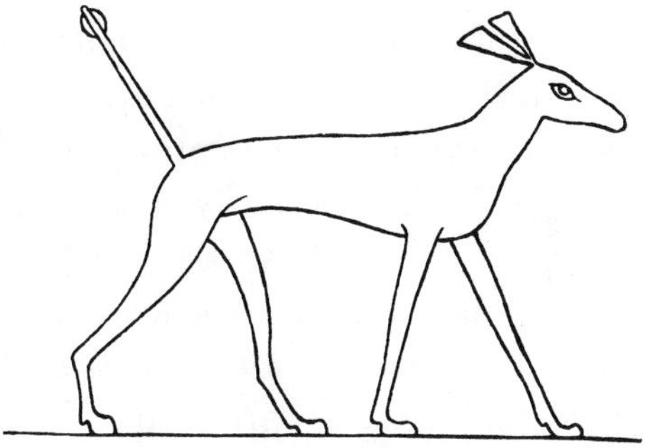
The animal *Sha*.

On the other hand, it is possible that the Egyptians really believed in the existence of composite animals, and that they never understood the impossibility of the head and neck of a serpent growing out of the body of a lion, or the head of a hawk out of the body of a lion, or a human head with the wings of a bird out of the body of a leopard. They were keen enough observers of the animals with which they came in contact daily, and their representations of them are wonderful for the accurate delineation of their forms and characteristics; but of animals which they had never seen, and could only know from the reports of travellers and others, naturally they could not give accurate representations. Man in all ages seems prone to believe in the existence of composite animals and monsters, and the most cultured of the most ancient nations, e.g., the Egyptians and the Babylonians, form no exception to the rule. The early seal-cylinders of the Babylonians reveal their belief in the existence of many a fabulous and mythical animal, and the boundary stones, or landmarks, of a later period prove that composite animals were supposed to watch over the boundaries of kingdoms and estates, which they preserved from invasion, and the winged man-headed bulls, which the Assyrians set up in the gates and doorways of their palaces to "protect the footsteps of the kings who made them," indicate clearly that they duly followed the examples set them by their kinsmen, the Babylonians. From the Assyrians Ezekiel probably borrowed the ideas which he developed in his description in the first chapter of his book of the four-faced and four-winged animals. Later, even the classical writers appeared to see no absurdity in solemnly describing animals, the existence of which was impossible, and in declaring that they possessed powers which were contrary to all experience and knowledge. Horapollo, i. 10, gravely states that the scarabaeus represents an *only begotten*, because the scarabaeus is a creature self-produced, being unconceived by a female, μονογενές μὲν ὅτι αὐτογενές ἐστι τὸ ζῶον, ὑπὸ θηλείας μὴ κυοφορούμενον; and in one form or another this statement is given by Ælian (*De. Nat. Animal.*, iv. 49), Aristotle (*Hist. An.*, iv. 7), Porphyry (*De Abstinentia*, iv. 9), Pliny (*Nat. Hist.*, xi. 20 ff.), etc. Of the man-headed lion at Gîzeh, i.e., the Sphinx, Pliny, Diodorus, Strabo, and other ancient writers have given long descriptions, and all of them seem to take for granted the existence of such a creature.

The second explanation, which declares that composite animals are the result of the imagination of peoples who have no knowledge, or at all events a defective one, of the common facts of natural history is not satisfactory, for the simple reason that composite animals which are partly animal and partly human in their powers and characteristics form the logical link between animals and man, and as such they belong to a certain period and stage of development in the history of every primitive people. If we think for a moment we shall see that many of the gods of Egypt are closely connected with this stage of development, and that comparatively few of them were ever represented wholly in man's form. The Egyptians clung to their representations of gods in animal forms with great tenacity, and even in times when it is certain they cannot have believed in their existence they continued to have them sculptured and painted upon the walls of their temples; curiously enough, they do not seem to have been sensible of the ridicule which their conservatism brought down upon them from strangers.

We have already said above that the common word given by the Egyptians to God, and god, and spirits of every kind, and beings of all sorts, and kinds, and forms, which were supposed to possess any superhuman or supernatural power, was NETER, 𓈖𓏏𓂋, and the hieroglyph which is used both as the determinative of this word and also as an ideograph is 𓊹. Thus we have 𓊹 or 𓊹𓀭, "god," and 𓊹𓏪, or 𓊹𓏥, or 𓊹𓊹𓊹, or 𓊹𓊹𓊹𓏥, "gods;" the plural is sometimes written out in full, e.g., 𓈖𓏏𓂋𓅃𓀭𓏥. The common word for "goddess" is NETERT, which can be written 𓊹𓏏𓆇, or 𓊹𓏏𓂋𓏏, or 𓊹𓏏𓂋𓏏𓆇; sometimes the determinative of the word is a woman, 𓁐, and at other times a serpent, e.g. 𓊹𓏏𓂋𓏏𓆗. The plural is NETERIT, 𓊹𓏏𓂋𓇌𓏏𓆗𓏥. We have now to consider what object is supposed to be represented by 𓊹, and what the word NETER means. In Bunsen's *Egypt's Place* (i., Nos. 556, 557, 623) the late Dr. Birch described 𓊹 as a hatchet; in 1872 Dr. Brugsch placed[1] 𓊹 among "objets tranchants, armes," in his classified list of hieroglyphic

[1] *Index des hiéroglyphes phonétiques*, No. 394.

characters; thus it is clear that the two greatest masters of Egyptology considered 𓊹 to be either a weapon or a cutting tool, and, in fact, assumed that the hieroglyphic represented an axe-head let into and fastened in a long wooden handle. From the texts wherein the hieroglyphics are coloured it is tolerably clear that the axe-head was fastened to its handle by means of thongs of leather. The earliest axe-heads were made of stone, or flint or chert, and later of metal, and it is certain that when copper, bronze, and iron took the place of stone or flint, the method by which the head was fastened to the handle was considerably modified. Recently an attempt has been made to show that the axe, 𓊹, resembled in outline "a roll of "yellow cloth, the lower part bound or laced over, the upper part "appearing as a flap at the top probably for unwinding. It is "possible, indeed, that the present object represents a fetish, e.g., "a bone carefully wound round with cloth and not the cloth "alone."[1] But it need hardly be said that no evidence for the correctness of these views is forthcoming. Whether the hieroglyphic 𓊹 was copied from something which was a roll of cloth or a fetish matters little, for the only rational determination of the character is that which has already been made by Drs. Birch and Brugsch, and the object which is represented by 𓊹 is, in the writer's opinion, an axe and nothing else.

Mr. Legge has collected[2] a number of examples of the presence of the axe as an emblem of divinity on the megaliths of Brittany and in the prehistoric remains of the funeral caves of the Marne, of Scandinavia, and of America, and, what is very much to the point, he refers to an agate cylinder which was published by the late Adrien de Longpérier, wherein is a representation of a priest in Chaldaean garb offering sacrifice to an axe standing upright upon an altar. Mr. Legge points out "that the axe "appears on these monuments not as the representation of an "object in daily use, but for religious or magical purposes," and goes on to say that this is proved by "the fact that it is often "found as a pendant and of such materials as gold, lead, and even "amber; while that it is often represented with the peculiar "fastenings of the earlier flint weapon shows that its symbolic use

[1] Griffith, *Hieroglyphs*, p. 46. [2] *Proc. Soc. Bibl. Arch.*, 1899, p. 310.

"goes back to the neolithic and perhaps the palaeolithic age." He is undoubtedly correct in thinking that the use of the stone axe precedes that of the flint arrow-head or flint knife, and many facts could be adduced in support of this view. The stone tied to the end of a stick formed an effective club, which was probably the earliest weapon known to the predynastic Egyptians, and subsequently man found that this weapon could be made more effective still by making the stone flat and by rubbing down one end of it to form a cutting edge. The earliest axe-head had a cutting edge at each end, and was tied by leather thongs to the end of a stick by the middle, thus becoming a double axe; examples of such a weapon appear to be given on the green slate object of the archaic period which is preserved in the British Museum[1] (Nos. 20,790, 20,792), where, however, the axe-heads appear to be fixed in forked wooden handles. In its next form the axe-head has only one cutting edge, and the back of it is shaped for fastening to a handle by means of leather thongs. When we consider the importance that the axe, whether as a weapon or tool, was to primitive man, we need not wonder that it became to him first the symbol of physical force, or strength, and then of divinity or dominion. By means of the axe the predynastic Egyptians cut down trees and slaughtered animals, in other words, the weapon was mightier than the spirits or gods who dwelt in the trees and the animals, and as such became to them at a very early period an object of reverence and devotion. But besides this the axe must have been used in sacrificial ceremonies, wherein it would necessarily acquire great importance, and would easily pass into the symbol of the ceremonies themselves. The shape of the axe-head as given by the common hieroglyphic 𓊹 suggests that the head was made of metal when the Egyptians first began to use the character as the symbol of divinity, and it is clear that this change in the material of which the axe-head was made would make the weapon more effective than ever.

Taking for granted, then, that the hieroglyphic 𓊹 represents an axe, we may be sure that it was used as a symbol of power and

[1] See my *History of Egypt*, vol. ii., p. 10, where it is figured and described.

divinity by the predynastic Egyptians long before the period when they were able to write, but we have no means of knowing what they called the character or the axe before that period. In dynastic times they certainly called it NETER as we have seen, but another difficulty presents itself to us when we try to find a word that will express the meaning which they attached to the word; it is most important to obtain some idea of this meaning, for at the base of it lies, no doubt, the Egyptian conception of divinity or God. The word NETER has been discussed by many Egyptologists, but their conclusions as to its signification are not identical. M. Pierret thought in 1879 that the true meaning of the word is "renewal, because in the mythological conception, the god assures "himself everlasting youth by the renewal of himself in engender-"ing himself perpetually."[1] In the same year, in one of the Hibbert Lectures, Renouf declared that he was "able to affirm "with certainty that in this particular case we can accurately "determine the primitive notion attached to the word," i.e., to NUTAR (NETER). According to him, "none of the explanations "hitherto given of it can be considered satisfactory," but he thought that the explanation which he was about to propose would "be generally accepted by scholars," because it was "arrived at as "the result of a special study of all the published passages in which "the word occurs."[2] Closely allied to NUTAR (NETER) is another word NUTRA (NETRA), and the meaning of both was said by Renouf to be found in the Coptic ⲛⲟⲩⲧⲉ or ⲛⲟⲩϯ, which, as we may see from the passages quoted by Tatham in his *Lexicon* (p. 310), is rendered by the Greek words ἰσχὺς, παράκλησις, and παρακαλεῖν. The primary meaning of the word ⲛⲟⲩϯ appears to be "strong," and having assumed that NETER was equivalent in meaning to this word, Renouf stated boldly that NETER signified "mighty," "might," "strong," and argued that it meant Power, "which is "also the meaning of the Hebrew El." We may note in passing

[1] "Le mot par lequel on rendait l'idée de Dieu  *nuter*, signifie au "propre, 'renouvellement,' parce que dans la conception mythologique, le dieu "s'assure une éternelle jeunesse par le renouvellement de lui-même, en s'engendrant "lui-même perpétuellement." *Essai sur la Mythologie Égyptienne*, Paris, 1879, p. 8.

[2] *Religion of Ancient Egypt*, p. 93.

that the exact meaning of "El," the Hebrew name for God, is unknown, and that the word itself is probably the name of an ancient Semitic deity.

The passages which were quoted to prove that NETER meant "strong, strength, power," and the like could, as M. Maspero has said,[1] be explained differently. M. Maspero combats rightly the attempt to make "strong" the meaning of NETER (masc.), or NETERIT (fem.), in these words: "In the expressions 'a town "*neterit*,' 'an arm *neteri*,' . . . . is it certain that 'a strong city,' "'a strong arm,' gives us the primitive sense of *neter?* When "among ourselves one says 'divine music,' 'a piece of divine "poetry,' 'the divine taste of a peach,' 'the divine beauty of a "woman' [the word] divine is a hyperbole, but it would be a "mistake to declare that it originally meant 'exquisite' because "in the phrases which I have imagined one could apply it as "'exquisite music,' 'a piece of exquisite poetry,' 'the exquisite "taste of a peach,' 'the exquisite beauty of a woman.' Similarly "in Egyptian 'a town *neterit*' is a 'divine town'; 'an arm "*neteri*' is 'a divine arm,' and *neteri* is employed metaphorically "in Egyptian as is [the word] 'divine' in French, without its "being any more necessary to attribute to [the word] *neteri* the "primitive meaning of 'strong,' than it is to attribute to [the "word] 'divine' the primitive meaning of 'exquisite.' The "meaning 'strong' of *neteri*, if it exists, is a derived and not an "original meaning."[2]

The view taken about the meaning of *neter* by the late Dr. Brugsch was entirely different, for he thought that the fundamental meaning of the word was "the operative power which "created and produced things by periodical recurrence, and gave "them new life and restored to them the freshness of youth (die "thätige Kraft, welche in periodischer Wiederkehr die Dinge "erzeugt und erschafft, ihnen neues Leben verleiht und die "Jugendfrische zurückgiebt."[3] The first part of the work from which these words are quoted appeared in 1885, but that Dr. Brugsch held much the same views six years later is evident

[1] *Études de Mythologie et d'Archéologie Égyptiennes*, tom. ii., p. 215.

[2] Maspero, op. cit., p. 215.

[3] *Religion und Mythologie*, p. 93.

from the following extract from his volume entitled *Die Aegyptologie* (p. 166), which appeared in 1891. Referring to Renouf's contention that NETER has a meaning equivalent to the Greek *δύναμις*, he says, "Es liegt auf der Hand, dass der Gottesname in "Sinne von Starker, Mächtiger, vieles fur sich hat, um so mehr "als selbst leblose Gegenstände, wie z. B. ein Baustein, adjek-"tivisch als *nutri* d. h. stark, mächtig, nicht selten bezeichnet "werden. Aber so vieles diese Erklärung für sich zu haben "schient, so wenig stimmt sie zu der Thatsache, dass in den "Texten aus der besten Zeit (XVIII Dynastie) das Wort *nutr* als "ein Synonym für die Vorstellung der Verjungung oder Erneue-"rung auftritt. Es diente zum Ausdruck der periodisch wieder-"kehrenden Jugendfrische nach Alter und Tod, so dass selbst dem "Menschen in den ältesten Sarginschriften zugerufen wird, er sei "fortan in einen Gott d. h. in ein Wesen mit jugendlicher Frische "umgewandelt. Ich lasse es dahin gestellt sein, nach welcher "Richtung hin die aufgeworfene Streitfrage zu Gunsten der einen "oder der anderen Auffassung entschieden werden wird; hier "sei nur betont, dass das Wort 𓊹 *nutr*, *nuṭe*, den eigentlichen "Gottesbegriff der alten Aegypter in sich schliesst und daher einen "ganz besonderen Aufmerksamkeit werth ist."

In this passage Dr. Brugsch substantially agrees with Pierret's views quoted above, but he appears to have withdrawn from the position which he took up in his *Religion und Mythologie*, wherein he asserted that the essential meaning of NETER was identical with that of the Greek *φυσις* and the Latin "natura."[1] It need hardly be said that there are no good grounds for such an assertion, and it is difficult to see how the eminent Egyptologist could attempt to compare the conceptions of God formed by a half-civilized African people with those of such cultured nations as the Greeks and the Romans.

The solution of the difficulty of finding a meaning for NETER is not brought any nearer when we consider the views of such distinguished Egyptologists as E. de Rougé, Lieblein, and Maspero.

[1] "Der Inbegriff dieses Wortes deckt sich daher vollständig mit der ur-"sprünglichen Bedeutung des griechischen *physis* und des lateinischen *natura*." (p. 93.)

The first of these in commenting on the passage 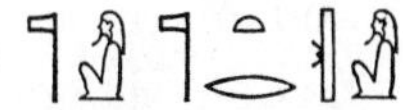 (variant ) , which he translates "Dieu "devenant dieu (en) s'engendrant lui-même," says in his excellent *Chrestomathie Égyptienne* (iii. p. 24), "One knows not exactly the "meaning of the verb *nuter*, which forms the radical of the word "*nuter*, 'god.' It is an idea analagous to 'to become,' or 'renew "oneself,' for *nuteri* is applied to the resuscitated soul which "clothes itself in its immortal form." Thus we find that one of the greatest Egyptologists thinks that the exact meaning of NETER is unknown, but he suggests that it may have a signification not unlike that proposed by Pierret. Prof. Lieblein goes a step further than E. de Rougé, for he is of opinion that it is impossible to show the first origin of the idea of God among any people hitherto known historically. "When we, for instance, take the Indo-"Europeans, what do we find there? The Sanskrit word *deva* is "identical with the Latin *deus*, and the northern *tivi*, *tivar;* as "now the word in Latin and northern language signifies God it "must also in Sanskrit from the beginning have had the same "signification. That is to say, the Arians, or Indo-Europeans, "must have combined the idea of God with this word, as early as "when they still lived together in their original home. Because, "if the word in their pre-historic home had had another more "primitive signification, the wonder would have happened, that "the word had accidentally gone through the same development "of signification with all these people after their separation. As "this is quite improbable, the word must have had the significa-"tion of God in the original Indo-European language. One could "go even farther and presume that, in this language also, it was "a word derived from others, and consequently originated from a "still earlier pre-historic language. All things considered it is "possible, even probable, that the idea of God has developed itself "in an earlier period of languages, than the Indo-European. The "future will perhaps be able to supply evidence for this. The "science of languages has been able partly to reconstruct an Indo-"European pre-historic language. It might be able also to "reconstruct a pre-historic Semitic, and a pre-historic Hamitic, "and of these three pre-historic languages, whose original connexion it not only guesses, but even commences to prove gradually, it will, we trust in time, be able to extract a still earlier pre-historic language, which according to analogy might be called Noahitic. When we have come so far, we shall most likely in this pre-historic language, also find words expressing the idea of God. But it is even possible that the idea of God has not come into existence in this pre-historic language either. It may be that the first dawning of the idea, and the word God should be ascribed to still earlier languages, to layers of languages so deeply buried that it will be impossible even to excavate them. Between the time of inhabiting caves in the quaternian period, and the historical kingdoms, there is such a long space of time, that it is difficult to entertain the idea, that it was quite devoid of any conception of divinity, so that this should first have sprung up in the historical time. In any case we shall not be able to prove historically where and when the question first arose, who are the superhuman powers whose activity we see daily in nature and in human life. Although the Egyptians are the earliest civilized people known in history, and just therefore especially important for the science of religion, yet it is even there impossible to point out the origin of the conception of the deity. The oldest monuments of Egypt bring before us the gods of nature chiefly, and among these especially the sun. They mention, however, already early (in the IVth and Vth Dynasties) now and then the great power, or the great God, it being uncertain whether this refers to the sun, or another god of nature, or if it was a general appellation of the vague idea of a supernatural power, possibly inherited by the Egyptians. It is probably this great God indicated on the monuments, from the the IVth Dynasty, and later on, who has given occasion to the false belief that the oldest religion of the Egyptians was pure monotheism. But firstly, it must be observed, that he is not mentioned alone but alongside of the other gods, secondly, that he is merely called 'The great God,' being otherwise without distinguishing appellations, and a God of whom nothing else is mentioned, has, so to speak, to use Hegel's language, merely an "abstract existence, that by closer examination dissolves into "nothing."

It is necessary to quote Professor Lieblein's opinion at length because he was one of the first to discuss the earliest idea of God in connection with its alleged similarity to that evolved by Aryan nations; if, however, he were to rewrite the passage given above in the light of modern research he would, we think, modify many of his conclusions. For our present purpose it is sufficient to note that he believes it is impossible to point out the origin of the conception of the deity among the Egyptians. The last opinion which we need quote is that of M. Maspero, who not only says boldly that if the word NETER or NETRI really has the meaning of "strong" it is a derived and not an original meaning, and he prefers to declare that the word is so old that its earliest signification is unknown. In other words, it has the meaning of god, but it teaches us nothing as to the primitive value of this word. We must be careful, he says, not to let it suggest the modern religious or philosophical definitions of god which are current to-day, for an Egyptian god is a being who is born and dies, like man, and is finite, imperfect, and corporeal, and is endowed with passions, and virtues, and vices.[2] This statement is, of course, true as regards the gods of the Egyptians at several periods of their history, but it must be distinctly understood, and it cannot be too plainly stated, that side by side with such conceptions there existed, at least among the educated Egyptians, ideas of monotheism which are not far removed from those of modern nations.

From what has been said above we see that some scholars take the view that the word NETER may mean "renewal," or "strength," or "strong," or "to become," or some idea which suggests "renewal," and that others think its original meaning is not only unknown, but that it is impossible to find it out. But although we may not be able to discover the exact meaning which the word had in predynastic times, we may gain some idea of the meaning which was attached to it in the dynastic period by an examination of a few passages from the hymns and Chapters which are found in the

[1] *Egyptian Religion*, by J. Lieblein, Leipzig, 1884.

[2] *La Mythologie Égyptienne* (*Études de Mythologie*, tom. ii., p. 215).

various versions of the *Book of the Dead.* In the text of Pepi I. (line 191) we have the words:—"Behold thy son Horus, to whom "thou hast given birth. He hath not placed this Pepi at the "head of the dead, but he hath set him among the gods *neteru*,"

 Now here *neteru*, ..., must be an adjective, and we are clearly intended to understand that the gods referred to are those which have the attribute of *neteru*; since the "gods *neteru*," ..., are mentioned in opposition to "the dead" it seems as if we are to regard the gods as "living," i.e., to possess the quality of life. In the text of the same king (line 419) a *bāk neter*, ..., i.e., a hawk having the quality of *neter* is mentioned; and in the text of Unȧs (line 569) we read of *baui netrui*, ..., or the two souls which possess the quality of *neter*. These examples belong to the Vth and VIth Dynasties. Passing to later dynasties, i.e., the XVIIIth and XIXth, etc., we find the following examples of the use of the words *neter* and *netri*:—

1. 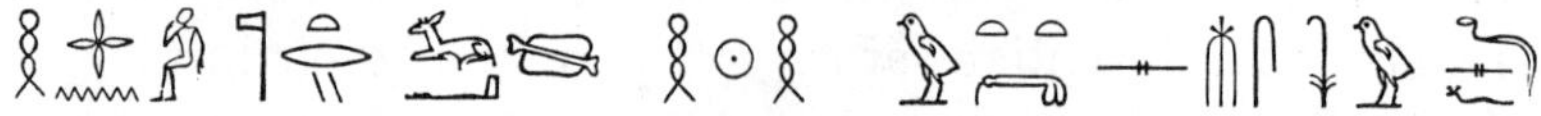 [1]

*ḥun* *netri* *aā* *ḥeḥ* *utet* *se-mes* *su* *tchesef*

Boy *netri*, heir of eternity, begetting and giving birth to himself.

2. 

*ṭā-ȧ* *tū* *em* *ȧb-ȧ* *ȧti* *bakai* *netri*

I am devoted in my heart without feigning, O thou *netri*

 [2]

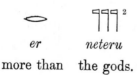

*er* *neteru*

more than the gods.

[1] See my *Chapters of Coming Forth by Day*, Text, p. 11, l. 10.

[2] *Ibid.*, p. 43, l. 4.

3.  [1]

*tchet - tu* *re* *pen* *her* *mahu* *en* *netràt*

Shall be said this chapter over a crown of *netràt*.

4.  [2]

*neter - kuà*

I have become *neter*.

5.  [3]

*àu - à* *khā - kuà* *em* *bàk* *netri*

I have risen up in the form of a hawk *netri*.

6. 

*āb - kuà* *neter - kuà* *khu - kuà*

I have become pure, I have become *neter*, I have become a spirit (*khu*),

 [4]

*user - kuà* *ba - kuà*

I have become strong, I have become a soul (*ba*).

7. 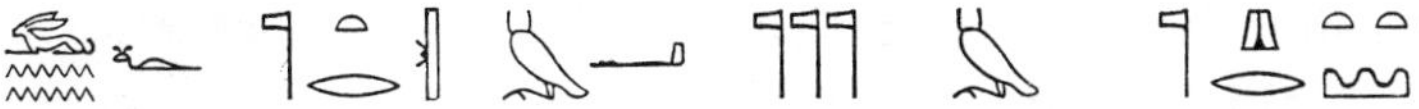 [5]

*unen-f* *neter* *mā* *neteru* *em* *Neter-khertet*

His being (or, he shall be) *neter* with the gods in the Neter-khertet.

8.  [6]

*àu - f* *netrà* *khat-f* *temtu*

He shall *netrà* his body all.

[1] See my *Chapters of Coming Forth by Day*, p. 80, l. 10.
[2] *Ibid.*, p. 154, l. 6.
[3] *Ibid.*, p. 168, l. 3.
[4] *Ibid.*, p. 174, l. 15.
[5] *Ibid.*, p. 417, l. 12.
[6] *Ibid.*, p. 419, l. 7.

9.  [1]

*netri* *u* *ba* - *k* *em* *per* *Sebut*

They make *neter* thy soul in the house of Sebut.

10.  [2]

*netri* - *f* *ba* - *k* *mȧ* *neteru*

He makes *neter* thy soul like the gods.

11.  [3]

*neter* *netri* *kheper tchesef* *paut*

God *netri*, self-produced, primeval matter.

Now, in the above examples it is easy to see that although the words "strong" or "strength," when applied to translate *neter* or *netri*, give a tolerably suitable sense in some of them, it is quite out of place in others, e.g., in No. 6, where the deceased is made to say that he has acquired the quality of *neter*, and a spirit, and a soul, and is, moreover, strong; the word rendered "strong" in this passage is *user*, and it expresses an entirely different idea from *neter*. From the fact that *neter* is mentioned in No. 1 in connection with eternal existence, and self-begetting, and self-production, and in No. 11 with self-production and primeval matter, it is almost impossible not to think that the word has a meaning which is closely allied to the ideas of "self-existence," and the power to "renew life indefinitely," and "self-production." In other words, *neter* appears to mean a being who has the power to generate life, and to maintain it when generated. It is useless to attempt to explain the word by Coptic etymologies, for it has passed over directly into the Coptic language under the forms *nouti* **ⲛⲟⲩϯ**, and *noute* **ⲛⲟⲩⲧⲉ**, the last consonant, *r*, having disappeared through phonetic decay, and the translators of the Holy Scriptures from that language used it to express the words "God" and "Lord." Meanwhile, until new light is thrown upon the subject by the discovery of inscrip-

[1] See my *Chapters of Coming Forth by Day*, Text, p. 509, l. 13.

[2] *Ibid*, p. 511, l. 13.

[3] *Ibid*, p. 49, l. 1.

tions older than any which we now have, we must be content to accept the approximate meaning of *neter* suggested above.

The worship of the gods (*neteru*), which began far away back in predynastic times, continued through the archaic and dynastic periods, and lasted until the IVth or Vth century of our era; it is tolerably certain that in respect of some of them the ideas of the Egyptians never changed, but, as regards others, their views did not remain as constant as some writers would have us imagine. In the earliest days every village community in Egypt had its local god, who shared the good or evil fortune of the community to which he belonged. His emblem or symbol was carried out to war, and was, of course, present at all great public gatherings when matters connected with the welfare of his devotees were discussed. A special habitation was set apart for him, and its upkeep was provided for out of common funds. As the riches of the people of the village increased, the rank and dignity of their god kept pace with them, but his revenues suffered in times of scarcity, and defeat, and war; his emblem might even be carried off into captivity and burnt, or smashed, when, of course, the spirit which dwelt in his symbol was also destroyed. The number of such early gods was legion, for many large communities possessed several gods, each of which was famed locally for some particular attribute. When a man left one village and settled in another he took his god or gods with him, but he would be obliged to acknowledge the god of the village or city in which he had made his new abode, and to contribute towards the maintenance of his house and its small compound. The reduction in the number of the gods of Egypt began when man first realized that certain gods were mightier than others, for he ceased gradually to worship those who had, in his opinion, failed to justify his belief in them, and transferred his allegiance to the gods who were able to give him the most help. In process of time the god or goddess of a certain village or town would obtain a fame and reputation for power which would outrival those of the deities of the neighbouring cities, and the growth of the worship of such god or goddess would be accompanied by a corresponding decline in that of the gods in the towns round about. The gods, in the first instance, grew by a process of selection out of the spirits who were well disposed towards man and were helpful to him, and the "great gods" of the Egyptians were evolved, practically, in a somewhat similar manner. It is at present hopeless to attempt to enumerate all the gods who were, from first to last, worshipped by the Egyptians, for it will not be possible to do this until every text extant has been published. Meanwhile an examination of the earliest Egyptian religious literature known to us proves that a number of gods who were of some importance in the polytheistic system of the Early Empire dropped out from it long before the period of the New Empire, and thus it is very doubtful if we shall ever be able to collect the names of all the gods who have been worshipped in the Valley of the Nile between the Archaic and Roman periods, whilst to make a list of all the predynastic gods is manifestly impossible.

Future discoveries in Egypt may produce texts that will tell us which were the favourite gods in the archaic period and give us some idea as to the pronunciation of their names, for we have reason to think that during the greater part of that period the Egyptians were able to write. If ever such texts are brought to light we shall probably find that the gods who were worshipped during the archaic period were those who were popular in the predynastic period, just as we find that the gods of the Egyptians of the Middle and New Empires were to all intents and purposes the same as those of the Egyptians of the Early Empire. Speaking generally, it may be said that the Egyptians of the greater part of the dynastic period of their history invented few new gods, and that they were well content to worship such deities as were known to their ancestors; we know that they admitted, at times, foreign gods into the assembly of the old Egyptian gods, but the religious texts prove that they were never allowed to usurp the functions of the indigenous gods. Political and other reasons might secure for them a certain amount of recognition in the country generally, and the people of the cities where their emblems and statues found resting-places treated them with the easy toleration which is so marked a characteristic of many countries in the East; but as soon as such reasons disappeared the foreign gods were quietly ignored, and in a short time their worship was forgotten. This statement is not intended to apply to the gods who were introduced from one city or district of Egypt into another, for we know that the Egyptian priesthood and people of a given city were ready to show hospitality to almost any god of any town, or city, or district, provided that he belonged to the same *company* as that of which the chief local god was a member.

We have, unfortunately, no long connected religious texts in the forms in which they must have existed under the first four dynasties, and we cannot therefore say what gods were worshipped during that period. There is, as has been shown elsewhere,[1] good reason for believing that some parts of the *Book of the Dead* were revised or edited during the early part of the period of the Ist Dynasty, and if this be so we may assume that the religious system of the Egyptians as revealed in the texts of a much later time closely resembled that which was in existence in the later part of the archaic period, i.e., during the first three dynasties. Under the Vth and VIth Dynasties we touch firmer ground, and we find abundant, though not complete, materials for the study of the gods of Egypt and their attributes in the lengthy hieroglyphic texts which were inscribed inside the pyramid tombs of Unȧs, Tetȧ, Pepi I., Mer-en-Rā-Meḥti-em-sa-f, and Pepi II. An examination of these texts reveals the existence of an established theological system in Egypt, and we find that even at that time the literature in which it was, more or less, expounded, contained innumerable layers of religious thought and expressions of belief which belonged to periods many of which must have been separated by long intervals of time. The gods are mentioned in such a way as to prove that the writers of the texts, or at least the copyists, assumed that the reader would be well acquainted with the subject matter of the compositions, and from first to last neither explanation nor gloss is to be found in them. The texts are, of course, sepulchral, and the greater number of the gods mentioned in them are referred to in their characters as gods who deal with the souls of the dead in the world beyond the grave.

The Sun-god Rā and the gods of his cycle, and Osiris, the god and judge of the dead, and the gods of his cycle, have definite

[1] See my *Book of the Dead*, London, 1901, vol. i., p. xxxiii.

positions and duties assigned to them, and it is very clear that both the texts which describe these and the ceremonies which were performed in connection with the words recited by the priests were, even under the Vth Dynasty, extremely ancient. Moreover, it is certain that the religious texts in use for funeral purposes under that dynasty are substantially those which were compiled several centuries before. We may note in passing that the funeral books were edited by the priests of Ȧnnu or Ȧnu, i.e., Heliopolis, and as a result they exhibit traces of the influence of the theological opinions of the great priestly college of that city; but at bottom the views and beliefs which may be deduced from them, and the fundamental conceptions to which they give expression are the products of the minds of the predynastic, indigenous Egyptians. To the consideration of the Heliopolitan religious system we shall return later, and we may therefore pass on to the enumeration of the principal gods who are made known to us by the Pyramid Texts at Ṣaḳḳâra. Among the great gods who were certainly worshipped in the early archaic period may be mentioned :—

| | |
|---|---|
| Ptaḥ (Tetȧ 88) 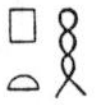 | Ḥeru,[3] or Horus (Mer-en-Rā 454)  |
| Nu (Unȧs 199)  [1] | Kheper (Unȧs 444)  |
| Net, or Neith (Unȧs 67)  [2] | Khepera (Pepi II. 856)  |
| Rā (*passim*)  | Khnemu (Unȧs 556)  |
| Ḥet-Ḥeru (Hathor)  | Sebek (Unȧs 565)  |

Of these gods Heru, or Horus, was the hawk-god, i.e., the spirit and personification of the "height" of heaven; Kheper was the beetle-god; Khnemu the ram-god; and Sebek the crocodile-god; Net or Neith was originally a wood-spirit, Rā and Ptah were two forms of the Sun-god, and Nu was the watery mass of heaven

1 Or,  (Unȧs, 399), or  (Teta, 78).

2 Or,  (Unȧs, 272).

3 Or,  Ḥeru-ur, "Horus the elder" (Unas, 358).

in which he lived. With Rā and Kheper the priests of Heliopolis associated the form of the Sun-god which was specially worshipped in their city, and thus we have mentioned the compound gods Rā-Tem (Unȧs 216, 224, Mer-en-Rā 458), and Tem-Kheprer (Pepi II. 662). In the text of Unȧs (line 626) Sebek is styled "son of Net," , and he is also called "lord of Baru," (line 565); but if the XVIIIth Dynasty texts be correct the name of this place is misspelt, and in any case it must be identical with the Bakhau, , or Mountain of the Sunrise of Chapter cviii. of the *Book of the Dead.* The following is a list of the other principal gods mentioned in the Pyramid Texts:—

Aḥu (Pepi II. 850) [1]

Aker (Unȧs 498, 614, Tetȧ 309)

Ȧpi (Unȧs 487)

Ȧp-uat (Unȧs 187)

Ȧmen (Unȧs 557)

Ȧment (Unȧs 557)

Ȧm-ḥenth-f (Pepi I. 666)

Ȧm-sepa-f (Pepi I. 666)

Ȧmsu or Min (Unȧs 377)

Ȧmset (Tetȧ 60, 197)

Ȧnȧ (Unȧs 272, 275)

Ȧnpu (Unȧs 71, 207, 219)

Ȧn-mut-f (Pepi II. 772)

Ȧn-tcher-f (Pepi I. 651)

Ȧkhet-nen-thȧ (Tetȧ 307)

Ȧsȧr, Osiris (*passim*)

Ȧst, Isis (Unȧs 181)

Ȧsken (Pepi II. 1324)

Ȧṭer-ȧsfet (Pepi II. 980)

Ānkh (Pepi I. 672)

[1] Aḥu appears to be identical with , who is Ȧmsu or Min ; see Pepi II., l. 1320.

I-en-ḥer-pes (Unȧs 392)

Uaḥu (Tetȧ 333)

Ur-sheps-f (Pepi I. 671)

Urt (Unȧs 272)

Urt-ḥekau (Unȧs 269)

Usert (Unȧs 229)

Uthes (Pepi II. 976)

Ba (Mer-en-Rā 784)

Babȧ (Unȧs 532)

Babi (Unȧs 644, 647)

Baȧbu (Pepi I. 568)

Babuȧ (Pepi I. 604) [1]

Bastet (Pepi I. 569) [2]

Ba-āshem-f (Mer-en-Rā 784)

Penṭ (Unȧs 280)

Pesetchet (Unȧs 417)

Maat-Khnemu (Pepi I. 445)

Maāt (Unȧs 220)

Mut (Unȧs 181). The variants are

Ment (Pepi II. 849)

Menṭef (Pepi II. 1228)

Menth (Mer-en-Rā 784)

Meḥt-urt (Unȧs 427, 623)

Meḥt-urt (Unȧs 427, 623)

Em-khent-maati (Pepi I. 645)

Em-khent-maati (Pepi I. 645)

Meskha (Unȧs 567)

Meskhaat (Pepi I. 671)

Metchetȧt (Pepi II. 956)

Nȧu (Unȧs 557)

Nubt (Unȧs 479)

Nebt-ḥet (Unȧs 220),

Nefer-Tem (Unȧs 395)

[1] This god is said to have a "red ear".   [2] Var.

Enen (Unȧs 557)
Enenet (Unȧs 240)

Nekhben (Unȧs 459)

Neḥebkau (Unȧs 559)

Nekhebet (Mer-en-Rā 762)

Neḥt (Unȧs 601)

Nesert (Unȧs 269)

Neṭi (Unȧs 279)

Netetthȧb (Unȧs 598)

Renenut (Unȧs 441)

Ruruthȧ (Pepi II. 976, 979)

Hep̦ath (Pepi I. 636)

Henenȧ (Pepi I. 636)

Hetchhetch (Pepi I. 173)

Heṭṭenuut (Tetȧ, 332)

Ḥu (Unȧs 439)

Ḥep (Unȧs 187)

Ḥep-ur (Unȧs 431)

Ḥep (Tetȧ 60, 197)

Ḥem (Pepi I. 641)

Ḥemen (Pepi II. 850)

Ḥen-pesetchti (Tetȧ 309)

Ḥent (Unȧs 417)

Ḥunt (Tetȧ 357)

Ḥeru (*passim*)

Ḥeru-ȧāḥ (Tetȧ 365)

Ḥeru-ȧm-ḥenu (Unȧs 211)

Ḥeru-khent-peru (Unȧs 202)

Ḥeru-khesbetch-maati(Unȧs369)

Ḥeru-khutthȧ (Unȧs 471)

Ḥeru-Sepṭ (Unȧs 465)

Ḥeru-ṭesher-maati (Unȧs 369)

Ḥeru-Ṭat (Unȧs 218)

Ḥeru-kharṭ (Tetȧ 301)

Ḥrȧ-f-ḥa-f (Pepi I.)

Ḥer-ḥepes (Unȧs 226)

Ḥesat (Pepi II. 976)

Ḥesmennu (Mer-en-Rā 670)

Ḥet-Ḥert (Unȧs 575)

Ḥeka (Pepi I. 583)

Ḥeqet (Pepi I. 570)

Khāȧta (Unȧs 536)

Khebetch (Unȧs 434)

Khent-Ȧmenti (Unȧs 201)

Khent-maati (Unȧs 218)

Khnemu (Unȧs 556, Pepi I. 455)

Khensu (Unȧs 510)

Khensu-Sepṭ (Unȧs 588)

Sȧa (Unȧs 439)

Sathet (Pepi I. 297)

Seb (Unȧs 234)

Sepḥu-urt (Pepi II. 976)

Sepṭ (Unȧs 219)

Sma-ur (Unȧs 280)

Smentet (Tetȧ 355)

Sunth (Pepi II. 854)[1]

Seref-ur (Tetȧ 309)

Serqet (Pepi I. 647)

Serqet-ḥetu (Tetȧ 207)

Seḥepu (Pepi I. 685)

Sekhemf (Pepi II. 978)

Sekhen-ta-en-ur (Unȧs 281)

Sekhet (Unȧs 390)

Sȧshsa (Pepi II. 975)

Seker (Pepi I. 641)[2]

Seksen (Pepi I. 650)[3]

Set (Unȧs 6)

Sethȧsethȧ (Pepi I. 265)

Seththa (Pepi I. 259)

Shu (Unȧs 185)

[1] Var. Pepi I., 352.

[2] He is identified with in Pepi II., 1320.

[3] Var.

Shesmu (Unȧs 511)

Sheskhentet (Unȧs 390)

Ḳenur (Pepi II. 979)

Ḳasut (Pepi II. 975)

Qebḥsennuf (Tetȧ 60)

Tait (Tetȧ 376)

Tebȧ (Unȧs 428)

Tefen (Unȧs 453)

Tefnut (Unȧs 453)

Tem (Unȧs 207)

Tem-khepercr (Pepi II. 662)

Tatet (Unȧs 67)

Ṭuamutef (Tetȧ 60)

Ṭenānu (Pepi I. 269)

Ṭenṭen (Unȧs 280)

Teḥuti (Unȧs 228)

Tchenṭ (Mer-en-Rā 773)

Tchenṭeru (Tetȧ 198)

Tchenṭtchenṭer (Pepi I. 301)

Besides the above gods are mentioned the "angel (or messenger) of the two gods," (Unȧs 408); and the "Āshem that dwelleth within Ȧru," (Tetȧ 351). Allusions are made to the following important stars:—

Nekhekh (Tetȧ 218), .

Sepṭet (Tetȧ 349), , i.e., the Dog Star.

Saḥ (Tetȧ 349), , i.e., Orion.

Seḥuṭ (Pepi II. 857), .

The Pyramid Texts show that in addition to the gods already enumerated there existed certain classes of beings to whom were attributed the nature of the gods, e.g.:—

The Āfu (Pepi II. 951), .

The Utennu (Pepi II. 951), .

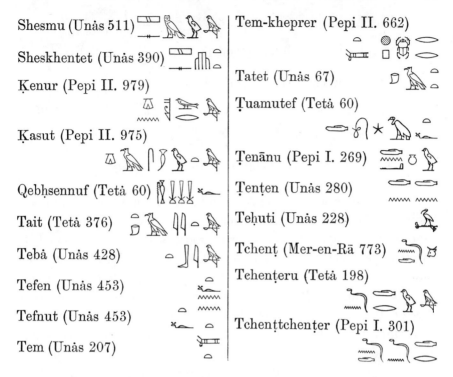

The Urshu of Pe (Pepi II. 849), 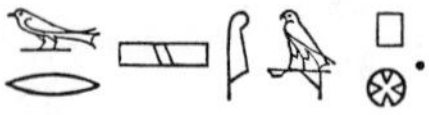.

The Urshu of Nekhen (Pepi II. 849), .

The Ḥenmemet (Unȧs 211), .

The Set beings, superior and inferior, (Pepi II. 951), .

The Shemsu Ḥeru (Pepi I. 166), .

Of the functions of the Āfu and Utennu nothing whatever is known. The Urshu, i.e., the Watchers, of Pe and Nekhen may have been groups of well-known gods, who were supposed to "watch over" and specially protect these cities; but, on the other hand, they may only have been the messengers, or angels, of the souls of Pe and Nekhen. The Ḥenmemet beings are likewise a class of divine beings about whom we have no exact information. In certain texts they are mentioned in connection with gods and men in such a manner that they are supposed to represent "unborn generations," but this rendering will not suit many of the passages in which the word occurs, and in those in which it seems to do so many other hypothetical meanings would fit the context just as well. The passage in which the Set beings are referred to must belong to the period when the god Set was regarded as a beneficent being and a god who was, with Horus, a friend and helper of the dead. The text quoted above shows that, like Horus, Set was supposed to be the head of a company of divine beings with attributes and characteristics similar to those of himself, and that this company was divided into two classes, the upper and the lower, or perhaps even the celestial and the terrestrial. Last must be mentioned the Shemsu Ḥeru, or the "Followers of Horus," to whom many references are made in funeral literature; their primary duties were to minister to the god Horus, son of Isis, but they were also supposed to help him in the performance of the duties which he undertook for the benefit of the dead. In the religious literature of the Early Empire they occupy the place of the "Mesniu," 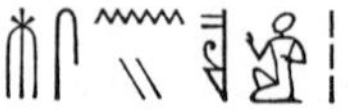, of Horus of Beḥuṭet, the modern

Edfû, i.e., the workers in metal, or blacksmiths, who are supposed to have accompanied this god into Egypt, and to have assisted him by their weapons in establishing his supremacy at Beḥuṭet, or Edfû. The exploits of this god will be described later on in the section treating of Horus generally.

In the text of Pepi I. (line 419) we have a reference to a god with four faces in the following words:—"Homage to thee, O thou "who hast four faces which rest and look in turn upon what is in "Kenset,[1] and who bringest storm . . . . .! Grant thou unto this "Pepi thy two fingers which thou hast given to the goddess Nefert, "the daughter of the great god, as messenger[s] from heaven to "earth when the gods make their appearance in heaven. Thou "art endowed with a soul, and thou dost rise [like the sun] in thy "boat of seven hundred and seventy cubits.[2] Thou hast carried in "thy boat the gods of Pe, and thou hast made content the gods of "the East. Carry thou this Pepi with thee in the cabin of thy "boat, for this Pepi is the son of the Scarab which is born in "Ḥetepet beneath the hair of the city of Iusāas the northern, and "he is the offspring of Seb. It is he who was between the legs of "Khent-maati on the night wherein he guarded (?) bread, and on "the night wherein he fashioned the heads of arrows. Thou hast "taken thy spear which is dear to thee, thy pointed weapon which "thrusteth down river banks, with a double point like the darts of "Rā, and a double haft like the claws of the goddess Mafṭet."

Throughout the Pyramid Texts frequent mention is made of one group, or of two or three groups, of nine gods. Thus in Unås (line 179) we read of "bowing low to the ground before the nine gods," ; and in line 234 we are told that the king's bread consists of "the word[3] of Seb which cometh

1 

2 

3  *tcheṭ* means literally "word," but it often is used to express "thing," "matter," like the Hebrew דָּבָר.

forth from the mouth of the nine male gods," . The god Seshaȧ, , is said in line 382 to have been "begotten by Seb and brought forth by the nine gods," ; and in line 592 Rā is said to be the "chief of the nine gods," . From several passages (e.g., Unȧs 251) we learn that one company of nine gods was called the "Great," , and that another company was called the "Little," , and the "nine gods of Horus" are spoken of side by side with "the gods,"[1] (line 443), but whether this group is to be connected with the Great or Little company of gods cannot be said. A double group of nine gods is frequently referred to, e.g., in Tetȧ, line 67, where it is said, "The eighteen gods cense Tetȧ, and his mouth is pure," ; and in Pepi I., line 273, where we read that the "two lips of Meri-Rā are the eighteen gods," ; and again in line 407, where Pepi I. is said to be "with the eighteen gods in Qebḥu," and to be the "fashioner of the eighteen gods," . We may perhaps assume that the eighteen gods include the Great and the Little companies of the gods, but, on the other hand, as "male and female gods" are mentioned[2] in the text of Tetȧ, nine of the eighteen gods may be feminine counterparts of the other nine, who must therefore be held to be masculine. But the texts of Tetȧ (line 307) and Pepi I. (line 218) show that there was a third company of nine gods recognized by the priests of Helio-

[1] Variant ; Tetȧ, l. 253.

[2] (l. 197).

polis, and we find all three companies represented thus: 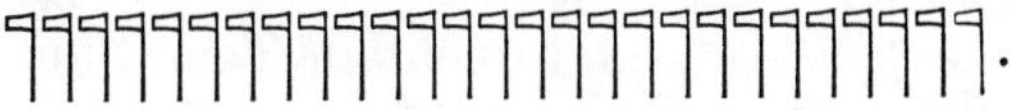.

The Egyptian word here rendered "company" is PAUTI or *paut*, which may be written either  or , and the meaning usually attached to it has been "nine." It is found in texts subsequent to the period of the pyramids at Ṣaḳḳâra thus written:—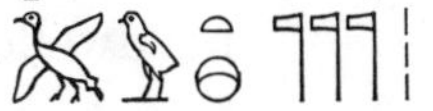 *paut neteru*, "*paut* of the gods"; the double company of the gods is expressed by  *pautti*, or we may have 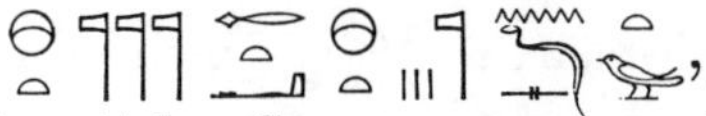, *paut neteru āat paut neteru netcheset*, i.e., "the Great company of gods and the Little company of the gods." The fact that a company of gods is represented by nine axes, , has led to the common belief that a company of the gods contained nine gods, and for this reason the word *paut* has been explained to mean "nine." It is quite true that the Egyptians frequently *assigned* nine gods to the *paut*, as we may see from such passages as Unȧs 235,[1] and especially from line 283, where it is said, "Grant thou that this Unȧs may rule the nine, and that he may complete the company of the gods," 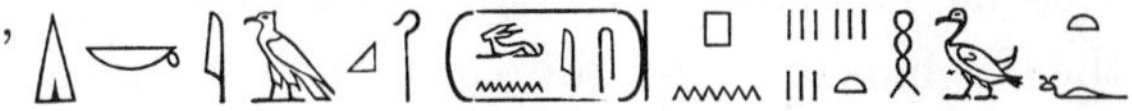 . But the last quoted passage proves that a *paut* of the gods might contain more than nine divine beings, for it is clear that if the intent of the prayer was carried out the *paut* referred to in it would contain ten, king Unȧs being added to the nine gods. Again, in a litany to the gods of the Great company given in the Unȧs text (line 240 ff.) we see that the *paut* contains Tem, Shu, Tefnut, Seb, Nut, Isis, Set, Nephthys, Thoth, and Horus, i.e., *ten* gods, without counting the deceased, who wished to be added to the number of the gods. In the text of Mer-en-Rā (line 205) the *paut* contains nine gods,[2] and it is described as the

1 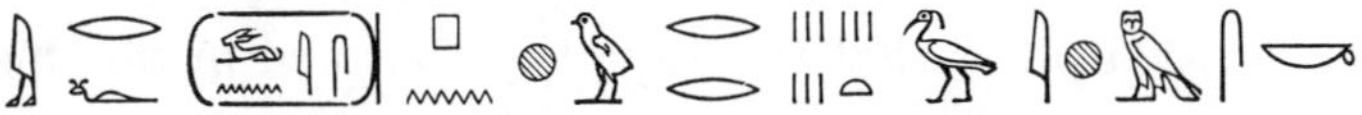.

2 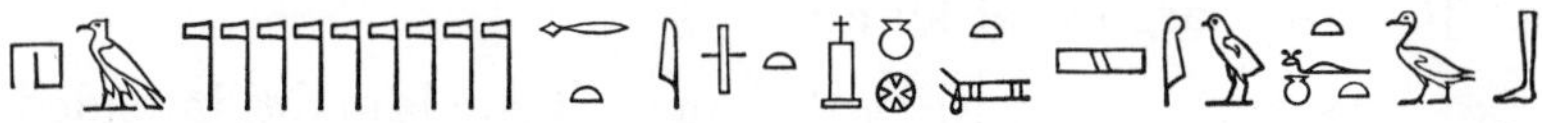 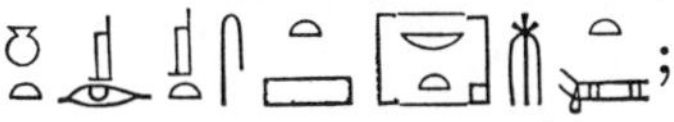; see also Pepi II., l. 665.

"Great *paut* which is in Ȧnnu" (Heliopolis), whilst in the text of Pepi II. (line 669) the same *paut* is said to contain Tem, Shu, Tefnut, Seb, Nut, Osiris, Osiris-Khent-Ȧmenti, Set, Horus, Ṙā, Khent̄-maati, and Uatchet, i.e., *twelve* gods. Similarly the gods of the Little *paut* are more than nine in number, and in Unȧs (line 253 f.) they are thus enumerated :—Ṙāt, , the dweller in Ȧnnu, 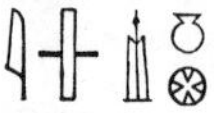, the dweller in Āntchet, 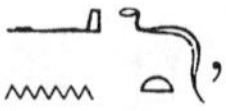, the dweller in Ḥet-Serqet, 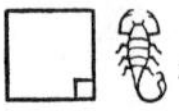, the dweller in the divine palace, , the dweller in Ḥetch-paār, 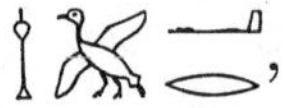, the dweller in Orion, , the dweller in Ṭep, 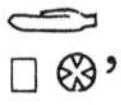, the dweller in Ḥet-ur-ka, , the dweller in Unnu of the South, , the dweller in Unnu of the North, 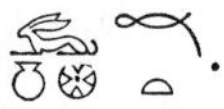.

Thus the Little *paut* contained *eleven* gods, not counting the deceased who desired to be added to their number. The fact that the *paut* contained at times more than nine gods is thus explained by M. Maspero[1]: "The number nine was the original number, "but each of the nine gods, especially the first and the last, could "be developed." Thus if it was desired to add the god Ȧmen of the Theban triad to the *paut* of Heliopolis, he could be set at the head of it either in the place of Temu, the legitimate chief of the *paut*, or side by side with him. Mut, the consort of Ȧmen, might be included in the *paut*, but Ȧmen and Mut would together only count as one god. Similarly, any one or all of the gods who belonged to the shrine of Ȧmen could be included with that god himself in the *paut* of Heliopolis, and yet the number of that *paut* was supposed to be increased only by one. In other words, the admission of one god into a *paut* brought with it the admission of all the gods who were in any way connected with him, but their names were never included among those of the original members of it. This explanation is very good as far as it goes, but it must not be taken as a proof that the Egyptians argued in this manner, or that they argued at all about it.

The nine axes  are, beyond doubt, intended to re-

[1] *La Mythologie Égyptienne*, p. 245.

present nine gods, i.e., a triad of triads, but the signs , *paut neteru*, must be translated not "Neunheit," as Brugsch rendered them,[1] but the "stuff of the nine gods," i.e., the substance or matter out of which the nine gods were made. The word *paut*, , means "dough cake," or cake of bread which formed part of the offerings made to the dead; similarly *paut* is the name given to the plastic substance out of which the earth and the gods were formed, and later, when applied to divine beings or things, it means the aggregation or entirety of such beings or things. Thus in the Papyrus of Ani (sheet i., line 6) the god Tatunen is declared to be "one, the maker of mankind, and of the "material of the gods of the South and the North, the West and "the East."[2] But there was a primeval matter out of which heaven was made, and also a [primeval] matter out of which the earth was made, and hence Kheperȧ, the great creator of all things, is said in Chapter xvii. (line 116) of the *Book of the Dead* to possess a body[3] which is formed of both classes of matter (*paut*). And again in Chapter lxxxv. (line 8) the deceased, wishing to identify himself with this divine substance, says, "I am the eldest "son of the divine *pautti*, that is to say, the soul of the souls of the "gods of everlasting, and my body is everlasting, and my creations are "eternal, and I am the lord of years, and the prince of everlasting-"ness." In the words which are put into the mouth of Kheperȧ, who is made to describe his creation of the world, the god says, "I produced myself from the [primeval] matter [which] I made,"

[1] "Der kosmogonische Lehre von der Ogdoas, deren aelteste Spuren sich bis "zu den Pyramidentexten verfolgen lassen, schloss sich die Doctrin 'der Neunheit' "(Enneas) oder der 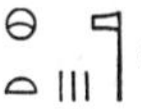 an. Sie umfasste die genetische Entstehung der neun "Theile und Kräfte, welche die zukünftige Wohnung der den Leib Gottes bildeten, "dessen Seele davon Besitz nahm, um alles mit ihr zu erfüllen." *Aegyptologie*, p. 170.

[2] 

[3] 

;[1] this is the only meaning which can be extracted from the Egyptian words, and the context, which the reader will find given in the section on the Creation, proves that it is the correct one. The word "primeval," which is added in brackets, is suggested by the texts wherein *pautti* is accompanied by  *tep*, i.e., "first," in point of time, compare ,[2] "first matter," that is to say, the earliest matter which was created, and the matter which existed before anything else. From the above facts it is clear that the meaning "Neunheit" must not be given to the Egyptian word *paut*.

We have now seen that, so far back as the Vth Dynasty, the priests of Heliopolis conceived the existence of three companies of gods; the first two they distinguished by the appellations "Great" and "Little," but to the third they gave no name. The gods of the first or "Great" company are well known, and their names are:—1. Tem, the form of the Sun-god which was worshipped at Heliopolis. 2. Shu. 3. Tefnut. 4. Seb. 5. Nut. 6. Osiris. 7. Isis. 8. Set. 9. Nephthys. Sometimes this company is formed by the addition of Horus and the omission of Tem. The names of gods of the second or "Little" company appear to be given in the text of Unȧs, line 253 ff., where we have enumerated :—1. Rāt. 2. Ȧm-Ȧnnu. 3. Ȧm-Āntchet. 4. Ȧm-Ḥet-Ṣerqet-ka-ḥetepet. 5. Ȧm-Neter-ḥet. 6. Ȧm-Ḥetch-paār. 7. Ȧm-Saḥ. 8. Ȧm-Ṭep. 9. Ȧm-Ḥet-ur-Rā. 10. Ȧm-Unnu-resu. 11. Ȧm-Unnu-meḥt. It must, however, be noted that whereas in the text the address to the Great company of the gods as a whole follows the separate addresses to each, the address to the Little company precedes the separate addresses to each; still there is no reason for doubting that the second group of names given above are really those of the Little company of the gods. The names of the gods of the third company are unknown, and the texts are silent as to the functions which the company was supposed to perform; the Great and Little companies of the gods are frequently referred to in texts of all periods, but

1 See *Archaeologia*, vol. lii., p. 557.
2 See my *Chapters of Coming Forth by Day*, Text, p. 348, l. 15.

the third company is rarely mentioned. Thus in the text of Pepi I. (line 43), the king is said to sit on an iron throne and to weigh words at the head of the Great company of gods in Ȧnnu; the two companies of the gods lift up the head of Pepi (line 97), and he takes the crown in the presence of the Great company (line 117); he sits at the head of the two companies (line 167), and in their boat (line 169); and he stands between the two companies (line 186). It has already been suggested[1] that the Great company of gods was a macrocosm of a primitive kind, and the Little company a microcosm; this view is very probably correct, and is supported by passages like the following:—"The son of his father is come with "the company of the gods of heaven, . . . the son of his father is "come with the company of the gods of earth."

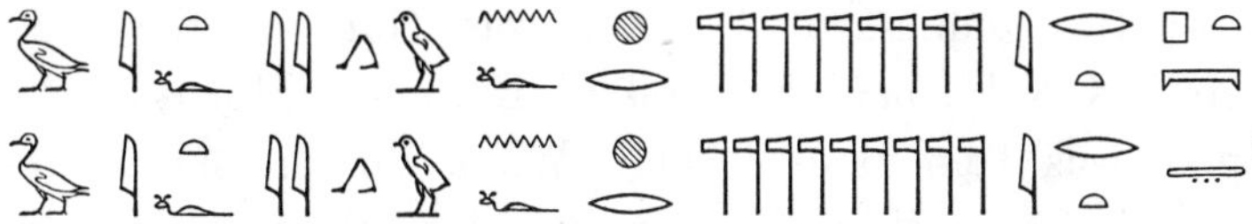[2]

From numerous passages in texts of all periods it is clear that the Egyptians believed that heaven was in many respects a duplicate of earth, and, as it was supposed to contain a celestial Nile, and sacred cities which were counterparts of those on the earth and which were called by similar names, it is only reasonable to assign to it a company of gods who were the counterparts of those on earth. And as there were gods of heaven and gods of earth, so also were there gods of the Ṭuat, or Underworld, who were either called *ṭuat*, , or , or *neteru en ṭuat*, 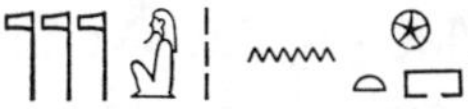. This being so, we may assume that when the writers of the Pyramid Texts mentioned three companies of the gods, , they referred to the company of the gods of heaven, the company of the gods of earth, and the company of the gods of the Underworld, meaning thereby what the writer of the XXIIIrd Chapter of the *Book of the Dead* meant when he spoke of "the

[1] Maspero, *La Mythologie Égyptienne*, p. 244.
[2] Pepi I., ll. 298–300.

"company of all the gods," . In the Pyramid Texts, however, and in the later Recensions of the *Book of the Dead* which are based upon them, the *pautti neteru*, , or 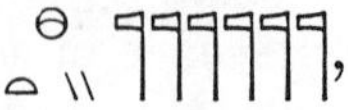, were intended to represent the Great and Little companies of the gods, and these only; the members of each company varied in different cities and in different periods, but the principle of such variation is comparatively simple. Long before the priests of Heliopolis grouped the gods of Egypt into companies certain very ancient cities had their own special gods whom they probably inherited from their predecessors, i.e., the predynastic Egyptians. Thus the goddess of Saïs was Nit, or Net, or Neith; the goddess of Per-Uatchet was Uatchet; the goddess of Dendera was Hathor; the goddess of Nekheb was Nekhebet; the god of Edfû was Horus; the god of Heliopolis was Tem; and so on. When the priests of these and other cities found that, for some reason, they were obliged to accept the theological system formulated by the priests of Heliopolis and its Great company of gods, they did so readily enough, but they always made the great local god or goddess the head or chief, 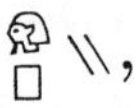, of the company.

At Heliopolis, where the chief local god was called Tem, the priests joined their god to Rā, and addressed many of their prayers and hymns to Tem-Rā or Rā-Tem. At Edfû the great local god Horus of Beḥutet was either made to take the place of Tem, or was added to the Heliopolitan company in one form or another. The same thing happened in the case of goddesses like Neith, Uatchet, Nekhebet, Hathor, etc. It was found to be hopeless to attempt to substitute the Heliopolitan company of gods for Neith in the city of Saïs, because there the worship of that goddess was extremely ancient and was very important. The fact that her name forms a component part of royal names very early in the Ist Dynasty proves that her worship dates from the first half of the archaic period, and that it is much older than the theological system of Heliopolis. But when the priests of Saïs adopted that system they associated her with the head of the company of the gods, and gave her suitable titles and ascribed to her proper attributes, in accordance with her sex, which would make her a feminine counterpart to the god Tem. The god Tem was the Father-god, and the lord of heaven, and the begetter of the gods, therefore Neith became "the "great lady, the mother-goddess, the lady of heaven, and queen of "the gods," . Elsewhere[1] she is called "mother of the gods," and just as Tem was declared to have been self-produced, so we find the same attribute ascribed to Neith, and she is said to be "the great lady, who gave birth to Rā, who "brought forth in primeval time herself, never having been "created,"[2] . The same thing happened at the cities of Per-Uatchet in the Delta and Nekhebet in Upper Egypt, for at one place Uatchet, the ancient and local goddess, became the head of the company of gods, and the goddess Nekhebet at the other. It is interesting to note that the priests of Heliopolis themselves included Uatchet in their Great company of the gods, as we may see from the text of Pepi II.,[3] where we find that the deceased king prays concerning the welfare of his pyramid "to the great *paut* of gods in Ȧnnu," i.e., Tem, Shu, Tefnut, Seb, Nut, Osiris, Set, Nephthys, Khent-Maati, and Uatchet.

The goddess Hathor at Dendera was treated by the priests there as was Neith at Saïs, for every conceivable attribute was ascribed to her, and her devotees declared that she was the mother of the gods, and the creator of the heavens and the earth, and of everything which is in them. In fact, both Neith and Hathor were made to assume all the powers of the god Tem, and indeed of every solar god.

The general evidence derived from a study of texts of all periods shows that the chief local gods of many cities never lost their exalted positions in the minds of the inhabitants, who clung to their belief in them with a consistency and conservatism which are truly Egyptian. In fact, the god of a nome, or the god of the

[1] D. Mallet, *Le Culte de Neit à Saïs*, Paris, 1888, p. 47.
[2] *Ibid.*, p. 146. [3] See ll. 669 ff.

capital city of a nome, when once firmly established, seems to have maintained his influence in all periods of Egyptian history, and though his shrine may have fallen into oblivion as the result of wars or invasions, and his worship have been suspended from time to time, the people of his city always took the earliest opportunity of rebuilding his sanctuary and establishing his priests as soon as prosperity returned to the country.

## CHAPTER III

# PRIMITIVE GODS AND NOME-GODS

DURING the predynastic period in Egypt every village and town or settlement possessed its god, whose worship and the glory of whose shrine increased or declined according to the increase or decrease of the prosperity of the community in which he lived. When the country was divided into sections which the Egyptians called *ḥespu*, , or "nomes," a certain god, or group of allied gods, became the representative, or representatives, of each nome, and so obtained the pre-eminence over all the other gods of the nome; and sometimes one god would represent two nomes. In this way the whole country of Egypt, from the Mediterranean Sea to Elephantine, was divided among the gods, and it became customary in each nome to regard the god of that nome as the "Great God," or "God," and to endow him with all the powers and attributes possible. We have, unfortunately, no means of knowing when the country was first split up into nomes, but the division must have taken place at a very early period, and the gods who were chosen to represent the nomes were undoubtedly those who had been worshipped in the large towns or settlements during the predynastic period. Thus in the earliest dynastic times of which we have inscriptions of any length we find that Neith was the chief deity of Saïs, Osiris of Busiris, Thoth of Hermopolis, Uatchet of Per-Uatchet, Ptaḥ of Memphis, Sebek of Crocodilopolis, Åmen of Thebes, Nekhebet of Nekheb, and Khnemu of Elephantine. The number of the nomes seems to have been different in different periods, so it is not possible to say with certainty how many the early nome-gods were in number. The Egyptian lists give the number of nomes as forty-two or forty-four, but the classical writers,

Strabo, Diodorus, and Pliny, do not agree in their statements on the subject. Strabo says[1] that the Labyrinth contained twenty-seven chambers, and if each one represented a nome the nomes must have been twenty-seven in number, i.e., ten in Upper Egypt, ten in Lower Egypt, and seven in the Heptanomis. On the other hand, Herodotus says[2] that the Labyrinth contained twelve halls. Pliny (Bk. v., chap. 9) enumerates the nomes as follows:—Ombites, Apollopolites, Hermonthites, Thinites, Phaturites, Coptites, Tentyrites, Diopolites, Antaeopolites, Aphroditopolites, Lycopolites, Pharbaethites, Bubastites, Sethroites, Tanites, the Arabian nome, the Hammonian nome, Oxyrynchites, Leontopolites, Athribites, Cynopolites, Hermopolites, Xoites, Mendesium, Sebennytes, Cabasites, Latopolites, Heliopolites, Prosopites, Panopolites, Busirites, Onuphites, Saïtes, Ptenethu, Phthemphu, Naucratites, Metelites, Gynaeopolites, Menelaites, Maraeotis, Heracleopolites, Arsinoïtes, Memphites, and the two nomes of Oasites. Diodorus Siculus (i. 54) gives the number of the nomes as thirty-six;[3] Herodotus (ii. 164) tells us that the country of Egypt was divided into districts[4] or nomes, but he does not say how many of them there were. These facts serve to show that the number of nomes when the country was first divided was smaller than in later times, and we may assume that it was the nomes of the Delta which increased in number rather than those of Upper Egypt. The following is a list of the nomes of Egypt according to inscriptions at Edfû and elsewhere, together with their capitals and the gods who were worshipped in them:—

UPPER EGYPT.

| | Nome. | Capital. | God. |
|---|---|---|---|
| 1. | TA-KHENT  | Ābu 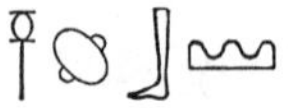 (Elephantine) | Khnemu  |
| 2. | THES-ḤERTU  | Ṭeb  (Apollinopolis Magna) | Ḥeru-Beḥuṭet  |

[1] xvii. l. § 37. [2] ii. § 148.

[3] Τὴν δὲ χώραν ἅπασαν εἰς ἓξ καὶ τρίακοντα μέρη διελών, ἃ καλοῦσιν Αἰγύπτιοι νομούς.

[4] κατὰ γὰρ δὴ νομοὺς Αἴγυπτος ἅπασα διαραίρηται.

| | Nome. | Capital. | God. |
|---|---|---|---|
| 3. | TEN | Nekheb (Eileithyia)<br>Senit (Esneh) | Nekhebet |
| 4. | UAST | Uast (Thebes) | Ȧmen-Rā |
| 5. | ḤERUI | Qebti (Coptos) | Ȧmsu, Min or Khem |
| 6. | ȦA-ṬĀ | Ta-en-tarert (Denderah) | Ḥet-Ḥeru (i.e., Hathor) |
| 7. | SESHESH | Ḥet (Diospolis Parva) | Ḥet-Ḥeru |
| 8. | ȦBṬ | Ȧbṭu[1] (Abydos)<br>Thenit (This) | Ȧn-Ḥer |
| 9. | ȦMSU, MIN or KHEM | Ȧpu (Panopolis) | Ȧmsu, Min or Khem |
| 10A. | UATCHET | Ṭebut (Aphroditopolis) | Ḥet-Ḥeru |
| 10B. | NETERUI | Ṭu-qat (Antaeopolis) | Ḥeru (Horus) |
| 11. | SET | Shas-ḥetep (Hypsele) | Khnemu |

[1] Var. *Ȧb-ṭut,* i.e., "the city of the mountain of the heart's desire"; see Dümichen, *Geschichte*, p. 143.

| | Nome. | Capital. | God. |
|---|---|---|---|
| 12. | Ṭu-f | Nut-en-bak (Antaeopolis) | Ḥeru |
| 13. | Ȧtef-khent | Saiut (Lycopolis) | Ȧp-uat |
| 14. | Ȧtef-peḥu | Qesi (Cusae) | Ḥet-Ḥert |
| 15. | Un | Khemennu (Hermopolis) | Teḥuti (Thoth) |
| 16. | Meḥ-maḥetch | Ḥebennu (Hipponon) | Ḥeru |
| 17. | Ȧnpu | Kasa (Cynopolis) | Ȧnpu |
| 18. | Sep | Ḥet-suten (Alabastronpolis) | Ȧnpu |
| 19. | Uab | Per-Mātchet (Oxyrynchus) | Set |
| 20. | Ȧtef-khent | Henensu (Herakleopolis Magna) | Ḥer-shefi |
| 21a. | Ȧtef-peḥu | Ermen-ḥert | Khnemu |
| 21b. | Ta-she | Sheṭ (Crocodilopolis) | Sebek |
| 22. | Māten | Ṭep-ȧḥet (Aphroditopolis) | Ḥet-Ḥert |

## LOWER EGYPT.

| | Nome. | Capital. | God. |
|---|---|---|---|
| 1. | ÅNEB-ḤETCH | Men-nefert (Memphis) | Ptaḥ |
| 2. | KHENSU[1] | Sekhemt (Letopolis) | Ḥeru-ur |
| 3. | ÅMENT | Nut-ent-Ḥāp (Apis) | Ḥet-Ḥeru |
| 4. | SÅPI-RES | Tcheqā | Sebek, Isis, Åmen |
| 5. | SÅP-MEḤ | Saut (Saïs) | Net (Neith) |
| 6. | KASET | Khasut (Xoïs) | Åmen-Rā |
| 7. | ... ÅMENT | Senti-nefert | Ḥu |
| 8. | ... ÅBT | Theket (Succoth)<br>Per-Åtem (Pithom) | Temu |
| 9. | ÅTI | Per-Åsår[2] (Busiris) | Osiris |

[1] Perhaps a variant is = = ; see Pleyte, *Aeg. Zeit.*, 1868, p. 17; and Dümichen, *Kalendarinschriften*, 118*b*, 106*d*.

[2] Or, (?).

| | Nome. | Capital. | God. |
|---|---|---|---|
| 10. | KA-QEM | Ḥet-ta-ḥer-àb (Athribis) | Horus |
| 11. | KA-ḤESEB | Ḥebes-ka (Cabasus) | Isis |
| 12. | THEB-KA | Theb-neter (Sebennytus) | Àn-ḥer |
| 13. | ḤEQ-ĀṬ | Ànnu (Heliopolis, On) | Rā |
| 14. | KHENT-ÀBT | Tchalu (Tanis) | Ḥeru |
| 15. | TEḤUT | Per-Teḥuti (Hermopolis) | Teḥuti (Thoth) |
| 16. | KHA (?) | Per-ba-neb-Ṭeṭṭu (Mendes) | Ba-neb-Tattu, or Ṭeṭṭeṭet |
| 17. | SAM-BEḤUṬET | Pa-khen-en-Àmen (Diospolis) | Àmen-Rā |
| 18. | ÀM-KHENT | Per-Bast (Bubastis) | Bast |
| 19. | ÀM-PEḤU | Per-Uatchet (Buto) | Uatchet |
| 20. | SEPṬ | Qesem (Goshen ?) | Sepṭ [1] |

[1] The authorities to be consulted on the nomes of Egypt are Brugsch, *Dict. Géog.* (see the list at the end of vol. iii.); Dümichen, *Geographie des alten Aegyptens* (in Meyer, *Geschichte des alten Aegyptens*), Berlin, 1887; and J. de Rougé, *Géographie Ancienne de la Basse-Égypte*, Paris, 1891.

Thus every nome of Egypt possessed a representative god whose temple was situated in the capital city of the nome, and attached to the service of each nome-god was a body of priests who divided among themselves the various duties connected with the service of the gods, the maintenance of the buildings of the temple, the multiplying of copies of religious works, and the religious education of the community. In Upper Egypt, where the care of the dead seems to have been the principal duty of the living, the lower orders of the priesthood probably carried on a lucrative business in mummifying the dead, and in funeral papyri and amulets, and in conducting funerals. The high-priest of each great city, and sometimes even the high-priestess, bore a special title. In Thebes the high-priest was called "first servant of the "god Rā in Thebes";[1] in Heliopolis the title of the high-priest was "Great one of visions of Rā-Ȧtem";[2] in Memphis, "Great chief "of the hammer in the temple of him of the Southern Wall, and "Setem of the god of the Beautiful Face (i.e., Ptaḥ)";[3] in Saïs, "governor of the double temple";[4] and similarly the high-priestess of Memphis bore the title of "Nefer-tutu";[5] in Sekhem the title of the high-priestess was "Divine mother";[6] in Saïs, "Urt," i.e., "great one";[7] in Mendes, "Utcha-ba-f";[8] and so on. The priests of every great god were divided into classes, among which may be mentioned "those who ministered at certain hours," ; "the servants of the gods," ; the "holy fathers," ; the "libationers," . The accounts of the temple were kept by the "scribe of the temple,"

1 .

2 .

3 .

4 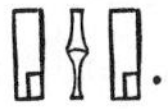. 5 . 6 .

7 . 8 .

, and, in large temples, one or more scribes kept a register of gifts to the temple and of the property of the god.[1] It is impossible to say how many priests of all classes ministered to any given nome-god; it seems that the highest permanent priestly officials were at all times and in all cities very few in number, and that the "servants of the god" were very many. The priests of each nome-god were subject to no external authority, and the high-priest of a great nome possessed a power which was hardly inferior to that of the nomarch himself.

The worship of each nome-god contained elements peculiar to itself, and the beliefs which centred in him represented all the ancient and indigenous views of the inhabitants of the nome, and these were carefully observed and cultivated from the earliest to the latest times. We may see from the list of nome-gods given above that many nomes worshipped the same god, e.g., Horus was worshipped in three nomes of Upper Egypt and two nomes of Lower Egypt, whilst one nome worshipped him under the special form of Horus of Beḥuṭet; three nomes of Upper Egypt worshipped Khnemu, two worshipped Åmsu (or Min or Khem ?), two worshipped Ånpu, and Hathor was worshipped in five nomes in Upper Egypt and one in Lower Egypt. The cults of the ram-headed god Khnemu at Elephantine, of the vulture goddess Nekhebet at Eileithyia, of the crocodile god Sebek in the district of Ta-she (Fayyûm), of the dog-headed god Ånpu at Cynopolis and Alabastronpolis, of the ibis-god Thoth at Hermopolis, of Horus the elder (Ḥeru-ur) at Letopolis, and of Uatchet at Buto (Per-Uatchet), were extremely ancient, and with them are probably to be grouped in point of antiquity the cults of the wolf(?)-headed god Åp-uat, the lioness goddess Sekhet, the cat-headed goddess Bast, and the god Set. The animal which was the type and symbol of this last god has not as yet been identified; it cannot have been the ass as was once thought, and it is hardly likely to have been the camel; at present, therefore, we can only tentatively assume that it belonged to some class of animal which became extinct at a very early period. The cults of the various forms of the sky-god Horus, and of the Sun-god, and of the

[1] For other temple officials see Brugsch, *Aegyptologie*, p. 218.

goddess Hathor, are the oldest of all. The goddess Neith, whose symbols were two arrows and a shield, appears to have been of Libyan origin, but, as has already been shown, the attributes of some of the oldest indigenous gods of Egypt were ascribed to her in early dynastic times. The origin of the god Osiris is obscure, but it is difficult, when all the statements made concerning him in the religious texts are taken into consideration, not to think that the original seat of his worship was in the Delta. Early in the dynastic period his most important shrine was at Abydos, which became the centre of his cult and the sacred city to which his worshippers flocked for countless generations. In spite of this, however, the nome-lists show that the nome-god was Ȧn-Ḥer, or Ȧnhur, and notwithstanding the special honour in which Osiris was held throughout Egypt, Ȧn-Ḥer was always regarded as the official god of the nome Ȧbṭ and of its capital of the same name.

The Elysian Fields, i.e., the Sekhet-ḥetepet, were situated in the Delta where the country was fertile, and where the land was traversed by canals and streams of water running in all directions; moreover, the "House of Osiris" *par excellence* ( Per-Ȧsȧr[1] = Busiris) was in the Delta, and the shrine of the god who was worshipped in the form of a ram which was said to contain the soul of Osiris, was also in the Delta. Everywhere in the texts Osiris is called the "lord of Abydos," and generally this title is followed by another, i.e., "lord of Ṭaṭṭu." Now Ṭaṭṭu is the city, and "The Ram, lord of Ṭaṭṭu,"  *Ba-neb-Ṭaṭṭu*, was its god. The name Ṭaṭṭu was corrupted into "Mendes" by the Greeks, and in this city the great local god was worshipped under the form of a ram, which is now commonly known as the "Mendesian Ram." The frequent use of the title "lord of Ṭaṭṭu" suggests that the worship of Osiris was grafted on to or was made to absorb that of the local ram-god, and that in consequence Osiris became the lord of the city in his stead. It may be urged that Ṭaṭṭu was merely the seat of the shrine of the god Osiris in the northern kingdom, just as Abydos was his

[1] The words *Ba-neb-Ṭaṭṭu* usually follow here, therefore the full name of the city is, "House of Osiris, the Ram, lord of Ṭaṭṭu."

sanctuary in the southern kingdom, but this explanation of the use of the title is insufficient. It may further be urged that, inasmuch as the titles "lord of Abydos," "lord of Ṭaṭṭu," occur in connection with others which have reference to Osiris in his capacity as governor of the Underworld, the Abydos and Ṭaṭṭu here mentioned are mythological cities and not cities upon earth. But even if this be so it matters little, for we know that the Egyptians fashioned their mythological or heavenly cities after the manner of their earthly cities, and that their conceptions of things spiritual were based upon things material.

Returning for a moment to the adoption of gods, we may note that from first to last the people of one nome were generally ready to offer hospitality to the gods of another, and also to the gods of strangers who had come to settle among them. At times, however, a new god, or a new group of gods, was forced upon the inhabitants of one or more nomes, and even upon a whole province, as the result of conquest, or by the wish of the king, or by the supremacy of the priesthood of a given city. Thus the priesthood of Rā or Rā-Tem at Heliopolis succeeded in making their theological system paramount in the country, and the whole of the religious philosophy of the Theban *Books of the Dead* is based upon their teaching. Until the conquest of the Hyksos by the Theban princes the god Åmen was a nome-god of no great importance, but when they became kings of the south and north, he immediately became the king of all the gods of the south and the north, and the titles and powers and attributes of the great gods of the country were ascribed to him by his priests. As the prince of Thebes was greater than any and every prince in the other nomes of Egypt, so the Theban nome-god was greater than any and every other god of Egypt. The extraordinary dislike which Åmen-ḥetep IV. exhibited towards this god, and the foolish attempt which he made to substitute for his worship that of Åten, or the Disk, furnishes us with an example of the imposition of a god upon a priesthood and province; the attempt was successful for a time over a limited area, but it had no chance of permanent success because the fundamental ideas of the worship of the god as Åmen-ḥetep interpreted them were foreign to the religious conceptions of the Egyptians generally.

From what has been said above it will be easy to imagine the remarkable spectacle which Egypt must have presented to a foreigner who went there and found the country split up into a series of nomes, each possessing its great god, who was ministered to by a body of priests and servants who were amenable to no general authority outside the nome, and who performed his worship when and as they pleased, and who claimed for him powers, and rights, and privileges without fear of opposition. The stranger would find that each college of priests in each nome asserted that its god was the father of all the other gods, and the creator of the heavens and the earth, and that, generally speaking, the priests of one nome-god and his divine companions were content to allow their neighbours in other nomes to declare anything they pleased about their nome-gods and their divine companions. As far as can be gathered from the religious texts, it seems that the priests of one company of gods never attempted to suppress the gods of another company if the fortune of war gave them paramount power in the nome wherein they were worshipped. Thus when the priests of Rā attained to the great power which they enjoyed at Heliopolis under the Vth and VIth Dynasties they did not suppress the local god Tem, but they associated their god with him, and produced the compound god Rā-Tem. Similarly, at a later period, when Ȧmen, as the nome-god of the victorious princes and kings of Thebes, was declared to be the greatest of the gods of Egypt, his priests did not declare that the other gods of Egypt were not gods and try to suppress them, but they asserted that all the powers of the other gods were assimilated in him, and that he was in consequence the greatest of the gods. In the texts of Unȧs and the kings who were his immediate successors we read of the Great and Little companies of the gods, but we also find mention of the company of gods of Horus and of the double company of gods of Tem;[1] the priests of Heliopolis claimed supremacy among the gods for Rā, but they took care to include as far as possible the name of every god and goddess to whom worship had been paid in past generations. The

[1]  . Unȧs, ll. 443, 444.

same characteristic is observable in the texts of the Theban priesthood, and we find that their god Åmen was even introduced into the *Book of the Dead* where, manifestly, he had little claim to be. The hymns in the chapters of that work are addressed either to Rā, in one form or another, or to Osiris, but in Chapter clxxi. we find the following address:—" O Tem, O Shu, O Tefnet, O Seb, O Nut, " O Osiris, O Isis, O Set, O Nephthys, O Ḥeru-khuti (Harmachis), " O Hathor of the Great House, O Kheperå, O Menthu, the lord of " Thebes, O Åmen, the lord of the thrones of the two lands, O " Great company of the gods, O Little company of the gods, O gods " and goddesses who dwell in Nu, O Sebek of the two *Meḥt*, O " Sebek in all thy manifold names in thine every place wherein thy " Ka (i.e., double) hath delight, O gods of the south, O gods of the " north, O ye who are in heaven, O ye who are upon the earth, " grant ye the garment of purity unto the perfect spirit of Åmen- " ḥetep."[1] The greater number of the gods whose names are given in the Pyramid Texts are also mentioned in the religious literature, especially in the *Book of the Dead* of later periods, and if we possessed copies of all the religious works of the New Empire we should probably discover that the names of all the gods, with perhaps the exception of Set, worshipped under the Early Empire were preserved in them. The Egyptians, certainly in dynastic times, rarely abandoned a god, and, speaking generally, it is remarkable how little the character and attributes of the gods vary in the period between the IVth and the XXVIth Dynasties. The obstinate conservatism of the Egyptians, which seems to have been inherited in an almost unaltered state by their descendants the Copts, induced the writers of religious texts to introduce into their works as many of the gods as possible, and they were moved to do this as much by motives of priestly policy and by self-interest as by feelings of reverence for the gods of Egypt.

In the Pyramid Texts the predominant gods are those of the company of Heliopolis, but we nevertheless find that the gods of remote towns and cities had duties assigned to them, and that one and all of them were supposed to minister to the deceased kings in the Underworld. The reason of this is not far to seek.

[1] See my *Chapters of Coming Forth by Day* (Translation), p. 315.

The heaven which the Egyptian conceived in his mind closely resembled Egypt in respect of its sub-divisions, and its various cities and districts were ruled by gods whom it was necessary to propitiate, and whose friendship must be gained at any cost. A man hoped that in the next life he would be able to wander about at will through the length and breadth of heaven, and the only way to obtain this privilege was to secure the goodwill of the gods of the four quarters of the sky by the recital of prayers of various kinds, and by the performance of certain ceremonies, which were always of a more or less magical character. To be able to pass at pleasure along the eastern Delta of heaven and without opposition presupposed the favour of Sepṭ and Temu; and to have power to drink of the waters of the celestial Nile presupposed the favour of the god Khnemu, the lord of the Island of Elephantine, close to which were situated, according to Egyptian belief, the sources of the Nile. The texts of all periods exhibit an almost childish anxiety to prove that every god of Egypt is interested in the welfare of the beings in the Underworld who were once mortal men, and it was a common belief also in all periods that the mere asserting in writing that the gods would minister to the deceased would produce the assistance desired. To enjoy the power to enter into certain cities in heaven the deceased was obliged to know the various gods or "Souls" who were worshipped in them. Thus the Souls of the West were Tem, and Sebek, the lord of the Mountain of Sunrise, and Hathor, the lady of the Evening;[1] the Souls of the East were Ḥeru-khuti (Harmachis), the Calf of the goddess Kherȧ, and the Morning Star;[2] the Souls of the city of Pe were Horus, Mesthȧ, and Ḥāpi;[3] the Souls of the city of Nekhen were Horus, Ṭuamutef, and Qebḥsennuf;[4] the Souls of Heliopolis were Rā, Shu, and Tefnet;[5] and the Souls of the city of Hermopolis were Thoth, Sa, and Tem.[6] Similarly every great heavenly city was held to contain a company of gods, and the beatified soul was thought to enjoy the duty of paying visits to their shrines just as, when in the body, it made offerings to their earthly counterparts.

[1] *Book of the Dead*, Chap. cviii. [2] *Ibid.*, Chap. cix. [3] *Ibid.*, Chap. cxii.
[4] *Ibid.*, Chap. cxiii. [5] *Ibid.*, Chap. cxv. [6] *Ibid.*, Chap. cxvi.

In the observations already made concerning the difficulty of assigning an exact meaning to the word for God and "god," neter, , we have seen that in dynastic times the chief attribute which was assigned to a god was the power to renew his life indefinitely, and to live for ever, and the text of Unȧs has shown us that in very early times the Egyptian thought he could obtain this power by eating his god or gods. Closely connected with this belief is another which finds expression in the Pyramid Texts, and also in the later Recensions of the *Book of the Dead* which are based upon them. In many passages scattered throughout the religious texts of all periods we find it stated that the deceased has acquired the powers of such and such a god, and that as a result he has become the counterpart or fellow of several gods, and that he takes his place among the company of gods in the proper persons of several of their number. A still further development of the idea makes every member of the body of the deceased to be, first, under the protection of a god, and secondly, to become that same member of the god its protector; hence his whole body becomes the "double company of the gods," and the "two great "gods watch, each in his place, and they find him in the form of "the double company of the gods weighing the words of every "chief like a chief, and they bow down before him, and they make "offerings to him as to the double company of the gods."[1] Moreover, the deceased is made in the texts to stand up at the head of the company of the gods as Seb, the "erpā," or hereditary chief, of the gods, and as Osiris, the governor of the divine powers, and as Horus, the lord of men and of gods.[2] His bones are the gods

[1] See Pepi I., ll. 317, 318.

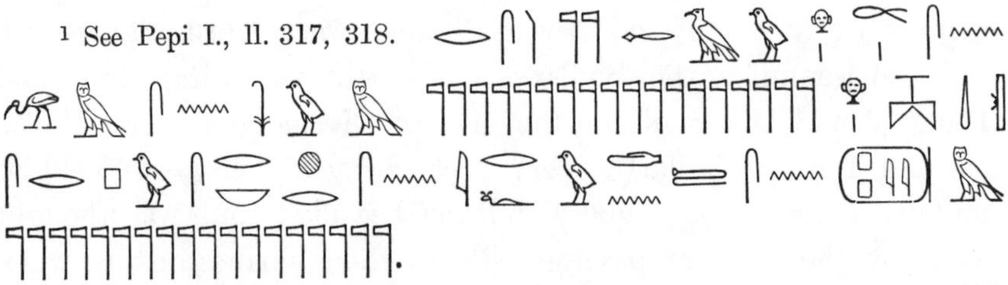

[2]

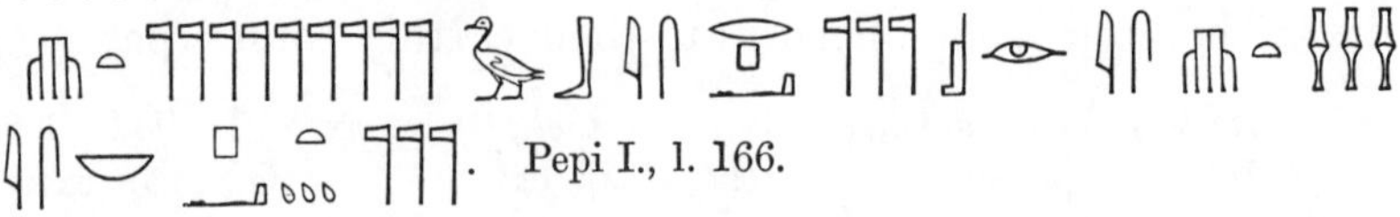

Pepi I., l. 166.

and goddesses of heaven;[1] his right side belongs to Horus, and his left side to Set; he becomes the actual son of Tem, or Tem-Rā, and Shu, Tefnet, Seb, and Nut, and he is the brother of Isis, Nephthys, Set, and Thoth, and the father of Horus.[2] The god Horus taketh his own Eye and giveth it to him,[3] and he bestoweth upon him his own *ka* or double,[4] and never leaveth him, and the Bull of the Nine[5] maketh wide his dominions among the gods.

The oldest copy of the prayer for the deification of the members of the body is found in the text of Pepi I. (line 565 ff.), and as it is very important from several points of view a version of it is here given:—"The HEAD of this Rā-meri is in the form "of [that of] the hawk; he cometh forth and raiseth himself up in "heaven. The SKULL, , of this Pepi is that of the divine "Goose; he cometh forth and raiseth himself up in heaven. The "[HAIR] of this Pepi is the . . . .  of Nu; he cometh forth "and raiseth himself up in heaven. The FACE of this Pepi is the "face of Åp-uat, 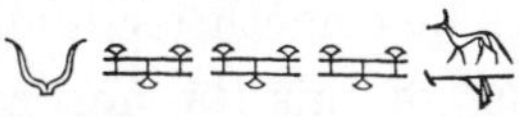; he cometh forth and raiseth "himself up in heaven. The TWO EYES of Rā-meri are the great "goddess (Hathor ?) at the head of the Souls of Ånnu; he cometh "forth and raiseth himself up in heaven. The MOUTH of this Pepi "is Khens-ur, 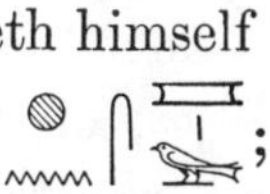; he cometh forth and raiseth himself up "in heaven. The TONGUE of this Pepi is the steering-pole (?) of the "boat of Maāt; he cometh forth and raiseth himself up in heaven. "The TEETH of this Pepi are the Souls [of Ånnu]; he cometh forth "and raiseth himself up in heaven. The LIPS of this Pepi are "the . . . . ; he cometh forth and raiseth himself up in heaven.

1 See Tetå, l. 209.

2 See Unås (*Recueil*), tom. iii, pp. 209–211.

3 . Pepi I., l. 457.

4 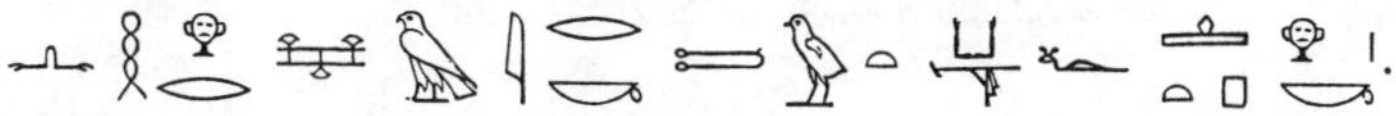. Tetå, l. 265.

5 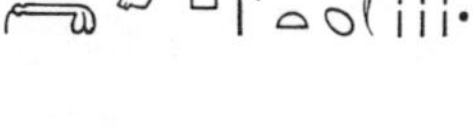.

"The CHIN of this Pepi is Khert-Khent-Sekhem, 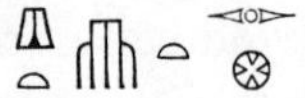; he "cometh forth and raiseth himself up in heaven. The BACKBONE of "this Pepi is [the Bull] Sma, ; he cometh forth and "raiseth himself up in heaven. The SHOULDERS AND ARMS of this "Pepi are Set; he cometh forth and raiseth himself up in heaven. "The [BREAST] of this Pepi is Baȧbu, ; he cometh "forth and raiseth himself up in heaven. The HEART of this "Rā-meri is Bastet; he cometh forth and raiseth himself up "in heaven. The BELLY of this Rā-meri is Nut; he cometh "forth and raiseth himself up in heaven. The [LOINS of "this Pepi are] the Great and Little companies of the gods; "he cometh forth and raiseth himself up in heaven. The "BACK of this Pepi is Ḥeqet; he cometh forth and raiseth "himself up in heaven. The BUTTOCKS, , of this Rā-meri are "the Semket and Māt boats;[1] he cometh forth and raiseth himself "up in heaven. The PHALLUS of this Pepi is Ḥāp;[2] he cometh "forth and raiseth himself up in heaven. The two THIGHS[3] of "Rā-meri are Nit and Serqet; he cometh forth and raiseth himself "up in heaven. The two LEGS[4] of this Rā-meri are the twin soul-"gods at the head of Sekhet-tcher;[5] he cometh forth and raiseth "himself up in heaven. The soles of the two FEET[6] of this Rā-"meri are the double Maāti boat; he cometh forth and raiseth "himself up in heaven. The HEELS (?), 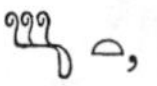, of this Pepi are the "Souls of Ȧnnu; he cometh forth and raiseth himself up in "heaven."

In the XVIIIth Dynasty versions of this interesting text were written in papyri containing the *Book of the Dead*, and of these the following exhibit variant readings which appear to indicate changes of belief.

FROM THE PAPYRUS OF NU.

(Brit. Mus., No. 10,477, sheet 6.)

"My hair is the hair of Nu.
"My face is the face of the Disk.
"My eyes are the eyes of Hathor.
"My ears are the ears of Åp-uat.
"My nose is the nose of Khenti-"khas.
"My lips are the lips of Ånpu.
"My teeth are the teeth of "Serqet.
"My neck is the neck of the "divine goddess Isis.
"My hands are the hands of "Ba-neb-Ṭaṭṭu.
"My fore-arms are the fore-arms "of Neith, the Lady of Saïs.
"My backbone is the backbone "of Suti.
"My phallus is the phallus of "Osiris.
"My reins are the reins of the "Lords of Kher-āḥa.
"My chest is the chest of Āa-"shefit.
"My belly and back are the "belly and back of Sekhet.
"My buttocks are the buttocks "of the Eye of Horus.
"My hips and legs are the hips "and legs of Nut.
"My feet are the feet of Ptaḥ.
"[My fingers] and my leg-bones "are the fingers and leg-"bones of the Living Gods.
"There is no member of my

FROM THE PAPYRUS OF ANI.

(Brit. Mus., No. 10,470, sheet 32.)

"The hair of Osiris Ani is the "hair of Nu.
"The face of Osiris Ani is the "face of Rā.
"The eyes of Osiris Ani are the "eyes of Hathor.
"The ears of Osiris Ani are the "ears of Åp-uat.
"The lips of Osiris Ani are the "lips of Ånpu.
"The teeth of Osiris Ani are the "teeth of Serqet.
"The neck of Osiris Ani is the "neck of Isis.
"The hands of Osiris Ani are "the hands of Ba-neb-Ṭaṭṭu.
"The shoulder of Osiris Ani is "the shoulder of Uatchet.
"The throat of Osiris Ani is the "throat of Mert.
"The fore-arms of Osiris Ani "are the fore-arms of the "Lady of Saïs.
"The backbone of Osiris Ani is "the backbone of Set.
"The chest of Osiris Ani is the "chest of the Lords of "Kher-Āḥa.
"The flesh of Osiris Ani is the "flesh of Āa-shefit.
"The reins and back of Osiris "Ani are the reins and "back of Sekhet.
"The buttocks of Osiris Ani are

"body which is not the
"member of a god. The
"god Thoth shieldeth my
"body wholly, and I am
"Rā day by day."[1]

"the buttocks of the Eye
"of Horus.
"The phallus of Osiris Ani is
"the phallus of Osiris.
"The legs of Osiris Ani are the
"legs of Nut.
"The feet of Osiris Ani are the
"feet of Ptaḥ.
"The fingers of Osiris Ani are
"the fingers of Orion.
"The leg-bones of Osiris Ani
"are the leg-bones of the
"Living Uraei."

The text which follows that describing the deification of the members in the inscription of Pepi I.[2] is perhaps of even greater interest, for it declares that :—

"This Pepi is god, the son of god; he cometh forth and raiseth "himself up to heaven. This Rā-meri is the son of Rā, who loveth "him; he cometh forth and raiseth himself up to heaven. Rā hath "sent forth this Rā-meri, who cometh forth and raiseth himself up "to heaven. Rā hath conceived this Pepi, who cometh forth and "raiseth himself up to heaven. Rā hath given birth to this Pepi, "who cometh forth and raiseth himself up to heaven. This [is] the "word of power which is in the body of Rā-meri, and he cometh "forth and raiseth himself up to heaven. This Rā-meri is the "Great Power among the great company of sovereign chiefs who "are in Ȧnnu, and he cometh forth and raiseth himself up to "heaven."

In the previous pages it has been shown that the Great company of the Gods of Heliopolis contained nine or more gods, and that whenever these were adopted by other cities and towns the attributes of the chief of the Heliopolitan gods were transferred to the local nome-god, and the identities of both gods were merged in each other. It will, however, be evident at a glance that there

1 See my *Chapters of Coming Forth by Day* (Translation), p. 94.
2 Line 574.

were very few localities which could afford to maintain in a proper state the worship of nine or more great gods in addition to that of the nome-god, and as a matter of fact we find that very few even of the great towns and cities adopted all the gods of the companies of Heliopolis, and that very few possessed companies of gods which contained as many members as nine. The city of Khemennu (Hermopolis) was famous as the sanctuary of the company of Eight Gods, indeed the name "Khemennu," , means "the city of the Eight Gods." The names of these gods were:—1. Nu, 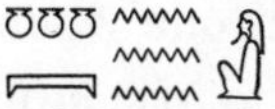. 2. Nut, 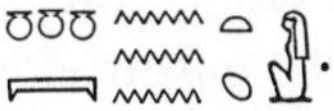. 3. Ḥeḥu, . 4. Ḥeḥut, . 5. Kekui, . 6. Kekuit, . 7. Ḳereḥ, . 8. Ḳereḥet, , and with their leader Teḥuti, or Thoth, they formed one of the oldest of the companies of gods in all Egypt. The names of the members of the *paut*, or company, of Hermopolis as here given are taken from the texts inscribed on the walls of the temple which Darius II. built at Ḥebet in the Oasis of Khârga,[1] and which is a comparatively late building, but there is reason for believing that they are copied from very ancient documents, and that taken together this group of gods represents the oldest form of the Hermopolitan *paut*. In some lists of the gods Åmen and Åment are made to take the places of Nu and Nut, and those of Ḳereḥ and Ḳereḥet are filled by Nenu and Nenut; in others Åmen and Åment are substituted for Ḳereḥ and Ḳereḥet.[2]

Throughout Egypt generally the company of gods of a town or city were three in number, and they were formed by the local deity and two gods who were associated with him, and who shared with him, but in a very much less degree, the honour and reverence which were paid to him. Speaking generally, two members of such a triad were gods, one old and one young, and the third was a goddess, who was, naturally, the wife, or female counterpart, of the older god. The younger god was the son of the older god and goddess, and he was supposed to possess all the

[1] See Brugsch, *Reise nach der grossen Oase el-Khargeh*, Leipzig, 1878, pl. 14.

[2] For the lists of the *paut* of Thoth at Edfû, Dendera, Karnak, Philae, etc., see Brugsch, *Religion und Mythologie*, p. 127.

attributes and powers which belonged to his father. The head of the triad was sometimes Rā, and sometimes a god of comparatively limited reputation, to whom were ascribed the power and might of the great Sun-god, which his devotees assumed that he had absorbed. The feminine counterpart or wife of the chief god was usually a local goddess of little or no importance; on the other hand, her son by the chief god was nearly as important as his father, because it was assumed that he would succeed to his rank and throne when the older god had passed away. The conception of the triad or trinity is, in Egypt, probably as old as the belief in the gods, and it seems to be based upon the anthropomorphic views which were current in the earliest times about them. The Egyptian provided the god with a wife, just as he took care to provide himself with one, in order that he might have a son to succeed him, and he assumed that the god would have as issue a son, even as he himself wished and expected to have a son. In later times, the group of nine gods took the place of the triad, but we are not justified in assuming that the ennead was a simple development of the triad. The triad contains two gods and one goddess, but the ennead contains five gods and four goddesses, being made up of four pairs of deities, and one supreme god. The ennead is, however, often regarded as a triad of triads, and the three enneads of Heliopolis, , as a triad of a triad of triads. The conception of the ennead is probably very much later than that of the triad.[1] Examples of triads are:—At Mendes, Ba-neb-Ṭaṭṭu , Ḥāt-meḥit , and Ḥeru-pa-khart 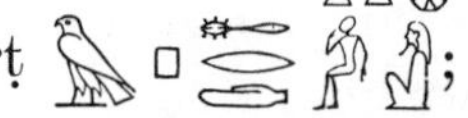; at Tcheqā, Sebek 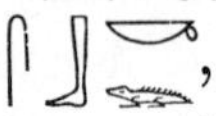, Isis 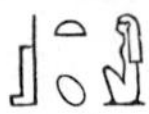, and Àmen 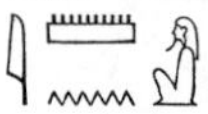; at Memphis, Ptaḥ 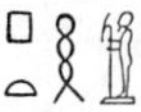, Sekhet 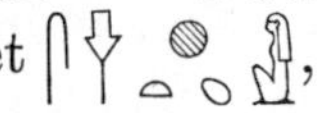, and I-em-ḥetep ; at Thebes, Àmen-Rā 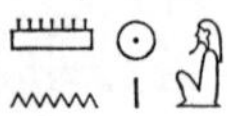, Mut , and Khensu ; and triads like Osiris, Isis, and Horus , 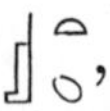, 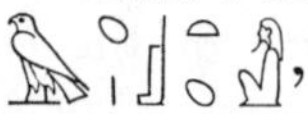, and Set, Nephthys, and Anubis 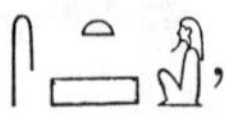, 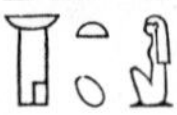,  were wor-

[1] An exactly opposite view is taken by M. Maspero (*La Mythologie Égyptienne*, p. 270).

shipped in several places in Egypt. The members of many triads in Egypt varied at different times and in different places, but variations were caused chiefly by assimilating local gods and goddesses with the well-known members of the companies of the gods of Heliopolis.

The facts recorded in the preceding pages show that the great gods of the dynastic period in Egypt were selected from a large number of local gods, who were in turn chosen from among the representatives of the gods of the desert, and mountain, and earth, and water, and air, and sky, who had been worshipped in predynastic times. Thus in the great company of the gods of Heliopolis we have Shu, a form of Ȧn-ḥer 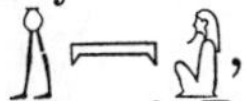, the local god of Sebennytus; Osiris, the local god both of Busiris and Mendes; Isis, a form of the still more ancient goddess "Uatchit, lady of Pe," , i.e., Buto; Tefnet, the goddess of a district in the fifteenth nome of Lower Egypt; etc. The gods of the later predynastic period were, of course, developed out of the multitude of spirits, good and bad, in whom the most primitive Egyptians believed, and it is clear that in general characteristics the gods of the dynastic period were identical with those of the predynastic period, and that the Egyptians rarely abandoned any god whose priests in the earliest times had succeeded in establishing for him a recognized position. The form of the worship of the gods must have changed greatly, but this was due rather to the increase in the general prosperity of the country than to any fundamental change in the views and beliefs of the Egyptians as to their gods; the houses of the gods, or temples, became larger and larger and more magnificent as increased wealth flowed into the country as the result of foreign conquest, but the gods remained the same, and the processions and ceremonies, though more magnificent under the New Empire, preserved the essentials of the early period. But if we examine the religious texts carefully it will be seen that the Egyptians were always trying to reduce the number of their gods, or, in other words, were always advancing from polytheism to monotheism. The priesthood and the educated classes must have held religious views which were not absolutely identical with those of the peasant who cultivated the fields, but such, I believe, were concerned chiefly with the popular forms of worship of the gods and with conceptions as to their nature. The uneducated people of the country clung with great tenacity to the ordinary methods of celebrating their worship, principally because the frequent festivals and the imposing ceremonies, which formed a large and important part of it, were regarded as essential for their general well-being; the priests and the educated, on the other hand, clung to them because their influence was not sufficiently powerful to establish a popular form of religion and worship which would be consistent with their own private views.

Every change which can be traced in the religion of the country proves that the priesthoods of the various great religious centres absorbed into the new systems whenever possible the ancient gods and the ancient beliefs in them; hence during the period of the highest culture in Egypt we find ideas of the grossest kind jostling ideas which were the product of great intellectuality and much thinking. Expressions which are the result of a series of beliefs in tree gods, desert gods, water gods, earth gods, and gods with human passions, abound, and it is these which have drawn down upon the Egyptians the contempt of the Hebrews, the Greeks, and the Romans, and even of modern skilled investigators of Egyptian religion and mythology. It has not been sufficiently realized that the polytheism of the Egyptians had aspects which were peculiar to itself, and the same may be said of one phase of the beliefs of this people which appears to be, and which, the writer thinks, undoubtedly is, monotheistic. When the priests of Heliopolis formulated their system of theogony they asserted that the god Tem produced the two gods that issued from himself, i.e., Shu and Tefnut, by masturbation,[1] and there is little doubt that in making this declaration they were repeating what the half savage and primitive Egyptians may really have believed; but it would be

[1] 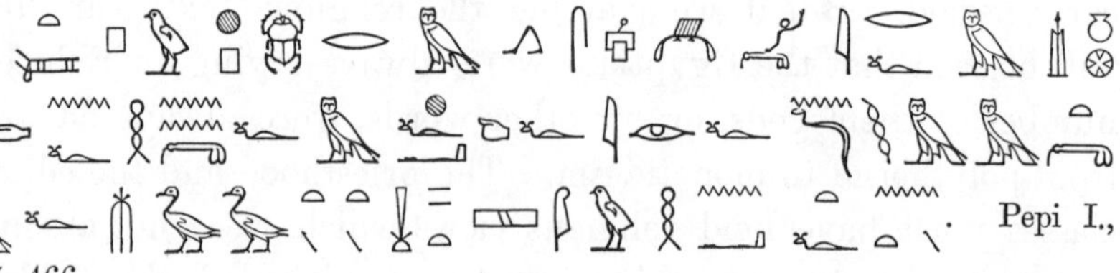 Pepi I., ll. 465, 466.

utterly wrong to declare that the priests themselves believed these things, or that such a statement represented the views of any educated person in Egypt on the subject of the origin of the gods. In Chapter xvii. of the *Book of the Dead*[1] is an allusion to the fight which took place between Horus and Set, but no Egyptian who accepted the refined beliefs which are found even in the same chapter could have regarded this allusion as anything more than the record of an act of savagery which had crept into religious texts at a time when acts of the kind were common.

The same might be said of dozens of expressions and allusions which are scattered throughout the texts of all periods, and no just investigator will judge the Egyptians, and their religion, and their beliefs by the phases of thought and expressions which reflect the manners and customs and ideas of the primitive dwellers in the Valley of the Nile. But yet it is precisely by such things that the Egyptian religion is judged by many modern writers. The eminent Egyptologist, M. Maspero, says that before he began to decipher Egyptian texts for himself, and so long as he was content to reproduce the teaching of the great masters of the science of Egyptology, he believed that the Egyptians had in the earliest times arrived at the notion of divine unity, and that they had fashioned an entire system of religion and of symbolic mythology with an incomparable surety of hand. When, however, he began to study the religious texts he found that they did not breathe out the profound wisdom which others had found. "Certainly," he says, "no one will accuse me of wishing to belittle the Egyptians; "the more I familiarize myself with them, the more I am persuaded "that they were one of the great nations of the human race, and "one of the most original and most creative, but at the same "time that they always remained half savage."[2] In other words,

1 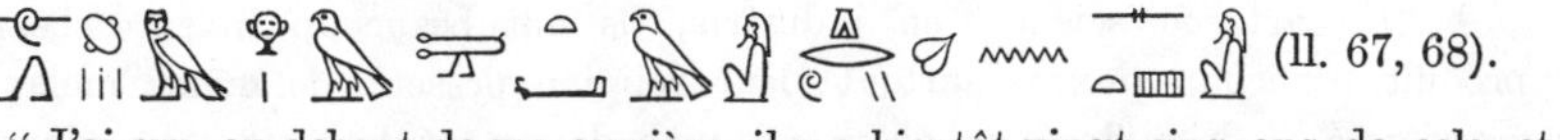
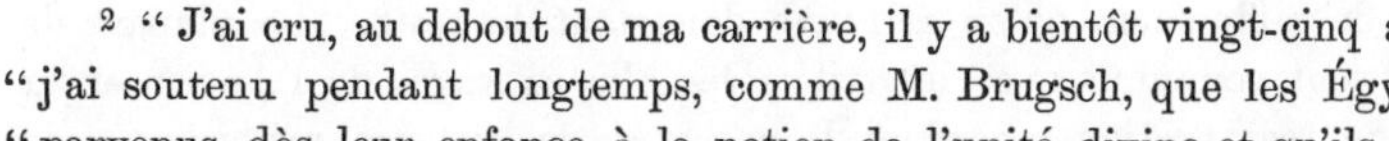 (ll. 67, 68).

2 "J'ai cru, au debout de ma carrière, il y a bientôt vingt-cinq ans de cela, et "j'ai soutenu pendant longtemps, comme M. Brugsch, que les Égyptiens étaient "parvenus, dès leur enfance, à la notion de l'unité divine et qu'ils en avaient tiré "un système entier de religion et de mythologie symbolique, agencé d'un bout à

the Egyptians, according to M. Maspero, never attained to the idea of the unity of God, and were at the best of times nothing but a half savage nation. It is easy to bring a charge of being half savage against a great nation, but in this case the charge is ill-founded, and is, in the writer's opinion, contradicted by every discovery which is made in Egypt; for the more we learn of the ancient Egyptians the more complete and far-reaching we find their civilization to have been. The evidence of the monuments of the Egyptians will, however, be sufficient to exhibit the character of this civilization in its true light, and, as the expression "half savage" is at best very vague, and must vary in meaning according to the standpoint of him who uses it, we pass on to consider the question whether the Egyptians attained to a conception of the unity of God or whether they did not.

We have seen that M. Maspero believes that they did not, but on the other hand some of the greatest Egytologists that have ever lived thought that they did. He thinks that the Egyptians possessed the greater number of their myths in common with the most savage of the tribes of the Old and New Worlds, that their practices preserved the stamp of primitive barbarism, that their religion exhibits the same mixture of grossness and refinement which is found in their arts and crafts, that it was cast in a mould by barbarians, and that from them it received an impression so deep that a hundred generations have not been able to efface it, nor even to smooth its roughnesses or to soften its outlines.[1] No

"l'autre avec une sûreté de main incomparable. C'était le temps où je n'avais pas "essayé par moi-même le déchiffrement des textes religieux et où je me bornais "à reproduire l'enseignement de nos grands maîtres. Quand j'ai été contraint "de les aborder, . . . . . j'ai dû m'avouer à moi-même qu'ils ne respiraient point "cette sagesse profonde que d'autres y avaient sentie. Certes on ne m'accusera pas "de vouloir déprécier les Égyptiens : plus je me familiarise avec eux, et plus je me "persuade qu'ils ont été un des grands peuples de l'humanité, l'un des plus originaux "et des plus créateurs, mais aussi qu'ils sont toujours demeurés des demi-barbares." *La Mythologie*, p. 277.

[1] "En art, en science, en industrie, ils ont beaucoup inventé, beaucoup "produit, beaucoup promis surtout; leur religion présente le même mélange de "grossièreté et de raffinement qu'on retrouve dans tout le reste. La plupart de "ses mythes lui sont communs avec les tribus les plus sauvages de l'Ancien et du "Nouveau-Monde; ses pratiques gardent le cachet de la barbarie primitive, et je "crois que les sacrifices humains n'en avaient pas disparu dans certaines circon-

one will attempt to deny that traces of half savage ideas and customs are to be found in Egyptian religious literature, but the real question is whether such traces render it impossible for the Egyptians ever to have attained to the conception of monotheism, whether the existence of such half savage ideas and customs is incompatible with it or not. Every one who is familiar with the literatures of oriental religions knows that the sublime and the ridiculous, spiritual ideas and material views, intellectuality and grossness, and belief and superstition, occur frequently in close juxtaposition, and illustrations of these statements may be found in the writings of the Arabs, and even in certain parts of the Hebrew Scriptures. Yet no one will deny that the Arabs as a people have been monotheists since the time of Muḥammad the Prophet, and no one will refuse to admit that the Hebrews, after a certain date in their history, became monotheists and have remained so. The literatures of both the Hebrews and the Arabs are full of extravagances of every kind, but no competent person has denied to these nations the right to be called monotheistic, and no one in the light of modern research will attempt to judge them by the coarsest expressions and materialistic thoughts which are found in their Scriptures. On the other hand, no one expects to find either in Hebrew or in Arabic literature the lofty spiritual and philosophical conceptions which modern highly educated thinkers associate with the idea of monotheism, and the same is, of course, to be said for the literature of the Egyptians; but it is not difficult to show that the idea of monotheism which existed in Egypt at a very early period is at least of the same character as that which grew up among both Hebrews and Arabs many centuries later.

To prove this statement recourse must be had to a number of extracts[1] from religious texts, and among such may be quoted the following:—To the dead king Unȧs it is said, "Thou existest at

"stances, même sous les grands Pharaons thébains. Elle a été jetée au moule "par des Barbares, et elle a reçu d'eux une empreinte si forte que cent générations "n'ont pu, je ne dirai pas l'effacer, mais en amollir les aspérités et en adoucir les "contours." *La Mythologie*, p. 277.

[1] See the group given in my *Papyrus of Ani*, London, 1895, p. lxxxiii. ff.

"the side of God," ; of Tetȧ it is said, "He weigheth words, and behold, God hearkeneth unto the words," ; of the same king it is said, "God hath called Tetȧ (in his name, etc.)," ; to Pepi I. it is said, "Thou hast received the "attribute (or, form) of God, thou hast become great therewith "before the gods," 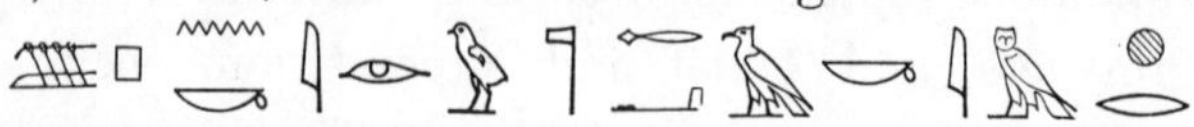 ; and "Thy mother Nut hath set thee to be as God to thine "enemy in thy name of God,"  ; and of the same king it is said, "This Pepi is, therefore, God, the son of God,"  . It may be argued that we should render *neter*, , in these passages by "a god" or "the god," but this would make nonsense of the passages in most cases. There is no point in telling a dead king that he will live "by the side of a god," or that "a god" will listen to his words when he is weighing words, i.e., giving judgment upon matters in the next world; what the writer said and what he meant his readers to understand was that Unȧs will live with the God, or God, and that he will have such an exalted position there that he will be appointed by God to act as judge, an office which belonged to God himself, and that God will listen to, i.e., obey his rulings. The above passages are taken from texts of the Vth and VIth Dynasties, but they are only copies of older documents, for there are good reasons for thinking that even so far back as the time when they were made, about B.C. 3300, the texts had already been revised two or three times, and changes and additions made in them as the result of modified beliefs and ideas.

The value of such passages, however, consists in the fact that they prove conclusively that so far back as B.C. 3300 some one god had become so great in the mind of the Egyptians that he stood out from among the "gods," , and was different from the First, Second, and Third companies of the gods,

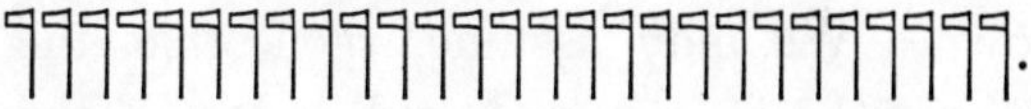. Another view which may be urged is that the *neter*, , here referred to is either the god Osiris or the god Rā, but even so it must be admitted that Osiris or Rā occupied a position in the mind of the Egyptian theologian which was far superior to that of any of the "gods." On the other hand, it must be pointed out that the Pyramid Texts are full of passages in which we are told what great things Rā will do for the deceased in the next world, and the honour which he will pay to him, and we must therefore conclude that the God referred to in the passages which we have quoted is not Rā, although he may be Osiris. But if we arrive at this conclusion we must admit that in the relatively remote period about B.C. 3300 Osiris was considered to be such a great god, and to occupy such an exalted position at the head of the "gods," that he could be spoken of and referred to simply as "God." We have already seen it implied that Osiris was the judge of those who were in the Underworld, and we know from the text of Unȧs (line 494) that he sat on a throne in heaven;[1] as the king is said to have become "god, and the messenger (or, angel) of God"[2] (line 175), and to "enter into the place which was more holy than any other place"[3] (line 178), it is perfectly clear that the God of the Pyramid Texts was an entirely different being from the "gods" and the "companies of the gods." The deceased is actually called "Osiris Pepi,"[4] and as he is said to have become an angel of God, if Osiris be that God and judge, he must have held a similar position to that of the God of the Hebrews, who is said to "judge among the gods,"[5] and must have been ministered to by "gods"

1 .

2 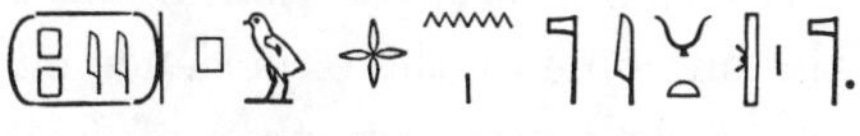.

3 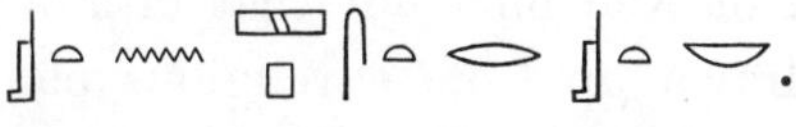.

4 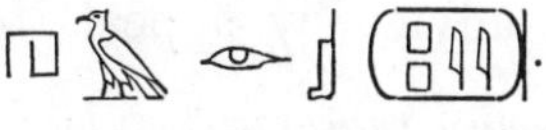. Pepi I., l. 60.

5 Psalm lxxxii. 1, בְּקֶרֶב אֱלֹהִים יִשְׁפֹּט.

of a rank inferior to his own. We may assume, then, that the God of the Pyramid Texts was Osiris, the god and judge of the dead, but it is clear that the only aspects of the God which are referred to are those which he bears as the god and judge of the dead. We have, unfortunately, no means of knowing how he was described by his earliest worshippers, for the priests of Heliopolis, when they absorbed him into their theological system, took care to give him only such characteristics as suited their own views; they have, however, shown us that he was the judge of the dead, and that he occupied a unique position among the gods, and enjoyed some of the powers possessed by the God of the nations which are on all hands admitted to be monotheistic.

But we may obtain further information about the conception of God among the Egyptians by an examination of certain passages in the famous Precepts of Kaqemna and the Precepts of Ptaḥ-ḥetep. The first of these works was composed in the reign of Seneferu, a king of the IVth Dynasty, and the second in the reign of Ȧssȧ, a king of the Vth Dynasty, but we only know them from the copies contained in the papyrus which was given to the Bibliothèque Royale in Paris by E. Prisse d'Avennes in 1847.[1] This document was probably written about the period of the XVIIth Dynasty, and may, of course, contain readings and additions reflecting the opinions of the Egyptians on religion and morals which were then current; but the foundations of both works belong to an earlier time, though whether that time fell under the XIIth Dynasty, as some think, or under the IVth and Vth Dynasties as the works themselves declare, matters little for our present purpose. In both sets of Precepts we have a series of moral aphorisms similar to those with which we are familiar in the Book of Wisdom, and Ecclesiasticus, and the Book of Proverbs, and they are given as the outcome of the experience of men of the world; neither the work of Kaqemna nor that of Ptaḥ-ḥetep can be said to have been drawn up from a religious point of view, and neither author supports his advice by appeals to religious

[1] See *Fac-simile d'un papyrus Égyptien en caractéres hièratiques*, Paris, 1847, folio.

authority. In these works we find the following admonitions and reflections:—

1. 

*àn* *rekhentu* *khepert* *àrit* *neter*

"Not [are] known the things which maketh God,"

i.e., the things which will come to pass by God's agency cannot be known, that is to say, God's ways are inscrutable.

2. 

*àu* *àm* *tau* *kher* *sekher* *neter*

The eating of bread is according to the plan of God,

i.e., a man's food comes to him through the providence of God.

3. 

*àm* - *k* *àri* *ḥer* *em* *reth*

Thou shalt not put terror into men and women;

*khesef* *neter*

is opposed [thereto] God.

4. 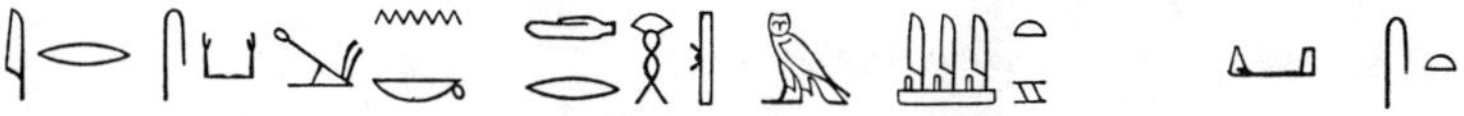

*àr* *seka* - *nek* *ṭer* *em* *sekhet* *ṭā* *set*

If thou hast land for ploughing labour in the field (which) hath given

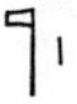

*neter*

God.

[1] The author of this observation was Kaqemna; the other ones are by Ptaḥ-ḥetep.

5. 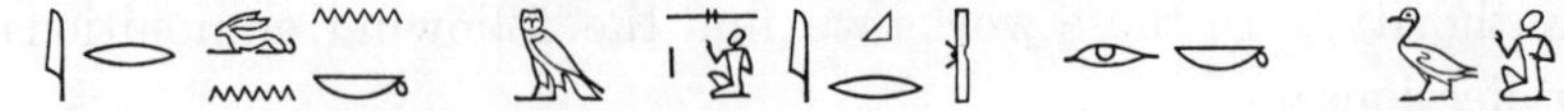

*ȧr un - nek em sa ȧqer ȧri - k sa*

If thou wouldst be a man perfect make thou [thy] son

*en smam neter*

to be pleasing unto God.

6. 

*seḥetep āqu - k em khepert-nek khepert*

Satisfy thy dependants by thy actions; it should be done

*en ḥesesu neter*

by him that is favoured by God.

7. 

*mertu neter pu setem ȧn setem*

What is loved of God is obedience; disobedience

*en mesṭetu neter*

hateth God.

8. 

*māk sa nefer en ṭāṭā neter*

Verily a son good [is] of the gifts of God.

And finally from the Prisse Papyrus may be quoted the exhortatation, "If having been of no account, thou hast become great, and "if, having been poor, thou hast become rich, when thou art "governor of the city be not hard-hearted on account of thy "advancement, because thou hast [only] become

9. 

| *mer* | *septu* | *neter* |
|---|---|---|
| "the guardian | of the provisions | of God." |

From this group of extracts we learn that the ways of the god referred to in the "Precepts" were inscrutable, that it was he who was supposed to give a man children, and property, and food, that he was opposed to any man tyrannizing over his fellow creatures; that he loved to be obeyed and hated disobedience, i.e., those who would not hearken unto him; that the perfect man was he who brought up his son in ways pleasing to God; that God expected the man who had been favoured by him to do good to those who were dependent upon him; and the writer of the "Precepts" urged the governor of a city to remember that he was only the guardian of goods and provisions which belonged to God. In all these extracts it is clear that the allusion is to some great and powerful being who rules and governs the world and provides according to his will for those who are in it. In the second extract we have the words *sekher neter*, i.e., the *sekher* of God. The word *sekher* , has many meanings, among them being "thought, plan, intention, scheme, design," and the like, and when Ptaḥ-ḥetep said that "the eating of bread is according to the *sekher* of God," there is no doubt that he intended his readers to understand that a man obtained bread, or food, to eat according to the plan or design which God had made, or decreed beforehand. A rendering which would very well represent the words *sekher neter* is "Divine providence;" but they do not justify the translation "fate" which has been proposed for them.

Now we know that both the writers Kaqemna and Ptaḥ-ḥetep lived in the neighbourhood of Memphis, because their tombs are at Ṣakḳâra, and if they lived at Memphis their great local god would be Ptaḥ of the Beautiful Face, or Ptaḥ of the White Wall, whose feminine counterpart was Sekhet and whose son was I-em-ḥetep. But in the group of extracts just given there is no mention of any of these gods, and the God referred to cannot be Osiris, first, because the texts are not funereal, and secondly, because the attributes ascribed to this God are not of those which we know from later texts belonged to the god of the dead. Who then is the God whose power, and providence, and government of the world are here proclaimed? The answer to this question is that the God referred to is God, Whose power men of the stamp of Ptaḥ-ḥetep discerned even at the remote period in which he lived, and Whose attributes they clearly distinguished; He was in their opinion too great to be called anything else but God, and though, no doubt, they offered sacrifices to the gods in the temple at Memphis, after the manner of their countrymen, they knew that God was an entirely different Being from those "gods."

Passing now to the period of the New Empire we have to consider a few extracts from the famous work commonly known as the "Maxims of Ani," or the "Precepts of Khensu-ḥetep," which was first described[1] by E. de Rougé in 1861, and was published in full fifteen years later by Chabas.[2] The text[3] is written upon a papyrus which was found in a box lying upon the floor of the tomb of a Christian monk at Dêr al-Medînet, and from considerations of palaeography it must probably be assigned to the period of the XXIInd Dynasty, but the original composition must be a great deal older, and it may well date from the XVIIIth Dynasty. The following extracts will illustrate the conception of God in the mind of the author of the "Maxims":—

1. 

*pa* *neter* *en* *sāauȧ* *ren - f*

The God is for making great his name.

[1] See *Moniteur*, 15 Août, 1861; and *Comptes Rendus*, Paris, 1871, pp. 340-350.

[2] See *L'Égyptologie*, Chalons-sur-Saône and Paris, 4to, 1876-1878.

[3] A facsimile was published by Mariette in *Papyrus Égyptiens du Musée de Boulaq*.

2. 

*pa* *neter* *àput* *pa* *maā*

The God [is] the judge of the right.

or, the God is the judge, the righteous one, i.e., the judge who passes sentence according to what is straight, *maā*, i.e., the law, the canon.

3. 

*àu* *ṭāu* *neter-ku* *unu*

Giveth thy God the means of subsistence.

4. "I have given thee thy mother," the writer says to his son, "and she carried thee even as she carried thee, and took upon "herself a heavy burden for thy sake, and did not lean upon me. "When at length thou wast born after having been carried by her "for months, she laid herself under thy yoke, and she nourished "thee for three years,[1] and was never weary of thee. . . . When "thou wast sent to school to be taught, she came every day "without fail to thy master [bringing] bread and beer [for thee] "from her house. Now thou hast become a man and hast married "a wife and hast a house, set thine eye upon thy child, and bring "him up as thy mother brought thee up. Wrong not thy mother "lest she lift up

*āāui-set* *en* *pa* *neter* *emtuf* *setemu* *sebḥu-set*

"her hands to the God [and] he hearken unto her prayers"

[and punish thee].

5. 

*àmmā* *su* *en* *pa* *neter*

"Let [a man] give himself to the God,

[1] Literally, "her breasts were in thy mouth for three years."

*sauu - k su em-ment en pa neter*

"keep thou thyself daily for the God,

*àu ṭuauu mà-qeṭi pa haru*

"to-morrow (?) being like the day (to-day ?)."

6. 

*khennu en neter betu-tuf pu seḥebu*

"The sanctuary of God its abomination is much speaking.

*senemeḥu-nek em àb mert àu meṭet - f*

"Make thou thy prayers with a heart of love all the petitions

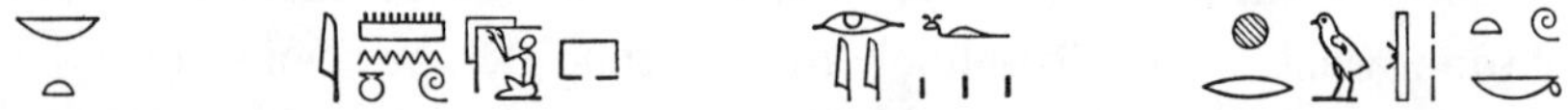

*nebt àmennu àri-f kheru-tuk*

"of which are in secret. He will perform thy affairs,

*setemu-f à tcheṭetu-k seshepu-[f] uṭennu-ṭuk*

"he will hear what thou sayest, he will accept thine offerings.

7. 

*uṭennu neter-ku sau-tu er*

"In making offerings to thy God guard thou thyself against

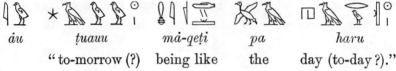

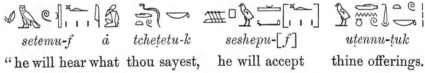

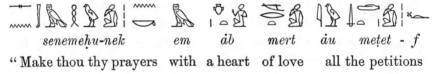

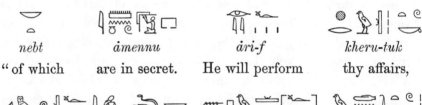

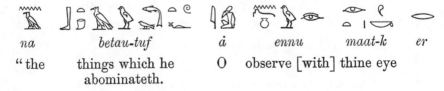

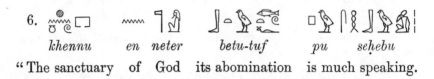

*na betau-tuf à ennu maat-k er*

"the things which he abominateth. O observe [with] thine eye

*paif sekheru qenṭet emtuk senenti-tu*

"his plans. Devote thyself to the adoration

*em ren - f su ṭāt baiu ḥeḥ*

"of his name. It is he who giveth souls to millions

*en ȧaru sāauȧ pa enti*

"of forms, and [he] magnifieth whosoever

*sāauȧ - f ȧr neter ta pen en*

"magnifieth him. Now the god of this earth is

*pa Shuu ḥer khut ȧu naif mȧtui*

"the god Shu, he who is over the horizons. His similitudes

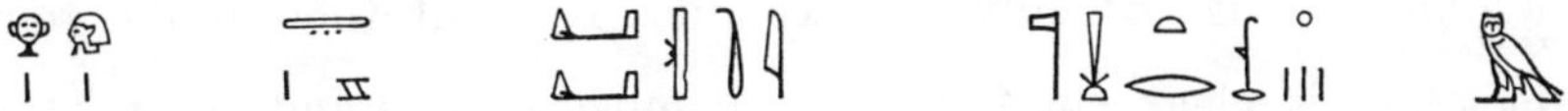

*ḥer ṭep ta ṭāṭā-thȧ senterȧ em*

"[are] upon earth, are given [to them] offerings of incense with

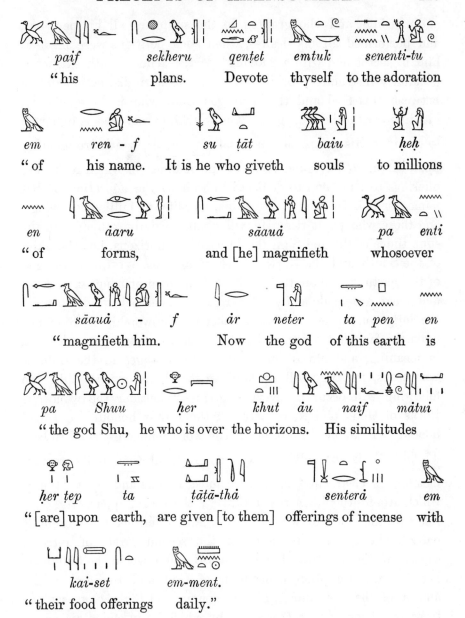

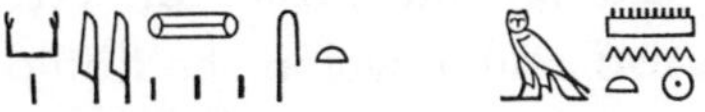

*kai-set em-ment.*

"their food offerings daily."

The group of passages given above supplies a new set of attributes ascribed by the Egyptians to God, and they show that they believed this Being to be one who judged according to right, who was jealous for the honour of his name, who received prayers and offerings, and who granted to the suppliant all his petitions, and performed all his desires, when such petitions were made to him in secret and with a "loving heart." The seventh extract is peculiarly instructive, for in it we have a sharp distinction drawn between this God and the solar god Shu, who is here, clearly, identified with the Sun-god. The worshipper of God is exhorted to consider His plans, or designs, , which are manifest upon earth, to pay good heed to the manner in which he makes offerings to Him, and to dedicate himself to the adoration of His name, for it is He who giveth souls, i.e., life, to millions of beings, and those who exalt Him He will exalt. On the other hand, the similitudes of the god Shu, the lord of the horizons, i.e., the skies of the South and the North, the East and the West, and the god of this earth, are upon the earth, and to them offerings of incense and meat are made daily. There is no need here to dwell upon the lofty conception of what is meet for the worship of God; nor upon the fact that many of the phrases in the extract are identical in meaning, and almost in words, with passages in the Hebrew Scriptures, for they will be familiar to all, and extracts like the following will occur to every reader:—"Consider the wondrous works of God" (Job xxxvii. 14); "them that honour me I will honour" (1 Samuel ii. 30), etc. The word rendered "similitudes," 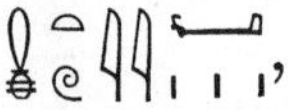, is difficult to explain in detail though its general meaning is clear enough, and we must understand by it "things which are in the likeness [of Shu]"; these can, apparently, only refer to the gods to whom incense and offerings were brought daily. The great importance of the second group of extracts consists in the fact that they emphasize and develop the difference between the Egyptian conception of God and the gods. The author of the "Maxims," like Kaqemna and Ptaḥ-ḥetep, set out to write a book of moral precepts by which he intended his son to mould his course of life and to be guided. This work is not of a funereal character, therefore the God who is referred to throughout cannot be Osiris, and the context proves beyond all doubt that the writer is alluding to the same Being as were the earlier writers of moral aphorisms already mentioned. In the case of the

"Maxims," however, the word for God, *neter* , is usually qualified by the emphatic article *pa* .

But in all the passages quoted above there is no distinct statement that the God alluded to therein is God alone, and that there is no other God besides Him, although this is clearly implied; we must therefore turn to another class of texts in which the attribute of oneness or unity is ascribed to one or more "great gods," and see how it is applied. The god Ta-tunen is called, "One, maker of mortals, and of the company of the gods";[1] the god Rā-Tem is called, "lord of heaven, lord of earth, maker of "beings celestial and of beings terrestrial, God One, who came "into being in primeval time, maker of the world, creator of "rational beings, maker of Nu (the sky), creator of the Nile, "maker of whatsoever is in the waters, and giver of life to the "same, knitter together of the mountains, making to come into "being men and women, and beasts and cattle, and creator of the "heavens and the earth";[2] the great Khu (Spirit) whom Tem created is described as the "only One in Nu";[3] Osiris is said to be "lord of the gods, god One";[4] and in a remarkable passage, in which the whole of the attributes of the Sun-god Rā have been transferred to Åmen-Rā, we have the following statement wherein this god is said to be "the holy (or, venerable) Soul which came

1 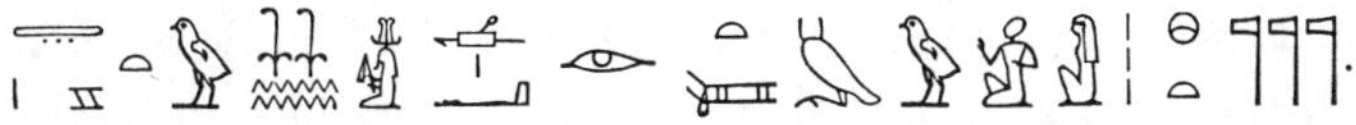. *Papyrus of Ani*, sheet 1, line 6.

2 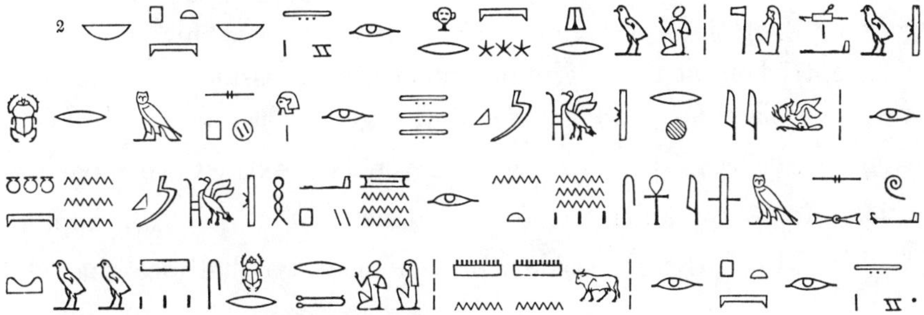.
*Papyrus of Hunefer*, sheet 1, line 5 ff.

3 *Book of the Dead*, Chap. lxxviii. 16.

4 *Ibid.*, Chap. clxxiii.

"into being aforetime, the great god who liveth in (or by) Maāt "(i.e., unfailing and unvarying order and regularity),

*pautti* — *ṭepi* — *mes* — *pautti*
"the *paut* — primeval [which] gave birth to — the two companies of gods,

*kheper* — *neter* — *neb* — *ȧm - f* — *uā* *uāui*
"came into being — god — every — through him, — one alone,

*ȧri - f* — *unen* — *shaā* — *ta* — *em* — *sep ṭepi*
"he made — what exists — when the earth began — in — primeval time,

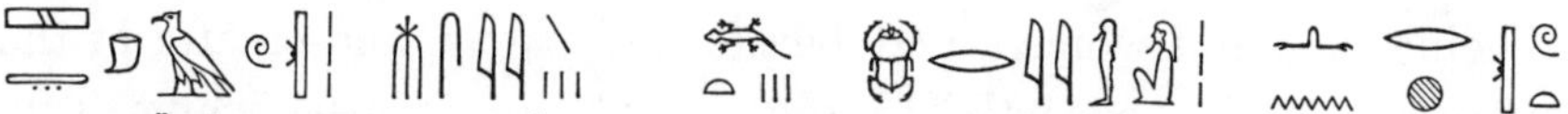

*shetau* — *mesi* — *āsht* — *kheperiu* — *ȧn rekhtu*
"hidden — of births, — manifold — of forms, — not is known

*bes - f*
"his growth."[1]

The text goes on to say that Ȧmen-Rā is the "holy Sekhem (i.e., "Power), the god who is beloved, and is terrible and mighty in "his risings, lord of space, the Power, Kheperȧ, the creator of "every evolution (or, thing) which belongeth to his existence,[2] "except whom at the beginning none other existed." Here then we have Ta-tunen, Rā-Tem, and the god Osiris all called "God One," *neter uā*, , and in the last extract we have the remarkable expression "God One alone," 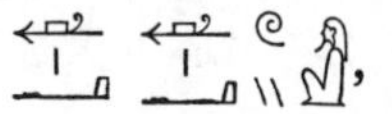, applied to Ȧmen-Rā. If we consider for a moment we shall see that the

[1] See Maspero, *Mém. Miss. Arch.*, tom i., p. 594.

[2] .

gods Tem and Kheperȧ are only forms of the Sun-god Rā, and as Tatunen was concerned in the production of the Sun-god he also is a solar god; at the time when the above extracts were written, i.e., under the XVIIIth Dynasty, we have abundant proof that the Egyptians were continually adding to the attributes which they ascribed to Osiris, and that such attributes were those which belonged to some form of Rā or to Rā himself. The word "One" then is applied in these cases to Rā, and to the forms of Rā, and to a god who had come to be regarded in one aspect at least as a solar god, and it will be found on examination of the texts that whenever a god or goddess is described as "One" it is because that deity has been endowed by the writer, whether rightly or wrongly is another matter, with some of the attributes of Rā.

It is easy to see from the hieroglyphic extract given above that to the god there described are attributed many of the creative qualities which we assign to God Almighty. Thus he is said to be the primeval *Paut* or divine substance who gave birth to the two companies of the gods (in this case we must understand the company of the gods of heaven and the company of the gods of earth, and not the Great and Little Companies of the gods of Heliopolis), and every god came into being by him or through him. Here it is quite clear that "every god" means only every inferior being who possessed something of the quality of a *neter* or "god," and every being who ministered to the great Paut, and who in the Hebrew Scriptures would be grouped under the name "Elôhîm," אֱלֹהִים, or among the "angels," and in Arabic literature among the good Jinn. The text goes on to say not only in primeval times, i.e., "in the beginning," he created whatever exists upon the earth, but also that in primeval time no other being existed with him. This is a definite statement of the unity or oneness of God which cannot be gainsaid, and it was this attribute of unity or oneness which the priests of various cities ascribed to their local god whenever they could. We have no means of saying whether this idea of oneness or unity was first applied to Rā or to some more ancient god such as Horus, but it is, in the writer's opinion, quite certain that it existed in the minds of the educated classes of Egypt in the earliest times, and that in all periods it was the central point of their conceptions of God. But the text goes on to say that the great Paut who created the companies of the gods is "hidden of births and manifold of forms," and that "his growth (or development) is unknown." This is only another way of saying that the manner in which the beings and things produced by the Paut came into being is unknown, and that he appears under many forms. We may here refer to the passage in the XVIIth Chapter of the *Book of the Dead* (line 9), wherein it is said:—

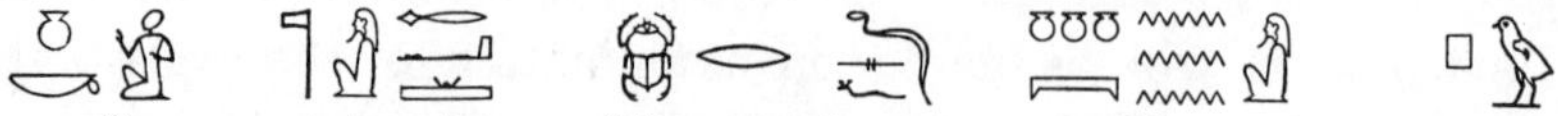

*nuk* *neter āa* *kheper tchesef* *Nu* *pu*

"I am the great god self-created, Nu, that is to say,

*qemam* *renu - f* *paut* *neteru*

"who made his names the company of the gods

*em* *neter*

"as god."

Concerning this being the question is asked, "Who then is this?" and the following answer is given:—

*Rā* *pu* *qemam* *renu* *en* *āt - f*

"It is Rā who created names for his members

*kheper* *enen* *pu* *em* *neteru*

"and these came into being in the form of the gods

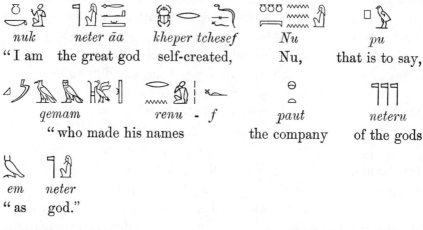

*ȧmi - khet* *Rā*

"who are in the following of Rā."

On the creative power of the great Paut special emphasis is laid in the extract on p. 132, for, after declaring that he created in the beginning whatsoever exists, the text adds that he created everything that had to do with his own coming into being; and in the passages from the *Book of the Dead* it is taught, according to one dogma, that the names of the great, self-produced god Nu became the company of gods under the form of God, and according to another that the gods who were in the train of Rā were the members or limbs of Rā, and that these limbs were, in turn, the names of Rā. The last text quoted is of considerable importance, for it gives us a direct proof that the attributes of the god Nu were transferred to Rā, and that Rā was identified absolutely with Nu, and the last text but one quoted shows how the attributes of Rā were transferred to Ȧmen, who was originally only the local god of Thebes, by means of the fusion of the two gods into Ȧmen-Rā. We know that to many gods were ascribed the attributes of Rā, and that all solar gods were, in the dynastic period at least, held to be forms of him; if we could identify them all we should be able to reduce the number of Egyptian gods considerably.

The attribute or quality of oneness or unity, which is ascribed first to the great God who was the creator of the heavens and the earth and all therein, and secondly to the Sun-god who was regarded as the visible type and symbol of God and his various forms, and thirdly, at a later period to the god Osiris, has been termed "henotheism" by many writers who asserted that it was a "phase of religious thought"[1] which was different from monotheism. According to the late Right Honourable Prof. Max Müller we have become acquainted with this phase of religious thought "for the first time through the Veda," and he goes on to say that "when these individual gods are invoked they are not "conceived as limited by the power of others, as superior or "inferior in rank. Each god is to the mind of the suppliant as "good as all the gods. He is felt at the time as a real divinity, "as supreme and absolute, in spite of the necessary limitations "which, to our mind, a plurality of gods must entail on every "single god. All the rest disappear from the vision of the poet, "and he only who is to fulfil their desires stands in full light "before the eyes of the worshippers." It is quite true that the

[1] Max Müller, *Hibbert Lectures*, p. 285.

Egyptian religion passed through a phase which has been identified as henotheism, but, assuming for a moment that we should be correct in calling that phase henotheism, the Egyptian religious texts prove that it was "not the henotheism of Max Müller or of "Hartmann, or of Asmus, but a practical henotheism, i.e., the "adoration of one God above all others as the specific tribal god or "as the lord over a particular people, a national or relative "monotheism, like that of the ancient Israelites, the worship of an "absolute sovereign who exacts passive obedience. This practical "monotheism is totally different from the theoretical monotheism, "to which the Aryans, with their monistic speculative idea of the "godhead, are much nearer."[1]

These words by the late Professor Tiele here quoted were not applied by him to the Egyptian religion, but they so well express the present writer's views about the monotheism of the Egyptians that they are adopted for that purpose. Professor Tiele was, undoubtedly, the greatest authority on comparative religion of his day, and although he was not an Egyptologist at first hand, he had discussed Egyptian religious texts with great experts like Chabas, Birch, de Rougé, and others, to such good purpose that his opinion on the subject is of peculiar value. According to him the Egyptian religion presents two apparently contradictory and irreconcilable phenomena:—1. A lively sentiment of the spirituality of God united to the coarsest materialistic representations of different divinities; and 2. A sentiment, not less lively, of the unity of God, united to an extremely great multiplicity of divine persons.[2] The best educated priests, he thinks, who were the most vigorous promoters of religious progress, were as much attached to forms and traditional symbols as the people themselves, and they were most unwilling to give up any part of them. The symbolism, being misunderstood by the ignorant folk, produced serious errors, and the forms under which the Egyptians represented their gods, and which are repellent to our refined taste, answered in their minds to the idea of divinity which was purer and more spiritual than the noble and beautiful forms of the gods of

[1] C. P. Tiele, in *Encyclopaedia Britannica*, vol. xx., p. 367.

[2] *Histoire Comparée des Anciennes Religions*, Paris, 1882.

Hellas. The ignorant felt no repugnance to monstrous representations because they appeared as representations having a profound and mysterious meaning; the learned understood the meanings of the symbols, and paid their adoration through them to the truth of which they were the coverings. In other words, the uneducated loved a plurality of gods, while the priests and educated classes who could read and understand books adopted the idea of One God, the creator of all the beings in heaven and on earth who, for want of a better word, were called "gods."

The priests and theologians saw nothing incompatible in believing that God was One, and that he existed under innumerable forms. We may note the existence of the same view in the Hebrew Scriptures where, in spite of the commandments, "Thou "shalt have no other gods before me. Thou shalt not make unto "thee any graven image, or any likeness [of anything] that [is] "in heaven above, . . . . Thou shalt not bow down thyself to "them, nor serve them . . . ." (Exodus xx. 3-5), the Israelites felt no scruple in representing God in the midst of His sons, and for a very long time they continued to adore a number of divine beings side by side with Yahweh.[1] Thus in Joshua xxii. 22, we read, "The Lord God of gods, the Lord God of gods, he knoweth and "Israel shall know;" in Exodus xxii. 28 is given the commandment, "Thou shalt not revile the gods nor curse the ruler of thy people;" in Psalm cxxxvi. 2, Israel is exhorted to "give thanks unto the "God of gods;" the "sons of God" we know from Genesis vi. 2; Job ii. 1; xxxviii. 7;[2] and that "gods" in some passages mean nothing but beings possessing some characteristic of God is clear from 1 Samuel xxviii. 13, wherein we read that the witch of Endor told Saul that she "saw gods ascending out of the earth." The allusion in this last passage is clearly to some kind of supernatural being or beings. Returning for a moment to the views of Professor Tiele, we admit that, judging from certain texts of the Dynastic Period, he is justified in asserting that in Egypt monotheism is anterior to polytheism; but judging from the evidence of the recently discovered monuments of the

[1] Tiele, *Hist. Comparée*, p. 138.

[2] Cf. also Deut. x. 17; Psalms xiv. 3; lxxxii. 1, 6; Job i. 6.

predynastic and archaïc periods, we must admit that polytheism appears to be older than monotheism. On the other hand, the monotheistic ideas which appear in the works of Kaqemna and Ptaḥ-ḥetep were certainly not invented during the period in which they lived, and there is every reason for believing that they originated at a much earlier date. If literary compositions belonging to the first three dynasties are ever brought to light from the tombs of Egypt, we shall probably find that the idea of the oneness of God is expressed with just as much force and certainty as it is under the following dynasties, and in the same works we shall also find mention of the various gods who were created by the great God who was proclaimed to be One, and expected to be worshipped with obedience.

The final opinion of Professor Tiele on the Egyptian religion was that from the beginning it was polytheistic, but that it developed in two opposite directions; in the one direction gods were multiplied by the addition of local gods, and in the other the Egyptian drew nearer and nearer to monotheism.[1]

We may now consider the opinions of some of the greatest Egyptologists on the monotheism of the Egyptians. Writing in the *Revue Archéologique* (1860, p. 73) E. de Rougé says, "The "unity of a supreme and self-existent being, his eternity, his "almightiness, and eternal reproduction thereby as God; the "attributing of the creation of the world and of all living beings "to the supreme God; the immortality of the soul, completed by "the dogma of punishments and rewards; such is the sublime

[1] "Een voorhistorisch monotheïsme onderstelt een graad van ontwikkeling "en een vordering in het wijsgeerig nadenken, die bij een nog barbaarsch volk "niet denkbaar zijn. Ook de egyptische godsdienst is van animisme en magisch "polydaemonisme uitgegaan en zoo eerst tot polytheïsme opgeklommen. Dit "polytheïsme ontwikkelt zich dan in twee geheel tegen o vergestelde richtingen. "Aan den eenen kant wordt de godenwereld, door bijeenvoeging van plaatselijke "godsdiensten, een gevolg van de onderwerping der verschillende gewesten met "hun godsdienstige middelpunten aan het gezag van éen koning, en door over- "neming van vreemde godheden, steeds rijker. Aan den anderen kant nadert "men het monotheïsme meer en meer, zonder het ooithelder en ondubbelzinnig uit "te spreken. De geleerden trachtten beide mit elkander overeen te brengen, onder "anderen door de vele goden voor te stellen als de openbaringen van den éenen, "ongeschapen, verborgen God, zijn leben, door hem zelnengeschapen." See *Geschiedenis van den Godsdienst in de Oudheid*, Amsterdam, 1893, p. 25.

"and persistent base which, notwithstanding all deviations and all "mythological embellishments, must secure for the beliefs of the "ancient Egyptians a most honourable place among the religions "of antiquity."[1] In an article on the "Religion of the Ancient Egyptians," written nine years later as a result of a close study of many of the great religious texts, he asserted that more than five thousand years before there existed in the Valley of the Nile the hymn to the unity of God, and the belief in the unity of a supreme God with the attributes of Creator of men, and Legislator of man, whom he has endowed with an immortal soul. In his description of the principal monuments at the Egyptian Museum at Bûlâk in Cairo, Mariette Bey said, "At the head of the Egyptian pantheon "soars a God who is one, immortal, uncreated, invisible and hidden "in the inaccessible depths of his essence; he is the creator of the "heavens and of the earth; he has made everything which exists "and nothing has been made without him; such is the God who "is reserved for the initiated of the sanctuary."[2] A similar view was held by Chabas,[3] who said, "The One God, who existed before "all things, who represents the pure and abstract idea of divinity, "is not clearly specialized by [any] one single personage of the vast "Egyptian pantheon. Neither Ptaḥ, nor Seb, nor Thoth, nor Rā,

[1] "L'unité d'un être suprême existant par lui-même, son éternité, sa toute- "puissance et la génération éternelle en Dieu; la création du monde et de tous "les êtres vivants attribuée à ce Dieu suprême; l'immortalité de l'âme, complétée "par le dogme des peines et des récompenses; tel est le fond sublime et persistant "qui, malgré toutes les déviations et toutes les broderies mythologiques, doit "assurer aux croyances des anciens Égyptiens un rang très honorable parmi les "religions de l'antiquité." . . . . . "Il y a plus de 5000 ans qu'a commencé, dans "la vallée du Nil, *l'hymne à l'Unité de Dieu et à l'Immortalité de l'âme;* et nous "voyons dans les derniers temps l'Égypte arrivée au *Polythéisme* le plus effréné. "*La croyance à l'Unité du Dieu suprême, à ses attributs de Créateur et de Législateur* "*de l'homme, qu'il a doué d'une âme immortelle;* voilà les notions primitives "enchâssées comme des diamants indestructibles au milieu des superfétations mytho- "logiques accumulées par les siècles qui ont passé sur cette vieille civilisation." *Annales de Philosophie Chrétienne*, Paris, 1869, p. 336.

[2] "Au sommet du panthéon Égyptien plane un Dieu unique, immortel, incréé, "invisible et caché dans les profondeurs inaccessibles de son essence; il est le "createur du ciel et de la terre; il a fait tout ce qui existe, et rien n'a été fait sans "lui; c'est le Dieu réservé à l'initié du sanctuaire." Mariette, *Notice*, Cairo, 1876, p. 17.

[3] *Calendrier des jours fastes et néfastes*, p. 107.

"nor Osiris, nor any other god is a personification of him at all "times; but of these sometimes one and at other times another is "invoked in terms which assimilate these intimately with the "supreme type; the innumerable gods of Egypt are only attributes "and different aspects of this unique type."

M. Pierret, in discussing the matter, holds the view that the texts prove that the Egyptians believed in a God who was One, and was without a second, and was infinite and eternal. At the very time, however, when the scribes were writing upon papyrus or cutting upon stone the inscriptions which affirmed this belief, the artists were making sculptures of the gods with heads of hawks, or rams, or crocodiles, or goddesses with the heads of lionesses, cats, or cows. Nevertheless the One God, who is without a second, is One even among the company of the gods, for he has numerous names and forms, and he appears under sacred and mysterious forms in the temples, that is to say under the figures[1] which were painted on the walls, and in the statues of the gods which were set up in the temples. The greatest supporter of the doctrine of ancient Egyptian monotheism was the late Dr. Brugsch, who assigned to the word for God, *neter* 𓊹𓀭, the highly philosophical meaning which has been quoted above. Accepting the view, which the Egyptians themselves held, that the gods were only names of the various attributes of the One God, he searched through the religious literature and collected from the hymns, prayers, etc., which were addressed to the various gods and goddesses in various periods, a number of epithets and attributes[2] which were bestowed upon them by their worshippers. These extracts he classified, and when they were grouped and arranged they formed a description of God such as it would be difficult to find a parallel for outside the Holy Scriptures. It has been contended that as these scattered epithets are never found together the ancient Egyptians had no conception of a God who was One, and was self-produced, and had existed, and would exist, always, and was hidden and unknown of form and name, and was the Creator of heaven and the gods, and earth, and man, and all

[1] Pierret, *Le Panthéon Égyptien*, Paris, 1881.

[2] They will be found in Brugsch, *Religion und Mythologie*, p. 96 ff.

things, and was at the same time merciful, and compassionate, and loving, and the protector of the weak against the strong, and the rewarder and protector of those who served him.

But this contention is not well founded, because, although these attributes were ascribed to a miscellaneous number of deities, we must remember that they would not have been thus associated unless the writers recognized such gods as phases or aspects of the Great God. The fact remains that such attributes were ascribed to gods who were created by God, and that the Egyptians arrived at such ideas as those described above is a lasting proof of the exalted character of their religion and of their conception of monotheism. The main point to keep in view is that the gods of Egypt were regarded by the Egyptians generally as inferior beings to the great God who made them, and that they were not held to be equal to him in all respects. Further, we must repeat that the God referred to in the moral precepts of the Early Empire holds a position similar to that held by Yahweh among the Hebrews and Allah among the Arabs, and that the gods and goddesses who were ministers of his will and pleasure find their counterparts in the angels, and archangels, and spirits of all kinds, both good and bad, of whom the Hebrew and Arabic literatures are full. No surer proof of this can be given than the well-known passage in Deuteronomy vi. 4, where it is said, "Hear, O Israel, Yahweh our "God (literally, gods), is Yahweh One,"[1] and the Egyptian *neter uā* 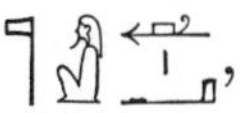, "One God," as far as the application and meaning of *uā* is concerned, is identical with that of the Hebrew word אֶחָד in the text quoted. We may note, too, the words, "Yahweh our gods," which show that Yahweh was identified with the gods, אֱלֹהִים, of the polytheistic period of the ancient Hebrew religion; it is, however, possible that when the verse in Deuteronomy was written the word Elôhîm had come to mean the great God of the Hebrews, although originally it had meant a collection of sacred or divine beings. In the Ḳur'ân, Sura cxii., the God of the Arabs is declared to be One, and from the commentaries on the Sura we know that this declaration was revealed to Muḥammad in answer to the people of

[1] Compare St. Mark xii. 29.

the Kurêsh, who asked him concerning the distinguishing attributes of the God he invited them to worship. If we had all the literature of the early Hebrews, and of the Arabs at the period of the propaganda of Muhammad we should probably find that many local gods in Palestine and Arabia were called One, but that only the God who had the moral aspects which were attributed to the great God of the Egyptians by the philosophers of the Early Empire succeeded in retaining it permanently.

The religion of the Egyptians has, however, always been regarded from two distinct and opposite points of view; a number of scholars, among whom may be mentioned Champollion-Figeac, de Rougé, Chabas, Mariette, Déveria, Birch, and Brugsch, have considered it to have been monotheistic, but others have declared unhesitatingly that it was polytheistic; this result is due probably to the way in which it is regarded. Speaking of the difference of opinion which existed on the subject between the late Dr. Brugsch and himself, M. Maspero says that he and Brugsch considered the Egyptian religion in two different ways. Time, he says, which has done so much harm to other nations, has shown itself favourable to the Egyptians. It has spared their tombs, their temples, their statues, and the thousand small objects which were the pride of their domestic life, and it has led us in such a way that we judge them by the most beautiful and the prettiest of the things which they made, and has at length caused us to place their civilization on the same footing as that of the Romans or the Greeks. But if it be looked at more nearly the point of view changes; to speak quite shortly, Thothmes III. and Rameses II. resemble Mtesa of Central Africa more closely than they do Alexander or Caesar. It is not their fault, but they arrived too soon in a period which was too early, and they must bear the penalty of their precociousness. In art, in science, in trade, they have invented much and produced much, and have, above all, promised much; their religion presents the same mixture of coarseness and refinement which is found in all else. Most of its myths it holds in common with the most savage tribes of the Old and the New Worlds. The Egyptian possessed the spirit of the metaphysician, a fact which he proved when Christianity furnished him with a subject worthy of his subtle powers. But, M. Maspero asks, what kind of metaphysics could proceed from so naïve a conception of the universe and of things which he has revealed? He thinks it must be true, at least in the main, because Brugsch depicted the Egyptian world in a manner very similar to his own, and deeming it true he cannot any longer admit the notion of the Egyptian Deity and his unity which several scholars have adopted. He takes the Egyptian religion for what it shows that it is, viz., a polytheism with its contradictions, and its repetitions, with its dogmas indecent sometimes, cruel sometimes, and ridiculous sometimes, according to modern ideas, and with its families of half-human gods which the worshipper cherished the more or understood the better the more closely they resembled himself.[1] The opinion thus expressed, though unfavourable to the character of the Egyptian, and directly opposed to the views of some of the greatest Egyptologists of the last century, is evidently honest, and coming from such a quarter is entitled to the greatest respect; but it seems that M. Maspero has judged the Egyptians of all periods according to the standard of religion which was in vogue in Egypt in predynastic times, when the primitive Egyptians were, no doubt, half savage.

The Egyptians, being fundamentally an African people, possessed all the virtues and vices which characterized the North African races generally, and it is not to be held for a moment that any African people could ever become metaphysicians in the modern sense of the word. In the first place, no African language is suitable for giving expression to theological and philosophical speculations, and even an Egyptian priest of the highest intellectual attainments would have been unable to render a treatise of Aristotle into language which his brother priests without teaching could understand. The mere construction of the language would make such a thing an impossibility, to say nothing of the ideas of the great Greek philosopher, which belong to a domain of thought and culture wholly foreign to the Egyptian. The allusion to the Christian metaphysics of the Egyptian is understandable, as everyone knows who has taken the trouble to read the literature of the Copts, who transferred much of the base and degraded Egyptian

[1] *La Mythologie Égyptienne*, p. 278.

mythology which was current during the first few centuries of the Christian era into their newly acquired belief in Jesus Christ. The lives of the Coptic martyrs show the use which the Egyptian made of his metaphysical spirit, and the history of the early Church in Egypt illustrates what happened when he tried to apply it to the consideration of the common theological terms in Greek and in Latin. Incidentally we may note that in order to express the various ideas connected with the Christian Deity and the Persons of the Trinity he was obliged to take over the actual Greek words into his language, which was poor in abstract ideas. In the picture which M. Maspero has given of the Egyptian's conception of the universe and of the origin of gods and things he has only dwelt upon the mythological side of the question, and has not set forth all the passages upon which other Egyptologists have based their views about Egyptian monotheism; moreover, no allowance appears to have been made for the peculiar religious and mental characteristics of the race. But when all is said against the Egyptian religion which can be said, the fact remains that it is not the religion itself which has cruel, ridiculous, and indecent dogmas, but the myths wherewith generations of foolish priests obscured the pure beliefs in monotheism and immortality which seem to have existed in Egypt from the earliest times. If modern oriental religions were judged in the adverse manner in which the religion of ancient Egypt has been judged, none would escape similar condemnation; the same thing may be said of some of the religions of the Western nations.

The superstitions which exist among many Eastern nations professing monotheism and even Christianity are as gross as those found among so-called Pagan nations; as examples may be quoted the Christians of St. John in Southern Mesopotamia, and many of the Arabic-speaking peoples of the Eastern Sûdân, yet among the former no one attempts to deny the existence of a sort of Christianity, though he would indeed be bold who would dare to compare it with the Christianity of such men as Canon Liddon or Cardinal Newman; similarly, the monotheism of the peoples of the Eastern Sûdân is universally admitted, but it does not prevent their indulging in the coarsest and most fantastic beliefs and practices, many of which, however, it must be admitted have descended to them from their pagan ancestors. Fortunately, however, the monotheistic character of the Egyptian religion rests on too firm a foundation to be easily overthrown, and notwithstanding the elaborate system of symbolic ceremonials which was so prominent a feature of Egyptian worship, Egyptian monotheism always maintained its place in the minds of those who were sufficiently educated to understand the ideas which the symbols thereof represented. The Egyptian never confounded God with the gods, and it would seem that he even discriminated between God and "the god of the "city," for in the Negative Confession (No. 38) the deceased says, "O Utu-rekhit, who comest forth from thy house, I have not cursed "God"; and in No. 42 he says, "Hail, Ȧn-ā-f, who comest forth "from Ȧukert (the Underworld), I have not thought scorn of (or, "belittled) the god who is in my city." Whence came the Egyptian conception of monotheism, or when it first sprang up, cannot be said, but in its oldest form it is coeval with the dynastic civilization of Egypt at least, and it may well date from far earlier times. The monotheistic idea is not the peculiar attribute of any one people or period. It may seem unnecessary to discuss Egyptian monotheism at such length, but the matter is one of great interest and importance because the literature of Egypt proves it to have been in existence in that country for more than three thousand five hundred years before Christ; in fact, Egyptian monotheism is the oldest form of monotheism known to us. It is easy enough to understand how anxious the priesthoods of the various cities would be to persuade the people who worshipped the local gods that this or that god was the being who united in himself the attributes of the original god of the city with those of the great cosmic god with physical aspects who created the heavens and the earth, and with those of the ethical god who was proclaimed by Kaqemna, Ptaḥ-ḥetep, Ani, and other writers of moral precepts.

In the earliest times it was the god Horus who was chosen in this manner, for under the form of a hawk he appears to have been the first god who was worshipped throughout the country generally, and the numerous forms of this god, and the fact that his attributes were at a later period ascribed to Horus the son of Isis, attest the antiquity and importance of his cult. The next god chosen to represent the great ethical God of the Egyptians was not a personification of the sky as was Horus, but the Sun-god Rā, on whom was bestowed every epithet of power and might which was known to the Egyptians, as well as the epithets and forms of the god Horus. But although his worship was common throughout Egypt, and his sanctuaries were for many centuries the most important in the land, there is abundant proof that the Egyptians never merged their conceptions of their great ethical God in their conceptions of Rā.

There seem to be traces of a belief that Rā as the spirit or god of the sun may have been a form or representative of him, but they are not very definite, and the worship of Rā's visible symbol, the sun, as the source of heat and light, and therefore of life—as the Egyptians recognized at an early period—was commoner than any abstract conception of his nature or existence. In a hymn to Ḥāpi, the Nile-god, we find a remarkable passage in which some of the chief attributes of God are ascribed to the power which causes the Inundation and who is addressed under the names of the gods Ptaḥ and Khnemu. To this Being it is said by the author of the hymn, "If thou wert overcome in heaven the gods, 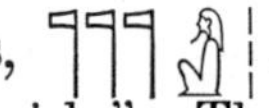, "would fall upon their faces and mankind would perish." The context shows that the author first pays a tribute of reverence to the local god of Memphis, Ptaḥ, whom he styles the "lord of fish," and the "creator of wheat and barley," and of whom he says with reference to the well-known attribute of Ptaḥ as the great artificer, "inactivity is the abomination of his fingers," i.e., the fingers of the god hate idleness. He then goes on to mention Khnemu, the local god of the First Cataract, wherein the sources of the Nile were at one time believed to be situated, and styles him "the bringer of "food and provisions, the creator of all good things, the lord of all "choice and pleasant meats, who maketh the herb to grow for the "use of the cattle, who filleth the storehouses and heapeth up high "[corn] in the granaries, who payeth heed to the poor and needy, "who maketh to grow crops which are sufficient for the desires of "all men and yet is not diminished thereby, and whose strength is "a shield." Now the author of the hymn goes on to declare that the true Ḥāpi, or god of the Nile, "cannot be figured in stone, he "is not to be seen in the images on which are set the crowns of the "south and the north with their uraei, offerings cannot be made to "him, he cannot be brought forth from his secret places, his dwell-"ing-place is not to be found out, he is not to be found in the "shrines which are inscribed with texts, there is no habitation "which is sufficiently large for him to dwell in, and the heart [of "man] is unable to depict him."[1]

The being here referred to is a physical and not an ethical god, and the simplest and, from this point of view, most natural explanation of these remarkable statements is that they are intended to describe the inaccessibility both of the Nile-god and of his shrine. The fact, however, remains that the declaration of the almighty strength and inscrutability, and invisibility, and the impossibility of a description of the power which moves the Nile-god being made by man in writing, or in drawing, or in sculpture, proves the existence in the minds of the Egyptian writers of a lofty conception of the attributes of God.

But side by side with the fundamental ideas of Horus and Rā and the conceptions which were at the root of the worship of these gods, there existed in the minds of the Egyptians a firm and continuous belief in the god Osiris, who held a position in the Egyptian religion which was quite distinct from that held by any other god. About his origin nothing can be said, but there is no reason for doubting that he was a god of the indigenous inhabitants of Egypt, and that his worship was firmly established in the country before the dynastic period. He was from the earliest times associated with the doctrine of immortality, and was, the writer believes, the symbol of monotheism in Egypt. It is impossible to say, or even to suggest, what was the original form of his worship, but we know that in the archaic period one great centre of his cult was at Abydos, and from the fact that he was included in the *paut*, or company of gods of Heliopolis, we may conclude that he was a very important god of Ṭaṭṭu, or of Busiris, in the Delta, and that his sanctuary was much visited by the peoples thereof. Under the Vth Dynasty, as we have already

[1] A transcript of this text will be found in my *First Steps in Egyptian*, p. 208.

seen, he was regarded as the judge of the dead, and it is clear that he was also the god of the dead *par excellence*; but it must be noted that the priests of Rā formed at that time the predominant priesthood of Egypt, and therefore care was taken to assign to Osiris a position inferior to that of Rā in heaven. When the VIth Dynasty of kings came to an end the power of the priesthood of Rā was greatly diminished, and the worship of Osiris grew and prospered. It is unnecessary to trace here step by step the growth of the cult of the god until the period of the XVIIIth Dynasty, and it will be sufficient to say that between the VIth and the end of the XVIIIth Dynasty nearly all the attributes of the Sun-god Rā were transferred to Osiris, and the name of Rā is joined to that of Osiris, just as in much earlier times it was joined to Tem and Ḥeru-khuti to indicate the compound gods Rā-Tem and Rā-Ḥeru-khuti. Thus in Chapter cxxx. of the *Book of the Dead*[1] the deceased says, "I shall not be turned back in the "horizon, for I am Rā-Osiris," and this passage is a proof that quite early in the XVIIIth Dynasty Osiris was considered to be a solar god. In Chapter xvii. (l. 110 ff.) the deceased is made to say, "I am the God-Soul which dwelleth in the Twin-gods, "." On this the question follows, "What does this "mean?" to which we have the answer, "It hath reference to "Osiris when he goeth into Ṭaṭṭu[2] and findeth there the soul of "Rā; there one god embraceth the other, and the divine Souls "spring into being within the Twin-gods." These lines of text are illustrated by a very interesting vignette in the Papyrus of Ani (see sheets 7-10), wherein we see a pylon-shaped building between the double , which represents Ṭaṭṭu, and upon it stand the god Rā, in the form of a hawk with a solar disk upon his head, and Osiris in the form of a human-headed hawk, wearing the White Crown. The two gods face each other in Ṭaṭṭu, and, according to the text, were absorbed or merged each in the other; thus Osiris obtained the attributes and characteristics of the Sun-god Rā, but was supposed at the same time to retain all his own peculiar attributes.

[1] Papyrus of Nu, Chap. cxxx., l. 18.

[2] Either Mendes in the Delta, or the heavenly Mendes.

The view here given is that which was favoured by the priests of Thebes who, however, only reproduced that which they had borrowed from the priests of Heliopolis, and having gained currency in the theological colleges of the South, it spread among the people to such an extent that almost every great city possessed a sanctuary dedicated to Osiris. A very important hymn to Osiris, which is certainly as old as the period of the XVIIIth Dynasty, shows us how this god assimilated to himself the old solar gods, and how he became Rā. His holy double ( *ka*) was said to live in Mendes, he was the god who dwelt in Sekhem (i.e., Horus), the lord of Qerert (i.e., the Underworld), the holy one in Memphis, the lord of the temple of Hermopolis, the local gods of which were Thoth and his *paut*, or company, and he was declared to be the "soul of Rā" and the very body of this god, . His essence was that of the primeval god Nu, and he was the great spirit and divine body in heaven. He was supposed to fight and to vanquish the traditional fiend Sebȧ, who dared to wage war against Rā, and he was the stablisher of right and truth, 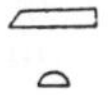 *maāt*, throughout the world. He made the earth with his own hands, and its winds, and its vegetation, and feathered fowl, and fish, and cattle and other quadrupeds, and to him belonged by right the mountains and the desert land throughout the world. The lands of Egypt rejoiced[1] to crown him upon his throne like his father Rā. The Great and the Little Companies of the gods loved him, he was the leader of every god, and the brother of the stars. Finally, as a proof of the absolute identity of Rā and Osiris may be quoted the opening lines of Chapter clxxxi. of the *Book of the Dead*, which read:—"Homage "to thee, O governor of Ȧmentet, Un-nefer, the lord of Ta-tchesert, "O thou who risest like Rā! Verily I come to see thee and to "rejoice at thy beauties. His disk is thy disk; his rays are thy "rays; his crown is thy crown; his majesty is thy majesty; his "risings are thy risings: his beauty is thy beauty; the awe which "is his is the awe which is thine; his odour is thy odour; his hall

[1] See the text, with a transliteration and translation, in my *First Steps in Egyptian*, p. 179 ff.

"is thy hall; his seat is thy seat; his throne is thy throne; his "heir is thy heir; his ornaments are thy ornaments; his command "is thy command; his mystery is thy mystery; his things are "thy things; his knowledge is thy knowledge; his attributes of "majesty are thy attributes of majesty; his magical powers are "thy magical powers; he died not and thou shalt not die; he was "not vanquished by his enemies and thou shalt not be vanquished "by thine enemies; no evil thing befell him, and no evil thing "shall befall thee for ever and for ever."

In such terms did the Egyptians extol the greatness and power of Osiris, but they make no mention of the aspect of the god which endeared him to countless generations of Egyptians. From hundreds of funeral and other texts we learn that Osiris was held to be partly divine and partly human, that is to say, unlike any other Egyptian god he possessed two natures, and two bodies, the one divine and the other human, and two doubles, the one divine and the other human, and two souls, the one divine and the other human, and two spirits, the one divine and the other human. The human body, according to the Egyptian tradition recorded by Plutarch,[1] once lived upon earth and was put to death in a cruel manner, and was mutilated by his brother; but his feminine counterpart, Isis, succeeded in obtaining from Thoth the knowledge of certain words and ceremonies, and having learnt from him the proper manner of reciting these words, and how to perform these ceremonies, by means of them she raised up to life the dead body of Osiris. The god Thoth was the personification of the intelligence of the whole company of the gods, and thus the words which he taught Isis were divine, and they were, presumably, names by the utterance of which the gods themselves maintained their existence. Now when Osiris had been raised from the dead he did not continue his life upon earth, but passed into the region of the Underworld, where he became the judge and god of the dead and, as we have seen, was made the possessor of all the attributes of the Sun-god Rā and of the great One God. But, the Egyptians in the early ages thought, Since Osiris was raised to life by the words and ceremonies which Thoth taught Isis, and since Osiris has gained

[1] *De Iside et Osiride*, ed. Didot (Scripta Moralia, t. iii., pp. 429–469), § xii. ff.

immortality by means of them, these same words and ceremonies will raise us to life and give us immortality also. Their priests therefore invented a number of magical ceremonies, which they led the people to believe were identical with those which Isis had performed at the bidding of Thoth, and they strung together magical words which they declared to be those which had raised Osiris to life, and the words were recited and the ceremonies performed by priests who appear to have dressed themselves in such a way as to resemble the divine beings who were concerned with the resurrection of Osiris.

At a later period, however, the Egyptians put their trust in Osiris himself, and addressed their prayers directly to him as the Being, partly divine and partly human, who had raised himself from the dead without having seen corruption, and who had bestowed upon his own earthly body, by means of his divine nature, the gift of an everlasting life which it enjoyed in an incorruptible and glorified form in heaven. The Egyptians "loved life "and hated death," and they worshipped Osiris as the Great God who not only possessed the power of maintaining his own life indefinitely—which was supposed to be the chief distinguishing characteristic of a god—but also of giving mortals the power to live after death in this world. What Osiris had effected for himself he could effect for man; hence Thothmes III. is made to address the god in these words, "Homage to thee, O my divine "father Osiris, thou hast thy being with thy members. Thou "didst not decay, thou didst not turn into worms, thou didst not "rot away, thou didst not become corruption, thou didst not "putrefy. . . . I shall not decay, I shall not rot, I shall not "putrefy. . . . I shall have my being, I shall live, I shall germinate, "I shall wake up in peace. . . . My body shall be stablished, and "it shall neither fall into ruin nor be destroyed off this earth."[1] Because the human body of Osiris rose from the dead, the body of every man could rise from the dead also, but man lacked what Osiris possessed, i.e., the divine body, soul, spirit, and nature, which had brought about the resurrection of his human body, soul, spirit, and nature. In the earliest times of the worship of the

[1] *Book of the Dead*, Chap. cliv.

god the Egyptians, as we have seen, invented magical words and ceremonies with the object of supplying the human body with the power necessary to raise itself from the dead, but as time went on they realized that both words and ceremonies were incapable of giving eternal life to the dead, and that only Osiris himself could give them that which they so earnestly desired, i.e., everlasting life, by supplying to their dead earthly bodies the power to rise again, a power which he himself possessed. Beyond all doubt the Egyptians realized that Osiris was the only God who could make them to inherit life everlasting, and that he alone had the power of making "men and women to be born again."[1]

We have already seen how the attributes of the great God who created all things were ascribed to him, and we now see that he was regarded as the god who had the power to vanquish death by raising up the bodies of the dead in glorified forms, and to reunite to them their souls and their spirits, and to give them eternal life in his dominions. These things were declared of no other god, and no other god united in his person the attributes of an ethical god, and an almighty, creative god, and a god who was the vivifier of the dead. The conception of Osiris included the conceptions of every other god, but the conception of no other god included that of Osiris during the period of the highest thought and civilization of Egypt. The Sun-god Rā was called "One," a few other gods who were made to usurp his attributes were also each called "One;" this in the earliest times was natural enough, because the Egyptians were only acquainted with one Sun, and whether the physical body of the sun as a symbol of the power which moved it or that power itself is referred to in the hymns matters little, for "One" was a suitable epithet both for the sun and its god. In connexion with this matter it is important to remember the unique position which Osiris occupies in the *Book of the Dead* and in funeral texts generally. In the texts of the Vth Dynasty we find that Osiris was believed "to weigh words," i.e., to inquire into the various words and deeds of the lives of

[1] ; see *Book of the Dead*, Chap. clxxxii., l. 15.

men when their souls left their bodies, in order that he might reward them according to their merits.

In later times this idea was illustrated by the vignette in which the heart of the deceased was seen being weighed in the Great Scales against the symbol of Maāt, or the Law and right and truth; at a still later period, when the heart was the symbol of the conscience, this scene became associated with the examination of the words and deeds of the dead which took place in the Hall of Maāti. In the large scenes of the weighing of the heart which were prefixed to the finest papyri of the *Book of the Dead* of the XVIIIth and XIXth Dynasties, and which were accompanied by suitable hymns and texts, the ceremony takes place in the presence of the gods of the Great and Little companies, but in the Hall of Maāti the Forty-Two Assessors are substituted for the gods. In both cases, however, the great judge of all is Osiris, and it was to him that all Egyptians returned after death. Why the Assessors were forty-two in number cannot be said, but it is very probable, as has been before suggested, that each of them represented a district in Egypt in the earliest dynastic times, and that the Hall of Maāti thus became a meeting place for the Assessors of the whole country when Osiris sat to judge the dead. It is, moreover, impossible to say why certain assessors were supposed to hear confessions about the non-committal of certain sins, and we have no knowledge of the circumstances which gave rise to their selection and to their admission into the Hall of Judgment. Some of them appear to have been originally the gods of cities, and others gods of nomes, but, on the other hand, a few of them are deities who, in the earliest times, were apparently hostile to the dead. Failing full information on the subject, the chief interest which attaches to the Assessors and the Hall of Maāti, in which they sit, consists in the fact that the vignette proves how completely Osiris had gained the ascendancy over all the gods of Egypt.

In the preceding pages an attempt has been made to trace the development of the conception of a supreme being in Egypt, from the earliest times to the period when Osiris became endowed with many of the attributes now ascribed to God Almighty. There is no doubt that in predynastic times the Egyptians worshipped stocks, and stones, and animals, and plants, and trees, and that they only arrived at the idea of gods which were partly animal and partly man at the end of a long period of what is called in modern times "gross idolatry." From the idea of animal-man gods they advanced to the idea of a man-god, and finally their minds developed the conception of monotheism. When we first gain any definite knowledge of them we find that as a people they had put away the worship of stocks and stones, and most of the things which that worship implies, but that certain animals were held to be sacred in certain cities, and that the literature contained allusions to savage habits and practices, as we have already seen. As time went on, many changes took place in the minds of the Egyptians concerning their gods, but little variation was made in their worship and ceremonial in the temples; in other words, the spirit of the religion changed whilst the observance of the letter remained unchanged. Thus the forms of worship and the literature preserved a great deal which no one believed in except the commonest folk, and in this way traces of the lowest forms of religion were preserved and handed down to posterity. The Egyptians, after the period of the IVth Dynasty, were the victims of conservatism and conventionality, and, we might almost add, of the priesthoods of Heliopolis and Thebes; but for these powerful and wealthy confraternities the history of the religion of Egypt would have been very different. The conception of monotheism, which is so clearly expressed in the moral precepts of the Early Empire, would have developed rapidly, and in its growth it would have obliterated the remains of the old and obsolete faiths which had crystallized, and which existed in layers side by side with the higher doctrine. But the decay which set in after the IVth Dynasty, and which stifled the development of painting and sculpture, also attacked the religion of the country, and the noble conception of monotheism, with its cult of the unseen, was unable to compete with the worship of symbols, which could be seen and handled, until the time when Osiris was recognized as the One God, who was also the giver of eternal life. The Egyptians were unlike other nations, and similarly their religion and their gods were unlike the religion and the gods of other nations; and as they must not be judged by the standard of any one foreign nation belonging to any one period, so their religion and their gods must not be judged by the standard of the religion and gods of any later civilized nation. We can only know what the Egyptians thought and believed by reading and studying the texts which they wrote, and a final opinion on their beliefs cannot be obtained until all their religious literature has been published; the general outline, however, of their religion is clear enough, and it shows us that they possessed a good, practical form of monotheism and a belief in immortality which were already extremely ancient even in the days when the Pyramids were built.

## CHAPTER IV

# THE COMPANIONS OF THE GODS IN HEAVEN

IN the preceding chapters, which are devoted to the consideration of general questions concerning God and the gods, no mention is made of the habitation of these divine beings or of their companions. The texts of all periods are silent as to the exact position of heaven, but it is certain that the Egyptians assigned to it a place above the sky, and that they called it *pet*; we must distinguish between the meanings of *pet* and *nut*, for the former means "heaven," and the latter "sky." We may also note that two skies are mentioned in the texts, i.e., , the day sky, and , the night sky. The hieroglyphic for heaven and sky represents a slab, each end of which rests on a support, and we may assume that the primitive Egyptians believed that each end of heaven rested upon a support (i.e., two mountains); out of one mountain came the sun every morning, and into the other he entered every night. The mountain of Sunrise was called Bakhau, , and the mountain of Sunset Manu, . In the earliest times the sky was divided into two parts only, the East and the West, but later another division was made, and heaven was split up into four parts, and each was placed under the care of a god. The latter division was made long before the Pyramid Texts were written, for in them it is always assumed that the flat slab of iron which formed the sky, and therefore the floor of the abode of the gods, was rectangular, and that each corner of it rested upon a pillar, . That this is a very ancient view concerning the sky is proved by the hieroglyphic

, which is used in texts to determine words for rain, storm, and the like; here we have a picture of the sky falling and being pierced by the four pillars of heaven.

At a later period, the four quarters of heaven were believed to be under the direction of four gods, and the four pillars of the sky were poetically described as the four sceptres which they held in their hands. Thus in the text of Tetà (l. 233) it is said, "As "Tetà goeth towards them they bring unto him the four gods "who stand with the sceptres of heaven, and they repeat the name "of Tetà to Rā, and they take up his name to Horus of the two "horizons."[1] In several texts[2] allusion is made to the lifting up of heaven upon its four pillars, e.g., 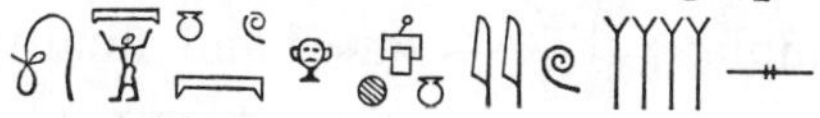, and in one place the four pillars are said to support that on which the four heavens rest, ; at a comparatively late period the idea arose that the sky needed support in the middle as well as at the corners, and the god who acted as the prop was called Ḥeḥ, . According to one myth which represented the heavens in the form of the head of a man, and which made the sun and the moon to be his eyes, the supports of heaven were supposed to be formed of his long flowing hair, and thus we have in the text of Unȧs (l. 473) an allusion to the "four elder spirits who dwell "in the locks of hair of Horus, who stand in the eastern part of "heaven grasping their sceptres."[3] The gods who grasped as sceptres the four pillars of heaven, which eventually became the

1 

2 See Brugsch, *Wörterbuch*, p. 1351.

3 

four cardinal points, were Ȧmset, , god of the southern point, Ḥāp, , the god of the northern point, Ṭua-mutef, , the god of the eastern point, and Qebḥsennuf, 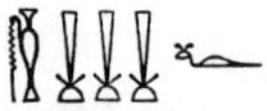, the god of the western point. These four gods played a prominent part in connexion with the deceased in the Pyramid Texts, where they are called the "children of Horus,"[1] for at one time they are called upon to bring him the boat of the Eye of Tem, , which is on the Lake of Kha, and at another they are exhorted to protect his life by their magical power and amulets, ,[2] and finally the deceased is said to become one of these four gods (Pepi I. l. 672), . The duties which are assigned to them as funereal gods in the *Book of the Dead* will be described later on.

Chief among the dwellers in heaven was the god Rā, who is said to sit upon an iron throne [the sides of which were ornamented] with the faces of lions and feet which resembled the hoofs of bulls.[3] Round about Rā, whether walking or sitting, were the gods who were "in his train," and these formed the nucleus of the inhabitants of heaven. Next to these came certain companies of the gods, and as the whole universe was divided into three portions, namely, heaven, earth, and the Ṭuat, or Underworld, and each portion had its own gods, we may assume that a place was reserved for them in the heaven of the Egyptians. But this heaven also contained several classes of beings, first and foremost among whom may be mentioned the Shesu-Ḥeru, or Shemsu-Ḥeru, a name which appears in the Pyramid Texts under the form  (Pepi I., l. 166), and may be translated "Followers of Horus." They are, in fact, beings who followed Horus, the son of Isis, in heaven, where they waited upon him, and performed his behests,

[1] 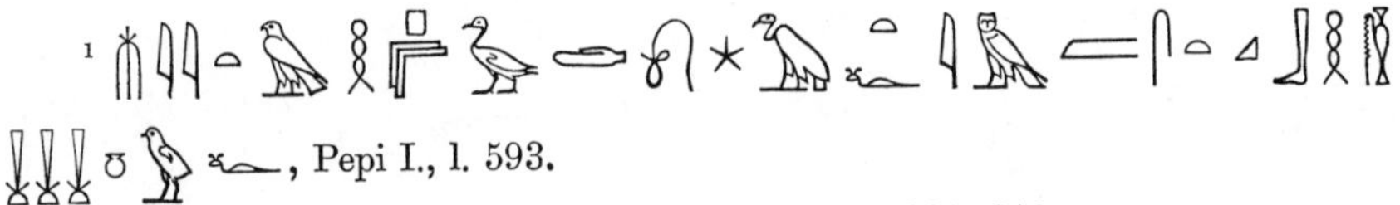, Pepi I., l. 593.

[2] Pepi I., l. 444.

[3] *Ibid.*, ll. 309, 310.

and when necessary defended and protected him. They occupied a position of great importance among the celestial hosts, and are mentioned in such a way as to suggest that they were almost equal to the gods; thus Pepi I. (l. 166) is said to "pacify them," but on the other hand it was they who "washed him, and who recited on "his behalf the Chapter of those who come forth, and [the Chapter "of those who] rise up."[1] Next may be mentioned the Āshemu, , a class of beings whose characteristics are not known, and who in the text of Tetȧ (l. 327) are referred to in connexion with the *sekhemu*. The word *āshem* is usually supposed to mean the "form in which a god is visible," but it must have another and an older meaning. The Ḥenmemet, ,[2] or hamemet, appear to have been a class of beings who either were to become, or had already been, human beings, but the Egyptians themselves seem to have had no very clear idea about their attributes, and the passages in the Theban *Book of the Dead* in which they are mentioned have been understood in different ways by different scholars.

In a hymn it is said of Rā, "when he riseth the *rekhit* (i.e., "rational beings) live, and the *hamemet*, , exult in "him"; Osiris is called "[lord of] the *hamemet*, , in "Kher-āḥa"; and the deceased says in Chapter xlii. of the *Book of the Dead*, "And shall do me hurt neither men, nor gods, , "nor spirits, , nor the dead (or damned), , "nor the *pāt*, , nor the *rekhit* (i.e., rational beings), nor "the *hamemet*." Elsewhere the deceased prays "that the com- "pany of the gods may hold their peace whilst the *hamemet* talk "with me";[3] and it seems from a passage in an inscription of

[1] Compare the variant .

[2] Tetȧ, l. 95.

[3] See the list of passages given in my *Vocabulary* to the *Book of the Dead*, p. 205.

Ḥātshepset[1] as if in the latter part of the dynastic period the word had come to mean a class of men and women, especially as it is determined by the signs , which usually indicate a number of human beings. Thus Rameses III. speaks of "all the gods and "goddesses of the South and the North, and all men, and all the "*pāt*, and all the *rekhit*, and all the *hamemet*"; finally, that the *hamemet* were believed to live upon grain is proved by the passage in a hymn to Åmen-Rā wherein this god is said to be the "maker "of the green herb which giveth life to the beasts and cattle, and "of the plant of life, , of the *hamemet*."[2] Of the characteristics of the classes of beings called Āfa, , and Utennu, , who are mentioned in the text of Pepi II. (l. 951), we know nothing, and the same must be said of the Set beings, , who were, however, divided into two classes, the Upper and the Lower, . The following extract will show how these beings are mentioned:— "O great heaven, stretch out thy hand to Pepi Nefer-ka-Rā! "O mighty heaven, stretch out thy hand to Pepi Nefer-ka-Rā, for "Pepi is thy divine hawk, . Pepi hath come "having come forth into heaven, and he hath penetrated Qebḥu; "Pepi hath paid homage to his father, and he riseth like Horus. "Pepi hath come to the place where he is, and he (his father) "granteth to him to rise like the sun, and he stablisheth for him his "two divine *utchats*, 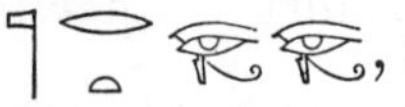, and when Pepi cometh forth "with him, great like Horus, son of Nut, and like the child with "the lock of hair (i.e., Harpocrates), and smiting the crowns, and "giving orders to the gods Utennu, the Āfa gods follow Pepi, and "those who are in the heavens and on the earth come to him pay- "ing homage, together with the two uraei guides, , "and the jackals, and the spirits, and the Set beings, both the

1 

2 Ed. Grébaut, section vi.

"Upper and the Lower." It is possible that the Set beings may have been of like nature to the god Set, who was the brother and associate of Horus in the earliest times, but who in later times lost his position as a god and became the type and symbol of all evil.

In addition to these the text of Pepi II. (line 849) mentions the "Watchers of the city of Pe," and the "Watchers of the city of Nekhen," 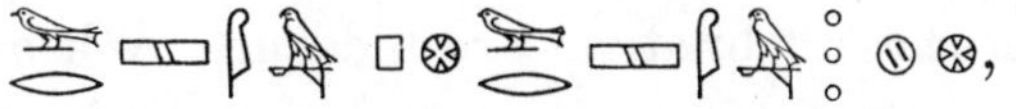, from which we may assume that certain cities were supposed to enjoy the protection of a number of gods whose duty it was to look after their interests in heaven. We know from several passages in the *Book of the Dead* that groups of gods were called the "souls" of such and such cities, and it is clear from the inscriptions that each city and town possessed a soul which had, like the soul of a man after death, the power to wander about at will. Thus on a wall in the temple which Cleopatra VII. built at Erment (now destroyed), was a scene in which the great queen was depicted in the act of giving birth to her son Caesarion. The goddess Neith holds up the queen's arms, and the midwife Netchemtchemt, 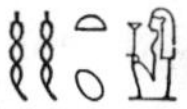, receives the boy in the presence of several gods and goddesses. Now in the upper part of the relief were two groups of souls of cities, seven on the right hand and seven on the left, who were supposed to have been present at the birth of the child, and to have taken him under their protection. Among the cities represented are Thebes, Ȧnt, , Het, 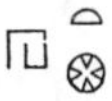, Qeset, Unt, Ȧhet, Ḥetep, Uauaā, 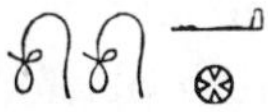, etc.[1] Each soul is in the form of a human-headed hawk, and each has on its head horns and a disk, , in the front of which is a uraeus.

Want of space does not allow of the mention of many obscure beings who are called gods, and who are practically innumerable, and we therefore pass on to refer to the spirits and souls, etc., of the righteous men and women who once lived upon this earth. To these, as well as to the divine beings, was given the name "living ones," , as may be seen from the passage in Unȧs (line 206), which reads, "Hail, Unȧs, behold thou hast not departed dead

[1] See Lepsius, *Denkmäler*, iv. pl. 60.

", but as one living  thou hast gone to "take thy seat upon the throne of Osiris. Thy sceptre *āb* "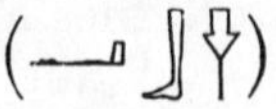 is in thy hand, and thou givest commands unto the "living ones; thy sceptre *mekes* , and thy sceptre "*Neḥebet*  are in thy hands, and thou givest thine "orders to those whose habitations are hidden." When king Tetȧ is in heaven the seat of his heart is declared to "be among the "living ones on this earth for ever," .[1] We have in this latter passage a proof that the Egyptians conceived it possible for a man to attain to all the attributes of a divine being, or, let us say, of an angel, and at the same time to enjoy an existence upon earth as well as in heaven. This idea probably arose because they wished to provide a future for the dead body just as they provided a habitation in heaven for the spirits and souls of the righteous. Heaven and earth were complements each of the other, the gods of heaven were the complements of the gods of earth, and *vice versâ*, and the existence of the spiritual and mental attributes of man with the gods in heaven was a complement of his continued life after death in some region on this earth. The Pyramid Texts show that the opinion of the Egyptians about the number and functions of the constituent parts of his economy, both physical and spiritual, changed as time went on and as they ascended the various grades which led up to the high platform of their civilization, and the result of the change, or rather changes, made itself manifest in their religious compositions. In the early predynastic period they thought that the life after death was a mere continuation of the life in this world, and when they had placed some food in or on the graves of their dead they were satisfied.

But they knew that the body of a man in the new life could

[1] Compare also 

, Pepi I., ll. 545, 546.

not be like that which he possessed on earth, although its form might be similar, and they therefore assumed the existence of another body. In his dreams the Egyptian saw a figure of himself or a duplicate, engaged in various occupations, and to this figure he gave the name *ka*, 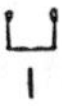; it was born with a man, it remained within him, usually inoperative, and survived him at death. It never left the body in the grave or tomb, and the offerings which were made in the halls of the tombs in all periods were intended to maintain its existence. Nevertheless the *ka* of Horus, , is in heaven (Tetà, line 88), and also the *ka* of Tetà (line 94), which is adjured to bring that which the king might eat with it; and as the *kau* of men and gods lived in heaven so there lived there also the *kau* of cities, e.g., of the city of Pe, 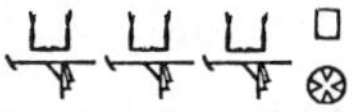 (Tetà, line 88), and the "lords of *kau* praised Rā both in the dominions of Horus "and in the dominions of Set."[1] King Unàs is declared to be the "chief of the doubles," , and he is said to "gather together "hearts for the great wise chief" (Unàs, line 395). Men and gods alike possessed shadows, and they also had an existence in heaven after the death of the bodies to which they belonged. When Unàs had eaten the bodies of the gods, and had absorbed all their souls and spirits, it is said that the "flame of Unàs is in their bones, for "their soul is with Unàs, and their shadows are with their forms" (Unàs, line 523, Tetà, line 330). The souls and the spirits of men had their abode in heaven with the gods, and the religious texts of all periods are so full of allusions to this fact that it is unnecessary to quote examples; the soul, *ba*, , is usually depicted in the form of a hawk with a human head, and the spirit, *khu*, , as a heron. Related intimately to the body, but with undefined functions, so far as we can discover, was the *sekhem*, , a word which has been translated "power," and "form," and even "vital force;" and finally the glorified body, to which had been

1  , Tetà, l. 192.

united the soul, and spirit, and power, and name of the deceased, had its abode in heaven. This new body of the deceased in heaven was called *sāḥu*, 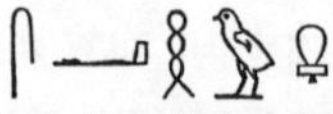, and may for all practical purposes be termed the spiritual body; it grew out of the dead body and was called into existence by the ceremonies which were performed, and the words which were recited by the priests on the day when the mummified body was laid in the tomb.

Thus we see that the denizens of heaven consisted of the Great, and the Little, and the other companies of the gods; and of a large number of beings, who may for convenience be called the "inferior gods," and of several orders of beings who possessed some characteristic which caused the Egyptians to assume that they were divine; and of the shadows, doubles, souls, spirits, powers, hearts, and spiritual bodies of those who had lived upon this earth. In Chapter lxiv. of the *Book of the Dead* (line 21) is a curious statement to the effect that the "spirits are four million, "six hundred and one thousand, two hundred,"  , in number, but whether this is intended to be an enumeration of the spirits of heaven, or of the spirits which once inhabited human bodies, cannot be said. Of the occupations of the denizens of heaven little is known, but to some of them was assigned the task of directing the affairs of this world, others directed the operations of the celestial bodies, and others were attached to the trains of the great gods, and accompanied them in their triumphant courses through the heavens. All these sang praises to Rā as the king and chief of the gods, and they sang hymns to him describing his greatness and glory just as men sang songs of joy to the sun when he rose and set. The gods nourished themselves with celestial food which was supplied to them by the Eye of Horus, that is to say, they supported their existence on the rays of light which fell from the sun which lit up heaven, and they became beings whose bodies were wholly of light. According to one myth the gods themselves lived upon a "wood, or plant of life,"  (Pepi I., line 430), which seems to have grown near the great lake in Sekhet-ḥetep, round which they were wont to sit,[1] but this idea belongs to the group of views which held that the beatified dead lived in a beautiful, fertile region, where white wheat and red barley grew luxuriantly to a great height, and where canals were numerous and full of water, and where material enjoyments of every kind could be found. In other places we read of "bread of eternity," and "beer of eternity," i.e., bread and beer which was supposed never to grow stale or to become spoiled,[2] and we also have mention of a heavenly fig-tree (), and a heavenly vine (), the fruit of which is eaten by the beatified. The bread upon which the blessed fed themselves was that bread which the Eye of Horus shed upon the branches of the olive-tree,  (Unȧs, line 200). Finally, the blessed were arrayed in apparel similar to that which was worn by the gods, but they also had white linen garments on their bodies, and white sandals on their feet.

All these details show the simple character of the heaven which the primitive Egyptian imagined, and prove that it was at first intended to be nothing but the celestial complement of a terrestrial farm or estate. He wished for a vine, and a fig-tree, and an olive tree, for wheat wherewith to make bread, and for barley wherewith to brew beer; he also desired clean white garments and white sandals. His celestial homestead he expected to be intersected with numerous canals, which would do away with the necessity of laboriously drawing water from the celestial Nile by means of some mechanical contrivance similar to the modern *shadûf;* the tillage would, of course, be provided for in the next world by the gods, who would take care that the crops did not fail. This simple material heaven is very different from the

1 
, Pepi, l. 431.

2 Tetȧ, l. 288, Pepi I., l. 442 and l. 390.

heaven of the Hebrew and Muḥammadan writers, with its sensual and sensuous joys of every kind, and its luxurious meats, and drinks, and delights. We know from one or two passages in the Pyramid Texts that there were women in heaven just as there were goddesses, but they are not spoken of as are the *Ḥur al-'uyûn* (houris), i.e., the women with large, black pupils of the eye set in large whites, who are mentioned in Arabic descriptions of Paradise, and they are not made to be one of the chief attractions of heaven. As far as can be seen, the heaven of the Egyptians had no musical instrument in it, and the only sounds heard in it must have been the songs of the ministering gods and of the beatified when they hymned the Great God. What the Egyptian gentleman who lives on his own land in places remote from towns is now, the Egyptian gentleman everywhere was then; he loved to wash and anoint himself, and having put on clean linen to sit in the sun in the morning, and to bear himself with dignity, and to be treated with respect by his neighbours and inferiors. He loved to have corn, and wine, and oil in abundance, and a sufficient number of slaves to minister to his wants and to maintain his dignity when he moved about from village to village. He honoured his mother, and usually married a very limited number of wives, among whom might be a sister, or half-sister, or cousin, and he took great interest in his male offspring; we note in the Pyramid Texts that the families of the deceased kings are never mentioned, and that nothing is said about their wives, although Unȧs (lines 628, 629) is said to carry off women from their husbands,  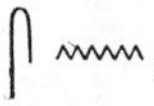, wheresoever he pleaseth, whensoever he pleaseth. On the other hand, Isis is said to come to king Tetȧ, who unites with her, and the goddess having conceived like the star Sepṭ gives birth to Horus Sepṭ,[1] and in another passage Unȧs is said to have

[1]  , Tetȧ, l. 276.

become the husband of the goddess Māuit, and also of the young woman who brought bread to him.[1]

But these beings were, after all, only the celestial waters described under the forms of a goddess and a woman, and the sensual idea conveyed by a literal interpretation of the text therefore disappears. The life of the primitive Egyptians in heaven was as simple as their life upon earth, and their chief wish was to enjoy a state of comfortable and dignified peace, without war and without tumult or strife. We hear nothing of a heaven with a floor of white flour or musk, with pearls for stones, and trees with trunks of gold, and houses covered with gold and silver, and rivers of milk, and honey, and wine, and innumerable maidens with bodies made of pure musk, who live in pavilions made of hollow pearls and are free from all defects of their sex. The idea of the means to be employed for reaching the heaven of the Egyptians was as primitive as that of the heaven itself, for the Egyptians thought that they could climb on to the iron floor of heaven by going to the mountains, the tops of which it touched in some places. At a later period it was thought that a ladder was necessary, certainly for those who did not live near the mountains whose tops touched heaven's floor, and in many tombs models of ladders were placed so that the deceased might make use of them at the proper time. The god Osiris even was believed to have needed a ladder, and to have been helped to ascend it by Rā and Horus, or by Horus and Set. The idea of the need of a ladder was deeply seated in the Egyptian mind, for when the custom of placing models of ladders in the tombs ceased, they drew

1 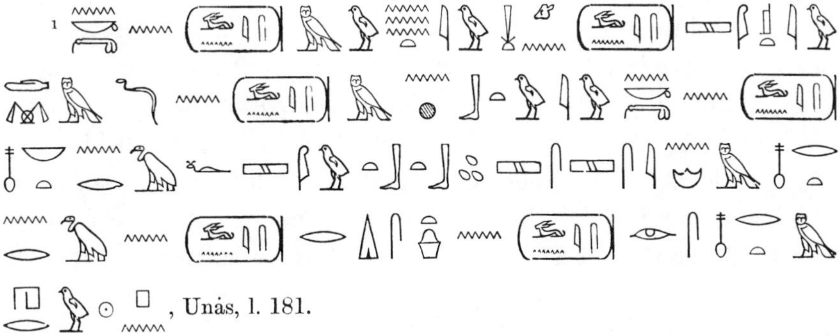, Unȧs, l. 181.

pictures of them in the papyri of the *Book of the Dead* which were placed in tombs.[1] The model of the ladder, , *maqet*, could be made as long as the deceased wished by reciting certain words of power over it, and by similar means the picture of the ladders given in the papyri could be turned into real ladders.

The above mentioned facts will show that in his conception of heaven the Egyptian never succeeded in freeing himself wholly from material ideas and the wish to make sure of eternal life and happiness by means of his own acts. In the latter part of the dynastic period the conception of heaven became more material, and at length, if we may judge by the texts, the belief in the resurrection of the actual physical body prevailed, and the life after death was regarded as nothing but a continuation of the life upon earth. Thus the title of Chapter cx. of the *Book of the Dead* declares that the text which follows will give a man the power of "doing everything even as a man doeth upon earth." As a result of this view the deceased prays thus:—"May I become a *khu* "(spirit) therein, i.e., in the Sekhet-ḥetep or Elysian Fields, may I "eat therein, may I drink therein, may I plough therein, may I "reap therein, may I fight therein, may I make love therein, may "my words be mighty therein, may I never be in a state of "servitude therein, but may I be in authority therein." He also wishes that he may have with him in Sekhet-ḥetep his father and mother, and presumably his wife and children, and also the god or gods of his city, but in these materialistic passages we find no mention of his desire to worship and praise the gods of heaven, or even the Great God who is said to "grow" therein. Thus in another place in the same chapter he says, "O Uakh, I have "entered into thee, I have eaten my bread, I have gotten the "mastery over choice pieces of the flesh of oxen and of feathered "fowl, and the birds of Shu have been given to me. I have "plunged into the lakes of Tchesert; behold me, for all filth hath "departed from me. The Great God groweth therein, and behold, "I have found [food therein]; I have snared feathered fowl and "I feed upon the best of them. . . . I have seen the Osiris [my

[1] See the *Papyrus of Ani*, 2nd edition, pl. 22.

"father], and I have gazed upon my mother, and I have made "love." In every division of the Elysian Fields the deceased, in the later period of dynastic history, found some fresh material pleasure, but, in spite of all its inconsistencies and his materialism, the heaven of the Egyptians was better and purer than that of many more modern nations which are credited with higher intelligence and better civilization.

## CHAPTER V

# THE UNDERWORLD

In the chapters on God and the gods it has already been said that the Egyptians in the earliest times believed that the gods were moved by the same passions as men and grew old and died like men; later, however, they believed that it was only the bodies of the gods which died, and they therefore provided in their religious system a place for the souls of dead gods, just as they provided a place for the souls of dead men and women. The writers of the religious texts were not all agreed as to the exact position of this place, but from first to last, whatever might be the conceptions entertained about it, it was called Ṭuat, . This word is commonly rendered "underworld," but it must be distinctly understood that the Egyptian word does not imply that it was situated under our world, and that this rendering is only adopted because the exact signification of the name Ṭuat is unknown. The word is a very old one, and expresses a conception which was originated by the primitive Egyptians, and was probably unknown to their later descendants, who used the word without troubling to define its exact meaning. To render Ṭuat by "hell" is also incorrect, because "hell" conveys to modern peoples ideas which were foreign to the Egyptians of most schools of religious thought. Whatever may be the moral ideas of the Ṭuat as a place of punishment for the wicked in later times, it is clear that at the outset it was regarded as the place through which the dead Sun-god Rā passed after his setting or death each evening on his journey to that portion of the sky in which he rose anew each morning. In the XIXth Dynasty we know that the Ṭuat was believed to be situated not below our earth, but away beyond the earth, probably in the sky, and certainly near the heaven wherein the gods dwelt; it was the realm of Osiris who, according to many texts, judged the dead there, and reigned over the gods of the dead as well as over the dead themselves.

The Ṭuat was separated from this world by a chain or range of mountains, and consisted of a great valley, which was shut in closely on each side by mountains; the mountains on one side divided the valley from this earth, and those on the other divided it from heaven. We may note in passing that the Hebrews separated the blessed from the damned by a wall,[1] and that Lazarus was separated from Dives in hell by a "great gulf,"[2] and that the Muḥammadans divide heaven from hell by the mountain Al-A'râf, الاعراف,[3] which, however, cannot be of any great breadth because those who stand upon it are supposed to be able to hold converse both with the blessed and the damned. It is pretty certain that both Hebrews and Muḥammadans borrowed their ideas of the partition between heaven and hell from the Egyptian Ṭuat, but there is no authority in the texts for the Muḥammadan view that it is a sort of limbo or purgatory for those who are too good for earth but not good enough for heaven. Those who stand on Al-A'râf are said to be angels in the form of men, patriarchs, prophets, and saints, and those whose good deeds on earth were exactly counterbalanced by their evil deeds, and who therefore merit neither heaven nor hell. Through the valley of the Ṭuat runs a river, which is the counterpart of the Nile in Egypt and of the celestial Nile in heaven, and on each bank of this river lived a vast number of monstrous beasts, and devils, and fiends of every imaginable kind and size, and among them were large numbers of evil spirits which were hostile to any being that invaded the valley.

On the sarcophagus of Seti I. is a representation of the Creation, which is reproduced on p. 204, and from it we see that the Ṭuat is likened to the body of Osiris, which is bent round like a hoop in such a way that his toes touch the back of his head.

[1] See Eisenmenger, "Was die Juden von der Höllen lehren" (*Entdecktes Judenthum*, tom. ii., p. 322 ff.

[2] St. Luke xvi. 26.

[3] See Ḳur'ân, Sura vii.

On the top of his head stands the goddess Nut, who supports with both hands the disk of the sun. From this we may conclude both that Osiris is the personification of the Ṭuat, and that the Ṭuat is a narrow circular valley which begins where the sun sets in the west, and ends where he rises in the east. The Ṭuat was a terrible place by reason of the monsters and devils with which it was filled, and its horrors were increased by the entire absence of light from it, and the beings therein groped about in the darkness of deep night. That the Ṭuat should be a place of blackness and gloom is quite natural when once we have realized that it was the path of the dead sun between the sunset of one day and the sunrise of the following day. The ideas about this region, which we find reproduced in papyri of the New Empire, belong to different periods, and we can see that the Theban writers who described it and drew pictures of the beings which lived in it, collected a mass of legends and myths from every great religious centre of Egypt, wishing to make them all form part of their doctrine concerning the great god of Thebes, Åmen-Rā. As the priests of Heliopolis succeeded in promulgating their theological system throughout the length and breadth of Egypt by identifying the older gods with their gods, and by proving that their views included those of all the priesthoods of the great cities of Egypt, so the priests of Thebes endeavoured to convince the priests of other great cities of the superiority and greatness of their God Åmen-Rā, and probably succeeded in so doing. The Theban writers and scribes knew perfectly well that originally every nome or great city possessed its own underworld just as it possessed its own company of gods, and that each underworld was designated by a special name; they, therefore, made the Ṭuat to include all these underworlds and all the various gods with whom they were peopled, and they gave it the most important of the names of the local underworlds. The best known of these was Åmentet, , i.e., the "hidden place," which appears to have been originally the place where Ån-ḥer, the local god of Abydos, ruled as god of the dead, under the title of "Khenti Åmentet," that is to say, "he who is the chief of the unseen land." When the importance of Ån-ḥer was eclipsed by the new-comer Osiris, the title of the former was assigned to Osiris, who, henceforth, was always called "Khenti Ȧmentet." But this usurpation of Ȧn-ḥer's title as god of the dead by Osiris must have taken place in very early times, for Ȧmentet was a common name for the underworld throughout Egypt, and is found in texts of all periods, even in those of the Vth and VIth Dynasties.

Yet long before even this remote period the priesthoods of certain nomes or cities must have developed the idea that the life of a man resembled the course of the sun during the day, and that setting was to the sun what death was to a man; the sun, however, reappeared each morning in apparently a new body, and as man wished to live again in a renewed, or new, body, the Egyptian theologians set to work to form a system of theology in which the souls of the blessed dead, i.e., those who had been buried with all the ceremonies prescribed by the religion of the period, were made to accompany the sun in his boat as he passed through the portion of the Ṭuat which had been assigned to them. As the sun passed through the Ṭuat large numbers of souls made their way into his boat, and although it was only the dead sun that was their guide and protector, and his passage was through the realms of the dead which were under the sovereignty of Osiris, the god of the dead, they were brought forth at length to renewed life and light as soon as the boat passed out from the eastern end of the Ṭuat into the day. This view was a very popular and widespread one, especially as it made Rā and Osiris work together, each after his own method, to secure eternal life and happiness for the souls of the dead. As soon as the priests had made up their minds that the Ṭuat existed, they began to people it with imaginary beings which were supposed to be hostile to the souls of the dead, and to invent descriptions of the various regions into which they declared it was divided; such descriptions were at length committed to writing, at first in a very simple form, and after the manner of every group of texts which were composed for the benefit of the dead, but finally they became more elaborate, and attempts were made to represent pictorially the creatures which were found in the Ṭuat. In fact, it was intended to compile a book which should contain such accurate descriptions of the Ṭuat, and such true pictures of the foes which the dead soul would have to meet there, together with lists of their names, that when a soul was once provided with a copy of it he would find it impossible to lose his way, or to be overcome by any monster which attempted to bar his way or to prevent his access to the boat of Rā.

The great work which the Egyptians called "Coming Forth by Day," , supplied the soul with a great many words of power, and prayers, and incantations, as well as hymns, but even in the Early Empire, about B.C. 3500, many of its doctrines were antiquated, and the priests found it necessary to add new chapters and to modify old ones in order to make it a funeral work suitable for the requirements of newer generations of men. Owing to the extreme antiquity of the "Book of Coming Forth by Day," the views expressed in many of its chapters were contrary to those held by Theban priests of the New Empire, about B.C. 1650, and as a result, whilst preserving, and holding in great reverence this work which they had borrowed from the ancient priesthood of Heliopolis, they compiled two works, which may be called "THE BOOK OF THAT WHICH IS IN THE ṬUAT," and the "BOOK OF THE PYLONS." In the first of these, the SHĀT ȦM ṬUAT," , were gathered together all the views held by the Heliopolitan priesthood on the life of man's soul after death, and though it contained all the doctrines as to the supremacy of Rā, their great Sun-god, these were so skilfully manipulated by the Theban priests, that the compilation actually became a work which magnified the grade and influence of Ȧmen-Rā, the great god of Thebes, and raised him to the position which the Thebans claimed for him, namely, "king of the gods, and lord of the thrones of the two lands." The thrones here referred to are not those of kings, but the shrines of all the gods on all the land on each side of the river Nile. In the Heliopolitan system of theology the god Osiris held a comparatively subordinate position in the *paut*, or company of the gods, and was in fact only the greatest of the gods of the dead who were worshipped in the Delta; in the "Book of that which is in the Underworld" he also holds a position subordinate to Rā, and his underworld is made to be a portion of the Ṭuat through which the dead sun passed nightly. In the Shāt en Sbau, , or "Book of the Pylons," the greatest god of all is the god Osiris, and the whole work is devoted to a description of the various sections of the region over which he presides, and is intended to form a guide to it whereby the souls of the dead may be enabled to make their way through it successfully and in comfort. The Shāt ȧm Ṭuat and the Shāt en sbau were, in fact, the outcome of two distinct schools of theology; the latter, in its most primitive form, was the older of the two, and described the life of man after death more as a continuation of his existence on this earth than as an entirely new life, while the former made the future life to be passed entirely with the Sun-god. The latter maintained the views about the Elysian Fields and their material delights, which found utterance in the "Book of Coming Forth by Day," and was to all intents and purposes an amplification of, and a companion volume to it, but it also contained doctrines which were inserted in it with the view of making it harmonize with the theories in the former which related to the absolute supremacy of Rā. The Theban priests had no wish, when once they had established the mastery of Ȧmen-Rā, but to bring all the doctrines of the various schools of religious thought into harmony with their own, for such a course could do nothing but contribute to the material prosperity of the great brotherhood of Ȧmen-Rā. They were tolerably sure of the offerings of the faithful of Thebes, but they were anxious to obtain a share of those of the devotees of Osiris who flocked to Abydos, which was, rightly or wrongly, celebrated as the burial-place of the god. The history of Egypt shows that the fight between the kings of the South and the kings of the North for the supremacy of the whole country was always going on, but as the fortunes of war had given victory to the kings of the South, who were the lords of all Egypt under the New Empire, the priests of the god of these kings determined that Ȧmen-Rā should be the king of the gods. Religious ambition was helped by the success of the great warrior kings of the XVIIIth Dynasty, and thus Ȧmen-Rā became the overlord of Osiris.

Both the "Book of that which is in the Underworld" and the "Book of the Pylons" divide the Ṭuat into twelve parts, each of which corresponds to one of the hours of the night, and the divisions are called "Field," , *sekhet*, or "City," , *nut*, or "Hall," *ārret*, or "Circle," *qerert*. In Chapter cxliv. of the *Book of the Dead*, according to the Papyrus of Nu (Brit. Mus., No. 10,477), the *Ārrets* are seven in number, and each is guarded by a doorkeeper, a watcher, and a herald with the following names:—

ĀRRET I. 1. Sekheṭ-ḥrȧ-āsht-ȧru, . 2. Semetu, . 3. Hu-kheru, .

ĀRRET II. 1. Ṭun-peḥti, . 2. Seqeṭ-ḥrȧ, . 3. Sabes, .

ĀRRET III. 1. Am-ḥuat-ent-peḥ-fi, . 2. Res-ḥrȧ, . 3. Uāau, .

ĀRRET IV. 1. Khesef-ḥrȧ-āsh-kheru, . 2. Res-ȧb, . 3. Neteqa-ḥrȧ-khesef-aṭu, .

ĀRRET V. 1. Ānkh-em-fentu, . 2. Ashebu, . 3. Ṭeb-ḥer-kehaat, .

ĀRRET VI. 1. Ȧken-tau-k-ha-kheru, . 2. Ȧn-ḥer, . 3. Meṭes-ḥrȧ-ȧri-she, .

ARRET VII. 1. Meṭes-sen, . 2. Āa-kheru, . 3. Khesef-ḥrȧ-khemiu, .

In Chapter cxlv. of the *Book of the Dead* according to the Theban and Saïte Recensions the domain of Osiris, i.e., Sekhet-Ȧarru, , or Sekhet-Ȧanre, , contains Twenty-one pylons, each of which has a name, generally a very long one, and each of which is guarded by a god. The names of the gods who guard the first ten of these pylons are:—1. NERI, . 2. MES-PEḤ, . 3. ERṬĀT-SEBANQA, . 4. NEḲAU, . 5. ḤENTI-REQU, . 6. SEMAMTI, . 7. ȦKENTI, . 8. KHU-TCHET-F, . 9. TCHESEF, . SEKHEN-UR, . These names are taken from the Papyrus of Nu already quoted (sheet 25), but the following come from the Turin Papyrus, which was edited by Lepsius so far back as 1842, and they illustrate the changes which have taken place in the names. 1. NERȦU, . 2. MES-PTAḤ, . 3. BEQ, . 4. ḤU-TEPA, . 5. ERṬĀ-ḤEN-ER-REQAU, . 6. SAMTI, . 7. ȦM-NIT, . 8. NETCHSES, . 9. KHAU-TCHET-F, . 10. SEKHEN-UR, . The names of all the pylons are given in both the Theban and Saïte Recensions,[1] but the names of the gods who guard pylons XI.—XXI. are given in neither. The domain of Osiris, or Sekhet-Ȧarru, was, according to Chapters cxlix. and cl., divided into fifteen Ȧats, which are thus enumerated:—ȦAT () I. Sekhet Ȧarru;

[1] See my *Chapters of Coming Forth by Day* (Text), p. 334 ff.

its god was Rā-Ḥeru-khuti. ÅAT II. ÅPT-ENT-KHET, ; its god was Fa-ākh, . ÅAT III. ṬU-QA-ĀAT, . ÅAT IV. "The Åat of the spirits," . ÅAT V. ÅMMEḤET, ; the god in it is called Sekher-remu, . ÅAT VI. ÅSSET, . ÅAT VII. HA-SERT, ; the god in it is Fa-pet, . ÅAT VIII. ÅPT-ENT-QAḤU, . ÅAT IX. ÅṬU, ; the god in it is Sepṭ, . ÅAT X. UNT, ; the god in it is Ḥetemet-baiu, . ÅAT XI. ÅPT-NET, ; the god in it is Āa-sekhemu, . ÅAT XII. KHER-ĀḤA, ; the god in it is Ḥāp, , i.e., the Nile. ÅAT XIII. ÅTRU-SHE-EN-NESERT-F-EM-SHET, . ÅAT XIV. ÅKESI, ; the god in it is Maa-thet-f, . ÅAT XV. ÅMENTET-NEFERT, "Beautiful Åmentet, ," wherein the gods live upon cakes and ale.

In connexion with these various divisions of the realm of Osiris here will follow naturally a brief description of the BOOK OF PYLONS. An excellent copy of its text, with illustrations, is to be found on the famous alabaster sarcophagus[1] of Seti I., now preserved in Sir John Soane's Museum in Lincoln's Inn Fields, and variants of several of the passages are given on the walls of the tombs of several kings of the XXth Dynasty, who were buried in the Valley of the Tombs of the Kings at Thebes. Curiously enough, the work, as M. Jéquier has remarked,[2] seems never to have become popular, and copies of it are only found in royal tombs; it is generally admitted that it represents an attempt on

[1] See Bonomi and Sharpe, *The alabaster Sarcophagus of Oimenephtah I., King of Egypt*, London, 1864.

[2] *Le Livre de ce qu'il y a dans l'Hades*, Paris, 1894, p. 13.

the part of the Theban priests to adjust the cult of Rā to that of Osiris, and if this be so there is little to wonder at if it failed. According to the BOOK OF PYLONS the Ṭuat is a long, narrow valley, with sandy slopes, and is divided into two equal strips by the river on which the boat of the sun sails; it is made to contain

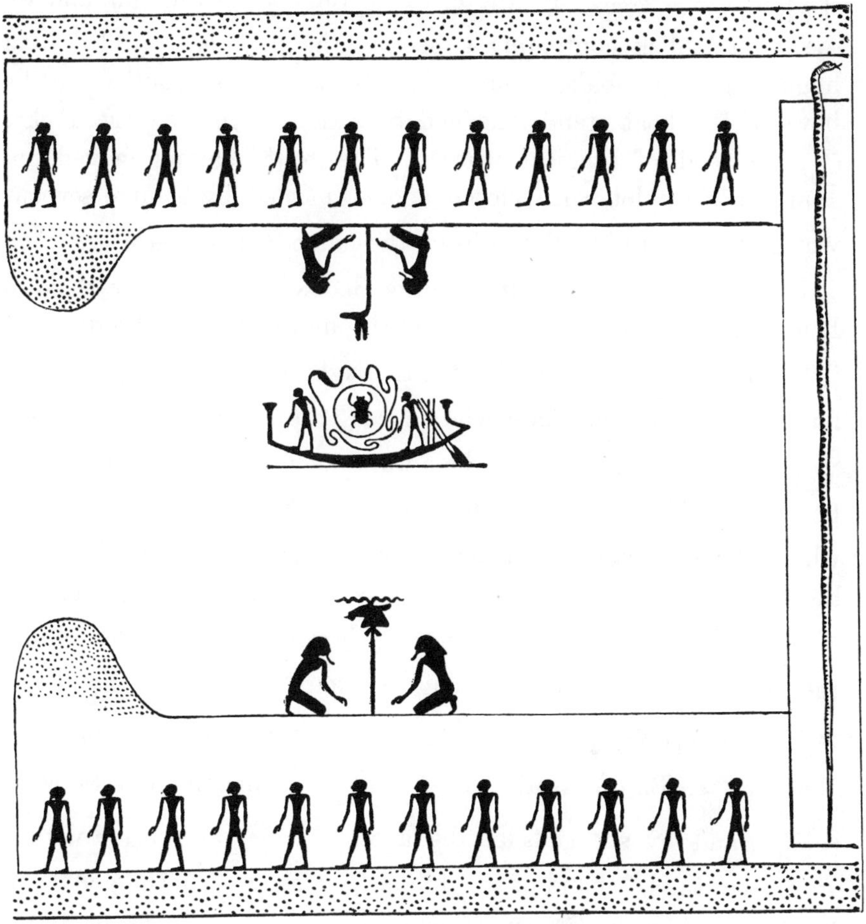

The First Hour of the Night.

twelve nomes or divisions, which correspond to the twelve hours of the night.

In the FIRST DIVISION, i.e., the FIRST HOUR, we have the Mountain of the West, ⌓, divided into two portions, and along its lowest part is a path which forms the entrance from this world to the Ṭuat. On the right-hand side is a jackal-headed standard,

, and on the left a ram-headed standard, ; each of these is adored by the god of the mountain, Set, , and the god of the Ṭuat, . On the right are the twelve gods of the mountain, and on the left the twelve gods of Set-Åmentet, . In the centre is the boat of the sun, and we see in it a disk containing a beetle; the disk is encircled by a huge serpent in folds, which holds its tail in its mouth. In the bows of the boat stands the god Sa, , and in the stern, Ḥeka, , the god of magical words. The boat, having moved on, approaches a pylon with closed doors, guarded by a huge serpent which stands on his tail and bears the name Saa-Set, . This pylon forms the entrance to the SECOND DIVISION, or SECOND HOUR, and when the god has passed through it "those who dwell in "their Set, , cry out."[1] On the right are twenty-four human forms, which represent those who praised Rā upon earth, , and who directed their words of power against the arch-fiend Apep, . In the centre is the boat of the sun, in which the god stands in a shrine; he is ram-headed, and holds in his hand a sceptre. The shrine is protected by the serpent Meḥen, , and a serpent stands upright on its tail before him; the boat is being towed along by four beings of the Ṭuat, , and is met by the seven gods called Nepmeḥ, , Nenḥā, , Ba (?), Horus, Uā-åb, , Khnemu, and Setchet, , and by six gods of the āqet, , and a god with a staff. On the left hand of the divine boat are:—(1) The god Tem, leaning on a staff, , (2) four dead men lying on their backs, and twenty men standing with their arms tied together behind their backs. These last are, according to M. Lefébure's rendering[2] of the text, "the criminals in Rā's great hall (the world), those "who have insulted Rā on the earth, those who have cursed that

[1] Bonomi and Sharpe, op. cit., pll. 5 and 4.

[2] See *Records of the Past*, vol. x., p. 85 ff.

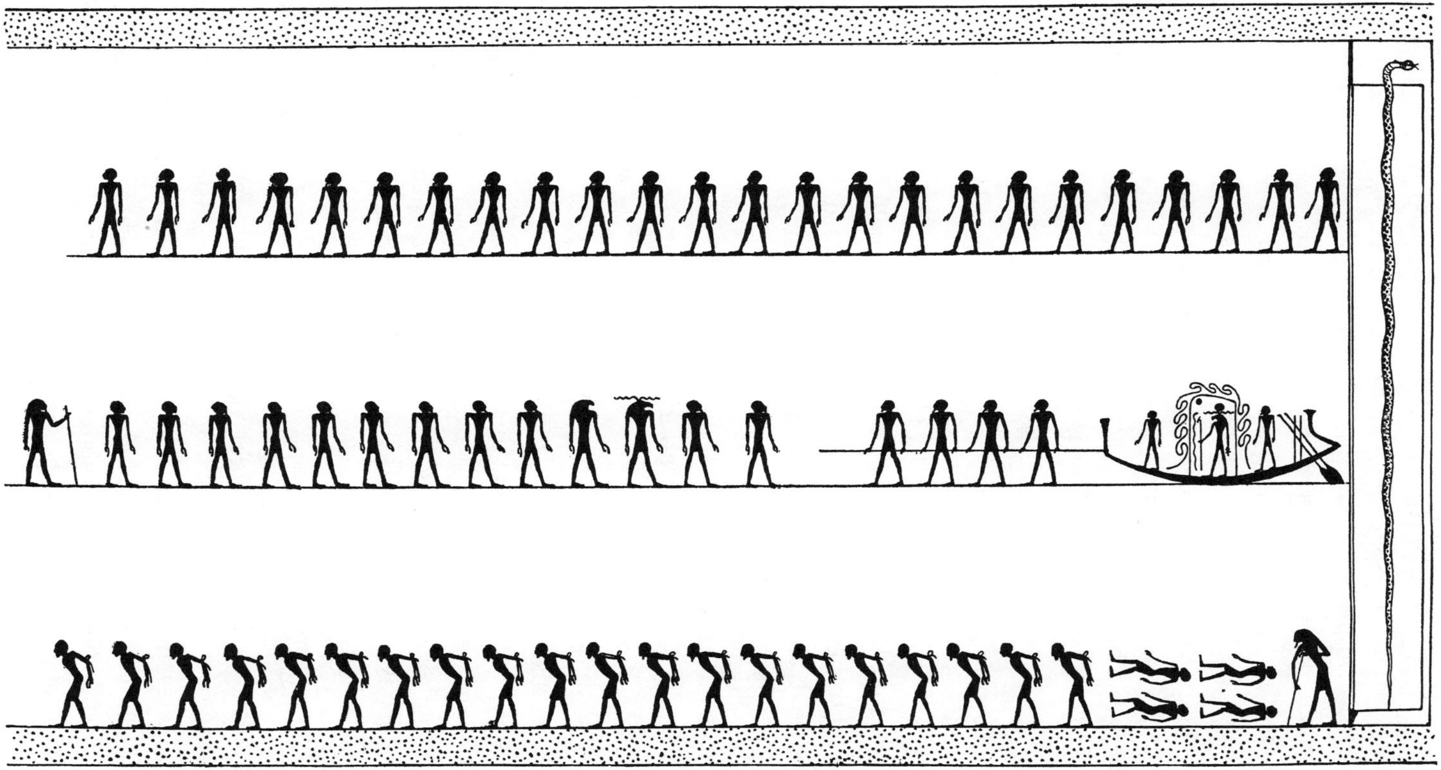

The Second Hour of the Night.

"which is in the Egg, those who have frustrated justice, those who "have uttered blasphemies against Khuti." The pylon which the god now approaches is quite different from the first, but it resembles all the others which have to be passed through. The opening is protected like a fortress by some advanced work, and through the wall is an entrance to a corridor which runs between two walls crowned with a series of spear heads. This corridor bends at right angles, and in each angle is a uraeus, from the mouth of which drop balls of fire that fill the whole length of it; at each end of the corridor is a god in the form of a mummy, one is called Ām-āua-qāḥ-f, , and the other, Sekhabsenfunen, . The pylon itself is called Sepṭet-uauau, , and the name of the snake which guards it and stands upon its tail is Aqebi, . The entrance to the pylon is also protected by nine gods, in mummied form, who represent the "Second Company" of the gods, .

The door of the pylon is opened towards the THIRD DIVISION OF THE ṬUAT, or the THIRD HOUR. The gate is called SEPṬET UAUAU SETET-SEN-RĀ, 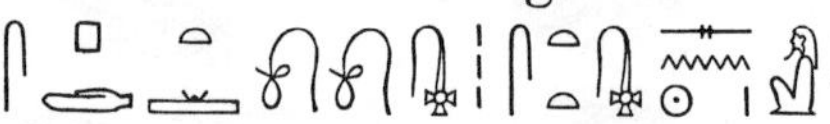. On the right hand of the boat of the god are twelve holy gods of the Ṭuat, each in his shrine, with the doors open, and twelve gods of the lakes of fire; a huge snake lies along the tops of all the shrines, and before each god of the basins of fire is an ear of corn. On the left hand are:—1. The god Tem; 2. the serpent Āpep; 3. the nine gods who are called the "chiefs who drive back Āpepi," ; and 4. Tem and the nine gods of things, 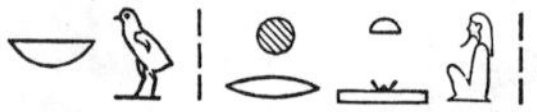. The boat of the sun is towed through this division by eight gods of the Ṭuat, and the middle of the rope is fastened to a long pole or beam, each end of which terminates in the head of a bull. This pole is supported by eight gods in mummied form, and upon it are seated seven gods; in front and behind these stands a bull, and at the end of the division stand four shrouded mummy forms. The gods who are

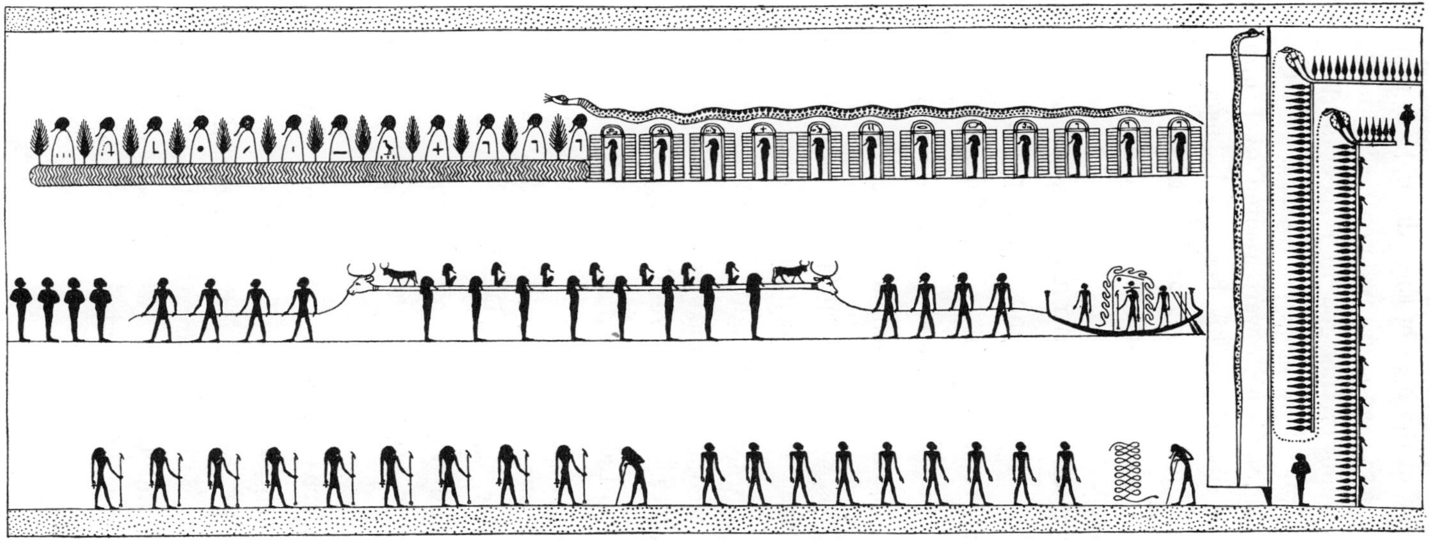

The Third Hour of the Night.

on the left hand of the boat of the sun, and are under the direction of Tem, form two companies, whose special duty it was to carry out the commands of this god in respect of the slaughter of the arch-fiend Åpepi. This monster was first of all to be enchanted by the incantations which were recited over him, and then his head was to be cut off, and his body to be hacked in pieces at the joints. As the god passes out of the Third Division and the door closes, all the beings who are fated to remain in it lift up their voices and weep.

The pylon of the FOURTH DIVISION or FOURTH HOUR is called Nebt-s-tchefau, , and the name of the serpent which guards it and stands upon its tail is Tcheṭbi, ; the gods in mummied forms who stand one at the beginning and one at the end of the corridor are called Nenuerbesta, , and Seṭa-ta, , respectively. The nine gods who guard the wall are the "the third company of the great god," . On the right side of the boat of the god are twelve gods, who are described as the "bringers of their doubles," , and twelve jackal-headed figures, who are walking on the Lake of Life,[1] and ten uraei, who rise out of the Lake of uraei;[2] to all these the Sun-god addresses words of comfort, and they respond suitably. The uraei, who are called "those who live," , are ordered to preserve their flames and fire for use against the enemies of Rā, and they answer the god, saying, "Come to us, unite thyself to Tanen," . On the left side of the boat of the god is Horus the Aged, who follows eleven human forms as they march behind the uraeus called Flame, , to a shrine in which the god Osiris, wearing the crown of the South, stands upon a serpent. Behind Osiris are the twelve gods, "who are behind the shrine," and four gods, who preside over pits in the earth, and the "prince of destruction," who holds a sceptre in his left

.

2 .

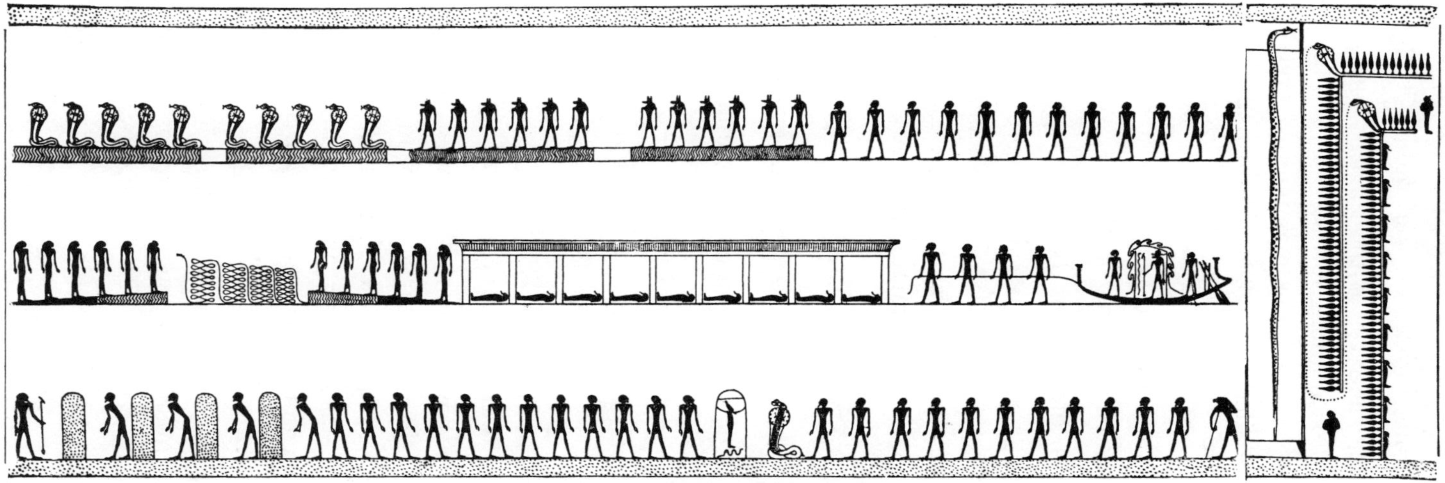

The Fourth Hour of the Night.

hand and  in his right. In the middle is the boat of the sun being towed along the river of the Ṭuat by four gods as usual, and it is made to approach a long low sepulchral building in which are nine chapels, each containing a mummied god lying flat on his back; these are called "the gods who are in the train of Osiris in their caves," 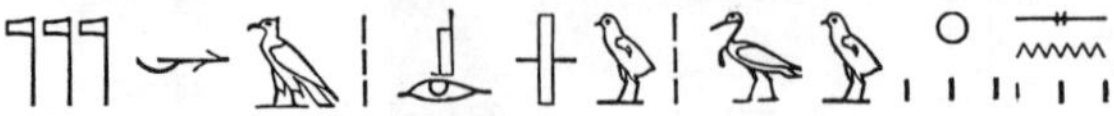. At the end of this building are two groups, each containing six women, who are the personifications of the twelve hours in the Ṭuat; between them is the serpent Ḥerert, , with multitudinous coils and windings, and he is said to give birth to twelve young ones to devour the hours. In this division, as in the others, Rā addresses the beings who are in it, and makes arrangements for their supply of food, and reminds them of their duties to him their creator.

The pylon of the FIFTH DIVISION or FIFTH HOUR is called Ȧrit, , and the serpent who guards it bears the name of Teka-ḥrȧ, 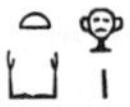; the jackal-headed mummy at one end of the corridor is Āau, , and he at the other is Tekemi, 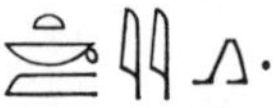. Along the front of the wall are nine gods in mummied forms who represent the fourth company of the gods. On the right hand of the boat of the god are:—1. The twelve worshippers in the Ṭuat; 2. Twelve bearers of cord, ; and 3. Four gods with sceptres. These beings are said to be those who knew Rā upon earth, and who made offerings to him, and in return for this Rā awarded them meat and drink in the most holy place in Ȧmentet, and said to them, "I am satisfied "with what you did for me, whether I was shining in the Eastern "heaven, or whether I was in the temple, , of my eye." Therefore they feed upon the food which Rā eats, and offerings are made to them upon earth on account of the praise which they ascribe to Rā in Ȧmenti. The beings who carry the cords are supposed to measure the "fields of the spirits," 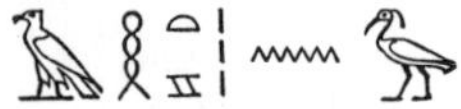, and their cords are supposed to represent the cord of law, i.e.,

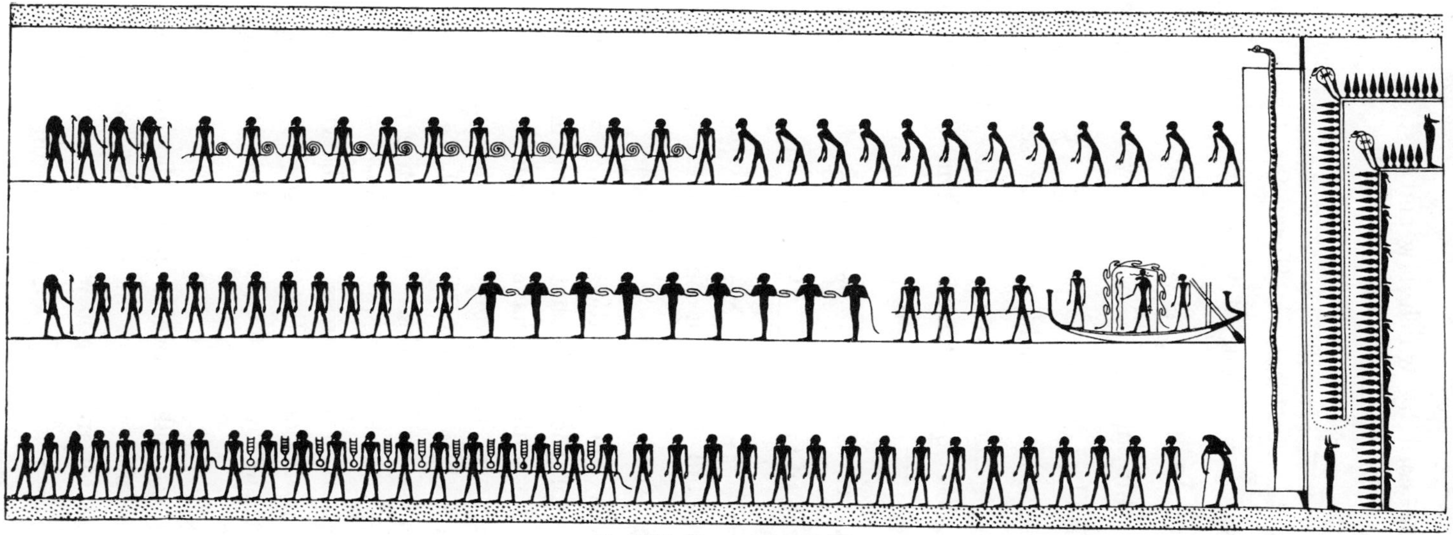

The Fifth Hour of the Night.

the measuring cord by which law and justice are represented, and "Rā says to them, Their law is the cord in Ȧmentet," . On the left side of the boat of the sun are:—1. Horus the Elder leaning upon a stick; 2. Sixteen men, four of whom are , i.e., Egyptians, four are Āamu, , four are Negroes, , and four are Libyans, ; 3. Twelve men, called "those who bear ladders (?) in Ȧment, , and who are holding a long serpent; and 4. Eight divine sovereign chiefs in Ȧment. To these four classes of men, whom Horus describes as being in the Ṭuat of Egypt and the Red Land, , it is said by the god, "Ye are the "tears from my Eye," , "in your name of 'men,'" . He then tells the Āamu, , and the Negroes and the Libyans that he has created them, and that it is the goddess Sekhet, , who redeems their souls, . Finally, the god addresses those who hold the ladder (?), and bids them take measurements of the souls that are appointed for destruction, and destroy the souls that have to be destroyed; in the hands of these beings was the power of determining the length of the period which had to be passed by souls in Ȧmentet, and it is undoubtedly passages like these which have given rise to the idea that the Egyptians believed in purgatory. In the centre of this Division the boat of the sun is being drawn along by four gods belonging to it as before. Before these are nine gods with projecting elbows and covered shoulders called "holders of Ennutchi," ; they are joined together by a rope; these gods follow twelve men who are described as the "souls of the men who are in the Ṭuat," and both groups of beings proceed towards a god who holds a sceptre, and is called Ḥer-qenbet-f, . The duty of this god was to call the souls of the righteous and put them in their dwellings, by the corner of those who lived near him. Rā addresses the gods who tow his boat along, and bids them to pull with vigour, and to be strong of arm and firm of limb, and swift of foot, and bold of soul to make a prosperous way for him to the hidden circles, . Next he addresses the figures with draped shoulders who bear the serpent Ennutchi, and bids them to draw him along; and then praises those who have spoken truth, , upon earth, and have magnified the forms of God, , and decrees for them cakes for their souls, wind for their nostrils, green herbs from Sekhet-Åaru, and a place among the gods of right and truth, , in the corner of the abode of Rā where the companions of the god pass sentences of doom. The doctrine here preached is essentially that of Osiris, and there is no wonder that the Book of Pylons was not popular with the priests of Åmen.

The name of the pylon of the SIXTH DIVISION[1] or the SIXTH HOUR is Nebt-āḥa, , the guardian at the entrance to the corridor is Maā-åb, , "Right of heart," and he who is at the end is Sheta-åb, , "Secret Heart." The wall is guarded by twelve gods in mummied forms, who are called "the gods and "goddesses who are in this Pylon," . Behind the wall is a chamber, the wall of which has upon it a row of spear heads, and inside we see the god Osiris

[1] The scene of the Sixth Division is so mutilated on the sarcophagus of Seti I. that it is not reproduced here.

seated upon the top of a flight of nine steps, on each of which stands a god; thus the whole company of the gods of Osiris are here represented. Osiris wears a double crown, , and holds in his hands the sceptre, , and the emblem of "life." Before him stands a mummied figure who forms the pillar of a pair of scales, and who may be regarded as the personification of the Great Balance with which we are familiar in the Judgment Scene as depicted in papyri. In the pan of the scales is the bird of evil, . Near the scales is a boat in which are an ape and a pig; the ape is urging the pig along with a stick. In the upper part of the scene are the heads of four oryxes and a figure of the god Anubis. The difficult texts which accompany this scene tell us that the "enemies of Osiris are beneath his feet, the gods and the spirits "are before him; he is the foe of the damned, he repulses the "enemies, and he destroys them, and effects their slaughter. "The bearer of the hatchet, and the supporter of the scales "protect him who is in Åmenti, who resteth in the Ṭuat, and who "passeth through darkness and shadow. Above is Joy, and below "are Right and Truth (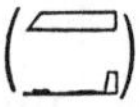). The god resteth and giveth forth "the light of Maāt which he hath made." The ape in the boat is said to hand over the pig to punishment "when the god riseth," and Anubis says, "O ye who bring words true or false to me "[remember] that it is Thoth who weigheth them." Concerning Osiris we read, "When the weighing of words taketh place he "smiteth evil; he hath a right heart, and he holdeth the words in "the Scales in the holy place wherein the trial of the secret things "of the secrets of the spirits taketh place. It is the god who riseth "who hath made all the beings who are in the Ṭuat." The text which relates to the four inverted heads of oryxes is not clear in its meaning, but it says that their dwelling-place is the Åmeḥet, a district in the Elysian Fields, and that they hide or protect the spirits. We must note in passing the position of the Sixth Division of the Ṭuat. Assuming that the Ṭuat was regarded as a nearly circular valley which curved round from the West, where the sun set, to the North, and curved round from the North to the East, where the sun rose, it follows if all the twelve divisions of the Ṭuat be equal in length, that the Sixth Division would be very near the most northerly part of the Ṭuat. And this is exactly where it was intended to be, for the most northerly part of the Ṭuat would include the greater part of the Delta, where the principal shrines of Osiris, i.e., Mendes and Busiris, were situated, and it was only right to make the position of the kingdom of Osiris on earth to correspond with that of his domain in the Ṭuat. Unlike the other divisions of the Ṭuat, the Sixth Division contains no representation of the god Rā, and the texts belonging to it do not even mention his name; the Book of Pylons made Osiris absolutely supreme in his own dominions, and the exclusion of Rā, or Åmen-Rā, from them was clearly the cause which made the work unpopular with all the worshippers of the great god of Thebes. The position of Osiris on the top of a flight of steps explains the allusions to the "god who is on his staircase" in the Book of the Dead, and it proves that it is this god who is represented on the wooden plaque of Semti,[1] and before whom the king is dancing. The Sun-god Rā, having arrived at the north of the Ṭuat, must now make his way towards the East.

The serpent who guards the pylon of the Seventh Division or the Seventh Hour[2] is called Ākhan-maati, 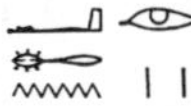, and the guardian at the end of the corridor is called Shepi, 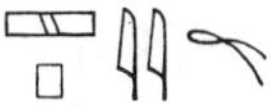; but the mutilated state of the scene renders it impossible to give the name of the pylon or of the guardian of the entrance to the corridor. On the right side of the boat of the god are a number of beings bearing a rope, which is usually made to resemble a serpent, and on the left side are:—1. A god bending over a staff; his name is Men-sheta, 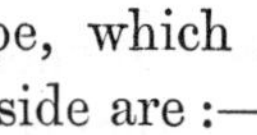, "Stablisher of what is secret." 2. A number of mummied forms extended on couches, who are described as the "mighty spirits." These beings are commanded by Rā to uncover themselves and to drive away darkness. In the centre is the boat of the Sun-god being towed along, presumably

[1] See *British Museum*, No. 32,650.

[2] The scene of the Seventh Division is so mutilated on the sarcophagus of Seti I. that it is not reproduced here.

by four gods of the Ṭuat as before. Marching in front of those who tow the boat are twelve gods with sceptres, and four mummied forms who cry out to the inhabitants of this Division of the Ṭuat to praise Rā, for he will weigh words and will destroy their enemy.

The pylon of the EIGHTH DIVISION or the EIGHTH HOUR is called Bekhkhi, , and the name of the snake-god, its guardian, is Set-ḥrȧ, ; the guardian of the entrance to the corridor is called Benen, , and the guardian at its end is Ḥept-ta, . The wall is protected by nine gods in mummied forms, . On the right side of the boat of the god are:—1. Twelve beings in human form, who are described as the "sovereign chiefs who give bread, Maāt, and green herbs to "the souls of Ta-neserser," . 2. Nine souls, in the form of bearded human-headed hawks, with their hands raised in adoration; these are the "souls of Ta-neserser," which are fed with bread and green herbs by the command of the god Rā. On the left hand side of the boat of Rā are:—1. Horus leaning on a staff. 2. Twelve men, who represent the enemies of Osiris that have been burnt in the fire, with their arms tied together behind their backs, each group of four in a different way. Opposite the first of these is a huge serpent called Kheti, , which belches forth a stream of fire into his face; on the back of the serpent stand seven gods. The twelve beings are those on whom punishment has been inflicted by Horus at the command of Rā, who has decreed the death both of their bodies and of their souls because of what they did against Osiris, whose mysteries they despised, and whose image they tore from the sanctuary. The serpent Kheti, which is commanded by Horus to consume the foes of his father Osiris, is adjured to burn up both the souls and the bodies of these wicked ones. In the centre of this division are:—1. The boat of the sun being towed by four gods as before. 2. "The dweller in Nu" leaning on a staff. 3. A rectangular lake in which

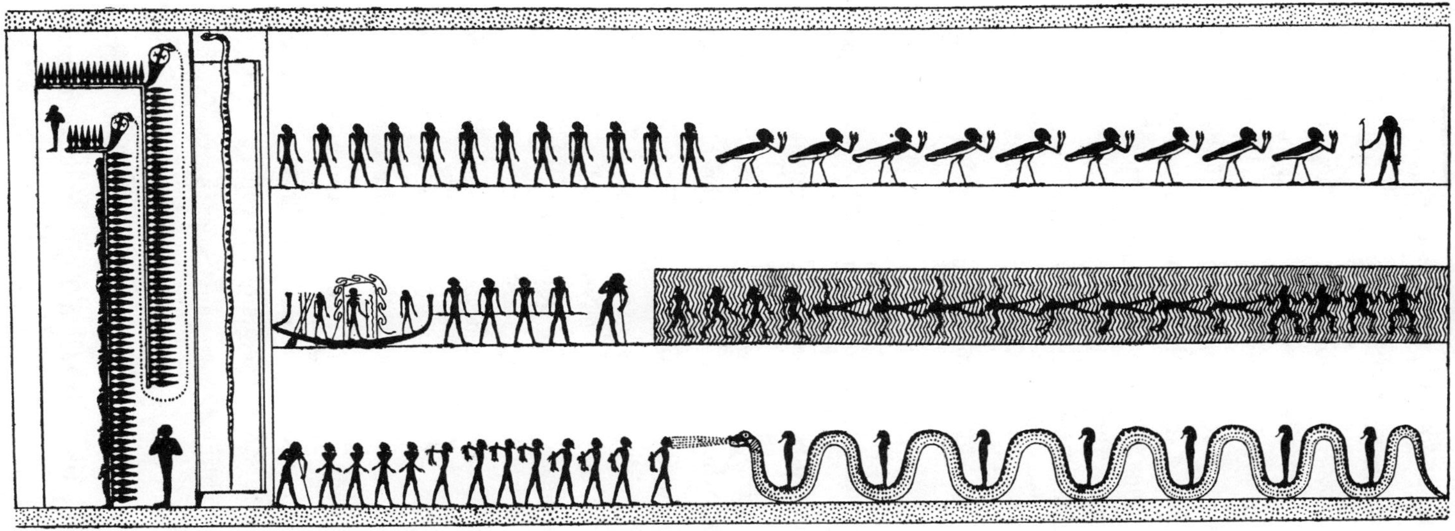

The Eighth Hour of the Night.

are sixteen men, four of whom bathe, ⟨hieroglyphs⟩, four float,
⟨hieroglyphs⟩, four swim, ⟨hieroglyphs⟩, and four dive, ⟨hieroglyphs⟩.
The gods who tow the boat say, " Let there be praise to the soul of
" Rā in heaven, and adoration to his body upon earth; for heaven
" is made new by his soul, and earth is made new by his body.
" Hail! We open for thee heaven, we make straight for thee the
" ways of Ȧḳert. Rest thyself, O Rā, upon thy hidden things;
" the hidden ones are adored in thy forms." He who dwelleth in
Nu also addresses those who are in the lake.

The pylon of the NINTH DIVISION or NINTH HOUR, is called
Āāt-shefsheft, ⟨hieroglyphs⟩; the serpent which guards it is
Āb-ta, ⟨hieroglyphs⟩; and the guardians of the corridor are Ȧnḥefta,
⟨hieroglyphs⟩, and Ermen-ta, ⟨hieroglyphs⟩. The wall is guarded by
nine gods in mummied forms, ⟨hieroglyphs⟩. On the right hand side of
the boat of the Sun-god are :—1. Four gods of the South, ⟨hieroglyphs⟩,
each wearing the white crown, and grasping a rope which is also
held by a man who is called " the master of the front," ⟨hieroglyphs⟩,
between the man and these four gods is a pillar surmounted by a
bearded head, with a white crown on it, which is being raised by
means of the rope. 2. A hawk-headed sphinx with the white
crown on his head, and a bearded head, with a white crown on it,
resting on his hind quarters. Standing on his back is a human
figure which is surmounted by the heads of Horus and Set.
3. Four gods of the North, ⟨hieroglyphs⟩, each wearing the red crown,
and grasping a rope which is also held by a man who is called " the
master of the back," ⟨hieroglyphs⟩; between the man and these four gods
is a pillar, surmounted by a bearded head with a red crown on it,
which is being raised by means of the rope. 4. A personage called
Ȧpu, ⟨hieroglyphs⟩, holding the serpent Shemti, ⟨hieroglyphs⟩, which has four
heads at each end of his body. 5. A personage holding the serpent
Bȧth, ⟨hieroglyphs⟩, with a head at each end of his body; on his back
stands a serpent which is called Ṭepi, ⟨hieroglyphs⟩, and which is provided

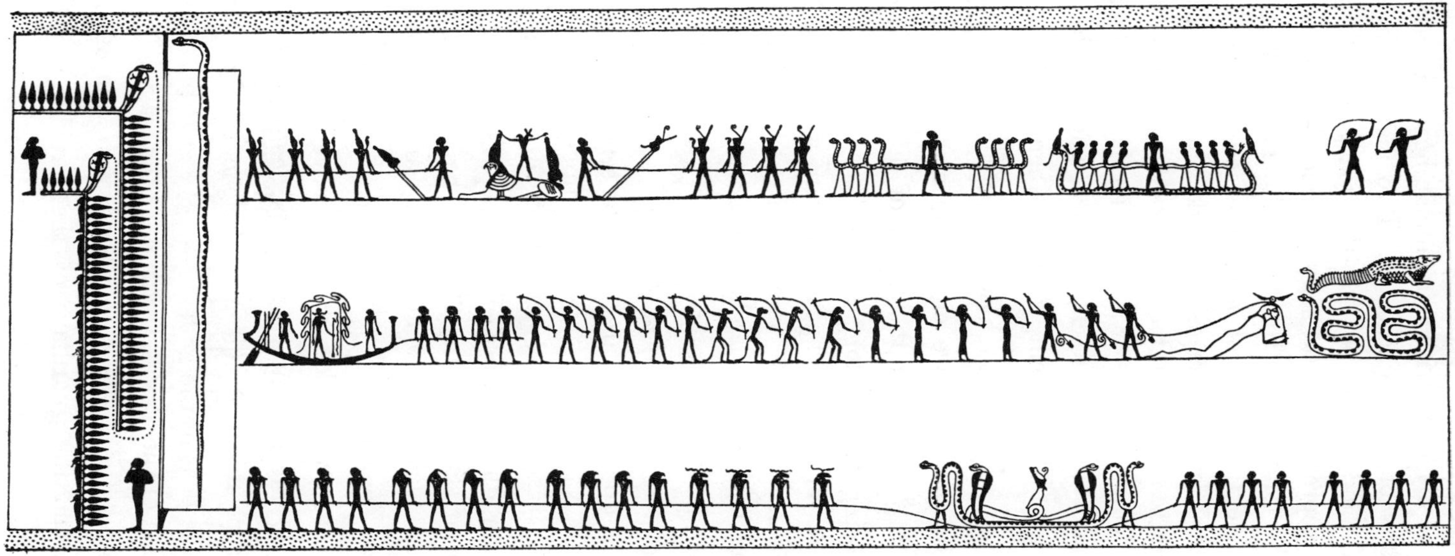

The Ninth Hour of the Night.

at each end of his body with four human heads, breasts, and arms, and four pairs of human legs. 6. Two men holding a rope (?). On the left hand of the boat of the god are:—Sixteen human forms which represent the (*a*) souls of Amentet, (*b*) the followers of Thoth, (*c*) the followers of Horus, (*d*) the followers of Osiris; the first four have the heads of men, the second four the heads of ibises, the third four the heads of hawks, and the fourth four the heads of rams. These sixteen beings draw a rope to which is attached a double serpent with four heads, two at each end of his body, and one pair of legs at each end which support the larger serpent. The serpent is called Khepri, , and on one of his folds is perched the hawk Ḥeru-ṭuati, . At the other end of the rope are eight human forms called Ȧkhmiu, . In the centre of this Division the boat of the god is being towed along as before. Before him march:—1. Six human forms, four apes, and four women, each holding a rope (?); and 2. Three men holding a rope which is thrown over the head and held in the hands by a prostrate man who has the ears of an ass, and who is called Ȧai, , i.e., "Ass." Each man holds a pike which he is about to drive into the prostrate body. In front of the man are:—1. The serpent Āpep, and 2. The crocodile, with a tail which terminates in a serpent's head, called Shesshes, 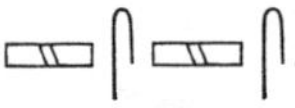. The beings here described are those who work magic for Rā on the arch-fiend Āpep, and they bid him come to the place of slaughter that he may be slain; they say, "the "slaughtering places are against thee, and the Ȧai gods are "against thee," 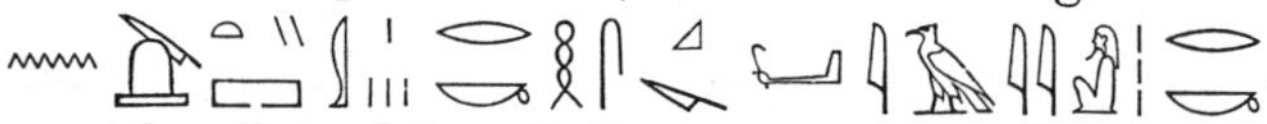. The three beings with pikes drive their weapons into Āpep, and destroy utterly the serpent Sesi, 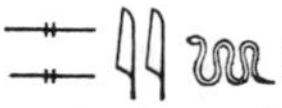; and they keep fast hold of the rope of Ai, , and do not let that serpent rise up towards the boat of the god.

The pylon of the TENTH DIVISION or the TENTH HOUR is called Tcheserit, ; the serpent-god who guards it is Sethu, ; and the guardians of the corridor are Nemi, ,

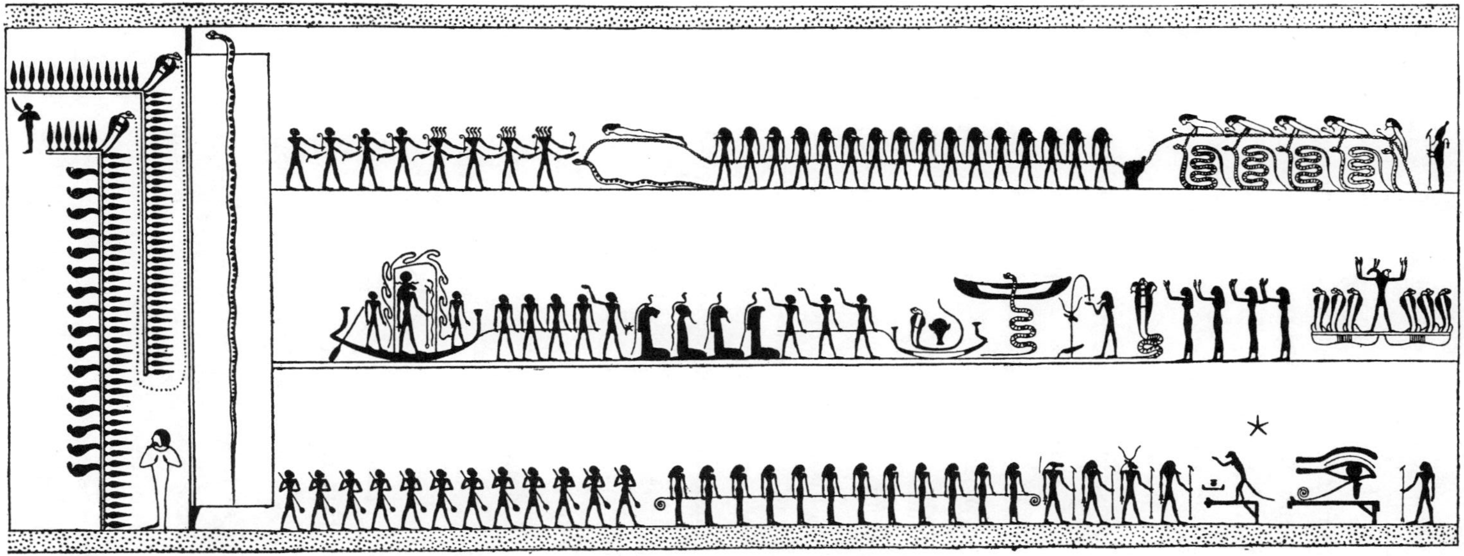

The Tenth Hour of the Night.

and Kefi, . The wall is guarded by sixteen uraei. On the right hand of the boat of the god are:—1. Four beings, each holding a knife and a rope (?). 2. Four beings, similarly armed, but each having four serpents' heads; these are called Ȧntiu, , and Ḥentiu, , respectively. 3. The serpent Āpep, "whose voice goeth round about in the Ṭuat," held by a chain which is grasped by four beings, Sṭefiu, , and twelve gods, and a mighty hand called the "hidden body," . On the chain, near Āpep's head, is stretched out the scorpion-goddess Serqet. Behind the hand, and growing out of the chain are:—(*a*) Seb, , who grasps a small chain to which is attached the serpent Uamemti, . (*b*) Mest, , Ḥāpi, , Ṭuamutef, , and Qebḥsennuf, . At the end stands Khenti-Ȧmenti, or Osiris. The beings on this side of the Ṭuat are engaged in destroying Āpep and the foes of the sun-god so that they may not attack the boat of the sun when it comes to a narrow passage. On the left hand side of the boat of Rā are:—1. The twelve Ȧkhmu-seku gods, , holding paddles. 2. Twelve women, who represent the hours. 3. Four gods with sceptres, Bānt, , Seshshȧ, , Ka-Ȧment, , and Renen-sebu, . 4. A monkey on a standard, , with a star over his head, described as the "god of Rethenu" (Syria), . 5. An eye (utchat) on a standard, . 6. A god with a sceptre. Along the middle of this division the boat of the god is towed as usual by four gods. Before it are:—1. The star god Unti, . 2. Four deities, Sekhet, Ābesh, , Serq, , and Horus. 3. Three star gods, who tow a small boat in which are the "face of the disk," , and a uraeus. 4. A winged uraeus called Semi, , standing upon its tail. 5. A god called Besi, , pouring flame upon a standard surmounted

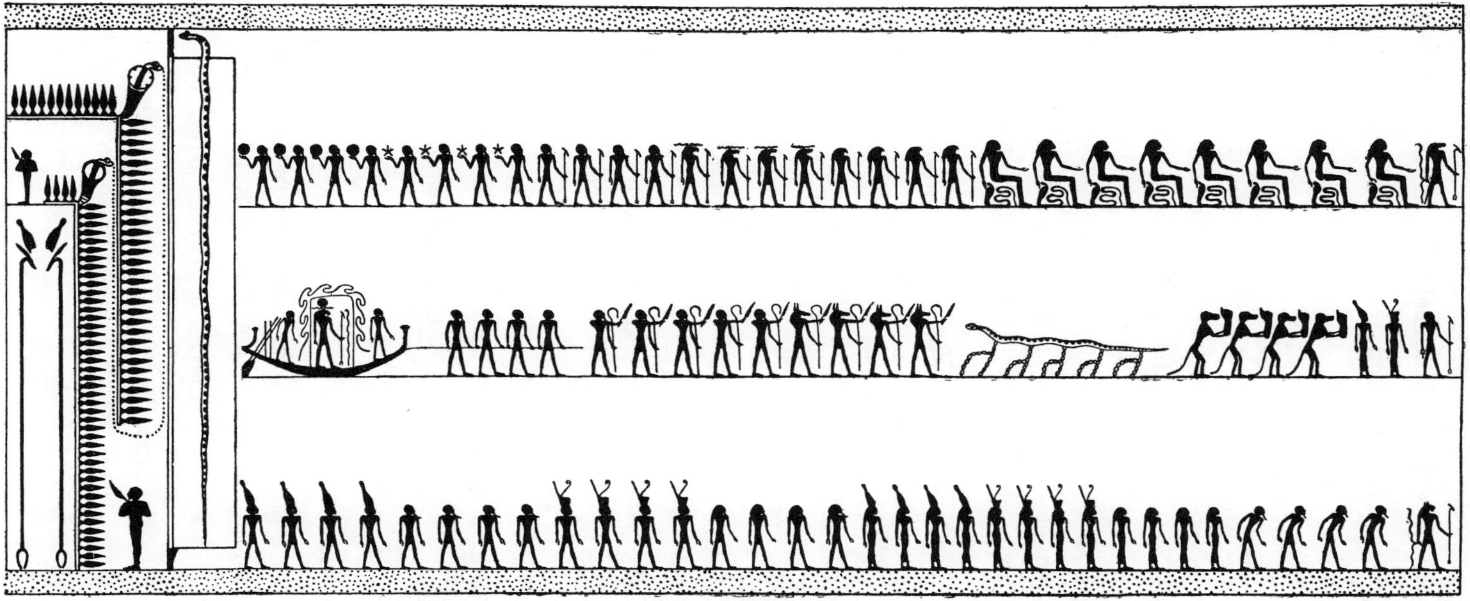

The Eleventh Hour of the Night.

by the head of a horned animal. 6. A serpent caled Ānkhi, , with a bearded god in mummied form growing out from each side of its body. 7. Four women, with hands raised in adoration, who are called "the adorers," . 8. The double god Horus-Set, with two heads and two pairs of arms and hands on one body, standing upon a platform which rests on two bows; from each end of the platform spring three uraei. All these beings are supposed to be employed in helping Rā to continue his course through the Tenth Division, and to make his way to the region of the sunrise; it is evident that most of them are personifications of the stars which herald the approach of the dawn.

The pylon of the ELEVENTH DIVISION or the ELEVENTH HOUR is called Shetat-besu, , and the serpent which guards it is called Åm-net-f, ; the guardians of the corridor are Meṭes, , and Sheṭāu, . Before the wall are two large sceptres surmounted by the white crown; one of these is called Sar, , i.e., Osiris, and the other Horus. On the right hand of the boat of Rā are:—1. Four gods, called "bearers of light," , holding disks on their right hands. 2. Four gods, called "bearers of stars," , holding stars in their right hands. 3. Four gods "who go out," . 4. The gods Ba, , Khnemu, , Penṭer, , and Ṭenṭ, , ram-headed. 5. Four gods, Horus, Horus-Sepṭ, Sepṭ, and "he who is in his double boat," , hawk-headed. 6. Eight women, the Hours, seated on coiled up serpents and each holding a star in her hand; these are the "protecting hours," . 7. The god Sebek-Rā, crocodile-headed. All these are personifications of stars which bear along the boat of Rā towards the day-break, for they wish to see it floating once more on the bosom of Nut, ; and when "the arms of the "sky-god Nu receive Rā they shout praises with the stars which "they carry, and go to him in the heights of heaven in the bosom of Nut."[1] In connexion with the idea of the stars praising Rā at sunrise we may note its similarity to that expressed in Job xxxviii. 7, "When the morning stars sang together, and all the "sons of God shouted for joy." On the left of the boat of Rā are:—1. Four beings, Setheniu-ṭep, , wearing white crowns. 2. Four bearded gods called Åkebiu, i.e., "wailers," . 3. Four beings, Khnemiu, 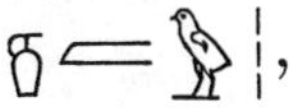, wearing red crowns. 4. Four bearded gods called Renniu, 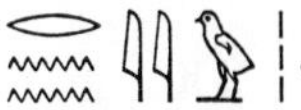. 5. Twelve goddesses, the female counterparts of the first three groups of gods. 6. Four gods, with bowed bodies, and 7. The cat-headed goddess Måti, . These beings were supposed to place white crowns on the heads of the gods in the train of Rā, and though their souls rose up, they were never able to leave this Division of the Ṭuat or pass out of the pylon. Their duty was to weep for Osiris after Rā had passed out of Åment,[2] and to be with him, as far as their souls were concerned, but their bodies had to stay in their places; they also had to raise up Maāt and to stablish it in the shrine of Rā.[3] It was they who "fixed the period of the "years which those who were decreed for the Ṭuat should pass "there, and the period of those who were to live in heaven;"[4] but they "tore their hair in grief before the great god in Åmentet, "for although they drove away Set from the pylon they themselves

1 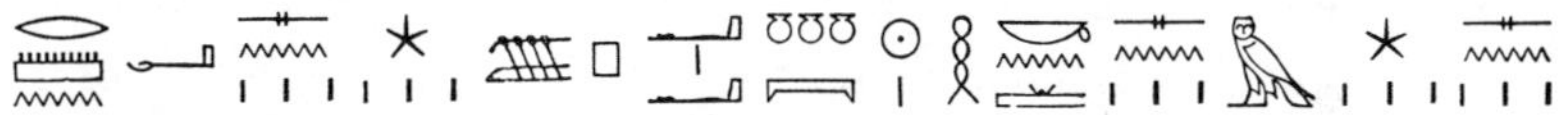
, Bonomi and Sharpe, op. cit., pl. 10.

2 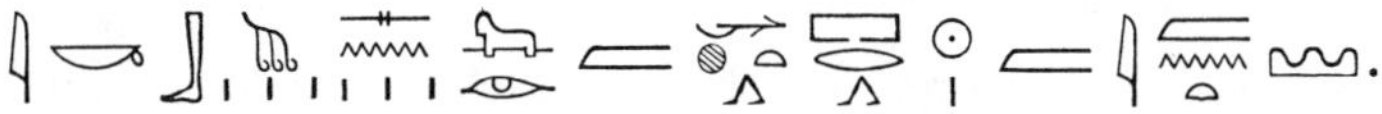

3 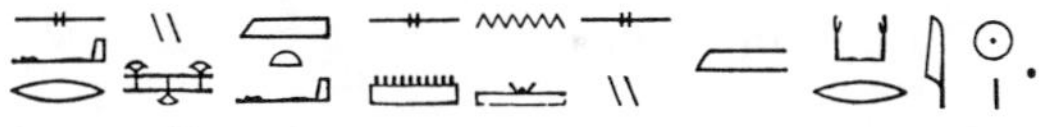

4 

"were not allowed to enter into the heights of heaven."[1] In the centre of this division we have the boat of Rā being drawn along by four of its gods as usual. Preceding these are:—1. A group of nine gods, each of whom holds a knife, , in the right hand, and a sceptre, , in the left; the first four are jackal-headed. They are described as the "nine gods who annihilate Āpep," . 2. The serpent Āpep chained to the earth by five chains which are called the "gods who produce winds," . 3. Four apes, , each holding before him a large hand. 4. The god of Àmenti, , wearing the crown of the South. 5. The goddess of the North, Ḥerit (?), (?) , wearing the crown of the North. 6. The god Sebekhti, . These gods of the Ṭuat say, "[This is] the exit from Àment, and the "place for rest in the two divisions of Nu, and [the god] maketh "his transformations in the hands of Nu. This god doth not enter "heaven ( ), but he openeth the Ṭuat upwards in his trans- "formations [which take place] in Nu. What openeth the Ṭuat "into heaven are the two hands of the god whose name is hidden, " . He existeth in the darkness which is a solid thing, " , and Rā cometh forth [in] it from the night, " . Those who are in this portion take their knives in "their hands, and grasp their weapons, and smite Āpep, and effect "his slaughter, and smash his joints which are in heaven. The "chains of this fiend are in the hands of the children of Horus, "they advance to the god with their fetters in their fingers. The "god counteth his members after the hidden one hath opened his "[arms] to the Eye of Horus. The Worm ( ) who is "in this scene is fettered by the children of Horus." The other gods "acclaim Rā in the Eastern horizon of heaven, and the four

1 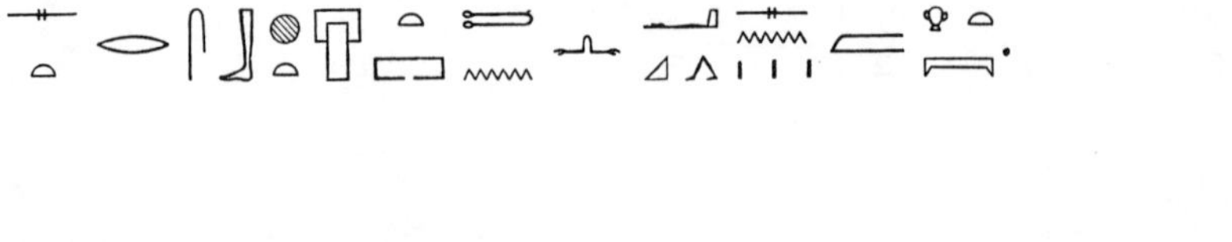

"apes guide him who created them, two on the right hand, and "two on the left, to the double *ȧtert* ( ) of this god."

The pylon of the TWELFTH DIVISION or TWELFTH HOUR is called Ṭesert-baiu, , i.e., "Red-Souls," and its serpent god is Sebi, ; the two guardians of the corridor are Pai, , and Ȧkhekhi, . In front of the wall are two poles, each of which is surmounted by a bearded head; on one head is the disk of the god Tem, and on the other the beetle of the god Kheperȧ, i.e., two forms of the Sun-god. Close to the pylon "Red-Souls" was the pylon of the serpent god Reri, , each side of which was guarded by the two uraei of Isis and Nephthys, one on each side. When Rā had passed through these doors he emerged triumphantly from the Ṭuat, and his boat floated on the waters of Nu, i.e., in the sky. In the scene in which this is depicted we see the boat containing the beetle of Kheperȧ and the disk of Rā, with the five gods Seb, Shu, Ḥek (for Ḥeka), Ḥu, and Sa, and the two goddesses Isis and Nephthys, and three gods of pylons. The god Nu, , is seen holding up the boat with his hands, which "come forth from the water, and bear up this god."

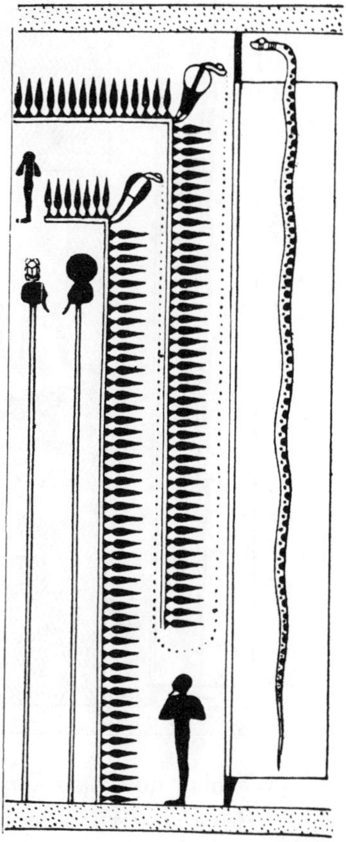

A little distance away from the boat is a sort of island which is formed by Osiris, the body of the god being bent round in such a way as to cause the tips of his toes to touch the back of his head; the text says that it is Osiris himself who forms the encircling border of the Ṭuat. On the head of the god stands the goddess

Nut, [hieroglyphs], with arms outstretched ready to receive Rā. Thus the god reaches the end of the Ṭuat and passes by an opening through its border, which is painted black, dotted everywhere with red spots. We have seen that Rā was omnipotent in all divisions of the underworld, except one, which was sacred to Osiris; in this neither Rā nor his name appears.

We may now pass on to the consideration of the contents of the "Book of that which is in the Underworld." The authorities for the text and vignettes of this work are numerous,[1] and from the copies of both which have come down to us it is

[1] See Sharpe, *Egyptian Inscriptions*, 1st series, pll. 28-32; 2nd series, pll. 1-21; Pierret, *Recueil*, tom. v., pp. 103 ff; Lanzone, *Domicile des Esprits*, Paris, 1879; Birch, *Papyrus of Naskhem*, London, 1863; Mariette, *Papyrus Égyptiens*, tom. ii., Cairo, 1878.

clear that the book was one of considerable length. But long before the end of the XXIst Dynasty (about B.C. 1100) the Egyptians found it impossible to obtain or to pay for complete copies with all the vignettes, and a shortened form of it consequently came into general use. This shortened form, which is called an "Abrégé" by M. Maspero, and a "Résumé" by M. Lefebure, was supposed to contain all that was absolutely necessary for the dead, and it became very popular throughout Egypt. In the tomb of Seti I.[1] we find a copy of the full text, with vignettes, of the first eleven hours, and also a copy of the "Abridgment." The space at our disposal will not admit of a detailed description of the longer work, and therefore a notice of the "Abridgment" only is given here. The complete work is entitled, "The beginning "of the horn of the West, the remote boundary of thick darkness," . The "horn of the West" means the most westerly point where the sun sets, and *keku samu*, i.e., "thick darkness," or "solid darkness," refers to the extreme end of the Ṭuat, which is painted to resemble a black wall, dotted everywhere with red spots, and which contains an opening through which the boat of Rā emerges every morning. The shorter work is entitled "Abridgment of this book," 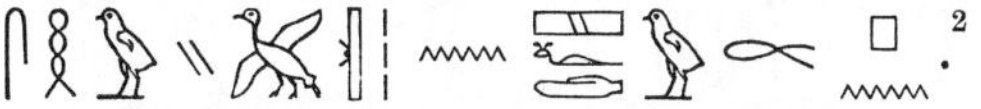.[2]

The FIRST HOUR of the night is called USHEMET ḤĀTU KHEFTI RĀ,[3] i.e., "Crusher of the forehead of the enemies of Rā," and the place through which the god passes in it is described as an *ārrit*, 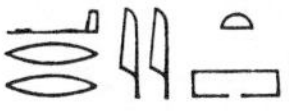, i.e., a hall, or a sort of ante-chamber of the Ṭuat. It is quite unlike any part of the Ṭuat, for when Rā is in this hall he

[1] See "Le Tombeau de Seti Ier," in *Mémoires de la Miss. Arch. Française*, Paris, 1886; First Hour, part iv., pll. 24-26; Second Hour, part iv., pll. 29-32; Third Hour, part iv., pll. 32-35; Fourth Hour, part i., pll. 23-25; Fifth Hour, part i., pll. 26-29; Sixth Hour, part iv., pll. 39-42; Seventh Hour, part iv., pll. 43-46; Eighth Hour, part iv., pll. 47-49; Ninth Hour, part ii., pll. 15-18; Tenth Hour, part ii., pll. 19-22; Eleventh Hour, part ii., pll. 23-26; and see Maspero, *Les Hypogées Royaux de Thèbes*, p. 29.

[2] See the edition of the hieroglyphic text, with a French translation, by Jéquier, op. cit., pp. 37 ff.

[3] 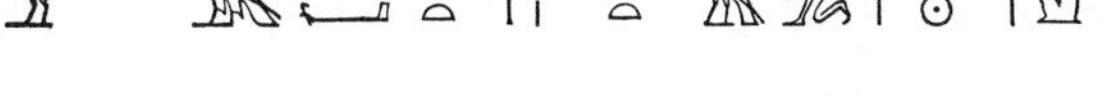.

has not yet arrived in that dismal valley. But even when here he is an entirely different being from what he was in the day-time, for instead of being the sun of day, he is the sun of night, i.e., a dead god, in fact a mere dead body which is called Åf, , i.e., "Flesh," and is represented with the head of a ram surmounted by a solar disk. In the day time he travelled in the Āṭet boat,

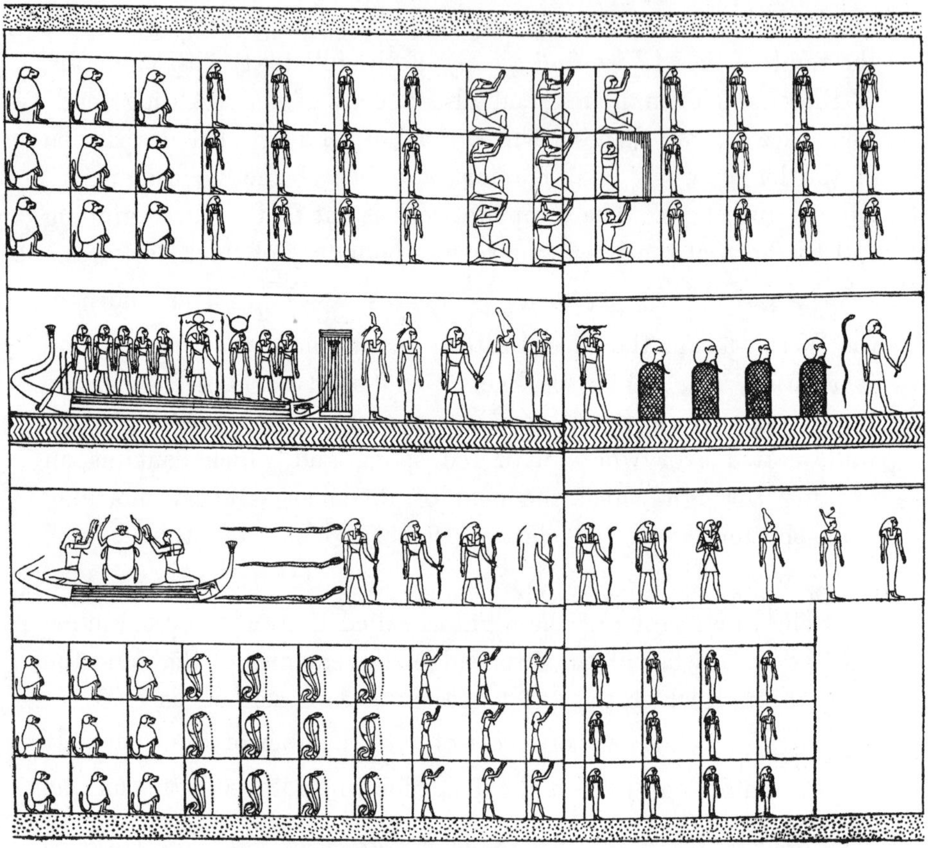

The First Hour of the Night.

, but at night he made his journey along the river of the Ṭuat in the Sektet boat, , in fact, in the same boat in which he sailed over the sky from noon to sunset. In the boat with the dead Sun-god Åf are Åp-uat, , "The Opener of the ways," Sa, , Ḥeru-Ḥekenu, , Nehes, , Ḥu, , the double of Shu, , the captain of the boat,

, and the "lady of the boat," 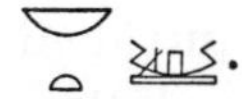. The last-named celestial personage changed every hour, for she represented the local goddess of one hour who was supposed to be the appointed guide of the god through one portion of the Ṭuat only; knowing the way through her own district, she was able to instruct the captain of the boat how and where to sail over difficult reaches of the river.

The dwellers in the First Hour of the night appear to have been the apes who opened the doors of the *ārrit* to the god, and the beings who were necessary for the singing of songs of praise to Rā, and for piloting his boat through this hall to the Ṭuat, and a large number of celestial beings who are mentioned in the text, but who are otherwise unknown, and the souls of the dead who had passed from the earth to this intermediate place and who were waiting for the opportunity of entering into the boat of Rā, wherein they would fain continue their journey. Why the last-named were here cannot be said, but it is probable that such souls belonged to men and women who, when living upon earth, were unable to avail themselves of all the costly and complicated ceremonies prescribed by the priests, and the numerous amulets which were thought to be necessary for the welfare of the soul in the Ṭuat. The descriptive text of the First Hour reads:—"This "god entereth from the earth into the *ārrit* of the horizon of "the West, and he must travel one hundred and twenty *ȧtru* " () in this *ārrit* before he arriveth at the gods "of the Ṭuat. Net-Rā (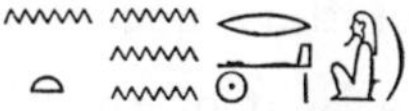) is the name of this first "country of the Ṭuat. Rā giveth fields to the gods who are in his "following, and he beginneth to pass decrees and to give commands "concerning the things which are done in the Ṭuat by the gods of "this country. Whosoever shall do these things according to this "similitude of the hidden things of the Ṭuat, and shall recognize "that they are similitudes of the great god himself, shall find them "of benefit to him on the earth, and they shall do him good in the "great Ṭuat." The fact that this region is called "country" shows that it was regarded almost as a part of this world, and it is definitely stated that it is 120 *ȧtru* in length; now, the *ȧtru* is said to be the equivalent of the Greek *σχοῖνος*, i.e., about an English furlong, and thus the region of the sunset traversed by Rā in his first hour would be fifteen miles in length. It is probable, however, that 120 *ȧtru* were intended to be a greater distance than fifteen miles, for the second hour brought Rā into the domain of Osiris, which is more than fifteen miles from Thebes.

The name of the SECOND HOUR is SHESAT MĀKET NEB-S, i.e., "She who knoweth how to protect her lord."[1] The country passed through is called Ur-nes, 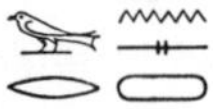, which the late Dr. Birch compared with, and believed to be equivalent to, the Greek *οὐρανός*; this name, however, seems to be that of the Nile in the second region of the Ṭuat, and in any case it is not applied to any other division or hour except by accident.[2] The descriptive text says, "This great god next arriveth in Ur-nes, which is three "hundred and nine *ȧtru* in length, and one hundred and twenty "*ȧtru* in width (i.e., this division measures about 50 miles by 15 "miles). The name of the gods who are in this country is 'Souls "of the Ṭuat,' , and he who knoweth their "name shall be with them. This great god will give to him fields, "the situation of which shall be in the country of Ur-nes; he shall "stand up with the gods who stand up, and he shall follow after "this great god. He shall make his way through the Ṭuat, he "shall see the tresses of the gods who wear long flowing hair, he "shall trample upon the Eater of the Ass (), "and after the division of the unoccupied land hath been made, "he shall eat bread in the Boat of the Earth (), "and there shall be given to him of the first things of Tatubȧ "()." The text adds that those who draw pictures of these Souls of the Ṭuat and make offerings to them upon earth will gain benefit therefrom a million fold after death; moreover, it will be extremely useful to them in the Ṭuat if they know what words are addressed by the gods to the great god.

1 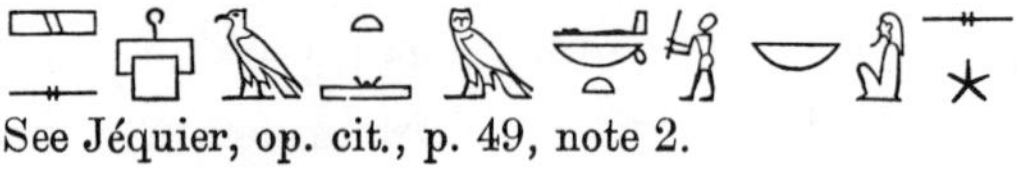.

2 See Jéquier, op. cit., p. 49, note 2.

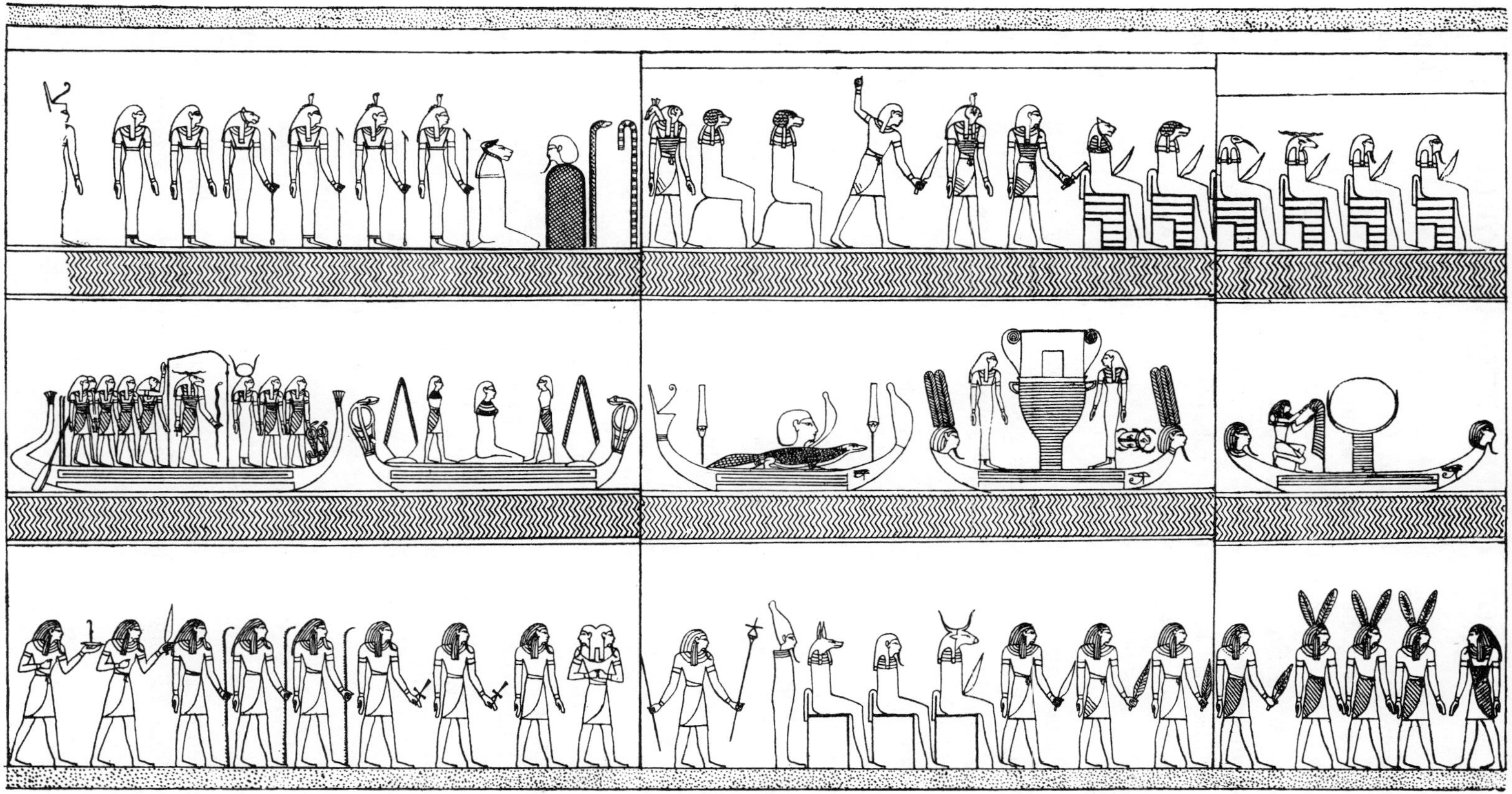

The Second Hour of the Night.

The gods with long flowing hair are the four children of Horus, Mesthȧ, Ḥāpi, Ṭuamutef and Qebḥsennuf, each of whom wore a lock or tress of hair, which became a pillar-sceptre, and supported one of the four corners of heaven; these four gods became at a later period the gods of the cardinal points and the lords of the four quarters of heaven. The Eater of the Ass is, of course, the great serpent of darkness, probably Āpepi, and the Ass is a form of the Sun-god, between whom and the serpent was continual war; the Ass was connected with the Sun-god by reason of his great virile powers. According to M. Maspero,[1] the Boat of the Earth is a name given to the Boat of Rā when it reaches the earth; Tatubȧ was probably an earth god.

The illustrated version of the SECOND HOUR shows that the boat of Rā was preceded by four boats. The first of these had a human head on each end, and on its side were the picture of heaven, , and the Utchat, . In the boat rests the moon on a pedestal, and behind it is the god who sets up the feather of Maāt. This is the boat of Osiris as the Moon, who is one of the Souls of the Ṭuat. The second boat has a human head surmounted by the plumes of Ȧmen, , on each end, and in it is a huge sistrum, the emblem of Hathor; on each side of it is a goddess. In the bows is a beetle, . This is the boat of Isis as Hathor, who is one of the Souls of the Ṭuat. The third boat has the white crown at the bows, and the red crown at the stern; in it, between the two standards, which are the symbols of the gods Ȧnpu (Anubis) and Ȧpuat, is a huge lizard, out of the back of which spring a human head and the white crown. This is the boat of the god who opens the ways, and who is one of the Souls of the Ṭuat. The fourth boat has a uraeus at the bows and stern. In the centre is a kneeling woman without arms, and on each side of her stands a woman also armless; at each end of the boat is a plant, or shrub. This is the boat of Nepr, 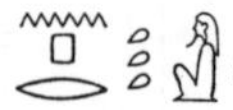, the god of grain and of vegetation, and a form of Osiris, and he is also one of the Souls of the Ṭuat. The gods who minister to

[1] *Les Hypogées*, p. 46.

Osiris in the Second Hour are:—Isis who avengeth, , Seb of the two corners, , Khnemu of the two corners, , Thoth on his stairs, , Åfu on his stairs, , Ketuit-ṭen-ba, , Kherp-ḥu-khefti, , Ḥeru-Ṭuat, , Seben-ḥesq-khaibit, , the two ape-gods Ḃenth, , and Ȧānā, , the god with two faces, , Horus-Set, Mest-en-Ȧsår, , Meṭ-en-Ȧsår, , the term of Osiris, and a lion-headed goddess Sesenet-khu, . Behind all these come seven goddesses, Mest-tcheses, , Āmām-mitu, , Ḥer-ṭuaiu, , Sekhet of Thebes, , Āmet-tcheru, , Ȧment-nefert, , and Nit-ṭep-Ȧment, . On the other side of the boat of the god are Nebui, , Besabes-uāa, , Nepr, , Ṭepu, , Ḥetch-ā, , Āb, , Nepen, , Ȧr-ȧst-neter, , Āmu-āa, , Ḥeru-khabit, , Anubis, Osiris-Unnefer, Khui, , Horus of the two faces, i.e., Horus and Set, Ḥen-Ḥeru, , Ḥun, , Ḥatchetchu, , Neḥr, , Makhi, , Renpti, , Āfau, , and Fa-tråu, . All these gods worship the great god, and guide him on his way, and weep when he has left them; some of them bear to him the prayers of those who are upon earth, and also lead disembodied souls to the forms which belong to them; others apparently mark the seasons of the year. When Rā addressed the beings there, they came to life at the sound of his voice, and they breathed again; he gave them food in abundance, and the gods gave water to the spirits to drink at his command, and the hearts of the rebels of Rā were burnt in the fire. It is, however, clear from the texts that although Osiris was the Lord of the Second Hour Rā was the overlord of Osiris, and that it was he who, like Osiris, made gifts to the dead. On the other hand, the followers of Osiris had to perform service for Rā, and one of their chief duties consisted in keeping in check his enemies, who were always attempting to prevent the progress of his boat; in a way the service of these followers was unrewarded, for they were condemned to remain always in the same place, and to perform the same duty.

From the above paragraph the reader will gain some idea of the difference between the illustrated version of the Second Hour and the abstract of it which is found in the "Abridgment." As the short version makes no attempt to supply the souls which were supposed to make use of it with the names of the various gods and beings in it, we can only assume that they learnt them when on earth in the body. The larger version of the Second Hour is extremely interesting in showing what a subordinate place the priests of Åmen-Rā made Osiris occupy in respect of Rā when passing through the Ṭuat.

The descriptive text of the THIRD HOUR, which is called ṬENT-BAIU,[1] says:—"This great god next arrives in the Country "of those who slay (), and he roweth over "the Stream of Osiris (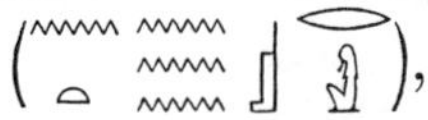), a space three hundred and "nine *åtru* long,[2] and one hundred and twenty *åtru* wide (i.e., "this portion of the Ṭuat measured about 38½ miles long by 15 "miles wide). This great god giveth commands to the gods who "are in the following of Osiris concerning this city, and he assigns "to them estates from this country. The name of the gods who "are in this field is 'Hidden Souls' (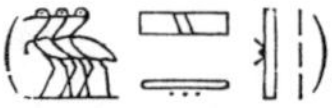), and whosoever "knoweth their name shall ascend to the place where Osiris is,

1 

2 A variant given by Jéquier gives 480 *åtru* as the length, i.e., about sixty miles.

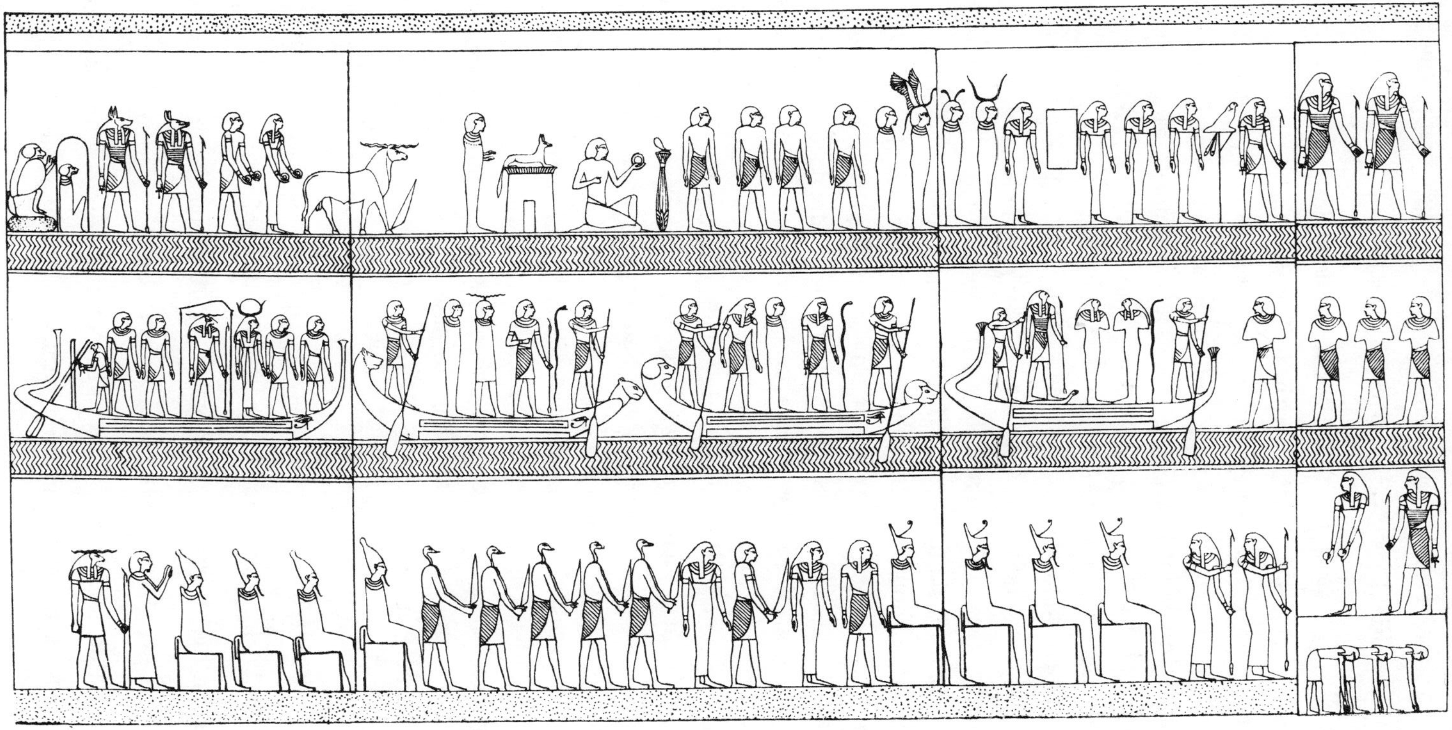

The Third Hour of the Night.

"and water shall be given unto him for his Field. The name "of this Field is Net-neb-uā-kheper-āutu ( "). Whosoever shall make drawings of these "Hidden Souls together with a representation of the hidden "things of the Ṭuat—beginning the same from the West—it shall "be of great benefit not only to him upon earth, but in the Under- "world, and indeed always. Whosoever knoweth them shall pass "[unhurt] by them as they roar, and shall not fall into their "cauldrons. Whosoever knoweth these things, being attached to "his place, shall have his bread with Rā. Whosoever, being a "soul and a spirit, knoweth these things shall have the mastery "over his legs, and he shall never enter into the place of destruc- "tion, and he shall come forth in his forms and smell the air at his "appointed hour." The illustrated version of the Third Hour represents the boat of Rā sailing over the "Stream of Osiris" preceded by three boats, each of which is moved onwards by two men with paddles; the beings in these boats are all forms of the god Osiris, and the gods who stand on each side of the stream belong to his cycle, or company. These latter had their bodies of flesh, to which their shadows had been re-united, and their souls talked in them, as soon as Rā had spoken to them; they made answer to the god, and sang his praise whilst he was with them, but their cries of joy changed to lamentations when he left them. They could not go with him, because it was their duty to guard their district, and to destroy the enemies of Rā, and to support the life of Rā, and to make the Nile to flow.

Among the gods in this Hour were the nine forms of the god Osiris:—Osiris, lord of Ȧment, ; Osiris Khenti-Ȧment, ; Osiris the Throne, ; Osiris, conqueror of millions, ; Osiris the double of Ȧment, ; Osiris on his staircase, ; Osiris prince of the gods, ; Osiris king of Lower Egypt, ; and Osiris-Saḥu, . The duties of the beings who are grouped with these are clear from their names, for these refer to destruction in one form or another, and the explanatory text tells us that they are employed in "hacking and cutting souls, in shutting up the "shadows of the dead, and in dragging the occupants of tombs to "their place of slaughter;" moreover, they shoot out flames, they cause fires to come into being, and the heads of the enemies of Rā are cut off by their swords. The master of the region traversed in the Third Hour is called Khatrȧ, , and we learn from the speech of Rā that the inhabitants of the mythological district over which he presides were created by Rā specially to follow and to protect Osiris. To these he says, "O ye whom I have hidden, "whose souls I have put in a secret place, whom I have set in the "following of Osiris to defend him; to accompany his images, to "make an end of those who attack him (even as the god Ḥu is "behind thee, O Osiris, to defend thee, to accompany thy images, "to destroy those who attack thee, even as Ḥu is to thee, O Osiris, "and even as Sa is to thee, O Khenti Ȧmentet), ye souls whose "forms are stablished, ye souls whose magical powers make "certain your coming into being, who breathe the air [through "your nostrils, who look] with your faces, who listen with your "ears, who are apparelled in your raiment, who are clothed with "your swathings, who have offerings made to you at stated seasons "by the priests of God, who have estates set apart for your own "behoof and benefit, whose souls are not cast down, whose bodies "are not overthrown: [O Hidden Souls, I say] open ye your "circles, and set ye yourselves in your own places, for I have "come to see my bodies, and to look upon the similitudes of myself "which are in the Ṭuat, and it is you who have brought me along "and have given me the opportunity of coming to them. And "now I lead thy soul to heaven, O Osiris, and thy soul to earth, O "Khenti Ȧuḳert, with thy gods behind thee, and thy spirits before "thee, and thy being and thy forms [about thee]. And thy spirit "hath its word of power, O Osiris, and you, ye spirits who are in "the following of Osiris, have your words of power. I go up on "the earth and the day is behind me; I pass through the night, "and my soul rejoins itself to your forms during the day, and I "fulfil the ceremonies of the night which are needful for you. I

" have created your souls for mine own use, so that they may be " behind me, and what I have done for them will preserve you " from falling down to the place of destruction." [1]

The FOURTH HOUR of the night, which is called SEKHEMUS,[2] conducts the boat of the Sun-god through a region of a very different character from the earlier divisions. The descriptive text says, "The majesty of this great god next arriveth in the hidden " Circle of Åmentet, and he performeth the designs of the gods " who are therein by means of his voice without seeing them. " The name of this Circle is Ānkhet-kheperu (), " and the name of the pylon of this Circle is Åment-sthau " (). Whosoever knoweth this plan " of the hidden paths of Re-stau (), and of the " winding roads of the Åmmeḥet (), and of the " hidden pylons which are in the Land of Seker, he who is on his " sand shall eat the bread which hath been prepared for the mouth " of the living gods who are in the temple of Tem. He who " knoweth these things shall [know] the paths rightly, and shall " have power to journey along the roads of Re-stau, and to see " the forms (or guides) in the Åmmeḥet." The Circle Åmmeḥet is, as we learn from Chapter cxlix of the *Book of the Dead*, the Sixth Åat, or district of the domain of Osiris which is presided over by the god Seker; the deceased addresses it thus:—" Hail, " thou Åmmeḥet which art holy unto the gods, and art hidden " for the spirits, and art baleful unto the dead; the name of the " god who dwelleth in thee is Sekher-Āṭ (?) [or Sekher-remu]. " Homage to thee, O Åmmeḥet, I have come to see the gods who " dwell in thee. Uncover your faces and put off your head-dresses " when ye meet me, for, behold, I am a mighty god among you, " and I have come to prepare provisions for you. Let not Sekher- " Āṭ (?) have dominion over me, let not the divine slaughterers

[1] See Maspero, *Les Hypogées*, p. 64.

[2] , or URT-SEKHEMU-S,  .

"come after me, let not the murderous fiends come after me, but "let me live upon sepulchral offerings among you."[1]

The illustrated edition of the Fourth Hour shows us the boat of Rā passing through an entirely new country, in fact a region

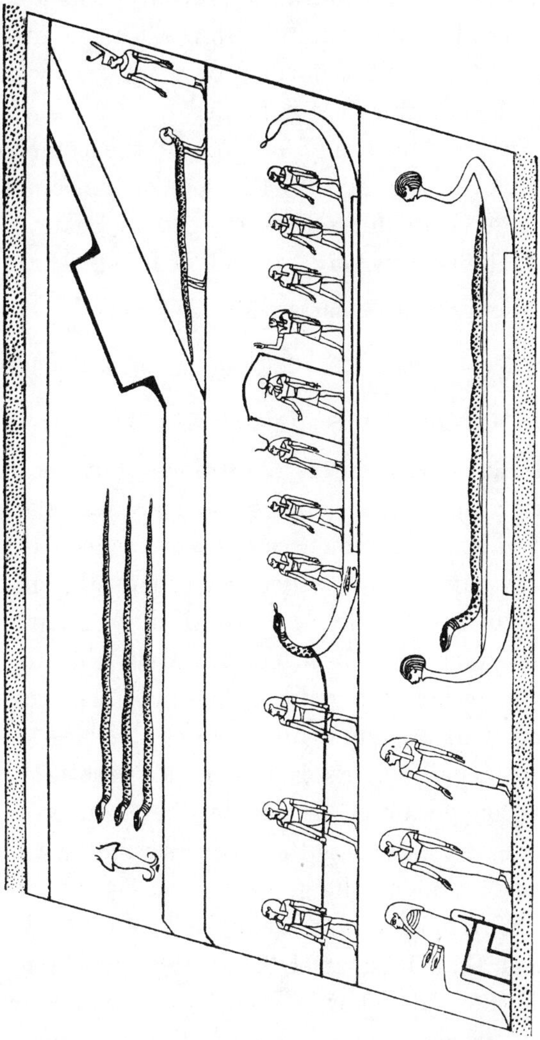

The Fourth Hour of the Night.

which is filled with huge and fearsome snakes, and represents the region over which the god Seker presides. Here there is no river with banks lined with the gods and the souls of the dead, and here

[1] See my *Chapters of Coming Forth by Day* (Translation), p. 267.

there are no fields to be distributed by Rā among the faithful followers of himself and of Osiris; indeed there are so few beings to render him service that he is obliged to betake himself to another kind of boat, and the god of day is compelled to glide through the passages of the dark and gloomy land almost without a following of gods. Rā stands within a shrine in his boat as before, but the boat itself is formed of a serpent with a head at each end of his body; this boat is hauled over the sandy ground of the god "who is upon his sand" by gods of the company of Osiris, with whom, however, are mingled the gods of the company of Ptaḥ of Memphis, and Osiris himself is merged in Seker and becomes Osiris Seker. The narrow way, or road, of Re-stau has three doors, which are called Māṭes-sma-ta, 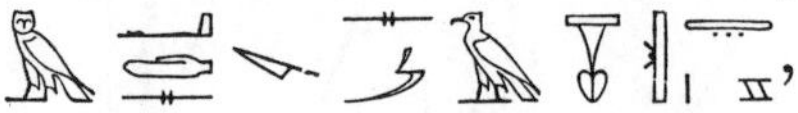, Meṭes-mau-āt, , and Meṭes-neḥeḥ,  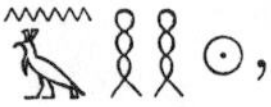, and by these it is divided into three parts. Into one part the god Rā neither enters nor travels, but the door thereof obeys his voice; in another part is the body of Seker, who is on his sand, the hidden form which can be neither looked at nor seen; another part is that through which Seker passeth, but neither the gods, nor the spirits, nor the dead go through it, and it is filled with the souls which have been consumed by the fire that comes forth from the mouth of the goddess Ām-mit. The region through which the boat of Rā travels is full of thick darkness, and the light which the god usually emits is unable to penetrate it; in this difficulty he is helped upon his way by the light of the flames of fire which issue from the mouth of the serpent which forms the body of his boat. Among the gods who march in front of the boat are Thoth and Horus, who stand facing each other with outstretched hands in which they hold an Utchat, , which is here to be identified with the god Seker. The serpents which are passed by the god are of various kinds and of different sizes. The first, called Ḥetch-nāu, 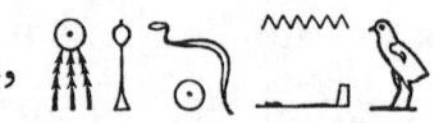, lies at full length in a boat, each end of which terminates in a human head, and is the guardian of Seker; the second is three-headed, and he moves over the ground on four human legs and feet; the third is called Åmen,

The Fourth Hour of the Night.

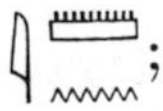; the fourth is Ḥekent, 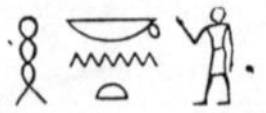, and has a human head growing out of its body just above the tail; and the fifth is Menmenu, 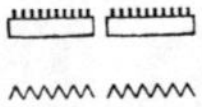, which has three heads, and bears on its back fourteen stars and fourteen human heads surmounted by disks. Next we have three huge serpents near the great scorpion Ankhet, , and a huge uraeus, to which libations are being poured out by a man; and a three-headed serpent, with wings, which moves along on four human feet and legs; and the serpent Neḥeb-kau, , which has two heads at one end of its body, and one head at the other. All these monsters are said to make their journey daily round about the region of the Fourth Hour, and they live upon what they find on their way.

The last hour, as we have seen, is a part of the dominions of Seker, but the FIFTH HOUR, which is called SEMIT-ḤER-ÅBT-UÅA-S,[1] contains his capital city. The descriptive text says, "This great "god is drawn along over the actual roads of the Ṭuat, and over "the hidden Circle of Seker, the god who is on his sand, and he "neither seeth nor looketh upon the hidden figure of the land "which containeth the flesh of this god. The gods who are with "this god hear the voice of Rā-Ḥeru (?), and they adore him at "the seasons of this god. The name of the pylon of this city is "Āḥā-neteru, , and the name of this Circle is "Åment, 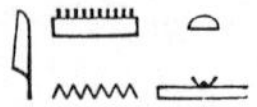. [Here are] the secret ways of Åment, and "the doors of the house of Åment, and the habitable house "(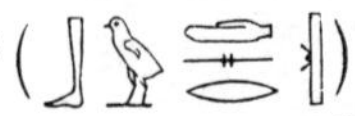) of the earth of Seker, and his flesh, and his "members, and his body, in their primeval forms. The name of "those who are in this Circle is 'Baiu åmu Ṭuat' (i.e., Souls in the "Ṭuat). The forms who are in their hours and their hidden beings "neither see nor look upon this form of Seker himself. Whosoever "maketh a picture of these things which are in Åment in the Ṭuat, "to the south of the hidden house, and whosoever knoweth these "things, his soul shall be at peace, and he shall be satisfied

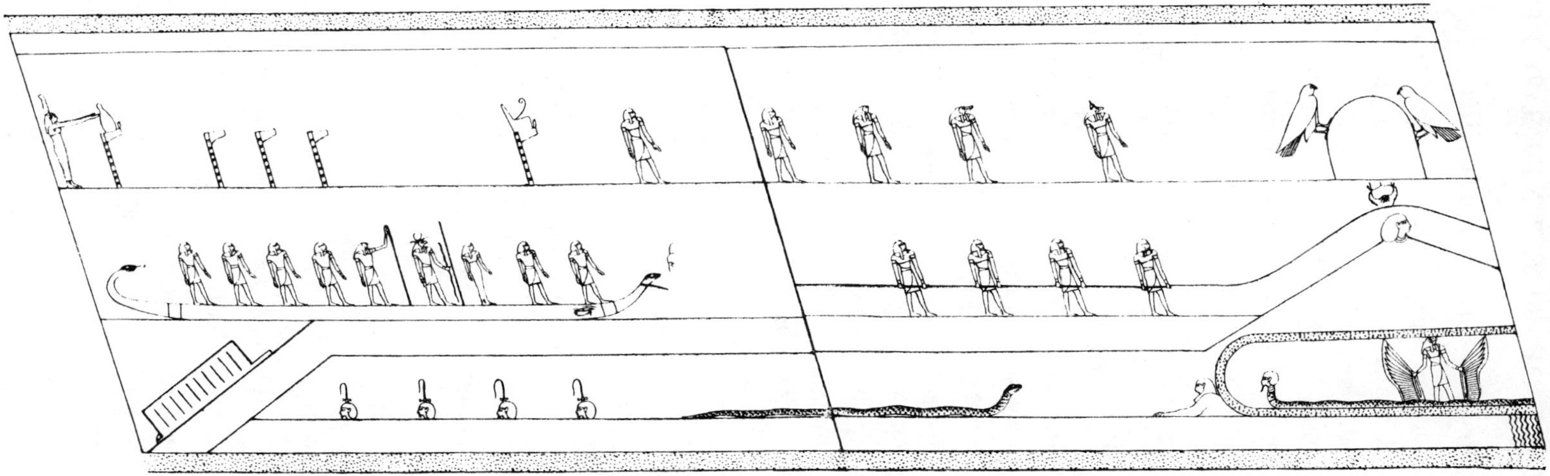

The Fifth Hour of the Night.

"with the offerings of Seker. And Khemit ( ) shall "not hack his body in pieces, and he shall go to her in peace. "Whosoever shall make offerings to these gods upon earth shall "[find] them of benefit to him in the Ṭuat."

The illustrated version of the Fifth Hour shows us Rā travelling in his serpent boat and being towed along by seven gods and seven goddesses, who represent the gods of fourteen days of the month; before these are the divine sovereign chiefs, i.e., Ḥer-khu, , Ȧn-ḥetep, , Ḥer-ḥequi, , and Ḥetch-met . Half way through the hour Rā comes to a mound of sand, the top of which is surmounted by the head of a woman, whereon rests the forepart of a beetle, only one half of which is visible, symbol of the god Kheperȧ; this head indicates the position of the hidden abode wherein is Seker, and when the beetle alights upon it the god Kheperȧ holds converse with that god. Immediately beneath the head is the "Land of Seker," which has the shape , and is described as the "hidden land of "Seker which guardeth the hidden flesh;" it is surrounded by a wall of sand, and at each end, outside the wall, is a sphinx with the head of a man and the body of a lion. Inside this land is a two-headed, winged serpent, with a tail which terminates in a human head; between the wings stands a figure of the hawk-headed god Seker; this serpent monster represents the god watching over his own image. The two sphinxes are watched by two serpents, Ṭepȧn, , and Ānkh-ȧapau, ; the first serpent enters into the presence of this god, and carries to him daily the offerings which are made by the living, but the second never leaves his place, and lives upon the flames which proceed from his own mouth. Before the second serpent are four seated gods, who bear on their knees the emblems of "hidden symbols" of Seker, i.e., , , , and , and rest by the side of a lake of water called Nut, ; for those who are in this lake its waters are like fire, and each of the heads of the four gods which rise above them bears upon it the symbol of fire. The lake is watched over by the company of gods of Rā, represented by nine axes, and five gods. But before Rā has passed through the Fifth Hour he arrives at a large vaulted chamber, filled with

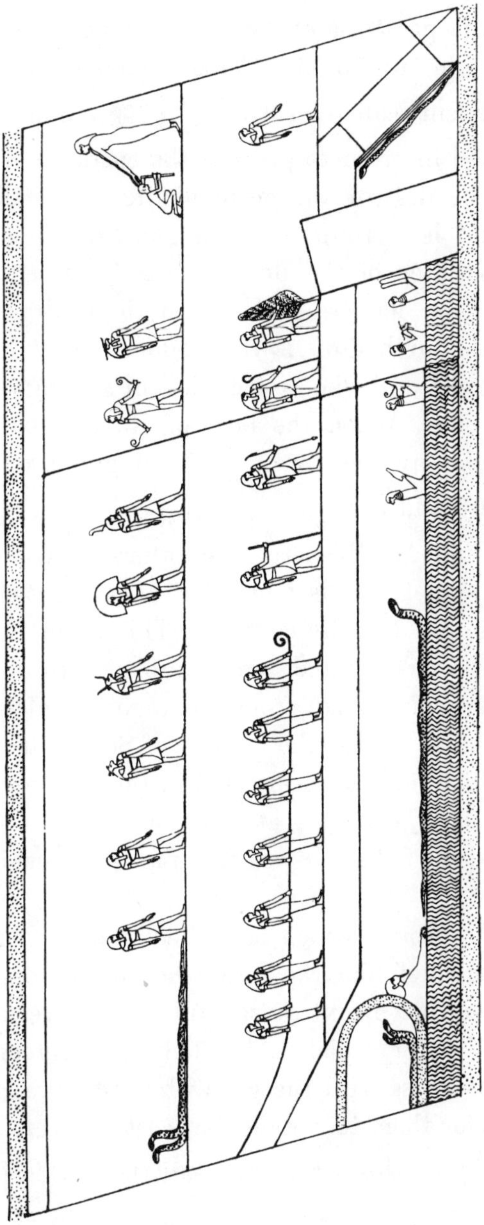

The Fifth Hour of the Night.

sand, and called 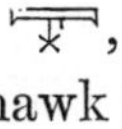, i.e., "Night," and on each side, clinging by its claws, is a hawk; from the lower part of it goes forth the beetle, only one half of which is visible. This beetle, or Kheperȧ, typified the germ of life, and when the boat of Rā was drawn on to the top of the mound of sand already described, it was supposed to stop on it as it passed, and having done so, it went to the dead god and raised him up to life. This chamber was guarded by a two-headed serpent called Ṭer, , and it had to be jealously watched in order to prevent the entrance of any one who would disturb or destroy the germ of life. A little beyond the chamber of sand is a group of seven gods, whose duty it was to inspect the slaughter of the dead in the Ṭuat, and to consume their bodies by the flames of their mouths in the course of each day; and a little further on is the goddess who "lives upon the blood of the dead," and who is occupied in slaying a man doomed to die by the gods. When the boat of Rā arrived at the end of the Fifth Hour he saw the star of the "living god, who journeyeth, "and journeyeth and passeth," 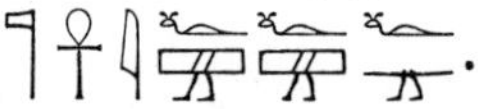. Dr. Brugsch, and following him M. Maspero, and others, have identified this star with the planet Venus, the star of the morning, and the identification is undoubtedly correct. This is an important fact, for, as M. Jéquier has pointed out,[1] coupled with the representation of the beetle going forth from the night to place itself in the boat of Rā, it shows us that the domain of Seker, although reduced to two hours which have been inserted in their proper geographical position in the Ṭuat, certainly at one time formed a complete hell, and that the rising of the sun was the final event which took place in it.

The Sixth Hour, which is called Mesperit-ȧrāt-maātu,[2] brings us to the neighbourhood of the shrines of Osiris in the Delta. The descriptive text says, "When this great god arriveth "at the abyss of water, which is the lady of the gods of the Ṭuat, "he holdeth discourse with the gods who are there, and he giveth "the command for them to obtain the mastery over their offerings "() in this city. He saileth in this [Field] being

[1] *Le Livre de ce qu'il y a dans l'Hades*, p. 76.

[2] .

"provided with his boat, and he commandeth them [to have] their "fields for their offerings, and he giveth them water for their "streams as they go about the Ṭuat each day. The name of the

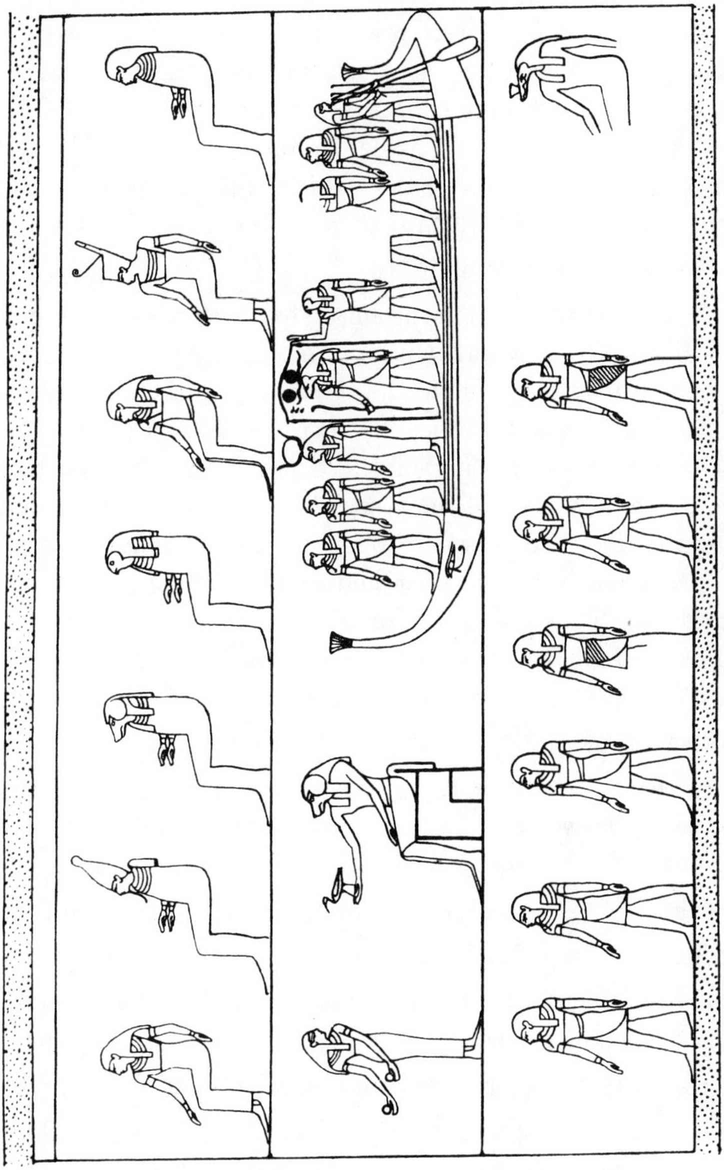

The Sixth Hour of the Night.

"pylon of this city is Sepṭ-metu ( ). The "hidden path of Àmentet, on the stream of which this great god 'journeyeth in his boat to perform the affairs of the gods of the "Ṭuat, and the collecting of their names, and the manner in which "their forms rest, and all that appertaineth to their hidden hours, "and the hidden similitude of the Ṭuat, are unknown . . . . The "majesty of this god uttereth words, and he giveth divine offerings "to the gods who are in the Ṭuat, and he standeth near them; "they see him, and they have the mastery over their fields and "over the gifts which are made to them, and they have their "beings through the command which this great god, who is "mighty of words, giveth unto them. The name of this district "is Metchet-nebt-Ṭuatiu ()." The third paragraph of the text promises to those who make pictures of the Sixth Hour a participation in the offerings which have been made to the gods in the train of Osiris, and also that offerings shall be made to them by their kinsfolk on earth.

The illustrated edition of the Sixth Hour shows us that Rā has no longer any need of the boat which was made of the body of a serpent wherein he passed through the realm of Seker, and that he is once again in his old boat and sailing over the waters of the stream in the Ṭuat. In front of his boat are:—1. Thoth, who is called Khenti-Ṭuat, and who is represented by a dog-headed god holding an ibis on his out-stretched right hand; and 2. the goddess Åment-semu-set, 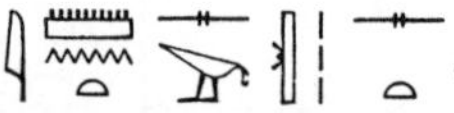. Beyond these is a large house with sixteen divisions, in each of which is a god in mummied form; these represent the mansions of Osiris, and four contain kings of the South, four contain kings of the North, four contain Ḥeteptiu, , and four contain Spirits. All these form the guardians of a huge five-headed serpent called Āsh-ḥråu, , the body of which is bent round into an irregular oval in such a way that his tail almost touches one of his heads. Lying on his back within this oval is a god who is called Āfu, , i.e., "Flesh," and as he is touching with his right hand the leg of a beetle which he holds on his head, we may assume that he represents the dead body of Kheperå, and is the opposite of the Sun-god in his boat, who is called "Flesh of Rā," . The sixteen gods mentioned

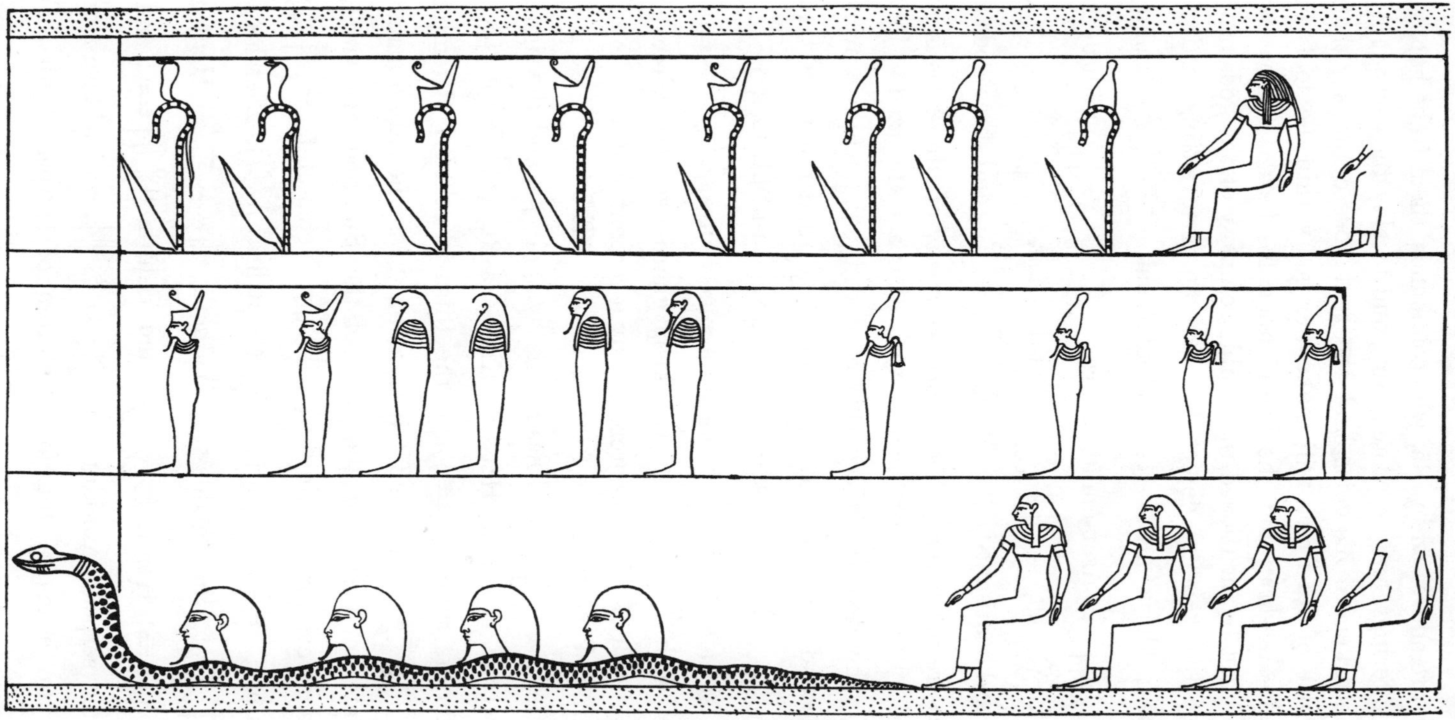

The Sixth Hour of the Night.

above are addressed by Rā, who commands them to be happy with their offerings, and to protect him, and to slay the serpent Āpepi; they hearken to his voice, and the text goes on to say that it is the voice of Rā which will make the god within the folds of the serpent Āsh-ḥrâu and the beetle upon his head to move. With these must be mentioned the double company of the gods of Osiris, one company being depicted in human form sitting on invisible thrones; these are:—Ḥetep-Ḥenti-Ṭuat, , Åst-åmḥit, , Åsår-åm-åb-neteru, , Ḥeru-khenti-åḥet-f, , Benti-år-åḥt-f, , Maā-åb-ḳhenti-åḥt-f, , and three gods whose names are not given. The second company of nine gods is represented by nine sceptres, each of which has a knife fixed at its base, ; the first three are surmounted by the white crowns, , the second three by the red crowns, , and the third three by uraei, . Next we have the lion god Ka-hemhem, , with Isis, and Horus, and the mummied figure, , armed with , and, , who keep guard over the three houses of Rā, each of which is protected by a serpent god standing upon its tail and emitting fire from its mouth. The first house is called Ḥet-ṭua-Rā , and has for its symbol , and the sign ; the second is called Ḥet-stau-Kher-āḥa-Rā, , and has for its symbol, ; and the third is called Ḥet-ṭemṭet-Rā, , and has for its symbol, , the head of a man. On the left hand side of the boat of the Sun-god are two gods whose names are wanting, Åḥi, , Netch-åtef, , Ānkh-ḥrå, , Meṭ-ḥrå, (Sepṭ-ḥrå ?), Netch-pautti, ; the goddesses Åntheth, , Ḥenḥenith, , Ḥemt, , and Seḥith, ; and the monster serpent Ām-khu, , which bears on its back the heads of the four Children of Horus, Mesthå, Ḥāpi,

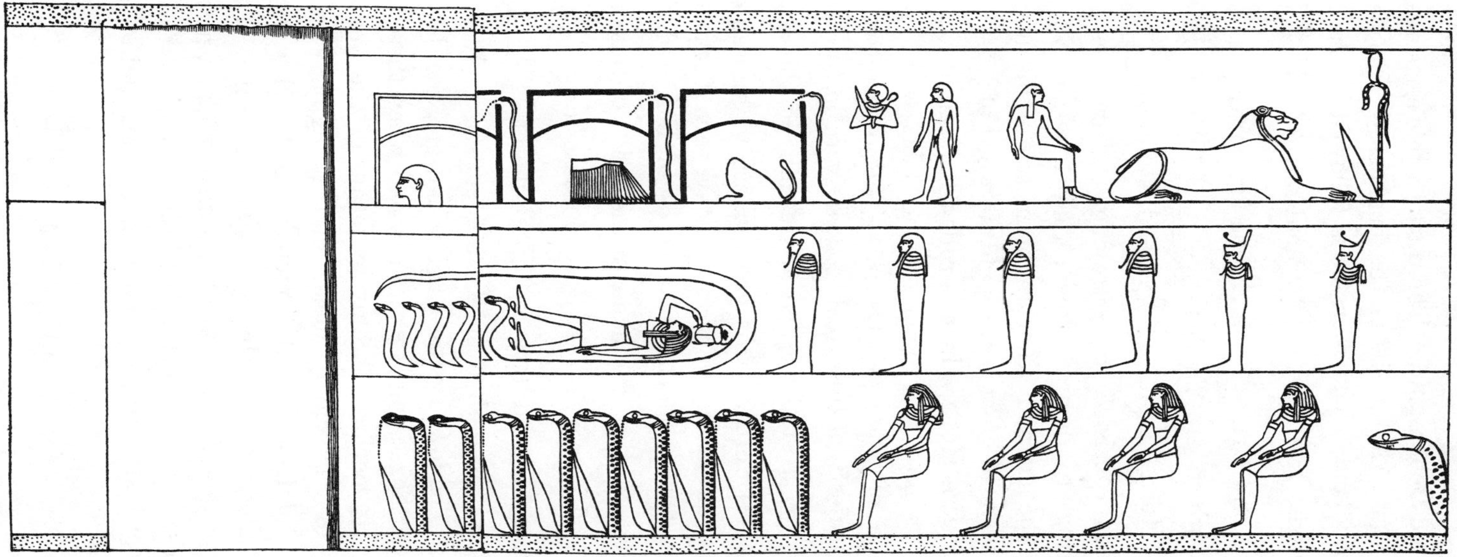

The Sixth Hour of the Night.

Ṭuamutef, and Qebḥsennuf. The duty of this serpent is to devour the shadows and the spirits of the enemies of Rā, who are overthrown in the Ṭuat. The monster is followed by the four earthly forms of Osiris, Ḳai, , Meni-reṭ, , Enen-reṭui, , and Urṭ, , and nine fire-spitting serpents armed with knives, which are Ta-thenen, , Tem, Kheperȧ, Shu, Seb, Osiris, Horus, Ȧpu, , and Ḥetepui, . The duty of these gods consisted in destroying the enemies of Kheperȧ, and in cutting up their shadows; they lived in Nu and in the water of Ta-thenen, and Kheperȧ by means of his magical power daily made them to breathe through the word of Rā.

The SEVENTH HOUR, which is called KHESEF-HȦA-ḤESEQ-NEḤA-ḤRȦ,[1] takes us into the region of the Ṭuat which contains the hidden abode of the god Osiris. The descriptive text says, "When the majesty of this great god arriveth in the hidden abode "(*Tepḥet* ) of Osiris, he addresseth to the gods who are "there [suitable] words. This god maketh to himself other forms "for this hidden abode, so that he may turn back the way for "Āpep by means of the magical words of Isis, and the magical "words of Ser, . The name of the pylon of this city through "which the god journeyeth is 'Gate of Osiris' ( ); "and the name of the city is Tepḥet-shetat ( ). "This great god passeth over the hidden way of Ȧmentet in his "boat which is endowed with magical powers, and he journeyeth "over it when there is no stream in it, and when there are none to "tow him. He performeth this by means of the words of power "of Isis and of Ser, and by means of the mighty words of power "which proceed from his own mouth, and in this region of the "Ṭuat he inflicteth with the knife wounds upon Āpep, whose "place is in heaven." The man who shall make a picture of the things which are to the north of the hidden house of the Ṭuat shall find it of great benefit to him both in heaven and on earth; and

1 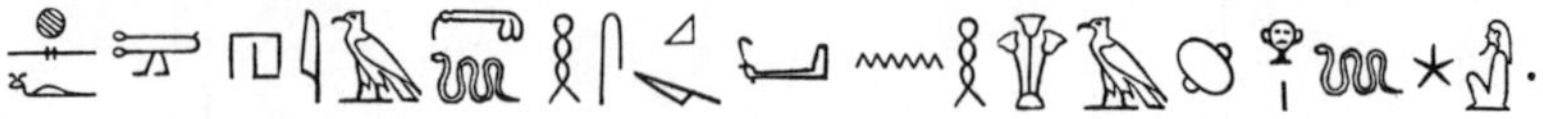

he who knows it shall be among the spirits near Rā, and he who recites the words of Isis and Ser shall repulse Āpep in Åmentet, and he shall have a place on the boat of Rā both in heaven and

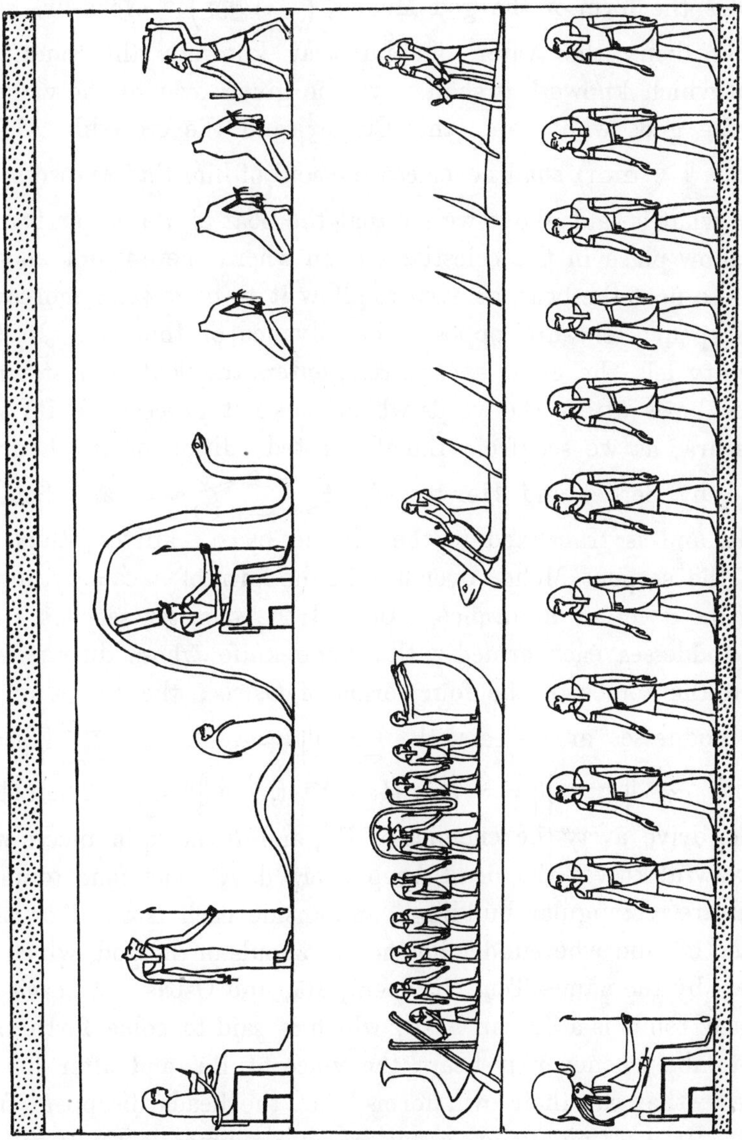

The Seventh Hour of the Night.

upon earth. The man who knows not this picture shall never be able to repulse the serpent Neḥa-ḥrȧ.

The text continues, "The shallows of the land of Neḥa-ḥrȧ are

"450 cubits long, and it is filled with his folds, but over one "portion thereof this great god journeyeth not when he travelleth "to the hidden abode of Osiris, for he journeyeth through this city "under the form of the god Meḥen, ( ). Neḥa-ḥrȧ shall "never drink the water of him that knoweth this, and the "soul which knoweth it shall never be given over to the violence "of the gods who are in this Circle; and the crocodile Āb-she "( ) shall never eat the soul of him that knoweth it." From what is said above we see that the boat of Rā has arrived at a shallow place in the celestial stream where there is not enough water to float the boat, or even to allow it to be towed; moreover, the serpent Neḥa-ḥrȧ opposes the advance of the god. In this difficulty Isis, the great enchantress, enters the boat, and standing in the bows utters the words which make it proceed on its way. Neḥa-ḥrȧ, as we see from the illustrated edition of the hour, is seized by Serqet and Ḥer-ṭesu-f, , and held in bonds, and is transfixed to the ground by six knives; thus Rā, with the serpent Meḥen over him in the form of a canopy, moves on without let or hindrance. Behind the monster serpent stand four goddesses, each armed with a huge knife, whose duty it is to guard the tombs of the four forms of Osiris; the names of the four goddesses are:—Ṭemṭith, , Ṭenith, , Nȧkith, , and Ḥetemitet, . Their duty was to drive away the enemies of Rā, and to hack in pieces with their awful knives the fiend Āpep every day. The four tombs of Osiris are rectangular buildings, and inside each is a bed or small mound of sand whereunder lie the dead souls of the god, which are known by the names Tem, Kheperȧ, Rā, and Osiris. At each end of each tomb is a human head, which is said to come forth from the tombs whenever it hears the voice of Rā, and after he has passed "they eat their own forms," i.e., the heads disappear from sight. It was, no doubt, a custom in predynastic times to slay slaves at the graves of kings and nobles, just as in many parts of the world it has been the custom to kill human beings and to lay their bodies beneath the foundations of buildings which were to

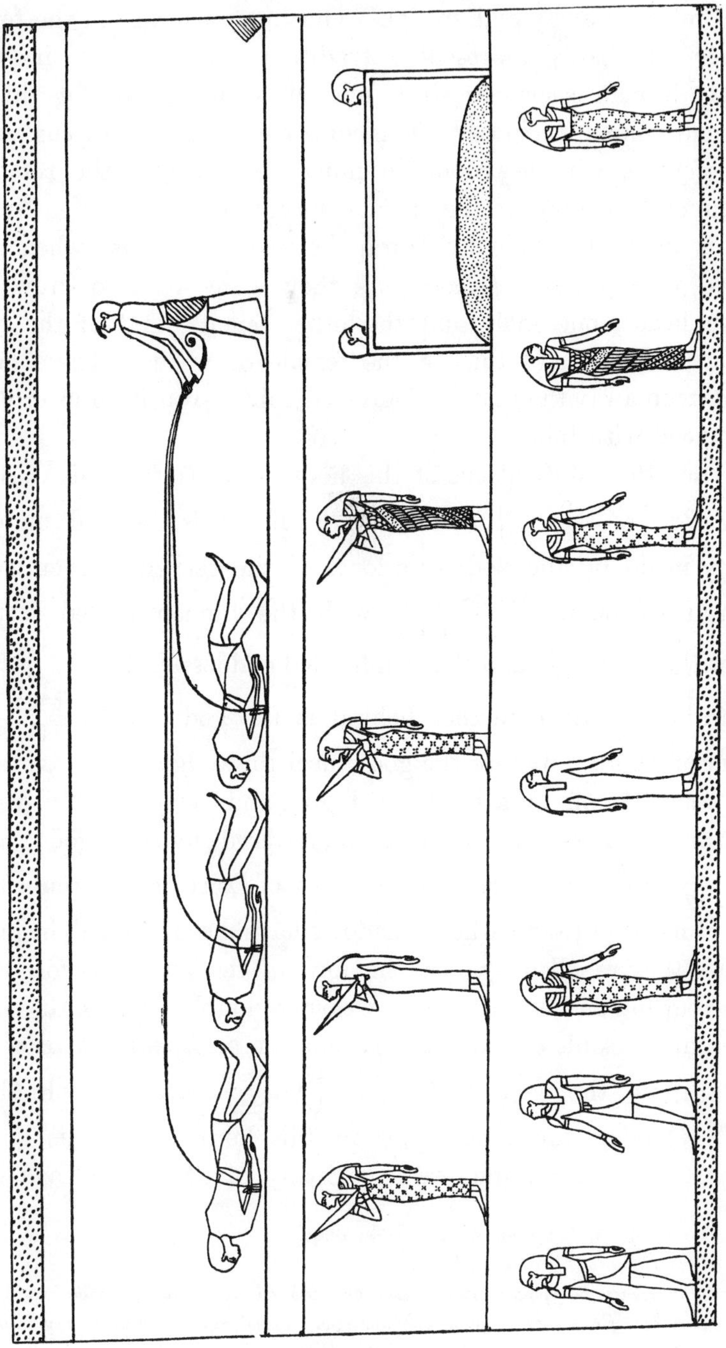

The Seventh Hour of the Night.

be erected in order that the souls of the slaughtered might protect them and keep away evil spirits. The human heads on the tombs of Osiris probably represent a tradition that, when Osiris was buried, human sacrifices were offered at his tomb for this or for some similar purpose.[1] This view has been well discussed by M. Lefébure, who has done so much to illustrate the religious and funeral customs of the ancient Egyptians,[2] and some allusion to it is probably made by Horapollo,[3] who says that when they wanted to represent *φυλακτήριον* they were wont to draw two human heads, one male and the other female, that of the male looking inwards, and that of the female outwards. These heads would keep away the attack of any evil spirit, even if no inscription was placed with them.

The other illustrations of this hour show us the god Åf-Åsår, , i.e., "Flesh of Osiris," seated under a canopy made by the body of a form of the serpent Meḥen called Ānkh-åru-tchefau, , with the human-headed serpent Ānkhtith, , and the lion-headed goddess Ḥekenth, , behind him; a little further behind is the god Shepes, , a form of Thoth. Before the god kneel three figures, whose heads have been cut off by a cat-headed god, and lying on the ground are three beings who have been fettered by the god Ånku, , these represent the enemies of Osiris whose souls have been plucked out, and whose shadows have been hacked in pieces because they rebelled against the lord of the Ṭuat. Before these are three human-headed hawks wearing double crowns, and they represent the souls of the "living;" and on a serpent near is seated on a throne the god Åf-Tem, , i.e., "Flesh of Tem." Among the other gods in this hour is "Horus on his throne," and before him are a company of gods who have been

[1] See Maspero, *Les Hypogées*, p. 104; Jéquier, op. cit., p. 94.

[2] *Rites Égyptiens*, pp. 4 ff., 18 ff.

[3] *Φυλακτήριον δὲ γραφειν βουλόμενοι, δύο κεφαλάς ανθρώπων ζωγραφοῦσι, τὴν μὲν τοῦ ἄρσενος ἔσω βλέπουσαν, τὴν δὲ θηλυκὴν ἔξω. ὄυτω γάρ φασιν οὐδὲν τῶν δαιμονίων ἐφαψεται, ἐπειδὴ καὶ χωρὶς γραμμάτων, κ.τ.λ.* *Hieroglyphica*, i. 24.

The Seventh Hour of the Night.

joined to their stars, and the goddesses of the twelve hours. Facing these companies is the crocodile "Āb-shā-ȧm-Ṭuat," 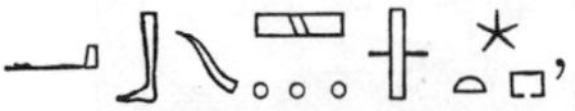, who acts as guardian of the tomb of Osiris and of what is in it. When Rā passes by the crocodile, which is described as "Osiris, the Eye of Rā," this beast is fascinated and made helpless by the words so long as the god is speaking to him, and the dead Osiris, who is in the ground under the crocodile, puts up his head that he also may look at the Sun-god; the

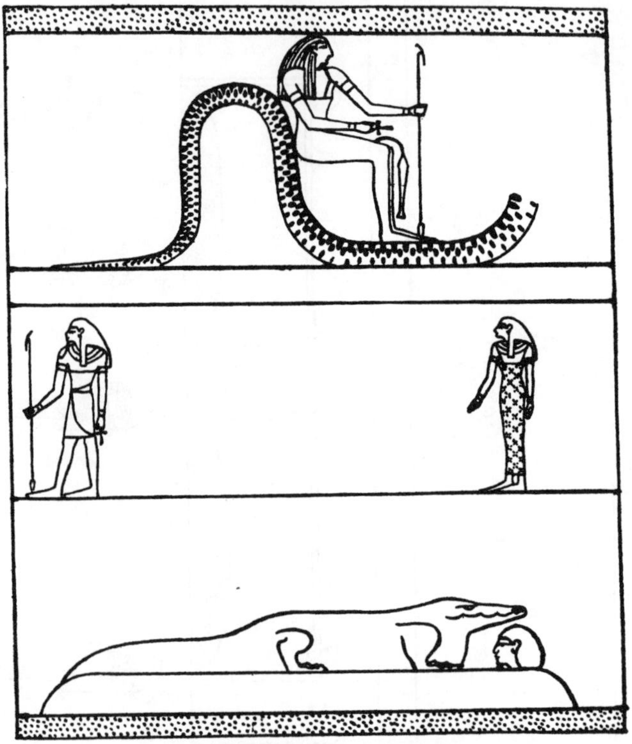

The Seventh Hour of the Night.

followers of Osiris also seize the opportunity of gazing upon Rā, and do so without risk of being devoured by the monster which is temporarily enchanted.

The Eighth Hour, which is called Nebt Ushau,[1] brings us into a very interesting division of the Ṭuat; the name of its pylon

[1] .

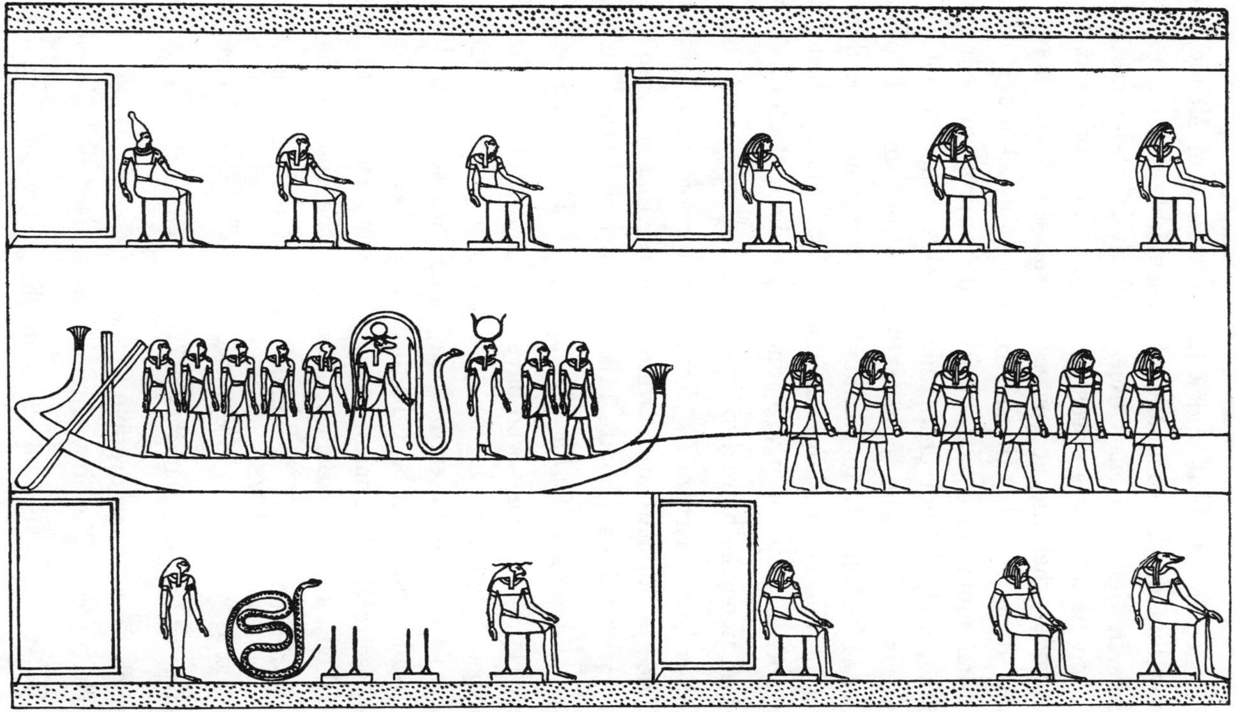

The Eighth Hour of the Night.

is Āḥā-en-urṭ-nef, , and the name of the city is Ṭebat-neteru-s, . Rā passes through this division in his boat under the protection of Meḥen, and its gods tow him at the command of this mighty snake; he sees all the gods in their various Circles, and those "who are on their sand," and he addresses words to them. They come out of their secret abodes when the god passes by, and the doors thereof open of their own accord. In this Hour only gods and spirits who have been mummified and buried with appropriate rites are to be found, and, though dead, they quickly come to life again at the words of Rā, who exhorts them to put an end to all the enemies of his who are to be found in that region. The illustrated edition of the Hour shows us the boat of the god being towed along, and in front of it are nine large signs, the forms of which are based upon the hieroglyphic character  *shesu* or *shemsu*, i,e., "follower" or "servant." From the top of seven of these is suspended a human head, which shows that we are actually dealing with beings who are in the following of Osiris, and before each is the hieroglyphic for "linen," 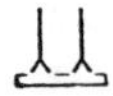. These nine remarkable objects represent beings who have been mummified in the manner prescribed by Horus, and who are suitably provided with funeral bandages; they are described as beings whose whole life is in their heads, and when Rā calls to them by their names they immediately seize his enemies everywhere and cut off their heads with their knives. Before these are the four forms of the god Ṭa-thenen, 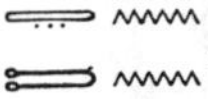, which are depicted as rams and are described as "form one," , "form two," , "form three," 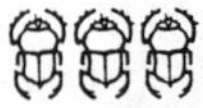, and "form four," 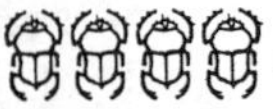. On each side of the way by which Rā journeys are five Circles.

The door of the first Circle, Sesheta, is called Ṭes-neb-ṭerer. . . . 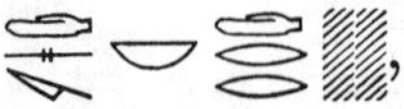, and shuts in the images of Tem, Kheperȧ, and Shu; when Rā speaks to them they answer in a voice which resembles the humming of bees. The door of the second Circle,

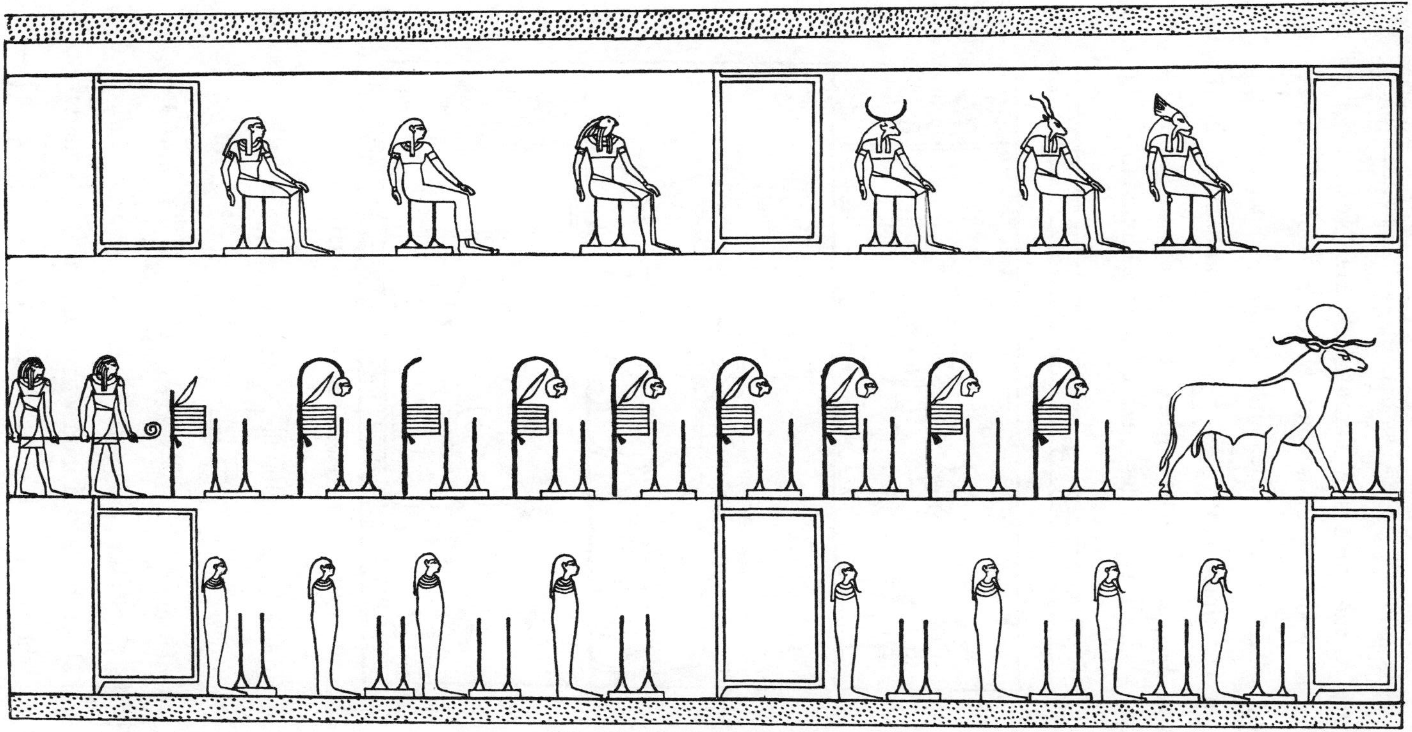

The Eighth Hour of the Night.

Ṭuat, , is called Ṭes-āḥā-Ta-thenen, , and shuts in the images of Tefnut, Seb, and Nut; when Rā speaks to them they answer in a voice which resembles that of weeping women. The door of the third Circle, Ȧs-neteru, , is called Ṭes-khem-baiu, , and shuts in the images of Osiris, Isis, and Horus; when Rā speaks to them they answer in a voice which resembles that of men who moan. The door of

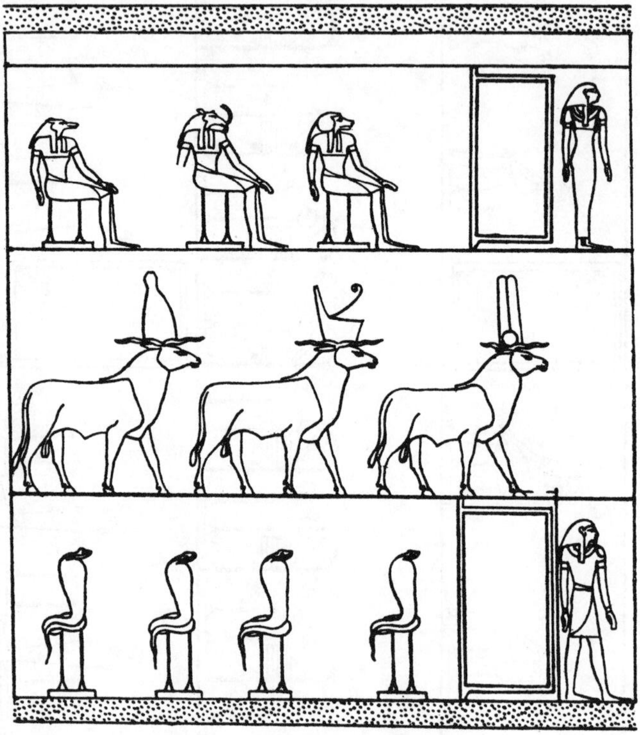

The Eighth Hour of the Night.

the fourth Circle, Ȧaḳebi, , is called Ṭes-sheta-em-theḥen-neteru, , and shuts in the images of Ka-Ȧmentet, , Ba-neteru, , and Rem-neteru, ; when Rā speaks to them they answer in a voice which is like that of bulls and men when they make lamentation. The door of the fifth Circle, Nebt-semu-nefu, , is called Ṭes-sma-kekui, , and shuts in the images of Khatri, , Åffi, , and Årānbfi, ; when Rā speaks to them they answer in a voice which is like unto that of him that maketh supplication in terror. These five Circles are shut in by a door called Ṭes-khaibit-ṭuatiu, . The door of the sixth Circle is called Ṭes-ermen-ta, , and shuts in some divine beings whose attributes are not yet all clearly defined; when Rā speaks to them they answer in a voice which is like that of male cats when they mew. The door of the seventh Circle, Ḥetemet-khemiu, , is called Ṭes - Rā - khefti - f, , and shuts in Nut, Ta, and Sebeq-ḥrå, ; when Rā speaks to them they answer in a voice which is like the roar of the living. The door of the eighth Circle, Ḥap - semu - s, , is called Ṭes - sekhem - åru, , and shuts in four gods;[1] when Rā speaks to them they answer in a voice which is like the shouts of war heard in the battle of Nu. The door of the ninth Circle, Seḥert-baiu-s, , is called Ṭes-sepṭ-nestu, , and shuts in four gods;[2] when Rā speaks to them they answer in a voice which is like that of the cry of the divine hawk of Horus. The door of the tenth Circle, Āāt-setekau, , is called Ṭes-khu, , and shuts in four gods in the form of uraei

[1] , Ḥebset , Senket; , Ṭebat; and Temṭet, .

[2] , Keku; , Menḥi; , Tcher-khu; and , Khebs-ta.

who rest upon ; when Rā speaks to them they answer in a voice which is like the twittering and chattering of water-fowl on a lake. The last five Circles are shut in by a door called Ṭes-am-mit-em-sheta-f, .

The NINTH HOUR, which is called ṬUATET-MĀKET-NEB-S,[1] brings us into a country which is called the "hidden Circle of "Åmentet"; the name of the city is Bes-åru, ,[2] and the name of its pylon is Sa-Aḳeb, . "When the great god arriveth in this "Circle he addresseth from his boat the gods who are therein, and "the sailors who are in his boat are content with this city." The man who shall make a copy of the scenes of this Hour, and shall know the names of the gods and their places in Åmentet shall attain to a position in Åmentet, and he shall stand up in the presence of the lord of affairs and shall enjoy the power of making what he says to come to pass with the divine assessors, , on the day of reckoning up accounts by Per-āa (Pharaoh). The illustrated edition of this Hour shows us the boat of the god travelling on as before, and in front of it are twelve divine rowers, each with his paddle; among these are Khenu, , Åkhem-sek-f, , Åkhem-urṭ-f, , Åkhem-ḥemi-f, , Åkhem-khemes-f, , Khen-unnut-f, , Ḥāpti-ta-f, , Ḥetep-uåa, , Neter-neteru, , Tcha-Ṭuat, , and Ṭepi, . The duty of these sailors is not only to row, but also to throw water with their paddles upon the spirits who stand on each bank of the river whereon the god sails, and they have to lead the soul of Rā to the place where he will reanimate the disk. Before these sailors, resting on baskets, are the three gods who give abundant

[1] .

[2] Some copies add .

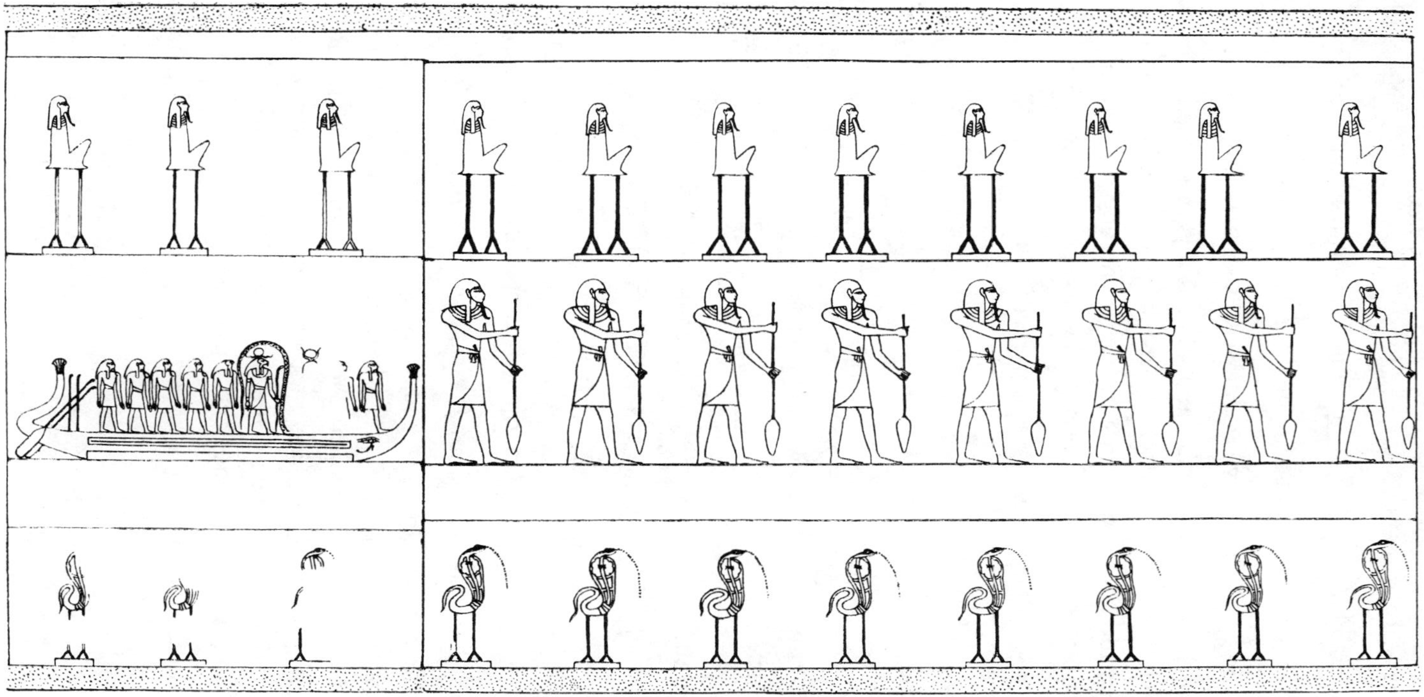

The Ninth Hour of the Night.

offerings, Muti-khenti-Ṭuat, , Nesti-khenti-Ṭuat, , and Nebt-āu-khent-Ṭuat, . On the right the boat of Rā passes twelve gods, each seated on , and twelve goddesses; these last are said to breathe after he has saluted them, and after they have heard his voice, and their duty is to utter words of power wherewith they are to surround the hidden soul, and thereby to cause life and strength to rise up in Osiris. The names of these are:—Nehata, , Ṭeba, , Ariti, , Menkhet, , Ḥebs, , Nebti, , Ȧsti-neter, , Ȧsti-paut, , Ḥetemet-khu, , Neb-pāt, , Temṭu, , Men-ā, , Perit, , Shemat-khu, , Nebt-shāt, , Nebt-shef-shefet, , Āat-ȧaṭet, , Nebt-seṭau, , Ḥent-nut-s, , Nebt-māt, , Ṭesert-ȧnt, , Āat-khu, , Sekhet-meṭu, , Netert-en-khentet-Rā, . On the left are twelve uraei, each of whom rests on , and sends out fire through his mouth; they are said to kindle the fire for the god who is in the Ṭuat with the fire which is in their mouths, and when the god has passed on his way they eat up the fire which they poured forth before Rā went by. The object of the fire was, of course, to show light on his path. Before these uraei come the nine gods of cultivation and of husbandry, who are under the direction of a god in mummified form; these nine are the *sekhtiu*, , or "field-labourers," of the god Ḥer-she-ṭuati, , their leader, and they perform all the works connected with the ploughing and watering of the fields.

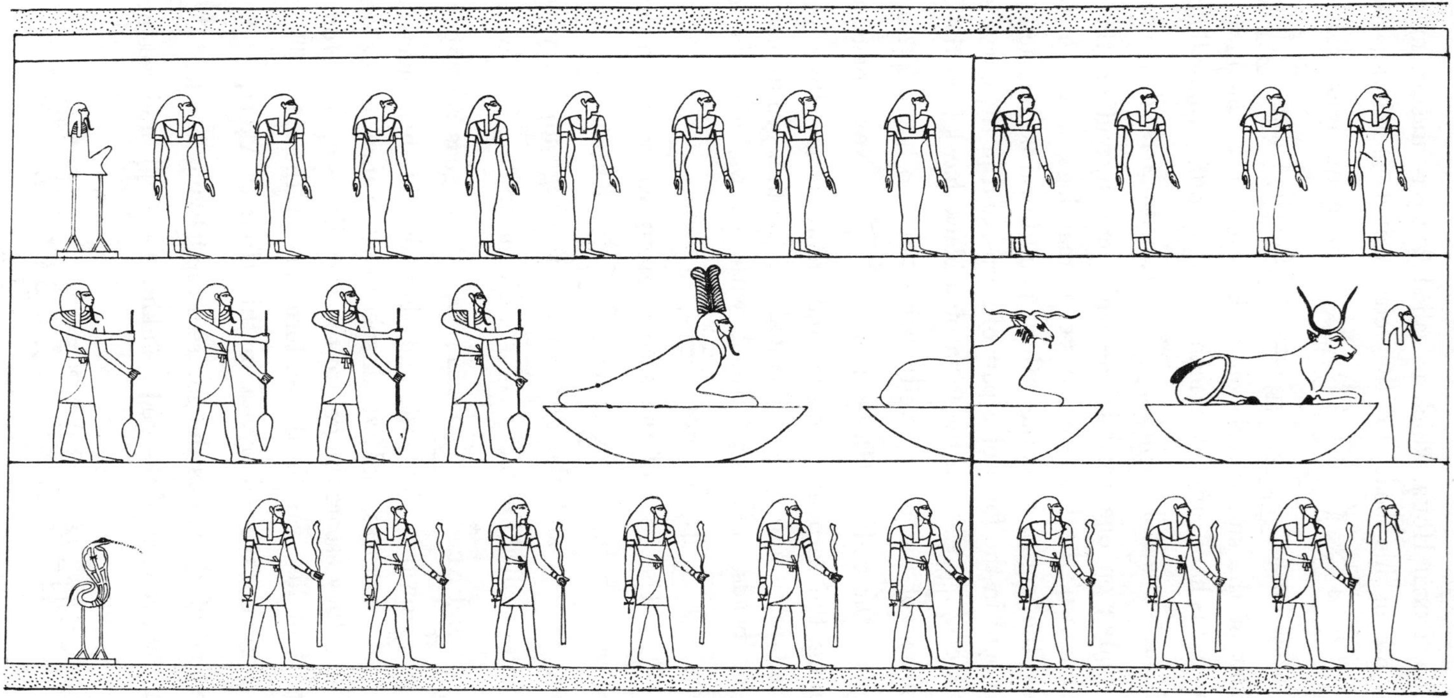

The Ninth Hour of the Night.

The TENTH HOUR, which is called ṬENṬIT-UḤESQET-KHAṬ-ȦB,[1] brings Rā in his boat to the city called Metchet-qat-uṭebu, , with its pylon called Āa-kheperu-mes-ȧru, . The boat of the sun travels on as before, but Rā again holds a serpent in his hand after the manner of a staff. Immediately in front is the serpent Thes-ḥrȧu, , with a head at each end of his body; on one head is the white crown, and on the other the red crown; he has two pairs of human legs, one pair turned towards the right, and the other pair towards the left. His body is bent in the form of a pair of horns, and in the curve stands Khent-Ḥeru, , in the form of a black hawk; on the left is the goddess of the north, Neith, with her two bows, , and on the right is the goddess Ḥert-ermen, . Next comes a boat containing the serpent Ānkh-ta, and before it are three groups, each containing four gods. The gods of the first group have solar disks for heads, and are armed with arrows, and are called Ṭeptherȧ, , Sheserȧ, . Ṭemau, , and Uṭu, . The gods of the second group carry each a javelin, and are called Setu, , Rāu, , Khesfu, , and Nekenu, ; and the gods of the third group carry each a bow, and are called Pesthi, , Shemerthi, , Ṭhesu, , and Khā-ā, . All these gods accompany Rā as he goes towards the east, and they slay all his enemies who live in the darkness, and wreak special vengeance on the serpent Neḥa-ḥrȧ; they escort the god to the very limits of the Hour, and form part of his train in the eastern part of the sky. The name of the region traversed by Ra in this Hour is Ȧkert, . As the boat of Rā passes the god sees the "living beetle," , born in the presence of the god P-ānkhi, , and sees how he

[1] 

The Tenth Hour of the Night.

pushes before him his zone, . Next we have the two serpents, Menenui, 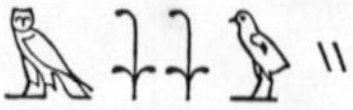, standing on their tails, and holding on their bent necks a solar disk; and two seated personifications of the South and North; and the two goddesses, Netheth, 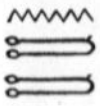, and Kenȧt, , one of whom supports the hatchet, and the other the solar disk, which rests upon it, . From the serpents go forth two goddesses, those of the East and West; and from the axe, called Sefṭit, 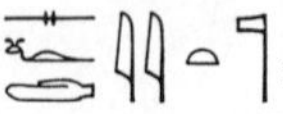, go forth the goddesses of the East and West also; i.e., these goddesses are the souls of the serpents and of the axe, which come forth to look upon the Sun-god, and as soon as he has passed they return into their material bodies.

Next Rā sees eight[1] goddesses advancing to a seated dog-headed god, who presents to them the Eye of Horus, , and their duty is to see that it is in good condition, and to take care of it and protect it, so that it may shine daily. Besides these there come the eight gods called Ermenui, , Neb-āqet, 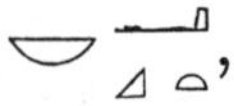, Ṭua-khu, , Ḥer-she-taiu, 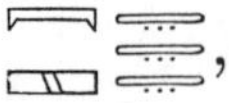, Sem-Ḥeru, , Ṭua-Ḥeru, , Khenti-ȧst-f, , and Khenti-ment, 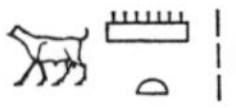; the duty of these gods, who lived by the breath of the great god, was to wreck the bodies and scatter the swathings of the enemies of Rā. On his left hand Rā passed in his journey through this Hour Horus, and twelve beings who dive and swim and perform evolutions in tanks of water. These are said to beat the water in their attempts to recover their breath, and Rā calls upon them to fill themselves with the water of the celestial Nile, and promises that their members shall not suffer corruption, and that their bodies shall not perish; he decrees that they shall

[1] I.e., Sekhet, 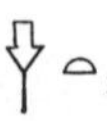, Menkert, 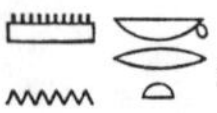, Ḥunṭheth, 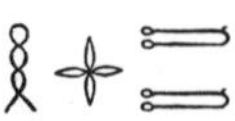, Usit, , Ābet-neteru-s, 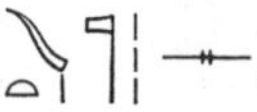, Ȧritatheth, 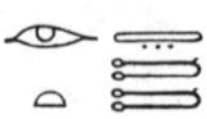, Āḥāt, , and Themath, 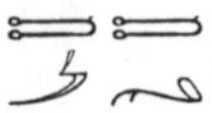.

be masters of their own arms in their water because they are the denizens of Nu, and that their souls shall live. Beyond these are

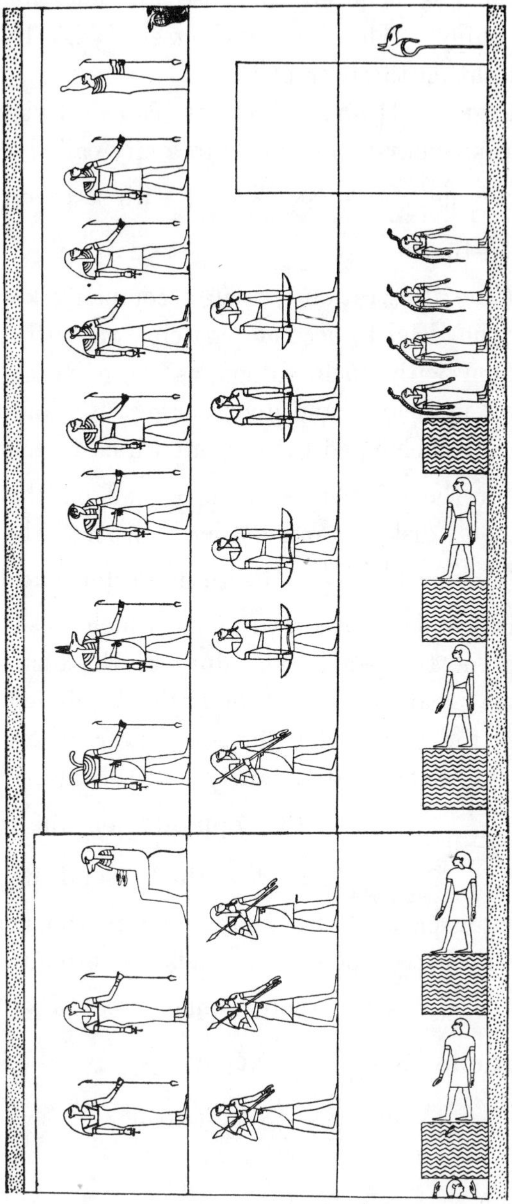

The Tenth Hour of the Night.

four goddesses, each with a serpent hanging down her back with its head above her own, and with them is a standard surmounted by the head of Set, . This god was the guardian of the Tenth Hour, and when Rā was about to pass from it into the eastern part of the sky, Set was believed to rouse himself and to make the journey with him. The four goddesses "who lived by their heads," shed light on the path of Rā.

The ELEVENTH HOUR, which is called SEBUIT-NEBT-UȦA-KHESFET-SEBȦU-EM-PERT-F,[1] brings us to a city called Re-qerert-ȧpt-khaṭ, , with a pylon bearing the name of Sekhen-ṭuatiu, ; the object of the texts and the illustrations which accompany it was to enable the spirits of the dead to become participators with the gods, and to provide them with such things as were necessary for their equipment both in heaven and upon earth. Rā stands as usual in his boat, but he has changed the serpent which he held in his hand as a sceptre for the ordinary sceptre, , and on the bows of the boat we see a solar disk, surrounded by a serpent; the name of this disk is  or , Pesṭu or Pesṭet, and it is probably connected with some well-known star which rose heliacally at certain seasons of the year. The duty of the disk was to guide the boat of the great god along the paths which led to that part of the Ṭuat, at the end of the Eleventh Hour, where the darkness faded away; the texts call the darkness at this point *keku ḳesḳesu*, , i.e., the opposite of the *kekui samui*, , or the thick, solid darkness which filled the greater part of the Ṭuat. Before the boat of Rā are twelve gods, who carry upon their heads the serpent Meḥen to the eastern part of the sky; their names are:—Fa, , Ermenu, , Athpi, , Neṭru, , Shepu, , Reṭā, , Amu, , Ȧma, , Sheṭu,

[1] 

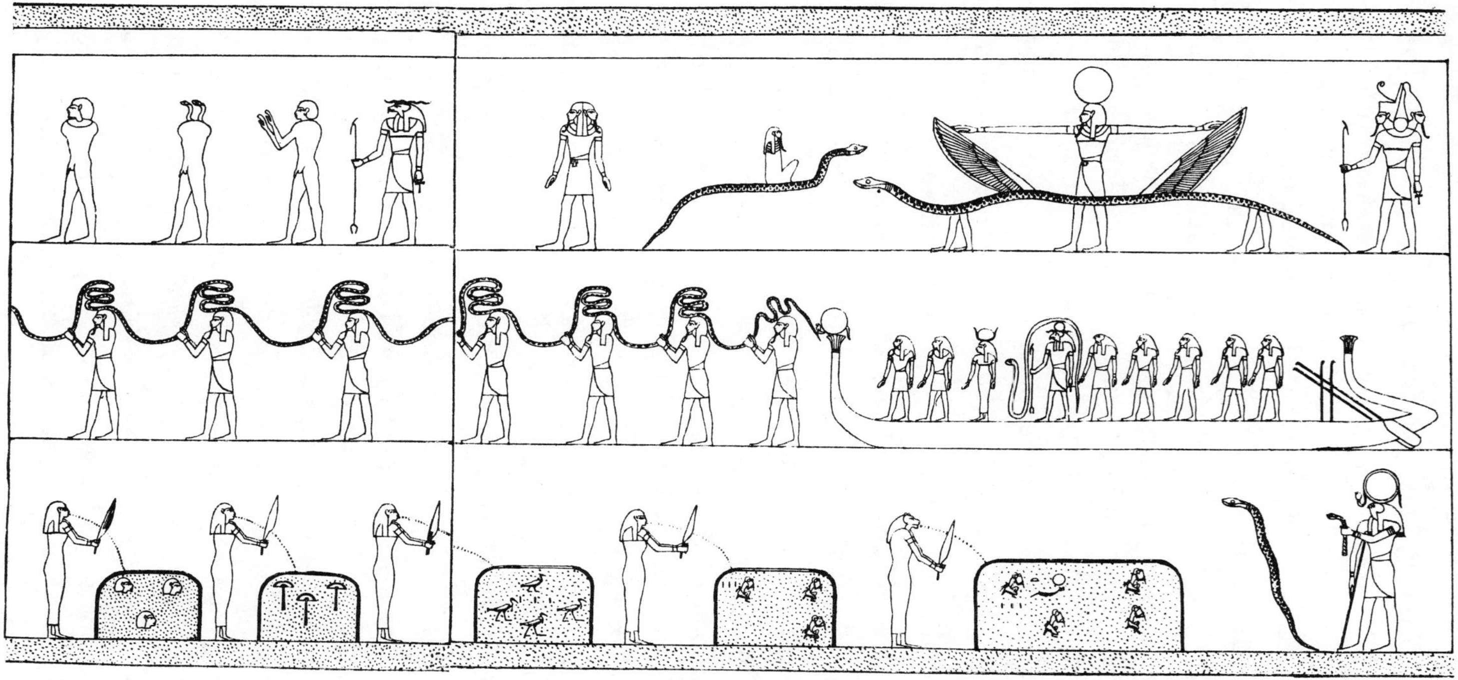

The Eleventh Hour of the Night.

, Sekhenu, , Semsem, , and Meḥni, . Before these are:—1. A uraeus wearing the crown of the North and a human head; and, 2. A uraeus from the back of which emerges the white crown, with a human head on each side of it.

The first of these is called Sem-shet, , and the second Sem-Nebt-ḥet, ; the human heads on the white crown only come forth when Rā is passing by, and when he has departed they disappear. Next we have figures of the four forms of the goddess Neith, two of them wearing the white crown, and two the red; they are called Neith the fecundator, , in allusion to the belief that this goddess begat herself, Neith of the red crown, , Neith of the white crown, , and Neith the child, ; these goddesses came into being as soon as they heard the voice of Rā, and their duty was to guard the gate of Saïs, , the unknown, the unseen, the invisible, . This Circle of the Ṭuat through which the god travels to appear in the mountain of the sunrise contains many wonderful beings, and it is said to "swallow always the forms therein in the presence of "the god who knoweth, , who is in this city, and afterwards "it giveth them for the births of those who are to come into being "on this earth." Among these are:—A god with the solar disk for a head; from it project two human heads, one wearing , and the other . He is called Āper-ḥrȧ-neb-tchetta, , and stands facing a god having two heads, but without crowns, whose name is Ṭepui, . In the space between we see a serpent provided with a pair of wings and four human legs and feet, facing the serpent Sheṭu, , upon the back of which is seated a god; the heads of both serpents are among a number of stars. Standing by the side of the winged serpent, which is called Tchet-s, , is a god called Petrȧ, , with his arms stretched out in such a way as to keep the wings wide apart; he has on his head a disk, and his neck is between the double *utchat*,

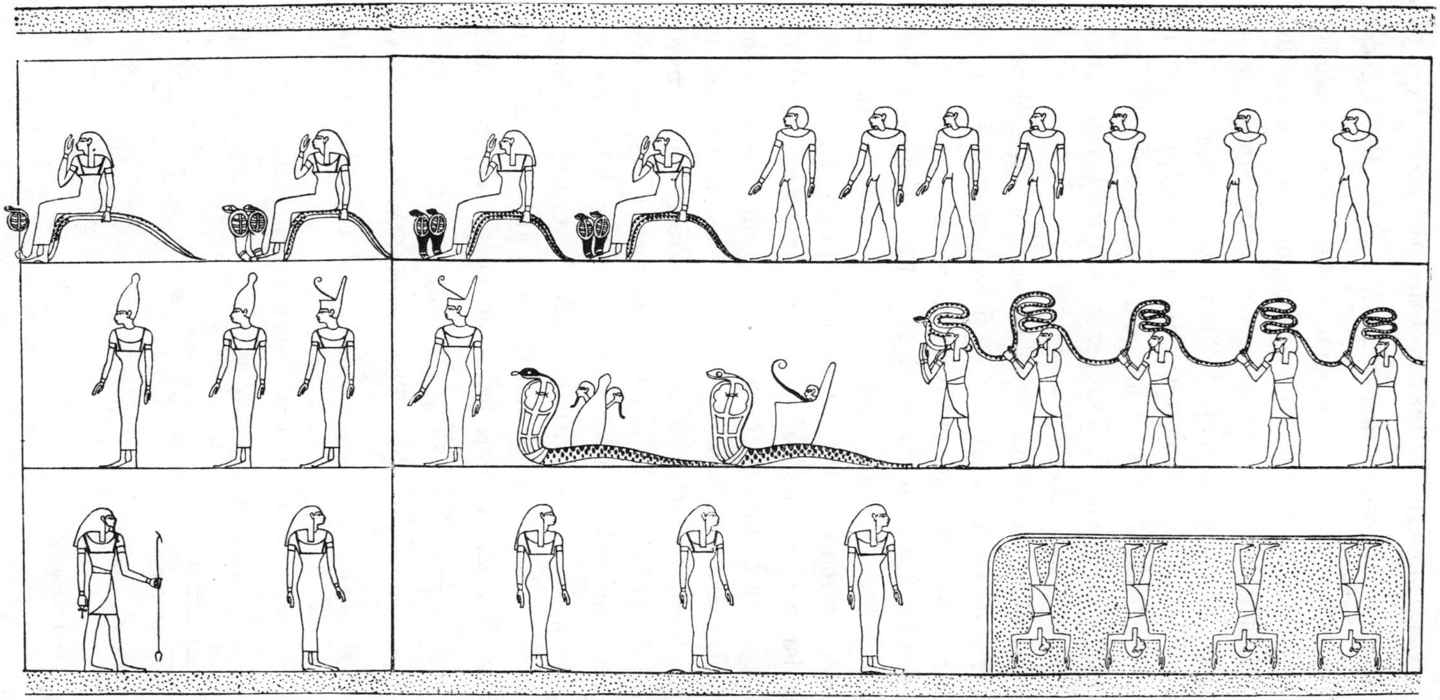

The Eleventh Hour of the Night.

. The descriptive text says that the god with a disk and two heads is "he who stands, , by Rā,"[1] and that he never leaves his place in the Ṭuat. The god who stands by the winged serpent is Temu, who springs out of the reptile's back when Rā addresses it; but as soon as the words cease Temu disappears into the serpent. The second serpent is the constellation Sheṭu, i.e., the Tortoise, and its soul appears in human form on its back as soon as Rā addresses it, but when the words have ceased like Temu it disappears into its body. The duty of Sheṭu was to "emit life for Rā every day."

Before these march Khnemu and ten gods, five of whom have no arms; from the neck of one of these project the heads of two serpents.[2] From the descriptive text we learn that the souls of these gods lived on the hidden light of Rā; that the breath of his mouth gave them life, and that their souls fed upon the provisions which were stored in his boat; their chief duty was to be with and in attendance upon the god. Besides these gods we also have in this Hour four goddesses, each of whom sits upon the bodies of two uraei, which are bent upwards in such a way as to form a seat; the heads of each pair of uraei are reared up in front of the knees of the goddess, who is sitting on their backs, and whose feet rest upon their necks. Each goddess has her right hand raised as if to hide her face, and with her left she grasps the body of one of the uraei. It is possible that the uraei are only four in number, and that they are two-headed; the goddesses are called Nebt-ānkhiu, . Nebt-khu, , Nert, , and Ḥent (?)-neteru, . The descriptive text says that the arms of these beings are on earth, and their feet in the thick

[1] M. Maspero speaks of him as the "agathodemon" of Rā.

[2] The names are:—Khnem-renit, , Nerta, , Āāiu-f-em-kha-nef, , Āpt-taui, , Mer-en-āāui-f, , Āunāāuif, , Rest-f, , Ṭua-Ḥeru, , Maā, , Meskhti, , and Ḥepā, .

darkness, and as long as the god is speaking to them they utter cries and acclaim him; they never move from their places, and their souls live upon the voices of the uraei which go forth from their feet daily. When the shadows depart the winds which arise in the Ṭuat are diverted from the faces of the four goddesses by their hands, which they hold up. In this statement we seem to have an allusion to the keen, fresh wind of dawn with which all travellers in the desert are well acquainted, and which usually blows about one hour before sunrise.

In the region on the left hand side of Rā we see how punishment is inflicted upon the enemies of Rā, and in it we have a country of blazing fire. At one end stands Horus with a disk, surrounded by a uraeus, upon his head, holding in his left hand a boomerang, one end of which terminates in the head of a serpent; the idea here suggested is that the weapon held by the god is a real serpent, which when thrown at an enemy will suddenly attach itself to his body after the manner of the vicious uraeus. The right arm of Horus rests on a staff wherewith the god usually supports himself, and before him rears itself a huge serpent called "Set of millions of years," , the duty of which was to devour any of the enemies of Rā, i.e., the dead, who succeeded in making their escape from the fires of the country of the Eleventh Hour. In front of these were the five awful chambers, or pits in the sky, which were filled with the red-hot materials of blazing fires, and employed to consume the enemies of Rā.

The first chamber or pit, Ḥaṭet, 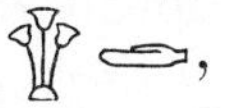, was filled with the bodies of fiends who were dashing out their own brains with axes, , and was under the charge of a lion-headed goddess, called Ḥert-Ketit-s, 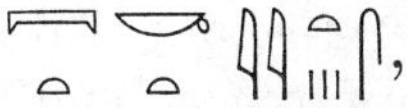, who stood by its side and belched fire into it through her mouth; when the fire had done its work on the wretched creatures they were hacked to pieces by the huge knife which she held in both her hands. The second chamber or pit was also filled with the bodies of fiends, and was under the charge of a woman called Ḥert-Ḥānṭuȧ, , who spat fire upon them and who was armed with a monster knife.

The third chamber or pit was filled with the souls, , of the fiends, and was under the charge of a woman called Ḥert-Nekeniṭ, , who spat fire upon them and who was similarly armed. The fourth and fifth chambers, which were under the charge of similar women, called Ḥert-Nemmȧt-set, , and Ḥert-sefu-s, , contained the shadows, , and heads, , of the damned. Passing by these chambers we come to the "Valley of those who are cast down headlong," , which is represented by a large hollow wherein four men are standing on their heads, ; next to this are four goddesses of the desert, each of whom has upon her head the emblem of desert; their names are Pesi, , Rekḥit, , Ḥer-shā-s, , and Sait, . Each name has a meaning something like "fiery," and refers to the goddesses in their character of mistresses of the blazing desert. Finally, behind these comes the god Ḥer-ut-f, , who was in some way connected with the embalming of the dead. The descriptive text which accompanies these scenes makes the great god Rā command "his father Osiris to hack in pieces the bodies of "the enemies and of the dead who are cast down headlong."

Then, addressing the enemies themselves, he tells them that when his father Osiris hath smitten them for destruction, and hath cut in pieces their spirits and souls, and hath rent asunder their shadows, and hath cut off their heads in such a way that existence in the future will be impossible for them, they will be cast down headlong into burning furnaces from which there is neither escape nor deliverance, and Set the everlasting snake will drive his flames against them, and the Lady of furnaces, and the Lady of fiery pits, and the Lady of slaughtering blocks, and the Lady of swords, will drive against them the flames which come forth from their mouths, that they will hack them in pieces in such wise that the wretched beings will never again see those who live upon the earth. The slaughter of the enemies is ordered to be performed by Horus, the god of those who are in the Ṭuat, and it is curious to note that the gods his companions are said to live upon the voices of the enemies who are slain, and on the shrieks and cries of the souls and shadows which are cast down into the blazing, fiery pits.

The TWELFTH HOUR, MAA-NEFERT-RĀ,[1] brings the god Rā into the Circle which is on the confines of thick darkness, and to a city called Khepert-kekui-khāāt-mest, , with its pylon called Then-neteru, 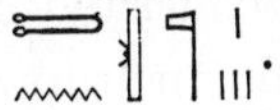. In this region the god is born under the form of Kheperȧ,  , and Nu, 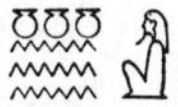, and Nut, , Ḥeḥu, , and Ḥeḥut, , come into the Circle when he is born, and when he goeth forth from the Ṭuat and resteth in the Mānṭit, , boat, and when he riseth on the body[2] of Nut. Rā journeys in his boat, as before, but the solar disk which was at the bows in the Eleventh Hour is no longer there, and its place is occupied by the beetle of Kheperȧ, the forerunner of the rising sun.[3] Twelve gods tow the boat, not over a river or over the back of a serpent or serpents, but completely *through* a serpent; in front the tow-rope is held by the hands of twelve women. This serpent is called Ka-en-Ānkh-neteru, 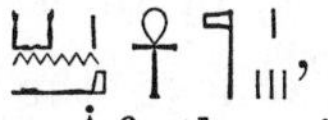, i.e., "the life of the gods," and the gods who draw Ȧf, that is to say, Rā, through it are his "loyal servants," , *Ȧmkhiu*. The boat enters the serpent at his tail in deep darkness, and passing through his body emerges through the mouth into the light of day; the god in his boat enters the snake in the form of a dead, old Sun-god, and he comes forth not only alive, but made young again, and appears in the sky under the form of Kheperȧ. The "loyal servants" of Rā are the souls of the blessed which have been so fortunate as to obtain admission into his boat; they were his devout adorers when upon earth, and the reward which they

1 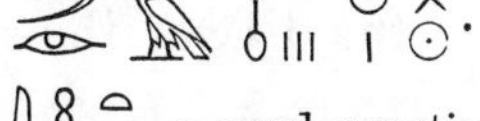.

2 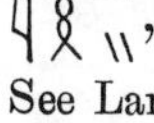, a word sometimes rendered by *vulva*, *pubis*, and *flank*.

3 See Lanzone, *Domicile des Esprits*, pl. v.

obtain for their fidelity is renewed youth and a new birth upon the earth. What they are to do upon earth is not made clear, but it is evident that they cannot remain there for an indefinite period, for since their master needs to be re-born daily they also must need re-birth each day. It is doubtful, if we judge by some passages, if they came to the earth at all, and it is far more likely that their enjoyment consisted in journeying about at will through the sky and looking down from some portion of it upon the scenes of their old life than in making hurried visits to the earth daily.

When the boat of Rā has passed through the serpent the twelve women or goddesses, mentioned above, take the rope from the gods and haul it on to the paths of the sky. The god is accompanied through the Twelfth Hour by:—1. Twelve goddesses, each bearing a serpent on her head and shoulders, and 2. Twelve gods, or men, with their hands raised in adoration; all these are on the right hand side. Each deity has a name, which is written in front of his or her figure. The uraei of the goddesses are said to proceed from them, and the flames which drive away Āpep come forth from their mouths. The goddesses travel with the god until he rises on this earth, but after this they return to their places. The duty of the twelve gods is to praise Rā. On the left of the boat we have the gods Nu, , Nuth, , Ḥeḥu, , Ḥeḥut, ; these gods are "in their own bodies," , and they go to Rā in heaven, to receive this great god as he cometh forth to them in the eastern part of heaven daily. They live in their *ārrit*, i.e., hall of the horizon, but their forms, , of the Ṭuat belong to this Circle. Next we have two human-headed gods, a bird-headed god called Nehui, , a god with two birds' heads called Ni, , the serpent Nesmekhef, , and four human-headed gods; all these carry paddles on their right shoulders. The duty of the gods is to raise up, , the disk of the sun daily, but the serpent Nesmekhef slaughters the enemies of Rā; they travel with Rā and receive their spirits, , in this

Circle. Before these are ten gods, with hands raised in adoration,[1] who are described as the *ḥentiu*, , of the forms of Osiris, the Governor of the thick darkness, , and they say to him, "Live, thou Governor of thy "darkness! Live, O thou who art great in all things! Live, O "thou Prince of Åmentet, Osiris, thou Governor of those who are "in Åmenti! Mayest thou live, mayest thou live, O thou who "art Governor of the Ṭuat, the wind of Rā is to thy nostrils, "the breath of Kheperå is with thee, thou livest and they live. "Hail, Osiris, lord of the living ones; the gods who are with "Osiris are those who were with him at the first time," etc.

The allusion here is to the death and burial of Osiris, when Horus carried out the arrangements which had to be made for the performance of the general ceremonies, and when every detail connected with mummification, etc., was thought out by the loving care of the son of Osiris. In the illustrated version of the Twelfth Hour, published by Signor Lanzone (tav. vii.), we have represented the semi-circular wall of thick darkness which forms the end of the Ṭuat and the division between it and this world. Against this wall, in the lower part of it, lies a mummied form, representing Osiris, and called Sem-Åf, , i.e., the "Image (or Form) of "Åf"; this is the object of the praises which the last two groups of gods lavish upon him. The descriptive text says concerning the mummy, "He who is in this picture in the hidden form of Horus of "thick darkness is the secret image which Shu makes to be under "Nut, and which cometh forth from Ḳeb-ur on earth in this form."[2]

[1] Ṭuati, , Ṭes-khu, , Themaru, , Aākhbu, , Sekhenu, , Ermenu, , Khennu, , Bunāu, , Āuru, , Åthep, , and Åm......, .

[2] 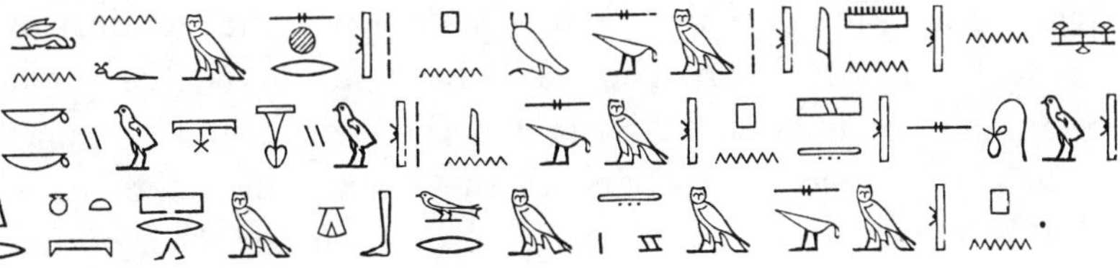

In the middle of the wall of thick darkness is a red disk, from which proceeds a human head; this is the "image of Shu," 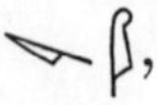, who extends his arms along the vaulted wall, and of whose body one part is in the Ṭuat and the other in this world. Immediately above the head of the god is the beetle of Kheperȧ, here spelt , which makes its way into this world through the opening which the head and shoulders of Shu have made in the wall of thick darkness. Through this opening the boat of Rā also was enabled to pass into this world, and the god continued his journey with the help of the deities who towed him along; there is no doubt about this because the tow-line is prolonged to the wall of thick darkness. As Ȧf, the dead body of Rā, passes into our world, his new life begins, and for men and women the night passes away, and a new day is born.

We have now traced the passage of the Sun-god through the Ṭuat as it was imagined by those who believed in the absolute supremacy of Osiris, and as it was described by the author of the BOOK OF PYLONS, and we have briefly passed through its divisions as described in the BOOK OF THAT WHICH IS IN THE ṬUAT, throughout which the absolute supremacy of Rā is maintained. It is now easy to see that these two works represent two opposite and conflicting theories as to the future life. The heaven of the devotees of Osiris was originally most materialistic, and the life which was led in it by the beatified was, to all intents and purposes, merely a continuation of the life led by men and women upon earth; the heaven of the priests of Rā was of a more refined character, and it lacked the grosser characteristics of the dwellers in the Elysian Fields of Osiris. Some have argued from the facts about the Ṭuat given above that the Egyptians believed in the existence of purgatory, and in the everlasting punishment of the wicked in a hell of fire, and in the reincarnation of souls, and in many other things which would presuppose the holding by them of doctrines which are commonly thought to be the products of the minds of modern nations; but the facts do not support these beliefs. Whichever doctrine of the future life we take, whether that of Osiris or that of Rā, we find no room in it for a purgatory.

In the Judgment which took place before Osiris only the righteous were permitted to enter into the Elysian Fields, and the wicked were destroyed immediately; in other words, annihilation was the punishment for sin. The Egyptians believed largely in the efficacy of works, and in addition to the deeds of love and charity which they performed in all periods, strict care concerning the ceremonies of religion, worship, and of the funeral, and a proper respect and reverence for words of power, and amulets, and sacred writings, and figures were demanded from them by priests and religious teachers at all times. There was, of course, a large class of people who could not afford costly burials, and who were too poor to buy even cheap amulets, but they were not condemned in the Judgment because of their poverty; on the contrary, they escaped annihilation and were admitted by Osiris into the first division of the Ṭuat, where, however, they were compelled to stay because they did not know the words of power which would enable them to continue their journey through the remaining divisions of the Underworld. But there was no punishment inflicted upon them because they had been both poor and ignorant in this world; they merely remained in the place to which their religious qualifications enabled them to attain, and each evening, or each night, they were made glad by the sight of the great god Rā as he sailed through the Ṭuat in his boat, and they rejoiced in his daily visit.

The beings in the Ṭuat of Osiris upon whom punishment was inflicted were the "enemies of Osiris," and these were usually the "enemies of Rā"; but in no text is it said that the punishment which they had to endure there ever obliterated their guilt, whatever it might be, or that when the proper time had arrived they would be allowed to proceed into another division of the Ṭuat where their punishment would be lighter, or where they would undergo none at all. Though a man could earn happiness in the realm of Osiris or in that of Rā by his good works on earth, and by ceremonies performed at his funeral by duly qualified priests, and by the presence of copies of religious texts which were buried with him, there is no reason to think that when once his soul reached the Underworld it could ever better its position there either by suffering punishment or by the performance of good works. The offerings made at the tombs of the dead were for the benefit of the *ka* or double, and perhaps for the animal soul which was at one time believed to exist in the human body, but neither the offerings nor the prayers which accompanied them seem to have been able to remove the spirits and souls of the dead from one division of the Ṭuat into another, or to modify the state or condition which had been decreed for them. Similarly, there is no evidence that prayers for the dead or offerings would ameliorate the condition of those who had successfully passed the ordeal of the Judgment, and had been sent by Osiris into one or other of the habitations of his kingdom.

CHAPTER VI

# HELL AND THE DAMNED

IF we examine the doctrine concerning the future life according to the priesthoods of Rā we find still less room for a purgatory in their theological system. According to this the souls of the dead assembled in Åmentet, i.e., the "hidden" region, the Egyptian Hades, where they waited for the boat of Rā to pass by. When the god appeared those who had been his worshippers and adorers on earth, and who were fortunate enough to have secured the words of power which would enable them to enter the boat did so, and they made their journey with him through the Ṭuat. Under his protection they passed through all the dangers which threatened to destroy them, and continued their journey through the realms of Osiris and Seker, and at length appeared with Rā in the eastern horizon of heaven at daybreak. Once there they were able to wander about heaven at will, and they did so, presumably, until the time of sunset, when they rejoined the god in his boat, and again made the journey through the Ṭuat with him. Each division of the Ṭuat, apparently, contained a host of beings who wished to enter the boat of Rā, but could not do so, either for want of the necessary words of power, or because they had reached the place to which their qualifications entitled them; these all, however, received great benefit from the nightly visit of Rā, and as he left each division to enter the next they were filled with great sorrow, and many of them ceased to exist until the following night, when they renewed their life for a brief period. Many divisions of the Ṭuat contained enemies of Rā, who were, of course, destroyed without mercy by the followers of the god; but there is no reason whatsoever for the view that these enemies were the damned, or that they were doomed to eternal punishment. At the end of the Ṭuat was a region where certain goddesses presided over pits of fire and superintended the destruction of the bodies, and spirits, and shadows, and heads of numbers of such enemies, and it would seem, judging by the knives in their hands, that they hacked the bodies to pieces before they were burnt. But even these were not punished eternally, for as soon as the god had passed through their region the fires went out, and the mere fact that he was able to appear in the eastern sky proved that all his enemies were destroyed. Each night and morning Rā destroyed the hosts of enemies who attempted to bar his progress, for such enemies perished instantly by the flames which went forth from the divine beings whom he had created.

Originally, too, such enemies were only the personifications of the powers of nature, such as twilight, darkness, night, gloom, the blackness of eclipses, fog, mist, vapour, rain, cloud, storm, wind, tempest, hurricane, and the like, which were destroyed daily by Rā and his fiery beams. Many, in fact the greater number of such personifications, were endowed by Egyptian artists with human forms, and the pictures of the scenes of their destruction by fire were supposed by many to represent the burning of the souls of the damned. The ignorant and the superstitious did not understand that the Sun-god slew and burned with fire the enemies of each night and morning during that same night and morning; each rising of the sun was the result of the annihilation of his foes of that day. It may be urged that these foes were always the same because they were always of the same kind, but the Egyptians did not think so, and they believed that a new host of foes appeared to attack Rā each night and morning. But even had they thought so, the punishment was only intermittent, and it was only renewed during that part of each night which immediately preceded the dawn, and during the interval between dawn and sunrise. The souls of the damned could have done nothing to hinder the progress of Rā, and the Egyptians never imagined that they did, but it is possible that in late dynastic times certain schools of theological thought in Egypt, being dissatisfied with and unconvinced of the accuracy of the theory of the annihilation of the wicked, assigned to evil souls dwelling-places with the personifications of the powers of nature already mentioned in the Ṭuat. The spears which pierced the enemies of Rā were the fiery rays of the sun, and the knives which hacked their bodies in pieces were his flames of fire; and the lakes and pits of fire were suggested to the minds of the primitive Egyptians by the fiery splendour which filled the eastern heavens at sunrise. They certainly did not believe in everlasting punishment, and there is nothing in the texts which will support the view that they did; in fact, the doctrines of purgatory and hell which were promulgated during the Middle Ages in Europe with such success find no equivalents in the ancient Egyptian religion. Apart from the general characteristics of their religion the Egyptians were too practical to entertain the idea of repeated destructions or consumings by fire of the same body, but had they done so we should certainly have found some texts which had been composed to avert such an awful doom. They mummified the bodies of their dead in the earliest times because they expected them to rise again, and they did so in later times because they believed that a spiritual body would grow out of them; they never expected to obtain a second physical body in the Underworld, and therefore they took the greatest care to preserve, by means of magical ceremonies and words, the bodies in which they lived in as complete a form as possible. The destruction of the body involved the ruin of the *ka*, or double, and of the shadow, and of many of the mental and spiritual constituents of man; and the Egyptians regarded the death of the body with such dismay that, fearing lest the spiritual body which sprang from it after death might be in danger of dying, they caused prayers to be composed for the purpose of averting from it the "second death" and the possibility of its dying a second time.

We may see, however, that although the Egyptians had no hell for souls in the mediaeval acceptance of the term, their fiery pits, and fiends, and devils, and enemies of Rā formed the foundations of the hells of later peoples like the Hebrews, and even of the descendants of the Egyptians who became Christians i.e., the Copts. Many proofs of this fact may be found in Coptic literature as the following instances will show. In "Pistis Sophia,"[1] we have the Virgin Mary asking Jesus, her Lord, to give her a description of "outer darkness,"[2] and to tell her how many places of punishment there are in it. Our Lord replies, "The "outer darkness is a great serpent, the tail of which is in its "mouth, and it is outside the whole world, and surroundeth the "whole world; in it there are many places of punishment, and it "containeth twelve halls wherein severe punishment is inflicted. "In each hall is a governor, but the face of each governor differeth "from that of his neighbour. The governor of the first hall hath "the face of a crocodile, with its tail in its mouth. From the "mouth of the serpent proceed all ice, and all dust, and all cold, "and every kind of disease and sickness; and the true name by "which they call him in his place is ENKHTHONIN. And the "governor of the second hall hath as his true face the face of a cat, "and they call him in his place KHARAKHAR. And the governor "of the third hall hath as his true face the face of a dog, and "they call him in his place ARKHARÔKH. And the governor of the "fourth hall hath as his true face the face of a serpent, and they "call him in his place AKHRÔKHAR. And the governor of the fifth "hall hath as his true face the face of a black ox,[3] and they call "him in his place MARKHOUR. And the governor of the sixth hall "hath as his true face the face of a goat, and they call him in his "place LAMKHAMÔR. And the governor of the seventh hall hath "as his true face the face of a bear, and they call him as his true "name LONKHAR. And the governor of the eighth hall hath as "his true face the face of a vulture, and they call him in his place "LARAÔKH. And the governor of the ninth hall hath as his true "face the face of a basilisk, and they call him in his place "ARKHEÔKH. And in the tenth hall there are many governors, "and there is there a serpent with seven heads, each head having "its [own] true face, and he who is over them all in his place they "call XARMARÔKH. And in the eleventh hall there are many

[1] See *Pistis Sophia. Opus Gnosticum Valentino adjudicatum*, ed. Schwartze, Berlin, 1851.

[2] ⲡⲕⲁⲕⲉ ⲉⲧ ϩⲓ ⲃⲟⲗ.

[3] ⲟⲩϩⲟ ⲙⲙⲁⲥⲉ ⲛ̅ ⲕⲁⲙⲉ.

"governors, and there are there seven heads, each of them having "as its true face the face of a cat, and the greatest of them, who is "over them, they call in his place RHÔKHAR. And in the twelfth "hall there are many great governors, and there are there seven "heads, each of them having as its true face the face of a dog, and "the greatest, who is over them, they call in his place KHRÊMAÔR. "These twelve governors are in the serpent of outer darkness, and "each of them hath a name according to the hour, and each of "them changeth his face according to the hour."[1]

It is quite clear that in the above extract from the famous Gnostic work we have a series of chambers in the outer darkness which has been borrowed from the twelve divisions of the Egyptian Ṭuat already described, and the reader has only to compare the vignettes to Chapters cxliv. and cxlv. of the *Book of the Dead* with the extract from "Pistis Sophia" to see how close the borrowing has been. An examination of another great Gnostic work, generally known as the "Book of Ieu,"[2] proves that the Underworld of the Gnostics was nothing but a modified form of the Åmentet or Åmenti of the Egyptians, to which were added characteristics derived from the religious systems of the Hebrews and Greeks. The Gnostic rivers and seas of fire are nothing but equivalents of those mentioned in the *Book of the Dead*, and the beings in Åmenti, and Chaos, and Outer Darkness are derived, in respect of form, from ancient Egyptian models. The great dragon of Outer Darkness and his twelve halls, and their twelve guardians or governors who change their names and forms every hour are, after all, only modifications of the old Egyptian system of the Twelve Pylons or Twelve Hours which formed the Underworld. The seven-headed serpent of the Gnostic system has his prototype in the great serpent Nāu, , which is called the "bull of "the gods," and has "seven serpents on his seven necks,"  ;[3] the seven-headed serpent, Nāu-shesmā,

[1] *Pistis Sophia*, Coptic text, p. 319 ff.
[2] See Schmidt, *Gnostische Schriften in Koptischer Sprache*, Leipzig, 1892.
[3] Tetå, l. 307.

, also had seven uraei for heads, and he had authority over seven archers, or seven bows,  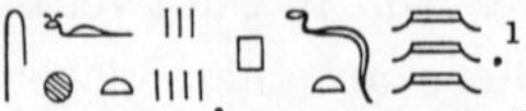.[1]

Of Àmentet and the Ṭuat in general we find many traces in the martyrdoms of Coptic saints, but, as was to be expected, the writers have made the demons and the pits of fire of the Egyptian Underworld instruments of punishment for the souls of those who did not embrace Christianity when upon this earth. Thus the writer of the Martyrdom of George[2] of Cappadocia makes the saint to raise up from the dead a pagan called Boês, who had been dead two hundred years, and who told Dadianus, the governor, that he had been on earth a worshipper of the "stupid, dumb, deaf, and "blind Apollo," and that when he departed this life he went to live in "a place in the river of fire until such time as I went to "the place where the worm dieth not." According to another writer, Macarius of Antioch restored to life a man who had been dead for six hours, and who stated that his miseries during that short time had been greater than those which he had endured throughout all his life upon earth. He confessed that he had been a worshipper of idols, and then went on to say that when he was dying the fiends crowded upon him, and that these had the faces of serpents, lions, crocodiles, and, curiously enough, of bears. They tore his soul from his body with great violence, and fled with it to a great river of fire wherein they plunged it to a depth of four hundred cubits; then they drew it out and set it before the Judge of Truth,[3] who passed sentence upon it. After this was done they took it to a "place of darkness, wherein there was no "light whatsoever, and they cast it down into the cold where "there was gnashing of teeth. Here," said the wretched man, "I "saw the worm which never slumbereth, and his head was like "unto that of a crocodile. He was surrounded by serpents of "every kind which cast souls before him, and when his own mouth

[1] Tetà, l. 306.

[2] See my *St. George of Cappadocia*, p. 20.

[3] ⲡⲓⲕⲣⲓⲧⲏⲥ ⲙ̄ⲙⲏⲓ. The word ⲙⲏⲓ is the old Egyptian , *maā*, which is commonly rendered by "law, right, truth, true, just," and the like.

"was full he allowed the other creatures to eat; in that place "they tore us to pieces, but we could not die. After that they "took me out of the place and carried me into Åmenti, where I "was to stay for ever."[1] In another work[2] a nameless mummy is made to tell how before he died the avenging angels came about him with iron knives and pointed goads, which they thrust into his sides, and how other angels came and tore his soul from his body, and having tied it to the similitude of a black horse they carried it off to Åmentet. Here he was tortured in a place filled with noxious reptiles, and having been cast into the outer darkness he saw a pit more than two hundred feet deep, which was filled with reptiles, each of which had seven heads, and had its body covered with objects like scorpions. In this place were several other terrible serpents, and to one of these, which had teeth like iron stakes, the poor soul was given to be devoured; this monster crushed the soul for five days of each week, but on Saturday and Sunday it had respite. This last sentence seems to suggest that the serpent respected the Sabbath of the Jews and the Sunday of the Christians.

In all these examples, and even in the words of Isaiah, who says (lxvi. 24), "their worm shall not die, neither shall "their fire be quenched," we have a direct allusion to the great serpent of the Egyptian Underworld, which was, in all periods of history, the terror of the worshippers of the Sun-god, and which was known by many names. The allies and companions of this serpent were serpents like itself, and to nearly every power which was hostile to the dead or the living the form of a snake or serpent was attributed. The type and symbol of all enmity to Rā, whether of a physical or moral character, was the arch-serpent Āpep or Āpepi, which attacked him daily, and was overcome daily. To this monster we have several allusions in the *Book of the Dead*, but these do not adequately convey an idea of the terror with which he was regarded, at all events in the latter part of the dynastic period.

[1] Hyvernat, *Les Actes des Martyrs de l'Égypte*, p. 56 f.

[2] Amélineau, *Monuments pour servir à l'Histoire de l'Égypte Chrétienne*, p. 167.

From a papyrus preserved in the British Museum[1] we learn that a special service was in use in Upper Egypt for the purpose of destroying the power of Āpepi and of making his attacks on the sun to have no effect. This service consisted of a series of chapters which were to be recited at certain times of the day during the performance of a number of curious ceremonies of a magical character. Thus one rubric orders that the name of Āpepi shall be written in green colour upon a piece of new papyrus, and that a wax figure of the fiend shall be made and his name inlaid upon it with green colour. Both papyrus and wax figure were to be burnt in the fire, the belief being that as the wax figure melted and as the sheet of papyrus burnt, the fiend Āpepi would also decay and fall to pieces. Whilst the wax figure was melting in the fire it was to be spit upon several times each hour, and when it was melted the refuse of it was to be mixed with dung and again burnt. It was imperative to do this at midnight, when Rā began his return journey in the Ṭuat, towards the east, and at dawn, and at noon, and at eventide, and in fact at any and every hour of the day. This might also be done with advantage whenever storm clouds appeared in the sky, or whenever the clouds gathered together for rain. The following extract will give an idea of the general import of the service for the destruction of Āpepi. The deceased says: "Āpepi hath fallen into the flame, a knife is stuck "into his head, his name no longer existeth upon this earth. It is "decreed for me to inflict blows upon him, I drive darts into his "bones, I destroy his soul in the course of every day, I sever his "vertebræ from his neck, cutting into his flesh with a knife and "stabbing through his skin. He is given over to the fire which "obtains the mastery over him in its name of 'Sekhet,' and it "hath power over him in its name of 'Eye burning the enemy.' "Darts are driven into his soul, his bones are burnt with fire, and "his limbs are placed therein. Horus, mighty of strength, hath "decreed that he shall come in front of the boat of Rā; his fetter "of steel tieth him up and maketh his limbs so that they cannot "move; Horus repulseth his moment of luck during his eclipse, "and he maketh him to vomit that which is inside him. Horus

[1] See *Archaeologia*, vol. lii.

"fettereth, bindeth, and tieth up, and Aker taketh away his "strength so that I may separate his flesh from his bones; that I "may fetter his feet and cut off his two hands and arms; that I "may shut up his mouth and lips, and break in his teeth; that I "may cut out his tongue from his throat, and carry away his "words; that I may block up his two eyes, and carry off his ears; "that I may tear out his heart from its seat and throne; and that "I may make him so that he existeth not. May his name never "exist, and may what is born to him never live; may he never "exist, and may his kinsfolk never exist; may he never exist, and "may his relatives never exist; may he never exist, and may his "heir never exist; may his offspring never grow to maturity; "may his seed never be established; moreover, may his soul, and "body, and spirit, and shade, and words of power, and his bones, "and his skin, never more exist."

The Rubric runs: "This Chapter is to be said over a figure "of Āpepi, inscribed upon new papyrus with green ink, and "placed inside a covering on which his name hath been written, "and thou shalt tie these round tightly with cord, and put such a "figure and covering into the fire every day. Thou shalt stamp "upon it and defile it with thy left foot, and thou shalt spit upon "it four times during the course of every day, and when thou "hast placed it upon the fire thou shalt say, 'Rā triumpheth over "'thee, Āpepi, and Horus triumpheth over his enemies, and P-āa "'(i.e., the deceased) triumpheth over his enemies.' Next thou "shalt write down the names of all the male and female devils of "which thy heart is afraid, the names of all the enemies of P-āa, "in death, and in life, and the names of their father, mother, and "children, [and place the papyrus] inside the covering, together "with a wax figure of Āpepi. These shall then be placed in the "fire in the name of Āpepi, and shall be burnt when Rā riseth in "the morning; this thou shalt repeat at noon and at evening "when Rā setteth in the land of life, whilst there is light at the "foot of the mountain. Over each figure of Āpepi thou shalt recite "the above chapter, in very truth, for the doing of this shall be "of great benefit [for thee] upon earth and in the Underworld."[1]

[1] *On the Hieratic Papyrus of Nesi-Amsu*, p. 52 (*Archaeologia*, vol. lii.).

To destroy the fiends which were associated with Āpepi it was necessary to make figures of them in wax, and having inscribed their names upon them to tie them round with black hair, and then to cast them on the ground, and kick them with the left foot, and pierce them with a stone spear. To obtain the full benefit of all the names of Āpepi a man had to make the figure of a serpent with his tail in his mouth, and having stuck a knife in its back, and cast it down upon the ground, to say, "Āpep, Fiend, "Betet." The faithful follower of Rā is also bidden to "make "another serpent with the face of a cat, and with a knife stuck in "his back, and call it HEMHEM. Make another with the face of "a crocodile, and with a knife stuck in his back, and call it "HAUNA-ÀRU-ḤER-ḤRÀ; make another with the face of a duck, "and with a knife stuck in his back, and call it ALUTI. Make "another with the face of a white cat, and with a knife stuck in "his back, and tie it up and bind it tightly, and call it 'Āpep "the Enemy.'" The papyrus which contains these interesting passages was written about B.C. 312-311, though the compositions in it are very much older, but it shows that, even at that period, when the Macedonians had begun to reign over Egypt, and Greek influence was making itself supreme in the country, the old beliefs still held sway over the minds of the Egyptians. In fact, in this matter as in nearly all others, they clung most tenaciously to the views and opinions of their forefathers.

The primitive Egyptians feared snakes and propitiated them, and the earliest dynastic people of the country employed charms, and incantations, and magical formulae to keep snakes, and serpents, and reptiles of every kind from their dead; the priests of Heliopolis respected the prevailing views of their countrymen, and ancient formulae against snakes were copied into their funeral texts. Every Recension of the *Book of the Dead* contained Chapters which were written to preserve the dead from the attacks of snakes; it is tolerably certain that some of them contain formulae which are not older than dynastic times, and these show that the fear of serpents was as great as ever, although these reptiles cannot have been so numerous as formerly. The priests of Àmen made snakes to play very prominent parts in the Underworld, and, curiously enough, they thought that the dead Sun-god, or the "Flesh of Rā," was re-born into the life of a new day, only after he had been drawn in his boat through the body of a serpent. The Egyptians usually had some reason for the things they said, and wrote, and depicted, and although it is not easy to find the reason in every case, there is, fortunately, little doubt about it here. They observed that snakes sloughed their skins from time to time, and that their bodies were much improved in appearance as the result, and it is pretty certain that they had this habit of snakes in their minds, when they made their god Rā as a new being to emerge in his boat out of the great serpent which lay in deep undulations between the end of the Ṭuat and this world.

Reference has already been made to the influence upon the hell of the Copts of the old Egyptian mythology about the Ṭuat, and it is right here to point out that the Hebrews appear to have borrowed from it many of their ideas concerning the abodes of the dead in the Underworld. It is quite certain that the hell of which they conceived the existence was not derived from the Babylonians, for we know from the story of Ishtar's descent into the "land of no return" that, although it had Seven Gates, it contained no pits of fire or monster serpents. Ishtar, we are told, found it to be a place of darkness, and she saw that the beings in it were dressed in garments of feathers, and that dust and mud were their food.[1] The commonest of the names which the Hebrews gave to the abode of the damned is GÊ HINNOM,[2] or Gehenna, which was originally the Valley of Hinnom, that lay quite near to Jerusalem,[3] where children were sacrificed to the god Moloch;[4] this name passed into the New Testament under the form *Γέεννα*, and into Arabic literature as "Jahannam."[5] The portion of the Valley of Hinnom where the sacrifices were burnt was called "Tôpheth." According to the Rabbis "Gehenna" was created on the second day of creation, with the firmament and the angels, and just as there were an Upper and a Lower Paradise so there were also two

[1] See L. W. King, *Babylonian Religion*, p. 179 f.

[2] גֵּי־הִנֹּם

[3] Now generally identified with the Wâdî er-Rabâbî.

[4] See 2 Kings xxiii. 10.

[5] جَهَنَّم

Gehennas, one in the heavens and one on the earth. As to the size of Gehenna we read that Egypt was 400 parassangs[1] long and 400 parassangs wide, i.e., about 1,200 miles long by 1,200 miles wide; that Nubia (כוש) was sixty times as large as Egypt; that the world was sixty times as large as Nubia, and that it would require 500 years to travel across either its length or its breadth; that Gehenna was sixty times as large as the world; and that it would take a man 2,100 years to reach it.[2]

In Gehenna, as in Paradise, there were seven "palaces" (היכלות), and the punishments which were meted out to their inhabitants varied both in kind and in intensity. In each palace there are 6,000 houses, or chambers, and in each house are 6,000 boxes, and in each box are 6,000 vessels fitted with gall. Gehenna is so deep that it would take 300 years to reach the bottom of it; according to another opinion it is 300 miles long, 300 miles wide, 1,000 miles thick, and 100 miles deep. The fire in each palace is fiercer and more destructive than that in the palace preceding, and the flames of the deepest portion of it are able to consume human souls utterly, which fire upon earth can never do. Each palace is, according to one view, under the command of an angel, who is subservient to Dûmâh, the prince of Gehenna, and who has with him tens of thousands of angels who are occupied in judging sinners and sealing their doom; but according to another the seven mansions are ruled, under Dûmâh, דומה, by three angels called Mashkhîth, Af, and Khêmâ. The voices of the beings in Gehenna rise up to heaven mingled with the cries of the wicked. Dûmâh, the prince of Gehenna, seems to have been of Egyptian origin, for we read, "At the time when Moses said, 'I will perform "'judgments on all the gods of Egypt,' Dûmâh, the prince of "Egypt, went 400 miles and God said unto him, 'This decree is "'decreed by me, even as it is written, I will visit the host of the "'height in the height;'[3] and in that same hour sovereignty was "taken away from him, and he was appointed prince over "Gehenna, and some say that he was set over the dead."

[1] The parassang = 30 stadia, and the stadion = 202 yards.
[2] Eisenmenger, *Entdecktes Judenthum*, part ii., p. 328.
[3] Isaiah xxiv. 21.

Another prince of Gehenna was called 'Arsîêl, and his duty was to stand before the souls of the righteous to prevent them from praying to God on behalf of the wicked. Opinions vary as to the number of gates or doors which are in Gehenna, some saying there are 50, others 8,000, and others 40,000; but the writers who followed the best traditions fixed the number at seven, and this agrees with the best Muḥammadan tradition also. Finally, as a river runs through the Ṭuat so a river or canal flows through Gehenna. The first division of Gehenna is 100 miles long and 50 miles wide, and it contains several pits wherein fiery lions dwell; when men fall into the pits the lions consume parts of them and the fire devours the remainder, but soon afterwards they come into being again and have to pass through the fire which is in the second division, when they are again consumed and again come to life. In this way they have to pass through the fire of all the seven divisions. According to another opinion one half of Gehenna is fire and the other half hail, and the angel who is in charge drives the souls of the damned from the fire into the hail and from the hail into the fire without ceasing. Another writer says that each of the seven divisions of hell contains seven streams of fire and seven streams of hail, and that each division is sixty times as large as that which is immediately above it. In each division are 7,000 small chambers, and in each chamber 7,000 clefts, and in each cleft 7,000 scorpions, and in each scorpion seven joints, and in each joint 1,000 vessels of gall; through it flow seven rivers filled with deadly poison, and the damned have to pass one half of the year in the fire, and the other half in the hail and snow, which are far more terrible than the fire. Moreover, from under the throne of God Almighty there goes forth a river of fire which empties itself upon the heads of the wicked, but most of these have a rest from their punishment for one hour and a half three times a day, i.e., at the times of morning, mid-day, and evening prayer, and they have rest the whole of each Sabbath and of each festival of the new moon. Some of the Rabbis believed that the punishment of the wicked would last for ever, but others thought that a period of punishment six or twelve months in length would suffice for their purification.

Those who are damned shall not remember the names which they bore upon earth, and although the angels beat them and call upon them to declare their names, they shall not be able to do so; this view was clearly held by the Egyptians, for we are specially told in the text of Pepi I. (line 169), "Pepi is happy with his "name," . From the facts recorded above it is easy to see how much the Hebrews were indebted to the Egyptians in the construction of their Gehenna, and how closely they fitted native beliefs into a framework of foreign conceptions. Some of their writers seem to have possessed a better insight into such matters than others, whilst a few of them unconsciously reproduced the original conception of the Ṭuat as the place of destruction for the enemies of the god, and believed that Gehenna, or hell, would be abolished. These thought that at some future time God would remove the sun from its place and would place it in the second firmament, in a hollow place or chamber specially prepared for it, and that having judged and condemned the wicked He would send them into this chamber, where the burning heat of the sun would consume them.[1] The Rabbis generally took no pains to say either how the fires of Gehenna were started, or how they were maintained, but Rabbi Yannai and Rabbi Shim'ôn ben-Lakîsh evidently thought it out, and so reduced Gehenna, unintentionally, to the place where a physical sun supplied the consuming fire, and did for the damned among the Hebrews exactly what it did for the enemies of Rā among the Egyptians.

It must be noted that the Gehenna of the Hebrew lacked the serpents of the Egyptian Ṭuat, but when we consider the difference between the physical characteristics of Egypt and those of Syria and Palestine this is not to be wondered at. In predynastic times Egypt was filled with serpents of every kind, and the terror which they inspired lived in the minds of the people of dynastic times long after the country had been practically cleared from these reptiles. In Palestine and Syria snakes were never very plentiful, but in the region of Southern

[1] Eisenmenger, op. cit., p. 366.

Babylonia, whence came Abraham and his companions, they must have existed in large numbers. It is a curious fact that the Hebrews, who borrowed so largely in their cosmogony from Babylonian sources, did not also borrow in some form or other the monster Tiamat, which played in their mythology the same part that Āpep or Āpepi played among the Egyptian gods. The Babylonian Tiamat waged war against Marduk, the champion chosen by the gods, and was held to be the incarnation of all evil, both physical and moral; and although the Hebrews assigned to the serpent cunning and guile, and declared that he was "more "subtle than any beast" (Gen. iii. 1), they hardly considered him to be a great physical power which waged war against the sun daily. Tiamat, as we learn from a cuneiform text,[1] was 50 *kasbu* long, and the height of its undulations was 1 *kasbu;* its mouth was one-half a *gar*, or six cubits wide, and it moved in water 9 cubits deep. Three other measurements are given, viẓ., 1 *gar*, 1 *gar*, and 5 *gar*, but as the text following them is broken it cannot be said to what they refer. Now, the *kasbu* was the distance usually passed over in a journey of two hours, and the cubit may be considered to be about 20 inches. Reckoning the *kasbu* at six miles we thus have a monster 300 miles long, which had a mouth 10 feet wide, and which moved in undulations six miles high! The measurements of 5 *gar* probably refers to its girth, and if this be so the creature was 100 feet round its body.

When Tiamat had been slain we are told that its blood flowed from its body for three years, three months, and one day, and we are able to obtain an idea of its huge size from the statement that when Marduk had smashed in its skull with his club, and had slit the channels of its blood, he split it, like a flat fish, into two halves, one of which he made use of to form the "covering of the "heavens."[2] There is no doubt that originally the Babylonian Tiamat was nothing but the rain clouds, and the mist and fog which lie over the Tigris and Euphrates in the early morning at certain seasons of the year, and which when looked at from the

[1] See King, *Cuneiform Inscriptions from Babylonian Tablets*, etc., part xiii., pl. 33 f., London, 1901; and King, *Seven Tablets of Creation*, vol. i., p. 119.

[2] King, *Babylonian Religion*, p. 77.

desert appear like a huge serpent stretched along the length of the stream, both up and down the river. The Hebrew Scriptures contain several allusions to a great nature serpent,[1] though he finds no place among the Seven Mansions of their hell. Thus the prophet Amos (ix. 3) refers to the serpent at the bottom of the sea, which Yahweh would command to bite the wicked if they attempted to hide there; in Psalm lxxiv. 13 f. God is referred to as the breaker of the heads of Leviathan and of the dragons in the waters; in Isaiah (li. 9) we have, "Awake, awake, put on strength, "O arm of Yahweh! Awake, as in the ancient days, in the "generations of old! Art thou not it that did slay the monster "Râhâbh, and wound the serpent (tannîn)?" Râhâbh may here, as some have argued, refer to Egypt, but if so, it is to Egypt as the home of the great serpent monster which we now know as Āpepi, and which was to the prophet Isaiah the type and symbol of the country, and not to the judgments which Yahweh meted out to that land.

The Hebrew writers refer to the nature serpent under several names, e.g., *tannîn*, *nâkhâsh*, *râhâbh*, but the monster referred to under them is, in reality, one and the same, i.e., Leviathan (לִוְיָתָן *livyâthân*), "the serpent of many twistings or folds," and both Nebuchadnezzar II. and the "King of Assyria" are identified with him (see Jeremiah li. 34; Isaiah xiv. 29). According to the Rabbis he was created on the fifth day of the week of creation,[2] and was hunted for slaughter by Gabriel, and with the assistance of Yahweh was slain by him; here we have a series of close resemblances to the history of Tiamat, for Gabriel is in every way the counterpart of Marduk, and Yahweh takes the place of Anshar as the head of the gods. Finally, Leviathan was slain by Gabriel, just as Tiamat was killed by Marduk, and out of the skin of Leviathan Gabriel made a tent wherein the righteous might dwell,[3] and a covering for the walls of the city of Jerusalem. This

[1] See Goldziher, *Mythology of the Hebrews*, pp. 27, 28; King, *Babylonian Religion*, p. 115.

[2] Eisenmenger, op. cit., p. 877.

[3] עתיד הקדוש ברוך הוא לעשות סוכה לצדיקים מעורו של לויתן: Eisenmenger, op. cit., p. 888.

covering was bright and shining, and it emitted light which was so strong that it could be seen from one end of the world to the other. The last statement recalls the words of the Fourth Tablet of the Creation Series, which tell how Marduk made a canopy in the heavens of one-half of the body or skin of Tiamat. In the Hebrew version of the story it is said that the righteous feed upon the body of Leviathan, but there is no equivalent passage in the cuneiform texts at present known. From the passage in the Psalm already quoted (lxxiv. 13) it would appear that Leviathan had many heads, but this view is not supported by any known description of Tiamat, and in the absence of any evidence on the subject we must assume that the idea of a plurality of heads came from Egypt. In the Book of Revelation (xii. 3; xiii. 1) mention is made of a "great red dragon, having seven heads and ten horns, and seven "crowns upon his heads," which appeared in heaven, and of a beast having seven heads and ten horns, with ten crowns upon his horns, which came up out of the sea, but the idea of these also was not derived from Babylonia. All the available evidence goes to show that whilst the Hebrew conception of Leviathan was of Babylonian origin that of a hell of fire was borrowed from Egypt.

Similarly, the seven-headed dragon and beast of the Book of Revelation, like the seven-headed basilisk serpent mentioned in "Pistis Sophia,"[1] have their origin in the seven-headed serpent which is mentioned in the Pyramid Texts. In Revelations ix. 19, horses are referred to which had tails "like unto serpents, and had heads," and here again we have an idea suggested by a monster which inhabited one of the Pylons of the Ṭuat, and which had the body of a crocodile and a tail formed of a writhing serpent's body with a serpent's head for the tip of it.

But although the Hebrews borrowed the framework of their hell from Egypt they appear to have made no use of the means by which the Egyptians hoped to escape from Åmentet and the Ṭuat, that is to say, there is no evidence to show that they had in early

ⲥⲓⲧ ⲛ̄ ϩⲟϥ ⲉⲣⲉ ⲥⲁϣϥⲉ ⲛ̄ ⲁⲡⲉ ⲉⲣⲟϥ; ed. Schwartze, pp. 136, 140, 147.

times any equivalent for the system of words of power which played such an important part in the magical side of the Egyptian religion. On the other hand, the Copts, at least those of them who belonged to Gnostic sects, retained the beliefs concerning the efficacy of magical words and names, and they introduced them into their writings in a remarkable manner. Thus in "Pistis Sophia" we are told[1] that after His resurrection Jesus stood up with His disciples by the sea, and prayed to His Father, whom He addressed by a series of magical names, thus:—Aeêiouô, Iaô, Aôi, Ôiapsinôther, Thernôps, Nôpsiter, Zagourê, Pagourê, Nethmomaôth, Nepsiomaôth, Marakhakhtha, Thôbarrabau, Tharnakhakhan, Zorokothora, Ieou, Sabaôth.[2] Whilst He was saying these names Thomas, Andrew, James, and Simon the Canaanite stood in the west with their faces towards the east; and Philip and Bartholomew stood in the south with their faces towards the north. In another passage[3] Jesus addresses His Father in these words and by these names:—Iaô Iouô, Iaô, Aôi, Ôia, Psinôther, Therôpsin, Ôpsither, Nephthomaôth, Nephiomaôth Marakhakhtha, Marmarakhtha, Iêana menaman, Amanêi tou ouranou, Israi Ḥamên Ḥamên, Soubaibai appaap Ḥamên Ḥamên, deraarai Ḥapaḥou Ḥamên Ḥamên, Sarsarsartou Ḥamên Ḥamên, Koukiamin miai Ḥamên Ḥamên, Iai, Iai, Toua Ḥamên Ḥamên Ḥamên, Mainmari, Mariê, Marei Ḥamên Ḥamên Ḥamên.[4] In another place[5]

Ed. Schwartze, p. 357.

[2] ⲁⲉⲏⲓⲟⲩⲱ· ⲓ̈ⲁⲱ· ⲁⲱⲓ̈· ⲱⲓ̈ⲁⲯⲓⲛⲱⲑⲉⲣ· ⲑⲉⲣⲛⲱⲯ· ⲛⲱⲯⲓⲧⲉⲣ· ⲍⲁⲅⲟⲩⲣⲏ· ⲡⲁⲅⲟⲩⲣⲏ· ⲛⲉⲑⲙⲟⲙⲁⲱⲑ· ⲛⲉⲯⲓⲟⲙⲁⲱⲑ· ⲙⲁⲣⲁⲭⲁⲭⲑⲁ· ⲑⲱⲃⲁⲣⲣⲁⲃⲁⲩ· ⲑⲁⲣⲛⲁⲭⲁⲭⲁⲛ· ⲍⲟⲣⲟⲕⲟⲑⲟⲣⲁ· ⲓ̈ⲉⲟⲩ· ⲥⲁⲃⲁⲱⲑ:

[3] Ed. Schwartze, p. 375.

[4] ⲓ̈ⲁⲱ ⲓ̈ⲟⲩⲱ· ⲓ̈ⲁⲱ· ⲁⲱⲓ̈· ⲱⲓ̈ⲁ ⲯⲓⲛⲱⲑⲉⲣ· ⲑⲉⲣⲱⲯⲓⲛ· ⲱⲯⲓⲑⲉⲣ ⲛⲉⲫⲑⲟⲙⲁⲱⲑ· ⲛⲉⲫⲓⲟⲙⲁⲱⲑ· ⲙⲁⲣⲁⲭⲁⲭⲑⲁ· ⲙⲁⲣⲙⲁⲣⲁⲭⲑⲁ· ⲓⲏⲁⲛⲁ ⲙⲉⲛⲁⲙⲁⲛ· ⲁⲙⲁⲛⲏⲓ̈· ⲧⲟⲩ ⲟⲩⲣⲁⲛⲟⲩ· ⲓⲥⲣⲁⲓ̈ ϩⲁⲙⲏⲛ ϩⲁⲙⲏⲛ· ⲥⲟⲩⲃⲁⲓ̈ⲃⲁⲓ̈· ⲁⲡⲡⲁⲁⲡ· ϩⲁⲙⲏⲛ· ϩⲁⲙⲏⲛ· ⲇⲉⲣⲁⲁⲣⲁⲓ̈ ϩⲁⲡⲁϩⲟⲩ ϩⲁⲙⲏⲛ ϩⲁⲙⲏⲛ· ⲥⲁⲣⲥⲁⲣⲥⲁⲣⲧⲟⲩ ϩⲁⲙⲏⲛ ϩⲁⲙⲏⲛ· ⲕⲟⲩⲕⲓⲁⲙⲓⲛ ⲙⲓⲁⲓ̈· ϩⲁⲙⲏⲛ· ϩⲁⲙⲏⲛ· ⲓ̈ⲁⲓ̈· ⲓ̈ⲁⲓ̈· ⲧⲟⲩⲁⲡ ϩⲁⲙⲏⲛ ϩⲁⲙⲏⲛ ϩⲁⲙⲏⲛ· ⲙⲁⲓⲛ ⲙⲁⲣⲓ· ⲙⲁⲣⲓⲏ· ⲙⲁⲣⲉⲓ· ϩⲁⲙⲏⲛ ϩⲁⲙⲏⲛ ϩⲁⲙⲏⲛ (p. 375).

[5] *Ibid.*, p. 375.

He addresses those who forgive sins by their names thus:—Siphirepsnikhieu, Zenei, Berimou, Sokhabrikhêr, Euthari, Nanaï Dieisbalmêrikh, Meunipos, Khirie, Entair, Mouthiour, Smour, Peukhêr, Oouskhous, Minionor, Isokhobortha;[1] and immediately afterwards He calls upon the Powers of His Father by these names:—Auêr, Bebrô, Athroni, Êoureph, Êone, Souphen, Knitousokhreôph, Mauônbi, Mneuôr, Souôni, Khôkheteôph, Khôkhe, Eteôph, Memôkh, and Anêmph.[2] An examination of the books of "Pistis Sophia" will show that many of the details of the "mysteries" which are there described are based upon ancient Egyptian beliefs, and that the whole of the doctrine of spiritual light which is expounded therein only represents a spiritualized conception of the far-reaching character of the powers of the light of the sun upon both the living and the dead, which the dynastic Egyptians recognized and described centuries before the Christian era. This was expressed in the terms of a highly artificial system wherein words of power, magical names, emanations, ranks of angels, gates, watchers, and purely Christian conceptions were mixed up together, with the Lord Christ as the central Figure. Much has yet to be done before all the comparisons and connections between the Egyptian and Christian systems can be fully worked out, but the facts quoted above will, perhaps, suggest the importance of the study.

[1] ⲥⲓⲫⲓⲣⲉⲯⲛⲓⲭⲓⲉⲩ· ⲍⲉⲛⲉⲓ· ⲃⲉⲣⲓⲙⲟⲩ· ⲥⲟⲭⲁⲃⲣⲓⲭⲏⲣ· ⲉⲩⲑⲁⲣⲓ· ⲛⲁⲛⲁⲓ̈· ⲇⲓⲉⲓⲥⲃⲁⲗⲙⲏⲣⲓⲭ· ⲙⲉⲩⲛⲓⲡⲟⲥ· ⲭⲓⲣⲓⲉ· ⲉⲛⲧⲁⲓⲣ· ⲙⲟⲩⲑⲓⲟⲩⲣ· ⲥⲙⲟⲩⲣ· ⲡⲉⲩⲭⲏⲣ· ⲟⲟⲩⲥⲭⲟⲩⲥ· ⲙⲓⲛⲓⲟⲛⲟⲣ· ⲓ̈ⲥⲟⲭⲟⲃⲟⲣⲑⲁ (p. 376).

[2] ⲁⲩⲏⲣ· ⲃⲉⲃⲣⲱ· ⲁⲑⲣⲟⲛⲓ· ⲏ̄ⲟⲩⲛⲉⲫ· ⲏ̄ⲱⲛⲉ· ⲥⲟⲩⲫⲉⲛ· ⲕⲛⲓⲧⲟⲩⲥⲟⲭⲣⲉⲱⲫ· ⲙⲁⲩⲱⲛⲃⲓ· ⲙⲛⲉⲩⲱⲣ· ⲥⲟⲩⲱⲛⲓ· ⲭⲱⲭⲉⲧⲉⲱⲫ· ⲭⲱⲭⲉ· ⲉⲧⲉⲱⲫ· ⲙⲉⲙⲱⲭ· ⲁⲛⲏⲙⲫ (p. 376).

## CHAPTER VII

# THE OLDEST COMPANY OF THE GODS AND THE CREATION

IN the earlier chapters of this work mention has been made of three companies of gods, the existence of which was formulated by the priests of Heliopolis, and it has been shown that a company of gods usually consisted of four pairs of deities, four gods and four goddesses, and a president or chief of the same. We have also shown that a *paut* or company of gods did not necessarily contain nine deities only, and that it as often as not was supposed to include more than nine gods. Originally, however, the Heliopolitan priests, or the authors of the theological system exhibited in the Pyramid Texts, intended the *paut* to consist of nine gods,

The Oldest Company of the Gods.

and it seems that they arrived at this decision as the result of the addition of their own local god Tem to a group of four pairs of deities, four gods and four goddesses, whom they had grouped together according to the plan followed by an older school of theologians in forming an older company of the gods. The company of the gods last mentioned is probably the oldest of all the companies in Egypt, although for various reasons it never seems to have attained to the popularity of the "great *paut* of the gods of Ȧnnu," or to have enjoyed such a prominent position in the minds of the religious philosophers of Egypt. This is not to be wondered at, for whilst the Heliopolitan company of the gods included the Sun-god Rā-Tem, or Rā-Tem-Kheperȧ, and Osiris, the god of the dead, the older company consisted of pairs of deities who represented religious conceptions, and faiths, and beliefs, which even at that remote period had been long dead, and the meaning of which had been forgotten. The very gods of the older company had been superseded, and their worship abolished, and the knowledge of their history and attributes was preserved only in the minds of priests and religious experts, who probably regarded the ancient views about these gods which had come down to them as the product of men belonging to a lower stage of civilization than their own. The older company of the gods here referred to have been described as personifications of aspects, or phases, or properties of primeval matter, and may be thus enumerated:—

| | |
|---|---|
| Nu, . | Nut, . |
| Ḥeḥu, . | Ḥeḥut, . |
| Kekui, . | Kekuit, . |
| Ḳerḥ, . | Ḳerḥet, . |

The character of the first pair of gods can be readily determined by the hieroglyphics which form their names; thus the name Nu, ,[1] is expressed by three vases of water which indicate the sound, and the outstretched heaven, , and the determinative for water, , and the sign for "god," all of which show that this deity was the god of the watery mass of the sky. The goddess Nut, , was merely his female counterpart, as the signs, , indicate. From various passages found in the religious, mythological, and funereal texts of all periods it is abundantly clear that in primeval times at least the Egyptians believed in the existence of a deep and boundless watery mass out of which had come into being the heavens, and the earth, and everything that is in them. The germs of all and every kind of life were in this watery mass, and they were supposed to have

[1] The old form is 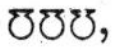, or  (Unȧs 199, 399), or  (Tetȧ 78).

been there from the beginning. They do not seem to have formulated any exact ideas about the position of this watery mass in the sky or heaven, and they certainly did not attempt to assign to it dimensions which could be expressed by the ordinary methods of measurements; in later times, however, Nu was frequently identified with the sky, *pet* , and with the heaven above it, *nut*, , though, strictly speaking, he represented the watery mass which was supposed to exist between the two. It must also be noted that the ocean and also the Nile [1] were identified with Nu, whose characteristics appear to have changed during the latter part of the dynastic period. The name of this god has been compared with the Coptic word **ⲛⲟⲩⲛ** "abyss," "deep," and the like, and it is possible that it may have some connection with it, but it is difficult to see how in that case it can mean "young," as the late Dr. Brugsch suggested.[2] The true meaning is much more likely to be suggested by the play on the words *Nu* and *nen* which we have on p. 309 in the passage, "I raised them up from out of the watery mass (*nu*) out of inactivity" (*nen*), i.e., Nu was the inert mass of watery matter from which the world was created. Of Nut, the female counterpart of Nu, little need be said here, except that she was regarded as the primeval mother, with whom in later dynastic times were identified several goddesses, e.g., Hathor, Mut, Nit, or Neith, and whose attributes were assigned to them. The forms in which Nu is depicted vary. Thus he is represented in human form holding a sceptre when he forms one of the company of the gods of Åmen, but he is also represented with the head of a frog, which is surmounted by a beetle,[3] and even with the head of a snake. The goddess Nut is also represented in human form, but sometimes she has the head of a uraeus, surmounted by a disk,[4] and at other times she has the head of a cat.[5]

[1] Compare Horapollo I. 21 (ed. Leemans; p. 28):—Νείλου δὲ ἀνάβασιν σημαίνοντες, ὃν καλοῦσιν Αἰγύπτιστι Νοῦν; attention was first drawn to this passage by Tattam.

[2] *Religion und Mythologie*, p. 129.

[3] Lanzone, *Dizionario*, pl. 167, No. 2.

[4] *Ibid.*, No. 3.

[5] *Ibid.*, pl. 170, No. 2.

The characteristics of the second pair of gods, Ḥeḥu, , and Ḥeḥut, , are not easy to determine. According to Signor Lanzone they are personifications of male and female elements of fire,[1] and from the ancient pictures of them we see that the Egyptian artists regarded them from different points of view. Thus in one group of the eight primeval gods Ḥeḥu is represented in one of the forms of Nu, i.e., frog-headed, already described, and Ḥeḥut in the form of Nut;[2] and in another group Ḥeḥu has the head of a serpent, and Ḥeḥut that of a cat. According to the late Dr. Brugsch[3] the name Ḥeḥ is connected with the word which indicates an undefined and unlimited number, i.e., *ḥeḥ*, ; when applied to time the idea suggested is "millions of years," and Ḥeḥ is equivalent to the Greek *αἰων*. In several passages quoted by Dr. Brugsch mention is made of a god Ḥeḥ, who seems to be a personification of the atmosphere which exists between heaven and earth, and to be identical with Shu, and that distinguished Egyptologist went so far as to compare his functions with those which were exercised by Aiôn, Eros, and Pneuma in Greek systems of philosophy. In a small scene reproduced by Signor Lanzone[4] we see the god Harpocrates in his usual attitude, , just above what appears to be a small tree. On the right kneels the goddess Ḥeḥut, who is making her outstretched hand and arm a support for the left hand of the young god which rests upon it; on the other side kneels Ḥeḥu, who is represented in the act of raising or supporting the feet of the god, above whose head are the beetle and disk.

The characteristics of the third pair of gods, KEKUI, , and KEKUIT, , are easier to determine, and it is tolerably certain that these deities represent the male and female powers of the darkness which was supposed to cover over the primeval abyss of water; they have been compared by Dr. Brugsch with the Erebos of the Greeks. In some aspects they appear to represent both the night and the day, that is to

[1] Lanzone, *Dizionario*, page 685.
[2] *Ibid.*, pl. 168 ff.
[3] *Religion*, p. 132.
[4] Op. cit., p. 685.

say, Kekui is called "the raiser up of the light," and Kekuit "the "raiser up of the night." It is not difficult to see how these deities obtained these names, for Kekui represents that period of the night which immediately precedes the day, and Kekuit is that period of the night which immediately follows the day. At one period Kekui and Kekuit were considered to be gods of Elephantine, and their attributes were identified with those of the Nubian god Khnemu and his female counterpart Sati; but this, no doubt, was a result of regarding Kekui and Kekuit as personifications of the Nile-god Ḥāpi, whose hidden fountains lay beneath the rocks at some part of the Island of Elephantine. According to another view the crocodile-god Sebek, one of whose chief seats of worship was at Kom Ombo, was a personification of the old primeval god Kekui, and in any case Sebek was certainly considered to be one of the principal forms in which the soul of the primeval darkness loved to array itself.[1] In the scenes in which the forms of the oldest *paut* or company of the gods are represented Kekui is usually given the head of a serpent, but Kekuit has the head either of a frog or a cat.[2] In one scene Kekui and Kekuit are identified with KA and KAIT, , 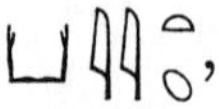, the former being called the "grandfather of all the gods," and the latter the "grandmother of the divine company," ; in this scene Ka or Kekui has the head of a frog surmounted by a beetle, and Kait or Kekuit the head of a serpent surmounted by a disk.

The characteristics of the fourth pair of gods, ḲERḤ, , and ḲERḤET, , are not easy to define, and the texts in some places give quite different names where we should expect to find theirs; thus we have Ni, , or Nenu, , or Nut, , or Åmen, 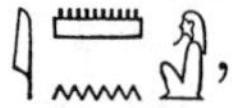, instead of Ḳerḥ, and Ennit, 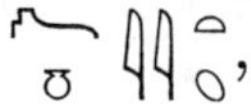, or Nenuit, , or Nut, , or Nit, , or 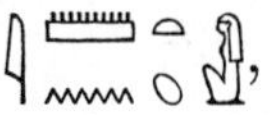, instead of Ḳerḥet. The common meaning of the word *ḳerḥ* is "night," and according

[1] Brugsch, *Religion*, p. 142. [2] Lanzone, op. cit., pl. 168 ff.

to this the deities Ḳerḥ and Ḳerḥet would represent the male and female powers of night; on the other hand, the determinative , which occurs in each name, shows that these gods were regarded as personifications of some apparently inactive powers of the primeval watery abyss, and we may, therefore, regard them as types of powers of nature in a state of repose either before or after a state of activity. In the scenes in which the forms of the oldest company of the gods are represented, Ni, that is to say, Ḳerḥ, has the head of a frog, with or without a beetle upon it, or the head of a snake, and Ennit, that is to say, Ḳerḥet, has either the head of a frog or that of a cat.

It is not easy to reconcile the various views which Egyptologists have held about the above four pairs of deities, and it certainly appears as if the ancient Egyptians themselves had no very clear ideas as to their functions. As to their antiquity there is no room for doubt, for although the oldest pictures of their forms do not date from a period anterior to the reign of Seti I., it is quite clear, from the way in which they are mentioned, that they represent traditional ideas of an extremely ancient character. One proof of this is the careful mention of the female counterparts of the four great primeval gods, for it was usual in the case of gods who were the product of the purely dynastic period to pay small attention to the goddesses who were regarded as their wives. Thus Rā and Ȧmen possessed female counterparts called Rāt, , and Ȧment, 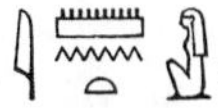, but they play no prominent parts in Egyptian mythology, and are rarely mentioned in the texts. Man always has fashioned, and probably always will, fashion his god, or gods, in his own image, and he has always, having reached a certain stage in development, given to his gods wives and offspring; but the nature of the position taken by the wives of the gods depends upon the nature of the position of women in the households of those who write the legends and traditions of the gods.

The gods of the oldest company in Egypt were, the writer believes, invented by people in whose households women held a high position, and among whom they possessed more power than is usually the case with Oriental peoples. Nut, Ḥeḥut, Kekuit, and

Ḳerḥet are the equals of the gods Nu, Ḥeḥ, Kekui, and Ḳerḥ, and not merely the bearers of offspring as were the later goddesses. The general drift of the texts wherein the four pairs of gods are mentioned indicates that three pairs were qualities, or characteristics, or attributes of the fourth pair personified, although some would make the four pairs represent the male and female elements of the Four Elements, Earth, Air, Fire, and Water, and others would make them stand for the primeval Matter out of which all things have been made, and primeval Space, and primeval Time, and primeval Power. To say definitely and exactly what they represent is in the present state of Egyptological knowledge impossible, for the evidence which would enable us to arrive at a final decision in the matter is not forthcoming.

Before we pass on to the consideration of the events which resulted in the creation of the sun and later of the world, it will be interesting to compare with the above four pairs of gods the group of gods that we meet with in the "Seven Tablets of Creation,"[1] which are written in cuneiform, and contain the views and beliefs of the Assyrians as to the origin of the gods, and of the world, and of mankind. The old company of primeval gods mentioned in these Tablets are also eight in number, and they fall readily into four pairs. The first pair consisted of APZÛ-RISHTÛ, , i.e., the "primeval abyss," and MÛMMU-TIAMAT, . The meaning of the word *mûmmu* is unknown,[2] but Tiamat is the name of the female counterpart of Apzû-rishtû, and she became the mother of offspring by him. These two deities, then, represent the male and female powers of the watery mass which contained the germs of all life, and of every kind of life, and they existed at a time "when of the "gods none had been called into being, and none bore a name, and "no destinies [were ordained]." When "their waters were

[1] The best copies of the cuneiform texts hitherto issued will be found in the publication of the Trustees of the British Museum, entitled *Cuneiform Texts from Babylonian Tablets*, part xiii., London, 1901. These, with many additional texts, are given in Mr. L. W. King's *Seven Tablets of Creation* with transliterations, translations, notes, etc., London, 1902. (Vol. I.)

[2] *Mûmmu* = the Μωϋμις of Damascus, and probably means "chaos."

"mingled together" then the work of creation began. We thus see that Apzû-rishtu and Mûmmu-Tiamat are the exact equivalents in the Babylonian cosmogony of Nu and Nut in the Egyptian, and that they are the originals of the Greek forms 'Απασὼν and Ταυθὲ, which are given in the scheme of Damascius.[1]

The next pair of gods in the Assyrian texts are LAKHMU, , and LAKHAMU, , but of their functions we know nothing, any more than we do of the Egyptian primeval gods Ḥeḥ and Ḥeḥut. The names of the third and fourth deities in the list of Damascius (ed. Kopp, p. 125) are Δαχός and Δαχή, but these are clearly mistakes for Λαχός and Λαχή, i.e., Lakhmu and Lakhamu.

According to the First Tablet of the Creation Series "ages increased,"[2] and then two more gods came into being, viz., ANSHAR, , and KISHAR, , i.e., the 'Ασσωρός and Κισσαρὴ of Damascius. Now up to this point the three pairs of gods of the Assyrians agree exactly with the first three pairs of gods of the oldest Egyptian company of the gods, and the points of resemblance are striking. We see from the table printed by Brugsch[3] that the Egyptian authorities differed as to the names of the god and goddess of the fourth pair of gods, some giving Ḳerḥ and Ḳerḥet, others giving Åmen and Åment, and others giving Enen and Enenet-ḥemset, and others Ni and Ennit; all, however, agreed that a fourth pair of deities were necessary to complete the company, and that one must be a god and the other a goddess.

The First Tablet of the Creation Series mentions a seventh deity called ANU, , who is clearly to be identified with the 'Ανός of Damascius, and an eighth deity called NUDIMMUD, , which is a title of the god EA; the context which would probably have supplied us with the name of a ninth god is broken away, and at present there is no means of restoring

[1] He was born in Syria, probably at Damascus, in the last quarter of the Vth century of our era. He studied at Alexandria and at Athens, and was a pupil of Marinus and Zenodotus, and when Justinian closed the schools at Athens he went to the court of the Persian king Khusrau (Chosroës). The best edition of his work on "First Principles" is that of Kopp, published in 1828.

[2] King, *Babylonian Religion*, p. 61.

[3] *Religion*, p. 127.

the passage. Both these deities are masculine, whereas one should be masculine and one feminine. In the list of the primeval gods given by Damascius following *Κισσαρὴ* we have *Ἀνός*, *'Ιλλινος*, and *'Αός*; the first of these is, as we have said, Anu; the second is the god Enlil, 𒀭𒂗𒆤; and the third is Ea, 𒀭𒂍𒀀. But all these are gods, and there is no goddess among them, and it is difficult not to think that in making the recension of the story which is preserved in cuneiform the Assyrian editors substituted the three gods Anu, Bel, and Ea, who represented heaven, and earth, and the abyss respectively, for those who were in the older recension. The Assyrian copy which we now have was made during the reign of Ashur-bani-pal, king of Assyria from B.C. 668 to B.C. 626, presumably from a Babylonian archetype, but it is impossible to say to what period the actual version which it represents is to be assigned. The Seven Tablets of Creation contain several Assyrianized forms of ancient Sumerian words, a fact which proves that the original traditions incorporated in the work must be of Sumerian origin, and must have been formulated in remote antiquity. It is surprising therefore to find so much similarity existing between the primeval gods of Sumer and those of Egypt, especially as the resemblance cannot be the result of borrowing. It is out of the question to assume that Ashur-bani-pal's editors borrowed the system from Egypt, or that the literary men of the time of Seti I. borrowed their ideas from the *literati* of Babylonia or Assyria, and we are therefore driven to the conclusion that both the Sumerians and the early Egyptians derived their primeval gods from some common but exceedingly ancient source. The similarity between the two companies of gods seems to be too close to be accidental, especially as there is every possibility that the Sumerian system was taken into Egypt by the same people who carried into the country the art of making bricks, the use of the cylinder seal, and the like.[1] Be this as it may, it is certain that the company of primeval gods, which, as we have seen, was common to the Sumerians and Egyptians, was quite different from the companies of gods of which Osiris and Rā-Tem were the heads in Egypt, and also from those which were formed

[1] See my *Egypt in the Predynastic and Archaic Periods*, p. 41.

in Babylonia and Assyria when these countries were inhabited by Semitic populations.

Now the First Tablet of Creation gives us to understand clearly that the work of creation began when the waters, or essences, of the first pair of primeval gods, Apzû and Tiamat, were mingled together, and that the offspring of this union were Lakhmu and Lakhamu, Anshar and Kishar, etc. What the views of the ancient Egyptians on this subject were we do not know, but it is quite clear from the allusions in many texts that the second, third, and fourth pairs of the gods already mentioned were the offspring of the union of the first pair Nu and Nut, i.e., that they were their attributes. We may also conclude that Nu and Nut were the male and female powers of the vast and inert watery mass, with its male and female counterparts Ni and Ennit, and that the second pair of gods, Ḥeḥ and Ḥeḥut, represented their eternal nature. The third pair of deities are nothing but the male and female counterparts of Darkness personified, and thus we have as the primeval material from which everything was made an eternal, boundless, watery mass wherein are the germs of life, male and female; this watery mass is, however, enveloped in thick darkness. The late Dr. Brugsch, basing his opinion upon certain statements made in the Egyptian texts, declared that the primeval spirit (Urgeist) felt the desire for creative activity, and that his word awoke the world to life in a form in which it had already been mirrored in his mind, and that the first act of creation began with the formation out of the primeval watery mass of an egg, wherefrom issued the light of day, i.e., Rā, which was the immediate cause of all life in the earthly world. In this light, that is to say, in the Rising Sun, the almighty power of the divine spirit incorporated itself in a brilliant form.[1]

[1] "Der göttliche Urgeist, unzertrennlich von dem Urstoff des Urwassers, "fühlte das Verlangen nach schöpferischer Thätigkeit und sein Wort erweckte die "Welt zum Leben, deren Gestalt und formenreiche Gebilde sich in seinem Auge "vorher abgespiegelt hatten. Ihre körperlichen Umrisse und Farben entsprachen "nach ihrer Entstehung der Wahrheit d.h. der Urvorstellungen des göttlichen "Geistes über sein künftiges Werk. Der erste Schöpfungsact begann mit der "Bildung eines Eies aus dem Urgewässer, aus dem das Tageslicht (Rā), die un-"mittelbare Ursache (rā) des Lebens in dem Bereiche der irdischen Welt heraus-"brach. In der aufgehenden Sonne verkörperte sich die Allmacht des göttlichen "Geistes in ihrer glanzvollsten Gestalt" (*Religion*, p. 101).

The opinion of the great Egyptologist is of great weight on all matters of this kind, but it must be remembered that we have no authority in the texts for all the details of his narrative of the events which are supposed to have taken place before the appearance of the sun in the heavens, and that for many of the ancient Egyptian views on the subject of the Creation our only authorities are compositions which, in the forms in which we know them, are not older than the period of the end of the Middle Empire and that of the beginning of the New Empire, and many of the views and opinions expressed in them date from the same periods. That the sun was the product of the primeval watery mass of Nu the Egyptians believed beyond doubt, because they declared repeatedly that Rā came forth from Nu, but they did not, as far as we know, make it to be the dwelling-place of a primeval spirit (Urgeist) which designed and planned the future world in its mind before it began to create it, and which carried out the various works of creation on the lines which it had evolved in its consciousness long before the darkness which lay on the watery mass was pierced by the light of the sun. We know that the priesthood of Hermopolis, the Khemennu of the Egyptian texts, i.e., the "city of the Eight Gods," where Nu, Nut, Ḥeḥu, Ḥeḥut, Kekui, Kekuit, Ḳerḥ, and Ḳerḥet were worshipped, placed at the head of their divine company the god Thoth, to whom certainly in later times were ascribed many of the attributes which Dr. Brugsch's "Urgeist" possessed. But there is no proof whatsoever that Thoth was the original leader of this company of gods; on the contrary, there is reason for thinking that if the Eight ever had a leader in the beginning of their existence he must have been a form of the Sun-god. The fact is that as the priests of Heliopolis formed their companies of gods from systems already in existence, and placed their own local gods at the head of them, so the priests of Hermopolis for some reason unknown to us adopted the primeval company of Eight, and appointed their own local god Thoth to be their head. The attempt to find any equivalent of the "spirit of Elohîm," which, according to the Book of Genesis, moved, or brooded, on the face of the waters before the creation of light, has nothing to support it in the Egyptian texts.

But although we do not know what the primitive Egyptians imagined to be the means by which the Sun came into being, we have a very good idea of what they thought about the creation of the gods, and of the world, and of the animals, birds, trees, fish, reptiles, etc., which are in it, and by whose agency it was brought about. We owe our knowledge of these things to a papyrus preserved in the British Museum (No. 10,188), which was written for a priest of Panopolis (the modern Akhmîm), of high rank and lineage, called Nes-Åmsu, or Nes-Min, during the thirteenth year of the reign of "Alexander, the son of Alexander," i.e., about B.C. 312. This remarkable document contains, among other valuable compositions, a series of Chapters of a long magical work which was written with the object of effecting the destruction of the arch-fiend Āpepi and his fiends and devils of darkness, and of keeping storms and hurricanes out of the sky; many of the Chapters are followed by rubrics which, as we have already shown in the description of the Ṭuat given above, contain directions for the performance of the ceremonies which were to accompany the recital of the words. Where the Chapters were to be recited is not clear, but as two out of three works in the papyrus were chanted in the temple of Amen-Rā, the king of the gods, at Thebes, we shall not be far wrong if we assume that the third was a service which was performed in the temple from time to time. The first work, the "Festival Songs of Isis and Nephthys," was a very important service, and the second, the "Lamentations of Isis," was probably a supplement to it; two priestesses, who dressed in the characters of Isis and Nephthys, and personified these goddesses, sang the sections, or "houses," of the Festival Songs in turn on the great commemorative festivals of Osiris, and as the "Lamentations" were rhythmical they were probably sung at the same service.

The rubric of the "Festival Songs" orders that they be sung in the temple of Åmen-Rā, and as the third work, the "Book of Overthrowing Āpepi," was devoted to the protection of the Sun-god Rā, the great lord of the temple, provision must have been made for reciting it there. Be this as it may, our present interest in the papyrus centres in the fact that it contains two copies of the story[1] of the Creation which are of the greatest interest. Curiously enough, each copy is inserted among the Chapters in the main body of the work, and it seems as if they represent two distinct versions, although in many places the text in each is identical. Each copy is entitled, "The Book of knowing the Evolutions of Rā, and of Overthrowing Āpepi." The word here rendered by "Evolutions" is *kheperu*, , being derived from the root *kheper*, , which means "to make, to fashion, "to produce, to form, to become," and in a derived sense "to roll," so that the title might be translated the "Book of knowing the "Becomings of Rā," i.e., the things which were made, or created, or came into being through Rā. In the text the words are placed in the mouth of the god Neb-er-tcher, , the lord of the universe and a form of the Sun-god Rā, who says, "I am he who "came into being in the form of the god Kheperȧ, , "and I was the creator of that which came into being, that is to "say, I was the creator of everything which came into being; now "when I had come into being myself, the things which I created "and which came forth from out of my mouth were very many." In these words Neb-er-tcher, or Rā, says that he took upon himself the form of Kheperȧ, i.e., that he was the god who was most intimately connected with the creation of things of every kind. Kheperȧ was symbolized by a beetle which belonged to the class of "Coprophagi," or "dung-eaters," which having laid its eggs in masses of dung rolled them about until they became circular in form. These balls, though made of dead, inert matter, contained the germs of life, which, under the influence of warmth and heat, grew, and in due course developed into living creatures which could move about and seek their food. At a very early period in their history the Egyptians associated the sun's disk with the dung ball of the beetle, partly on account of its shape, and partly because it was the source of heat, and light, and life to man, even as the dung ball was to the young beetles. Having once got the idea that the disk of the sun was like the ball of the beetle, they went a step farther, and imagined that it must be pushed across the sky

[1] The first copy is in column xxvi. and the second in column xxviii.

by a gigantic beetle just as the dung ball was rolled over the ground by a beetle on earth, and in pictures of the sunrise we actually see the disk being pushed up or forward into the sky by a beetle. Gradually the ideas of new life, resurrection, life in a new form, and the like, became attached to the beetle, and the god with the attributes of the beetle, among which in later days was included the idea of self-production, became one of the most important of the forms of Rā, and the creator of heaven, and earth, and the Ṭuat and all that is in them.

Having declared under what form he had come into being Kheperȧ goes on to say that his power was not exhausted by one creative act, but that he continued to create new things out of those which he had already made, and he says that they went forth from his mouth. The word "mouth" may be here a figurative expression, but judging from other parts of the text we are probably intended to understand it literally. The god continues his narrative thus:—"Heaven did not exist, and earth had not "come into being, and the things of the earth (plants?) and "creeping things had not come into existence in that place (or, at "that time), and I raised (or, built up) them from out of Nu from "a state of inactivity." Thus it is clear that Kheperȧ himself was the one thing besides the watery abyss of Nu which was then in existence, and it is evident that we are to understand that he performed the various acts of creation without the help of any female principle, and that Nu had nothing to do with them except to supply the primeval matter, the "Urstoff" of Brugsch, from which all things were made. The word rendered above by inactivity is *enen*, , and it ought to refer to the things which Kheperȧ says he raised up out of Nu, in which case we must understand that everything in heaven and in earth was at that time existing in a quiescent state in the watery mass of Nu.

The narrative continues: "I found no place there whereon I "could stand. I worked a charm upon my own heart (or, will), "[and] I laid a foundation in Maā, [and] I made every form (or, "attribute). I was one by myself, [for] I had not emitted from "myself the god Shu, and I had not spit out from myself the goddess

"Tefnut; there was no other being who worked with me." The things made clear by this passage are that Kheperȧ alone was the creator, and that he had no place to stand upon in performing the various acts of creation. The words, *Khut-nȧ em ȧb-ȧ*, here rendered "I worked a charm upon my heart," present difficulty, but this or something very like must be their meaning.

The word  in texts of the kind generally means "to "perform a magical rite or ceremony," and the author of the story of the creation before us found himself obliged to make the god resort to magical powers to get himself out of a difficulty; that Kheperȧ worked in some way and by some means upon his heart or will is clear, and as a result he laid a foundation for himself and the work which he was about to do in Maā. The name  may be read either as Maā or Shu, but Shu cannot be the reading here because in the next sentence Kheperȧ tells us that he had not at that time emitted Shu from himself. From the texts of all periods we learn much about the conceptions which the Egyptians had arrived at concerning Maā, and it is clear that the word primarily meant "what is straight," and that it also came to mean "straightness, rectitude, uprightness, right, law, order, "regularity, justice," and other significations of like character; the goddess Maāt, , was the personification of "Truth." The idea which the text is intended to convey here is that Kheperȧ laid the foundation of the future world according to a clear, well-defined, and unalterable plan, wherein there was no error; *Maā* was with Kheperȧ exactly what Ḥᴏᴋʜᴍâʜ, חָכְמָה (a word somewhat inadequately rendered "wisdom" in Proverbs viii. 2 ff.), was to Yahweh. Wisdom says that she was set up from everlasting, from the beginning, or ever the earth was, when there were no depths, before the mountains were settled, and before the hills was she brought forth when as yet Yahweh had made neither the earth, nor the fields, nor the highest part of the dust of the earth, and that she was there when he prepared the heavens and placed a circle upon the face of the depth (Proverbs viii. 23 ff.).

The narrative continues: "I made a foundation in (or, by) "my own heart, and there came into being multitudes of things, "of things from the things of what was produced from the things "which they produced." This sentence is both involved and redundant, but about its meaning there is fortunately no difficulty, for the writer only makes the god assert in an emphatic manner that everything that is came into being as a result of the act of the god in laying a foundation in his own heart, and that when once the creative processes had been set in motion they continued their operation of their own accord, apparently without any direct interference from the original creative power. In the next sentence we have a reference to a curious belief which was already current in the VIth Dynasty, but at that period it had reference to the god Tem and not to Kheperȧ, and occurs with the following context:—"This Pepi washeth himself in the Lake of Ȧaru wherein "Rā washeth himself; Horus hath brought the back of this Pepi, "and Thoth hath brought his legs, and Shu hath lifted him up "to heaven; O Nut, stretch out thy hand to Pepi. Tem hath "departed to Ȧnnu to satisfy his love of pleasure; he hath thrust "his member into his hand, and hath performed his desire, and "hath produced the two children Shu and Tefnut,[1] and these two "children put Pepi between them, and they set him among the "gods which are in Sekhet-ḥetepet." In the story of the creation Kheperȧ is made to say, "I had union with my hand, and I "embraced my shadow in a love embrace; I poured seed into my "own mouth, and I sent forth from myself issue in the form of "the gods Shu and Tefnut." Now a myth of this character can only be the product of a people at a low level of civilization, and it is difficult to understand the character of the mind of an author who in one sentence helps Kheperȧ out of a difficulty by ascribing to him the possession and use of magical powers, and in another reduces him to the necessity of committing an act of masturbation in order to begin the generations of the gods, and yet assigns to

[1]  Pepi I., l. 465 ff.

him at the same time many of the powers which are assigned by Christian nations to God. The only possible way of accounting for this gross passage is to assume either that it was copied into the papyrus of Nesi-Åmsu, or Nesi-Min, by the scribe simply because he found it in the archetype from which he was working, or that the author, knowing that Shu and Tefnut were held to be the children of Kheperȧ, and that this god was unaccompanied by any female counterpart, explained the origin of his children in the manner described above. But in any case this brutal example of naturalism was not intended to be obscene, and it must be regarded as a survival in literature of the dynastic period of one of the coarse habits of the predynastic Egyptians, that is to say, of one of the indigenous African tribes from which dynastic Egyptians were partly descended.

The next section of the narrative is difficult to translate and explain, for it contains words which Kheperȧ puts into the mouth of his "father" Nu, who says that his eye, i.e., the Sun, was covered up behind Shu and Tefnut, but that after *ḥenti* periods, , had passed[1] that he had become three gods instead of one, and after he had come into being in this earth, Shu and Tefnut were raised up from out of the watery mass wherein they were, and they brought his eye in their train. The general meaning of these words seems to be that when Kheperȧ was existing in Nu by himself the sun, in which he afterwards incorporated himself, was hidden in the watery deep; but as soon as Kheperȧ had produced Shu and Tefnut the sun emerged from the deep and followed in their train. In other words, we learn that the Eye, , of Nu was unable to make itself seen until after Shu and Tefnut had come into being. We need not tarry to consider all the various attributes of these twin gods, and it will be sufficient to say here that Shu represents the daylight and, in some cases, the atmosphere which supports the heavens and keeps them above the earth, whilst Tefnut, the female

[1] The *ḥen* period = 60 years, but when two such periods are referred to the writer does not mean necessarily 120 years, but some long, indefinite period of time.

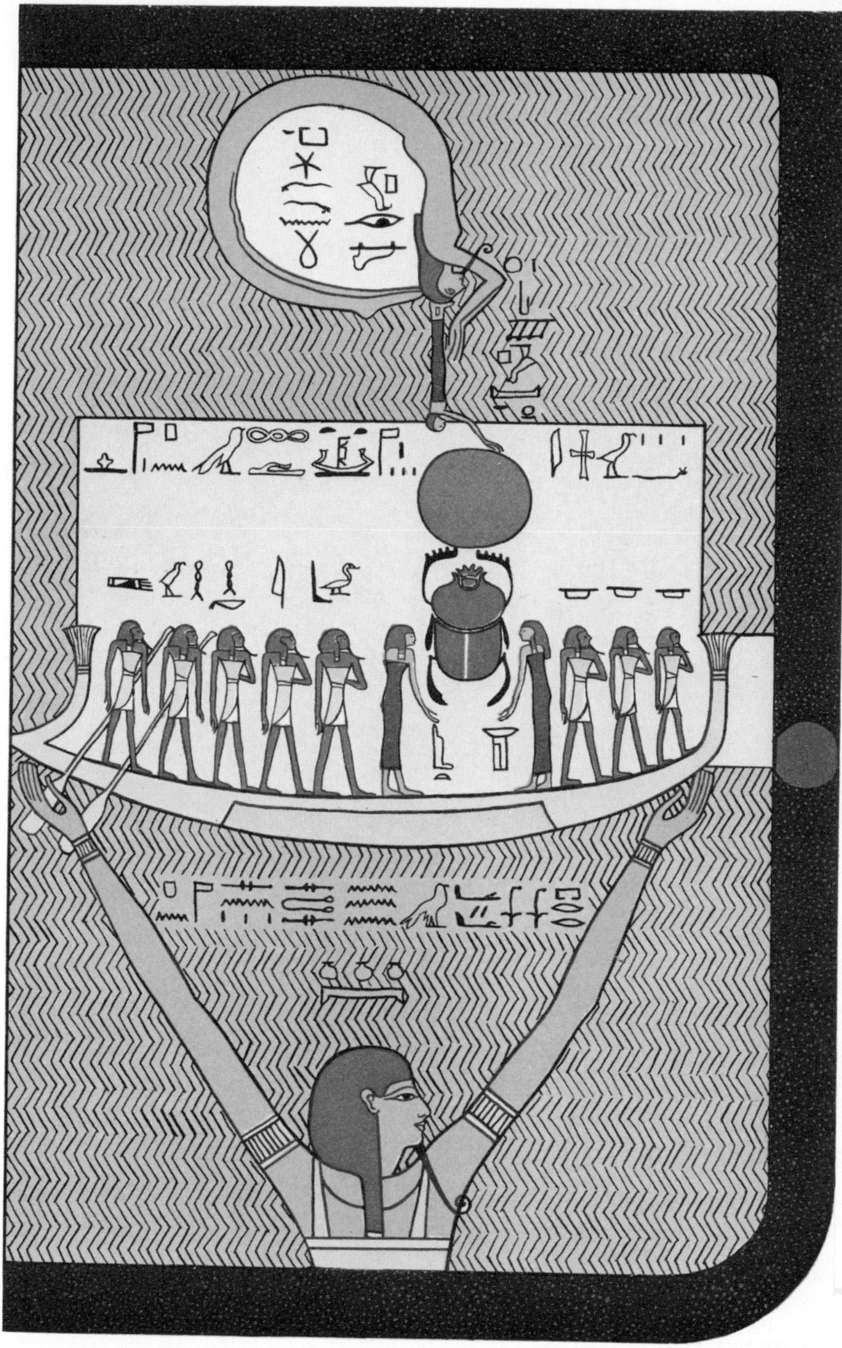

THE CREATION

counterpart of Shu, represents rain, dew, and moisture. We have already seen that these twin gods proceeded from Kheperȧ, and the words which are used to express the idea of emission, i.e., *ȧshesh* 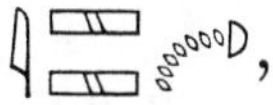, and *tef* , indicate the processes by which they came into being as separate entities. The creation of Shu made a space between the heavens and the earth into which the Eye of Nu could rise from out of the waters and shine, and because the sunlight immediately followed the creation of Shu that god is sometimes identified with light, and is regarded as its personification. The general sense of the passage under discussion makes it necessary to assume that Nu is identified with Kheperȧ, and *vice versâ*.

The next passage refers to the creation of man, and the god, presumably Kheperȧ, says, "Now after these things, I united my "members, and I wept over them, and men and women came into "being from the tears which came forth from my eye." Of this passage there are two interpretations possible. We may either assume that the tears which fell from the Eye of Nu, or Kheperȧ, are the rays of light which fell from the sun, and that men and women are the offspring of the light, or what is far more probable, that men and women are the product of the tears of water which fell from the eye of the god upon his members,[1] and that they turned into human beings straightway. Meanwhile the god Nu or Kheperȧ had made another Eye, by which we are, no doubt, to understand the Moon, and it is said that when the first Eye found that a second had been made it raged at the god; now when the god saw this he endowed the second Eye with some of the power (or, splendour) which he had made, and having made it take up its position in his face it henceforth ruled the whole earth. After this the god brought about the creation of plants, and herbs, and reptiles, and creeping things. Finally, the gods Shu and Tefnut produced the gods and goddesses Seb and Nut, Osiris and Isis, Set and Nephthys, and Ḥeru-khent-ȧn-maati, i.e., the "Blind Horus," one after the other at one birth, and these deities multiplied

1 

offspring in this earth. Thus we have a complete account of how a male god who existed alone in the watery abyss of Nu produced from himself by unnatural means a pair of deities, one male and one female, and how this pair produced three other pairs, i.e., three gods and three goddesses, and one male deity in addition, in fact the *paut* or company of the great gods of Heliopolis, which in this instance was made to include ten gods. It is interesting to note the order in which the acts of creation took place. The self-existent god who had lived for ever created: 1. The light. 2. The firmament, or home of moisture, i.e., clouds and rain. 3. Mankind. 4. The second (?) Eye, i.e., the Moon (?). 5. Plants, and herbs, and reptiles, and creeping things. 6. Seven deities, four being male and three female.

In the second version of the story of creation which we shall now describe some interesting variants will be found, and we shall see that the god Osiris is made to usurp the position which in the first version is occupied by the god Kheperà. The opening words are:—Neb-er-tcher saith, "I am the creator of what hath come "into being, and I myself came into being under the form of the "god Kheperà, and I came into being in primeval time. I came "into being in the form of Kheperà, and I was the creator of what "came into being, that is to say, I formed myself out of the "primeval matter, and I formed myself in the primeval matter. "My name is ÀUSÀRES,  (i.e., Osiris), [who] is the "primeval matter of primeval matter. I have done all my will in "this earth, I have spread abroad therein, and I have made strong "(or, lifted up) my hand." In this passage we have Neb-er-tcher, who came into being in the form of Kheperà, identifying himself with Osiris, who is described as the *pautet pautti*,  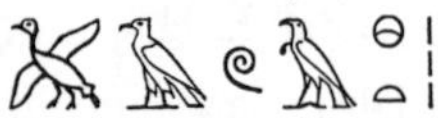, i.e., the very essence of primeval matter, and the source of all created things. This is a remarkable attribute to ascribe to the god of the dead, and it is only understandable when we remember that it was a common belief of the Egyptians that life rose out of death. The narrative continues, "I was alone, for "they (i.e., the gods) were not born, and I had emitted from "myself neither Shu nor Tefnut. I brought my name into my "own mouth, that is to say [I uttered it as] a word of power, " *ḥekau*, and I forthwith came into being under "the form of things which were created and under the form of "Kheperȧ."

Here we have an interesting statement, for the god tells us how he came into being, and he is not content with merely saying that he existed. We know from the literature of Egypt how great a part words of power played in its magical and religious systems, and how the believer hoped to obtain all his desires by the utterance of special names, or words, or formulæ. Here, however, we have the god Osiris transforming himself from the essence of primeval matter into the active principle of creation by merely uttering his own name. The belief in the potency of certain names is very old in Egypt, and rests upon a still older idea that no creature, animate or inanimate, could be said to have an existence until it possessed a name, an idea with which every one is familiar from Genesis ii. 19 f., where we read that Adam gave names to every beast of the field and to every fowl of the air, and to all cattle. Every god and goddess and supernatural being were believed to possess a hidden name by, and through, and in which he and she lived. The man who could find out these names was able to command the help of the gods who bore them, and the man who could obtain by any means a hidden name for himself thought he would be the equal of the gods. On the other hand, to destroy or "blot out" a name was to wipe out of existence the being who bore it, and it was for this reason that in the earliest days of civilization in Egypt services in which the name, or names, of the dead were commemorated, and were mentioned with laudatory epithets, were established. We may note in passing that one of the greatest gifts which was to be given to the true believers of the Church of Pergamos was "a white stone, and in "the stone a new name written, which no man knoweth saving he "that receiveth it" (Revelation ii. 17). Here is a direct allusion to the old belief in the efficacy of an amulet which was made of a certain stone, and inscribed with a name, by and through and in which its owner would enjoy life and happiness.

Returning to our narrative we find that the god continues, "I came into being from primeval matter, and I appeared under "the form of multitudes of things from the beginning. Nothing "existed at that time, and it was I who made whatsoever was "made. I was alone, and there was no other being who worked "with me in that place. I made all the forms under which I "appeared by means (or, out of) the god-soul which I raised up "out of Nu, 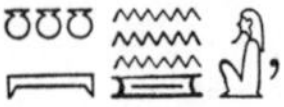, out of a state of inertness (or, out of the "inert mass)." In this passage we have a new element introduced, that is, a "god-Soul," , or, in other words, the Soul which possessed the quality of *neter*, and was existent in a quiescent state in the inactive watery mass of Nu. When we consider the general ideas of the Egyptians about the soul this statement need not surprise us, for we know that they endowed every object in nature with a soul, and if they assumed the existence of a mass of primeval matter they were bound, logically, to give it a soul. Thus we have in the second version of the story of the creation an idea which is wholly wanting in the first. We next read, "I "found there (i.e., in Nu) no place wherein I could stand. I "worked a spell on my heart, and I laid a foundation before me, "and I made whatsoever was made. I was alone. I laid a "foundation in (or, by) my heart, and I made the other things "which came into being, and the things of Kheperȧ which were "made were manifold, and their offspring came into existence "from the things to which they gave birth. It was I who emitted "Shu, and it was I who emitted Tefnut, and from being one god "(or, the one god) I became three, that is to say, the two other "gods who came into being on this earth came from myself, and "Shu and Tefnut were raised up from out of Nu wherein they had "been. Now, behold, my Eye,  (i.e., the Sun), did they "bring to me (or, I brought to them) after a double *ḥen* period "[had passed since] they went forth from me. I gathered "together my members which came forth from my own person "after I had union with my hand, and my heart (or will) came "unto me from out of my hand. The seed fell into my mouth, "and I sent forth from myself the gods Shu and Tefnut, and from "being one god (or, the one god) I became three, that is to say, "the two other gods who came into being, 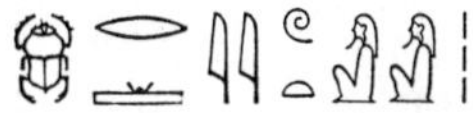, "on this earth came from myself, and Shu and Tefnut were raised "up from out of Nu wherein they had been."

The repetitions in the above passage are due to the fact that the scribes possessed many variant readings of portions of it, these representing, no doubt, the opinions of different schools, and the scribe of the papyrus of Nes-Åmsu, with characteristic reverence for what was written, incorporated them all into his text.

The next passage contains a very interesting addition and variant reading, which makes "father" Nu declare that his Eye, i.e., the sun, was covered over with large numbers of "bushes" for an indefinite number of periods, each containing sixty years; now "bushes," otherwise called "hair," is the name given to the clouds which hang round the sun at sunrise, and obscure his rays, and it seems as if the god intends to complain that his sight was impeded by them for centuries. The words following seem to indicate that vegetation and reptiles, including worms or serpents, proceeded from the god Rem, and that they were the product of the tears which fell from Kheperå, but this rendering is not wholly certain. The vegetation and worms here mentioned are forms of mist and cloud which wholly or partially hide the sun, and the line is probably added to the text to account for the "bushes" of which "father" Nu spoke above. Of the god Rem, , we know nothing, but as the word *rem* means "to weep," and an allusion to "crying or weeping," , is contained in the line in which the name of the god occurs, we may assume that he was the personification of Rā's tears. Mention is made in the *Book of the Dead* (lxxxiii. 4) of a god called Remi, , who seems to have been the Fish-god, and to have been identified in some way with Sebek, the personification of Nu, but it is not clear that Rem and Remi are one and the same god.

We next arrive at the description of the making of man, and each version of the story of the creation gives a different account. According to the first, Kheperå joined, or united, his members and wept upon them, and men and women came into being from these tears; according to the second, Kheperȧ wept with his Eye, and men and women came into being forthwith. It is impossible to say decidedly which is the older view, but it is probably the former. The difference between the methods employed in creating gods and men must be noted; the gods are the seed of Kheperȧ, and they came forth from his mouth, whilst men are only the tears of the god, and they came forth from his Eye. The older version makes the tears of Kheperȧ to fall upon his genital organs, and it is only after they have been in contact with the god's virility that they turn into human beings. In late dynastic times the Egyptians divided mankind into four classes, namely, the Egyptians, the Āamu, the Neḥesu, and the Themeḥu. Thus in the Book of Pylons[1] Horus says to the "chiefs of Rā," , who are in the Ṭuat of the Black Land and the Red Land (i.e., Egypt and the deserts to the South), "Ye are the tears made by my Eye in your name of 'Men.'"[2] The Āamu, , (i.e., the Semitic nomad tribes of the Eastern Desert), were created by Horus and Sekhet, , and this goddess protected their souls; the Themeḥu, or Libyans, , were also created by Horus and Sekhet, and the goddess protected their souls. Of the Neḥesu,  (i.e., the Negroes), Horus says, "I "masturbated for you, and I have been content at the millions "who have come forth from me in your name of Neḥesu; Horus "hath created you, and it is he who hath protected their souls."[3] This last statement is of interest, for it connects the idea of masturbation with the Negroes, that is to say, with the dark or black-skinned races of Nubia who lived on the banks of the Nile

1 See Bonomi and Sharpe, *Sarcophagus of Oimenepthah*, pll. 7 and 6D.

2 
.

3 
 (lines 16-20).

so far south as the Sixth Cataract, and, as we have already said, the legend as to the origin of the gods Shu and Tefnut is far more likely to have been the product of some indigenous dark-skinned race than of the group of mixed peoples whom we call Egyptians. It will be noticed that only the Egyptians, or offspring of Rā, are said to have been produced by the tears of Rā, which are the same as the tears of the Eye of Horus, i.e., the sun.

According to one version of the story of the creation, men and women were created *after* the gods Shu and Tefnut, and *before* the plants and reptiles, but according to the other, they were created *after* the plants and reptiles; neither version mentions the creation of beasts and cattle. A point of interest is that men and women were not fashioned by Kheperȧ, or Neb-er-tcher, himself, and that they seem to have come into being almost, as it were, by accident; in making the gods Kheperȧ showed both will and design, but men and women were only the tears which fell, apparently without volition, from his Eye. But it must also be noted that in both versions of the Egyptian creation legends it is Rā the Sun-god, the Eye of Temu, who is in reality the creator of man, and this is exactly what we find in the Mesopotamian creation legends. After Marduk had defeated Tiamat and her eleven fiends, and had split up her body, like a fish, and made heaven out of one half of her skin, he conversed with Ea, the lord of the great deep, and declared his intention of making man, in the following words:—"My blood will I take, and bone will I build up, and I will make "man, that man may . . . .; and I will build up man who "shall inhabit [the earth]." This very important passage proves that the statement of Berosus to the effect that man was made out of the blood of Bel, i.e., Marduk, was based upon a genuine Assyrian tradition; unfortunately the cuneiform text,[1] which was

[1] The tablet is No. 92,629 (obv. ll. 5-7). The text reads:—

 *da-mi lu-uk-ṣur-ma iṣ-ṣi-im-tum lu-*[*ub-ni*] *lu-ush-ziz-maa amêla*[*a*] *lu a-me-lu* [. . . .] *lu-ub-ni-ma amêla*[*a*] *a-shib irṣitim.* See L. W. King, *The Seven Tablets of Creation*, vol. i., pp. 86 ff., and vol. ii., pl. xxxv.

first identified by Mr. L. W. King, is incomplete, but when the inevitable duplicate is found we shall probably find the equivalent of the rest of the story according to Berosus, who says that the blood of which man was made was obtained from Bel himself after his head had been cut off.

The passage which follows the mention of the creation of man in the Egyptian story refers to the Eye of Nu, which, Kheperȧ says, he endowed with power or splendour, or with the serpent *khut*, 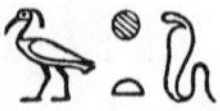, which possessed both these attributes. The Eye raged at him when it found "another growth" in its place, by which, apparently, the moon is referred to, and it made an onslaught upon the "bushes," i.e., the light clouds, which Kheperȧ had placed over it to adorn it, or to keep order in it; but finally it took up its position in the god's face, and henceforth ruled the whole earth. The text concludes with the statement that Shu and Tefnut gave birth to Seb, Nut, Osiris, Ḥeru-khenti-ȧn-maati, Set, Isis, and Nephthys, and that their offspring increase and multiply in the earth, and that they invoke the name of Kheperȧ and so overthrow their enemies, and that they create words of power, , whereby they overthrow Āpepi. We may now summarize briefly the results of the two versions, and we shall find that the Egyptians thought that a self-begotten and self-existent god lived alone in a primeval watery mass, which was itself part male and part female, and which was the abode of two living powers, the one male and the other female, and also of a soul, and that this mass was of unlimited extent, and was eternal, and was enveloped in thick darkness. The self-existent god, at some unknown time and for some unknown reason, uttered his own name as a word of power, and he straightway came into being under the form of the god Kheperȧ. He next roused the soul of the watery abyss out of inactivity, and then having brought some influence, probably by the utterance of certain words, to bear upon his heart, he produced some material place, probably the earth, whereon he could stand. From this place he produced the gods Shu and Tefnut, which act resulted in the immediate creation of light and in the dispersion of darkness, and in the formation of the sky or firmament. These acts were followed either by the creation of men and women, or by the creation of vegetation and creeping things and reptiles of every kind; of the creation of stars and of birds and beasts nothing is said. The above statement represents one of the earliest of the opinions of the Egyptians about the creation in its simplest form, the one in fact which was first adopted by the priests of Heliopolis, and was then modified to suit the theological system which they formulated. The texts on which it was based are transcribed into hieroglyphics with interlinear transliterations and translations in the following chapter.

CHAPTER VIII

## THE HISTORY OF THE CREATION OF THE GODS AND OF THE WORLD. VERSION A.

xxvi. 21.

| | | | | | |
|---|---|---|---|---|---|
| *Shāt* | *enti* | *rekh* | *kheperu* | *nu* | *Rā* |
| The Book | of | knowing | the evolutions | of | Rā, |

| | | | | |
|---|---|---|---|---|
| *sekher* | *Āpep* | *tcheṭtu* | *Neb-er-tcher* | *tcheṭ - f* |
| [and] of over-throwing | Āpep. | The words of | Neb-er-tcher | [which] he spake |

| | | | | |
|---|---|---|---|---|
| *em-khet* | *kheper - f* | *nuk* | *pu* | *kheper* |
| after | he had come into being. | I am | he who | came into being |

| | | | | |
|---|---|---|---|---|
| *em* *Kheperȧ* | | *kheper-nȧ* | *kheper* | 22. *kheperu* |
| in the form of Kheperȧ, | | I was (or, became) | the creator | of what came into being, |

| | | | | | |
|---|---|---|---|---|---|
| *kheper* | *kheperu* | *neb* | *em-khet* | *kheper-ȧ* | *āsht* |
| the creator | of what came into being | all; | after | my coming into being | many |

*kheperu* — *em per* — *em* — *re-ȧ* — *ȧn*

[were] the things which came into being — coming forth — from — my mouth. — Not

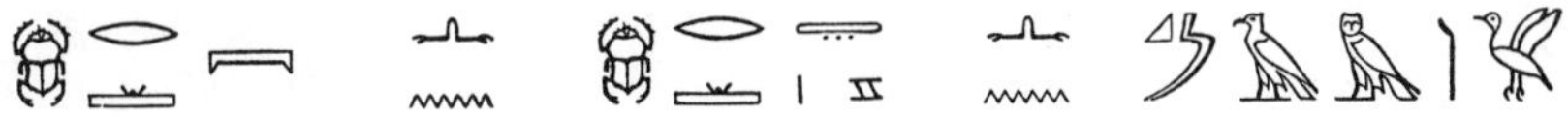

*kheper pet* — *ȧn* — *kheper ta* — *ȧn* — *qemam*

existed heaven, — not — existed earth, — not — had been created

*satat* — *tchetfet* — *em* — *bet* — *pui*

the things of the earth, (i.e., plants) — and creeping things — in place — that;

*thes - nȧ* — *ȧm - sen* — *em* — 23. *Nu*

I raised up them — from out of — Nu (i.e., the primeval abyss of water)

*em* — *enen* — *ȧn* — *qem-nȧ* — *bet* — *āḥā-nȧ*

from a state of inactivity. — Not — found I — a place — I could stand

*ȧmi* — *khut-nȧ* — *em* — *ȧbt-ȧ*

wherein. — I worked a charm — upon (or, with) — my heart.

*senti-nȧ* — *em* — *Maā* — *ȧri-nȧ* — *ȧru* — *nebt*

I laid a foundation — in — Maā — [and] I made — attribute — every.

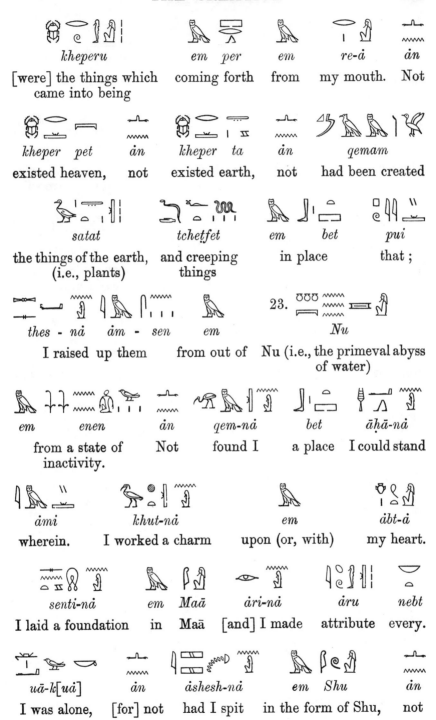

*uā-k[uȧ]* — *ȧn* — *ȧshesh-nȧ* — *em* — *Shu* — *ȧn*

I was alone, — [for] not — had I spit — in the form of Shu, — not

| *tef-nà* | *em Tefnut* | *àn* | *kheper* | *ki* |
|---|---|---|---|---|
| had I emitted | Tefnut,[1] | not | existed | another |

24. 

| *àri-nef* | *ḥenā-à* | *senti-nà* | *em* | *àbt-à* | *tches-à* |
|---|---|---|---|---|---|
| who worked | with me. | I made a foundation | in my | heart | my own, (or, by means of my own will) |

| *kheper* | *āsht* | *kheperu* | *nu* | *kheperu* |
|---|---|---|---|---|
| [and] there came into being | the multitudes of things | which came into being | of the things which came into being | |

| *em* | *kheperu* | *nu* | *mesu* | *em* |
|---|---|---|---|---|
| from out of | the things which came into being | of | births, | from out of |

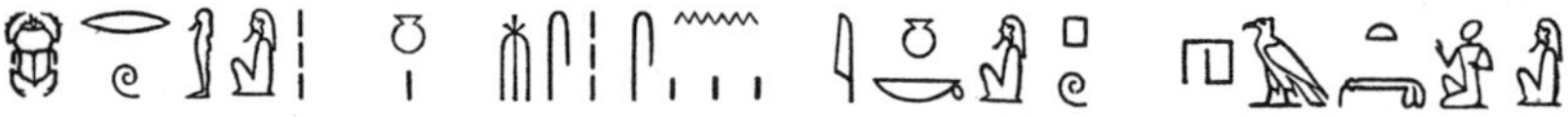

| *kheperu* | *nu* | *mesu-sen* | *ànuk pu* | *hat-à* |
|---|---|---|---|---|
| the things which came into being | of | their births. | I, even I, | had union |

 Col. xxvii. 1. 

| *em* | *khefā-à* | *tataàt-nà* | *em* |
|---|---|---|---|
| with | my clenched hand, | I joined myself in an embrace | with |

| *khaibit-à* | *kher-nà* | *em re-à* | *tches-à* |
|---|---|---|---|
| my shadow, | I poured seed | into my mouth | my own, |

[1] I.e., I had not sent forth from my body the emanation which took the form of Shu, nor the moisture which took the form of Tefnut.

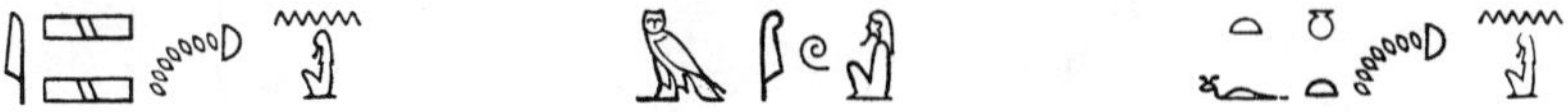

*àshesh-nà* · *em Shu* · *tefnet-nà*

I sent forth issue in the form of Shu, I sent forth moisture

*em Ṭafnut* · *àn* · *àtef-à* · *Nu* · *satet-sen*

in the form of Tefnut. Saith my father Nu, "They make to be weak

*maat-à* · *em-sa-sen* · *tcher* · *ḥenḥenti* · *uau-sen*

my eye behind them, because for double *ḥenti* periods they proceeded

*er-à* · *em-khet* · *kheper-à* · *em* · *neter* · 2. *uā* · *neter* · *khemt*

from me after I became from god one gods three,

*pu* · *er-à* · *kheper-nà* · *em* · *ta* · *pen* · *ḥāā*

that is from out of myself, [and after] I came into being in earth this. Were raised up

*àref* · *Shu* · *Ṭāfnut* · *em* · *enenu*

therefore Shu [and] Tefnut in the inert watery mass

*un-sen* · *àmi - f* · *àn-sen* · *nà* · *maat-à*

wherein they were, brought they to me my eye

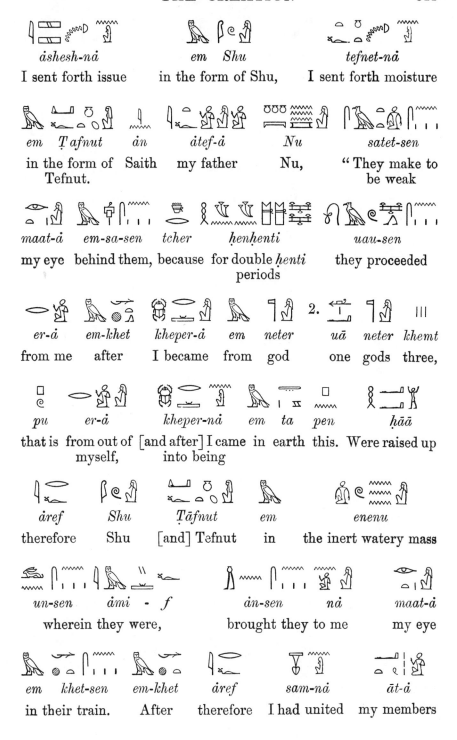

*em* · *khet-sen* · *em-khet* · *àref* · *sam-nà* · *āt-à*

in their train. After therefore I had united my members

*rem-nȧ* *ḥer-sen* *kheper* 3. *reth* *pu em*

I wept over them, [and] came into being men and women from

*remu* *per* *em* *maat-ȧ* *khāru-s*

the tears [which] came forth from my eye, [and] it raged

*er-ȧ* *em khet* *i-s* *qemi-s* *ȧri-nȧ* *ket*

against me after it came [and] found [that] I had made another

*em* *ȧst-s* *ṭebi-s* *em* *khut* *ȧru-nȧ*

in its place. [I] endowed it with the power (or, splendour) which I had made.

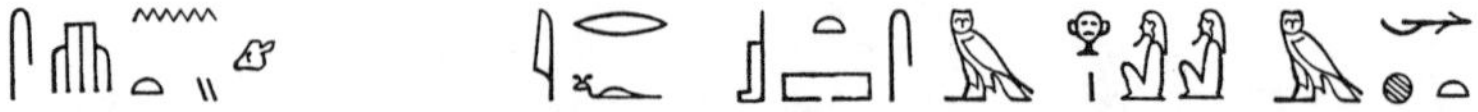

*sekhenti* *ȧref* *ȧst-s* *em* *ḥrȧ-ȧ* *em-khet*

Having made to approach therefore its place in my face, afterwards

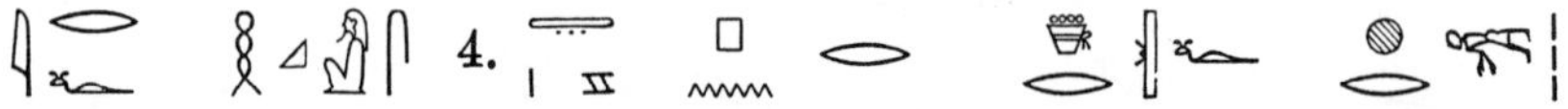

*ȧref* *ḥeq-s* 4. *ta* *pen* *er* *tcher-f* *kher*

therefore it ruleth earth this to its whole extent. Fall

*en at-sen* *ȧu uabu-sen* *ṭebui-nȧ*

their moments (or, seasons) upon their plants, I endowed it

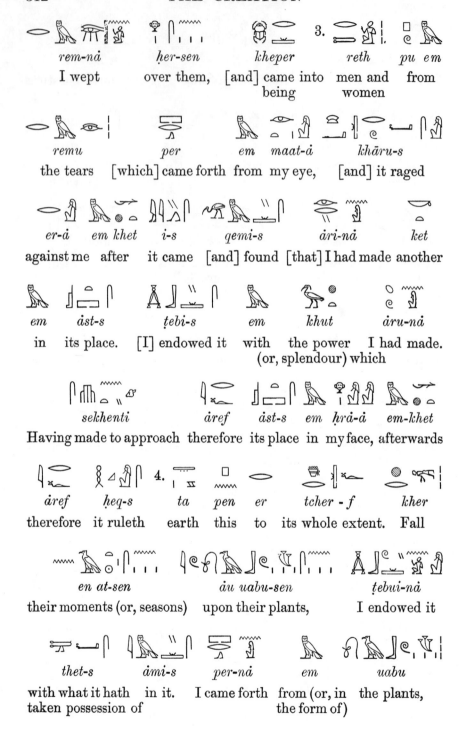

*thet-s* *ȧmi-s* *per-nȧ* *em* *uabu*

with what it hath taken possession of in it. I came forth from (or, in the form of) the plants,

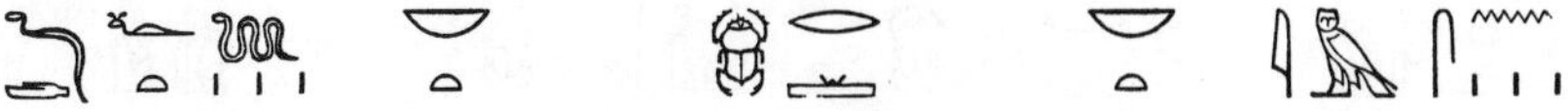

*tchetfet* · *nebt* · *kheper* · *nebt* · *åm-sen*

creeping things all, [and] things which came into being all [are] in them.

 5. 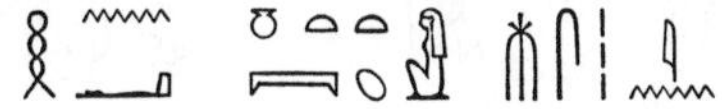

*mesu ån* · *Shu Tāfnut* · *ḥenā* · *Nut* · *mesu ån*

Give birth Shu [and] Tefnut [Seb] and Nut. Give birth

*Seb Nut* · *Åsår* · *Ḥer Khent-ån-maa* · *Set* · *Åst*

Seb and Nut to Osiris, Horus-Khent-ån-maati, Set, Isis,

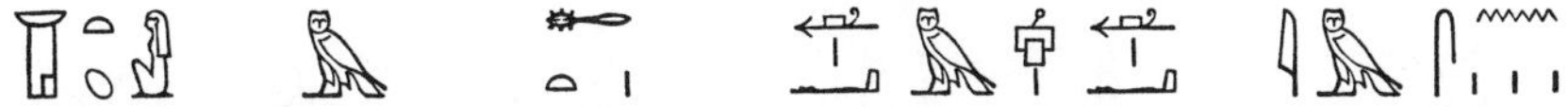

*Nebt-ḥet* · *em* · *khat* · *uā* · *em-sa* · *uā* · *åm-sen*

Nephthys from the womb, one after the other of them,

*mes-sen* · *āsht-sen* · *em* · *ta* · *pen*

they give birth [and] they multiply in earth this.

## THE HISTORY OF THE CREATION OF THE GODS AND OF THE WORLD. VERSION B.

xxviii. 20. 

*Shāt* · *ent* · *rekh* · *kheperu* · *nu* · *Rā*

The Book of knowing the evolutions of Rā

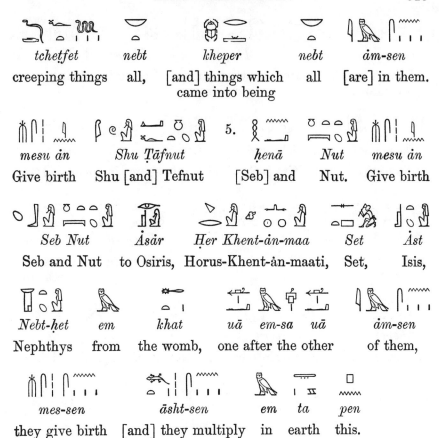

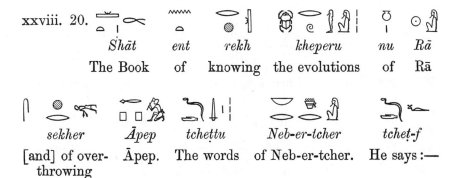

*sekher* · *Āpep* · *tchettu* · *Neb-er-tcher* · *tchet-f*

[and] of overthrowing Āpep. The words of Neb-er-tcher. He says:—

*kheper-ȧ* *kheper* *kheperu* *kheperu-k[u]ȧ* *em*

"I was (or, became) the creator of what came into being. I came into being in

*kheperu* *en* *Kheperȧ* *kheper* *em* *sep ṭepi*

the forms of Kheperȧ coming into being in primeval time.

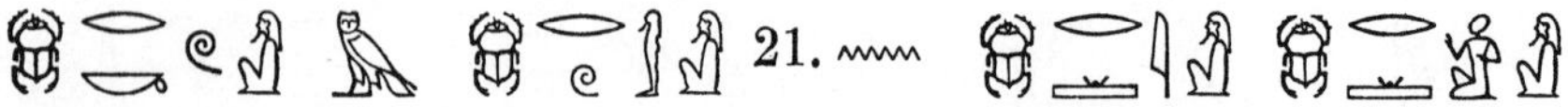

*kheper-kuȧ* *em* *kheperu* 21. *en* *Kheperȧ* *kheper-ȧ*

I came into being in the forms of Kheperȧ. I was (or, became)

*kheper* *kheperu* *pu en* *pa-nȧ*

the creator of what came into being, that is to say, I produced myself

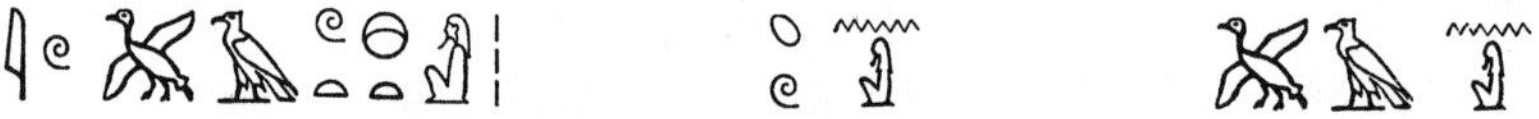

*ȧu* *pautet* *ȧru-nȧ* *pa-nȧ*

from the primeval matter [which] I made. I produced myself

*em* *pautet* *pa* *ren-ȧ* *Ȧusȧres*

from primeval matter. My name is Osiris,

*pautet* *pautit* 22. *ȧri-ȧ* *mertu-ȧ* *nebt*

the primeval matter of primeval matter. I have done my will all

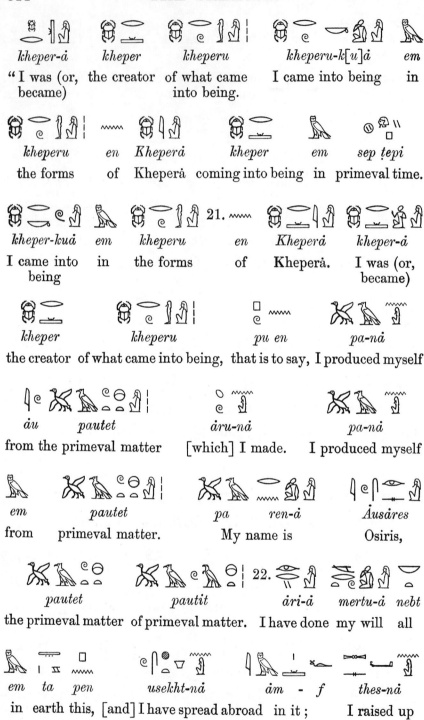

*em* *ta* *pen* *usekht-nȧ* *ȧm - f* *thes-nȧ*

in earth this, [and] I have spread abroad in it; I raised up

*ṭet-ȧ* *uāu-kuȧ* *ȧn* *mes-sen* *ȧn*

my hand. I was alone; not born [were] they. Not

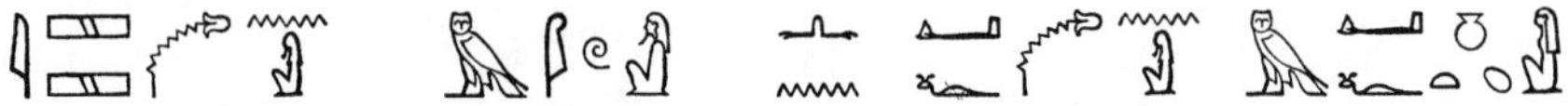

*ȧshesh-nȧ* *em Shu* *ȧn* *ṭāf-nȧ* *em Ṭāfnut*

had I spit in the form of Shu, not had I emitted Tefnut

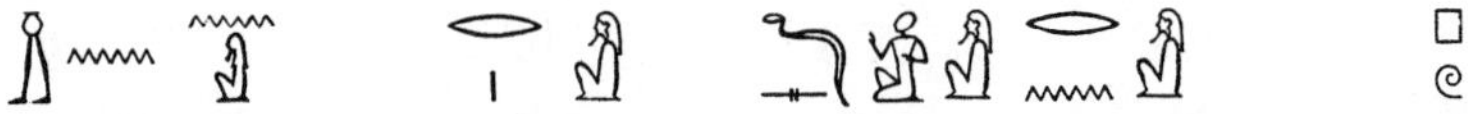

*ȧn-nȧ* *re-ȧ* *tches-ȧ* *ren-ȧ* *pu*

I brought [into] my mouth my own my name, that is to say,

*ḥekau* *ȧnuk pu kheper - nȧ* *em*

a word of power, and I, even I, came into being in the form

*kheperu* *kheper-kuȧ* *em* *kheperu* *en* *Kheperȧ*

of things which came into being, and I came into being in the forms of Kheperȧ.

*kheper-nȧ* *em* *pautti* *kheper*

I came into being from the primeval matter, coming into being

*āsht* *kheperu* *em* *ṭep-ā* *ȧn* *kheper*

[in] multitudes of forms from the beginning. Not existed

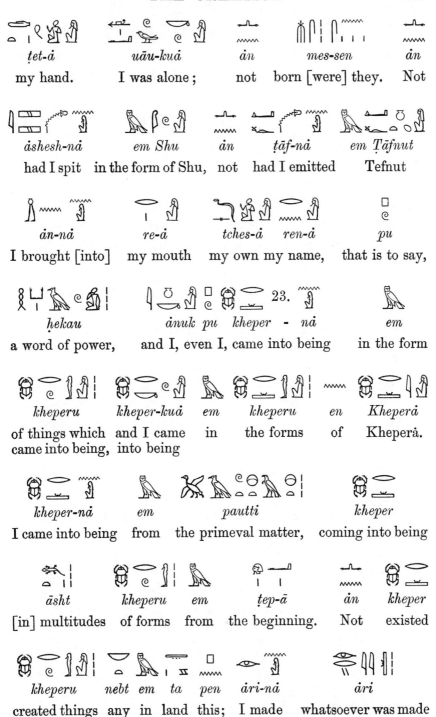

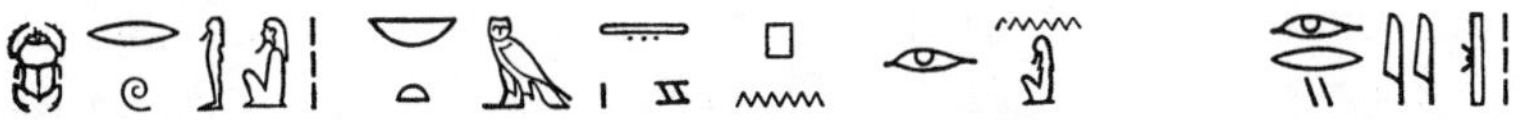

*kheperu* *nebt* *em* *ta* *pen* *ȧri-nȧ* *ȧri*

created things any in land this; I made whatsoever was made

*nebt* *uāu-k[uȧ]* *ȧn* *kheper* 24. *ki* *en* *ȧru-nef*

everything. I was alone, not existed [any other] who worked

*ḥenā-ȧ* *em* *bet* *pui* *ȧri-ȧ* *kheperu-ȧ*

with me in place that; I made what I made

*ȧmi* *em* *ba* *pui* *thes-nȧ*

therein by means of divine soul that [which] I raised up

*ȧmi* *em* *Nu* *em* *enen* *ȧn*

therein out of Nu (i.e., the primeval abyss of water) from a state of inertness, not

*qemi-nȧ* *bet* *āḥā-nȧ* *ȧmi* *khut-nȧ*

found I a place whereon I could stand. I worked with the spirit [which] was

*em* *ȧb-ȧ* *senti* - 25. *nȧ* *em ḥrȧ-ȧ* *ȧri-nȧ* *ȧri*

in my heart, I laid a foundation before me, I made whatsoever was made

*nebt* *uāu-k[uȧ]* *senti-nȧ* *em* *ȧb-ȧ* *qemam-nȧ*

all. I was alone, I laid a foundation in my heart, I made

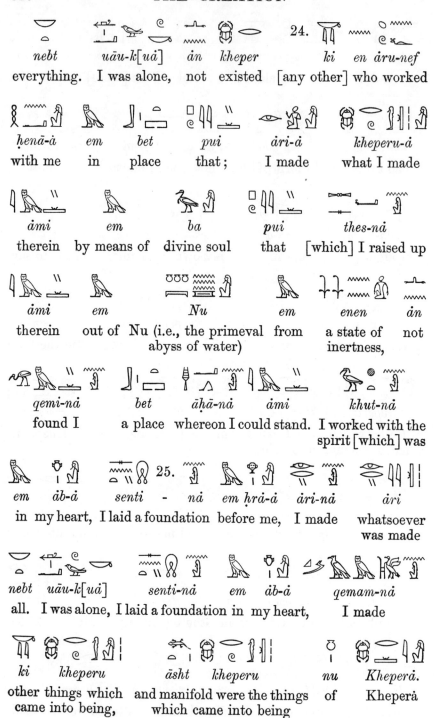

*ki* *kheperu* *āsht* *kheperu* *nu* *Kheperȧ.*

other things which came into being, and manifold were the things which came into being of Kheperȧ

*kheper* *ȧn* *mesu-sen* *em* *kheperu* *nu* *mesu-sen*

Came into being what they gave birth to out of the creations of their offspring.

26. 

*ȧnuk pu* *ȧshesh-nȧ* *em Shu* *ṭāf-nȧ*

I, even I, spat in the form of Shu, [and] I emitted

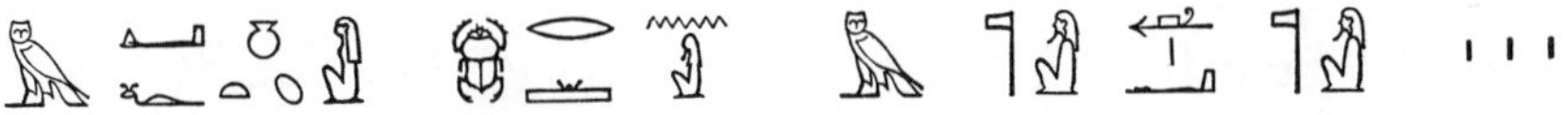

*em Ṭāfnut* *kheper-nȧ* *em* *neter* *uā* *neter* *khemt*

Tefnut, [and] I became from god one gods three,

*pu* *er-ȧ* *kheperiut* *em* *ta* *pen*

that is to say, from myself two gods came into being on earth this.

*ḥāā* *ȧref* *Shu* *Ṭāfnut* *em* *Nu*

Were raised up therefore Shu and Tefnut in Nu (i.e., the primeval watery abyss)

 27. 

*unen-sen ȧmi* *ȧn* *maat-ȧ* *ȧn-nȧ* *sen*

wherein they were. Behold, my eye brought to me they

*em-khet* *ḥenti* *uau-sen* *er-ȧ*

in the train of a ḥenti period, they proceeded from me.

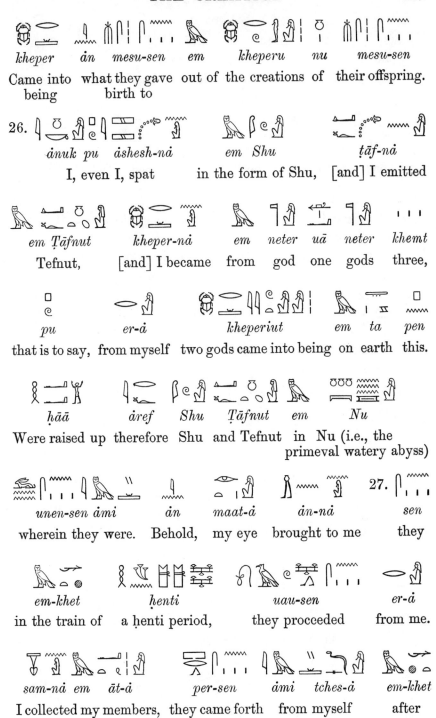

*sam-nȧ em* *āt-ȧ* *per-sen* *ȧmi* *tches-ȧ* *em-khet*

I collected my members, they came forth from myself after

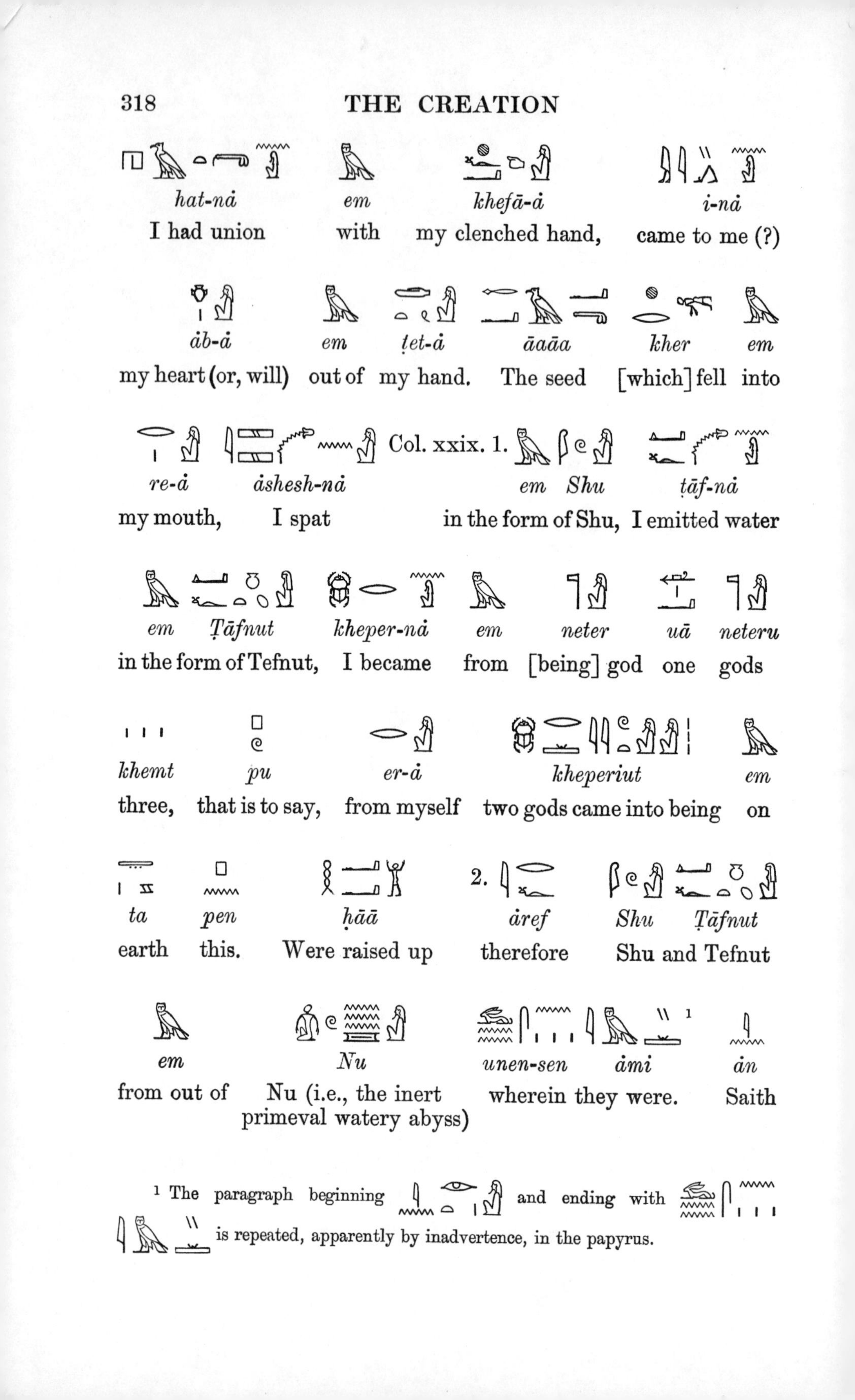

| | | | |
|---|---|---|---|
| *hat-nȧ* | *em* | *khefā-ȧ* | *i-nȧ* |
| I had union | with | my clenched hand, | came to me (?) |

| | | | | | |
|---|---|---|---|---|---|
| *ȧb-ȧ* | *em* | *ṭet-ȧ* | *āaāa* | *kher* | *em* |
| my heart (or, will) | out of | my hand. | The seed | [which] fell | into |

| | | | | |
|---|---|---|---|---|
| *re-ȧ* | *ȧshesh-nȧ* | Col. xxix. 1. | *em Shu* | *ṭāf-nȧ* |
| my mouth, | I spat | | in the form of Shu, | I emitted water |

| | | | | | |
|---|---|---|---|---|---|
| *em* *Ṭāfnut* | *kheper-nȧ* | *em* | *neter* | *uā* | *neteru* |
| in the form of Tefnut, | I became | from | [being] god | one | gods |

| | | | | |
|---|---|---|---|---|
| *khemt* | *pu* | *er-ȧ* | *kheperiut* | *em* |
| three, | that is to say, | from myself | two gods came into being | on |

| | | | | | |
|---|---|---|---|---|---|
| *ta* | *pen* | *ḥāā* | 2. *ȧref* | *Shu* | *Ṭāfnut* |
| earth | this. | Were raised up | therefore | Shu and Tefnut | |

| | | | | |
|---|---|---|---|---|
| *em* | *Nu* | *unen-sen* | *ȧmi*[1] | *ȧn* |
| from out of | Nu (i.e., the inert primeval watery abyss) | wherein they were. | | Saith |

[1] The paragraph beginning and ending with is repeated, apparently by inadvertence, in the papyrus.

3.

*ȧtef-ȧ* *Nu* *ati-sen* *maat-ȧ* *em-sa* *sen*

my father Nu, "They covered up [or, made weak] my eye after them

*uabu* *sep sen* *ḥentiu* *uabu*

[with] bushes, twice, for ḥen periods. Vegetation

*ḥefi* *em* *Rem* *em* *rem-th*

and reptiles [came] from the god Rem, from the tears

*er-ȧ* *ka* *en* *maat-ȧ* *kheper* *ret*

[falling] from me. Cried my eye, came into being mankind.

4.

*pu* *ṭebu-nȧ* *su* *em* *khut* *khāru-nes* *er-ȧ*

I endowed it with power. It raged at me

*em-khet* *i-s* *ket* *reṭ* *em khennu en ȧst-s*

after it came [finding] another growth within its place.

*kher* *en* *ṭen-ṭen-s* *ȧu* *uabu-s* *ḥer*

Fell its vigorous power upon its bushes, upon

5.

*uabu* *ṭebui-nȧ* *ȧm* *se-nāā* *ȧm-s*

the bushes [which] I placed there to make adornment in it.

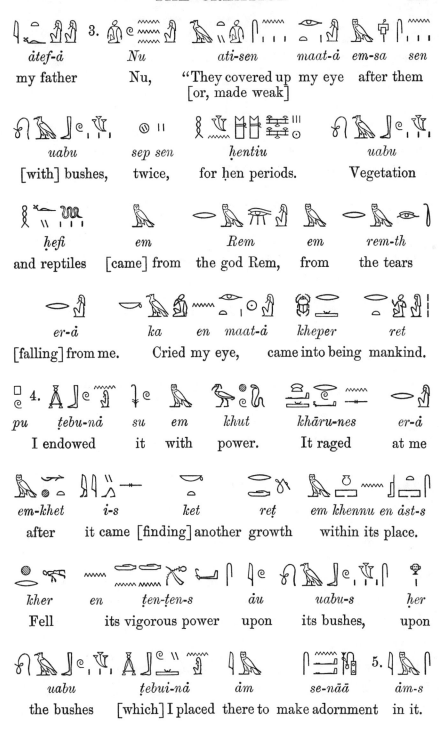

*khenti áref ást-s ḥrá-á ḥeq-nes ta tcher-f*

Ruling therefore [on] its seat in my face it ruleth the whole earth.

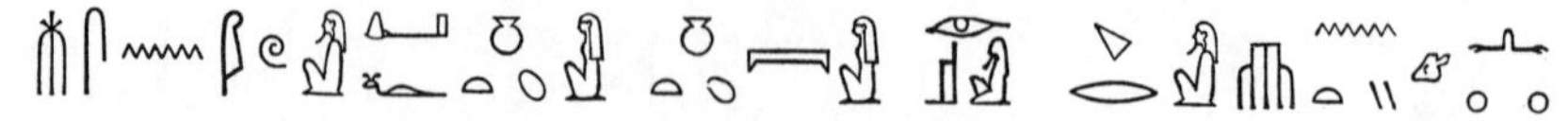

*mes en Shu Ṭāfnut Nut Ásár Ḥeru-khenti-án-maati*

Gave birth Shu [and] Tefnut to Nut, Osiris, Ḥeru-khenti-án-maati,

*Set Ást Nebt-ḥet án mesu-sen*

Set, Isis, Nephthys, [and] behold, their children

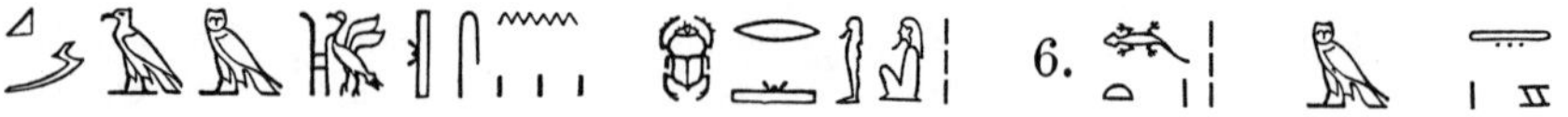

*qemam-sen kheperu* 6. *āsht em ta*

they create beings manifold in earth

*pen em kheperu nu mesu em kheperu nu*

this from the beings of children, from the beings of

*mesu-sen shent-sen ren-á sekher-sen*

their children. They invoke my name, they overthrow

*kheft-sen qemam-sen ḥekau en*

their enemies, they create words of power for

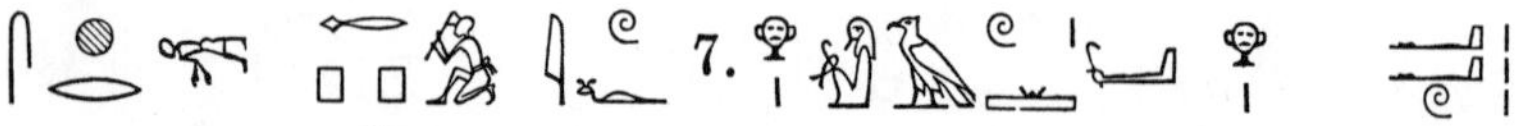

*sekher Āpep áu-f* 7. *ḥer sau ḥer āāui*

the overthrow of Āpep, who is to be bound by the two hands

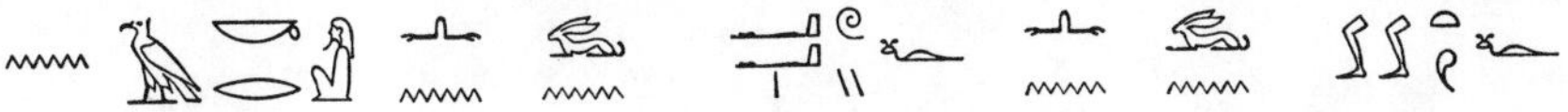

*en Aker àn un āāui - f àn un reṭui - f*

of Aker, not may be his two hands, not may be his two feet,

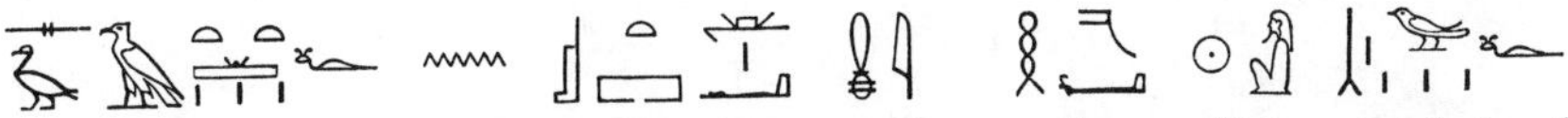

*satet - f en àst uā mà ḥu Rā setchebu-f*

may he be chained to one place even as inflicteth Rā his blows

*utu-nef àu sekher-tuf ḥer sati-f pui ṭu*

decreed for him. He is overthrown on his back wicked,

8. 

*senpu ḥrà-f ḥer àri-nef meni su*

slit is his face for what he hath done, and he remaineth

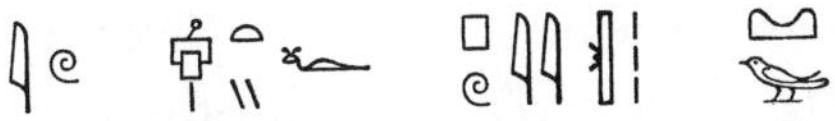

*àu sati - f pui ṭu*

upon his back evil.

## CHAPTER IX

# RĀ, THE SUN-GOD, , AND HIS FORMS

RĀ is the name which was given by the Egyptians of the dynastic period to the god of the sun, who was regarded as the maker and creator of everything which we see in the visible world around us, and of the gods in heaven, as well as of heaven itself, and of the Ṭuat or underworld and the beings therein; the original meaning of his name is unknown, but at one period of Egyptian history it seems to have been thought that the word *rā* indicated "operative and creative power," and that as a proper name it represented in meaning something like "Creator," this epithet being used much in the same way and with the same idea as we use the term when applied to God Almighty, the Creator of heaven and earth and of all things therein. The worship of the sun in Egypt is extremely ancient and appears to have been universal; at a very early period adoration of him was associated with that of the hawk-god Ḥeru, who was the personification of the "height" of heaven, and who appears to have been a type and symbol of the sun. The worship of the hawk-god Ḥeru, , is the oldest in Egypt, and, strictly speaking, he should have been discussed before Rā, but as Rā and the personifications of his various forms are the greatest of the gods of the Egyptians, he must be regarded as the true "father of the gods," and his attributes, and the myths which grew up round him must be considered before those of Horus. The god Rā is usually depicted with the body of a man and the head of a hawk, but sometimes he is represented in the form of a hawk; on his head he wears his symbol, , i.e., the disk of the sun encircled by the serpent *khut*, , of which mention has already been made. When he has a human body he holds the emblem of life, , in his right hand, and a sceptre, , in his left, and from the belt of his tunic hangs down the tail, which is a survival of the dress of men in predynastic times, and probably later. Viewed from a practical point of view Rā was the oldest of all the gods of Egypt, and the first act of creation was the appearance of his disk above the waters of the world-ocean; with his first rising time began, but no attempt was ever made to say when, i.e., how long ago, his first rising took place. When the Egyptians said that a certain thing had been in existence "since the time of Rā"[1] it was equivalent to saying that it had existed for ever.

The Egyptians, knowing that the sun was a fire, found a difficulty in assuming that it rose directly into the sky from out of the watery mass wherein it was brought forth, and they, therefore, assumed that it must make its journey over the waters in a boat, or boats, and as a matter of fact they believed that it passed over the first half of its course in one boat, and over the second half in another. The morning boat of the sun was called Māṭet, , i.e., "becoming strong," and the name of the evening boat was Semktet, , i.e., "becoming weak"; these are appropriate names for the rising and the setting sun.[2] The course which Rā followed in his journey across the sky was thought to have been defined at creation by the goddess called Maāt, who was the personification of the conceptions of rectitude, straightness, law, order, unfailing regularity, and the like, and there is no doubt that it was the regular and unfailing appearance of the sun each morning, as much as its light and heat, which struck wonder into primitive man, and made him worship the sun. In passing through the Ṭuat, or underworld, at night Rā was supposed to be obliged to leave his boat at certain places, and to make use of others, including even one which was formed by the body of a serpent; according to one opinion he changed his

[1] .

[2] See Unȧs, l. 292.

boat every hour during the day and night, but the oldest belief of all assigned to him two boats only. Rā was accompanied on his journey by a number of gods, whose duties consisted in navigating the boat, and in helping it to make a successful passage from the eastern part of the sky to the place where the god entered the Ṭuat; the course was set by Thoth and his female counterpart Maāt, and these stood one on each side of Horus, who acted as the steersman and apparently as captain also. Before the boat of Rā, one on each side, swam the two pilot fishes called Ȧbṭu, , and Ȧnt, , respectively.[1] But, judging from the religious and mythological texts which have come down to us, not all the power of Rā himself, nor that of the gods who were with him, could ward off the attacks of certain fiends and monsters which endeavoured to obstruct the passage of his boat.

Chief among such were the serpent Āpep, , and Sebȧu, , and Nȧk, , and of these the greatest and most wicked was Āpep. In dynastic times Āpep was a personification of the darkness of the darkest hour of the night, against which Rā must not only fight, but fight successfully before he could rise in the east in the morning; but originally he was the thick darkness which enveloped the watery abyss of Nu, and which formed such a serious obstacle to the sun when he was making his way out of the inert mass from which he proceeded to rise the first time. In the *Book of the Dead* he is frequently mentioned,[2] but rather from a moral than a physical point of view. Thus in the xxxixth Chapter the deceased says: "Get thee back, "Fiend, before the darts of his beams. Rā hath overthrown "thy words, the gods have turned thy face backwards, the Lynx "(Mafṭet, ), hath torn open thy breast, the "Scorpion goddess, , hath cast fetters upon thee, and "Maāt hath sent forth thy destruction. Those who are in the "ways have overthrown thee; fall down and depart, O Āpep,

[1] *Book of the Dead.* (*Papyrus of Ani*, pl. 1, line 15.)

[2] See the *Vocabulary* to my *Chapters of Coming Forth by Day*, under Āpep (p. 61).

"thou Enemy of Rā." A little further on the deceased says: "I "have brought fetters to thee, O Rā, and Āpep hath fallen because "thou hast drawn them tight. The gods of the South, and of the "North, of the West and of the East have fastened chains upon "him, and they have fastened him with fetters; the god "Rekes (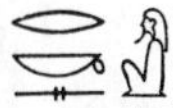) hath overthrown him, and the god Ḥertit "(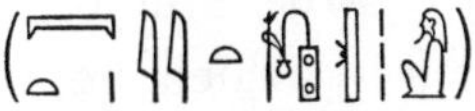) hath put him in chains. O Āpep, thou "Enemy of Rā, thou shalt never partake of the delights of love, "thou shalt never fulfil thy desire! He maketh thee to go back, "O thou who art hateful to Rā; he looketh upon thee, get thee "back. He pierceth thy head, he slitteth up thy face, he divideth "thy head where its bones join and it is crushed in thy land, thy "bones are smashed in pieces, thy members are hacked off thee, "and the god Aker () hath passed sentence of doom "upon thee."

From the "Books of Overthrowing Āpep,"[1] we obtain further information as to the destruction of the monster, and we find that this work was recited daily in the temple of Åmen-Rā at Thebes. The first Book was divided into Chapters, which were entitled:—1. Chapter of spitting upon Āpep. 2. Chapter of defiling Āpep with the left foot. 3. Chapter of taking a lance to smite Āpep. 4. Chapter of fettering Āpep. 5. Chapter of taking a knife to smite Āpep. 6. Chapter of putting fire upon Āpep. The following Books describe with great minuteness the details of the destruction which was to fall upon Āpep, and they are insisted on to a wearisome degree; according to these the monster, which is referred to at one time as a crocodile and at another as a serpent, is first to be speared, then gashed with knives, and every bone of his body having been separated by red-hot knives, and his head, and legs, and tail, etc., having been cut off, his remains were to be scorched, and singed, and roasted, and finally shrivelled up and consumed by fire. The same fate was to come upon Āpep's confederates, and everything which formed parts of him and of them, i.e., their shadows, souls, doubles, and spirits, were to be

[1] See *Archaeologia*, vol. lii. (*The Papyrus of Nesi-Åmsu*).

wiped out of existence, including any offspring which they might possess. Not content with reciting the words of power which would have the effect of destroying Āpep and his fiends, great care was taken to perform various ceremonies of a magical character, which were supposed to benefit not only Rā, but those who worshipped him on earth. Āpep was both crafty and evil-doing, and like Rā, he possessed many names; to destroy him it was necessary to curse him by each and every name by which he was known. To make quite sure that this should be done effectively the Papyrus of Nesi-Åmsu adds a list of such names, and as they are the foundation of many of the magical names met with in later papyri they are here enumerated:—1. NESHṬ. 2. ṬUṬU. 3. ḤAU-ḤRÅ. 4. HEMHEMTI. 5. QEṬṬU. 6. QERNERU. 7. IUBANI. 8. ĀMAM. 9. ḤEM-TAIU. 10. SÅAṬET-TA. 11. KHERMUTI. 12. KENEMEMTI. 13. SHETA. 14. SEREM-TAUI. 15. SEKHEM-ḤRÅ. 16. UNTI. 17. KARÅU-ÅNEMEMTI. 18. KHESEF-ḤRÅ. 19. SEBA-ENT-SEBA. 20. KHAK-ÅB. 21. KHAN-RU . . . . UĀA. 22. NĀI. 23. ĀM. 24. TURRUPA (?) 25. IUBAU. 26. UAI. 27. KHARUBU, THE FOUR TIMES WICKED. 28. SAU. 29. BEṬESHU.[1]

In the Egyptian texts we have at present no account of the

1 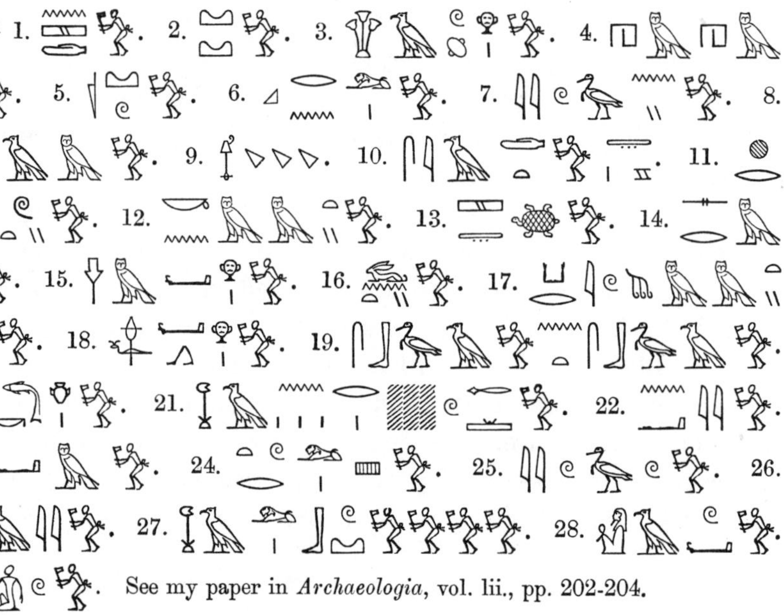

See my paper in *Archaeologia*, vol. lii., pp. 202-204.

first fight which took place between Rā and Āpep, but it is clear from several passages in the "Books of Overthrowing Āpep" that such a thing must have occurred, and that the means employed by the Sun-god for destroying his foe resembled those made use of by Marduk in slaying Tiamat. The original of the Assyrian story is undoubtedly of Sumerian origin, and must be very old, and it is probable that both the Egyptians and the Sumerians derived their versions from a common source. In the Assyrian version[1] Marduk is armed with the invincible club which the gods gave him, and with a bow, spear, net, and dagger; the lightning was before him, and fierce fire filled his body, and the four-fold wind and the seven-fold wind went with him. Marduk grasped the thunderbolt and then mounted his chariot, drawn by four swift and fiery horses which had been trained to beat down under their feet everything which came in their way. When he came to the place where Tiamat was, Kingu, whom she had set over her forces, trembled and was afraid, but Tiamat "stood firm with unbent neck." After an exchange of words of abuse the fight began, and Tiamat pronounced her spell, which, however, had no effect, for Marduk caught her in his net, and drove the winds which he had with him into her body, and whilst her belly was thus distended he thrust his spear into her, and stabbed her to the heart, and cut through her bowels, and crushed her skull with his club. On her body he took his stand, and with his knife he split it "like a flat fish into two halves," and of one of these he made a covering for the heavens. With the exception of the last, every detail of the Assyrian account of the fight has its equivalent in the Egyptian texts which concern Rā and Āpepi. An allusion to the fight is found in the apocryphal work of "Bel and the Dragon," wherein we are told that both the god and the monster were worshipped in Babylon; but the narrative says that the dragon was destroyed by means of lumps of pitch, and fat, and hair seethed together, and that these having been pushed into the creature's mouth he burst asunder. In Egyptian papyri Āpep is always represented in the form of a serpent, in each undulation of which a knife is stuck,

[1] See King, *Babylonian Religion*, p. 71 ff.

; in the "Book of the Gates" (see above p. 197) we see him fastened by the neck with a chain (along which is stretched the scorpion goddess Serqet), the end of which is in the hands of a god, and also chained to the ground by five chains.

It has already been said that Rā was the "father of the gods," and we find that as early as the Vth Dynasty a female counterpart, who was the mother of the gods, was assigned to him. This goddess is called in the text of Unȧs (l. 253) Rāt, , and in later times her title appears to have been "Rāt of the two lands, the "lady of heaven, mistress of the gods," ; she is also called "Mistress of Heliopolis." Her full name was, perhaps, Rāt-taiut, 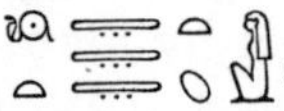, i.e., "Rāt of the world." She is depicted in the form of a woman who wears on her head a disk with horns and a uraeus, and sometimes there are two feathers above the disk;[1] the attributes of the goddess are unknown, but it is not likely that she was considered to be more important than any other great goddess.

The home and centre of the worship of Rā in Egypt during dynastic times was the city called Ȧnnu, , or Ȧn by the Egyptians, On by the Hebrews, and Heliopolis by the Greeks; its site is marked by the village of Maṭarîyeh, which lies about five miles to the north-east of Cairo. It was generally known as Ȧnnu meḥt, i.e., Annu of the North, to distinguish it from Ȧnnu Qemāu, i.e., Annu of the South," or Hermonthis. Among the early Christians great store was set upon the oil made from the trees which grew there, and in the famous "Fountain of the Sun" the Virgin Mary is said to have washed the garments of her Son; the ancient Egyptians also believed that Rā bathed each day at sunrise in a certain lake or pool which was in the neighbourhood. Of the origin and beginnings of the worship of Rā at Heliopolis we know nothing, but it is quite certain that under the Vth Dynasty, about B.C. 3350, the priests of Rā had settled themselves there, and that they had obtained great power at that remote period. The

[1] See Lanzone, op. cit., pl. 186, Nos. 1-4.

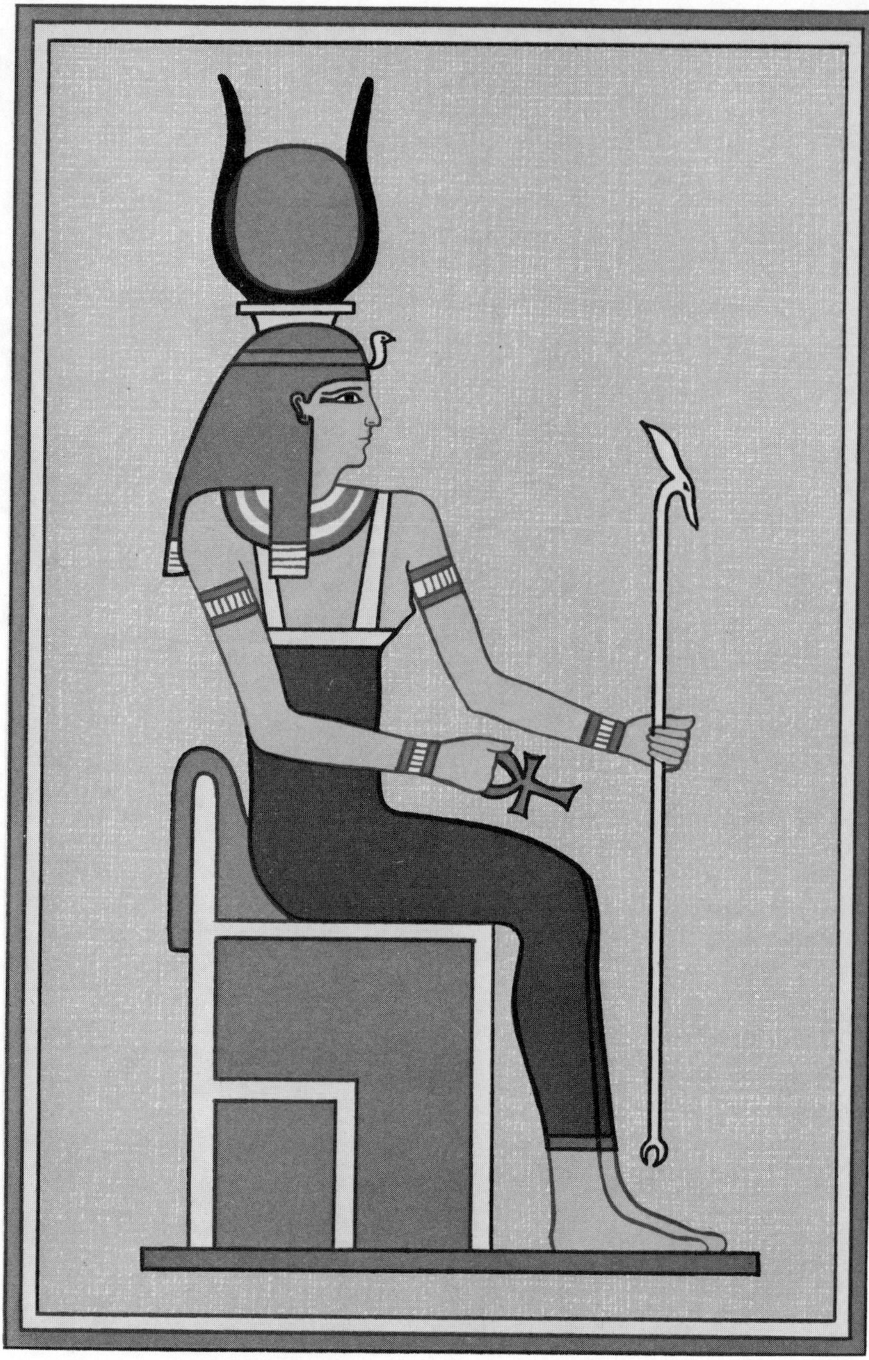

THE GODDESS RĀT.

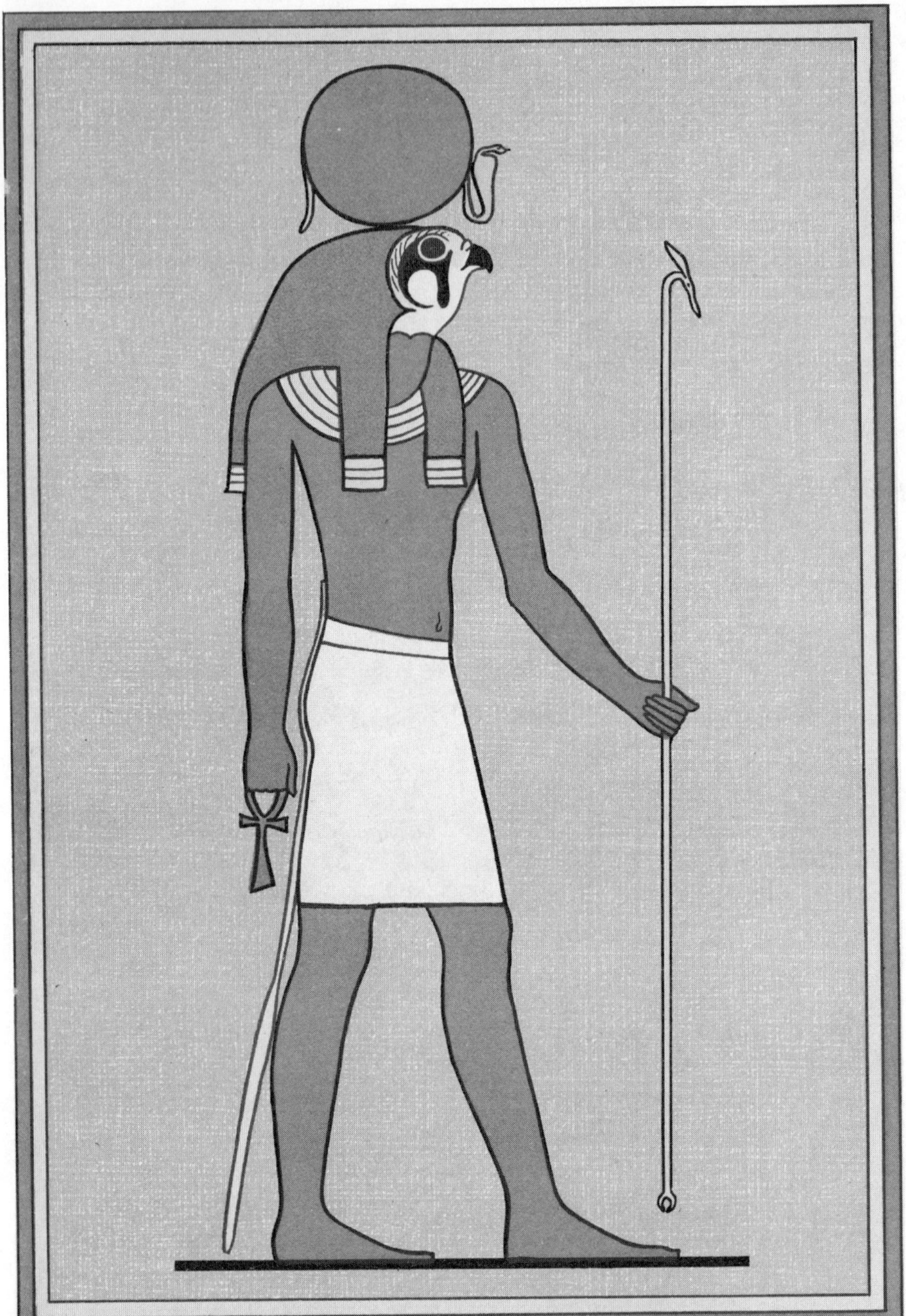

AMEN-RĀ – ḤERU – KHUTI.

AMEN-RĀ – (HARMACHIS).

evidence derived from the Westcar Papyrus[1] indicates that User-ka-f, the first king of the Vth Dynasty, was the high-priest of Rā, and that he was the first to add "son of the Sun" to the titles of Egyptian monarchs. Up to that time a king seems to have possessed :—1. A name as the descendant or servant of Horus. 2. A name as the descendant or servant of Set. 3. A name as lord of the shrines of Nekhebet and Uatchit, . 4. A name as king of the North and South, . User-ka-f, however, introduced the title of "son of the Sun," , which was always followed by a second cartouche, and it was adopted by every succeeding king of Egypt. According to the Westcar Papyrus User-ka-f and his two immediate successors Saḥu-Rā and Kakaȧ were the sons of the god Rā by Ruṭ-ṭeṭeṭ, the wife of a priest of the god Rā of Sakhabu, ; these were brought into the world by the goddesses Isis, Nephthys, Meskhenet, and Ḥeqet, and by the god Khnemu, and it was decreed by them that the three boys should be sovereigns of Egypt.

This legend is of importance, not only as showing the order of the succession of the first three kings of the Vth Dynasty, but also because it proves that in the early Empire the kings of Egypt believed themselves to be the sons of Rā, the Sun-god. All chronological tradition affirms that Rā had once ruled over Egypt, and it is a remarkable fact that every possessor of the throne of Egypt was proved by some means or other to have the blood of Rā flowing in his veins, or to hold it because he was connected with Rā by marriage. The bas-reliefs of Queen Ḥātshepset at Dêr al-Baḥarî, and those of Ȧmen-ḥetep III. at Luxor, and those of Cleopatra VII. in the temple at Erment (now destroyed, alas!) describe the process by which Rā or Ȧmen-Rā became the father of the kings and queens of Egypt. From these we see that whenever the divine blood needed replenishing the god took upon himself the form of the reigning king of Egypt, and that he visited the queen in her chamber and became the actual father of the child who was subsequently born to her. When the child was born it

[1] See Erman, *Westcar Papyrus*, pl. ix. ff.

was regarded as a god incarnate, and in due course was presented, with appropriate ceremonies, to Rā or Åmen-Rā, in his temple, and this god accepted it and acknowledged it to be his child. This clever priestly device gave the priests of Rā great power in the land, but their theocratic rule was not always the best for Egypt, and on one occasion they brought about the downfall of a dynasty. The first rise to power of the priests of Rā took place at the beginning of the Vth Dynasty, when the cult of Rā became dominant in the land. About the time of Userkaf we find that a number of shrines, which united the chief characteristics of the low rectangular tomb commonly known by its Arabic name of *masṭaba*, i.e., "bench," and of the pyramid, , were built in honour of the god;[1] but, according to Prof. Sethe, the custom of building such only lasted for about one hundred years, i.e., from the reign of Userkaf to that of Men-kau-Ḥeru. Be this as it may, the priesthood of Heliopolis succeeded in making their worship of Rā to supersede generally that of almost every other god of Egypt, and in absorbing all the local gods of importance throughout the country into their theological system, wherein they gave them positions subordinate to those of Rā and his company of gods.

Originally the local god of the city was Tem, who was worshipped there in a special temple, but they united his attributes to those of Rā and formed the double god Rā-Tem, 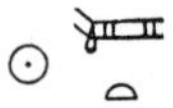 (Unȧs, l. 222). With the close of the VIth Dynasty the power of the priests of Rā declined, and it was not until the reign of Usertsen I., about B.C. 2433, that the sanctuary at Heliopolis was rebuilt, or perhaps entirely refounded. This king dedicated the temple which he built there to Rā and to two forms of this god, Horus and Temu, who were supposed to be incarnate in the famous Bull of Mnevis, which was worshipped at Heliopolis as Apis was worshipped at Memphis. In front of the temple he set up two massive granite obelisks, each 66 feet high, the pyramidions of which were covered with copper; these were still *in situ* about A.D. 1200. Between the XIIth and the XXth Dynasties we hear little of Heliopolis, but

[1] See an interesting paper on this subject by Sethe in *Aegyptische Zeitschrift*, 1889, p. 111 ff. (*Die Heiligthümer des Re' im alten Reich*).

a further restoration of the temple buildings took place under Rameses III., who set apart large revenues for the maintenance of the worship of Rā and the dignity of his priests and servants. When Piānkhi invaded Egypt, about B.C. 750, he visited Heliopolis after the capture of Memphis, going by way of the mountain of Kher-āḥa, 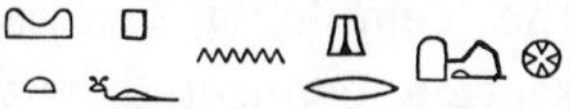, and he performed certain ceremonial ablutions in the "Lake of cold water," 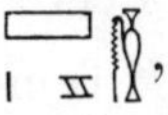, and washed his face in the "milk of Nu wherein Rā was wont to "wash his face;"[1] this "Lake" is clearly the fountain of the sun which we have already mentioned.

At a place called Shāi-qa-em-Ȧnnu[2] he "made great offerings "at Shā-qa-em-Ȧmen to Rā at sunrise, viz., white oxen, milk, *ānti* "unguent, incense, and sweet-smelling woods, and then he passed "into the temple of Rā, which he entered bowing low in "adoration to the god. The chief *kher ḥeb* priest, , "offered up prayer on behalf of the king, that he might be able to "repulse his enemies, and then having performed the ceremony "connected with the 'Star-room,' , he took the seṭeb girdle, "and purified himself with incense, and poured out a libation, "when one brought to him the flowers which are offered up in the "Ḥet-Benbenet,[3] . He took the flowers and went "up the steps [leading to] the 'great tabernacle,' 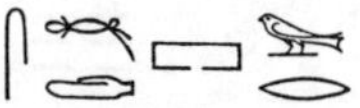, "to see Rā in Ḥet-Benbenet. He stood [on the top] there by "himself, he pushed back the bolt, he opened the doors [of the "tabernacle], and he saw his father Rā in Ḥet-Benbenet. He "made adoration to the Māṭet Boat of Rā (i.e., the boat of the "rising sun), and to the Sektet boat of Tem (i.e., the boat of the "setting sun). He then drew close the doors again, and having "affixed thereto the clay for a seal he stamped it with the seal of

1 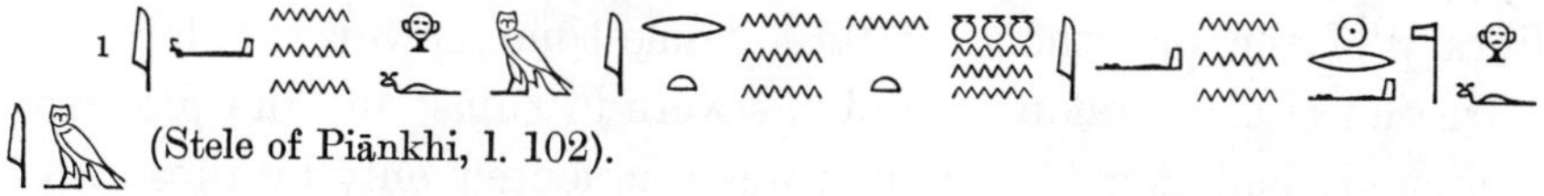 (Stele of Piānkhi, l. 102).

2 .

3 I.e., the shrine or holy of holies of the temple of Rā.

"the king himself. He then admonished the priests [saying], 'I "have set [my] seal here, let no other king enter herein [or] stand "here.' And they cast themselves on their bellies before his "majesty, saying, 'May Horus who loveth Ȧnnu (Heliopolis) be "firm and stable, and may he never come to an end.' And the "king went into the Temple of Tem, and he performed all the "ceremonies and service connected with the worship of father "Tem-Kheperȧ, , the prince of Ȧnnu."

From the above it is certain that the sacred boats of Rā were kept in a sort of wooden tabernacle with two doors, , that could be fastened by a bolt, and from what we know from pictures of these boats it is equally certain that the Māṭet boat contained a hawk-headed figure of Rā, and that the Sektet boat contained a man-headed figure of Rā. The text says that the tabernacle, , was situated on the top of a flight of steps, and this is what we should expect, for we know that the support was intended to represent the high ground in or near the city of Khemennu, (Hermopolis), whereon Rā established himself on the day when he proceeded from the watery abyss of Nu, before the pillars of Shu were set up. In the *Book of the Dead* this high ground is called "Qaqa in Khemennu," . During the period of the Persian invasion the prosperity of the priesthood of Heliopolis declined, and it is said that later, during the reign of Ptolemy II. (B.C. 285-247) many of its members found an asylum at Alexandria, where their reputation for learning caused them to be welcomed. A tradition says Solon, Thales, and Plato all visited the great college at Heliopolis, and that the last-named actually studied there, and that Manetho, the priest of Sebennytus, who wrote a history of Egypt in Greek for Ptolemy II., collected his materials in the library of the priesthood of Rā. Some time, however, before the Christian era, the temple buildings were in ruins, and the glory of Heliopolis had departed, and it was frequented only by those who went there to carry away stone or anything else which would be useful in building or farming operations.

We have now to consider briefly what was the nature of the doctrine which was the distinguishing characteristic of the teaching of the priests of Heliopolis. In the first place it proclaimed the absolute sovereignty of Rā among the gods, and it made him the head of every company of the gods, but it did not deny divinity to the older deities of the country. The chief authorities for the Heliopolitan doctrine are the Pyramid Texts, to which allusion has so often been made, and from these we see that the priests of Rā displayed great ingenuity and tact in absorbing into their form of religion all the older cults of Egypt, together with their magical rites and ceremonies. Apparently they did not attempt to abolish the old, indigenous gods; on the contrary, they allowed their cults to be continued, provided that the local priesthoods would make their gods subordinate to Rā. Thus Osiris and Isis, and their companion gods, were absorbed into the great company of the gods of Heliopolis, and the theological system of the priests of Osiris was mixed with that of the priests of Rā. Nothing is known of the origin of Osiris worship, but the god himself and the ceremonies which accompanied the celebration of his festivals suggest that he was known to the predynastic dwellers in Egypt. The belief in the efficacy of worship of the Man-god, who rose from the dead, and established himself in the underworld as judge and king, was indelibly impressed on the minds of the Egyptians at a very early period, and although the idea of a heaven of material delights which was promised to the followers of Osiris did not, probably, commend itself in all particulars to the imaginations of the refined and cultured folk of Egypt, it was tacitly accepted as true and was regarded as a portion of their religious inheritance by the majority of the people. On the other hand, the priests of Rā declared that the souls of the blessed made their way after death to the boat of Rā, and that if they succeeded in alighting upon it their eternal happiness was assured. No fiends could vex and no foes assail them successfully, so long as they had their seat in the "Boat of Millions of Years;" they lived upon the food on which the gods lived, and that food was light. They were apparelled in light, and they were embraced by the god of light. They passed with Rā in his boat through all the dangers of the Ṭuat, and when the god rose each morning they were free to wander about in heaven or to visit their old familiar habitations on earth, always however taking care to resume their places in the boat before nightfall, at which time evil spirits had great power to injure, and perhaps even to slay, the souls of those who had failed to arrive safely in the boat.

But although the priests of Rā under the Early Empire, and the priests of Ȧmen-Rā under the Middle and New Empires, were supported by all the power and authority of the greatest kings and queens who ever sat upon the throne of Egypt, in their proclamation of a heaven, which was of a far more spiritual character than that of Osiris, they never succeeded in obliterating the belief in Osiris from the minds of the great bulk of the population in Egypt. The material side of the Egyptian character refused to be weaned from the idea of a Field of Peace, which was situated near the Field of Reeds and the Field of the Grasshoppers,[1] where wheat and barley grew in abundance, and where a man would possess a vine, and fig trees, and date palms, and be waited upon by his father and his mother, and where he would enjoy an existence more comfortable than that which he led upon this earth. The doctrine of a realm of light, where the meat, and drink, and raiment were light, and the idea of becoming a being of light, and of passing eternity among creatures of light did not satisfy him. The result of all this was to create a perpetual contest between the two great priesthoods of Egypt, namely, those of Rā and Osiris; in the end the doctrine of Osiris prevailed, and the attributes of the Sun-god were ascribed to him. In considering the struggle which went on between the followers of Rā and Osiris it is difficult not to think that there was some strong reason for the resistance which the priests of Rā met with from the Egyptians generally, and it seems as if the doctrine of Rā contained something which was entirely foreign to the ideas of the people. The city of Heliopolis appears always to have contained a mixed population, and its situation made it a very convenient halting-place for travellers passing from Arabia and Syria into Egypt and *vice*

1  (*Book of the Dead*, cxxv. 19).

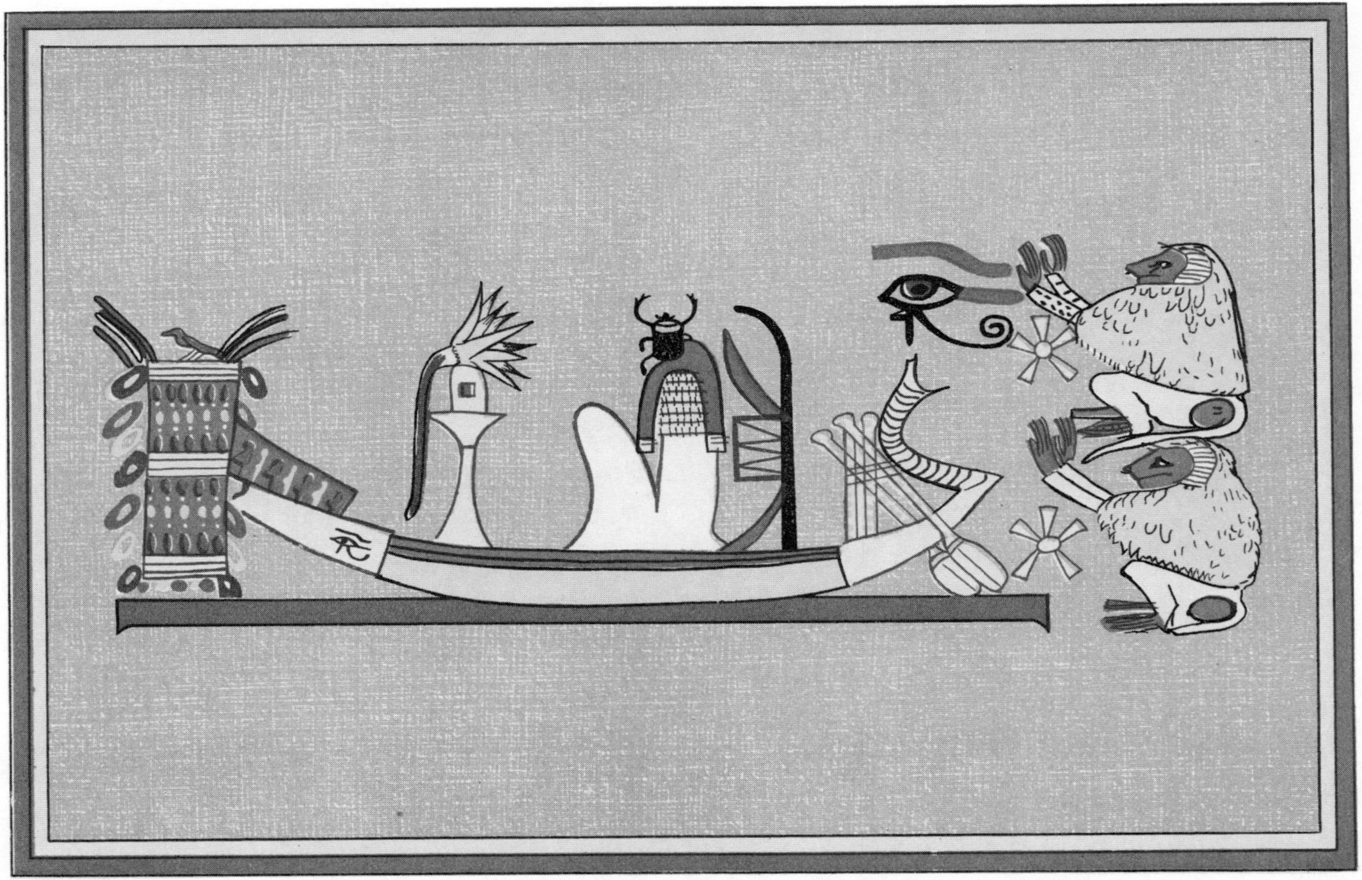

The God KHEPERA seated in his Boat.

*versâ;* it is, then, most probable that the doctrine of Rā as taught by the priests of Heliopolis was a mixture of Egyptian and Western Asiatic doctrines, and that it was the Asiatic element in it which the Egyptians resisted. It could not have been sun-worship which they disliked, for they had been sun-worshippers from time immemorial.

The above paragraphs contain a statement of the facts concerning the worships of Rā and Osiris which appear to be fairly deducible from the extant religious literature of the Egyptians, but it is time to let the hymns to these gods declare the attributes which were assigned to them during the most flourishing period of Egyptian history. More hymns were addressed to these two than to any other gods, a fact which proves that they were considered to be the chief means of salvation for the Egyptians. The following hymns are taken from the Papyri of Hunefer, and Ani, and Nekht[1]:—

"Homage to thee, O thou who art Rā when thou risest, and "Temu when thou settest. Thou risest, thou risest, thou shinest, "thou shinest, thou who art crowned king of the gods. Thou art "the lord of heaven, thou art the lord of earth; thou art the "creator of those who dwell in the heights and of those who "dwell in the depths. Thou art the God One who didst come "into being in the beginning of time. Thou didst create the earth, "thou didst fashion man, thou didst make the watery abyss of the "sky, thou didst form Ḥāpi (the Nile), thou didst create the "watery abyss, and thou dost give life unto all that therein is. "Thou hast knit together the mountains, thou hast made mankind "and the beasts of the field to come into being, thou hast made "the heavens and the earth. Worshipped be thou whom Maāt "embraceth at morn and at eve. Thou dost travel across the sky "with heart swelling with joy; the Lake of Testes becometh "contented thereat. The serpent-fiend Nȧk hath fallen, and his "two arms are cut off. The Sektet boat receiveth fair winds, and "the heart of him that is in the shrine thereof rejoiceth. Thou art "crowned prince of heaven, and thou art the One dowered [with

[1] See my *Chapters of Coming Forth by Day* (Translation), pp. 8, 36.

"all attributes] who comest forth from the sky. Rā is he whose "word when uttered must come to pass. O thou divine Youth, "thou heir of everlastingness, thou self-begotten one, thou who "didst give thyself birth! O thou One, thou mighty [one] of "myriad forms and aspects, King of the world, Prince of Ȧnnu "(Heliopolis), lord of eternity and ruler of everlastingness, the "company of the gods rejoice when thou risest and when thou "sailest across the sky, O thou who art exalted in the Sektet "boat." (From the Papyrus of Hunefer, sheet 1.)

"Hail, thou Disk, thou lord of rays, who risest on the horizon "day by day! Homage to thee, O Ḥeru-khuti, who art the god "Kheperȧ, the self-created; when thou risest on the horizon and "sheddest thy beams of light upon the lands of the North and "of the South, thou art beautiful, yea beautiful, and all the gods "rejoice when they behold thee, the King of heaven. The goddess "Nebt-unnut is stablished upon thy head; and her uraei of the "South and of the North are upon thy brow; she taketh up her "place before thee. The god Thoth is stablished in the bows of "thy boat to destroy utterly all thy foes. Those who are in the "Ṭuat come forth to meet thee, and they bow in homage as they "come towards thee to behold thy beautiful form. And I have "come before thee that I may be with thee to behold thy Disk "every day. May I not be shut up in [the tomb], may I not be "turned back, may the members of my body be made new when I "view thy beauties, even as [are those of] all thy favoured ones, "because I am one of those who worshipped thee upon earth. May "I come in unto the land of eternity, may I come even unto the "everlasting land, for behold, O my lord, this hast thou ordained "for me.

"Homage to thee, O thou who risest in the horizon as Rā, "thou restest upon law unchangeable and unalterable. Thou "passest over the sky, and every face watcheth thee and thy "course, for thou hast been hidden from their gaze. Thou dost "show thyself at dawn and at eventide day by day. The Sektet "boat, wherein is thy Majesty, goeth forth with light; thy beams "are upon all faces; the [number] of thy red and yellow rays "cannot be known, nor can thy bright beams be told. The lands "of the gods, and the lands of Punt must be seen, ere that which "is hidden [in thee] may be measured. Alone and by thyself thou "dost manifest thyself when thou comest into being above Nu. "May I advance, even as thou dost advance; may I never cease to "go forward as thou never ceasest to go forward, even though it be "for a moment; for with strides thou dost in one little moment "pass over the spaces which would need millions and millions of "years [for men to pass over; this] thou doest and then thou dost "sink to rest. Thou puttest an end to the hours of the night, and "thou dost count them, even thou; thou endest them in thine "own appointed season, and the earth becometh light. Thou "settest thyself therefore before thy handiwork in the likeness of "Rā [when] thou risest on the horizon.

"Thou art crowned with the majesty of thy beauties; thou "mouldest thy limbs as thou dost advance, and thou bringest them "forth without birth-pangs in the form of Rā, as thou dost rise "up into the upper air. Grant thou that I may come unto the "heaven which is everlasting, and into the mountain where dwell "thy favoured ones. May I be joined unto those shining beings, "holy and perfect, who are in the Underworld; and may I come "forth with them to behold thy beauties when thou shinest at "eventide and goest to thy mother Nu. Thou dost place thyself "in the west, and my two hands are [raised] in adoration of thee "when thou settest as a living being. Behold, thou art the "maker of eternity, and thou art adored when thou settest in the "heavens. I have given my heart unto thee without wavering, "O thou who art mightier than the gods. A hymn of praise to "thee, O thou who risest like unto gold, and who dost flood the "world with light on the day of thy birth. Thy mother giveth "thee birth, and thou dost give light unto the course of the Disk. "O thou great Light, who shinest in the heavens, thou dost "strengthen the generations of men with the Nile-flood, and thou "dost cause gladness in all lands, and in all cities, and in all "temples. Thou art glorious by reason of thy splendours, and "thou makest strong thy Double with divine foods. O thou "mighty one of victories, thou who art the Power of Powers, who "dost make strong thy throne against evil fiends; who art glorious "in majesty in the Sektet boat, and who art exceedingly mighty "in the Ātet boat, make thou me glorious through words which "when spoken must take effect in the Underworld; and grant thou "that in the nether world I may be without evil. I pray thee to "put my faults behind thee; grant thou that I may be one of thy "loyal servants who are with the shining ones; may I be joined "unto the souls which are in Ta-tchesertet, and may I journey "into the Sekhet-Åaru by a prosperous and happy decree." (From the *Papyrus of Ani*, sheet 20 f.)

"Homage to thee, O thou glorious being, thou who art "dowered with all attributes, O Tem-Ḥeru-khuti, when thou risest "in the horizon of heaven, a cry of joy cometh forth to thee from "the mouth of all peoples. O thou beautiful being, thou dost "renew thyself in thy season in the form of the Disk within thy "mother Hathor; therefore in every place every heart swelleth "with joy at thy rising for ever. The regions of the North and "South come to thee with homage, and send forth acclamations at "thy rising in the horizon of heaven; thou illuminest the two "lands with rays of turquoise light. O Rā, thou who art Ḥeru-"khuti, the divine man-child, the heir of eternity, self-begotten "and self-born, king of earth, prince of the Ṭuat, governor of "the regions of Åuḳert; thou comest forth from the water, thou "hast sprung from the god Nu, who cherisheth thee and ordereth "thy members. O thou god of life, thou lord of love, all men live "when thou shinest; thou art crowned king of the gods. The "goddess Nut doeth homage unto thee, and Maāt embraceth thee "at all times. Those who are in thy following sing unto thee "with joy and bow down their foreheads to the earth when they "meet thee, thou lord of heaven, thou lord of earth, thou king of "Right and Truth, thou lord of eternity, thou prince of ever-"lastingness, thou sovereign of all the gods, thou god of life, thou "creator of eternity, thou maker of heaven wherein thou art firmly "established.

"The company of the gods rejoice at thy rising, the earth is "glad when it beholdeth thy rays; the peoples that have been "long dead come forth with cries of joy to see thy beauties every "day. Thou goest forth each day over heaven and earth and art "made strong each day by thy mother Nut. Thou passest "through the heights of heaven, thy heart swelleth with joy; and "the Lake of Testes is content thereat. The Serpent-fiend hath "fallen, his arms are hewn off, the knife hath cut asunder his "joints. Rā liveth by Maāt the beautiful. The Sektet boat "draweth on and cometh into port; the South and the North, the "West and the East turn to praise thee, O thou primeval "substance of the earth who didst come into being of thine own "accord. Isis and Nephthys salute thee, they sing unto thee "songs of joy at thy rising in the boat, they protect thee with their "hands. The souls of the East follow thee, the souls of the West "praise thee. Thou art the ruler of all the gods, and thou hast "joy of heart within thy shrine, for the serpent fiend Nȧk hath "been condemned to the fire, and thy heart shall be joyful for "ever." (From the *Papyrus of Nekht*, sheet 21.)

Even more instructive, however, than these are the Seventy-five Praises of Rā which are found inscribed on the walls of royal tombs of the XIXth and XXth Dynasties at Thebes. In these we find enumerated a large number of most remarkable epithets and attributes, some idea of the meaning of which will be gathered from the following rendering:—

1. "Praise be to thee, O Rā, exalted Sekhem,[1] lord of the hidden "circles [of the Ṭuat], bringer of forms, thou restest in secret "places and makest thy creations in the form of the god Ṭamṭ "(, i.e., the universal god).
2. "Praise be to thee, O Rā, exalted Sekhem, thou creative force "(), who spreadest out thy wings, who restest in "the Ṭuaṭ, who makest the created things which come forth "from his divine limbs.
3. "Praise be to thee, O Rā, exalted Sekhem, Ta-thenen, begetter "of his gods. Thou art he who protecteth what is in him, and "thou makest thy creations as Governer of thy Circle.
4. "Praise be to thee, O Rā, exalted Sekhem, looker on the "earth, and brightener of Ȧmenti. Thou art he whose forms

[1] Literally, "Power."

"() are his own creations, and thou makest thy "creations in thy Great Disk.

5. "Praise be to thee, O Rā, exalted Sekhem, the Word-soul, "that resteth on his high place. Thou art he who pro-"tecteth thy hidden spirits (), and they have form "in thee.

6. "Praise be to thee, O Rā, exalted Sekhem, mighty one, bold of "face, the knitter together of his body. Thou art he who "gathereth together thy gods when thou goest into thy hidden "Circle.

7. "Praise be to thee, O Rā, exalted Sekhem. Thou dost call to "thine Eye, and dost speak to thy head, and dost give breath "to the souls in their places, and they receive it and have "their forms in him.

8. "Praise be to thee, O Rā, exalted Sekhem, destroyer of thy "enemies; thou art he who doth decree destruction for the "dead ().

9. "Praise be to thee, O Rā, exalted Sekhem, the sender forth "of light into his Circle; thou art he who maketh the "darkness to be in his Circle and thou coverest those who are "therein."

10. "Praise be to thee, O Rā, exalted Sekhem, the illuminer "of bodies in the horizons; thou art he who entereth into "his Circle.

11. "Praise be to thee, O Rā, exalted Sekhem, support (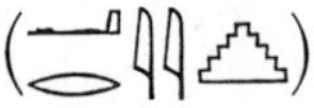) "of the Circles of Åment; thou art indeed the body of Temu "().

12. "Praise be to thee, O Rā, exalted Sekhem, the hidden support "of Ånpu (); thou art indeed the body of "Kheperå ().

13. "Praise be to thee, O Rā, exalted Sekhem, whose duration of "life is greater than that of her whose forms are hidden; "thou art indeed the bodies of Shu (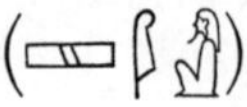).

14. "Praise be to thee, O Rā, exalted Sekhem, the guide

"( *sebi*) of Rā to his members; thou art indeed the "bodies of Tefnut ( ).

15. "Praise be to thee, O Rā, exalted Sekhem; thou dost make "to be abundant the things which are of Rā in their seasons, "and thou art indeed Seb ( ).

16. "Praise be to thee, O Rā, exalted Sekhem, the mighty one "who doth keep count of the things which are in him; thou "art indeed the bodies of Nut.

17. "Praise be to thee, O Rā, exalted Sekhem, the lord who "advancest; thou art indeed Isis ( ).

18. "Praise be to thee, O Rā, exalted Sekhem, whose head "shineth more than the things which are in front of him; "thou art indeed the bodies of Nephthys ( ).

19. "Praise be to thee, O Rā, exalted Sekhem, united is he in "members, One, who gathereth together all seed; thou art "indeed the bodies of Horus ( ).

20. "Praise be to thee, O Rā, exalted Sekhem, thou shining one "who dost send forth light upon the waters of heaven; thou "art indeed the bodies of Nu ( ).

21. "Praise be to thee, O Rā, exalted Sekhem, the avenger of Nu "who cometh forth from what is in him; thou art indeed the "bodies of the god Remi ( ).

22. "Praise be to thee, O Rā, exalted Sekhem; thou art the two "Uraei who bear their two feathers [on their heads]; thou art "indeed the bodies of the god Ḥuaaiti ( ).

23. "Praise be to thee, O Rā, exalted Sekhem; thou goest in "and comest out and thou comest out and goest in to thy "hidden Circle, and thou art indeed the bodies of Āaṭu "( ).

24. "Praise be to thee, O Rā, exalted Sekhem, the Soul who "departeth at his appointed time; thou art indeed the bodies "of Nethert ( ).

25. "Praise be to thee, O Rā, exalted Sekhem, who standeth up,

"the Soul One, who avengeth his children; thou art indeed "the bodies of Netuti ().

26. "Praise be to thee, O Rā, exalted Sekhem; thou raisest thy "head and thou makest bold thy brow, thou ram, mightiest "of created things.

27. "Praise be to thee, O Rā, exalted Sekhem, the light of Shu at "the head of Åkert (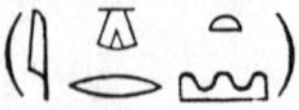); thou art indeed the bodies "of Åment (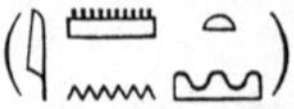).

28. "Praise be to thee, O Rā, exalted Sekhem, the soul that "seeth, the governor of Åment; thou art indeed the bodies "of the double Circle (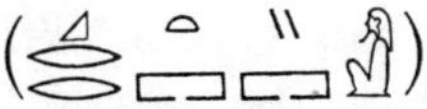).

29. "Praise be to thee, O Rā, exalted Sekhem; thou art "the Soul that mourneth, and the god that crieth "(); thou art indeed the bodies of "Åakebi (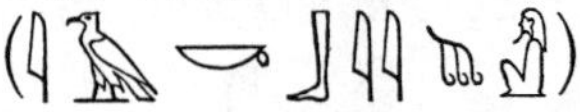).

30. "Praise be to thee, O Rā, exalted Sekhem; thou makest thy "hand to pass and praisest thine Eye, and thou art indeed "the bodies of the god of hidden limbs (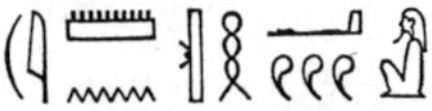).

31. "Praise be to thee, O Rā, exalted Sekhem; thou art the Soul "exalted in the double hidden place (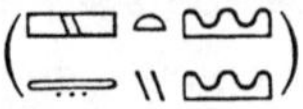); thou art "indeed Khenti-Åmenti (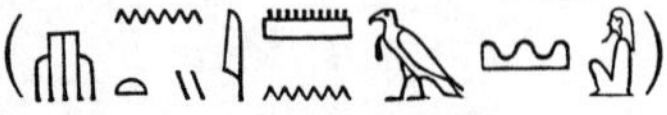).

32. "Praise be to thee, O Rā, exalted Sekhem, of manifold "creations in the holy house; thou art indeed the bodies of "the god Kheprer (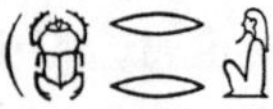).

33. "Praise be to thee, O Rā, exalted Sekhem; thou placest "thine enemies in their strong fetters, and thou art indeed the "bodies of Måti (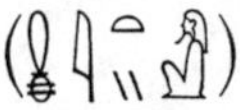).

34. "Praise be to thee, O Rā, exalted Sekhem; thou givest forth "light in the hidden place, and thou art the bodies of the god "of generation (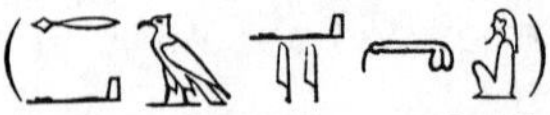).

35. "Praise be to thee, O Rā, exalted Sekhem; thou art the "vivifier of bodies; thou makest throats to inhale breath, and

"thou art indeed the bodies of the god Ṭebati (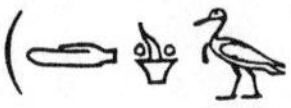
"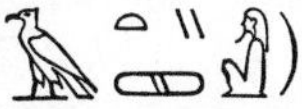).

36\. "Praise be to thee, O Rā, exalted Sekhem; thou assemblest "bodies in the Ṭuaṭ, and they gain the form of life, thou "destroyest foul humours, and thou art indeed the bodies of "the god Serqi (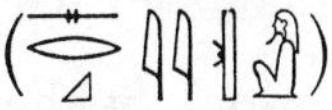).

37\. "Praise be to thee, O Rā, exalted Sekhem, Hidden-face "(), Seshem-Nethert (); thou "art indeed the bodies of Shai ().

38\. "Praise be to thee, O Rā, exalted Sekhem, lord of might; "thou embracest the Ṭuat and thou art indeed the bodies of "Sekhen-Ba (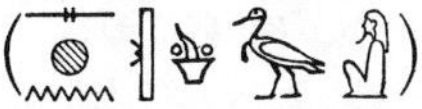).

39\. "Praise be to thee, O Rā, exalted Sekhem; thou hidest thy "body in that which is within thee, and thou art indeed the "bodies of Åmen-khat ().

40\. "Praise be to thee, O Rā, exalted Sekhem, more strong of "heart than those who are in his following; thou sendest fire "in the house of destruction, and thou art indeed the bodies "of the Fire-god Rekḥi (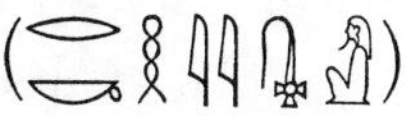).

41\. "Praise be to thee, O Rā, exalted Sekhem; thou sendest forth "destruction, and thou makest beings to come into existence "in thy creations in the Ṭuat, and thou art the bodies of "Ṭuati (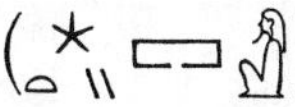).

42\. "Praise be to thee, O Rā, exalted Sekhem, Bua-ṭep (
"), governor of his Eye; thou sendest forth light into "the hidden place, and thou art indeed the body of Shepi "(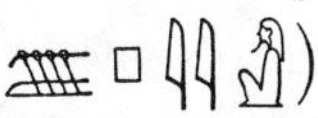).

43\. "Praise be to thee, O Rā, exalted Sekhem, Ṭemṭ-ḥātu, "stablisher of Åmta (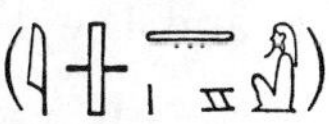); thou art indeed the bodies "of Ṭemṭ-ḥātu (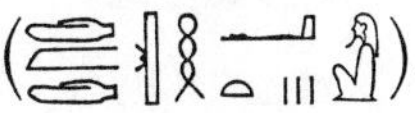).

44\. "Praise be to thee, O Rā, exalted Sekhem, creator of hidden "things, generator of bodies; thou art indeed the bodies of "the god Seshetai (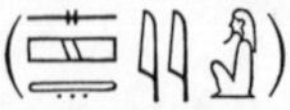).

45. "Praise be to thee, O Rā, exalted Sekhem; thou providest "those who are in the Ṭuat with what they need in the "hidden Circles, and thou art indeed Āper-ta (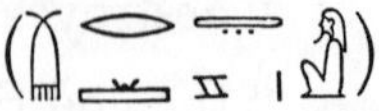).

46. "Praise be to thee, O Rā, exalted Sekhem; thy limbs rejoice "when they see thy body, O Uash-Ba (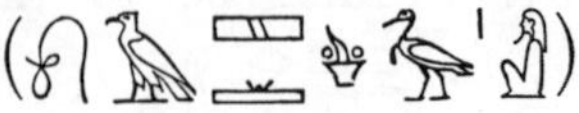), "when thou enterest thy body, and thou art indeed the bodies "of Ḥāi (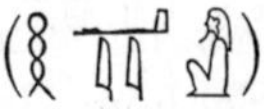).

47. "Praise be to thee, O Rā, exalted Sekhem, aged one of the "pupil () of the Utchat, Bai (); thou "makest full thy splendour, and thou art indeed the bodies of "Thenti ().

48. "Praise be to thee, O Rā, exalted Sekhem; thou makest "straight ways in the Ṭuat, and openest up roads in the "hidden place, and thou art indeed the bodies of Maā-uat "().

49. "Praise be to thee, O Rā, exalted Sekhem; thou art the Soul "who movest onwards, and thou hastenest thy stéps, and "thou art indeed the bodies of Åkhpå (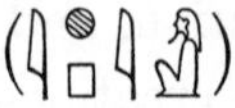).

50. "Praise be to thee, O Rā, exalted Sekhem; thou sendest "forth thy stars and thou illuminest the darkness in the "Circles of those whose forms are hidden, and thou art indeed "the god Ḥetchiu ().

51. "Praise be to thee, O Rā, exalted Sekhem; thou art the "maker of the Circles, thou makest bodies to come into being "by thine own creative vigour. Thou, O Rā, hast created "the things which exist, and the things which do not exist, "the dead (), and the gods, and the spirits; thou art "indeed the body that maketh Khati () to come "into being.

52. "Praise be to thee, O Rā, exalted Sekhem; thou art the "doubly hidden and secret god (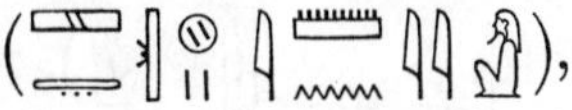), and "the souls go where thou leadest them, and those who follow "thee thou makest to enter in; thou art indeed the bodies of "Ȧmeni (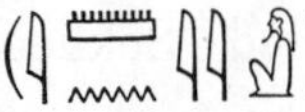).

53. "Praise be to thee, O Rā, exalted Sekhem; thou art Uben-"Ȧn () of Ȧment, and the light of the "lock of hair on thee . . . .; thou art indeed the bodies of "the god Uben.

54. "Praise be to thee, O Rā, exalted Sekhem; thou art the "Aged One of forms who dost go about through the Ṭuat, to "whom the souls in their Circles ascribe praises; and thou "art indeed the bodies of Then-ȧru ().

55. "Praise be to thee, O Rā, exalted Sekhem; when thou dost "unite thyself to the Beautiful Ȧment, the gods of the Ṭuat "rejoice at the sight of thee; thou art indeed the bodies of "Ȧāi ().

56. "Praise be to thee, O Rā, exalted Sekhem; thou art the "Great Cat, the avenger of the gods, and the judge of words, "and the president of the sovereign chiefs (or, assessors), and "the governor of the holy Circle; thou art indeed the bodies "of the Great Cat ().

57. "Praise be to thee, O Rā, exalted Sekhem; when thou fillest "thine eye, and speakest to the pupil thereof, the divine dead "bodies shed tears; thou art indeed the bodies of Meṭu-"khut-f ().

58. "Praise be to thee, O Rā, exalted Sekhem; thou art the Soul "on high and thy bodies are hidden; thou sendest forth the "light, and thou lookest upon thy hidden things (or, places); "thou art indeed the bodies of Ḥer-ba (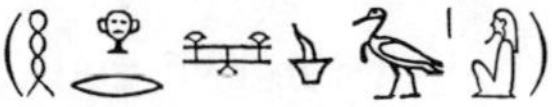).

59. "Praise be to thee, O Rā, exalted Sekhem, exalted of "Soul; thou destroyest thine enemies, thou sendest fire on "the wicked, and thou art the bodies of Qa-Ba ().

60. "Praise be to thee, O Rā, exalted Sekhem,· Åuaiu "(), who hidest in purity; thou hast gained "the mastery over the souls of the gods, and thou art indeed "the bodies of Åuai.

61. "Praise be to thee, O Rā, exalted Sekhem, Oldest one "(), Great one, Governor of the Ṭuat, Creating "one (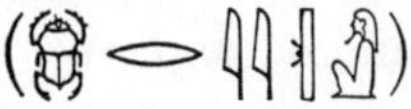); thou didst create the two Setchet "(), and thou art indeed the bodies of the two "Setchet gods ().

62. "Praise be to thee, O Rā, exalted Sekhem, Mighty One of "journeyings; thou orderest thy steps by Maāt, thou art the "Soul that doeth good to the body, thou art Senk-ḥrå "(, i.e., Face of Light), and thou art indeed the "bodies of Senk-ḥrå.

63. "Praise be to thee, O Rā, exalted Sekhem; thou dost protect "(or, avenge) thy body, and thou dost hold the balance "[among] the gods as the hidden Amå (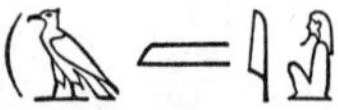), [and] "as Åm-ta (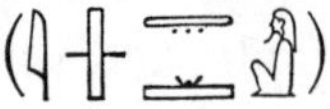), and thou art indeed the bodies of "the double god Amå-Åmta ().

64. "Praise be to thee, O Rā, exalted Sekhem; thou art the lord "of the fetters of thine enemies, the One, the Prince of the "Apes (), and thou art indeed the bodies of "Åntetu ().

65. "Praise be to thee, O Rā, exalted Sekhem; thou sendest "forth flames into thy furnaces (), and thou "cuttest off the heads of those who are to be destroyed "(), and thou art indeed the bodies "of the two gods Ketuit ().

66. "Praise be to thee, O Rā, exalted Sekhem; thou art the "god of generation (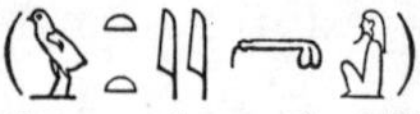), thou destroyest [thy] "offspring, thou art One, thou stablishest the two lands by

"[thy] spirit (), and thou art indeed the bodies "of the god Ta-Thenen ().

67. "Praise be to thee, O Rā, exalted Sekhem; thou stablishest "the gods who watch the hours () on their "standards, and who are invisible and secret, and thou art "indeed the bodies of the Watcher gods ().

68. "Praise be to thee, O Rā, exalted Sekhem; thou art the "double Tchent god () of heaven, and the gate of "the Ṭuat, and the god Besi () [with] his "spiritual bodies (), and thou art the bodies "of Besi.

69. "Praise be to thee, O Rā, exalted Sekhem; thou art the "Apes () . . . . ., and thou art the true creative "Power of [thy] divine attributes (), and "thou art indeed the bodies of the Ape-god in the Ṭuat.

70. "Praise be to thee, O Rā, exalted Sekhem; thou makest new "the earth, and thou openest a way for that which is therein, "thou that art the Soul which giveth names unto his limbs, "and thou art indeed the bodies of Sma-ta ().

71. "Praise be to thee, O Rā, exalted Sekhem; thou art Neḥi "() who burnest up thine enemies, the Fire-"god Setcheti (), who burneth up fetters, and "thou art indeed the bodies of Neḥi ().

72. "Praise be to thee, O Rā, exalted Sekhem; thou art the god "of motion (), the god of light (), "who travelleth, thou makest the darkness to come into "being after thy light, and thou art indeed the bodies of "Shemti.

73. "Praise be to thee, O Rā, exalted Sekhem; thou art the lord "of souls who art in the house of thy obelisk (), "thou art the chief of the gods who are supreme in their

"districts (), and thou art indeed "the god Neb-baiu (, i.e., Lord of souls).

74. "Praise be to thee, O Rā, exalted Sekhem; thou art the "double Sphinx-god, the Double obelisk-god ( " 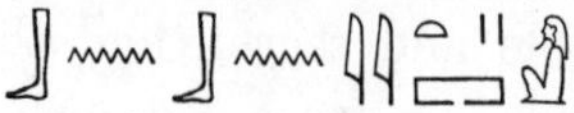), the Great God who lifteth up his "two Eyes, and thou art indeed the bodies of the double "Sphinx god Ḥuiti (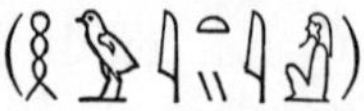).

75. "Praise be to thee, O Rā, exalted Sekhem; thou art the lord "of light and declarest the things which are hidden, and thou "art the Soul that speaketh with the gods who are in their "Circles, and thou art indeed the bodies of Neb-Senku "(, i.e., the Lord of light)."[1]

An impartial examination of the above translation will show the reader the lofty conceptions which were associated by the Egyptians with Rā the Sun-god, and there is not room for any reasonable doubt that they ascribed to the god, whose symbol was the sun, all the attributes which modern nations are wont to regard as the properties peculiar to God Almighty. He was One, and the maker of "gods" and men; he was the creator of heaven, earth, and the underworld; he was self-begotten, self-created, and self-produced; he had existed for ever and would exist to all eternity; he was the source of all life and light; and he was the personification of right and truth, and goodness, and the destroyer of darkness, night, wickedness, and evil. There is scarcely an attribute of importance ascribed to our God for which there is no equivalent in the hymns and texts which relate to Rā and describe his greatness and power, for he was not only the god of the living but also the god of the dead, and the god of everything unborn. His relations with Osiris, who was part god and part man, and was the cause and type of immortality for man, were at once those of a god, a father, and an equal, and when we consider that Osiris was a king who reigned over Egypt, and that every king was an

[1] For the hieroglyphic texts from the tombs of Seti I., Seti II., and Rameses IV., and a French translation, see Naville, *La Litanie du Soleil*, Leipzig, 1875.

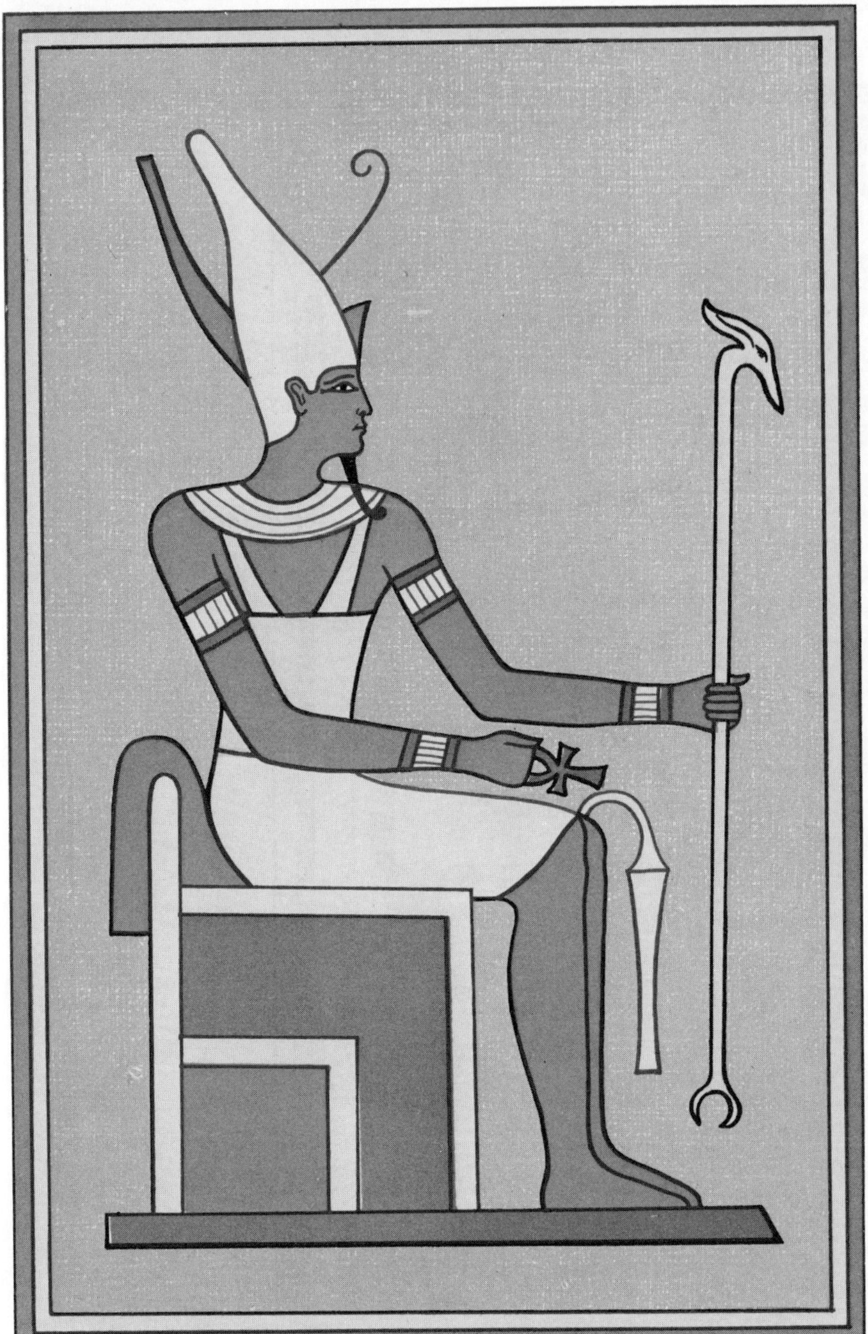

The God TEMU.

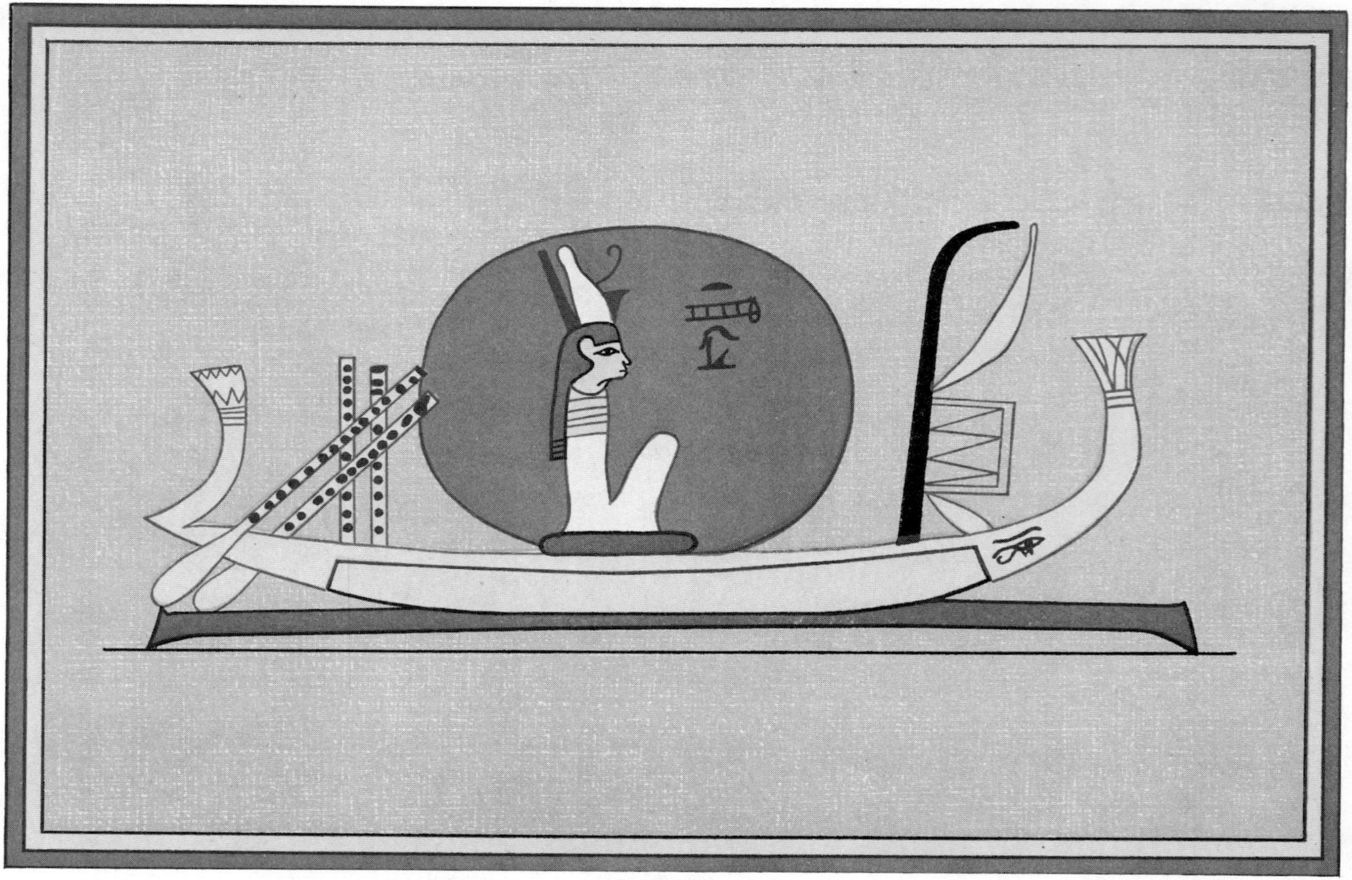

The God TEM Seated in his Boat.

incarnation of Rā, it is easy to understand how he came to have the power to rise from the dead, and to act as the judge of the dead on behalf of his father Rā.

## TEM, or TEMU, ,  or ÅTEM, .

TEM, or TEMU, or ÅTEM, was originally the local god of the city of Ånnu, or Heliopolis, and in the dynastic period at all events he was held to be one of the forms of the great Sun-god Rā, and to be the personification of the setting sun. In the predynastic period, however, he was, as M. Lefébure has pointed out,[1] the first man among the Egyptians who was believed to have become divine, and who was at his death identified with the setting sun; in other words, Tem was the first *living* man-god known to the Egyptians, just as Osiris was the first *dead* man-god, and as such was always represented in human form and with a human head. It is important to note this fact, for it indicates that those who formulated the existence of this god were on a higher level of civilization than those who depicted the oldest of all Egyptian gods, Horus, in the form of a hawk, or in that of a hawk-headed human body. In the papyri and on the monuments he usually wears , the crowns of the South and North, upon his head, and he holds , the emblem of life, in his right hand, and the sceptre, , in his left. In the boat of Rā he is depicted in human form even when Rā is symbolized by a disk which is being rolled along by a beetle, and the god Kheperȧ is represented by a beetle, and the rising sun Ḥeru-Khuti is shown under the form of a hawk's head, from which fall rays of light.[2] Tem was, in fact, to the Egyptians a manifestation of God in human form, and his conception in their minds marks the end of the period wherein they assigned animal forms to their gods, and the beginning of that in which they evolved the idea of God, almighty, inscrutable, unknowable, the maker and creator of the universe. It is useless to attempt to assign a date to the period when the Egyptians began to worship

[1] *Trans. Soc. Bibl. Arch.*, ix., p. 175. [2] Lanzone, op. cit., pl. 398.

God in human form, for we have no material for doing so; the worship of Tem must, however, be of very great antiquity, and the fact that the priests of Rā in the Vth and VIth Dynasties united him to their god under the name of Rā-Tem, 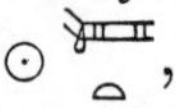, proves that his worship was wide-spread, and that the god was thought to possess attributes similar to those of Rā.

The Pyramid Texts show that the attributes of Temu were confounded with those of Rā, and that the protection and favour of this god were all essential for the well-being of the deceased in the Underworld; indeed, it is Tem the father who stretches out his hand to Pepi I. and sets him at the head of the gods, where he judges the great and the wise.[1] This passage shows that Tem was regarded as the father of the human race, and as he was also divine his powers to help the dead were very great. In many respects he was held to be the equal of Rā, and the prayers and hymns which were addressed to him frequently show that the Egyptians were very anxious to propitiate him. This is not difficult to understand if we remember the dogmas of the Heliopolitan priesthood about the means by which the souls of the blessed departed from this world. They taught that souls when they left this world went to the region which lay between the earth and the beginning of the Valley of the Ṭuat, and which was called Åmentet, and that they waited there until the Boat of the Setting Sun, i.e., the boat of Rā in his form of Temu, made his appearance there; as soon as it arrived the souls flocked to it, and those who had served Rā upon earth and whose bodies had been buried with the orthodox rites, and ceremonies, and prayers of the priesthood of Rā, and were, therefore, provided with the necessary words of power, were admitted to the boat of Tem, where they enjoyed the protection and favour of the god in his various forms to all eternity.

There was, moreover, another aspect of Tem which gave the god a position of peculiar importance in the minds of the Egyptians,

1 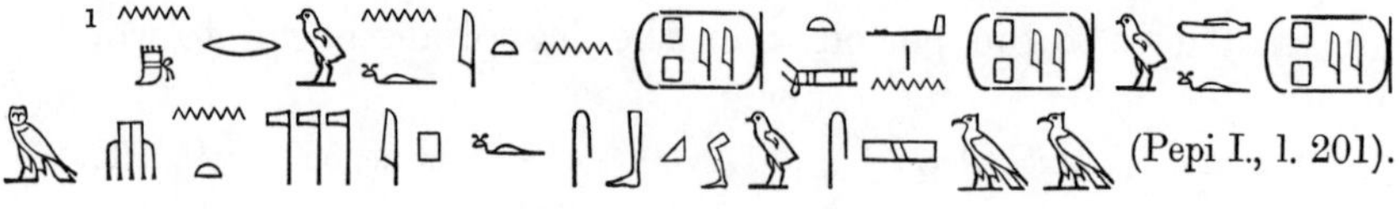 (Pepi I., l. 201).

i.e., he was identified not only with the god of the dead, Osiris, but also with the young Horus, the new and rising sun of the morrow. All these ideas are well expressed in a hymn to Tem which is found in the Papyrus of Mut-ḥetep (Brit. Mus., No. 10,010, sheet 5), and which was composed to enable every spirit who recited it to "come forth by day" and in any form he pleased and to have great power in the Ṭuat. The lady Mut-ḥetep says, "O Rā-Tem, in thy "splendid progress thou risest, and thou settest as a living being "in the glories of the western horizon; thou settest in thy "territory which is in the Mount of Sunset (Manu, ). "Thy uraeus is behind thee, thy uraeus is behind thee. Homage "to thee, O thou who art in peace; homage to thee, O thou who "art in peace. Thou art joined unto the Eye of Tem, and it "chooseth its powers of protection [to place] behind thy members. "Thou goest forth through heaven, thou travellest over the earth, "and thou jonrneyest onward. O Luminary, the northern and "southern halves of heaven come to thee, and they bow low in "adoration, and they do homage unto thee, day by day. The "gods of Åmentet rejoice in thy beauties, and the unseen places "sing hymns of praise unto thee. Those who dwell in the Sektet "boat go round about thee, and the Souls of the East do homage "to thee, and when they meet thy Majesty they cry: 'Come, "come in peace!' There is a shout of welcome to thee, O lord "of heaven and governor of Åmentet! Thou art acknowledged "by Isis who seeth her son in thee, the lord of fear, the mighty "one of terror. Thou settest as a living being in the hidden "place. Thy father [Ta-]tunen raiseth thee up and he placeth "both his hands behind thee; thou becomest endowed with divine "attributes in [thy] members of earth; thou wakest in peace and "thou settest in Manu. Grant thou that I may become a being "honoured before Osiris, and that I may come to thee, O Rā-Tem! "I have adored thee, therefore do thou for me that which I wish. "Grant thou that I may be victorious in the presence of the "company of the gods. Thou art beautiful, O Rā, in thy western "horizon of Åmentet, thou lord of Maāt, thou being who art "greatly feared, and whose attributes are majestic, O thou who art "greatly beloved by those who dwell in the Ṭuat! Thou shinest "with thy beams upon the beings that are therein perpetually, "and thou sendest forth thy light upon the path of Re-stau. "Thou openest up the path of the double Lion-god, thou settest "the gods upon [their] thrones, and the spirits in their abiding-"places. The heart of Naȧrerf (i.e., Ȧn-rutͅ-f, a region of the "Underworld) is glad [when] Rā setteth; the heart of Naȧrerf is "glad when Rā setteth. Hail, O ye gods of the land of Ȧmentet "who make offerings and oblations unto Rā-Tem, ascribe ye glory "[unto him when] ye meet him. Grasp ye your weapons and "overthrow ye the fiend Sebȧ on behalf of Rā, and repulse the "fiend Nebtͅ on behalf of Osiris. The gods of the land of Ȧmentet "rejoice and lay hold upon the cords of the Sektet boat, and they "come in peace; the gods of the hidden place who dwell in "Ȧmentet triumph." In the opening words of another hymn Tem is addressed as "Rā, who in thy setting art Tem-Ḥeru-khuti "(Tem-Harmachis), thou divine god, thou self-created being, thou "primeval matter,"[1] from which we see that the attributes of self-creation, etc., which, strictly speaking, belonged to Kheperȧ, were ascribed to Tem.

In the Myth of Rā and Isis Rā is made to say, "I am Kheperȧ "in the morning, and Rā at noonday, and Temu in the evening."[2] From which we may understand that the day and the night were divided into three parts, each of which was presided over by one of the three forms of Rā here mentioned. In the time of the Middle Empire Tem is often mentioned with Ḥeru-khuti, Rā, and Kheperȧ, and the priests of Heliopolis always attempted to prove that he was the ancestor of all the other forms of the Sun-god.

In the *Book of the Dead* (xvii. 5 ff.) the deceased is made to identify himself with Tem as the oldest of the gods, and he says, "I am Tem in rising; I am the only One; I came into being in "Nu. I am Rā who rose in the beginning." The statement is followed by the question, "Who then is this?" and the answer is,

[1] Naville, *Todtenbuch*, Bd. i., pl. 19.

[2] 

"It is Rā when at the beginning he rose in the city of Suten-"ḥenen, crowned like a king in rising. The pillars of Shu were "not as yet created when he was upon the high ground of him "that dwelleth in Khemennu" (i.e., Thoth). Thus it is clear that the Heliopolitans made out that it was Tem who was the first god to exist in primeval matter, and they consistently coupled him with Harmachis, , and with Kheperȧ, , as forms of the rising sun; on the other hand, they often, with fine inconsistency, identified him with the setting sun, and made the wind of evening, which gave refreshment to mortals and breath to the dead, to go forth from him.

It is difficult to say definitely where the original shrine of Tem was situated, but it appears to have been in the Eighth Nome of Lower Egypt,(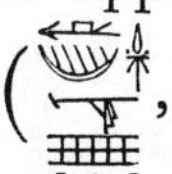, Nefer Ȧbt, the Heroopolites of the Greeks), at the place which is called both Thuket, 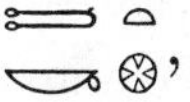, and Pa-Ȧtemt, 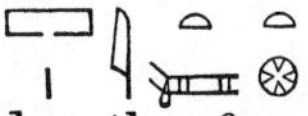, and it is described as the "gate of the East." Under the form "Pithom" the sacred name of the city Pa-Ȧtemt is familiar to all from the Bible. The site of Pa-Ȧtemt or Pithom was long thought to be buried beneath the ruins called by the Arabs Tell al-Maskhûtah,[1] which are situated close to the modern village of Tell el-Kebîr, and the excavations made on the spot by M. Naville prove that this view is correct. The inscriptions prove beyond all doubt that the great god of Pithom was Tem, and from the allusions which are made in them to the "Holy serpent" therein, and from the fact that one part of the temple buildings was called Pa-Qerḥet,[2] 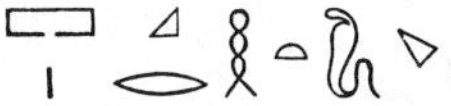, or Ȧst-qerḥet, 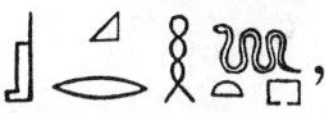, that is, "the house of the snake-god Qerḥet," it is tolerably certain that one of the forms under which Tem was worshipped was a huge serpent. A town situated as Pithom was on the large canal joining the Red Sea and the Nile, and on the highway from Arabia to Heliopolis must have contained a very mixed population, which would include a number of merchants and others from Western Asia. These probably brought in with them a number of strange

1 تل المسخوطة.

2 This is the Pi-hahiroth of the Bible.

practices connected with the worship of their own gods, which having been adopted by the indigenous peoples in the district modified their worship. From a passage in the Pyramid Texts already quoted it seems that the original form of the worship of Tem was phallic in character, but if it was nothing is known about it; some scholars have regarded obelisks as phallic emblems, and have pointed to their earliest forms, in which their tops were surmounted by disks, in proof of the correctness of their view.

Attached to the god Tem were two female counterparts called respectively IUSĀASET, , and NEBT-ḤETEP, 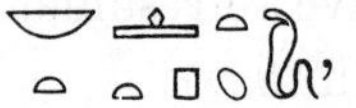, and they formed members of the company of the gods of Heliopolis, being mentioned with Tem, lord of the two lands of Ȧnnu, Rā, and Ḥeru-khuti.[1] Iusāaset, the Σαωσις of Plutarch, is called the "mistress of Ȧnnu," and the "Eye of Rā," 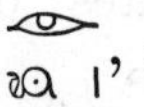, and she is regarded as the mother, and wife, and daughter of Tem according to the requirements of the texts;[2] as the wife of Tem she is said to be the mother of Shu and Tefnut. She is depicted[3] in the form of a woman who holds the sceptre, , in her right hand, and "life," , in her left; on her head she wears the vulture head-dress surmounted by a uraeus, and a disk between a pair of horns. In this form she is called the "mistress of Ȧnnu," 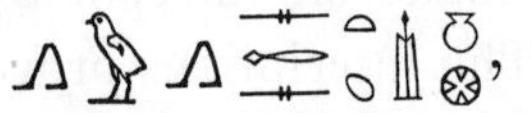, and was the wife of Tem-Ḥeru-khuti. The goddess Nebt-ḥetep appears to have been nothing but a form of Iusāaset, for in the scene in which she is represented in the form of a cow she is called "mistress of the gods, Iusāaset-Nebt-ḥetep."

According to Brugsch[4] Tem was joined to the god Osiris under the phase Tem-Ȧsȧr, and formed with Hathor of Ānnu, or Ānt, 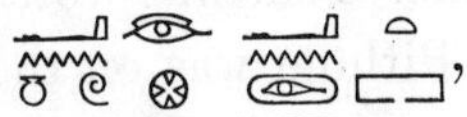, and Ḥeru-sma-taui, 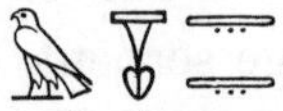, the head of the triad of Heroopolis. As local forms of the god Tem-Rā he enumerates Khnemu in Elephantine, Khnemu-Ḥeru-shefit in Heracleopolis Magna, and Khnemu-Ba-neb-Ṭeṭṭeṭ in Mendes.

[1] *Great Harris Papyrus*, sheet i., line 4.
[2] Brugsch, *Religion*, p. 284.
[3] Lanzone, op. cit., pl. 51.
[4] Op. cit., p. 290.

THE GODDESS IUSĀSET.

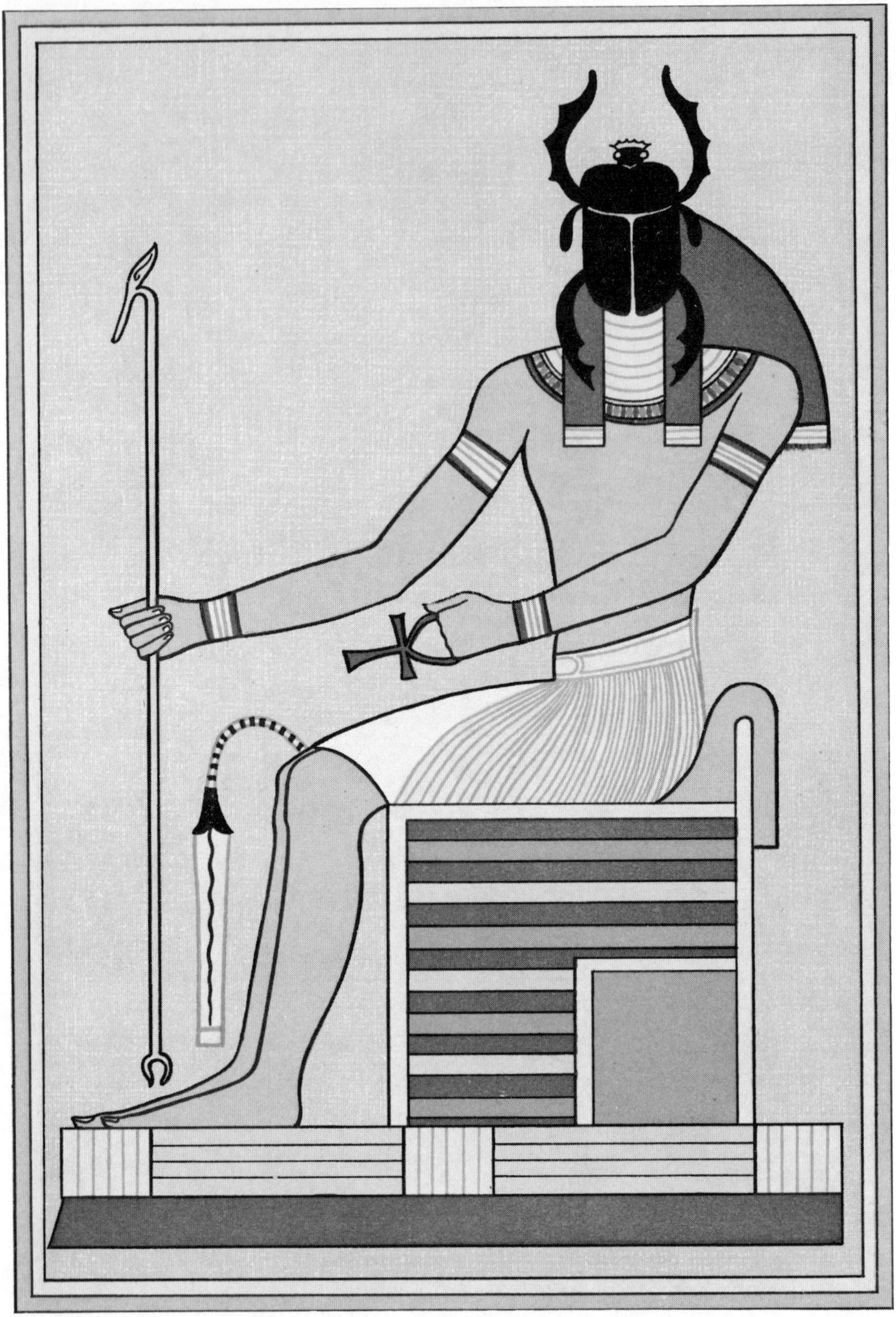

The God KHEPERA.

## KHEPERÅ 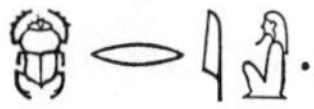.

The third form of Rā, the Sun-god, was KHEPERÅ KHEPER-TCHESEF, , i.e., Kheperå the self-produced, whose type and symbol was a beetle; he is usually represented in human form with a beetle upon the head, but sometimes a beetle takes the place of the human head. In one scene figured by Lanzone he is represented seated on the ground, and from his knees projects the head of the hawk of Horus, which is surmounted by ☥, "life."[1] In the section which treats of the Creation we have already translated and discussed the text which tells how the Sun-god Rā came into being under the form of Kheperå from out of the primeval watery mass of Nu, and how by means of his soul, which lived therein with him, he made a place whereon to stand, and straightway created the gods Shu and Tefnut, from whom proceeded the other gods. The worship of the beetle was, however, far older than that of Rā in Egypt, and it is pretty certain that the identification of Rā with the beetle-god is only another example of the means adopted by the priests, who grafted new religious opinions and beliefs upon old ones. The worship of the beetle, or at all events, the reverence which was paid to it, was spread over the whole country, and the ideas which were associated with it maintained their hold upon the dynastic Egyptians, and some of them appear to survive among the modern inhabitants of the Nile valley. The particular beetle which the Egyptians introduced into their mythology belongs to the family called *Scarabæidae* (Coprophagi), of which the *Scarabaeus sacer* is the type. These insects compose a very numerous group of dung-feeding Lamellicorns, of which, however, the majority live in tropical countries; they are usually black, but many are adorned with bright, metallic colours. They fly during the hottest hours of the day, and it was undoubtedly this peculiarity which caused the primitive Egyptians to associate them with the sun. Thus as far back as the VIth Dynasty the dead king Pepi is said "to fly like a bird, and to alight like a

[1] Lanzone, op. cit., pl. 329.

"beetle upon the empty throne in the boat of Rā."[1] According to Latreille[2] it was the species of a fine green colour (*Ateuchus Aegyptiorum*) which was first identified with the sun. The insect lays a vast numbers of eggs in a mass of dung, which it proceeds to push about with its legs until it gradually assumes the form of a ball, and then rolls it along to a hole which it has previously dug.

A ball of dung containing eggs varies in size from one to two inches in diameter, and in rolling it along the beetle stands almost upon its head, with its head turned away from the ball; in due course the larvae are hatched by the heat of the sun's rays beating down into the hole wherein it has been placed by the beetle, and they feed upon the covering of dung which protected them. The mind of the primitive Egyptian associated the ball of the beetle containing potential germs of life with the ball of the sun, which seemed to be rolled across the sky daily, and which was the source of all life. The beetle shows great perseverance in conveying the egg-laden balls of dung to the holes in which the larvae are to be hatched, and they frequently carry them over rough ground on the broad, flat surface of their heads, and seek, when unable singly to complete the work, the assistance of their fellows. It is this habit of the beetle which is represented in mythological scenes where we see the disk or ball of the sun on the head of the beetle, . A curious view was held by the ancient writers Aelian,[3] Porphyry,[4] and Horapollo[5] to the effect that beetles were all males (Κάνθαρος γὰς πᾶς ἄῤῥην), and that as there were no females among them, the males were, like the Sun-god Rā, self-produced. This erroneous idea probably sprang up because the male and female scarabaeus are very much alike, and because both sexes appear to divide the care of the preservation of their offspring equally between them, but in any case, it is a very ancient one, for in the Egyptian story of the Creation the god, whose type and symbol

1 
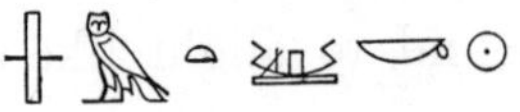 (Unȧs, l. 477).

2 Cailliaud, *Voyage*, tom. ii., p. 311.

3 *De Nat. Animal.*, x. 15.

4 *De Abstinentia*, iv. 9.

5 Ed. Leemans, p. 11.

was a beetle, not only produced himself, but also begot, conceived, and brought forth two deities, one male (Shu), and the other female (Tefnut).

In the Egyptian texts Kheperà is called the "father of the gods," 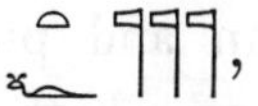, and in the *Book of the Dead* (xvii. 116) the deceased addresses him, saying, "Hail, Kheperà in thy boat, the "double company of the gods is thy body," but the form of the Sun-god with which he is most closely allied is that of Ḥeru-khuti, or Harmachis. In the *Book of the Dead* Kheperà plays a prominent part in connection with Osiris; he is called the "creator of the gods" (Ani, 1, 2); "Ḥeru-khuti-Temu-Ḥeru-Kheperà" (Qenna, 2, 15), and whatever forms he takes, or has taken, the deceased claims the right to take also. Moreover, the god Kheperà becomes in a manner a type of the dead body, that is to say, he represents matter containing a living germ which is about to pass from a state of inertness into one of active life. As he was a living germ in the abyss of Nu, and made himself to emerge therefrom in the form of the rising sun, so the germ of the living soul, which existed in the dead body of man, and was to burst into a new life in a new world by means of the prayers recited during the performance of appropriate ceremonies, emerged from its old body in a new form either in the realm of Osiris or in the boat of Rā. This doctrine was symbolized by the germs of life rolled up in the egg-ball of the beetle, and the power which made those to become living creatures was that which made man's spiritual body to come into being, and was personified in the god Kheperà. Thus Kheperà symbolized the resurrection of the body, and it was this idea which was at the root of the Egyptian custom of wearing figures of the beetle, and of placing them in the tombs and on the bodies of the dead; the myriads of scarabs which have been found in all parts of Egypt testify to the universality of this custom. As to its great antiquity there is no doubt whatsoever, for the scarab was associated with burial as far back as the period of the IVth Dynasty. Thus in the Papyrus of Nu (Brit. Mus., No. 10,477, sheet 21) we are told in the Rubric that Chapter lxiv. of the *Book of the Dead* was found inscribed in letters of real lapis-lazuli inlaid in a block "of iron of the south" under the feet of the god (i.e., Thoth), during the reign of Men-kau-Rā (Mycerinus), by the prince Ḥeru-ṭā-ṭā-f in the city of Khemennu.

At the end of the second paragraph this Chapter is ordered to be recited by a man "who is ceremonially clean and pure, who "hath not eaten the flesh of animals or fish, and who hath not had "intercourse with women." The text continues, "And behold, "thou shalt make a scarab of green stone, with a rim of gold, and "this shall be placed in the heart of a man, and it shall perform "for him the 'Opening of the Mouth.' And thou shalt anoint it "with *ānti* unguent, and thou shalt recite over it the following "words of power." The "words of power" which follow this direction form Chapter XXX B. of the *Book of the Dead*, wherein the deceased addresses the scarab as "my heart, my mother; my "heart, my mother! My heart whereby I came into being." He then prays that it will not depart from him when he stands in the presence of the "guardian" of the Balance wherein his heart is to be weighed, and that none may come forward in the judgment to oppose him, or to give false or unfavourable evidence against him, or to "make his name to stink." Curiously enough he calls the scarab "his double" (*ka*). Another Rubric makes the lxivth Chapter as old as the time of Ḥesepti (SEMTI), the fifth king of the Ist Dynasty, and the custom of burying green basalt scarabs inside or on the breasts of the dead may well be as old as his reign. Be this as it may, scarabs were worn by the living as protective amulets, and as symbols of triumphant acquittal in the Judgment Hall of Osiris, and as emblems of the resurrection which was to be effected by the power of the god Kheperå whom they represented, and the words of power of Chapter XXX B made them to act the part of the *ka* or double for the dead on the day of the "weighing of words" before Osiris, and his officers, and his sovereign chiefs, and Thoth the scribe of the gods, and the two companies of the gods. If scarabs were placed under the coffin no fiend could harm it, and their presence in a tomb gave to it the protection of the "father of the gods."

## CHAPTER X

# THE MYTHS OF RĀ

IN the preceding pages it has been shown how among theologians and thoughtful Egyptians Rā was regarded as God, but among certain classes, that is to say magicians, and astrologers, and soothsayers, quite other views were held about his nature and attributes. It will be remembered that among such men in ancient times it was customary to prescribe as antidotes to poison and sicknesses the recital or wearing of certain magical texts; the power of such texts was thought to be very great, especially if it contained a narrative of how some god or divine being had been delivered by the power of a great being from death by poison or by a sickness caused by poison. We may note in passing that such beliefs were not confined to the Egyptians, and that we find exactly the same ideas existent in Babylonia and Assyria; this is illustrated by the following interesting extract from a Babylonian tablet recently published by Mr. R. Campbell Thompson.[1] The text reads:—"From Anu [came the heavens], the heavens created "[the earth], the earth created the rivers, the rivers created the "canals, the canals created the marshes, and the marshes created "the Worm. Then came the Worm before Shamash, the Sun-god, "weeping, and before Ea came up her tearful plaint, [saying], "'What wilt thou give me to eat? What wilt thou give me to "gnaw?' [The gods said], 'I will give thee dry bones [to eat], "'and the pungent *khashkhar* wood.' [The Worm said], 'What "'are thy dry bones to me? Or, what is thy *khashkhar* wood to "'me? Let me drink among the teeth [of men], and give me "'my place in [their] gums, that I may suck the blood of the teeth,

[1] *Cuneiform Texts from Babylonian Tablets*, part xvii., pl. 50; and see R. C. Thompson, *The Devils and Evil Spirits of Babylonia*, vol. i., Introduction, at the end.

"'and that I may tear asunder the flesh of the gums. In this wise "'I shall have power over the bolt of the door' (i.e., the mouth of a "man). Therefore, O sick man, shalt thou say the following words, "'O Worm, may Ea smite thee with all his might.'" Following these words come the rubrical directions which order the patient to mix together a prescription compounded of beer, oil, and the juice of a certain plant, and when the incantation has been recited over the man with the toothache three times, the mixture is to be rubbed on the tooth. In the one case the object of the narrative was to cure the man who had been bitten by a venomous serpent, and in the other to ease the pain in the teeth and the inflammation of the gums which were supposed to be caused by a worm, a descendant of the original Worm which claimed before Ea the right to make teeth decay and to suck the blood of the gums.

The Egyptian texts which were written for magical purposes have preserved for us some very curious and interesting myths of Rā, and among these may be quoted the following story about him and the goddess Isis.[1] The title reads:—"The Chapter of the divine "god, the self-created being, who made the heavens and the earth, "and the winds which give life, and the fire, and the gods, and men, "and beasts, and cattle, and reptiles, and the fowl of the air, and the "fish of the sea; he is the king of men and of gods, he hath but "one period to his life, and with him a double *hen* period (i.e., one "hundred and twenty years) is as a single year; his names are "manifold and unknown, the gods even know them not." The story runs:—"Now Isis was a woman who possessed words of "power; her heart was wearied with the millions of men, there-"fore she chose the millions of the gods, but she esteemed more "highly the millions of the spirits. And she meditated in her "heart, saying, 'Cannot I by means of the sacred name of God "'make myself mistress of the earth and become a goddess of like "'rank and power to Rā in heaven and upon earth?' And

[1] The hieratic text will be found in Pleyte and Rossi, *Le Papyrus de Turin*, 1869-1876; pll. 31-37, and 131-138; and a transcript into hieroglyphics with a transliteration and translation in my *First Steps in Egyptian*, 1895, pp. 241-256. A French translation by Lefébure was published in *Aeg. Zeit.*, 1883, pp. 27 ff.; and for English renderings see my *Papyrus of Ani*, 1895, p. lxxxix., and *Egyptian Magic*, p. 137.

"behold, each day Rā entered at the head of his holy mariners "and established himself upon the throne of the two horizons; "but the divine one (i.e., Rā) had grown old, he dribbled at the "mouth, his spittle fell upon the earth, and his slobbering dropped "upon the ground. And Isis kneaded [some] thereof with earth "in her hand, and formed therewith a sacred serpent in the form "of a dart; she did not set it upright before her face, but let it "lie upon the ground in the path whereby the great god went "forth, according to his heart's desire, into his double kingdom. "Now the holy god arose, and the gods who followed him as "though he were Pharaoh went with him; and he came forth "according to his daily wont; and the sacred serpent bit him. "The flame of his life departed from him; and he who dwelt "among the cedars was overcome. The holy god opened his "mouth, and the cry of his majesty reached unto heaven; his "company of the gods said, 'What hath happened?' and his "gods exclaimed, "What is it?' But Rā could not answer, for "his jaws trembled and all his members quaked, the poison spread "swiftly through his flesh just as Nile rusheth through all his "land. When the great god had stablished his heart, he cried "unto those who were in his train, saying, 'Come unto me, O ye "'who have come into being from my body, ye gods who have "'come forth from me, make ye known unto Kheperȧ that a dire "'calamity hath fallen upon me. My heart perceiveth it, but my "'eyes see it not; my hand hath not caused it, nor do I know "'who hath done this unto me. Never have I felt such pain, "'neither can sickness cause more woe than this. I am a prince, "'the son of a prince, the sacred essence which hath proceeded "'from God. I am the great one, the son of the great one, and "'my father planned my name; I have multitudes of names, and "'multitudes of forms, and my being is in every god. I have "'been proclaimed by the heralds Temu and Horus; and my father "'and my mother uttered my name; but it hath been hidden "'within me by him that begat me, who would not that the words "'of power of any seer should have dominion over me. I came "'forth to look upon that which I had made, I was passing through "'the world which I had created, when lo! something stung me, "'but what I know not. Is it fire? Is it water? My heart is "'on fire, my flesh quaketh, and trembling hath seized all my "'limbs. Let there be brought unto me my children, the gods "'who possess the words of power and magical speech, and mouths "'which know how to utter them, and also powers which reach "'even unto the heaven.'

"Then the children of every god came unto him uttering "cries of grief. And Isis also came, bringing with her her words of "magical power, and her mouth was full of the breath of life; for "her talismans vanquish the pains of sickness, and her words make "to live again the throats of those who are dead. And she spake, "saying, 'What hath come to pass, O holy Father? What hath "'happened? Is it that a serpent hath bitten thee, and that a "'thing which thou hast created hath lifted up his head against "'thee? Verily it shall be cast down by my effective words of "'power, and I will drive it away from before the sight of thy "'sunbeams.' The holy god opened his mouth and said, 'I was "'passing along my path, and I was going through the two "'regions of my lands according to my heart's desire, to see that "'which I had created, when lo! I was bitten by a serpent which "'I saw not. Is it fire? Is it water? I am colder than water, "'I am hotter than fire. All my flesh sweateth, I quake, mine "'eye hath no strength, I cannot see the sky, and the sweat "'rusheth to my face even as in the time of summer.' Then said "Isis unto Rā, 'O tell me thy name, holy Father, for whosoever "'shall be delivered by thy name shall live.' And Rā said, 'I "'have made the heavens and the earth, I have knit together "'the mountains, I have created all that is above them, I have "'made the water, I have made to come into being the goddess "'Meḥt-urt, and I have made the Bull of his mother, from whom "'spring the delights of love, I have made the heavens, I have "'stretched out the two horizons like a curtain, and I have placed "'the souls of the gods within them. I am he who, if he openeth "'his eyes, doth make the light, and, if he closeth them, darkness "'cometh into being. At his command the Nile riseth, and the "'gods know not his name. I have made the hours, I have "'created the days, I bring forward the festivals of the year, I "'create the Nile-flood. I make the fire of life, and I provide "'food in the houses. I am Kheperȧ in the morning, I am Rā at "'noon, and I am Temu at even.' Meanwhile the poison was not "taken away from his body, but it penetrated deeper, and the "great god could no longer walk.

"Then said Isis unto Rā, 'What thou hast said is not thy "'name. O tell it unto me, and the poison shall depart; for "'he shall live whose name shall be revealed.' Now the poison "burned like fire, and it was fiercer than the flame and the "furnace, and the majesty of the great god said, 'I consent that "'Isis shall search into me, and that my name shall pass from me "'into her.' Then the god hid himself from the gods, and his "place in the Boat of Millions of Years was empty. And when "the time had arrived for the heart of Rā to come forth, Isis spake "unto her son Horus, saying, 'The god hath bound himself by "'oath to deliver up his two Eyes (i.e., the Sun and the Moon).' "Thus was the name of the great god taken from him, and Isis, "the lady of words of magical power, said, 'Depart, thou poison, "'go forth from Rā. O Eye of Horus, go forth from the god, and "'shine outside his mouth. It is I who work, it is I who make to "'fall down upon the earth the vanquished poison, for the name "'of the great god hath been taken away from him. Let Rā live, "'and let the poison die! Let the poison die, and let Rā live!' "These are the words of Isis, the mighty lady, the mistress of the "gods, who knew Rā by his own name." The above text was to be recited over figures of Temu, "the Bull of his mother," and Horus, and Isis and Horus, and there is little doubt that these figures were made to represent the various scenes which took place when Rā was poisoned, and when the goddess Isis succeeded in taking from him his name.

Another myth of Rā of considerable interest is that which describes the destruction of mankind, and tells how men scorned the great Sun-god because he had become old;[1] the text of this,

[1] For the hieroglyphic text see Lefébure, Tombeau de Seti I., part iv., pll. 15-18; Brugsch, *Die neue Weltordnung*, Berlin, 1881; Naville in *Trans. Soc. Bibl. Arch.*, iv., pp. 1 ff.; viii., pp. 412 ff.; Bergmann, *Hist. Inschrift.*, pll. 75-82; and my *First Steps in Egyptian*, pp. 218-230.

in a mutilated condition, is found inscribed upon the walls of the tombs of Seti I. and Rameses IV. at Thebes, and from it the following is clear. " [Rā is] the god who created himself after he " had risen in sovereignty over men, and gods, as well as over " things, the One. And mankind was uttering words of complaint, " saying, 'Behold now, his Majesty, life, strength, and health [to " 'him]! hath become old, his bones are like silver, his limbs are " 'like gold, and his hair is like unto real lapis-lazuli.' Now his " majesty heard the words which mankind spake [concerning " him], and he said unto those who were following him, 'Cry out, " 'and bring ye unto me mine Eye, and Shu, and Tefnut, and " 'Seb, and Nut, and the fathers and the mothers who were with " 'me when I was in Nu, together with my god Nu. Let him " 'bring his ministers with him, and let them be brought silently, " 'so that mankind may not perceive it and take to flight with " 'their hearts. Come thou with them to the Great House, and " 'let them declare their plans, for I will go forth from Nu unto " 'the place wherein I performed creations, and let those [gods] be " 'brought unto me there.' Now the gods were on both sides of " Rā, and they bowed down even to the ground in presence of his " Majesty, and he spake his words in the presence of the father of " the firstborn gods, the maker of men, and the king of those who " have knowledge. And they spake before his Majesty, [saying], " 'Speak unto us, for we are listening'; and Rā spake unto Nu, " saying, 'O thou firstborn god, from whom I came into being, O " 'ye gods [my] ancestors, behold ye what mankind is doing, they " 'who were created by mine Eye are uttering murmurs against " 'me. Give me your attention, and seek ye out a plan for me, " 'and I will not slay them until ye shall say [what I am to do] " 'concerning it.'

" Then the Majesty of the god Nu, the son of Rā, spake " [saying], 'Thou art the god who art greater than he that made " 'thee, and who art the sovereign of those who were created by " 'him, thy throne is set, and the fear of thee is great; let " 'then thine Eye be upon those who have uttered blasphemies " 'against thee.' And the Majesty of Rā spake [saying], " 'Behold ye how they have taken flight into the mountain!

"'Their hearts are afraid because of what they have said.' "'Then the gods spake before his Majesty, saying, 'Make "'thine Eye to go forth, and let it destroy for thee those who "'utter evil words of blasphemy against thee. There is not an "'eye upon all this earth which can resist thine when it "'descendeth in the form of Hathor.' And the goddess [Hathor] "went forth and slew the people on the mountain, and the Majesty "of this god spake, [saying], 'Come, come in peace, Hathor, the "'work is accomplished.' And the goddess said, 'Thou livest for "'me. When I had gained the mastery over men it was well "'pleasing to my heart.' And the Majesty of Rā spake, [saying], "'I will gain the mastery over them as king, and [I] will destroy "'them'; and it came to pass that Sekhet waded about in the "night season in their blood, beginning at Suten-ḥenen (Herakleo-"polis Magna). Then the Majesty of Rā spake, [saying], 'Cry out "'and fetch me swift and speedy messengers who can run like the "'wind'; and straightway one brought these messengers. And "the Majesty of this god spake, [saying], 'Let them go to Ābu "'(Elephantine), and bring me mandrakes in great number'; and "one brought to him these mandrakes, and the Majesty of this god "gave them to Sekhet who [dwelleth] in Ȧnnu (Heliopolis) to "crush. And behold, when the women were crushing the barley "to [make] beer, he placed these mandrakes in the vessels which "were to hold the beer, and some of the blood of the men [who "had been slain]. Now they made seven thousand vessels of "beer.

"Now when the king of the South and North, Rā, had come "with the gods to look at the beer, and the daylight appeared "after the goddess had slaughtered mankind in their season as she "sailed up the river, the Majesty of Rā said, 'It is doubly good, "'but I must protect mankind against her.' And Rā spake, "[saying], 'Let them take up the vases and carry them to the "'place where men and women are being slaughtered.' Then the "Majesty of the king of the South and North, Rā, commanded "them to pour out from the vessels during the [time of the] "beauty of the night the beer which made [men] wish to lie down, "and the regions of the four heavens were filled therewith even "according to the Will of the Majesty of this god. Now when the "goddess Sekhet came in the morning and found the regions flooded, "her face beamed with joy, and she drank of the beer and blood, "and her heart was glad, and she became drunk, and she took no "further heed of mankind. And the Majesty of Rā spake unto "this goddess, [saying] 'Come, come in peace, O fair and gracious "'goddess;' [and henceforth] there were young and beautiful "women in the city of Amen.[1] Then the Majesty of Rā said unto "this goddess, 'There shall be prepared for thee vases of drink "'which shall make thee wish to sleep at every festival of the New "'Year, and the number thereof shall be in proportion to the "'number of my handmaidens;' and from that day until this "present men have been wont to make on the occasions of the "festival of Hathor vases of beer which will make them sleep, in "number according to the number of the handmaidens of Rā. "And the Majesty of Rā spake unto this goddess, [saying], "'Behold, the pain of the burning heat of sickness hath come "'upon me; whence cometh [this] pain?' Then the Majesty of "Rā said, 'I am alone, but my heart hath become exceedingly "'weary of being with them (i.e., with men); I have slain [some "'of] them, but there is a remnant of worthless ones, and the "'destruction which I wrought among them was not commensurate "'with my power.' And the gods who were in his train said "[unto him], 'Tarry not in thy weariness, for thy might is in "'proportion to thine own will.' Then the Majesty of this god "said unto the Majesty of Nu, 'For the first time my limbs have "'lost their power, and I will never permit this thing to happen "'a second time.'"

At this point the inscription becomes much broken, and it is difficult to make out the general meaning which is to be attached

[1] Here there is a pun on the appellation of the goddess *Amit* 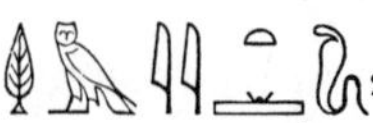, and on the name of the city Amen, , i.e., the capital of the nome, , Ȧment, where the goddess Hathor was worshipped. The city is also called , and the "city of Apis."

to the scattered words; according to the late Dr. Brugsch,[1] the myth ends somewhat as follows:—When Rā had described his weariness to Nu, this god commanded Shu to perform the work of Rā and to take the place of his Eye, and directed the sky goddess Nut to help Rā. Nut asked Nu how this was to be done, and he told her to take Rā upon her back; thereupon Nut took the form of a cow, and Rā seated himself upon her back. In due course mankind saw Rā on the back of Nut, and they were filled with remorse at their former behaviour towards him, and they wished to see slain his enemies who had blasphemed him, but his Majesty did not tarry, and he went on into the temple. On the following day as soon as the morning had come, men went forth armed with bows and spears in order to do battle with the enemies of Rā, and as soon as the god saw this he said to them, "Your sins are "forgiven you, for the sacrificial slaughters which ye have made "have done away with the murders [which mine enemies have "committed]." Then Rā raised himself from the back of the goddess Nut into the sky, where he made for himself a kingdom in which all people were to be assembled. Finally he ordered a Field to come into being, 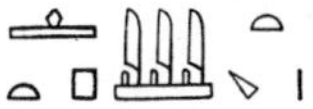 *ḥetep sekhet*, and straightway the Field of Ḥetep ("Peace"), 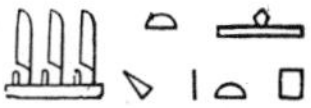 *Sekhet-ḥetep*,[2] came into being, and the Majesty of the god said, "I will plant "( *àaràṭ-à*, literally, I will make to grow) "green herbs therein," and straightway there came into being Sekhet-àaru,[3] , "and I will plenish "it with objects which sparkle,[4] that is to say with stars." Thereupon the goddess Nut quaked in all her members, and Rā declared that he would make supports to come into existence to strengthen her, and straightway supports appeared. Rā next

[1] *Die Neue Weltordnung nach Vernichtung des sündigen Menschengeschlechtes*, von H. Brugsch, Berlin, 1881, p. 23.

[2] Note the jingle in the words *sekhet* and *ḥetep*.

[3] Note the play on the verbal *àaraṭ-à* and the noun *àaru*.

[4] Note the jingle in 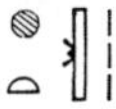 *khet*, "objects," and  "things which sparkle."

The Cow-goddess Nut.

ordered his son Shu to place himself beneath the goddess Nut, who was trembling, in such a way as to support her body, and he ordered him to take heed to the supports, or pillars, whereon the goddess rested, and to protect them, and to keep Nut stayed upon his head.

Near this place in the text we have a representation of the great cow-goddess Nut, i.e., the heavens and the sky (see opposite). Along the belly of the cow, which is emblematic of the sky, and is supported by the god Shu, are thirteen stars, and immediately below are the two boats of the Sun-god. In the Māṭet boat stands a figure of Rā as god of the day, with a disk upon his head, and in the Sektet boat we see the god seated in a shrine; the former boat is between the fore-legs of the cow of Nut, and the latter by her udders. Each leg of the cow is supported by two gods, one in front and one behind, and each god who is with the cow has a special name, which is duly set forth in the text which runs in vertical columns on each side of the scene.[1]

When the narrative recommences (line 56) we are told that the Majesty of the god Rā commanded Thoth to give the order that the god Seb, or Sab,  (whom Brugsch calls "Keb"), should come into his presence forthwith, and when he had done so, and Seb had appeared before him, Rā told him that strife had arisen by reason of the worms (or snakes), , which were in his (i.e., Seb's) territory, and, he added, "May they fear me as long as I am alive." Rā also told him to find out what their plans were, and then to go to the place wherein was his father Nu, and to warn him to be careful about what was on the earth and in the water. The text which immediately follows is full of difficulty, but its general meaning seems to be that Rā expects Seb to keep watch on the serpents in the earth, and that although he is about to betake himself to the uppermost regions of heaven his light will find them in their holes, and will watch them. Moreover, Rā promises that he will give the men who have knowledge of words of power, 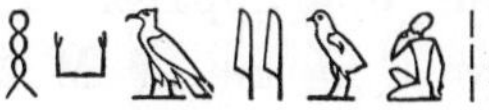, dominion over them, and that he

[1] See Lefébure, *Tombeau de Seti I.*, part iv., pl. 16, ll. 47 ff.

will furnish them with spells and charms which shall draw them from their holes. After these things the Majesty of the god Rā ordered that Thoth should come into his presence speedily, and when he had arrived he said to him, "Come, let us depart "from heaven, and from my place, because I am about to create "a thing of light ( ) of the god of light ( ), "in the Ṭuat ( ) and in the Land of Babat ( ). "And there thou shalt write down for punishment among the "dwellers therein those who have committed deeds of rebellion, "and those whom my heart hateth. And thou shalt be in my "place ( *ȧst*), and thou shalt be called Ȧsti ( ), "that is to say, the deputy of Rā. And it shall be permitted to "thee to send for thy messenger ( *hab*), and at "these words the ibis ( *habi*), which is the envoy "of Thoth, came into being." Rā next tells Thoth that he will give him the power to lift up his hand before the great companies of the gods, , and makes a play on the words *khen* , and *Tekhni* , a bird sacred to Thoth; he also promises to make Thoth to embrace *ȧnḥ*, the two heavens with his beauties, and straightway the Moon, , came into being. Thoth is to drive back, *ān*, the Ḥa-nebu, , and straightway the Ape, *ānān*, of the god came into being; and finally Thoth is to be wholly the representative of Rā upon earth.

From the observations which follow the words of Rā we can see how holy these words were considered to be. Any one who wished to repeat them must anoint his face with oil, and rub his hands and the places behind his ears with incense, and cleanse his mouth with natron, and wash his new apparel in Nile water, and put on white sandals, and lay a figure of Maāt upon his tongue; and he must cleanse himself with a sevenfold cleansing each day for three whole days. Finally, the king (Seti I.) for whom these texts were written declares that his soul is the soul of Shu, and [Khnemu], and Neḥeḥ, 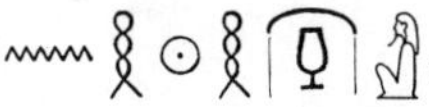, and Kek, 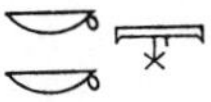, and Ḳerḥ, 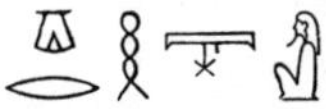, and Nu, and Rā, and Åsår-Ba-Ṭeṭṭeṭ, and the souls of the Sebåk gods, , and of the Crocodiles, and the soul of every god in the form of a serpent, , and the soul of Āpep, and of Rā in all the earth.

# CHAPTER XI

## THE LEGEND OF RĀ AND ISIS

### HIEROGLYPHIC TEXT WITH TRANSLITERATION AND TRANSLATION

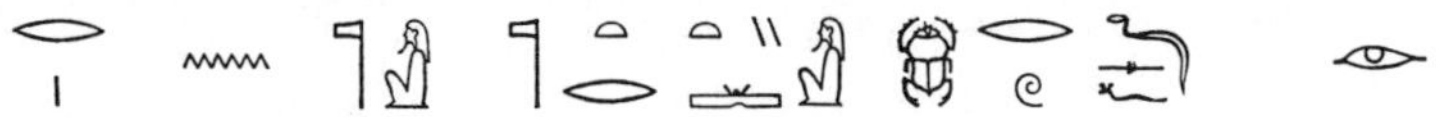

| | | | | | | |
|---|---|---|---|---|---|---|
| *Re* | *en* | *neter* | *neterti* | *kheperu* | *tchesef* | *ȧri* |
| Chapter | of | the god | divine (?) | self-produced, | | the maker |

| | | | | | |
|---|---|---|---|---|---|
| *pet* | *ta* | *māu* | *en* | *ānkh* | *khet* |
| of heaven, | [and] earth, | [and] the breath | of | life, | of fire, |

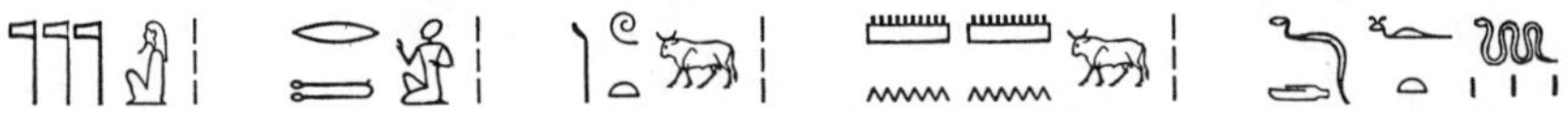

| | | | | |
|---|---|---|---|---|
| *neteru* | *reth* | *āut* | *menmen* | *tchetfet* |
| of gods, | of men, | of beasts, | of cattle, | of reptiles and creeping things, |

| | | | | | |
|---|---|---|---|---|---|
| *apṭ* | *remu* | *suten* | *reth* | *neteru* | *em* |
| of the fowl of the air, | [and] of fishes, | the king | of men | [and] of gods, | in |

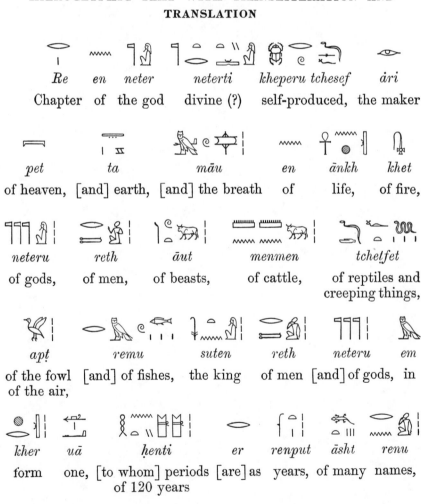

| | | | | | | |
|---|---|---|---|---|---|---|
| *kher* | *uā* | *ḥenti* | *er* | *renput* | *āsht* | *renu* |
| form | one, | [to whom] periods of 120 years | [are] as | years, | of many | names, |

*àn rekh pefi àn rekh pefi neteru*

not known is that [god], not known is that [god to] the gods.

*àstu Àst em set saa en*

Behold, Isis was in the form of a woman [who was] skilled in

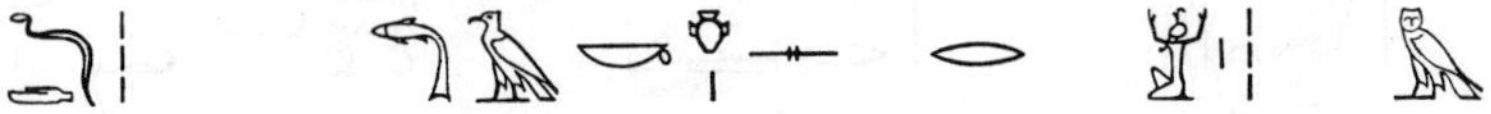

*tcheṭu khak-àb-s er ḥeḥu em*

words (i.e., matters). Her heart rebelled at the millions of

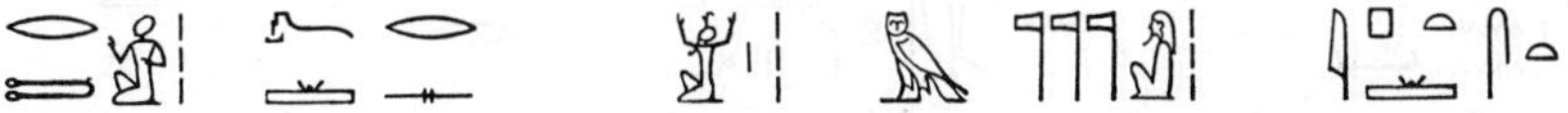

*reth setep eres ḥeḥu em neteru àpt-set*

men, she chose rather the millions of the gods, and she esteemed

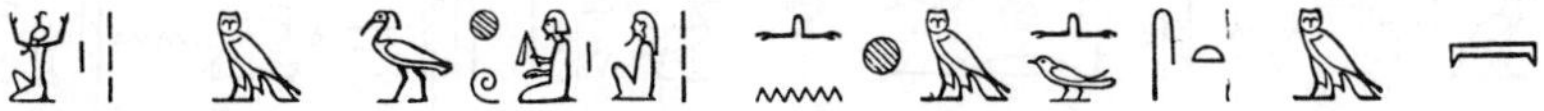

*ḥeḥu em khu àn khem set em pet*

the millions of the spirits [of more value]. "Could she not be in heaven

*ta mà Rā àri ḳert ta*

[and] earth like Rā [and] make herself mistress of the earth

*netert ka-set em àb-set er rekh*

and a goddess," she meditated in her heart, "by knowing

*ren neter shepsi*

the name of the god holy?"

*åstu āq en Rā hru neb em ḥāt qet - [f]*

Behold, came in Rā every day in front of [his] sailors,

*smen-thå ḥer nest khuti*

and was stablished upon the throne of the two horizons.

*åaut netri ennu - nef re - f*

Had become old the divine one, he dribbled at his mouth,

*sat - f nebåut - f er ta*

he poured out his exudations upon the ground,

*peḳas en su sekher ḥer sat sek-nes Åst*

and his spittle fell upon the earth. Isis she kneaded [it]

*em ṭet-set ḥenā ta unenet ḥer-set qeṭ-nes-set*

in her hand with earth which was on it, she fashioned it

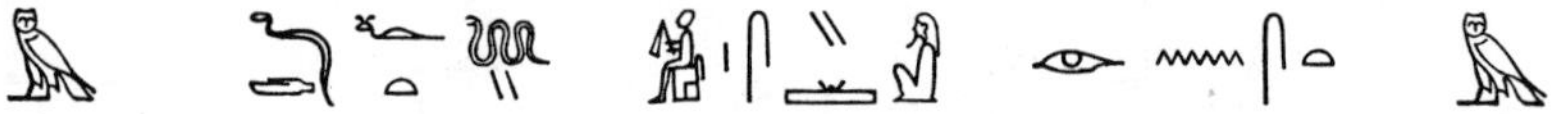

*em tchetfeti shepsi åri en set em*

in the form of a serpent sacred, [and] she made [it] in

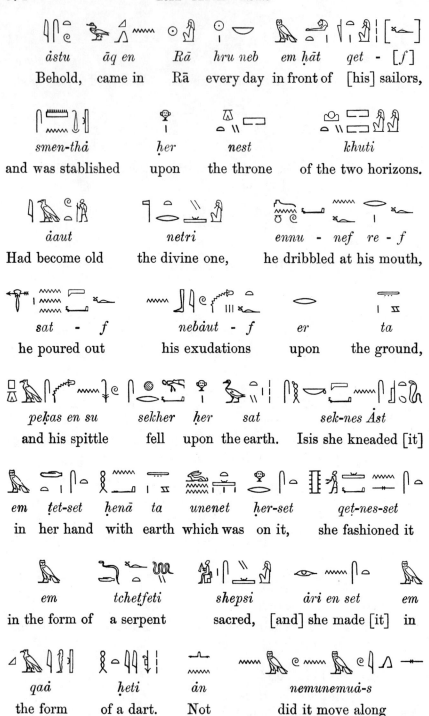

*qaå ḥeti ån nemunemuå-s*

the form of a dart. Not did it move along

*ānkh-thȧ* *er kheft-set* *khaā-set* *ḥamu* *ḥer*
alive before her, [and] she left [it] lying on

*uat* *āpep neter āa ḥer-s* *er* *ȧba - f*
the path whereon journeyed the great god according to his desire

*em khet* *taui - f*
through his two lands.

*neter* *shepsi* *khā - f* *er ḥa* *neteru*
The god holy rose up, behind the gods

*em* *Āa-perti* *ānkh* *utcha* *senb* *em* *khet- f*
in the great double house, life, strength, health! [were] following him,

*seftseft - f* *mȧ* *hru neb* *unkhu-set* *em*
[and] he marched on as [he did] every day [when] bit [him]

*tchetfeti* *shepsi* *khet* *ānkhet* *per-thȧ*
the serpent sacred; the fire of life was coming out

*ȧm - f* *tchesef* *ṭer-nes* *ȧmi* *na* *āshu*
from him himself, it destroyed the dweller in the cedars.

*neter netri [un] - f re - f kheru en*
The god divine he opened his mouth, the voice of

*ḥen - f ā. u. s. peḥ-nef er pet Paut*
his Majesty L. S. H.! reached unto heaven. The company

*neteru tuf ḥer mā pu-u neteru - f*
of the gods was for [saying], "What is it?" His gods [were]

*ḥer petrȧ-u ȧn qem - f*
for [saying] "What is the matter?" Not found he

*meṭtu er ushebt ḥer - f ȧrti-fi*
words to answer about it. His two jaws

*ḥer khetkhet āt - f neb ȧstiti metu*
rattled, his limbs all trembled, the poison

*thetet-nef em ȧufi mȧ thetet Ḥāp*
took possession of his body as taketh possession the Nile

*em khet - f neter āa smen-nef ȧb - f*
of his river bed. The god great stablished his heart,

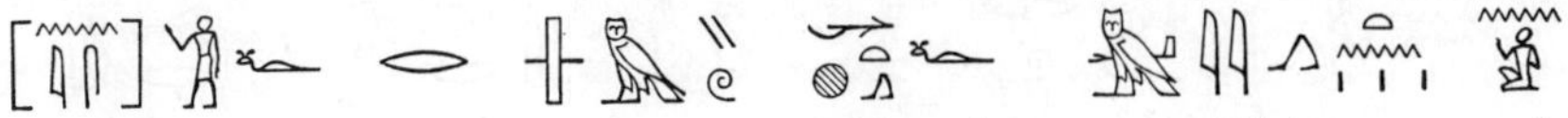

*[nȧs] - f* *er* *ȧmiu* *khet - f* *māi-ten* *nȧ*

he [cried] out to those in his train:— "Come to me,

*khepert* *em* *ḥāt-ȧ* *neteru*

O ye who have come into being from my members, [ye] gods

*peru* *em-ȧ* *ṭāt* *rekh-ten*

who have proceeded from me, and I will make you to know

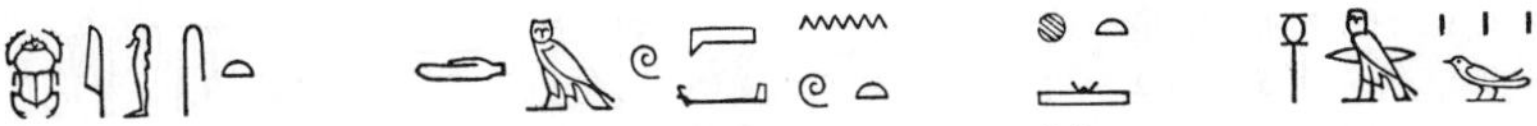

*kheperȧ-set* *ṭemu-entu* *khet* *meru*

what hath happened: I am wounded by something deadly,

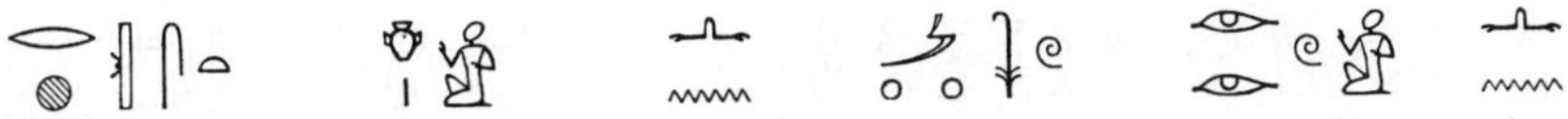

*rekh-set* *ȧb-ȧ* *ȧn* *maa su* *maa-ȧ* *ȧn*

knoweth it my heart. Not have seen it my eyes, not

*ȧri* *set* *ṭet-ȧ* *ȧn* *rekh-set* *em ȧri-nȧ* *nebt*

made it my hand, not know [I] it who hath done [this] to me anyone,

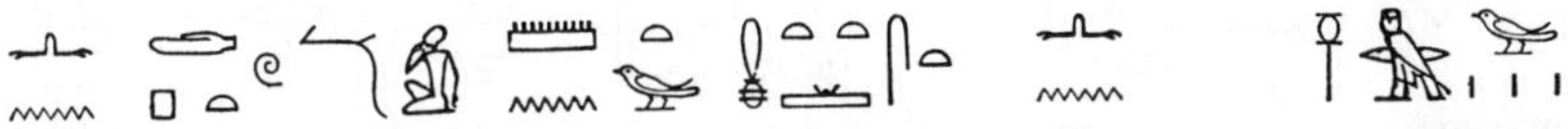

*ȧn* *ṭeptu-ȧ* *ment* *mȧtet-set* *ȧn* *meru*

not have I tasted pain like it, never was deadly [anything]

*er-s* *ȧnuk* *ser* *sa* *ser*

more than it. I am a prince, the son of a prince,

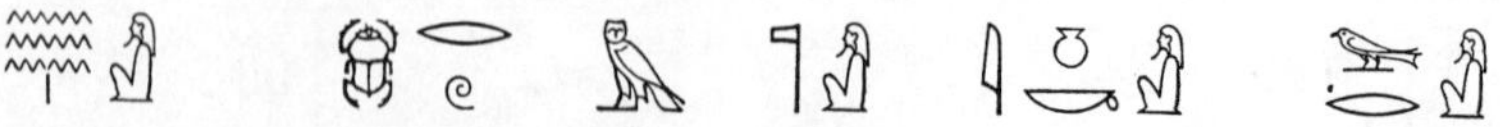

*mu kheperu em neter ȧnuk ur*

the divine issue produced by a god. I am a great one,

*sa ur maut en ȧtef-ȧ ren-ȧ*

the son of a great one, thought out my father my name.

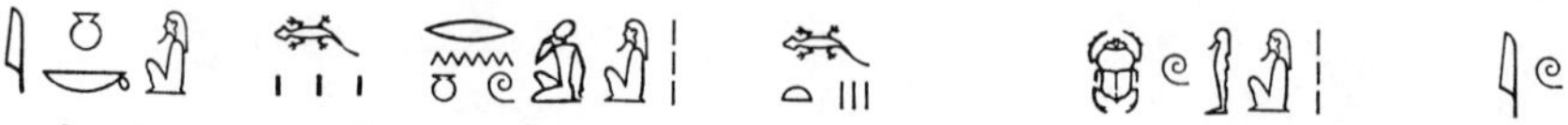

*ȧnuk āshu rennu āsht kheperu ȧu*

I am of many names, of many forms (or, existences) is

*kheperȧ-ȧ unu em neter neb nȧs-ȧ-tu*

my form (or existence) living in god every. I have proclaimed

*Temu Ḥeru ḥekennu ȧu tcheṭ ȧtef-ȧ*

Temu and Ḥeru Ḥekennu. Have uttered my father

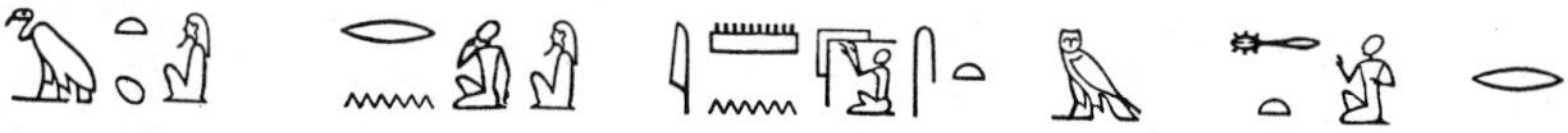

*mut-ȧ ren-ȧ ȧmen-set em khat-ȧ er*

and my mother my name, hidden was it in my body by

*mes-ȧ en meri tem erṭāt kheperu peḥti*

my begetter who wished not to let have power

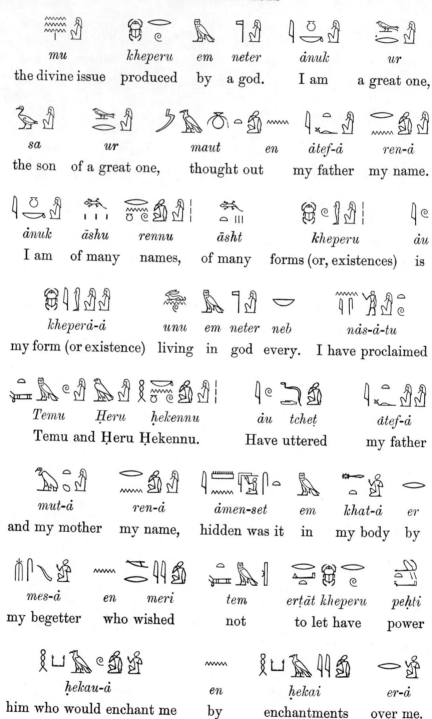

*ḥekau-ȧ en ḥekai er-ȧ*

him who would enchant me by enchantments over me.

*peru-k er ḥa er maa ȧri-nȧ*

I had come forth from the abode to see what I had made

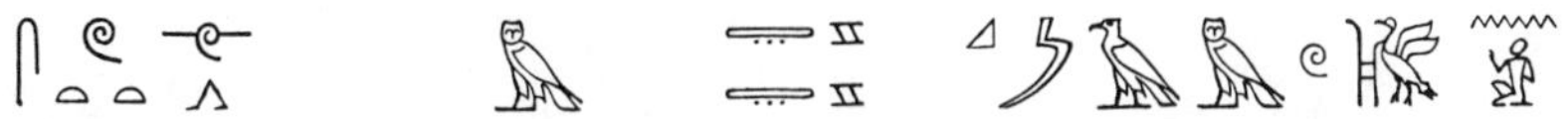

*sutet em taui qemamu-nȧ*

[and] was being led through the lands [which] I had created,

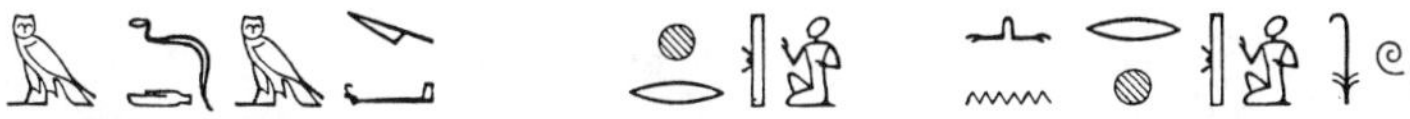

*em tcheṭem kher-ȧ ȧn rekh-ȧ su*

when [something] aimed a blow at me [and] I know not what it is.

*ȧn khet ȧs pu ȧn mu ȧs pu ȧb-ȧ kheri*

Behold it is not fire, behold it is not water. My heart contains

*[khet]u ḥāt-ȧ ȧstiti āt-[ȧ] kheri*

fire, my limbs [are] trembling, [my] members contain

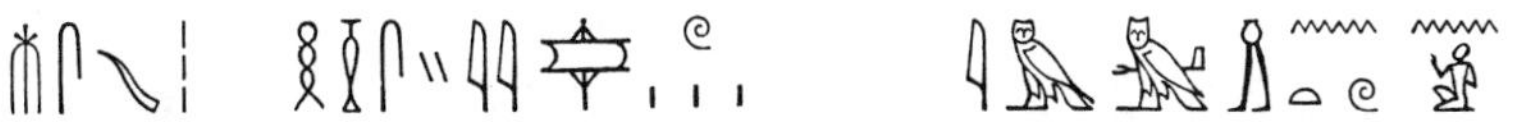

*mesu ḥesiu ȧmmā ȧntu-nȧ*

the children of quakings. I pray you let be brought to me

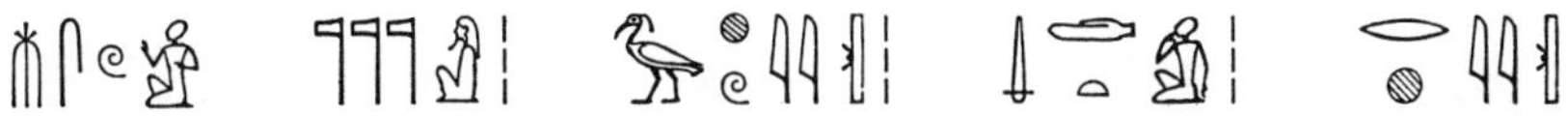

*mesu-ȧ neteru khui meṭet rekhi*

my children, the gods mighty of words, skilful

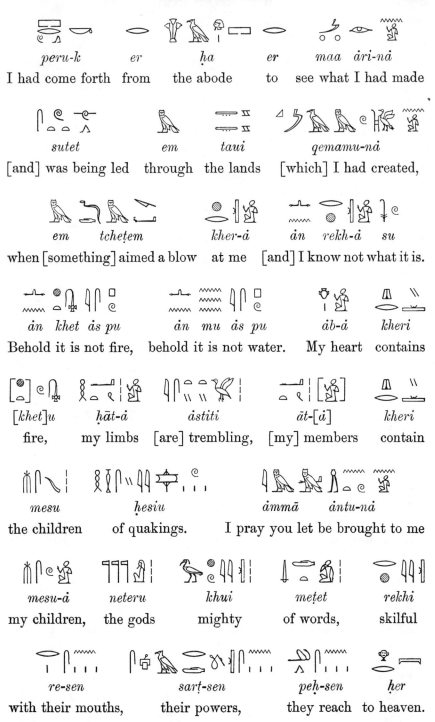

*re-sen sarṭ-sen peḥ-sen ḥer*

with their mouths, their powers, they reach to heaven.

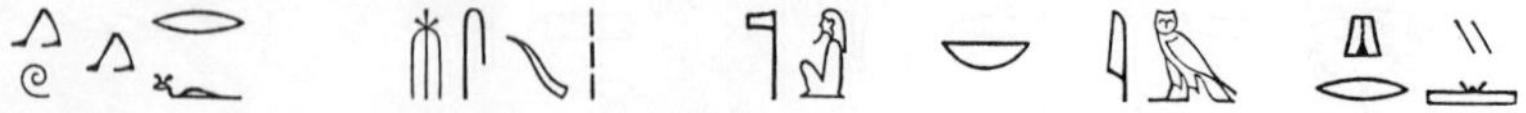

*iu-eref* *mesu* *neter* *neb* *ȧm* *kheri*

Came to him [his] children, god every there with

*ȧkebu-nef* *iu* *en Ȧst* *kheri* *khut-set*

his cries of weeping. Came Isis with her power

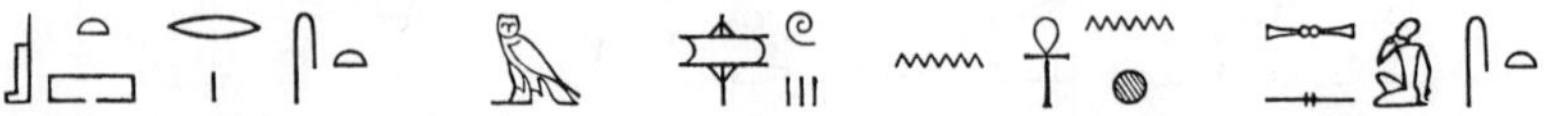

*ȧst* *re-set* *em* *nifu* *en* *ānkh* *thes-set*

and her skilled mouth, with the breath of life, her incantations

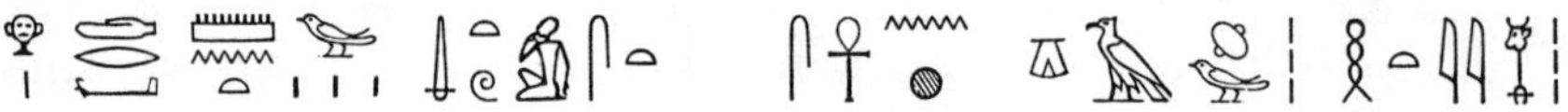

*ḥer* *ṭer* *ment* *meṭtu-set* *sānkh* *ḳa* *ḥeti*

destroy diseases, her word maketh to live stinking throats (i.e., throats of the dead).

*tcheṭ-set* *mā* *pu-u* *ȧtef* *neter* *petrȧ* *tcheṭfi*

She said, What is this, O father god? What is it? A snake

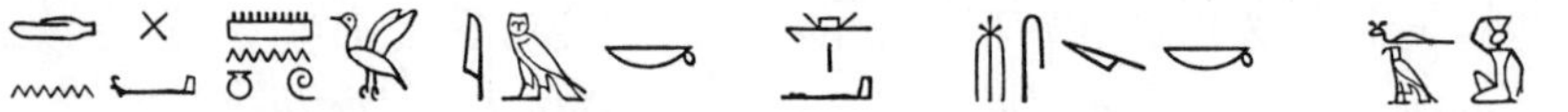

*ṭen* *mennu* *ȧm-k* *uā* *mes-k* *fa*

hath shot sickness into thee. A thing made by thee hath lifted up

*ṭep - f* *erek* *ka* *sekher-set* *em*

its head against thee. Verily it shall be overthrown by

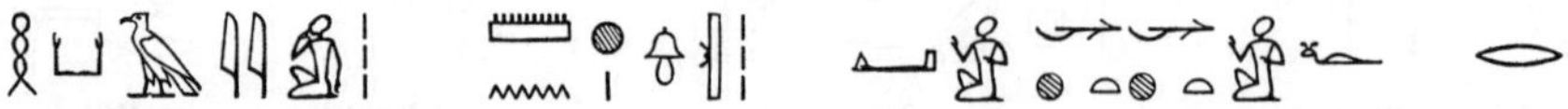

*ḥekaiu* *menkhiu* *ṭā-ȧ* *khetkhet - f* *er*

words of power beneficent, I will make it to depart from

*maa sati-k neter tcheseri ȧpu-nef re - f*

the sight of thy rays. The god holy opened his mouth:

*ȧnuk pu shemi ḥer uat sutut em*

I was passing over the way going through

*taui set-ȧ ȧba en ȧb-ȧ er maa*

the two lands of my country, wished my heart to see

*qemamu-nȧ khunen-nȧ em tchetfi*

what I had created [when] I was bitten by a snake

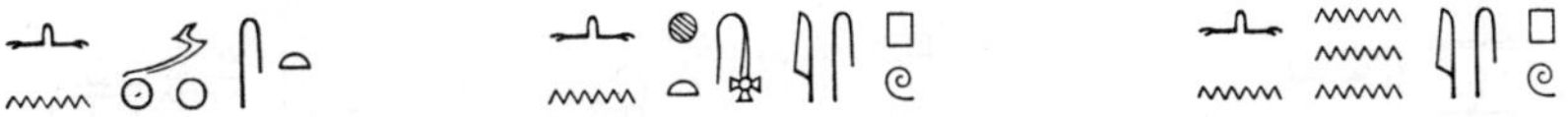

*ȧn maa set ȧn khet ȧs pu ȧn mu ȧs pu*

invisible. Behold it is not fire, behold it is not water.

*qebebḥ-kuȧ er mu shemem-kuȧ er*

I am colder than water, I am hotter than

*seshet ḥāt-ȧ neb er kheri fetet tuȧ*

fire, my limbs all are full of sweat, I

*ȧstiti maat-ȧ ȧn smen ȧn qemḥu-ȧ*

tremble, my eye is without stability, I cannot see

*pet ḥu mu ḥer ḥrȧ-ȧ em shemu*

the heavens, bursteth out water on my face [as] in summer.

*tcheṭ ȧn Ȧst en Rā ȧ tcheṭ-nȧ ren-k*

Said Isis to Rā, O tell me thy name,

*ȧtef neter ānkh sa ṭemu-tu ḥer*

father god; liveth the person who hath declared

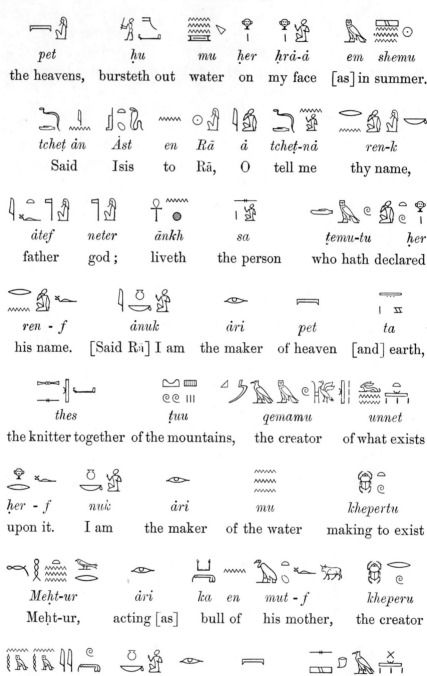

*ren - f ȧnuk ȧri pet ta*

his name. [Said Rā] I am the maker of heaven [and] earth,

*thes ṭuu qemamu unnet*

the knitter together of the mountains, the creator of what exists

*ḥer - f nuk ȧri mu khepertu*

upon it. I am the maker of the water making to exist

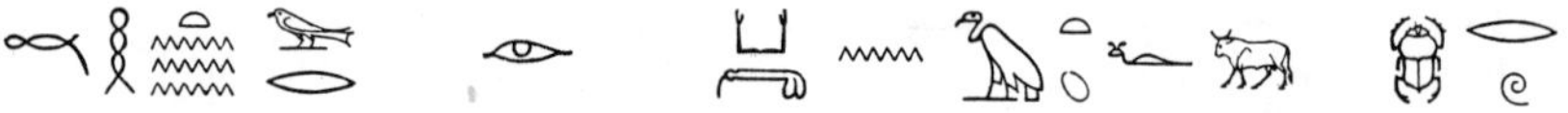

*Meḥt-ur ȧri ka en mut - f kheperu*

Meḥt-ur, acting [as] bull of his mother, the creator

*netchem netchemiu nuk ȧri pet sesheta*

of the joys of love. I am the maker of heaven and have covered over

*khuti* *ṭā-à* *ba* *nu* *neteru* *em-khennu-set*

the two horizons, I have set the soul of the gods within them

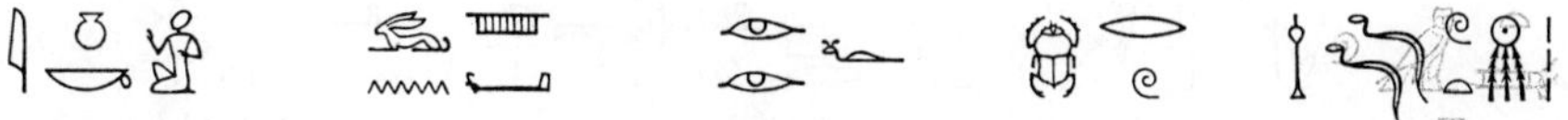

*ànuk* *un* *maati-f* *kheperu* *ḥetchetchtu*

I am he who openeth his eyes, becometh the light;

*ākhennu* *maati-f* *kheperu* *kekui* *ḥu* *mu*

shutteth [he] his eyes, becometh the dark. Riseth the flood

*Ḥāp* *kheft* *utu-nef* *àn*

of Ḥāp (Nile) when he giveth the command, not

*rekh* *en* *neteru* *ren* - *f* *nuk* *àri* *unnu*

know the gods his name. I am the maker of hours,

*kheperu* *hru* *nuk* *àpu* *ḥebu* *renpit*

the creator of days, I am the opener of the festivals of the year,

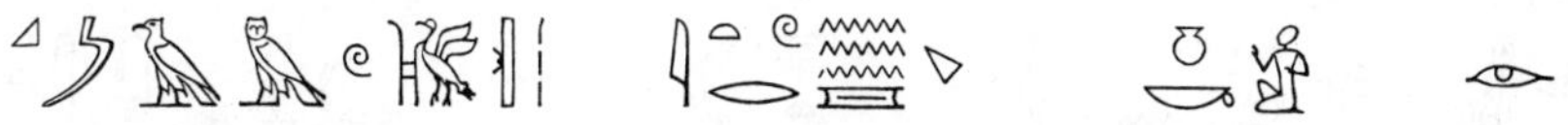

*qemamu* *àtru* *nuk* *àri*

the creator of streams of water. I am the maker

*khet* *ānkhet* *er sekheperu* *kat* *en* *amu*

of flame of life making to be performed works in the houses.

*nuk* *Kheperȧ* *em* *ṭuauu* *Rā* *em* *āḥāu-f*
I am Kheperȧ in the morning, Rā in his noontide,

*Temu* *ȧmi* *māsheru* *ȧn* *khesef*
Temu in the evening. [But] not was driven

*met* *em* *shemi-set* *ȧn* *netchem* *neter āa*
the poison out of its course, not was relieved the great god.

*tcheṭ ȧn* *Ȧst* *en* *Rā* *ȧn* *ren-k* *ȧpu*
Said Isis to Rā:—Thy name is not enumerated

*em* *na* *tcheṭu-k-nȧ* *ȧ* *tcheṭ-k* *set* *nȧ*
among the things which thou hast said to me; O tell thou it to me,

*peri* *ta* *metu* *ānkh* *sa*
and shall come out the poison. Shall live a person

*ṭemu-tu* *ren - f* *metu* *tcheṭemu-set*
having uttered his name. The poison it burned

*em* *tcheṭemu* *sekhemu-nes* *er* *nebȧu* *en*
with burnings, it was stronger than the flame of

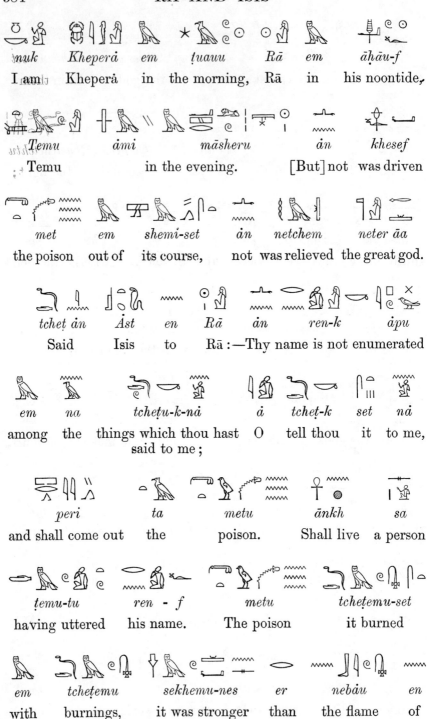

*ārt* *tcheṭ* *ȧn* *ḥen* *en* *Rā* *ṭāt-nȧ*

fire. Said the majesty of Rā, I give myself

*ḥeḥui* *mā* *Ȧst* *per* *em* *ren-ȧ* *em*

to be searched out by Isis, shall come forth my name from

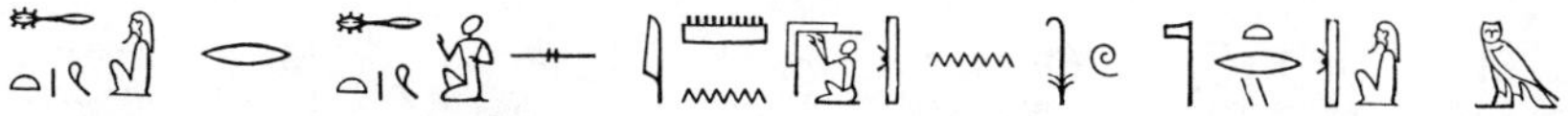

*khat-ȧ* *er* *khat-s* *ȧmen* *en* *su* *netri* *em*

my body into her body. Hid himself the divine one from

*neteru* *usekh* *ȧst* *em* *uȧa* *en* *ḥeḥ* *renput*

the gods, empty was the place in the Boat of millions of years.

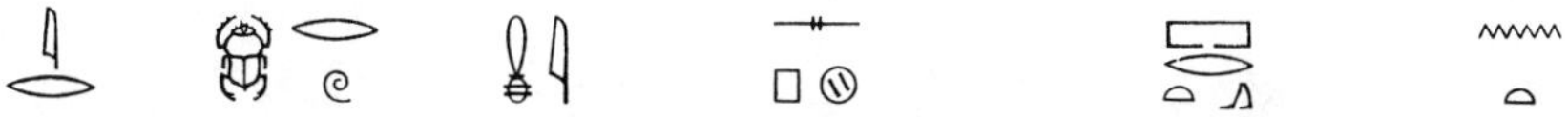

*ȧr* *kheperu* *mȧ* *sep* *pert* *ent*

When it became about the time of the coming forth of

*ȧb* *tcheṭ-s* *en* *sa* *Ḥeru* *senḥa* *ent* *su*

the heart she said to [her] son Horus:—Let him bind himself by an oath

*em* *ānkh* *neter* *erṭāt* *neter* *maati-f*

sworn by the life of thc god that the god will give his two eyes.

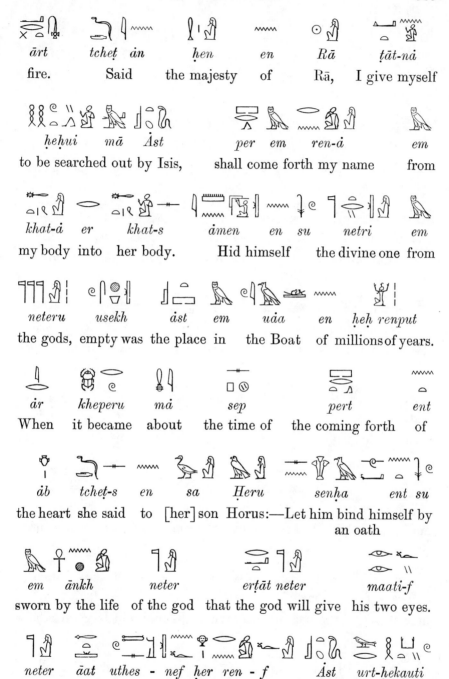

*neter* *āat* *uthes* - *nef* *ḥer* *ren* - *f* *Ȧst* *urt-ḥekauti*

The god great was removed from his name, Isis, great in words of power [said]:—

*shept metu per em Rā maat Ḥeru*

Run out, poison, come forth from Rā, Eye of Horus,

*peri em neter nubȧu en re - f*

come forth from the god, and shine without his mouth.

*nuk ȧri-ȧ nuk hau er māāi ḥer ta*

I, I have worked, I make to fall down upon the ground

*er metu sekhemu māki uthes en neter*

the poison which is defeated, verily was removed from the god

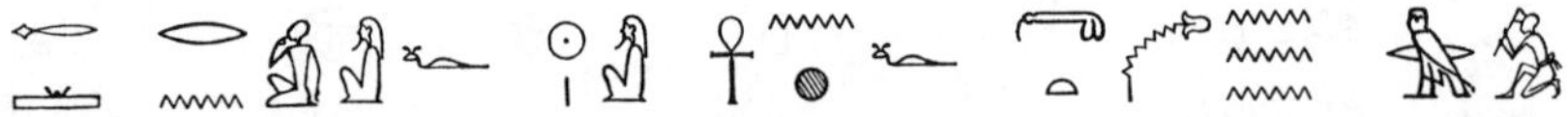

*āa ren - f Rā ānkh - f met mit*

great his name. Rā may he live, the poison may it die

*thes rer men mes en ment*

and conversely. A certain one, the son of a certain woman,

*ānkh - f metu mit tcheṭ en Ȧst ur*

may he live, the poison may it die. [Thus] said Isis, great lady,

*ḥent neteru rekh Rā em ren - f tchesef*

mistress of the gods, who knew Rā by his name his own.

*tcheṭ ḥer tut en Temu ḥenā Ḥeru-ḥekennu*

To be said over an image of Temu and Ḥeru-ḥekennu,

*erpit Ȧst tut Ḥeru*

and [over] a figure of Isis, and an image of Horus.

## CHAPTER XII

# THE DESTRUCTION OF MANKIND

### EGYPTIAN TEXT WITH TRANSLITERATION AND TRANSLATION

. . . . . . . *neter* *kheper* *tchesef* *em-khet* *un-nef* *em*

. . . . . . . god, who created himself. After he was in

*sutenit* *reth* *neteru* *em khet*

the sovereignty of men, and of gods, and of creation,

*Uāti* *un* *ȧn* *reth* *ḥer* *kat* *meṭet*

the One, men and women were blaspheming and saying,

*ȧstu* *eref* *ḥen* *ānkh* *utcha* *senb* *ȧauu*

Behold, his majesty, life, strength, health, has grown old,

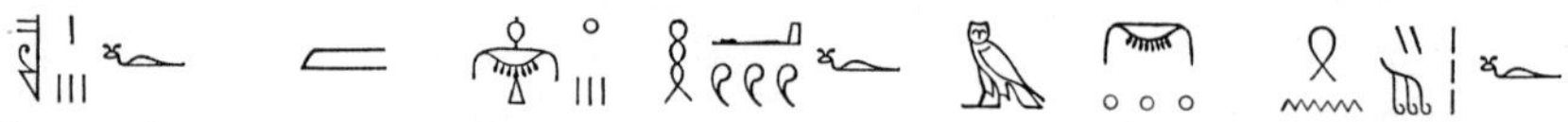

*kesu-f* *em* *ḥetch* *ḥāu - f* *em* *nub* *sheni - f*

his bones are like silver, his limbs like gold, his hair

*em* *khesbeṭ* *maāt* *un* *ȧn* *ḥen-f* *ḥer* *setem*

is like lapis-lazuli real; was his majesty listening to

*meṭet ȧn reth tcheṭ ȧn ḥen-f ānkh utcha senb*

what said mankind. Said his majesty, life, strength, health,

*er enti emkhetti-f nȧs mā-nȧ er maat-ȧ*

to those who were in his train. Call, bring me my Eye,

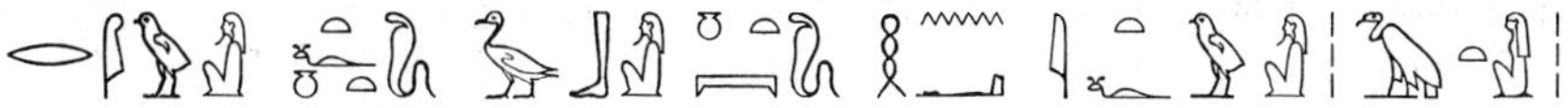

*er Shu Tefnut Seb Nut ḥenā ȧtefiu mut*

and Shu, Tefnut, Seb, Nut, and the father and mother gods

*uneniu ḥenā-ȧ ȧstu-ȧ em Nu ḥenā kher*

who lived with me when behold I was in Nu, together with

*neter-ȧ Nu ȧn-nef shenthi - f ḥenā - f*

my god Nu. Let him bring his ministers with him.

*ȧn-nek set em ketket ȧm maa*

Bring thou them in silence, that not may see

*reth ȧm uār ȧb-sen i-k*

mankind, not may flee their hearts. Come thou

*ḥenā-sen er ḥet-āat tcheṭ-sen sekheru-sen*

with them into the great temple, let them declare their counsel

*tchertu* *iu-à* *em* *Nu* *er* *bu*
fully; I will enter into Nu to the place

*kheper-nà* *àm* *àn-nà* *àn-tu* *enen* *neteru* *un* *àn*
wherein I was born, let be brought to me those gods. Were

*enen* *neteru* *àpen* *ḥer* *ḳesui-f* *ḥer* *ṭehen* *ta* *em-baḥ*
those gods on both sides of him, bowing to the earth before

*ḥen-f* *tchet-f* *meṭet-f* *em-baḥ* *àtef*
his majesty. He spake his words before the father

*semsu* *àri* *reth* *suten*
of the firstborn gods, the maker of men, the king

*rekhit* *tchet* *àn* *sen* *kheft* *ḥen-f*
of rational beings. They said before his majesty,

*meṭu-en-n* *er* *setem-en-set* *tchet* *àn* *Rā*
Speak to us, for we are listening to them. Said Rā

*en* *Nu* *neter* *semsu* *kheper-nà* *àm-f*
to Nu, O god firstborn, from whom I came into being,

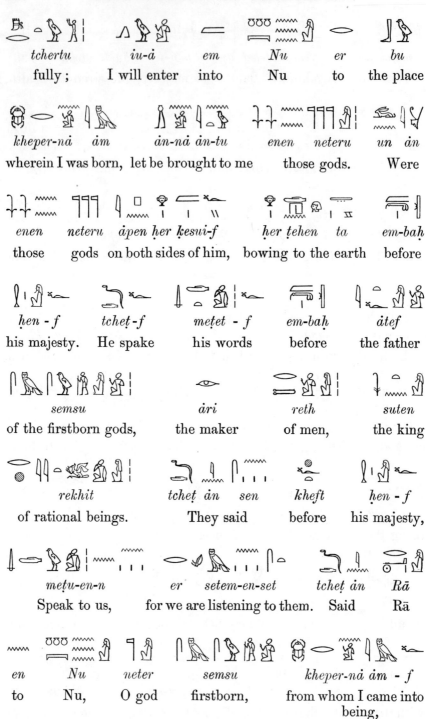

*neteru ṭep-āu mā-ten reth kheperu*

and ye ancestor gods, take ye heed to mankind who came into being

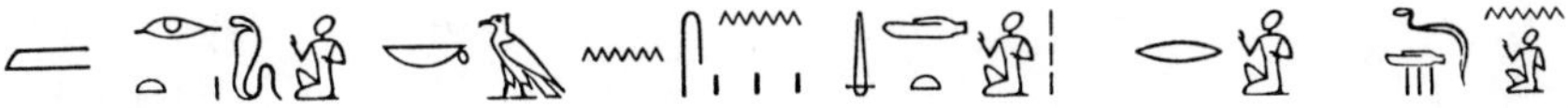

*em maat-ȧ ka-en-sen meṭet er-ȧ tcheṭ-nȧ*

from my eye, they speak words against me. Tell me

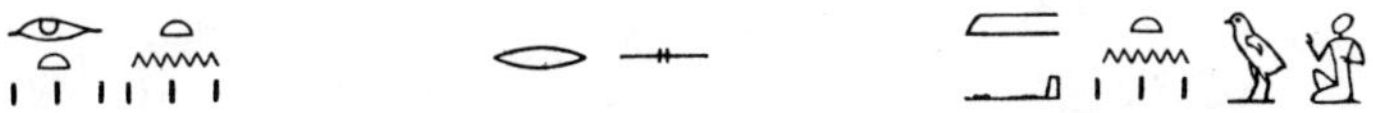

*ȧrit-ten er-s mā-ten-uȧ*

[what] ye would do about it, take ye heed to it for me,

*ḥeḥi-ȧ ȧn sma-nȧ set er setemu-ȧ*

seek out a plan for me. Not will I slay them until I hear

*tcheṭ-thȧ ten er-s tcheṭ ȧn ḥen en Nu*

what ye say concerning it. Said the majesty of Nu,

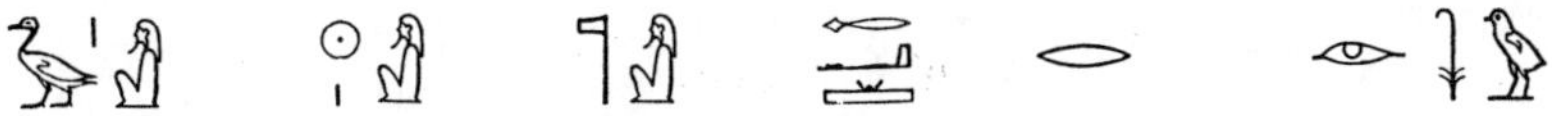

*sa Rā neter āa er ȧri su*

the son of Rā :— God greater than he who made him,

*ur er qema[m]-iu-su ḥems*

mightier than those who were created with him, sit on

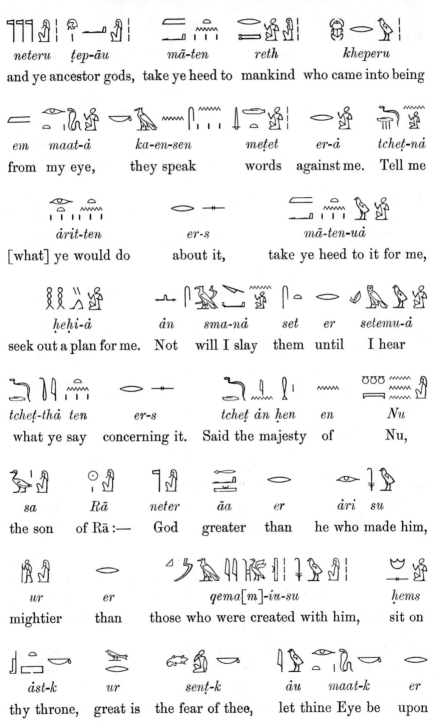

*ȧst-k ur senṭ-k ȧu maat-k er*

thy throne, great is the fear of thee, let thine Eye be upon

*uaiu* *ȧm-k* *tcheṭ* *ȧn* *ḥen* *en* *Rā*

those who blaspheme thee. Said the majesty of Rā:—

*mā-ten* *set* *uār* *er* *set* *ȧb-sen*

Behold ye them fleeing into the mountain, their hearts

*senṭu* *ḥer* *tcheṭ* *en* *sen* *tcheṭ* *ȧn-sen*

are afraid because of what they have said. They said

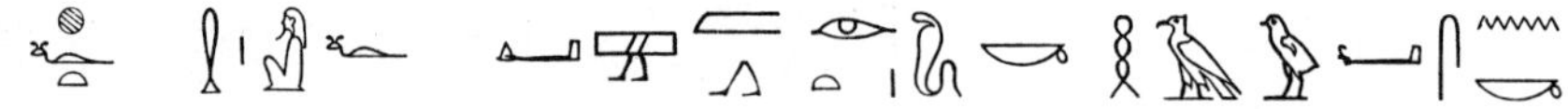

*kheft* *ḥen - f* *ṭā shem* *maat-k* *ḥau-s-nek*

before his majesty:— Let go forth thine Eye, let it destroy for thee

*set* *uaiu* *em* *ṭu* *ȧn* *maat*

those who blaspheme with wickedness, not an eye

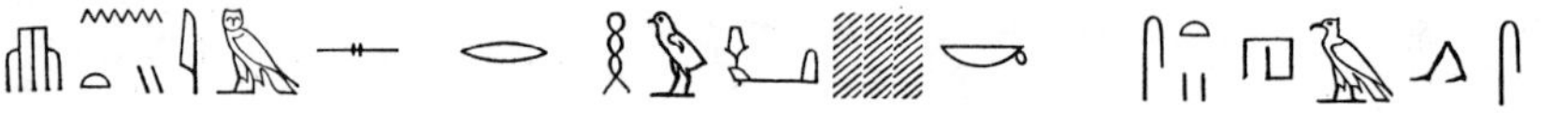

*khenti* *ȧm-s* *er* *ḥu . . . . .-k* *set* *ha-s*

can precede it in resistance . . . . . [when] it goeth down

*em* *Ḥet-Ḥert* *iu* *ȧn* *eref* *netert* *ten*

in the form of Hathor. Went forth then goddess this,

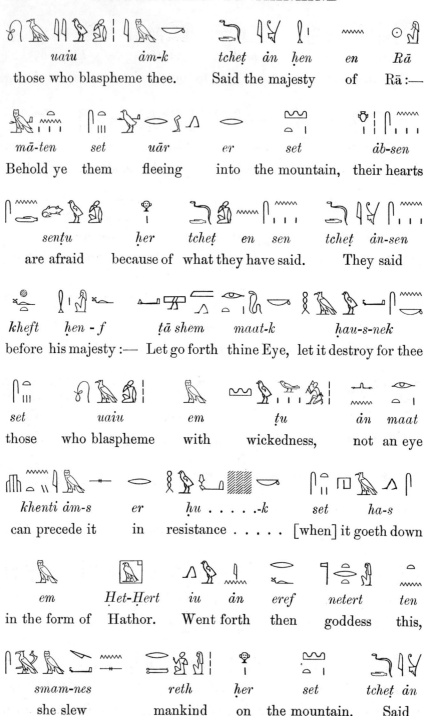

*smam-nes* *reth* *ḥer* *set* *tcheṭ* *ȧn*

she slew mankind on the mountain. Said

*ḥen en neter pen iāi-ui em ḥetep Ḥet-Ḥert*

the majesty of this god:— Come, come in peace, Hathor,

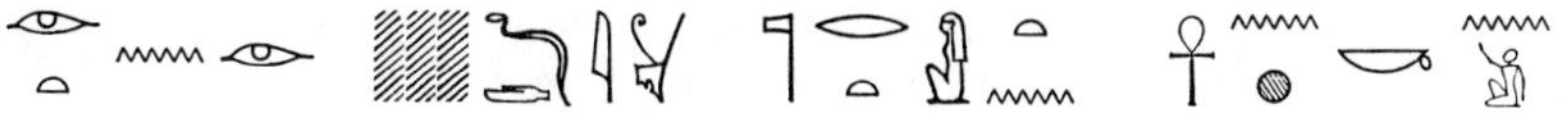

*ȧrit en ȧrit tcheṭ ȧn netert ten ānkh-k nȧ*

for the deed is done. Said this goddess :—Thou gavest me life,

*ȧu sekhem-nȧ em reth ȧu netchem ḥer*

when I had power over mankind it was pleasing to

*ȧb-ȧ tcheṭ ȧn ḥen en Rā ȧu-ȧ er sekhem*

my heart. Said the majesty of Rā :— I will be master

*em sen em suten em sānṭu-set kheper*

over them as king destroying them. It came to pass that

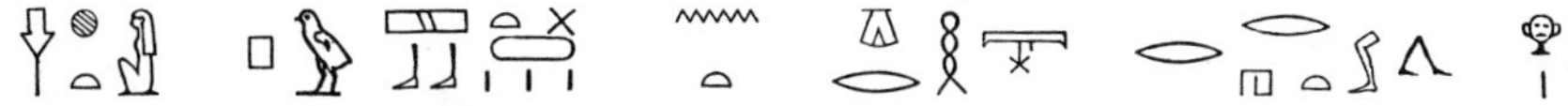

*Sekhet pu shebebet ent ḳerḥ er rehet ḥer*

Sekhet of the offerings of the night waded about in

*senf-sen shaā em Suten-ḥenen tcheṭ ȧn Rā*

their blood beginning in Suten-ḥenen. Said Rā:—

*nȧs mā-nȧ ȧputi khau sȧnnu*

Call, bring to me messengers swift [and] speedy,

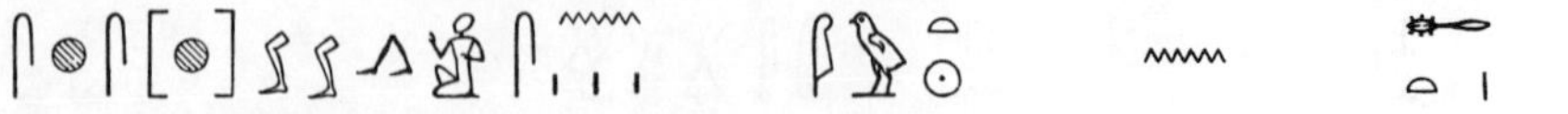

*sekhsekh-sen* *shut* *en* *khat*

they shall run [like] the wind of the body;

*ȧn* *ȧn-tu* *enen ȧputi* *ȧpen* *ḥer āui*

one brought messengers these straightway.

*tcheṭ* *ȧn* *ḥen* *en* *neter pen* *sha-sen* *er*

Said the majesty of this god:— Let them go to

*Ābu* *ȧn* *nȧ* *ṭāṭāȧt* *er ur*

Elephantine [and] bring me mandrakes in great number.

*ȧn ȧn-tu* *nef* *enen* *ṭāṭāȧt* *erṭāt ȧn* *ḥen*

One brought to him these mandrakes, gave the majesty

*en* *neter pen* *Sektet* *enti* *em* *Ȧnnu* *ḥer* *netch*

of this god to Sektet who is in Heliopolis to crush

*ṭāṭāȧt* *ȧpen* *ȧstu* *kher* *ḥent* *ḥer* *tesh*

mandrakes these. Behold, when the women were bruising

*pertu* *er* *ḥeqt* *erṭā* *ȧn-tu* *ṭāṭāȧt* *ȧpen*

the barley for beer, and they were placing mandrakes these

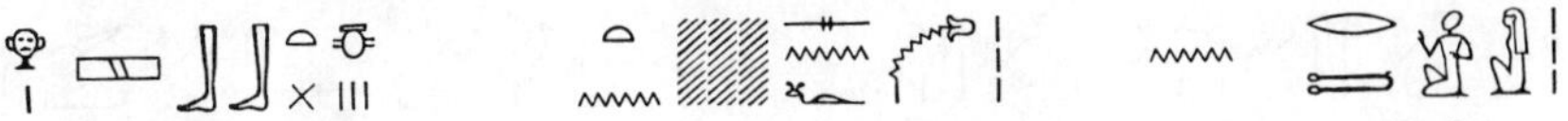

*ḥer shebebet* | *ten senf* | *en* | *reth*

in the beer vessels, [they became] blood of men.

*ȧrit-ȧn-ʻu* | *ḥeqt* | *ārnet* | 7000 | *iu* | *ȧn*

Having been made of beer vessels seven thousand, came

*eref* | *ḥen* | *en* | *suten bȧt* | *Rā* | *ḥenā*

therefore the majesty of the king of the South and North Rā with

*neteru* | *ȧpen* | *er* | *maa* | *enen* | *ḥeqet* | *ȧstu*

gods these to see this beer. Behold,

*ḥetch ta* | *en* | *smama* | *reth*

when it was dawn, after had slaughtered men

*ȧn* | *netert* | *em* | *sesu-sen* | *nu* | *khentithit*

the goddess during their period of sailing up the river,

*metch ȧn* | *ḥen* | *en* | *Rā* | *neferui* | *set*

said the majesty of Rā :— It is good, it is good.

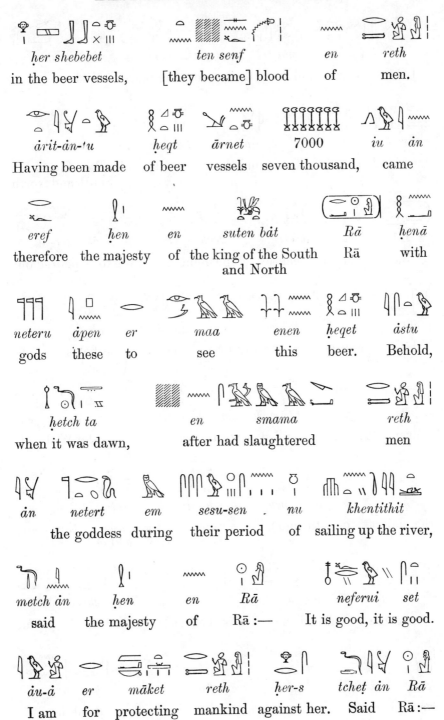

*ȧu-ȧ* | *er* | *māket* | *reth* | *ḥer-s* | *tcheṭ ȧn* | *Rā*

I am for protecting mankind against her. Said Rā :—

*fai* | *mā set* | *er* | *bua* | *nes sma*

Let them carry and bring them to the place she slew

*reth* | *ȧm* | *hep ȧn* | *ḥen* | *en* | *suten bȧt*

mankind therein. Commanded the majesty of the king of the South and North

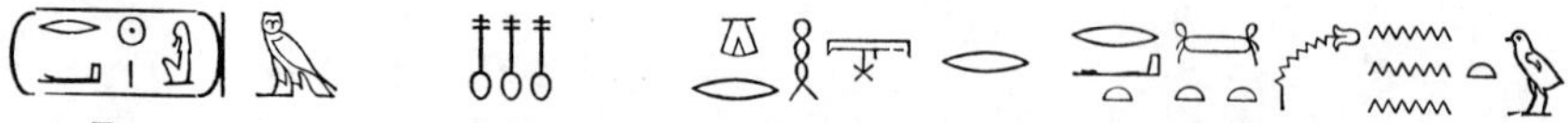

*Rā* | *em* | *neferu* | *ḳerḥ* | *er* | *erṭāt satet-tu*

Rā during the beauties of the night to cause to be poured out

*enen* | *setchert* | *un ȧn* | *aḥet* | *enti*

these vases of sleep-causing beer, were the fields of

*pet* | *fṭu* | *ḥer meḥ* | *em* | *mu* | *em* | *baiu* | *en*

heaven the four filled with water by the Will of

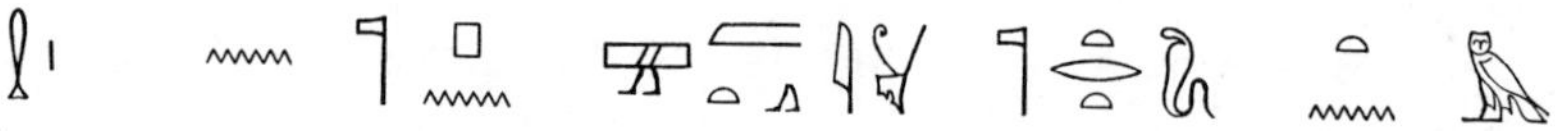

*ḥen* | *en* | *neter pen* | *shemt ȧn* | *netert* | *ten* | *em*

the majesty of this god. Came goddess (i.e., Sekhet) this in

*ṭuaiu* | *qem-nes* | *enen* | *ḥer meḥt* | *nefer*

morning, found she this [heaven] flooded, joyful

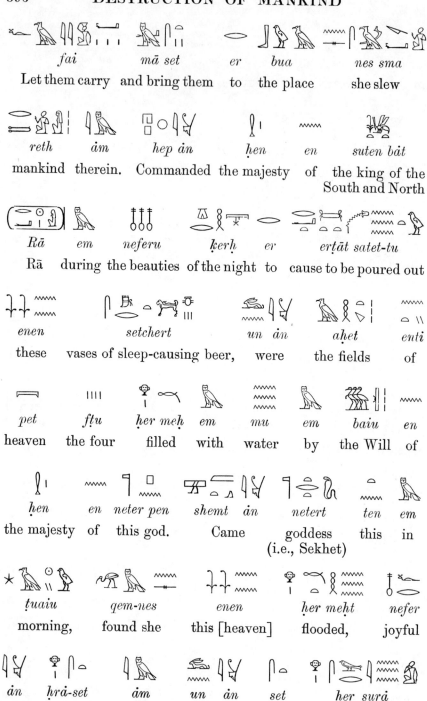

*ȧn* | *ḥrȧ-set* | *ȧm* | *un ȧn* | *set* | *ḥer surȧ*

was her face because of it, was she drinking,

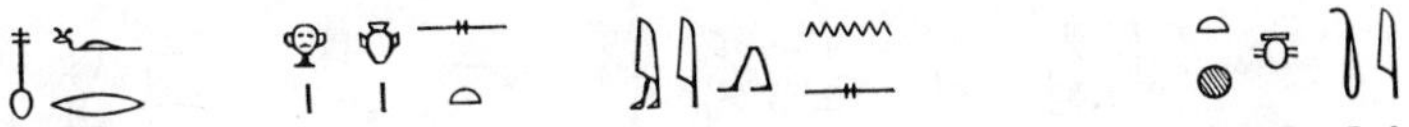

*nefer her áb-set i-nes tekh-thȧ*

merry was her heart, she came to a condition of drunkenness,

*ȧn sa-nes reth tchet ȧn hen en Rā*

not knew she mankind. Said the majesty of Rā

*en netert ten it-ui em hetep Amit*

to goddess this:— Come, come in peace, O Beautiful one;

*kheper nefert em Am tchet ȧn*

and there became beautiful young women in Am. Said

*hen en Rā en netert ten ȧri en set*

the majesty of Rā to goddess this:— Let be made for her

*setchertet em trȧiu renpet ȧpen*

vases of sleep-causing beer at seasons of the year these;

*set er hent-ȧ kheper ȧrit*

they [shall be] in proportion to my handmaidens. There were made

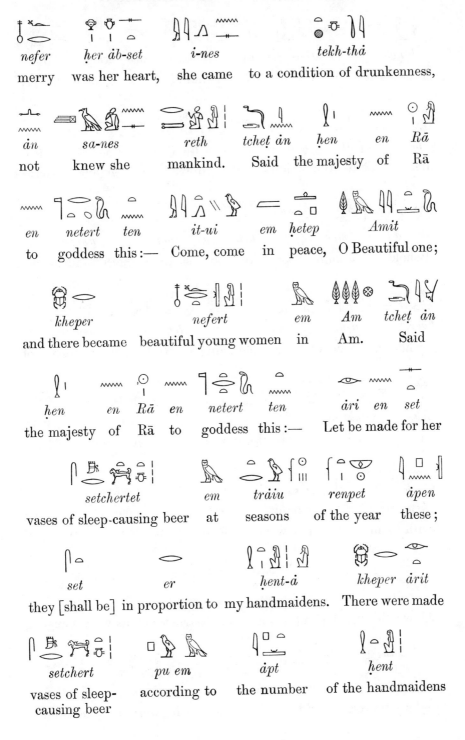

*setchert pu em ȧpt hent*

vases of sleep-causing beer according to the number of the handmaidens

*ḥeb en Ḥet-ḥert ȧn reth neb tcher hru*
of the festival of Hathor by mankind all since the day

*ṭepi tcheṭ ȧn ḥen en Rā en netert ten*
first. Said the majesty of Rā to goddess this:—

*ȧn ȧu mer en heh en mer kheper*
Behold a pain of fire of sickness hath come [on me],

*kher trȧ-ui ȧn mer tcheṭ ȧn ḥen en*
whence, O whence is the pain? Said the majesty of

*Rā ānkh-nȧ ȧu ȧb-ȧ urṭu ur unen*
Rā:— I live, [but] my heart is very weary of being

*ḥenā-sen smam-ȧ set sep en*
with them. I slew them, [but] there remain of

*ȧti ȧn un ānṭ āutu*
the worthless, for not was the destruction as wide-spreading

*ā-ȧ tcheṭet en neteru enti am- khet-f*
[as] my power. Said the gods who were in his train:—

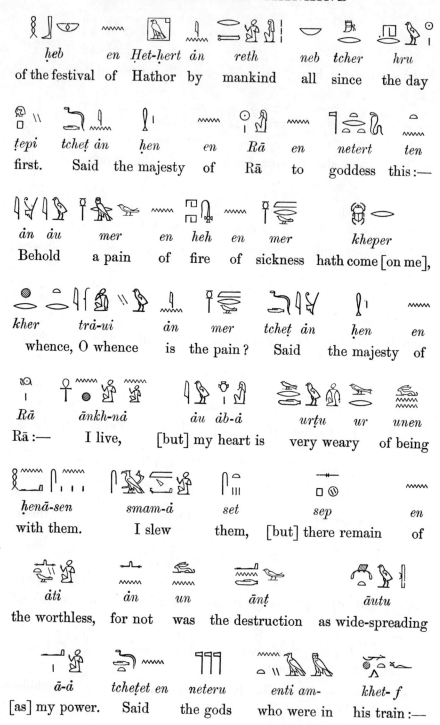

*em beh* *em* *urṭ-k* *àu-k* *sekhem-thà*

Tarry not in thy weariness [for] thou art mighty

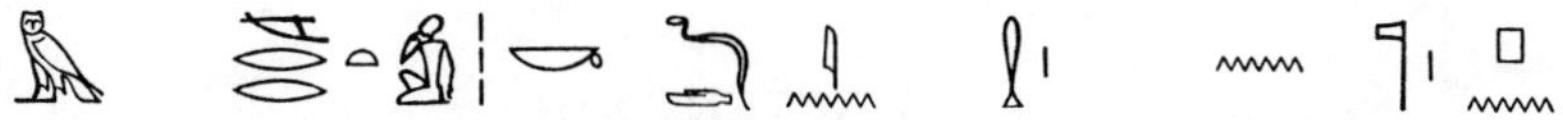

*em* *merret-k* *tcheṭ àn* *ḥen* *en* *neter pen*

according to thy will. Said the majesty of this god

*en* *ḥen* *en* *Nu* *ḥāu-à* *aheṭ* *em*

to the majesty of Nu:— My members are weak for

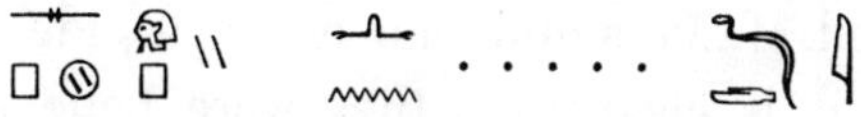

*sep ṭepi* *àn* . . . . .

the first time, not . . . . .

## CHAPTER XIII

# THOTH  (TEḤUTI), AND MAĀT, 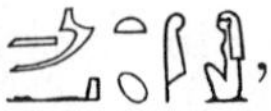, AND THE OTHER GODDESSES WHO WERE ASSOCIATED WITH HIM

THE hymns to Rā which are found in the *Book of the Dead* and in other funeral works of the ancient Egyptians state that the deities THOTH and MAĀT stand one on each side of the great god in his boat, and it is clear that they were believed to take some important part in directing its course; and as they were with Rā when he sprang up from the abyss of Nu their existence must have been coeval with his own. The conceptions which the Egyptians formed about Thoth and Maāt were both material and spiritual, and it is impossible to arrive at any conclusion concerning the functions of these deities without enumerating the facts about them which may be derived from the texts; speaking generally, Maāt may be considered the female counterpart of Thoth. In the Pyramid Texts, our earliest authorities, the functions of Thoth are of a purely funereal character, that is to say, he appears only as a god who is willing to be a helper of the deceased kings, and, although it is certain from many passages that his assistance was eagerly awaited by souls in the Underworld, there is no description given in these early works of the functions of the god. We must, then, rely upon the inscriptions of the later dynastic period for our knowledge of the powers of Thoth, and from these we learn that he was called, "Lord of "Khemennu, self-created, to whom none hath given birth, god "One;" "he who reckons in heaven, the counter of the stars, the "enumerator of the earth and of what is therein, and the measurer "of the earth;" and the "heart of Rā which cometh forth in the

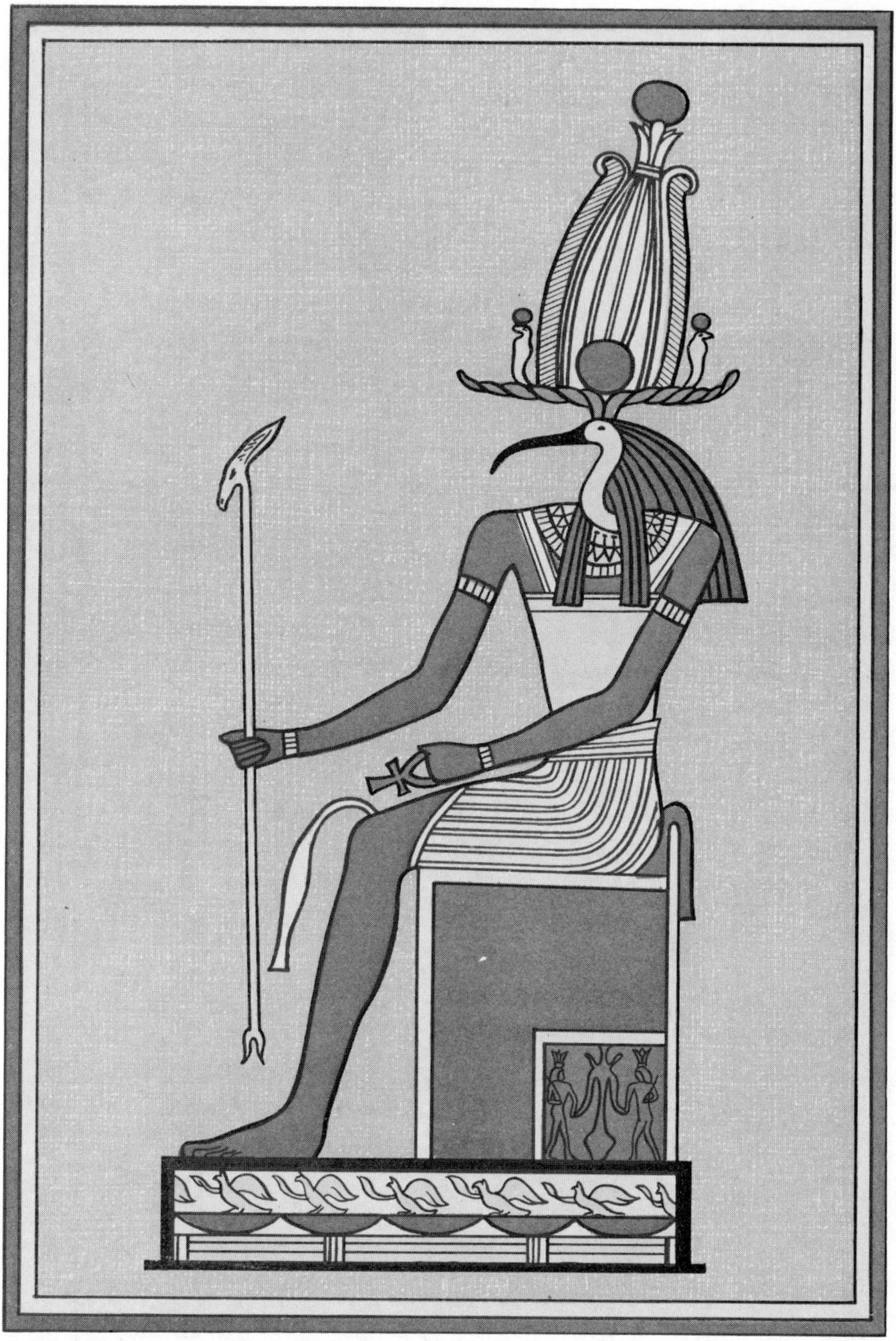

THOTH, THE SCRIBE OF THE GODS.

ÀĀḤ-TEḤUTI AND HIS ASSOCIATE THE APE.

"form of the god Thoth."[1] The chief shrine of the god was in Khemennu, 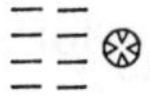, called Hermopolis by the Greeks, and Eshmûnên by the Arabs, but he also had shrines in Abydos, Ḥesert, 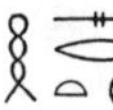, Urit, 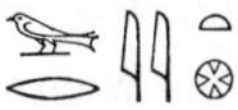, Per-āb, , Reḥui, , Ta-ur, , Sep, , Ḥāt, , Pselket, , Talmis, , Āa-tcha-Mutet, , Bāḥ, , Āmen-heri-āb, , and Ta-kens, 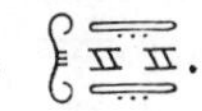. As lord of these places he was "lord of divine words," , "lord of Maāt," , and "judge of the two combatant gods," 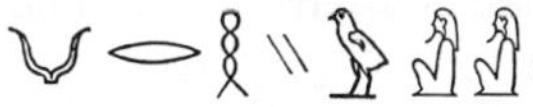, i.e., Horus and Set; and among other titles we find him called "Twice great," 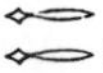, and "Thrice great," . From this last were derived the epithets "Trismegistos" and "ter maximus" of the classical writers.

The above facts prove that Thoth was regarded as a god who was self-begotten and self-produced, that he was One, that he made the calculations concerning the stablishing of the heavens, and the stars, and the earth, that he was the heart of Rā, that he was the master of law both in its physical and moral conceptions, and that he had the knowledge of "divine speech." From many passages we see also that he was the inventor and god of all arts and sciences, that he was the "lord of books," and the "scribe of the gods," and "mighty in speech," i.e., his words took effect, and he was declared to be the author of many of the funeral works by which the deceased gained everlasting life. In the *Book of the Dead* he plays a part which gives him a unique position among the gods, and he is represented as the possessor of powers which are greater than those of Osiris, and even those of Rā himself. Before, however, we go on to consider these the forms in which he appears on the monuments must be mentioned. Usually he appears in human form with the head of an ibis, but he also appears as an ibis. When in human form he holds in his hands

[1] See Lanzone, op. cit., p. 1265.

the sceptre and emblem of "life" common to all gods, but his headdress varies according to the particular form of the god in which the artist wishes to depict him. As the reckoner of times and seasons he has upon his head the crescent moon and disk, ; as a form of Shu and Ȧn-Ḥer he wears the headdresses of these gods; he is also seen wearing the *atef* crown, , and the united crowns of the South and the North.[1] In the *Book of the Dead* he appears as the "scribe of Maāt of the company of the gods," , and then he holds in his hands the writing reed and palette of the scribe; but his connection with Rā and his first rising in primeval times is indicated sometimes by the *utchat* , i.e., the power or strength, of the Eye of Rā, which he is seen carrying along in his hands.

The name of the god Thoth, , Teḥuti, appears to be derived from the supposed oldest name of the ibis in Egypt, i.e., *teḥu*, to which the termination *ti* has been added, with the idea of indicating that the king called Teḥuti possessed the qualities and attributes of the ibis.[2] A derivation of the name which appears to have been favoured by the Egyptians connected it with the word *tekh*, , "a weight," and in passages quoted by Lanzone[3] we find the god actually called *tekh*, . Now the determinative for the word *tekh*, a weight, is the sign for "heart," , and we know that the bird called *tekh* or *tekhnu*, which closely resembled the ibis, the bird sacred to Thoth, was in the opinion of some ancient writers connected with the heart. Thus Horapollo says (i. 36) that when the Egyptians wish to write "heart" they draw an ibis, for this bird was dedicated to Hermes (i.e., Thoth) as the lord of all knowledge and understanding; and Ælian (*De Nat. Animal.* x. 29) supports his testimony by adding several curious and interesting facts about the habits of the ibis. Other names given to Thoth were,[4] Ȧ, , and Sheps, lord of Khemennu, , Ȧsṭen, , Khenti, , Meḥi, ,

[1] See Lanzone, op. cit., pl. 402 f.

[2] Compare Brugsch, *Religion*, p. 439.

[3] Op. cit., p. 1265.

[4] See Brugsch, *Religion*, p. 441.

etc. The commonest name given to Thoth is *hab*, , "ibis," a word which finds its equivalent in the Coptic ϩⲓⲃⲱⲓ, and one of his commonest forms is the dog-headed ape, , which occupies such a prominent position in the Judgment Scene in the *Book of the Dead*. Here we see him seated on the top of the support of the beam of the Balance in which the heart of the deceased is weighed, where his duty is to watch the pointer, and tell the ibis-headed Thoth when the beam is exactly level; according to Brugsch, this ape is a form of Thoth as the god of "equilibrium," [1] and he appears to be a symbol of the equinoxes. The ape *āān* is also connected with the moon, for he is often seen with the lunar crescent and disk, ◯, upon his head; but there is no doubt that he represented Thoth in his character of "lord of divine words and the scribe [of the gods]," for in a scene reproduced by Lanzone [2] we see him holding in one paw the god's palette and writing reeds, and these titles are given to him. Besides these forms of Thoth may be also mentioned those in which he possesses the attributes of other gods. Thus as a god of Mendes he has a human body with the head of a bull surmounted by a disk and uraeus; as Shu he is depicted in the form of a man wearing the crown of Shu; as Ȧn-ḥer he is depicted in the form of a man wearing the crown of this god; as Sheps he has the head of a hawk; [3] the ibis and the ape *āān* are his commonest forms.

The principal seat of the worship of Thoth was Khemennu, or Hermopolis, a city famous in Egyptian mythology as the place containing the "high ground," , on which Rā rested when he rose for the first time. Here he was regarded as the head of the company of the gods of the city, who were eight in number: Nu and Nut, Ḥeḥu and Ḥeḥut, Kek and Keket, and Ḳerḥ and Ḳerḥet (or Nau and Nait), i.e., four pairs of deities, each pair consisting of a male and a female deity. As to the importance of this company of the gods two eminent Egyptologists have held directly opposite opinions, for the late Dr. Brugsch thought that

[1] *Religion*, p. 443. [2] Op. cit., pl. 404, No. 1.
[3] *Ibid.*, pll. 402 ff.

the four pairs of deities formed the oldest example of the *ogdoad*, while M. Maspero is of opinion that we must join the four pairs to Thoth, when the nine gods will form an independent *paut*, constructed partly on the model of the *paut* of Heliopolis. Dr. Brugsch thought that the eight gods of Hermopolis were primordial deities, but M. Maspero thinks that their character is entirely artificial, and that they are only "gods formed according to the laws of grammar, "four being masculine, and four feminine."[1] The latter argues that because the high priest of Hermopolis was called by a title which indicates that he served "him that is chief of five," the gods of the city were only five in number, i.e., Thoth and the four gods of the cardinal points; to the four gods of the cardinal points were then assigned female counterparts, hence the "Eight gods" . Thoth, according to M. Maspero, is to these what Tem or Rā-Tem was to the *paut* of Heliopolis, and the Hermopolitan *paut* was constructed after the model of the Heliopolitan *paut*; thus Nu and Nut = Shu and Tefnut, Ḥeḥu and Ḥeḥut = Seb and Nut, Kek and Keket = Osiris and Isis, and Ḳerḥ and Ḳerḥet (or, Nau and Nait) = Set and Nephthys. This view is, however, not supported by the evidence of the texts, which, in the writer's opinion, indicates, as has already been said, that the four pairs of gods of Hermopolis belong to a far older conception of the theogony than that of the company of gods of Heliopolis. Another point to be remembered is that Thoth was intimately associated with the ape, as were also the gods of his company; this takes us back to a very remote period when supernatural powers were assigned to the particular class of ape which was the companion of Thoth, and when the primitive Egyptian regarded the knowledge and cunning of the dog-headed ape as proofs of his divine nature. Between the period when this took place and the development of the Heliopolitan theogony, a very long interval of time must have passed; the two conceptions belong not only to different stages of civilization, but probably to two distinct races of men.

One of the most interesting titles of Thoth is "Judge of the

[1] *La Mythologie Égyptienne*, p. 257.

"Reḥeḥui, the pacifier of the gods, who dwelleth in Unnu "(Hermopolis), the great god in the Temple of Åbtiti."[1] A very early Egyptian tradition made a great fight to take place between the god of light and the god of darkness, and in later days Rā himself, or some form of him, generally one of the Horus gods, was identified with the god of light, and Set, in one form or other, was identified with the god of darkness. Thus the fights of Rā and Āpep, and Ḥeru-Beḥuṭet and Set, and Horus, son of Isis, and Set, are in reality only different versions of one and the same story, though belonging to different periods. In all these fights Thoth played a prominent part, for when the Eye of Rā, i.e., the Sun, was doing battle with Set, this evil power managed to cast clouds over it, and it was Thoth who swept them away, and "brought the Eye alive, and whole, and sound, and without defect "to its lord" (*Book of the Dead*, xvii. 71, ff.); he seems also to have performed the same office for Rā after his combat with Āpep. At the contest between Horus, son of Isis, who fought with Set in order to avenge the murder of his father Osiris, Thoth was present, and when Horus had cut off his mother's head because of her interference in the fight at the moment when victory was inclining to him, it was Thoth who gave her a cow's head in place of her own. In all these fights Thoth was the arbiter, and his duty was to prevent either god from gaining a decisive victory, and from destroying the other; in fact, he had to keep these hostile forces in exact equilibrium, the forces being light and darkness, or day and night, or good and evil, according to the date of the composition of the legends, and the objects which the scribes intended to secure by writing them down. In the group of titles of Thoth quoted in this paragraph we see that he is called "great god in Ḥet-Åbtit," or the Temple of Åbtit, which was one of the chief sanctuaries of the god, and was situated in Hermopolis.

The hieroglyphics with which the name "Ḥet Åbtit" are written prove that they mean the "House of the Net," i.e., the

1 

temple where a net was preserved and venerated, but the questions naturally arise, what was this net, and what was its signification? We know from the two versions of Chapter cliii. of the *Book of the Dead* that a net was supposed to exist in the Underworld, and that the deceased regarded it with horror and detestation. Every part of it, its poles, and ropes, and weights, and small cords, and hooks, had names which he was obliged to learn if he wished to escape from it, and would make use of it to catch food for himself, instead of being caught by "those who laid snares." Thus in a prayer we read, "Hail, thou 'god who lookest behind thee,' thou 'god who "hast gained the mastery over thine heart,' I go a-fishing with "the cordage of the 'uniter of the earth' (Horus?), and of him "that maketh a way through the earth. Hail, ye fishers who have "given birth to your own fathers, who lay snares with your nets, "and who go round about in the chambers of the waters, take ye "not me in the net wherewith ye ensnared the helpless fiends, and "rope me not in with the rope wherewith ye roped in the "abominable fiends of earth, which had a frame which reached "unto heaven, and weighted parts that rested upon the earth." From this passage it is clear that the Egyptians possessed a legend in which one power or the other in the mythological combats was armed with a net wherein he tried to ensnare his adversary. In Chapter cxxxiii. the deceased says, "Lift thyself up, O thou Rā, "who dwellest in thy divine shrine, draw thou into thyself the "winds, inhale the north wind, and swallow thou the *beqesu* "() of thy net () on the day wherein thou "breathest Maāt." The meaning of *beqesu* is not quite clear in this passage, because from its determinative, , we should naturally connect it with some organ of the human body, but it is evident from its context that Rā possessed a net, and we are certain from the former extract that it was one of the weapons which he employed in his war against the god and fiends of darkness.

An interesting parallel is afforded by the Assyrian and Babylonian versions[1] of the fight between the Sun-god Marduk and the monster Tiamat and her fiends, for it is said in them,

[1] See L. W. King, *Babylonian Religion*, p. 71.

"He (i.e., Marduk) set the lightning in front of him, with burning "fire he filled his body. He made a net to enclose the inward "parts of Tiamat, the Four Winds he set so that nothing of her "might escape; the South wind, and the North wind, and the "East wind, and the West wind, he brought near to the net which "his father Anu had given him." It is interesting to note that in the passage from the cxxxiiird Chapter the winds are also mentioned in connexion with the net of Rā, and it is difficult not to arrive at the conclusion that the use to which the Sun-god put his net was the same in each legend; whether this be so, however, or not matters little for our purpose here. It is quite clear that in the Egyptian legend the god Thoth was supposed to have some connexion with the net of Rā, and it is equally clear that in his temple, which was called the Temple of the Net, the emblem of a net, or perhaps even a net itself, was venerated.

We are now able to sum up the attributes ascribed to Thoth, and to consider how he employed them in connection with the dead. In the first place, he was held to be both the heart and the tongue of Rā, that is to say, he was the reason and the mental powers of the god, and also the means by which their will was translated into speech; from one aspect he was speech itself, and in later times he may well have represented, as Dr. Birch said, the λόγος of Plato. In every legend in which Thoth takes a prominent part we see that it is he who speaks the word that results in the wishes of Rā being carried into effect, and it is evident that when he had once given the word of command that command could not fail to be carried out by one means or the other. He spoke the words which resulted in the creation of the heavens and the earth, and he taught Isis the words which enabled her to revivify the dead body of Osiris in such wise that Osiris could beget a child by her, and he gave her the formulae which brought back her son Horus to life after he had been stung to death by a scorpion. His knowledge and powers of calculation measured out the heavens, and planned the earth, and everything which is in them; his will and power kept the forces in heaven and in earth in equilibrium; it was his great skill in celestial mathematics which made proper use of the laws (*maāt* ) upon which the foundation and maintenance of the universe rested; it was he who directed the motions of the heavenly bodies and their times and seasons; and without his words the gods, whose existence depended upon them, could not have kept their place among the followers of Rā. He was the "scribe of the gods," and possessed almost unlimited power in the Underworld; the god Osiris was in many ways wholly dependent upon his good offices, and the ordinary mortal sought his words and help with great earnestness. In the Judgment Scene in the *Book of the Dead* it is Thoth who acts the part of the recording angel, and it is his decision which is accepted by the gods, who ratify the same and report it to Osiris; for when once Thoth said that the soul of the deceased had been weighed, and that it had been found true by trial in the Great Balance, and that there was no wickedness whatsoever in it, the gods could not fail to answer, "That which cometh forth from thy mouth is true, "and the deceased is holy and righteous"; and in consequence they straightway award him a place with Osiris in the Sekhet-Ḥetepu, or Elysian Fields. Thoth as the great god of words was rightly regarded as the judge of words, and the testing of the soul in the Balance in the Hall of Osiris is not described as the judging or "weighing of actions," but as the "weighing of words,"  *utchā meṭet.*[1]

To words uttered under certain conditions the greatest importance was attached by the Egyptians, and in fact the whole efficacy of prayer appears to have depended upon the manner and tone of voice in which the words were spoken. Thoth could teach a man not only words of power, but also the manner in which to utter them, and the faculty most coveted by the Egyptian was that which enabled him to pronounce the formulae and Chapters of the *Book of the Dead* in such a way that they could not fail to have the effect which the deceased wished them to have. After the names of deceased persons we always find in funeral papyri the words *maā kheru* , or , which mean "he whose word is *maā*," that is to say, he whose

[1] See the passages enumerated in my *Vocabulary* to the *Book of the Dead*, p. 96.

THOTH, THE SCRIBE OF THE GODS.

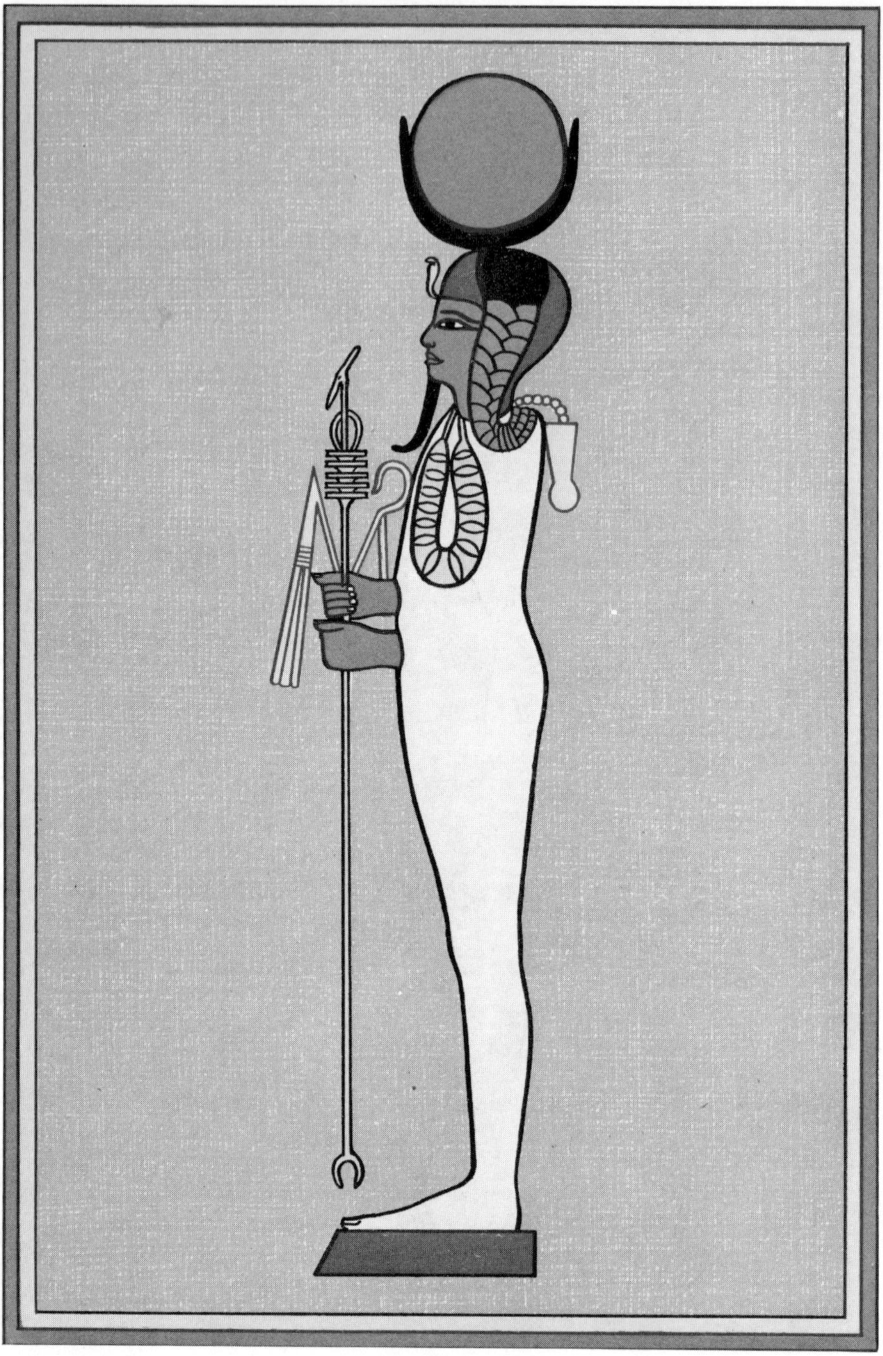

THE MOON GOD ÅĀH.

words possess such power that whenever they are uttered by him the effects which he wished them to produce unfailingly come to pass. The words, however, here referred to are those which must be learned from Thoth, and without the knowledge of them, and of the proper manner in which they should be said the deceased could never make his way through the Underworld. The formulae of Thoth opened the secret pylons for him, and provided him with the necessary meat, and drink, and apparel, and repelled baleful fiends and evil spirits, and they gave him the power to know the secret or hidden names of the monsters of the Underworld, and to utter them in such a way that they became his friends and helped him on his journey, until at length he entered the Fields of Peace of Osiris or the Boat of Millions of Years. These are the words referred to in the title of Thoth, "lord of divine words," or "lord of the words of god." The whole of the *Book of the Dead* was assumed to be the composition of Thoth, and certain chapters of it he "wrote with his own fingers." In the late work called the "Book of Breathings" it is said, "Thoth, the most mighty god, "the lord of Khemennu, cometh to thee, and he writeth for thee "the 'Book of Breathings' with his own fingers. Thus thy "soul shall breathe for ever and ever, and thy form shall be "endowed with life upon earth, and thou shalt be made a god "along with the souls of the gods, and they shall be the heart "of Rā, and thy members shall be the members of the great god."[1] In later times the epithet *maā kheru* appears to have had a somewhat different meaning from that given to it above, and at times it may well be rendered "he whose word is right," and have reference to the words of Thoth in the Judgment, when he informs the gods that the heart of Osiris has been weighed with the strictest care on the part of himself and his ape, which sits on the support of the Balance, and that at the weighing the heart in one pan of the Scales was able to counterbalance exactly the feather of Right or the Law in the other, and that the case of the individual under examination was a "right" one.

From many passages in the *Book of the Dead* we learn of the

[1] *Chapters of Coming Forth by Day* (Translation), p. cxcvii.

services which Thoth performed for Osiris, and which he was to repeat for the benefit of every man who was acquitted in the Judgment. In the xviiith Chapter is a list of calamities which were averted from Osiris by Thoth, who gave words to the dead god and taught him to utter them with such effect that all the enemies of Osiris were vanquished. Thus he made him to triumph (semaā-kheru ) "in the presence of the great assessors "of every god and of every goddess; in the presence of the assessors "who are in Ȧnnu on the night of the battle and of the overthrow "of the Sebȧu-fiend in Ṭaṭtu; on the night of making to stand up "the double Ṭeṭ in Sekhem; on the night of the things of the "night in Sekhem, in Pe, and in Ṭepu; on the night of stablishing "Horus in the heritage of the things of his father in Rekhti; on "the night when Isis maketh lamentation at the side of her "brother Osiris in Ȧbṭu; on the night of the Haker festival when "a division is made between the dead and the spirits who are on "the path of the dead; on the night of the judgment of those who "are to be annihilated at the great [festival of] the ploughing and "the turning up of the earth in Ȧn-ruṭ-f ịn Re-stau; and on the "night of making Horus to triumph over his enemies." In the clxxxiiird Chapter the deceased Hunefer says to Osiris, "I have "come unto thee, O son of Nut, Osiris, Prince of everlastingness; "I am in the following of the god Thoth, and I have rejoiced at "every thing which he hath done for thee. He hath brought unto "thee sweet (i.e., fresh) air for thy nose, and life and strength to "thy beautiful face, and the north wind which cometh forth from "Tem for thy nostrils, O lord of Ta-tchesert. He hath made the "god Shu to shine upon thy body; he hath illumined thy path "with rays of splendour; he hath destroyed for thee [all] the evil "defects which belong to thy members by the magical power of "the words of his utterance. He hath made the two Horus "brethren to be at peace for thee; he hath destroyed the storm-"wind and the hurricane; he hath made the Two Combatants to be "gracious unto thee, and the two lands to be at peace before thee; "he hath put away the wrath which was in their hearts, and each "hath become reconciled unto his brother."

In the xcivth Chapter the deceased addresses the "guardian of the book of Thoth," and says, "I am endowed with glory, I am "endowed with strength, I am filled with might, and I am "supplied with the books of Thoth, and I have brought them to "enable me to pass through the god Aker, who dwelleth in Set. "I have brought the palette and the ink-pot as being the objects "which are in the hands of Thoth; hidden is that which is in "them! Behold me in the character of a scribe! O Ḥeru-khuti, "thou didst give me the command, and I have copied what is "right and true, and I do bring it unto thee each day." In the vignette of the chapter we see the deceased seated with a palette and an ink-pot before him.

In the Pyramid Texts there is evidence[1] that Thoth was connected with the western sky just as Horus was identified with the eastern sky, and this idea is amplified in an interesting fashion in the clxxvth Chapter of the *Book of the Dead*, where we find that the deceased addresses Thoth both as Thoth and as Temu, the setting sun, or god of the west. He is disturbed about that which "hath happened to the divine children of Nut," for "they have done "battle, they have upheld strife, they have done evil, they have "created the fiends, they have made slaughter, they have caused "trouble; in truth, in all their doings the mighty have worked "against the weak . . . . And thou regardest not evil, nor art "thou provoked to anger when they bring their years to confusion "and throng in and push to disturb their months; for in all that "they have done unto thee they have worked iniquity in secret." The deceased adds, "I am thy writing palette, O Thoth, and I "have brought unto thee thine ink-jar," and as he declares that he is not one of those who work iniquity in secret places, at the same time he clearly dissociates himself from those who do. These words are followed by a very remarkable passage in which the deceased, addressing Thoth under the name of Temu, asks the god what the place is into which he has come, and he says that it is without water, that "it hath not air, it is depth unfathomable, it "is black as the blackest night, and men wander helplessly therein.

[1] Brugsch, *Religion*, p. 451.

"In it a man may not live in quietness of heart; nor may the "longings of love be satisfied therein." A little further on in the Chapter he asks the lord Tem, i.e., Thoth, "How long have I to live?" i.e., how long will my existence in this new world be? and the god replies, "Thou art for millions of millions of years, "a period of life of millions of years,"  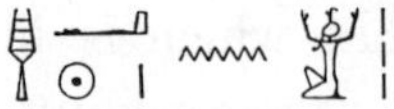. It is a remarkable fact that it is not Osiris, the lord of life everlasting, but Temu-Thoth who promises the deceased this coveted gift.

In the first part of the Chapter from which the above extracts have been made Thoth is, clearly, appealed to in his capacity of measurer and regulator of times and seasons, that is to say, as the Moon-god, who is commonly called ÅĀḤ-TEḤUTI, , or 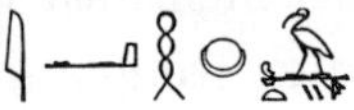, "the great god, the lord of heaven, the king of the gods," and "the maker of eternity and creator of everlastingness." Under this form the god Thoth is depicted:—1. As a mummy, standing upon the symbol of *maāt* , and holding in his hands the emblems of "life," , "stability," , "sovereignty and dominion," , and the sceptre 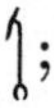; on his head is the crescent moon, , and by the side of his head he has the lock of hair, symbolic of youth, . 2. As a bearded, mummied human figure with the crescent moon on his head, and the lock of hair symbolic of youth. The head, however, has two faces, which are intended, presumably, to represent the periods of the waxing and the waning of the moon.[1] In some scenes we have Åāḥ-Teḥuti represented in the form of a disk resting between the horns of the crescent moon, and placed upon a pedestal in a boat similar to that in which Rā is usually seen; sometimes an *utchat*, , is placed over each end of the boat. In one interesting scene the god Åāḥ-ḥetep is represented with the head of an ibis surmounted by the lunar disk and crescent seated in a boat, and a dog-headed ape stands before him and presents an *utchat*; it is noteworthy that the curved end of the boat is notched like the notched palm branch which symbolizes "years," . In the narrowest sense

[1] For the figures see Lanzone, op. cit., pll. 36 ff.

Aāḥ-Teḥuti symbolizes the new moon, and this is only natural, for, as is well known, all calculations made by the moon in the East from time immemorial have been based upon the first appearance of the new moon in the sky; but, generally speaking, Thoth as the Moon-god represents the moon during the whole month. On the other hand, the *Utchat* of Thoth, , indicates the full moon, just as the *Utchat* of Rā  stands for the mid-day sun; this fact is proved by an interesting scene reproduced by Signor Lanzone[1] from Brugsch, *Monuments* (Berlin, 1857). Here we see the god Thoth, ibis-headed, standing by the side of a lotus pillar which supports heaven, , resting on heaven is a crescent, and in it is the *Utchat* of Thoth, . Leading up to the top of the pillar is a flight of fourteen steps, of unequal length, which are intended to represent the first fourteen days of the month, and at the foot of it stand fourteen gods,[2] the first of these being Tem, who has his right foot resting on the first step, which is the shortest of the whole flight. The gods who stand behind him are:—Shu, Tefnut, Seb, Nut, Horus, Isis, Nephthys, Ḥeru-em-ḥet-Āa, Åmseth, Ḥāp, Ṭua-mut-f, Qebḥ-sennuf, and a god without a name.

In a more extended sense the *Utchat* of Thoth represented the left eye of Rā, or the winter half of the year, when the heat of the sun was not so strong, nor its light so great, and when darkness remained in the skies for a longer period. This *Utchat* of Thoth, or of Thoth-Horus, as it should more correctly be called, is mentioned in the Pyramid Texts,[3] where it is called the "Black Eye of Horus"; thus of King Unås it is said, "Thou hast seized "the two Eyes of Horus, the White Eye and the Black Eye, "and thou hast carried them off and set them in front of thee and "they give light to thy face."[4] The White Eye here referred to

[1] Op. cit., pl. 39.

[2] The head and name of the fourth god are wanting.

[3] Unås, l. 37; the reference given by Brugsch is, like many others in his *Religion*, incorrect.

[4] 

is, of course, the sun. Thus we see that Thoth not only brought the Eye of Rā to the god, as we have already said, but that he also established the Eye of the Moon-god, who was indeed only a form of himself, and that Thoth was also in certain aspects identified with Osiris, , and with Horus, , and with Tem, and therefore with Kheperȧ. One other attribute of Thoth remains to be noticed, i.e., that which is made known to us by the xcvth Chapter of the *Book of the Dead*, wherein the deceased says, "I am he who sendeth forth terror into the powers of rain "and thunder, . . . . I have made to flourish my knife along with "the knife which is in the hand of Thoth in the powers of rain and "thunder." The short composition in which this passage occurs is called the "Chapter of being nigh unto Thoth," and in the vignette the deceased is seen standing before Thoth with both hands raised in adoration.

From the above facts it is quite clear that the Greeks were generally correct in the statements which they made about the wisdom and learning of Thoth, whom they identified with their own Hermes. They described him as the inventor of astronomy and astrology, the science of numbers and mathematics, geometry and land surveying, medicine and botany; he was the first to found a system of theology, and to organize a settled government in the country; he established the worship of the gods, and made rules concerning the times and nature of their sacrifices; he composed the hymns and prayers which men addressed to them, and drew up liturgical works; he invented figures, and the letters of the alphabet, and the arts of reading, writing, and oratory in all its branches; and he was the author of every work on every branch of knowledge, both human and divine. According to Clemens Alexandrinus (*Stromata*, vi.) the "Books of Thoth"[1] were forty-two in number, and they were divided into six classes; books i.-x. dealt with the laws, and the gods, and the education of

[1] On the Books of Thoth, see some interesting remarks by Brugsch in *Religion und Mythologie*, pp. 448 ff.; this distinguished Egyptologist thought he had discovered the original hieroglyphic titles of many of these inscribed on the walls of the temple of Edfû.

the priests; books xi.-xx. treated of the services of the gods, i.e., sacrifices, offerings, forms of worship, etc.; books xxi.-xxx. related to the history of the world, geography, and hieroglyphics; books xxxi.-xxxiv. formed treatises on astronomy and astrology; books xxxv. and xxxvi. contained a collection of religious compositions; and books xxxvii.-xlii. were devoted to medicine. An attempt was made some years ago to include the *Book of the Dead* among the "Books of Thoth," but it is now quite certain that, although Thoth was declared to have written some of its Chapters, it must be regarded as an entirely separate work and as one which enjoyed a much greater reputation than they. How Thoth was able to perform all the various duties which were assigned to him by the ancients it is difficult to understand, until we remember that according to the Egyptian texts he was the heart, i.e., the mind, and reason, and understanding of the god Rā. The title given to him in some inscriptions, , "three times great, great," from which the Greeks derived their appellation of the god ὁ τρισμέγιστος, or "ter maximus," has not yet been satisfactorily explained, and at present the exact meaning which the Egyptians assigned to it is unknown.[1] It is, however, quite clear that Thoth held in their minds a position which was quite different from that of any other god, and that the attributes which they ascribed to him were unlike the greater number of those of any member of their companies of the gods. The character of Thoth is a lofty and a beautiful conception, and is, perhaps, the highest idea of deity ever fashioned in the Egyptian mind, which, as we have already seen, was somewhat prone to dwell on the material side of divine matters. Thoth, however, as the personification of the mind of God, and as the all-pervading, and governing, and directing power of heaven and of earth, forms a feature of the Egyptian religion which is as sublime as the belief in the resurrection of the dead in a spiritual body, and as the doctrine of everlasting life.

[1] A number of valuable facts have been collected on the subject generally by Pietschmann, in his *Hermes Trismegistus, nach aegyptischen, griechischen und orientalischen Ueberliefungen*, 1875.

THE GODDESS MAĀ, OR MAĀT, , OR ,
OR .

Closely connected with Thoth, so closely in fact that she may be regarded as the feminine counterpart of the god, is the goddess Maāt, who stood with Thoth in the boat of Rā when the Sun-god rose above the waters of the primeval abyss of Nu for the first time. The type and symbol of this goddess is the ostrich feather, , which is always seen fastened to her head-dress, and is sometimes seen in her hand. She is represented in the form of a woman seated, or standing, , and she holds the sceptre, , in one hand, and , the emblem of "life," in the other; in many pictures of her she is provided with a pair of wings which are attached one to each arm, and in a few cases she has the body of a woman with an ostrich feather for a head.

The reason for the association of the ostrich feather with Maāt is unknown, as is also the primitive conception which underlies the name, but it is certainly very ancient, and probably dates from predynastic times. The hieroglyphic , which also has the phonetic value of Maāt, is described by some as a "cubit," i.e., the measure of a cubit, and by others as a "flute," which would, presumably, be made of a reed. We see, however, that the god Ptaḥ usually stands upon a pedestal made in the shape of , and that figures of the god Osiris stand upon pedestals of similar form, and as we have no reason for supposing that the figures of these two gods were placed upon flutes it is tolerably certain that  must mean something else besides flute. We know that Ptaḥ of Memphis was the god of artificers in general and of workers in metal and of sculptors in particular; it is far more likely that the form of his pedestal, , was intended to represent some tool which was used by sculptors and carvers, e.g., a chisel, or the identification of the object as a "cubit" may be correct if it means that it was some instrument used for measuring purposes. About the meaning of the word *maāt* , there is, fortunately, no difficulty, for from many passages in texts of all periods we

learn that it indicated primarily "that which is straight," and it was probably the name which was given to the instrument by which the work of the handicraftsman of every kind was kept straight; as far as we can see the same ideas which were attached to the Greek word κανών (which first of all seems to have meant any *straight rod* used to keep things straight, then a *rule* used by masons, and finally, metaphorically, a rule, or law, or canon, by which the lives of men and their actions were kept straight and governed) belong to the Egyptian word *maāt*. The Egyptians used the word in a physical and a moral sense, and thus it came to mean "right, true, truth, real, genuine, upright, righteous, just, steadfast, unalterable," etc.; *khesbet maāt* is "real lapis-lazuli" as opposed to blue paste; *shes maāt* means "ceaselessly and regularly," *em un maāt* indicates that a thing is really so, the man who is good, and honest is *maāt*, the truth (*maāt*) is great and mighty, and "it hath never been broken since the time of Osiris"; finally, the exact equivalent of the English words "God will judge the right" is found in the Egyptian *pa neter āpu pa maāt*, 
.

The goddess Maāt was, then, the personification of physical and moral law, and order and truth. In connexion with the Sun-god Rā she indicated the regularity with which he rose and set in the sky, and the course which he followed daily from east to west. Thus in a hymn to Rā we read, "The land of Manu (i.e., the West) "receiveth thee with satisfaction, and the goddess Maāt embraceth "thee both at morn and at eve;" "the god Thoth and the goddess "Maāt have written down thy daily course for thee every day;" "may I see Horus acting as steersman [in the boat of Rā] with "Thoth and Maāt, one on each side of him."[1] In another hymn Qenna says, "I have come to thee, O Lord of the gods, Temu-"Ḥeru-khuti, whom Maāt directeth;" Āmen-Rā is said to "rest upon Maāt," i.e., to subsist by Maāt; Rā is declared to "live by Maāt;" Osiris "carries along the earth in his train by Maāt in his name of Seker." In her capacity of regulator of the path of the

[1] *Papyrus of Ani*, sheet 1.

Sun-god Maāt is said to be the "daughter of Rā," and the "eye of Rā," and "lady of heaven, queen of the earth, and mistress of the Underworld," and she was, of course, "the lady of the gods and goddesses." As a moral power Maāt was the greatest of the goddesses, and in her dual form of Maāti, , i.e., the Maāt goddess of the South and the North, she was the lady of the Judgment Hall, and she became the personification of justice, who awarded to every man his due; judging by some vignettes which represent the weighing of the heart she took at times the form of the Balance itself. The hall in which Maāt sat in double form to hear the "confession" of the dead is often depicted in connection with the cxxvth Chapter of the *Book of the Dead*, and we see that it was spacious, and that the cornice thereof was formed of uraei and of feathers symbolic of Maāt. In the centre of it is a god with both hands stretched out over a lake, and at each end of the hall is seated an ape before a pair of scales.

Anubis was the guardian of the door at the end by which the deceased entered, and which was called Khersek-Shu, 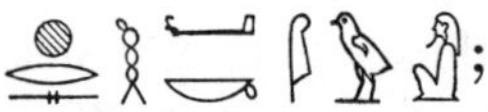; one leaf of the door was called Neb-Maāt-ḥeri-ṭep-reṭui-f, , and the other leaf Neb-peḥti-thesu-menmenet, 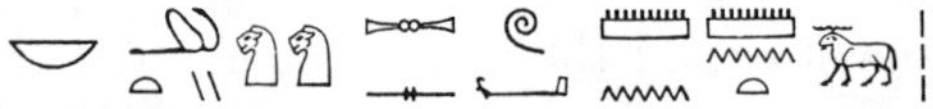. These names had to be learnt and uttered by the deceased before he was allowed to enter the Hall of the Maāti goddesses, 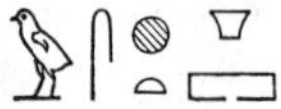  (or, ). When he arrived inside the Hall he found assembled there the Forty-two Assessors or Judges drawn up in two rows, each of which contained twenty-one Judges, one on each side of the length of the Hall. Before each of these he was obliged to make a solemn declaration that he had not committed a certain sin; these forty-two denials are commonly known as the "Negative Confession."[1] The names of the Assessors

[1] An English translation will be found in my *Chapters of Coming Forth by Day*, p. 193 ff.

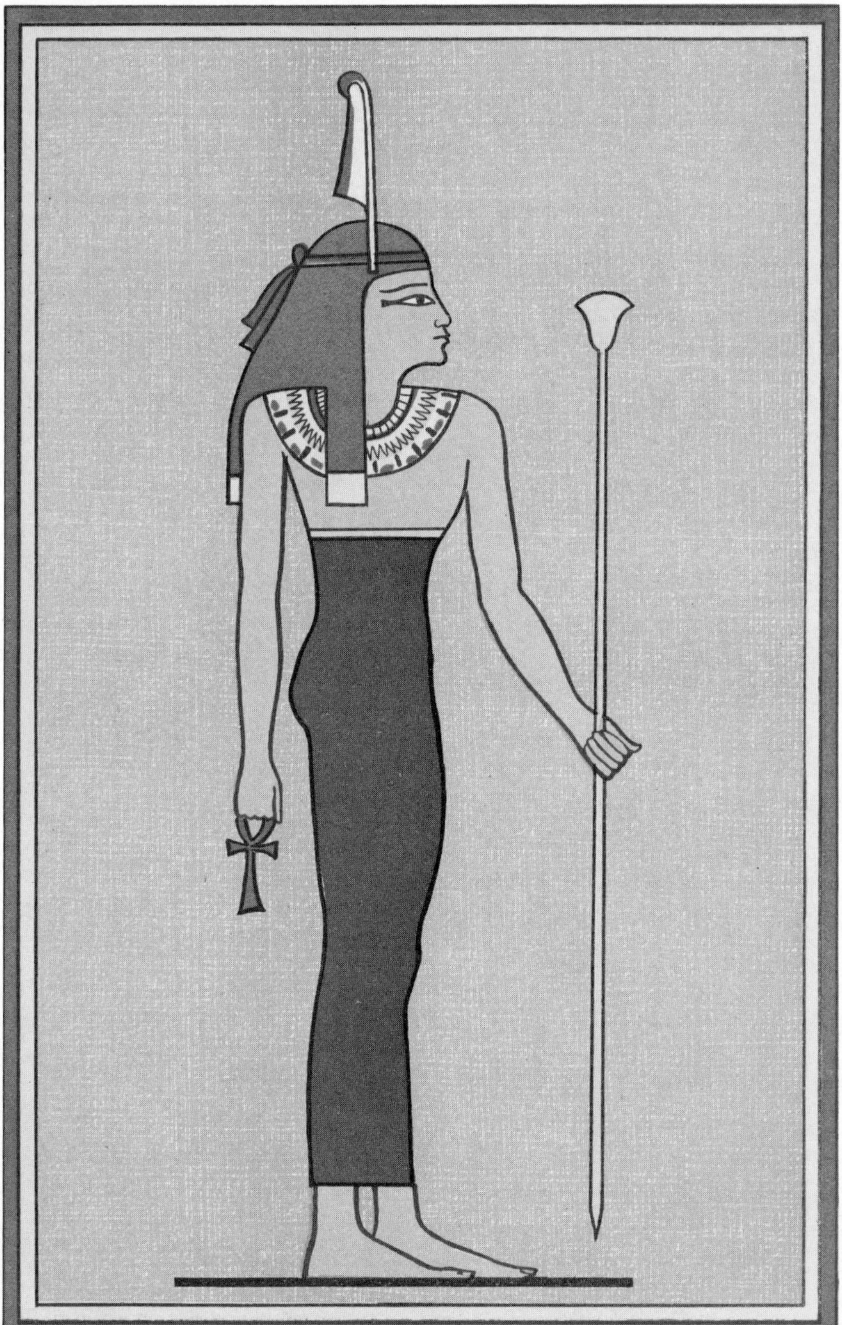

The Goddess Maāt.

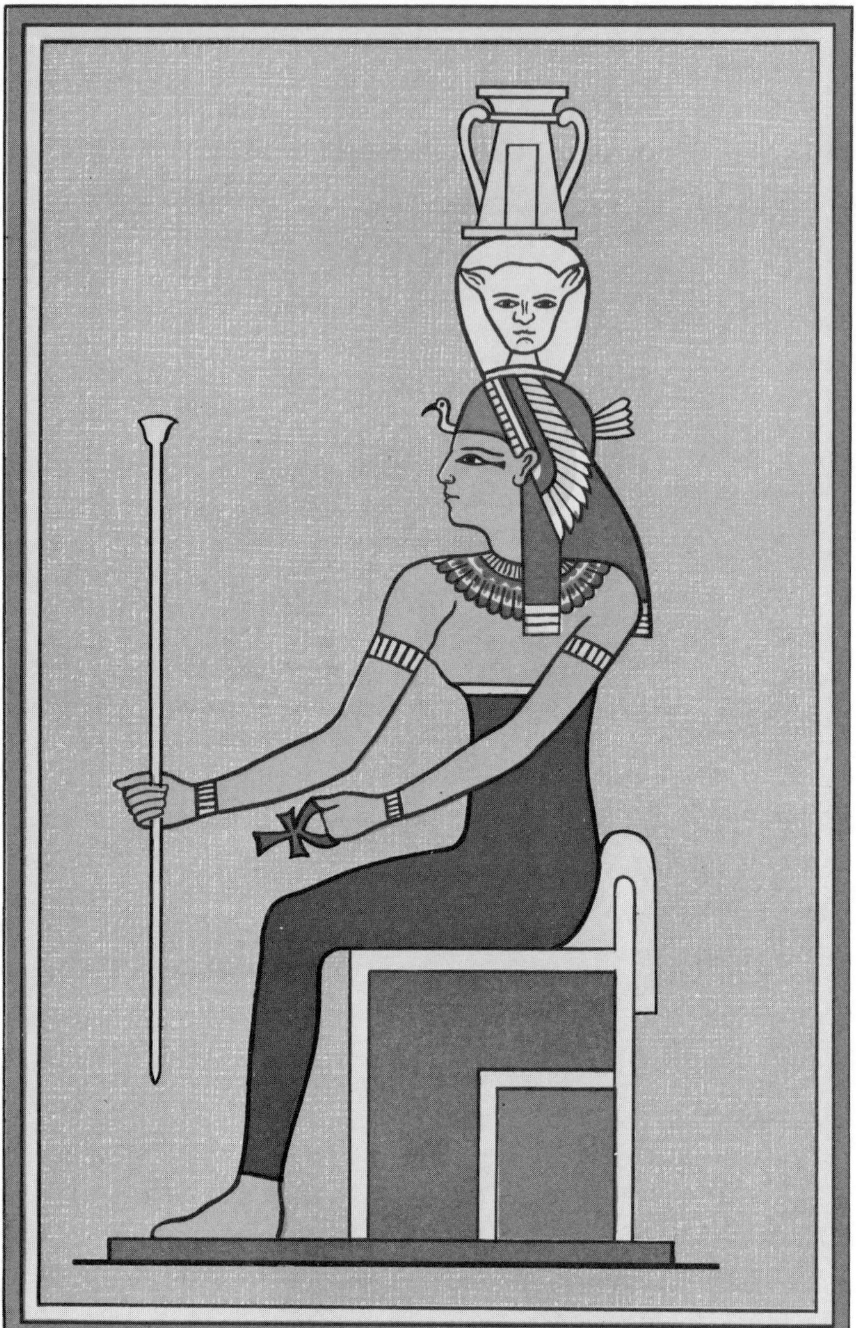

THE GODDESS NEKHEMĀUAIT.

according to the Papyrus of Nebseni (Brit. Mus., No. 9,900, sheet 30) are as follows:—

1. Usekht-nemmat,
2. Ḥept-shet,
3. Fenṭi,
4. Ām - khaibetu,
5. Neḥa-ḥāu,
6. Rerti,
7. Maati-f-em-ṭes,
8. Nebȧ-per-em-khetkhet,
9. Seṭ-ḳesu,
10. Uatch-nes,
11. Qerti,
12. Ḥetch-ȧbeḥu,
13. Ȧm-senf,
14. Ȧm - beseku,
15. Neb-Maāt,
16. Thenemi,
17. Āaṭi,
18. Ṭuṭu-f,
19. Uamemti,
20. Maa-ȧn-f,
21. Ḥeri-seru,
22. Khemi,
23. Sheṭ-kheru,
24. Nekhen,
25. Ser-kheru,
26. Basti,
27. Ḥrȧ-f-ḥa-f,
28. Ta-ret,
29. Kenemti,
30. Ȧn-ḥetep-f,
31. Neb-ḥrȧu,
32. Serekhi,
33. Neb-ābui,
34. Nefer-Tem,
35. Tem-sep,
36. Ȧri-em-ȧb-f,
37. Ȧḥi-mu (?),
38. Utu - rekhit,
39. Neḥeb - nefert,
40. Neḥeb-kau,
41. Tcheser-ṭep,
42. Ȧn-ā-f,

Even when the deceased had satisfied the Forty-two Assessors he could not pass out of the Hall of Maāti unless he knew the magical names of the various parts of the door which opened into the regions of the blessed. In the address which he makes to the gods collectively, and which is usually considered to have been made after the Negative Confession, he summarizes his good deeds, and declares to the god Osiris, whom he calls the "lord of the *Atef* crown," that he has done *Maāt*, and purified himself with *Maāt*, and that none of his members lack *Maāt*. He tells how he has been to the "Field of the Grasshoppers," and how he has bathed in the pool wherein the sailors of Rā bathe, and describes all the things which he has done, including the finding of a sceptre of flint in the "furrow of Maāt." Finally, having satisfied all the various parts of the door by declaring to them their magical names, he comes to the god MĀU-TAUI, , who acts as guardian of the Hall of Maāti, and who refuses to allow him to pass unless he tells his name. The deceased says, "Thy name is Sa-âbu-tchār-khat," 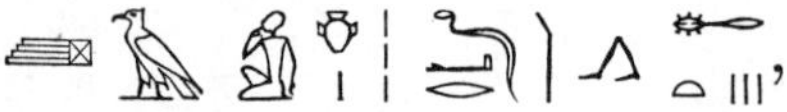, and demands to be admitted, but the god is not satisfied, and asks him, "Who is the god that dwelleth in his hour?" In reply the deceased utters the name MĀU-TAUI, whereupon he is at once asked by the god, "And who is this?" and in answer the deceased says, "Māu-taui is Thoth." On this Thoth asks the reason of his coming to the Hall, and when the deceased has told him that he has come because he wished his name to be written down by him, Thoth questions him further as to the fitness of his condition and as to the identity of the being "whose heaven is of fire, whose walls are living uraei, "and the floor of whose house is a stream of water." In answer to these questions he says that he is "purified from evil things," and that the being whose house is described is Osiris, whereupon Thoth calls upon him to enter, saying that his name shall be "mentioned" or recorded.

Thus we see how closely the attributes of Maāt merge into those of Thoth, and how the fate of the deceased depends ultimately upon these deities. It was not, however, sufficient for him to pass the Assessors, for beyond them stood Thoth with his final, searching questions; Thoth spake the word which caused the universe to come into being, and it was he who had the power to utter the name of the deceased in such a way that his new spiritual body would straightway come into being in the realm of Osiris. Thoth in one respect was greater than Rā, and in another he was greater than Osiris, but both from a physical and a moral point of view he was connected inseparably with the Maāt, which was the highest conception of physical and moral law and order known to the Egyptians.

### THE GODDESS NEḤEMĀUAIT .

Now besides Maāt or the Maāti goddesses we find that there were other goddesses who were associated with Thoth in different parts of Egypt, and among these is NEḤEMĀUAIT, who is described as the dweller in Ȧat-tchamutet, , and as the "holy and mighty lady in Khemennu" (Hermopolis),[1] and the "mistress of Per-Khemennu," and the "lady of Bāḥut," , and "the dweller in Dendera," . Thus we see that she was the goddess of the great temple in the city of Thoth, i.e., Hermopolis, and that she had a shrine in Dendera, and in the metropolis of the fifteenth nome of Lower Egypt, which is here mentioned under its civil name "Bāḥut"; the sacred name of the city was Per-Teḥuti-ȧp-reḥuḥ, , i.e., "Temple of Thoth, the judge between the *Reḥui* (Horus and Set)." The texts described her as the "daughter of Rā," and the manner in which she is depicted proves that she was regarded as a form of the goddess Hathor. In the examples given by Signor Lanzone[2] she has the form of a woman, and she wears upon her head either the sistrum, , or a disk resting between a pair of horns; in one picture a papyrus sceptre, , rests on the palm of her right hand, and a figure of Maāt, , on that of her left. A very interesting

[1] 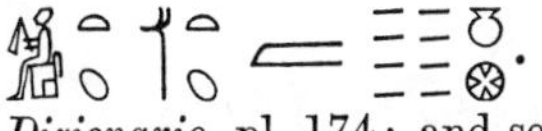.

[2] *Dizionario*, pl. 174; and see Brugsch, *Religion*, p. 471.

sketch also given by Signor Lanzone shows that her emblem was a Hathor-headed standard, on the top of which was a sistrum; on each side of the sistrum is a uraeus with a disk on its head, , and from each side of the face of the goddess hang two similar uraei. The standard is held up in a vertical position by two men who stand one on each side. Plutarch, as Brugsch has noted, says that Typhon was driven away by a sistrum, which seems to indicate that the rattling of the wires produced a sound that had a terrifying effect upon that evil beast; ladies of high rank and priestesses are often depicted with sistra in their hands, and though this fact is usually explained by assuming that those who hold sistra assisted in the musical parts of the services in the temples, it is very probable that they carried them both as amulets and as musical instruments. Dr. Brugsch quotes two passages from texts in which a royal personage declares that demoniacal powers are kept away from him by means of the sistrum which he holds in his hand. Neḥemāuait is not mentioned in the *Book of the Dead*, and it seems that she is not an ancient deity; she is probably a comparatively modern form of some well known older goddess.

From the texts of the late dynastic period we find that she was identified with MEḤ-URT [1] and with the goddess whose name is variously read Sefekh-āābu and Sesheta. Meḥ-urt, 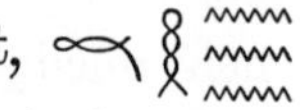 , is mentioned but rarely in the *Book of the Dead* (xvii. 76, 79; lxxi. 13; cxxiv. 17), but the passage in the xviith Chapter tells us exactly who she is. The deceased says there, "I behold Rā who was born yesterday from the buttocks of "the goddess Meḥ-urt," and as answer to the question, "What "then is this?" we have the words, "It is the watery abyss of "heaven, or (as others say), It is the image of the Eye of Rā in "the morning at his daily birth. Meḥ-urt is the Eye (Utchat) of "Rā." Meḥ-urt was originally a female personification of the watery matter which formed the substance of the world, and her name, which means "mighty fulness," indicates that she was the

[1] The Methyer (Μεθύερ) of Plutarch.

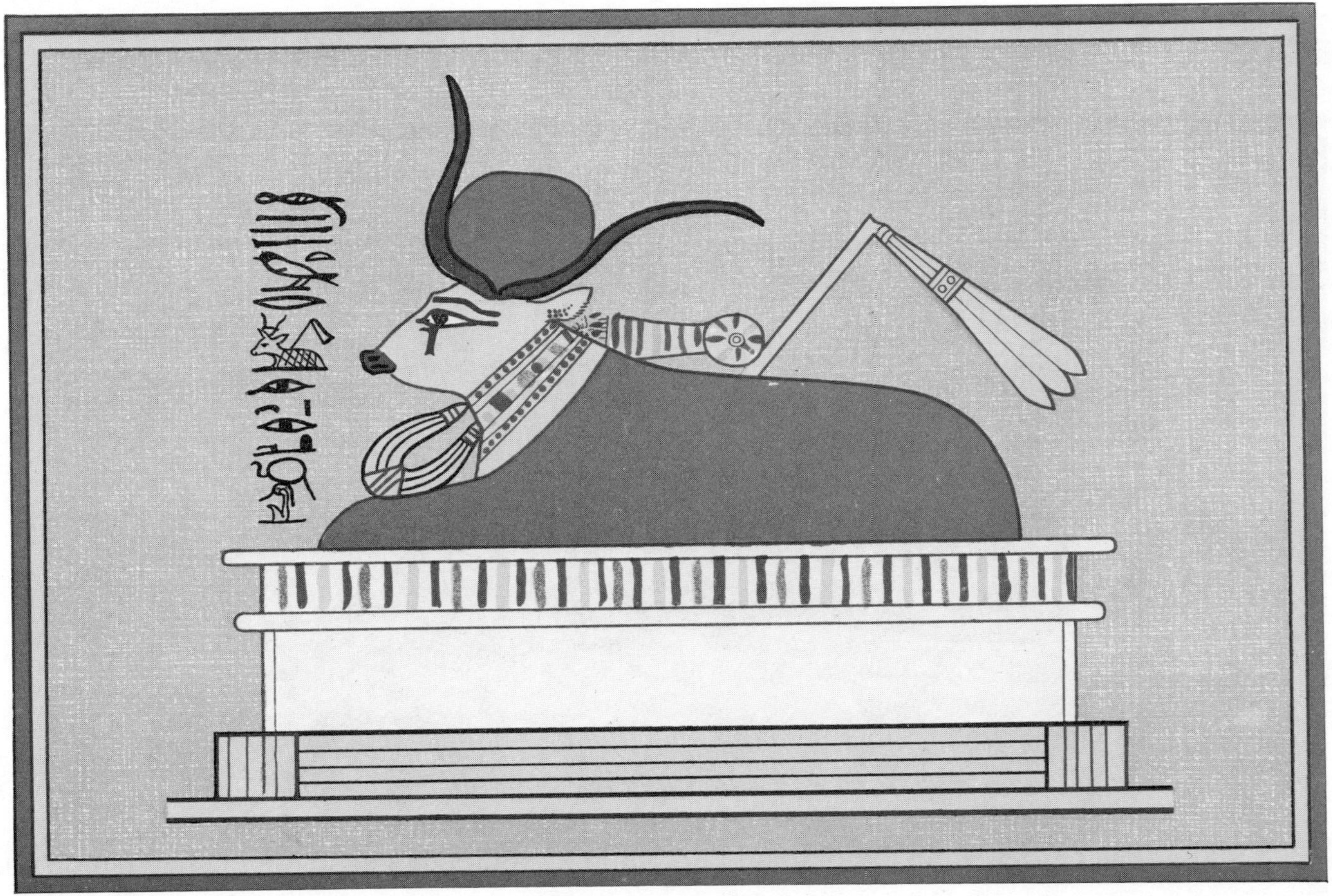

THE GODDESS MEH-URIT.

NUT, THE GODDESS OF HEAVEN, AS A COW.

abundant and unfailing source of the matter of every kind which was fecundated by the male germs of life of every kind; she was, in fact, a form of the primeval female creative principle, and in some aspects was identified with Isis and Hathor. She, of course, is a later conception than Nut, or Nit (Neith), of both of whom she was also a form. In one of the representations of the goddess figured by Signor Lanzone[1] she is depicted in the form of a pregnant woman with full, protruding breasts, emblem of fertility, but she usually appears as the great cow of the sky, either in the form which is illustrated on p. 368, or in that given in the accompanying plate. Sometimes she has the body of a woman and the head of a cow, and then she holds in her right hand a sceptre round which is twined the stalk of a lotus flower which she appears to be smelling; the flower itself is between , the symbols of the South and the North, and is supposed to represent the great world lotus flower, out of which rose the sun for the first time at the Creation. The usual titles of the goddess are "lady of heaven, "mistress of all the gods, mistress of the two lands," but she is also said to have "existed from the beginning," and to have helped Thoth to create the first things which appeared in Khemennu or Hermopolis. In primitive times the "weighing of words," i.e., the examination and judgment of the dead, was believed to take place in the Hall of Meḥ-urt, which seems to prove that in very early times the attributes of Maāt were ascribed to the great goddess, whose form was the cow, and that the souls of the dead were thought to be judged in the sky. The first conception of the Judgment was probably physical, and it was not until the period when the cult of Osiris became predominant that it assumed the character with which we are familiar from the *Book of the Dead.* It would seem that in the very ancient times it was the body and not the soul that was the subject of examination by the celestial powers, and this is what is to be expected in predynastic times when the theory of the resurrection then current demanded a renewed or revivified physical body.

Closely associated with Thoth in the performance of certain of

[1] Op. cit., pl. 131 ff.

his duties as the god of letters and learning, was thė goddess 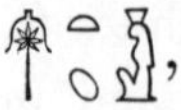, whose name is generally read SEFKHET-ĀĀBUT,  ; the reading "Sesheta" has also been proposed for the hieroglyphic sign, , which forms the symbol of this goddess, but both readings are merely guesses, for the phonetic value of the sign has not yet been ascertained, and even the sign itself has not been identified. All that is certain about it is that in some pictures of the goddess the sign seems to be compounded of a pair of horns inverted over a seven-rayed star, or flower with seven petals, supported on a standard. Dr. Brugsch believed that Sefkhet-āābut was the correct reading of the name, and that it either meant, "she who has inverted her horns," or, "she who is provided with seven horns," the latter meaning being suggested by the similarity of the first part of the name *Sefkhet* with the ordinary word for "seven." From the pictures of the goddess and the titles which accompany them it is quite certain what her functions were. We see her wearing her characteristic symbols on her head, with a close-fitting panther skin garment upon her body, and in her hands she holds a scribe's palette and writing reed; in this form she is called "the great one, the lady of the house of books," 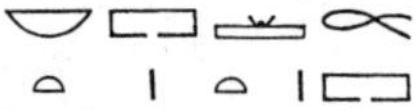. Thus she was a goddess of literature and the library.

Elsewhere we see her without her panther skin garment, holding a writing reed in the right hand, and the *cartouche* , symbolic of "name" in her left; in this form she suggests the idea of being a kind of recording angel, not so much of the deeds committed by man, but of their names, of which she, presumably, took note, that her associate Thoth might declare them before Osiris. In the title which accompanies this picture she is called "great one, lady of letters, mistress of the house of books," 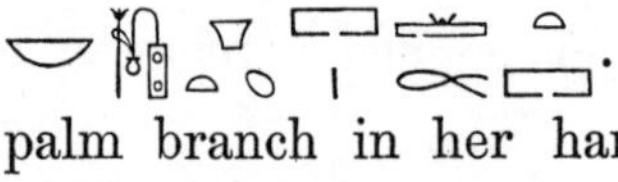. In another scene[1] she holds a notched palm branch in her hand, and she appears to be counting the notches; the lower end of the branch rests on the back of a frog,

[1] For all these pictures see Lanzone, op. cit., pl. 340.

seated upon , the emblem of "eternity," and from the upper end hangs the symbol of the double Seṭ festival, . Thus she appears in the character of the chronographer and chronologist; the use of the notched palm-branch as a symbol of the counting of years takes us back to a custom which was probably prevalent in predynastic times. In yet another scene we find the goddess standing before a column of hieroglyphics meaning "life," and "power," and "thirty-year festivals," which rest upon a seated figure who holds in each hand ☥, "life," and who typifies "millions of years." In connection with this must be noted a passage in a text in which she declares to a king that she has inscribed on her register on his behalf a period of life which shall be "hundreds of thousands of thirty-year periods," and has ordained that his years shall be upon the earth like the years of Rā, i.e., that he shall live for ever. In the *Book of the Dead* (lvii. 6) the deceased says, "My mouth and my nostrils are opened in Ṭaṭṭu, and I have "my place of peace in Ȧnnu, wherein is my house; it was built "for me by the goddess Sefekh-āābut (or Sesheta), and the god "Khnemu set it up for me upon its walls." And again he says (clii. 3), "The goddess Sefekh-āābut hath brought the god Nebṭ, "and Ȧnpu (Anubis) hath called unto the Osiris Nu (i.e., to me) "to build a house on the earth. Its foundation is in Kher-āḥa, "its shrine is the god Sekhem, who dwelleth in Sekhem, according "to that which I have written the renewal thereof, and men and "women bring offerings, and libations, and ministrants. And "Osiris saith unto all the gods who are in his train, and who "journey [with him], 'Behold ye the house which hath been built "'for a spirit who is well-equipped, and who cometh daily to "'renew himself among you.'" In the clxixth Chapter (line 18) the goddess is said to be seated before the deceased, and the goddess Sa protects his members.

These passages show that Sefekh-āābut was supposed to be the "goddess of construction," 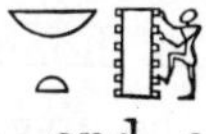, and she would thus be a suitable counterpart of Thoth, and one fitted to carry out his commands concerning the Creation. It is, however, certain from many passages that her chief duties were connected with the writing of history, and happy was the king who was fortunate enough to have his deeds recorded by the fingers of the goddess herself, and his abode in the next world built on the plan which she drew up in accordance with her attributes as the inventor of letters, the lady of the builder's measure, and the founder of architecture.[1] In a text quoted by Brugsch she declares to Seti that her words concerning him shall never be gainsaid, that her hand shall set down in writing his fame after the manner of her brother Thoth, and all according to the decree of Tem. She was identified with the goddess Renenet, , and with Isis, and at Dendera she is called the "daughter of Nut;" at Lycopolis she was regarded as the sister of Osiris, and the mother of Ḥeru-nub, , or the "Horus of gold."

Yet another goddess must be mentioned in connection with Maāt and Thoth, that is to say, Unnut, , the lady of Unnu, , who must not be confused with Unnut, the goddess of the hours, who is depicted in the form of a woman with a star upon her head. The former goddess has, on the other hand, the body of a woman with the head of a hare, and she usually holds in each hand a knife, ;[2] sometimes she holds a sceptre in one hand, and , "life," in the other. One aspect of her, i.e., that of the goddess who destroys with her knives, was identified with Sekhet, , and in this form she was the deity of the city Menḥet, . From a passage in the cxxxviith Chapter of the *Book of the Dead* we may gain some idea of the antiquity of the goddess Unnut, for towards the end of the rubric (line 38) it is said that the Chapter was found in the handwriting of the god Thoth in the temple of "Unnut, lady of Unnu," , by Ḥeru-ṭāṭā-f, the son of Khufu, i.e., Cheops, a king of the IVth Dynasty. Thus it is clear that even in that remote period a temple in honour of the goddess existed at Unnu, i.e., Hermopolis, or the city of Thoth. Unnu, as we know, was the chief city of the nome Un, the chief local god of which

1 See Brugsch, *Religion*, p. 474.

2 See Lanzone, op. cit., pl. 52.

The Goddess SESHETA.

(ḤET-ḤERT) HATHOR THE COW-GODDESS LOOKING FORTH FROM THE FUNERAL MOUNTAIN AT THEBES.

was depicted in the form of a hare, , and Unnut is the female counterpart of the god Unnu, and was the old local goddess of the metropolis of the nome.

In the vignette of the cxth Chapter of the *Book of the Dead* (Papyrus of Ani, pl. 35) we see the deceased standing with hands raised in adoration before three seated deities, the first having the head of a hare, the second that of a snake, and the third that of a bull; behind him stands the god Thoth with palette and reed, but whether he is in any way connected with the three gods cannot be said. A hare-headed god is also seen as one of the group of three gods who preside over one of the Ārits in the Underworld; according to the Papyrus of Ani it is the first Ārit, and according to the Papyrus of Nu it is the second. At Dendera a hare-headed god is seen wrapped in mummy swathings, with his hands in such a position that they suggest his identification with Osiris, and an attempt has been made[1] to show in connexion with this representation that the hare-headed god was called UN, that this name appears in the compound name "Un-nefer," the well-known title of Osiris, that the hare-god Un was only another form of Osiris, and that the name Un was applied to Osiris because he "sprang up," like the hare, which, as the rising sun, is said to be the "springer." According to this view the goddess Unnut would be a female form of the hare-god Un or Unnu, but Brugsch's opinion which makes her to be the goddess of the city of Unnu, or Hermopolis, is more correct, especially when we remember that the cities Ȧn, and Ȧpt, and Beḥuṭet, etc., possessed goddesses of the city which were called Ȧnit, and Ȧpit, and Beḥuṭit. We have already seen that the goddess Maāt had two forms, i.e., Maāt of the South and Maāt of the North, and similarly we find that Unnut had two forms, one of which belonged to Hermopolis of the South, and the other to Hermopolis of the North, the 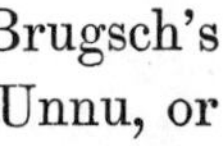 *Unnu meḥt* of the text, i.e., Hermopolis Parva, wherein Thoth was worshipped under the form of ȦP-REḤUI, 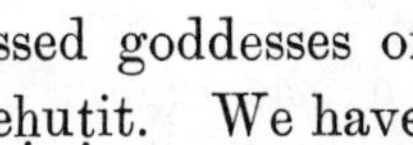, together with his female counterpart Neḥemāuait.[2]

[1] See Renouf in *Trans. Soc. Bibl. Arch.*, vol. ix., pp. 281-294.

[2] Brugsch, *Religion*, p. 477; de Rougé, *Géographie*, pp. 30, 102.

CHAPTER XIV

# HATHOR, , ḤET-ḤERT, AND THE HATHOR GODDESSES

THE goddess HATHOR is one of the oldest known deities of Egypt, and it is certain that, under the form of a cow, she was worshipped in the early part of the archaic period, because a flint model of the head and horns of the cow, which was her type and symbol, has been found among the early archaic, or late predynastic flints in Egypt.[1] The forms in which the goddess is depicted are numerous, but this is not to be wondered at, because during the course of the dynastic period she was identified with every important local goddess, and all their attributes, of whatever class and kind, were ascribed to her. The oldest form of all is probably that of the cow, and this was preserved, though chiefly in funeral scenes and in the *Book of the Dead*, until the beginning of the Roman period. ḤET-ḤERT, , the name of the goddess, means the "House above," i.e., the region of the sky or heaven, and another form of it, , which is to be read ḤET-ḤERU, and which means "House of Horus," shows that she was a personification of the house in which Horus the Sun-god dwelt, and that she represented the portion of the sky through which the course of the god lay. In the earliest times Hathor, the Ἁθωρ of the Greek writers, typified only that portion of the sky in which Horus, the oldest form of the Sun-god, had been conceived and brought forth, and her domain was in the east of the sky; but at length she came to represent the whole

[1] This is preserved in the British Museum, No. 32,124.

sky, and in so doing, she, no doubt, absorbed many of the attributes of predynastic goddesses. In the text of Pepi I. (line 593) it is said, "Every god will take the hand of Rā-meri in heaven, and "they will conduct him to Ḥet-Ḥeru ( ), which is in the "heaven of Qebḥu ( ), and his double shall be able "to make his voice (or word) take effect upon Seb." From this passage it seems as if the House of Horus was only one special part of the great watery mass of heaven which is generally known by the name of "Qebḥ."

At the time when the Egyptians first formulated their theogony Hathor was certainly a cosmic goddess, and was associated with the Sun-god Rā, of whom she was the principal female counterpart. In the theological system of the priests of Heliopolis she became, as Brugsch says,[1] the "mother of the light," the birth of which was the first act of creation; her next creative act was to produce Shu and Tefnut, that is to say, certain aspects of these gods, for according to a very old tradition Temu was their begetter and producer. Of the various forms in which Hathor is depicted may be mentioned the following[2]:—As the "chieftainess," , of Thebes and the mistress of Åmentet she is usually represented in the form of a woman who wears upon her head a pair of horns within which rests the solar disk; as the lady of Ḥetepet, , she wears the vulture tiara, with a uraeus in front and five uraei on the top of it; as the lady of Senemet, , she appears in the form of a woman with the headdress , or with plumes and horns; as the lady of Åbshek, , she wears a disk between horns; as the great goddess of Dendera, , she appears in the form of a lioness, with a uraeus on her head, and as a woman wearing and , or , or and , or and , or the sistrum, , or and , or and , or and , and , and , and she usually carries a sceptre, or ,

[1] *Religion*, p. 312.

[2] Lanzone, op. cit., pl. 314 ff.

in one hand, and "life," , in the other; as the lady of the "southern sycamore," , she has the head of a cow; as the lady of Ȧnnu she has on her head ; as the goddess of turquoise [land], i.e., the Sinaitic Peninsula, called "Māfek," , she wears the crown of the north, , or and ; and in another form she wears the vulture head-dress surmounted by a tiara formed of uraei, and above these is a pylon set among a mass of lotus flowers and buds. As the "lady of the Holy Land," i.e., the Underworld, and Ȧmentet, , she appears in the form of a cow walking out from the funeral mountain, and she is sometimes represented in the form of a cow standing in a boat surrounded by papyrus plants which are growing up to a considerable height above her body. As the cow-goddess of the Underworld, however, she wears a long, pendent collar, and on the back of her neck is the *Menȧt*, , an emblem of joy and pleasure. On her back also is a kind of saddle-cloth with a linear design, and the whole of her body is sometimes marked with crosses, which are probably intended to represent stars. Two other interesting forms of the goddess which are illustrated by Signor Lanzone[1] represent her holding in her hand the notched palm branch, which is usually the characteristic of the goddess Sefekh-āābut, who acted as assistant chronographer and chronologist to the god Thoth, and from this point of view Hathor must be regarded as a female counterpart of Thoth. Finally, she is represented as a sphinx, wearing on her head the vulture head-dress, with uraeus and disk; the side of her body is made to resemble a part of a *menȧt*, and she rests upon a pylon. The titles which accompany this last form call her "lady of Ḥetep, the eye of Rā, dweller in his disk, lady of "heaven, mistress of all the gods," .

We have already seen that the worship of Horus was universal in Egypt, probably from the earliest period, and that in dynastic times shrines which were specially consecrated to his worship were

[1] Op. cit., pl. 325 ff.

common throughout the country; the texts prove that the worship of Hathor was also universal, and that her shrines were even more numerous than those of Horus. She was, in fact, the great mother of the world, and the old, cosmic Hathor was the personification of the great power of nature which was perpetually conceiving, and creating, and bringing forth, and rearing, and maintaining all things, both great and small. She was the "mother of her father, "and the daughter of her son," and heaven, earth, and the Underworld were under her rule, and she was the mother of every god and every goddess. In all the important shrines of the local goddesses she was honoured with them, and she always became the chief female counterpart of the head of the company or triad in which she had been allowed to enter as a guest. A clear proof of this fact is given in the list compiled by the late Dr. Brugsch, which showed the various names and forms she took in all the large cities in Upper and Lower Egypt, and from this we see that she was identified with Satet, , and Ānqet, , in Elephantine; with Ta-sent-nefert, , in Ombos; with Beḥuṭet, , in Apollinopolis Magna; with Nit, , Nebuut, , and Menḥit, , in Latopolis; with Mut, , and Nekhebet, , in Eileithyiaspolis; with Rāt-tauit, , and Thenenet, , in Hermonthis; with Mut, , and Ȧmenthet, , in Thebes; with Ḥeqet, , in Apollinopolis Parva; with Isis, , and Ȧnit, , in Coptos; with Sefkhet-Āābut, in Diospolis Parva; with Meḥit-Tefnut-Khut-Menḥit, , in This; with Isis and Khent Ȧbtet, , in Panopolis; with Ḥeqet and Ānthȧt, , in Aphroditopolis; with Nit, Uatchet, , Sekhet, , etc., in Hypselis; with Maāt and Isis in Hierakonpolis; with Mut and

Sefkhet-āābut in Lycopolis; with Sekhet and Maāt in Cusae; with NEḤEMĀUAIT, , and Sefkhet-āābut, and Meḥ-urt, , in Hermopolis; with Ḥeqet and ASHET, , in Ibiu; with PAKHTH, 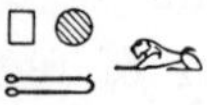, at the Speos Artemidos; with ÅNPET, 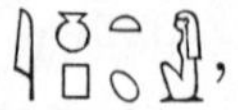, in Cynopolis; with UATCHET in Alabastronpolis; with HATHOR of Oxyrinchus; with ĀNTHÅT and MERSEKHENT 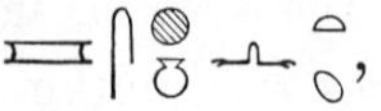, in Herakleopolis Magna; with RENPIT, , in Crocodilopolis; with KHERSEKHET in Ptolemaïs; with Isis and ṬEP-ÅḤET in Aphroditopolis; with Bast, , Sekhet, and Renpit in Memphis; with NEBUAREKHT-ĀAT,  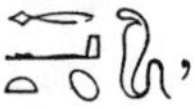, in Letopolis; with USERT-ḤEQET, , in Prosopis; with Nit (Neith) in Saïs; with Urt-Åpset, 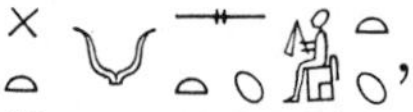, in *Xoïs*; with Isis in Canopus; with Uatchet in Buto; with Tefnut in Pa-Tem (Pithom); with TATET OR TAIT, 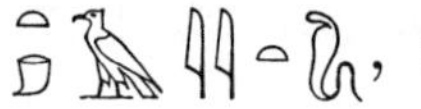, in Busiris; with KHUIT, 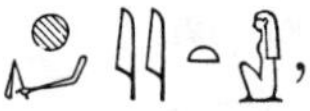, in Athribis; with ṬEṬET, daughter of Rā, , and Tefnut, in the form of a lion, 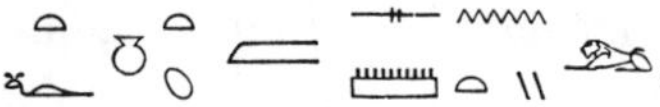, and ḤERT, , i.e., the female counterpart of Horus, and NESERT, 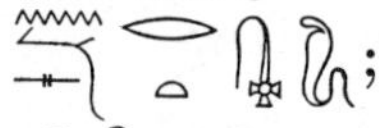; with IUSĀSET, 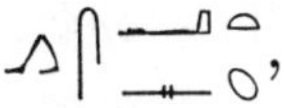, and NEBT-ḤETEP, 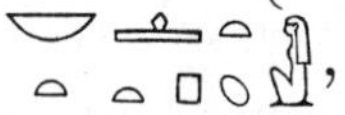, and MENÅT, 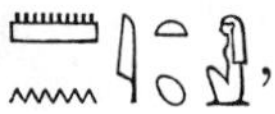, and REPIT, ; with KHENT-ÅBTET, , in Sele (?); with Neḥemāuait, Tefnut, and Isis in Hermopolis; with ḤĀT-MEḤIT, 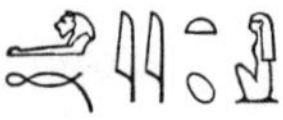, in Mendes; with Mut, Tefnut, and Khent-Åbtet, in Diospolis; with Bast, , in Bubastis; with Isis and Uatchet in Åmmet, 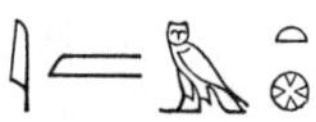; and with Septit, 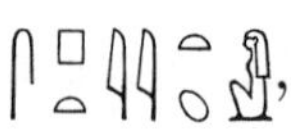, and Khekhsit, , in the nome of Sepṭ. It is, then, quite certain that in late dynastic times, at least, Hathor became the representative of all the great goddesses in Egypt, and that shrines in her honour were built in most great cities there. In his valuable *Dizionario di Mitologia Egizia* (p. 875), Signor

Lanzone has collected the names of a number of cities which contained shrines of Hathor, but the enumeration of them all[1] here would serve no useful purpose, because the identifications of the goddess described above are sufficient to indicate the universality of her worship.

A little consideration of the texts shows us that it was quite impossible for any worshipper of Hathor, however devout, to enumerate all the forms of the goddess which existed, and also that some of them were considered of greater importance than the others; as a result we find that at a comparatively early period a selection of the Hathors was made, and that it usually contained seven. The SEVEN HATHORS who were worshipped at Dendera were:—1. Hathor of Thebes, . 2. Hathor of Heliopolis, . 3. Hathor of Aphroditopolis, . 4. Hathor of the Sinaitic Peninsula, . 5. Hathor of Momemphis (Ammu), . 6. Hathor of Herakleopolis, . 7. Hathor of Keset, . These were represented[2] in the form of young and handsome women arrayed in close-fitting tunics, and wearing

[1] The following selection may, however, be of interest:—Ārit, , Åkent, , Sekhet-Rā, , Keset, , Senmet, , Khauit, , Mātcheṭ, , Sheṭenu, , Āḳenu, , Khakhat (?), , She-Ṭesher, , Kepenut (in Syria), , Per-ṭennu in Ānkh-tauit, , Reḥesu, , Feka, , Ṭep-åḥet, , Alkat, , Ån-Menthu, , Maāti, , Sebti, , Ḳennu, , Tcherutet, , Seḳ, , Per-Utchat, , Ḥes, , Kenset, , Neferus, , Khekhuit, , Åntet, , Sennut, .

[2] Brugsch, *Mythologische Inschriften*, Leipzig, 1884, p. 801 ff.

vulture head-dresses surmounted by , and holding tambourines in their hands. In the "Tale of the Two Brothers"[1] we find the Seven Hathors acting the part of prophetic fairies, for in that entertaining narrative they are made to come and look upon the wife whom Khnemu had fashioned for the younger brother Bata, and who "was more beautiful in her person than any other woman "in all the earth, for every god was contained in her;" but when they had looked upon her, they said with one voice, "Her death will be caused by the knife." Unfortunately we do not know the districts which these Seven Hathors, , represented. The Seven Hathors mentioned by Mariette[2] comprise the Hathors of Dendera, , Keset (Cusae), Nehet , the Two Mountains, (i.e., the modern Gebelên), Eileithyiaspolis, , and Māfek (Sinai), Kepenut (Byblos), and Ḥet-seshesh, (Diospolis Parva); thus it is clear that the company of the Seven Hathors did not always include the same forms of the goddess. In the Litanies of Seker[3] we have also a "Litany of the Hathors," wherein are mentioned the Hathors of:—1. Ṭep-āḥet. 2. Māfek and Thebes. 3. Thebes. 4. Nebt-ḥetep. 5. Suten-ḥenen. 6. Memphis. 7. She-Ṭesher; here, then, is a different group of Seven Hathors. In the six lines of text which follow, Hathor is identified with the goddesses:—1. Bast. 2. Sati. 3. Uatchet. 4. Sekhet. 5. Lady of Ammu. 6. Nit (Neith); and after this we have addresses to the Hathors of Thebes, Suten-ḥenen, Ṭep-āḥet, Nehau, Reḥsau, Shet-Teshert, Māfek, Åneb, Uaua, Ammu, Amem, and Hathor, lady of the "City of Sixteen," , i.e., Lycopolis, in all Twelve Hathors. If we had full information on the subject we should probably find that each great city possessed its own selection of Hathors, and that the forms of the goddess whose names were inscribed on funeral papyri were only those which were popular with those who caused such documents to be made.

[1] Page ix., l. 8. (Birch, *Select Papyri.*)

[2] See *Denderah*, tom. 1, pl. 27; Brugsch, *Dict. Géog.*, p. 972.

[3] See my paper in *Archaeologia*, vol. lii. (Papyrus of Nesi-Amsu).

The Goddess HATHOR.

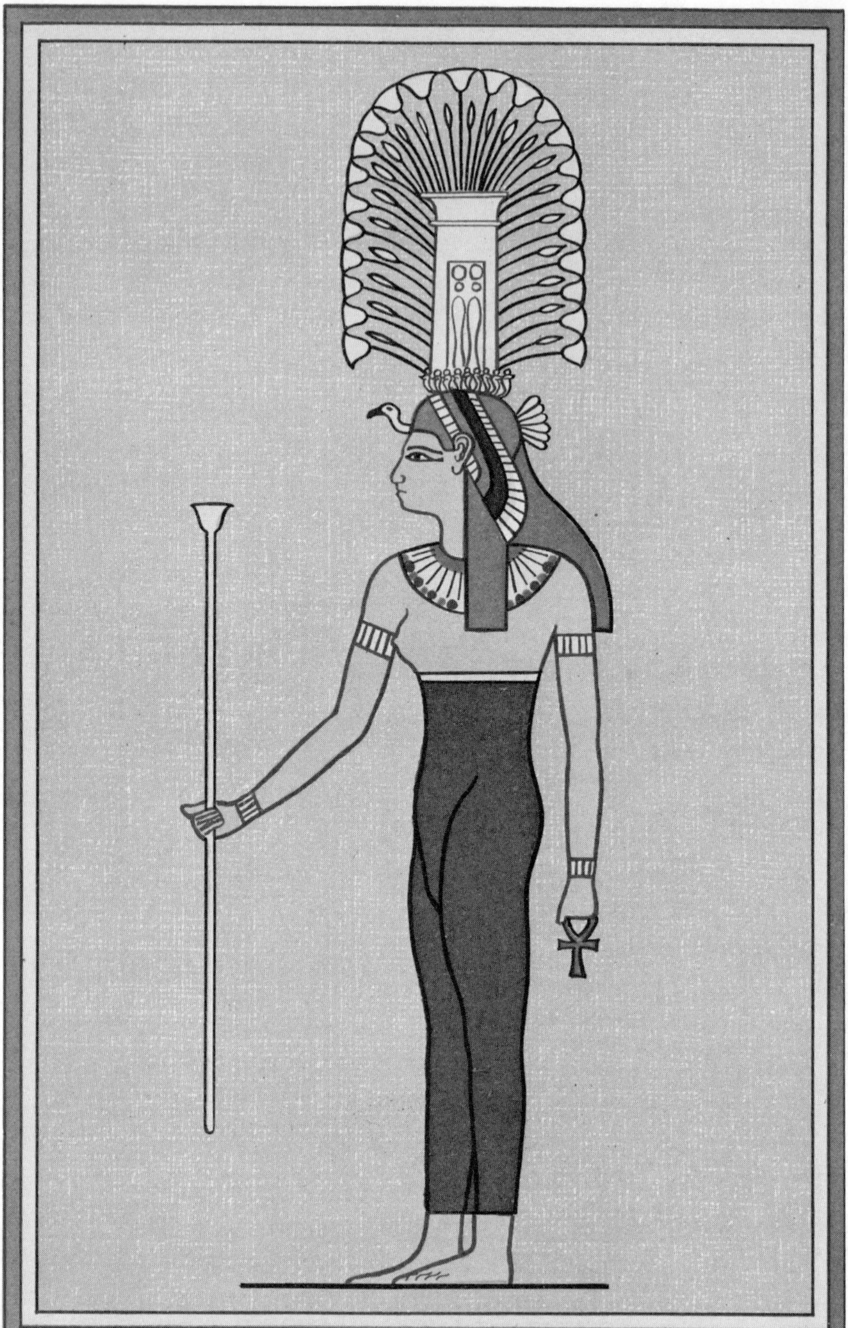

THE GODDESS ḤET-ḤERT (HATHOR).

The Greeks identified Hathor with their goddess Aphrodite, and there are many passages in the Egyptian texts which show that they were justified in doing so. She represented not only what was true, but what was good, and all that is best in woman as wife, mother, and daughter; she was also the patron goddess of all singers, dancers, and merry-makers of every kind, of beautiful women, and of love, of artists and artistic works, and also of the vine and wine, and ale and beer, and, in fact, of joy and happiness, and of everything which contributed thereto. She was identified astronomically with the star Sepṭ, , or Sothis, which was called the "second sun" in heaven, she was thereby connected with the rise of the Nile preparatory to the Inundation, and she appeared in the form of this star in the heavens in the neighbourhood of the sun in the second half of July. Sothis rose heliacally on the first day of the Egyptian New Year, and when the Sun-god Rā had entered his boat, Hathor, the goddess of the star Sothis, went with him and took up her place like a crown upon his forehead.[1] She was, as we have seen, both the wife of Rā, and the daughter of Rā; she herself was brought forth by the goddess Nut in the form of a black-skinned, 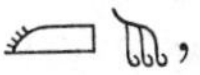, or blackish-red skinned child and received as her name that of the last hour of the day, Khnemet-ānkh, 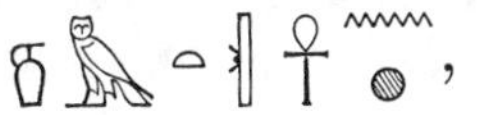, or .[2] Hathor, as lady of the Underworld, played a very prominent part in connection with the welfare of the dead, for without her friendly help and protection the deceased could never attain to everlasting life.

The position which Hathor held among the gods of the Underworld is well illustrated by the following passages from the *Book of the Dead*. In his hymn to Rā the deceased officer Nekht says, "O thou beautiful being, thou dost renew thyself in thy "season in the form of the Disk within thy mother Hathor," with which words he refers to the goddess as a nature power. In the Judgment Scene we find that she is one of the company of the gods who watch the "weighing of words," and who afterwards decree joy and felicity for the heart which has been weighed and

1 Brugsch, *Religion*, p. 318; Lanzone, op. cit., p. 865.

2 Brugsch, *Mythologische Inschriften*, p. 844 (Twelfth Hour of the Day).

found just. When the deceased is face to face with the monster Āpep, Hathor is one of the group of gods consisting of NETCHEB-ÅB-F, , Tem, Nentchā, 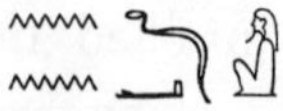, Seb, Nut, and Kheperå, who encourage the deceased to do battle with him, and she cries out to the deceased, "Take your armour;" but she, like the deceased, is in terror of Āpep and "she quaketh" thereat (xxxix. 22). In the Chapter (xlii.) which describes the deification of the members of the deceased, she becomes his two eyes, and he declares, "My eyes are the eyes of Hathor." Now Hathor was, according to one myth, the star Sothis, , *Sept*, and she took up her place in the face of Horus or Rā as his right eye; another myth which made her the night sky also made her the moon therein; hence the eyes of Hathor are the sun and moon, and the deceased regards these as his own eyes in the text. In other Chapters (lii., lxiii.A, lxviii.), she appears as the goddess who provides the deceased with meat and drink, and thus we find the following:—"Let me eat my food under the sycamore tree of my "lady Hathor, and let my times be among the divine beings who "have alighted thereon;" and again, "In a clean place I shall sit "on the ground beneath the foliage of the date palm of the goddess "Hathor, who dwelleth in the spacious Disk as it advanceth to "Ånnu, having the books of the divine words of the writings of "the god Thoth;" and again, "Let me have power over cakes, "and let me eat of them under the leaves of the palm tree of the "goddess Hathor, who is my divine lady" (lxxxii. 7).

In the Hall of Maāti the name of the left foot of the deceased was "Staff of Hathor" (cxxv. 35), and a special Chapter (ciii.) was composed with the view of enabling the deceased to "be among those who are in the following of Hathor." Thus we see that she was held to be sufficiently important to have a train of attendant gods, or ministering angels, about her. In the vignette of Chapter cxxxiv. Hathor forms one of the company of the gods of Heliopolis, which here consists of Tem, Shu, Tefnut, Seb, Nut, Osiris, Isis, Nephthys, Hathor, and Horus, the last named taking the place of Set or Suti; and in Chapter cxl. Hathor, with Tem, Utchatet, , Shu, Seb, Osiris, Suti, Horus,

Menth, , Bāḥ, , Rā-er-neḥeḥ, , Thoth, Nāāu-tchetta (?) , Nut, Isis, Nephthys, Nekht, , Mert, (?) , Maāt, Ȧnep, and Ta-mes-tchetta, , are said to be "the soul and body of Rā." In Chapter cli.A Nephthys addresses the deceased and says, "Rā hearkeneth unto thy cry; thou, O daughter of Hathor, art "made to triumph, thy head shall never be taken away from thee, "and thou shalt be made to rise up in peace." It was Hathor in the form of a cow who received the dead when they entered the Underworld, she gave them new life, and celestial food wherewith to maintain it, and in the Roman period the personality of the deceased is merged in that of the goddess in the funeral texts, just as during the dynastic period it was merged in that of Osiris. Finally, it is said in a passage quoted from a papyrus by M. Maspero[1] which prescribes the placing of the "swathing of Hathor" on the face of the deceased, "She (i.e., Hathor) shall make thy face "perfect among the gods, she shall make thy thighs large among "the goddesses, she shall open thine eye so that thou shalt see "each day, she shall enlarge thy place in Ȧmentet, she shall make "thy voice to prevail over thy adversaries; and she shall make "thy legs to walk with ease in the Underworld in her name of "Hathor, lady of Ȧmentet."

In an interesting text in the Ptolemaïc temple at Dêr al-Medîna,[2] on the western bank of the Nile opposite Thebes, we find that Hathor is called NUBT, , i.e., the "Golden One," and that she is addressed as the "queen of the gods," and her adorer says, "thou standest high in the south as the lady of Teka (Eileithyias-"polis), and thou illuminest the west as lady of Saïs. Thou "appearest and thou art commemorated in festivals as Hathor, "the great lady, the beloved of Rā in [thy] seven forms." Thoth, we are told, comes to look upon her face, and he praises her according to her desire, and she is built up by his words. As

1 *Mémoire sur quelques Papyrus du Louvre*, Paris, 1875, p. 104.

2 The Egyptian name of the place was , Kheft-ḥrȧ-en-neb-s, and the Greek Pasêmis; Brugsch, *Dict. Géog.*, p. 574.

NEBT-ḤETEPET she is glorious in heaven, and mighty upon earth, and queen of the Underworld. As the goddess TEMT she is the lady of the "two lands," and of the red covering, and she shines in the cities of Buto and Bubastis. It is evident from the above that as the goddess of the Underworld Hathor was identified with the four great and ancient goddesses, Nekhebet of Nekhebet (Eileithyiaspolis), Uatchet of Per-Uatchet, Bast of Bubastis, and Nit (Neith) of Saïs, i.e., with the four typical goddesses of the four quarters of the world and of the four cardinal points, and it is also quite evident that this identification is the product of a late period, when the earliest attributes of Uatchet and Nekhebet, etc., were forgotten. It is, however, convenient to consider these goddesses under the head of Hathor, and they will, therefore, be described here, not because the writer regards the Ptolemaïc identification as the correct one, but because there is something to be said for it.

## NEKHEBET, 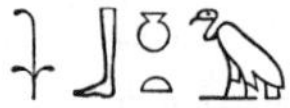, THE GODDESS OF THE SOUTH.

From the hieroglyphic inscriptions which belong to the archaïc period we find that the kings of Egypt were in the habit of placing before their names the sign , by which they intended to indicate their sovereignty over the South and the North; it is uncertain how these signs are to be read, but there is no doubt whatsoever about their meaning. The vulture is the symbol of the goddess of the South, and the uraeus is the symbol of the goddess of the North, and down to very late dynastic times the kings of Egypt gloried in declaring that they were sovereigns of the country by virtue of the favour of the goddesses whose emblems were the vulture and uraeus. It is tolerably certain that in predynastic times the vulture was worshipped generally throughout Upper Egypt, and that a particular form of the serpent was venerated in the Delta; the centre of the worship of the vulture was in the city called Nekhebet, , or, , which was named Eileithyiaspolis by the Greeks, and "Civitas Lucinæ" by the Latins, and formed the capital of the third nome of Upper Egypt, and the centre of the worship of the serpent was

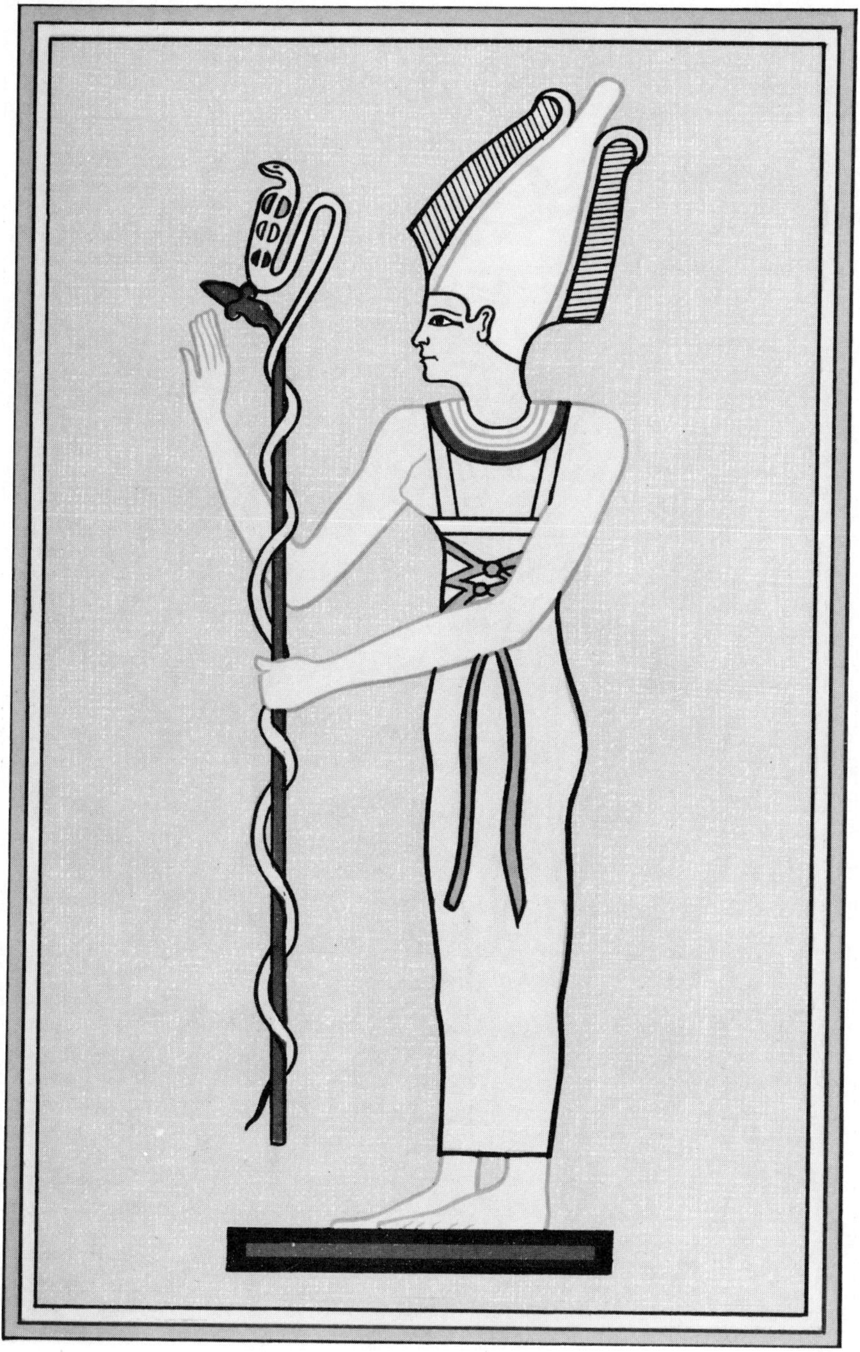

The Goddess NEKHEBIT.

The Goddess UATCHIT.

Per-Uatchet, , the Βοῦτος of the Greeks and the Buto of the Latins, and the capital of the seventh nome of Lower Egypt. Nekhebet was declared to be the daughter of Rā, , and also the "divine wife of Khent Åmenti," . The shrine of the goddess was Nekhent, , or, , or, , and its site is represented by the modern Arab village of El-Kâb; in late times Nekhebet lost all its political importance, and the neighbouring towns of Åni, , and Senit, , came into prominence in its place.[1] Nekhen, also written, , i.e., the "White Nekhen," was the town which contained the sanctuary of the "venerable (or, holy) vulture," , and the vulture goddess Nekhebet in the land of the South is distinctly, in later texts, identified with Hathor.[2]

Nekhebet is usually represented in the form of a woman who wears on her head the vulture head-dress surmounted by the white crown, , the sign of sovereignty over Upper Egypt, to which are attached two plumes; sometimes she holds in one hand the sceptre, , and sometimes , and in the other we see the symbol of "life," . Occasionally the sceptre is formed of a long-stemmed flower, which seems to be a water-lily, with a serpent twined round it; this serpent is none other than the winged serpent, with the crown of the South upon its head, which is as symbolic of the goddess as the vulture. Nekhebet is also represented in the form of a woman with the head of a vulture, and in a picture of her reproduced by Signor Lanzone[3] she stands upon *maāt* , and holds a bow and an arrow in her left hand. In the form of a uraeus Nekhebet took her place, with her twin sister Uatchet, upon the brow of Rā, and both goddesses devoted themselves to destroying the enemies of the god; this idea is alluded to in the winged disks which are seen

[1] Brugsch, *Dict. Géog.*, p. 352 ff.

[2] .

[3] Op. cit., pl. 348.

sculptured over the doors of temples in Egypt, for on each side is a serpent, that on the right, or south side, being Nekhebet, and that on the left, or north side, being Uatchet. Nekhebet was, astronomically, the western or right eye of the sun during his journey in the Underworld, and Uatchet was his eastern or left eye. As a nature power Nekhebet was a form of the primeval abyss which brought forth the light,[1] and she is therefore called the "father of fathers, the mother of mothers, who hath existed from "the beginning, and is the creatrix of the world." In the bas-reliefs in Egyptian temples she is usually represented with her twin sister Uatchet, and also in coronation scenes, for it was most important for a king to be crowned with the double crown, , by these deities.

According to Brugsch, special rooms or chambers were set apart in the temples of Egypt, near the sanctuaries of the gods wherein Uatchet and Nekhebet were supposed to abide; the chamber of the former was on the west, or right side of the sanctuary, and was called *per nesert* 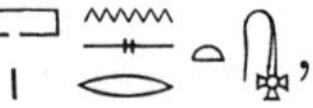, or "house of fire," and that of the latter was on the east, or left side of the sanctuary, and was called *per ur*, or "great house," . And it is very probable that at the time of the coronation of a king priestesses dressed themselves in the character of the two goddesses, and that the one declared the South had been given to him whilst the other asserted the same concerning the North. In coloured pictures of Nekhebet Fāḳit, , we find that she is painted of a light yellow, or almost white colour, which is probably intended to represent the colour of the desert regions of the South, and of the white light of the newly risen sun or moon. From one aspect she was identified with Isis, the fertile nature goddess, just as Uatchet was identified with Nephthys, who was supposed to act the part of nurse to the offspring whom Isis brought forth; in other words, Nekhebet was the mother of the Sun-god, and therefore also of the king of Egypt, his son, and Uatchet was his nurse. A passage in the text of Mer-en-Rā

[1] Brugsch, *Religion*, p. 324.

(line 762) seems to connect Nekhebet with Ȧnnu, for we read, "Thou protectest Mer-en-Rā, O Nekhebet, thou hast protected "Mer-en-Rā, O Nekhebet, in the House of the Prince in Ȧnnu; "thou hast committed him to ȦM-ḤENT-F, and Ȧm-ḥent-f hath "committed him to ȦM-SEPA-F;"[1] if this be so it is probable that Nekhebet was identified with one or other of the local goddesses Iusāaset or Nebt-ḥetep. In an interesting text published by M. Maspero[2] an allusion is made to the natron of the city of Nekheb, which was apparently much used in embalming the dead, and it was believed that in consequence the goddess Nekhebet would watch over them in the Underworld, and would change their faces into things of beauty with two brilliant eyes of light. To make certain of this result the "bandage of Nekheb" was laid upon the forehead of every carefully prepared mummy.

### UATCHET, 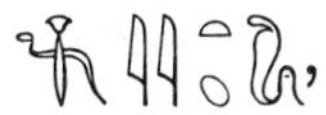, THE GODDESS OF THE NORTH.

UATCHET, or Uatchit, as we have already said above, is a goddess who was worshipped under the form of a serpent, and the oldest seat of her cult was at Per-uatchet, , the Βοῦτος of the Greeks, a city which was situated in the "land of Uatchet," ,[3] i.e., in the seventh nome of Lower Egypt, or Nefer-Ȧment, 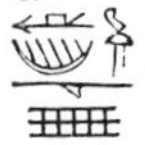. The temple in which Uatchet was venerated and its precincts are known in texts of all periods by the name Pe-Ṭep, 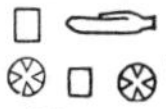, and from the frequent mention of this double name in the Pyramid Texts it is clear that the shrine was both very famous and very old. Uatchet was identified with Isis

1 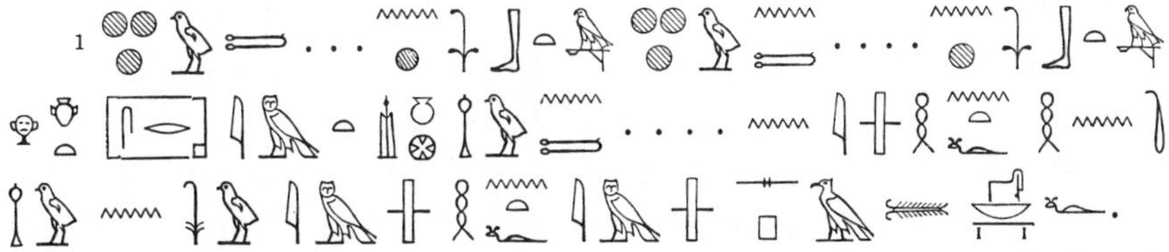

2 The Φθενότης of Ptolemy, and the Ptenetu of Pliny; see de Rougé, *Géographie*, p. 41.

3 *Mémoire sur quelques Papyrus*, pp. 50, 83.

at a very early period, and there is abundant proof that Horus, the son of Isis, was worshipped with Isis at Per-Uatchet; we are, then, driven to the conclusion that Pe-Ṭep was a city with two distinct divisions, in one of which Uatchet-Isis was worshipped, and in the other Horus, and that Horus dwelt in Pe, and Uatchet-Isis in Ṭep. Among the variants of the name worthy of mention are Pi-Tchepet, 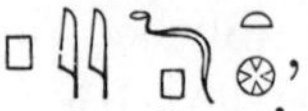, and Pi-Tep, .[1] In late dynastic times Uatchet was called Åp-taui, i.e., "opener of lands," 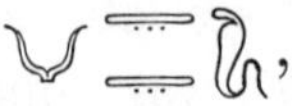, but the exact meaning of this title is not quite certain. Near the city of the goddess was situated the Island of Khebit, 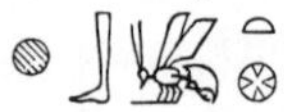, or , or 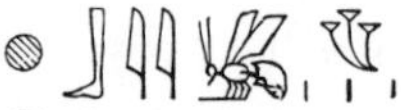, which has been rightly identified with the island called Χέμμις and Χέμρες[2] by classical writers, and round about which were the papyrus swamps , Na-åṭeḥ, the Natho of the Greeks, which play such a prominent part in the legends of Isis and Horus. According to these, Isis retreated to the papyrus swamps after she had conceived her child, and she remained hidden in them until her months were fulfilled, when she brought forth Horus, who afterwards became the "avenger of his father;" Set never succeeded in finding her hiding place, because the great goddess had found some means whereby she caused the papyrus and other plants to screen her from his view, and the goddess Uatchet visited her and helped her in her retreat.

In pictures and reliefs the goddess is represented in the form of a woman who wears upon her head the crown of the North, , and she holds in one hand the papyrus sceptre, round which is sometimes twined a long snake; in some examples she is seen bearing in her right hand the crown of the North, , which she is about to place upon the head of a king. Occasionally we find her in the form of a large winged serpent[3] with the crown of the North upon her head; her titles are "Uatchet, lady of heaven;" "Uatchet, lady of Pe, mistress of Ṭep, the august one, the mighty

[1] Brugsch, *Dict. Géog.*, p. 215.
[2] *Ibid.*, p. 568.
[3] See Lanzone, op. cit., pl. 58 f.

one;" "Uatchet, lady of heaven, mistress of all the gods;" "Uatchet, lady of Nebiui, , lady of Neter-"ta, , lady of Per-Menāt, , and lady of Åmemt, " ." Besides her shrines in these last named cities one built in her honour seems to have existed in Sepṭ, . The views held about the goddess in connexion with the dead are well illustrated by certain allusions made to her in the *Book of the Dead*. In the xviith Chapter she is mentioned in connexion with a god called Reḥu, , and she is definitely identified with Isis who is said to have protected her son Horus by shaking her hair out over him, although Uatchet appears in the form of a serpent twined round the stalk of a papyrus plant and is called the "eye of Rā." In the xliind Chapter the shoulder of the deceased is said to be the shoulder of Uatchet; in the lxvith Chapter the deceased says, "I have knowledge. I was conceived by Sekhet, and the "goddess Nit (Neith) gave me birth. I am Horus, and I have "come forth from the Eye of Horus (i.e., Rā). I am Uatchet who "came forth from Horus. I am Horus, and I fly up and perch "myself upon the forehead of Rā in the bows of his boat which is "in heaven." In Chapter cxxxvi.A the deceased is said to be the "lord of Maāt (), which the goddess Uatchet worketh;" in Chapter cxxxvi.B he says, "I am the spiritual body (*sāḥ* " ) of the lord of Maāt which is made by the goddess "Uatchet;" and in Chapter clxxix. he says, "The Enemy hath "come to an end beneath me in the presence of the Assessors, "and I eat him in the great field on the altar of Uatchet;" finally, in Chapter clxxii. (l. 19) certain bones in the head of the deceased are identified with those of the Uatchti goddesses, i.e., Nekhebet and Uatchet. During the ceremonies connected with embalming, the operator or priest addressed the mummy, saying, "The goddess Uatchet cometh unto thee in the form of the "living Uraeus (, *Ārāt*), to anoint thy head with their

1 Their = Uatchet and Nekhebet.

"flames. She riseth up on the left side of thy head, and she "shineth from the right side of thy temples without speech; they "rise up on thy head during each and every hour of the day, even "as they do for their father Rā, and through them the terror "which thou inspirest in the holy spirits is increased, and because "Uatchet and Nekhebet rise up on thy head, and because thy brow "becometh the portion of thy head whereon they establish them- "selves, even as they do upon the brow of Rā, and because they "never leave thee, awe of thee striketh into the souls which are "made perfect."[1]

In the *Book of the Dead* Uatchet generally plays the part of destroyer of the foes of the deceased, but her connexion with Maāt shows that she was identified with some one of the female counterparts of Thoth. In a calendar published by Brugsch[2] we see that under the name of Ȧpt, , or, , Uatchet was regarded as the goddess of the eleventh month of the Egyptian year (Epiphi).

### Bast, , the Lady of the East.

Bast was the goddess *par excellence* of the eastern part of the Delta, and the centre of her worship was at Per-Bast, or Pa-Bast, , or, , or Bubastis, the capital of the Ȧm-khent, , the seventh nome (Bubastites) of Lower Egypt; this city is often referred to by classical writers (Herodotus ii. 137, 156; Diodorus 16, 51; Strabo xvii.; Pliny v. 9), and is mentioned in the Bible under the name Pibeseth, פִּיבֶסֶת (Ezekiel xxx. 17). The site is marked by the ruins at Tell-Basta which were carefully excavated by M. Naville, who made some interesting discoveries concerning the great antiquity of the city of Bubastis, and who published the inscriptions which are still to be found upon the ruins of the great buildings which once stood there.[3]

1 Maspero, *Mémoire sur quelques Papyrus*, p. 82.

2 *Astronomische und Astrologische Inschriften*, p. 473, No. 11.

3 See *Bubastis*, Eighth and Tenth Memoirs of the Egypt Exploration Fund, 1891 and 1892.

THE GODDESS BAST.

In the version of Manetho according to Julius Africanus (Cory's *Ancient Fragments*, p. 98), it is said that in the reign of Boethus, the first king of the IInd Dynasty, a chasm opened at Bubastis, and that many persons perished, but M. Naville found no historical remains so old as this period on the site; he has, however, discovered on blocks of stone there the names of Khufu and Khāf-Rā, kings of the IVth Dynasty, written in such a way as to prove that the inscriptions were cut during the period of the Early Empire. Of the kings of the VIth Dynasty only the name of Pepi I. is found at Bubastis, and in connection with this king it is interesting to note that in his funeral inscription (line 569) his heart is said to be the heart of Bestet, i.e., Bast, . This fact shows that the worship of Bast was already very old in Egypt, at all events in the Delta, and that a definite position was assigned to her in the theological system of the priests of Heliopolis. In the text of Pepi II. 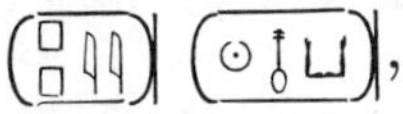, it is said, "O god of the double town  the double of Pepi is for thy "two fingers; Pepi hath swept off towards the heavens like a crane, "Pepi hath scented out the heavens like a hawk, Pepi hath flown "up to heaven like the grasshopper of Rā; Pepi must not be "repulsed, O king, there is no green herb for Pepi, O Bast "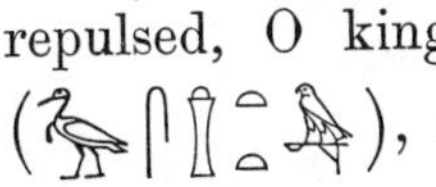, and none hath made dances for Pepi [who "standeth] like a great man at the door" (line 869). To find the name of Bast in the Pyramid Texts is natural enough, for their Heliopolitan editors introduced many local, and even foreign deities into the companies of their gods; in the Theban Recension of the *Book of the Dead*, however, Bast and her city are very rarely mentioned, and her name is entirely omitted from the list of the gods mentioned in connexion with the deification of members (Chapter xlii.).

In the "Negative Confession" (line 16) of the cxxvth Chapter we have the mention of the assessor called Thenemi, , i.e., he who goes backwards, who is said to come forth from Bast, , and an assessor called Basti,  (line 26), is said to come forth from the city of Shetait.

The goddess Bast is usually represented in the form of a woman with the head of a cat, but she also has, at times, the head of a lioness surmounted by a snake; in her right hand she holds a sistrum, and in her left an aegis with the head of a cat or lioness on the top of it. The form in which the goddess was worshipped in the earliest times was that of a cat, and her identification with a lioness probably belongs to a comparatively late period. From the inscription we find that she was also identified with Rāt, , the female counterpart of Rā, and with Temt, , the female counterpart of Tem; she is often called the "eye of Rā," and the "eye of Tem," and the Shetat, , i.e., the "Hidden one." According to one legend Bast was the personification of the soul of Isis, , and was worshipped as such in Bubastis, and it was only at "Bubastis of the South," , i.e., Dendera, that she was regarded as the female counterpart of Tem. From the fact that she is associated with the god Sepṭ, "the lord of the East," it is tolerably certain that in one aspect as least she was regarded as a foreign goddess, whose attributes and characteristics had been transferred to her. As Temt, , at Dendera, she was said to be the mother of the lion-headed god Åri-ḥes, , the lord of Aphroditopolis, , the holy Sekhem, , who dwelt in the temple of Bast of Dendera;[1] her husband in this case was the god Ån, , who was a form of Osiris.

At Thebes Bast was identified with Mut, the lady of Asheru; at Memphis with Mut and Uatchet, at Heliopolis with Iusāaset, and in Nubia with Sekhet and Menḥet, at a town in the Delta called Sekhet, , her name appears to have been Bare-Åst, .[2] If we are to seek for the derivation of the name Bast in Egyptian we must connect it with the word for

[1] See Brugsch, *Dict. Géog.*, p. 208; *Religion*, p. 332.
[2] Lanzone, op. cit., p. 226.

"fire," *bes* , and regard the goddess as a personification of a power of the sun which made itself manifest in the form of heat. That this view is correct is certain from several passages in Egyptian texts, wherein both Bast and Sekhet are described as closely connected forms of a female personification of the heat and light of the Sun-god, and wherein they are made to act as the destroyers both of the enemies of the Sun-god, and of the deceased. Thus of Sekhet it is said in the "Book of Overthrowing Āpep" (xxvii. 15), "The Eye of Horus falls upon him cutting and "hacking his head from his neck; the goddess Sekhet tears out "his intestines and kicks them on the fire with her left leg; she "places them on the fire and burns into him in her name of 'Set-"usert-āa' (); she burns into him and "drives out his soul from his body; she obtains the mastery over "him in her name of 'Sekhet' (); and she overpowers "him in her name of 'Khut-nebȧt' (, "i.e., Eye of Flame); she consumes his interior and blazes in it "with the flame of her mouth." Speaking generally, Sekhet personified the burning, fiery, and destructive heat of the sun, and Bast represented the milder heat which at certain periods of the day and year encouraged the growth of vegetation, and the germination of seeds.

That Sekhet and Bast are goddesses of fire is quite clear, for they accompany Hathor in her character of the "Eye of Rā," and as forms of the Sun-god they symbolize the heat of the late and early summer respectively. It has already been said that Bast is identified with Mut at Thebes, but we also find that at Thebes Mut-Bast[1] is depicted as Isis, and we see her wearing upon her head the feathers of the god Shu, , and horns with the sun's disk between them. The god of whom she is the female counterpart is in this case Ȧmen-Rā-Temu-Kheperȧ-Ḥeru-khuti, who is represented with the head of a hawk wearing the crown of Shu; the offspring of the two deities is Khensu, . These

[1] See Brugsch, *Religion und Mythologie*, p. 334.

considerations lead us to the conclusion that Bast was, at all events in dynastic times, a personification of the moon, especially when we remember that Khensu was a lunar god. With the head of a lioness, which is usually painted green, she symbolized the sunlight, but when she is given the head of a cat her connexion with the moon is undoubted; Dr. Brugsch refers to Plutarch's remark that the pupils of the eyes of cats become full and very large at the time of the full moon, and it is probable that the primitive Egyptians held the same view, and that as a result they identified the cat-headed goddess Bast with the moon. From another aspect Bast was regarded as exercising a special influence over women who were with child, and she appears on several occasions as one of the goddesses of the birth-chamber; her son Khensu was declared "to make women fruitful, and make "the human germ to grow in his mother's womb," and he was supposed to do this especially in his character of the "moon, the light-bearer."

According to the Stele of Canopus, the chief festivals of the goddess Bubastis were celebrated in the months of April and May, and of one of these Herodotus (ii. 60) furnishes some interesting information. He says:—"Such of this people as with entyre and "affectionate zeale most religiously obserue the feast at Bubastis, "behaue and beare themselues on this maner. Certayne shippes "being addressed, wherein infinite numbers of men and women "sayle towards the city, in the meane season whiles they be in "voiage on ye water, certaine of the women play upon drums and "tabers, making a great sound and noyse, ye men on pipes. Such "as want these implements, clap their hands and straine their "uoice in singing to ye highest degree. At what city soeuer they "ariue, happely some of the women continue their mirth and dis-"port on ye timbrels, some others raile, reuile, and scold at the "dames of ye city beyond measure: many trauise and daunce "minionly: other cast up their clothes, and openly discouer and "bewray their shame, doing this in all those cittes yt are neere "adioyning to the riuers side. Being assembled and gathered "together at Bubastis, they honour the feast day with principall "solemnity, making large offerings to Diana, wherein is greater "expence and effusion of grape wine than all the yeare besides. "To this place by the voice of ye countrey are wont to repayre "7000 men and women, besides children, and thus they passe the "time at Bubastis."[1] Of the city of Bubastis itself the same writer says[2] (ii. 137, 138):—"The noble city of Bubastis seemeth "to be very haughty and highly planted, in which city is a temple "of excellent memory dedicate to the goddesse Bubastis, called in "our speech Diana, then the which, albeit there be other churches "both bigger and more richly furnished, yet for the sightly grace "and seemelynesse of building, there is none comparable unto "it. Besides, the very entrance and way that leadeth unto the "city, the reste is in forme of an Ilande, inclosed round about with "two sundry streames of the river Nilus, which runne to either "side of the path way, and leauing as it were a lane or causey "betweene them, without meeting, take their course another way. "These armes of the floud are each of them an hundred foote "broade, beset on both sides the banckes with fayre braunched "trees, ouershadowing ye waters with a coole and pleasant shade. "The gate or entry of the city is in heighth 10. paces, hauing in "the front a beautifull image, 6. cubites in measure. The temple "it selfe situate in the middest of ye city, is euermore in sight to "those yt passe to and fro. For although ye city by addition of "earth was arrered and made higher, yet ye temple standing as it "did in ye beginning, and neuer mooued, is in maner of a lofty "and stately tower, in open and cleare viewe to euery parte of ye "city. Round about the which goeth a wall, ingrauen with "figures and portraitures of sundry beasts. The inner temple is "enuironed with an high grove of trees, set and planted by the "hande and industrie of men: in the whiche temple is standing an "image. The length of the temple is in euery way a furlong. "From the entrance of the temple Eastward, there is a fayre large "causey leading to the house of Mercury, in length, three furlongs "and four acres broade, all of faire stone, and hemmed in on each "side with a course of goodly tall trees planted by the hands of "men, and thus as touching the description of ye temple."

[1] B. R.'s Translation, fol. 86*a*.

[2] B. R.'s Translation, fol. 108*a*.

According to Brugsch,[1] the great triad of the city of Bubastis consisted of Osiris, Bast, and their offspring, who was called Ḥeru-ḥekennu, , or Nefer-Tem, or Bast; their equivalents in Heliopolis were Tem, Iusāaset, and Nefer-Tem; in Memphis, Ptaḥ-Sekhet, and Nefer-Tem; in Thebes, Åmen-Rā-Ḥeru-khuti, and Mut-Bast, and Khensu, or Horus, or Neb-āut-åb; in Aphroditopolis, Osiris-Ån, and Bast-Temt, and ·Åri-ḥes. In the Bubastite nome were many temples and localities in which the worship of Bast was paramount, and among such may be mentioned Bairåst, , the modern Belbês, and Netert, , or , where was preserved a thigh of Osiris, , shut up in a "hidden chest."[2]

NET, , OR , OR , OR ,
THE LADY OF THE WEST.

NET, or NEITH, was one of the oldest of all the Egyptian goddesses, and it is tolerably certain that her worship was wide-spread even in predynastic times; many attempts have been made to arrive at a decision about her earliest attributes by means of etymological processes, but they are unsatisfactory because they only illustrate the views which the Egyptians held concerning her in comparatively late dynastic times, and several of them only explain the objects which the goddess is seen holding in her hands in pictures. The examples reproduced by Lanzone represent the goddess in the form of a woman, who wears upon her head the crown of the North, ; she often holds a sceptre, , or , in one hand, and the symbol of life in the other, but sometimes the hand which holds the sceptre also grasps a bow and two arrows, which are her characteristic symbols. She once[3] appears in the form of a cow with eighteen stars on one side, and a collar round her neck from which hangs ; on her back is a ram-headed lion with horns and plumes, , upon his head. The cow stands in a boat, the

[1] *Religion*, p. 336.
[2] See de Rougé, *Géographie*, p. 122.
[3] Op. cit., pl. 175 ff.

THE GODDESS NIT (NEITH).

prow of which terminates in a lion's head with a disk upon it, and is provided with wings; the stern of the boat terminates in a ram's head, and by the fore feet of the cow, which is described as "Net, the Cow, which gave birth to Rā," , is an *utchat*, . In one scene she is represented with a crocodile sucking at each breast.[1] In late dynastic times there is no doubt that Net or Neith was regarded as nothing but a form of Hathor, but at an earlier period she was certainly a personification of a form of the great, inert, primeval watery mass out of which sprang the Sun-god Rā, and it is possible, as Brugsch has suggested, that the name Net may be akin in meaning to Nut. On the other hand, if we connect her name with the root *netet*, , "to knit, to weave," and the like, we may accept the view of those who describe Net as the goddess of weaving, and who identify the signs, , and , which are often seen upon her head, with a shuttle. It is, however, quite clear that the oldest and most characteristic symbols of the goddess were two arrows and a shield, which at a very early period became the recognized emblems, not only of Net herself, but also of the city in which her chief temple was situated, and they also served as the symbols which formed the name of the nome of which the city Saïs was the capital. Now since Net was represented by a bow and two arrows, there is no good reason for doubting that she was originally either a goddess of war or of the chase, and it is probable that she was identified with a local wood-spirit, or hunting-spirit, which was worshipped in the east of the Delta in the predynastic period. In any case it is quite certain, when we consider the attributes which are ascribed to her in the texts, that she represents several goddesses who were the conceptions of quite different periods of history and of stages of civilization. Thus, at times, her attributes cannot be distinguished from those of Isis, Uatchet, Sekhet, Bast, Mut, Nekhebet, and other goddesses, and she was identified with one and all of them by turns.

The most ancient and famous sanctuary of Net was at Saïs, , *Saut*, the capital of the fifth nome of Lower Egypt,

[1] Lanzone, op. cit., pl. 175, No. 3.

which bore the name of "Sȧpi-meḥt," i.e., "Sȧpi of the North," and which was also called Ḥet Net, , i.e., "House of Net," and "Ȧst-Net," , i.e., "The seat of Net;" a rare name of the city quoted by Brugsch[1] and de Rougé[2] is "Sȧpi," , or . The texts often mention the "temples of Net," , that is to say, the temples of the gods who were worshipped with Net at Saïs; the names of these temples are:—Ḥet-khebit, , Resenet and Meḥenet, , , Per-Rā, , and Per-Tem, . The great temple of Net at Saïs must, of course, not be confounded with that of Saïs of Upper Egypt, i.e., Esneh, which was called Per-Net-mut-kheper-ḥetch, ; the names of Esneh are Ȧni, , and Seni, . At Saïs was held the great annual festival in honour of Isis-Net, as recorded by Herodotus (ii. 59), and it is this which is described by the same writer (ii. 62) in the following words[3]:—"In like manner meeting (as before) at the city Sais, "there to accomplishe the rites and ceremonies due to the day, at "the approche and neere poynt of the euening, they furnish and "beset their houses with torches and lampes, which being re-"plenished with pure oyle mingled with salte, they giue fire to the "weike, and suffer them to continue burning till the next "morning, naming the day by the feast of lampes. Such as "resort not to this feast, do neuerthelesse at their owne homes giue "due honour to the night, placing in euery corner of theyr house "an infinite number of tapers and candles, the custome being not "only kept at Sais, but spread and scattered throughout the "whole region. But for what ende this night is held solemne by "lighting of lampes, a certayne mysticall and religious reason is "yeelded which we must keepe secret."

After describing the place in the temple of Saïs where Apries

[1] *Dict. Géog.*, p. 1323. [2] *Géographie de la Basse Égypte*, p. 24.
[3] B. R.'s translation, fol. 86*b*.

was buried, and mentioning the "fayre Chamber builte of stone, "beautyfied with sundry Pyllers ingrauen like unto Palme-trees, "being otherwyse very sumptuously and royally garnished," and the two "mayne posts in the middest of the chamber, betweene "the which standeth a Cophine," and the "toumbe in the same, "the name whereof," he says, "I may not descry without breache "of Religion," Herodotus goes on to speak of other matters connected with Saïs, and says (ii. 170):—"At Saïs in the Temple "of Minerva, beneath the Churche and neere unto the walle of "Minerva, in a base Chappell, are standinge certayne greate "brooches of stone, whereto is adioyninge a lowe place in manner "of a Dungeon, couered over wyth a stone curiously wroughte, the "vaute it selfe being on euery side carued with most exquisite "arte, in biggnesse matchinge with that in Delos, which is called "Trochoïdes. Herein euery one counterfayteth the shadowes of "hys owne affections and phantasies in the nyghte season, which "the Aegyptians call Mysteryes; touchinge whiche, God forbid, I "should aduenture to discouer so much as they vouchsafed to tell "mee."[1] The "Mysteries" here referred to were probably the ceremonies performed in connexion with the annual commemoration of the sufferings and death of Osiris, who, according to an old legend, was buried at Saïs.

Passing now to consider the antiquity of the cult of Net at Saïs we find much to prove that the worship of this goddess dates from the latter part of the predynastic period. The earliest form of Net's name is found on an ivory cover of a box and on an ivory vase,[2] where it occurs in connexion with *ḥetep*, and so serves as a constituent part of the proper name Net-ḥetep, . Now, Net-ḥetep, we know, was connected with the early king Sma, and she appears to have been the wife of king , Āḥa, who has been commonly, but on insufficient evidence, identified with Menȧ, the first historical king of Egypt. But whether Āḥa is Menȧ or not matters little for our purpose here, for it is quite certain that both he and Sma flourished about the beginning of the period of the

[1] B. R.'s translation, fol. 116*b*.

[2] See Petrie, *Royal Tombs*, ii., pp. 4-20, and pl. ii.

Ist Dynasty, and this being so the name of the goddess which forms part of the name of the queen Net-ḥetep must also be as old. Thus it is clear that even in the Ist Dynasty the cult of Net must have been of considerable antiquity. During the first four dynasties the goddess possessed sanctuaries in many parts of Egypt, and several of her priests and priestesses were buried in maṣṭaba tombs in and near Ṣaḳḳâra. M. Mallet quotes[1] an interesting passage from the sarcophagus of Apa-ānkh in which she is addressed together with Ȧnunu, , and Nesert, 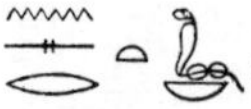, who are two very ancient goddesses, and in which it is declared that she came forth from the god, and that the god came forth from her.[2] We thus see that in the IVth Dynasty she was thought to be at once the mother and the daughter of the Sun-god Rā, and that she had more than one form, and possessed also the power to conceive and bring forth the new Sun-god daily by means of the divine and magical formulae with which she was provided. Among her early titles is that of Ȧpt-uat, i.e., "Opener of the ways," 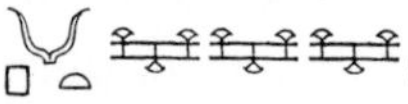, which seems to suggest that she was in some way a female counterpart of Anubis.

In the text of Unȧs (line 67) we find the "temples of Net," 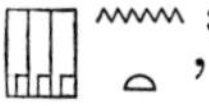,[3] mentioned, side by side with the city of Ṭep, , and the name of the goddess is coupled with that of Tatet, , who was supposed to dress the dead; thus the passage clearly proves that Net was believed to perform some important ceremonies in connexion with the preservation of the dead, and it would seem that these were of a magical character. We may note in passing that in the late "Ritual of Embalmment," published by M. Maspero,[4] it is directed that a piece of linen, upon which were drawn or painted figures of Ḥāpi and Isis, be placed in the hand of the deceased, and that Isis is identified with Neith. This piece

1 *Le Cult de Neit à Saïs*, Paris, 1888, p. 104.

2 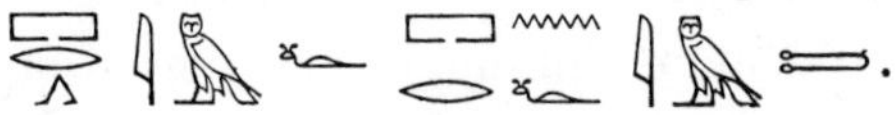.

3 Compare also .

4 *Mémoire sur quelques Papyrus du Louvre*, p. 90.

of linen was intended to serve as an amulet, and to bring to the mummy the protection of Net, who is referred to under the name of Isis. In the text of Unȧs (line 597) we have the following address:—"Homage to thee, O Horus, in the regions of Horus; "homage to thee, O Set, in the regions of Set; homage to thee, "O Ȧarer ( ) in Sekhet-Ȧarer;[1] homage to thee, O "Netetthȧȧb ( ), thou son of these four gods who are in "the Great Temple, wherefrom the voice of Unȧs goeth not out. "Take off your apparel in order that Unȧs may see you as "Horus seeth Isis, and that Unȧs may see you as Neḥebu-kau "( ) seeth Selqet; and that Unȧs may "see you as Sebek seeth Net, and that Unȧs may see you as Set "seeth Netetthȧȧb." A little further on (lines 620-627) we have another reference to Net and her son Sebek in these words, "Unȧs "hath come in the form of Khent-em-meḥt-aḳebȧ ( "), and this Unȧs is Sebek with the green "feather ( ), who watcheth and who raiseth up his "forehead, and who is the white one who cometh forth from the "thigh[s] of Khebset-urt ( ), who is in the light. "Unȧs hath come to his pools which are on the banks of the canal "( ) of Meḥt-urt ( ), at the place where "offerings flourish, and in the fields which are in the horizon, and "he hath made to flourish his garden on the banks of the horizon. "Unȧs hath brought the crystal ( ) to the Great "Eye which is in the field. Unȧs hath taken his place in the "horizon, he riseth like Sebek, the son of Net ( ), he "eateth with his mouth, he voideth water," etc. In the text of Tetȧ (line 204) Net is mentioned in connection with Isis, Nephthys, and Serqet-Ḥetu, , as one of the four goddesses who shot forth flame, ,

1 .

and worked "protection," , on behalf of the god Nu, , when he was seated on his throne.

These same four goddesses also appear in connection with the Four Children of Horus, whom they assisted in protecting by magical means the various parts of human bodies which were placed in "Canopic jars." Thus Isis says, "I conquer the foe, I "make protection for Åmseth who is in me"; Nephthys says, "I hide the hidden thing, and I make protection for Ḥāpi who is "in me"; Net says, "I pass the morning and I pass the night of "each day in making protection for Ṭuamutef who is in me"; Serqet says, "I employ each day in making protection for Qebḥ-"sennuf who is in me."[1] The Egyptian word used here to express the meaning of "protection" is *sa*, , and the character represents a knot of a peculiar kind; the part which knots and cords tied in various ways have always played in magical ceremonies is too well known to need description, and it need only be pointed out here that the sign  indicates that the protection which Net exercised on behalf of the dead must have been of a magical character. This view is supported by a passage in the text of Unȧs (l. 271 ff.) in which we find Net mentioned in connection with the goddesses Ȧnȧ, , Urt, , Nesert, , and Urt-ḥekau, ; now Urt-ḥekau is distinctly said to be the "protective power of the Eye of Horus," and thus the attributes of Net and of the other goddesses must be of a kindred nature. In the text of Pepi I. (l. 572), in the passage relating to the deification of the members of the deceased it is said that the thighs of Pepi are "Net and Serqet," ; but in the Theban Recension of the *Book of the Dead* (Chapter xlii. 11), it is the fore-arms of the deceased which are identified with the fore-arms of the lady of Saïs, i.e., Net. In the Theban Recension the deceased declares (lxvi. 2) that he was conceived by the goddess Sekhet, and that the goddess Net gave birth to him. In Chapter lxxi. 15, we read, "Behold, the god of "One Face is with me. The god Sebek hath stood up within his

[1] For the texts see my *Mummy*, p. 199 ff.

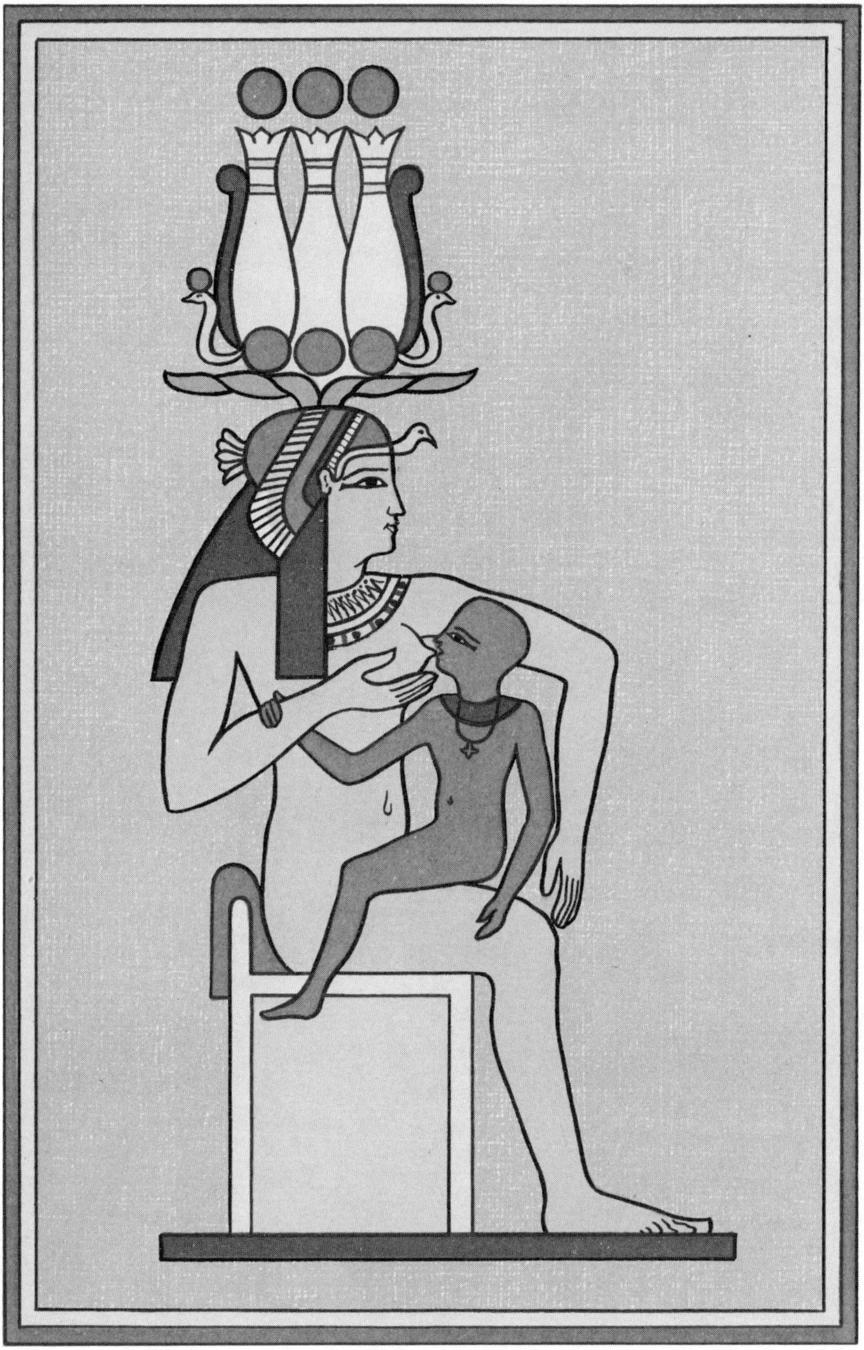

THE GODDESS SEBEK-NIT SUCKLING HORUS.

"ground, and the goddess Net hath stood up within her plantation"; and elsewhere (cxiv. 5; cxvi. 2) we read that she shineth in the city of Matchat, or Mentchat. In Chapter cxvi. 4, the deceased says, "O ye gods who dwell in Khemennu, ye know me even as I know the goddess Net"; and in Chapter cxlv. 81, he says, "I have entered into the house of Åstes, and I have made "supplication to the Khati gods and to Sekhet in the Temple of "Net." In the Rubric to Chapter clxiii., which has for its vignette a serpent on legs, and two *utchats* on legs, it is ordered that in the pupil of one *utchat* there shall be drawn a figure of the "god of the lifted hand" with the face of Net, and having plumes and a back like unto a hawk. From one aspect at least it is clear that Net must have been a form of the power of the Eye of Horus, as well as of Isis, his mother; her son Sebek is a local form of Horus, and it is probable that the two crocodiles, which are seen accompanying her, and which have been already mentioned, are in some way connected with the god Ḥenti, , whose symbols are two crocodiles. Ḥenti, there is every reason to believe, was a form of Osiris. It is, however, possible that one of the crocodiles may represent Horus, or Osiris, and the other Ḥetch-nefer-Sebeq, , the son of Net.

We have, unfortunately, no description of the ceremonies connected with the worship of Net, but there is good reason for believing that they were of a mystic character, and that they were modified from time to time in accordance with the change of beliefs of the priests in respect of the attributes of the goddess. Originally its chief characteristics must have been those of a local Delta or Libyan goddess of nature, and it is probable that it included ceremonies which were intended to represent the various processes of generation and reproduction. This view is supported by several of the titles which are given in Egyptian texts to her and to her kindred goddesses. Thus as Isis she was the first to give birth to a god, 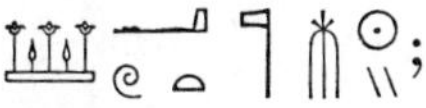;[1] as Hathor she was the "great cow which gave birth to Rā;" and she is called "the great goddess, the mother

[1] See Mallet, *Le Culte de Neït*, p. 140.

"of all the gods," and "Rāt (i.e., the female Sun), the lady of "heaven, the mistress of all the gods, who came into being in the "beginning." In a text quoted by M. Mallet she is actually called "One," 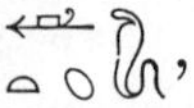, a fact which proves that at a certain period of her history she was to goddesses what Rā was to gods. A certain amount of light is thrown upon the history of Net by the inscription[1] on the famous shrine-bearing statue of Utchat-Ḥeru now preserved in the Vatican, but it must be remembered that this monument is not older than the early part of the Persian period. Utchat-Ḥeru was an official of very high rank in Saïs, and he was high-priest of Net, and as such bore the official title of *Ur-sun*, 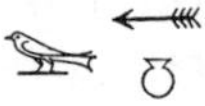, i.e., "great one of knowledge." He was commander of the vessels of Ȧāḥmes II. (Amasis), and when Cambyses came to Egypt and visited Saïs after his conquest of the country, it was Utchat-Ḥeru who received him, and explained to him the antiquity and greatness of the goddess Net, and conducted him through the various sanctuaries which were grouped together in her temple. In the course of his conversation with the king he told him that it was Net, the mighty mother, who had given birth to Rā, and that she was the first to give birth to anything, and that she had done so when nothing else had been born, and that she had never herself been born. For some reason or other Utchat-Ḥeru found favour in the sight of Cambyses, and the text tells us that the king made offerings "even as every other good king had done." The funds provided by Cambyses were spent by Utchat-Ḥeru in reviving the schools which had fallen into decay, and in refounding colleges for the priests of Saïs. The fame and traditions of the antiquity of Net and her worship were current among the late Greek writers, and it will be remembered that Plutarch (*De Iside et Osir.*, ix.) refers to an inscription on a statue of Pallas which he renders, "I am everything which hath been, and which is, and "which shall be, and there hath never been any who hath un-"covered (or revealed) my veil."[2] Elsewhere (Chapter lxii.) he

[1] See Revillout in *Revue Égyptologique*, tom. i., p. 72 ff.

[2] Ἐγώ εἴμι πᾶν τὸ γεγονὸς, καὶ ὄν, καὶ ἐσόμενον, καὶ τὸν ἐμὸν πέπλον οὐδείς πω ἀπεκάλυψεν.

says that the Egyptians often called Isis by the name Athene, which signifies, "I have come from myself." [1]

Up to the present no hieroglyphic inscription has been found which can be regarded exactly as the original of the Greek words, but there is no doubt that Plutarch only turned into words the opinions about the goddess Net which were current when he wrote his famous treatise on Isis and Osiris. In a passage of Proclus, who gives a Greek rendering of an Egyptian text in terms closely resembling those of Plutarch, after the words *Τὸν ἐμὸν χιτῶνα οὐδεὶς ἀπεκάλυψεν*, the goddess Net is made to say, *ὅν ἐγὼ καρπὸν ἔτεκον, ἥλιος ἐγένετο,* which beyond all doubt reflects with considerable exactitude the meaning of the Egyptian title of "Net, the mighty mother, who gave birth to Rā." [2] The words put into the mouth of the goddess, "I am what has been, what is, and what shall be," are, as M. Mallet has remarked,[3] only a development of a play upon her name Net and the word *ent* , or *entet* , i.e., a person or thing which is, or which exists, or which has being. In other words, the Egyptians regarded Net as the "Being" *par excellence*, i.e., the Being who was eternal and infinite, and was the creative and ruling power of heaven, earth, and the underworld, and of every creature and thing in them. Plutarch, however, was not without authority when he made Net say, *καὶ τὸν ἐμὸν πέπλον οὐδείς πω ἀπεκάλυψεν*, for in an Egyptian text published by Pierret [4] under the title of "lady of the sycamore house," 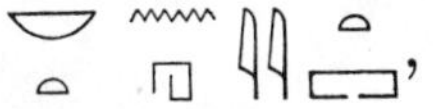, the goddess Net is addressed in the following words:—

| *à* | *mut* | *ur* | *àn* | *sefekh* | *mesu-s* |
|---|---|---|---|---|---|
| Hail, | mother | great, | not | hath been uncovered | thy birth! |

[1] ἦλθον ἀπ' ἐμαυτῆς.

[2]  *Net urt mut mes Rā.*

[3] Op. cit., p. 191.

[4] *Études Égyptologiques, etc.*, Paris, 1873, p. 45 ff.

*à netert āat em khen en Ṭuaut shetat sep sen*

Hail, goddess great, within the underworld which is doubly hidden,

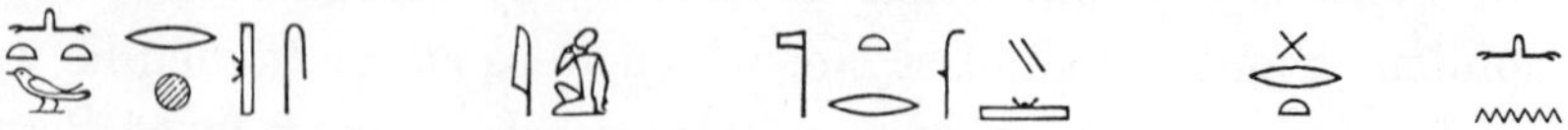

*àtet rekh-s à netrài urt àn*

thou unknown one! Hail, thou divine one great, not

*sefekh-tu qeràs-s à sefekh senḥu-s*

hath been unloosed thy garment! O unloose thy garment.

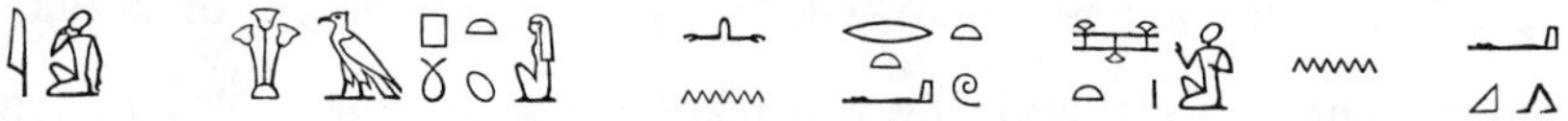

*à Ḥapt àn ertā-tu uat-à en āq*

Hail, Ḥapt (Hidden one), not is given my way of entrance

*er-es māāt shept ba en Àsàr khui-s*

to her, come, receive thou the soul of Osiris, protect it

*em khen en āāui*

within [thy] two hands.

These lines form a prayer which is put into the mouth of Ānkh-f-en-Khensu, and, in the form in which we have it here, is not older than the Saïte period, i.e., about B.C. 550; but the petition refers very distinctly to the mysterious character of the births of Net, and to her attribute of inscrutability in the doubly hidden underworld, and whilst the deceased declares that none has ever penetrated the cloak wherewith she is shrouded, he beseeches her to unloose it for him. Two words are used to express "cloak," i.e., *qeràs* and *senḥu* and , a fact which calls to mind the two words πέπλος and χιτῶν which are used by Plutarch and Proclus respectively to express the same word. It is, however, quite certain that the ideas and beliefs expressed in the above prayer are far older than the time of the Psammetici, and in one form or other they may be actually traced back to the period of the Early Empire.

Another proof of the mysterious and remarkable powers which were attributed to Net by Greek writers is given by Horapollo, who in his "Hieroglyphica" (i. 12) says that when the Egyptians wish to depict a figure of Hephaistos they draw a scarab and a vulture, and when they want to represent Athene (i.e., Net) they draw a vulture and a scarab, for they believe that the world is composed of two elements, the one male and the other female, these two being the only gods whom they believe to be both male and female.[1] We have already seen that the god Kheperà was supposed to possess the powers of begetting and conceiving, and giving birth, and, in fact, to be at once both male and female, "and other forms of the Sun-god were said to be self-begotten, self-produced, and self-born;" these characteristics are, however, not applied to any goddess except Net. Since the Egyptians declared that she was eternal, and was self-produced, it followed as a matter of course that both a masculine and a feminine nature must be attributed to her. We have already described how Kheperà produced his son Shu and his daughter Tefnut, the information on these points being derived from ancient Egyptian writings, but details of the birth of Rā by Net have not come down to us, and as far as can be seen the Egyptian conception of the manner in which this goddess exerted her reproductive powers is of a far loftier character than that which appertained to the creation of Shu and Tefnut by Kheperà. It is customary to say that the Egyptians possessed no philosophical conceptions until the arrival of the Greeks in their country, but this view is a mistaken one, for there is much evidence extant which proves that already under the Early Empire Egyptian philosophers were constantly engaged in thinking out the

[1] οὗτοι γὰρ μόνοι θεῶν παρ' αὐτοῖς, ἀρσενοθήλεις ὑπάρχουσι (ed. Leemans, p. 19).

problems which are connected with cosmogony and theogony. The reason why they did not advance as a nation further in such matters is that they allowed themselves to be hampered by traditional opinions and beliefs, and by the rituals and ceremonies which the people in general demanded should be integral portions of the public worship of the gods. The statements of Greek writers, taken together with the evidence derived from the hieroglyphic texts, prove that in very early times Net was the personification of the eternal female principle of life which was self-sustaining and self-existent, and was secret, and unknown, and all-pervading; the more material thinkers, whilst admitting that she brought forth her son Rā without the aid of a husband, were unable to divorce from their minds the idea that a male germ was necessary for his production, and finding it impossible to derive it from a power or being external to the goddess, assumed that she herself provided not only the substance which was to form the body of Rā but also the male germ which fecundated it. Thus Net was the prototype of partheno-genesis.

When, however, as Horapollo says, the Egyptians represented Net by a vulture they referred to her in her character of the universal mother, and as such many allusions are made to her in the texts. Certain passages, it is true, speak of her having set her arrow to her bow,[1] and of her enemies falling daily under her darts, but usually she is said to provide clothing for the dead, just as the house-mother arrays her dead in linen. Thus in the form of Meḥenit, 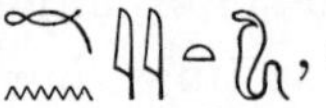, she brought linen apparel and coverings of white, green, red, and purple linen to deck the face of the deceased, and an ancient legend declared that she arrayed Osiris in the apparel which had been specially woven for him by the two Rekhti goddesses, , i.e., Isis and Nephthys. And because of the part which she had taken in arraying Osiris in his grave-clothes Net was made to preside over the "good house," 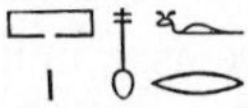, i.e., the chamber in which the dead were embalmed and swathed in linen, and over the chambers of the temples in which the unguents which were employed in public worship were

[1] See Brugsch, *Religion*, p. 340.

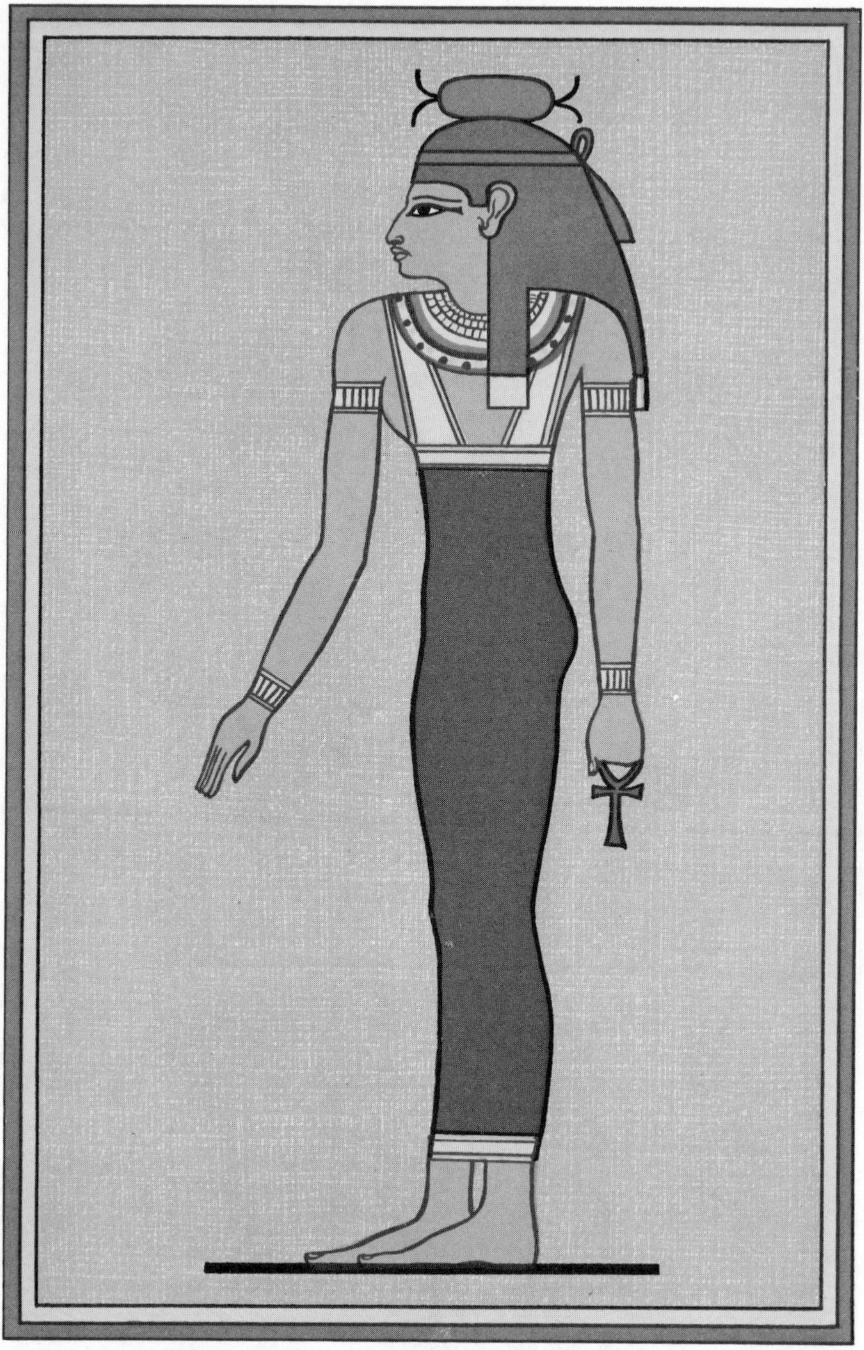

The Goddess NIT (Neith).

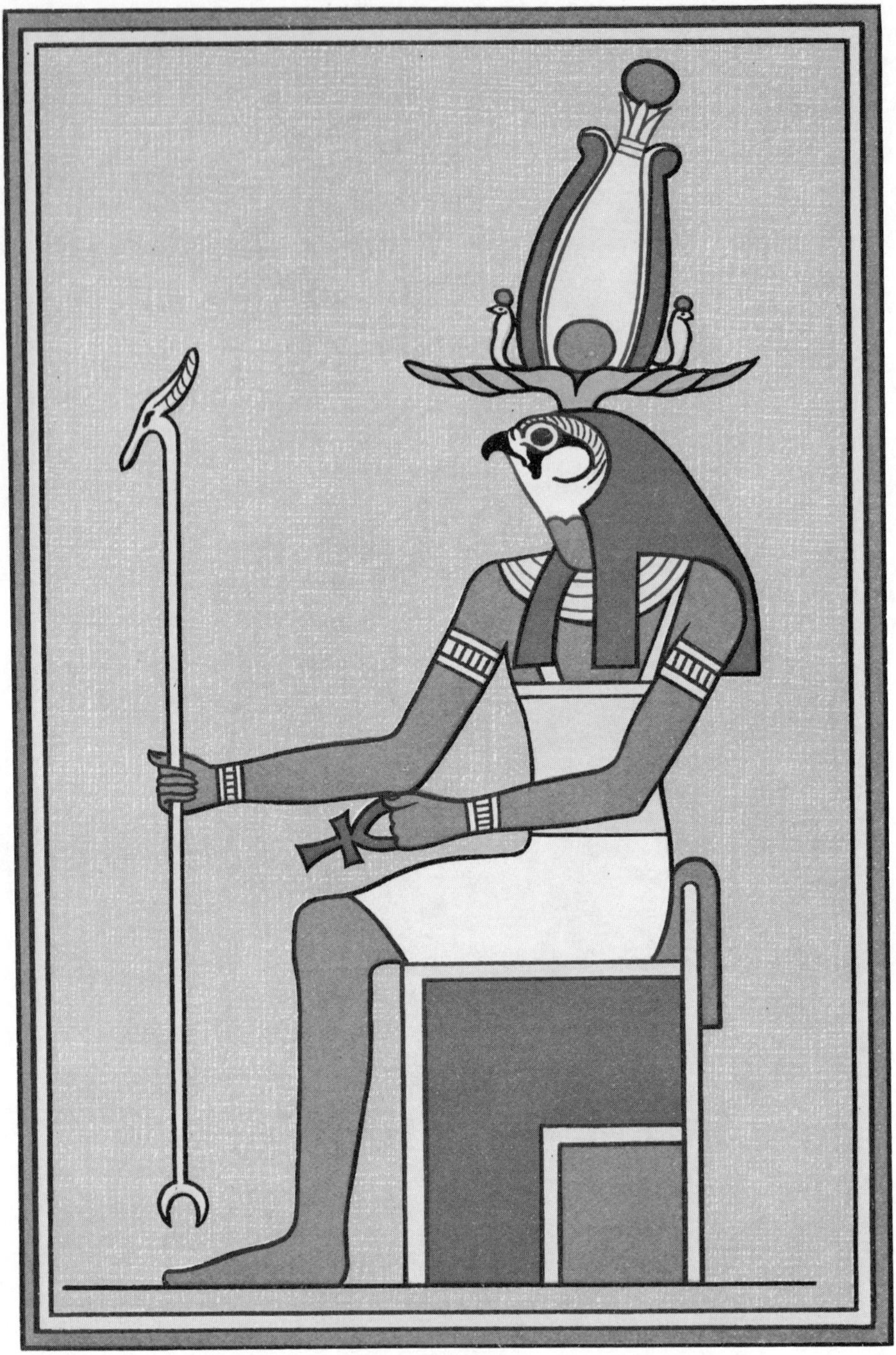

The God Ḥeru-ur.

compounded. The unguents which she mixed for Osiris proved to be the means by which the body of the god was preserved from destruction and made young again, and happy were the dead who were able to secure the ministrations of Net. We must note in connexion with these facts that many of the attributes of Net as a goddess of the dead were assigned to her because of her association with Osiris, and it is clear from the texts of the late dynastic period that Net was regarded in the light of a mother of Osiris, and Saïs was actually called the city of Osiris. At certain seasons of the year, festivals were celebrated there in commemoration of the embalming, and bandaging, and burial of this god, and the great feast of lamps, which is also referred to by Herodotus, was one of the most important. Another very important festival was that kept in the spring, on the birthday of Osiris, the son of Isis-Net, which the late Dr. Brugsch identified with the birthday of the spring sun.[1]

In Upper Egypt Net was chiefly worshipped at Seni (Esneh), the Latopolis of the Greeks, which is called in the texts, "the house of Net in the land of the south." Here she was identified with Nebuut, , Menḥit, Sekhet, and Tefnut, and was represented with the head of a lioness painted green; and her titles were, "Father of fathers, and Mother of mothers," and "Net-Menḥit, the great lady, lady of the south, the great cow "who gave birth to the sun, who made the germ of gods and "men, the mother of Rā, who raised up Tem in primeval time, "who existed when nothing else had being, and who created that "which exists after she had come into being." The people of Seni (Latopolis) assigned to her as husband the ram-headed god Khnemu, , the lord of the First Cataract, and she became therefore "lady of Ābu" (Elephantine), and the mother of Tutu, a form of the god Shu, whose symbol was a lion walking. Tutu, ,[2] is also known by the names Ḥer-ka, ,[3] and

[1] *Religion und Mythologie*, p. 347.

[2] Variants, , or .

[3] Or, *Ḥer-ka-p-khart.*

ḤETCH-NEFER-SEBEQ, , and he is depicted in the form of a young man[1] wearing on his head the crown of the North, and the *Atef* crown with uraei and disks; the forefinger of his right hand is raised to his mouth, which suggests that he had something in common with the Harpocrates gods. According to Dr. Brugsch he is the personification of the sun when he enters the zodiacal sign of Leo, and the same scholar would connect the lion-headed rain-spouts of the temples of Dendera, Khensu at Thebes, Edfû, and Philae, with the summer sun.[2] In the texts which describe these spouts they are called "Lion," the "Strong one of strength," "mighty of strength," "possessor of two-fold strength," "the mighty one of roarings," "fiery-face," and "lion of the face which enchanteth (or terrifieth)." A form of Tutu, the son of Net and Khnemu, called ÅR-ḤES-NEFER, 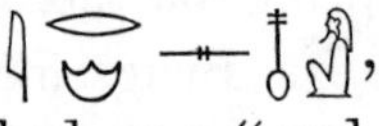, often appears in inscriptions wherein he is described as a "god of the south," and he must be identified with the crocodile-headed god who appears in the temple at Esneh under the names SEBEK-RĀ and ḤES-NEFER-SEBEK, the son of Net.

From certain passages in the texts quoted by Dr. Brugsch[3] it is clear that Åmen-Rā, the "king of the gods," was the son of Net, and in the hymn which Darius II. caused to be inscribed on the walls of the temple of Hebt, in the Great Oasis, it is said that the Cow, , i.e., Net, rejoiceth in the "Bull of his mother." Here the Sun-god is described as the husband who maketh fertile with his seed,[4] and he is said to come to the town of Såpi, , i.e., Saïs. The hymn continues,[5] "Thine image reposeth "in Ḥet-khebit, in the nest of the lady of Saïs. Thy mother Net "uniteth herself unto thee (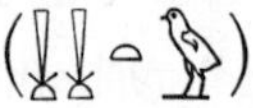) in the form of Nu, and with "thy body arrayed in the veil [which she hath woven] thy body "dwelleth in the temples Resenet and Meḥenet. Thy raiment is

1 Lanzone, op. cit., pl. 407, No. 3.

2 *Religion*, p. 349. 3 *Ibid.*, p. 353.

4 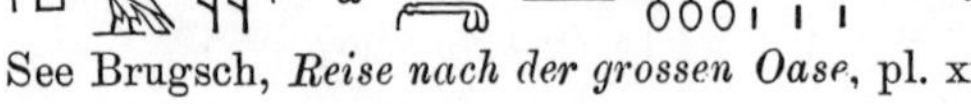

5 See Brugsch, *Reise nach der grossen Oase*, pl. xxvi., l. 28 f.

"upon the hands of the two crocodile gods," 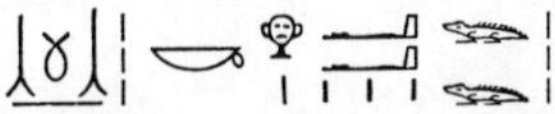. The crocodile gods here mentioned are, of course, the two crocodiles which are seen one on each side of the goddess in certain pictures of her. Finally, we find that in Thebes Net, as the mother and wife of Åmen-Rā, was known under the form and name of the ancient goddess Åment. She is represented as a young woman who wears upon her head the crown of the North, and holds in each hand the emblem of water, 𓈖; as such she is called "Åment, the dweller in Åpt, Nini," . Under the name of Åment-Rā, 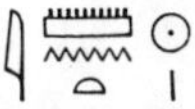, she is seen suckling Horus, and she also appears as a ram-headed goddess wearing the *Atef* crown.[1] All the attributes of Net were ascribed to Åment, who was originally the female counterpart of the local god Åmen, and of necessity a deity of little importance. Thus Åment is styled, "the Cow, the "great lady, who fashioned the company of the gods, the mother "of Rā, who gave birth to Horus." It is very difficult to harmonize all the various statements which are made in the texts concerning the attributes of Net, and the above paragraphs on this goddess will illustrate the difficulty. They prove, however, that the opinions which the Egyptians held concerning her varied from time to time, and that contradictions in their statements are due, not so much to inconsistency or ignorance on the part of the priests and copyists, as to the attempt made to harmonize every new religious system of belief with every one which had existed before it.

[1] See Lanzone, op. cit., pl. 25.

## CHAPTER XV

# THE HORUS GODS

IT has already been stated that the hawk was probably the first living creature which was worshipped generally throughout Egypt, and that as the spirit of the heights of heaven, and as the personification of the god who made the sky he was called Ḥeru, , i.e., "he who is above," or, "that which is above." It appears, however, that at a very early period this conception of Ḥeru was partly lost sight of, and whether as a result of the different views held by certain early schools of thought, or whether due to the similarity in sound between the name "Ḥeru" and the word for "face," Ḥer or Ḥrȧ, the idea which became associated with the god Ḥeru was that he represented the Face of heaven, i.e., the Face of the head of an otherwise unknown and invisible god. We can see that this view was an ancient one even in the time when the Pyramids were built, for several allusions are made in the funeral texts of the Vth and VIth Dynasties to the "hair" or "tresses," , of the Face of Ḥeru as the Face of heaven, and four gods who are called the "children of Horus," ,[1] are declared to have their abodes in these tresses.[2] The Face of heaven was supported by the four gods by means of the four sceptres which they held in their hands, and these four sceptres took the place of the four pillars, 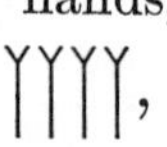, of the god Shu which, according to an older myth, supported the four corners, i.e., the four cardinal points of the great iron plate that formed the floor

[1] Pepi I., ll. 593, 600; and see Maspero, *La Mythologie Égyptienne*, p. 227.
[2] The "Children of Horus" will be described later.

of heaven and the sky above the earth. That the heavens, or the skies, were considered to be a Face is evident from many allusions. Thus the Sun is frequently called "Eye of Horus," and the Moon is also an "Eye of Horus," the Sun being the right eye, and the Moon the left; a well known title of the Face is "Horus of the Two Eyes," , and when neither Eye is visible it is called "Horus dwelling without Eyes," 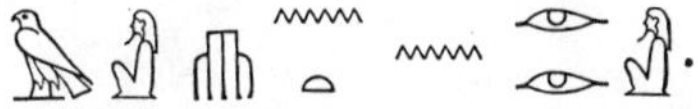. The forms of Horus mentioned in Egyptian texts are numerous, but the following are the most important:—

1. Ḥeru-ur, , i.e., Horus the elder" (or the "aged"), the Ἀρωῆρις of the Greeks, so called to distinguish him from Ḥeru-pa-khart̥, or, "Horus the younger." He is depicted in the form of a man with the head of a hawk, and also as a lion with the head of a hawk; he usually wears the crowns of the South and North united, but he is once seen with the horns of Khnemu upon his head, and above them are a crown with plumes, uraei, disks, etc.[1] According to the Egyptian texts Ḥeru-ur was the son of Rā and Hathor; the Hathor here referred to is the form of the goddess which was specially worshipped at Qesqeset, 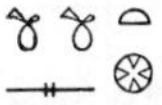, i.e., Apollinopolis Parva; but Plutarch declared him to be the son of Kronos and Rhea, i.e., Seb and Nut, and therefore the brother of Osiris. This statement was probably correct enough in late dynastic times, when men had wholly identified Horus, the son of Isis, with Horus the Elder. Originally Ḥeru-ur represented a phase or aspect of Horus, the Face of heaven, and it was he who was the twin god of Set; Ḥeru-ur was the Face by day and Set the Face by night. There was also a Ḥeru-ur of the South, as we learn from the picture of the god given by Lanzone,[2] the seat of whose worship was at Mākhenut, , near El-Kâb in Upper Egypt, and a Ḥeru-ur of the North, the seat of whose worship was at Sekhemet, , or 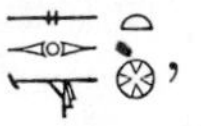, or Seshemet, 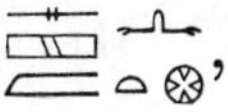, the Latopolis of the Greeks, and the ⲟⲩϣⲉⲙ of the Copts, which lay a

[1] See Lanzone, op. cit., pl. 226. [2] *Ibid.*, No. 3.

few miles to the north of Memphis; other shrines of Ḥeru-ur were at Ombos, , at Smennut, , and at Apollinopolis. The most important shrine of the god was at Sekhem, where stood the sanctuary Pa-Ȧit, ; in its shrine was preserved the shoulder, *mākhaq*, , of the god Osiris, and close by grew the famous Nebes, , and Shent, , trees. Ḥeru-ur of Sekhem is called "lord of the *Utchati*, ," i.e., lord of the Sun and Moon. In the *Book of the Dead* (xviii.*c*) it is said that the sovereign princes in Sekhem are Ḥeru-khent-ȧn-maati and Thoth, but it is clear that locally the great gods of the city were Isis, Osiris, and Horus. The form in which Ḥeru-ur was worshipped at Sekhem and other places was a lion. The inscriptions on the walls of the temple at Ombos[1] prove that he was called the "lord of the south," the "lord of Nubti (Ombos)," and that he was identified with Shu, son of Rā; with "Ḥeru-temā, the "great god and lord of heaven, of two-fold strength, mighty one "among all the gods, whose power hath vanquished the foes of his "father Rā"; with Ȧmen-ur, or Ȧmen the Elder; and in fact with several gods who were regarded as gods of light and of aspects of the rising Sun, and also with the various gods who were connected with them. At Ombos Ḥeru-ur was the head of a triad which consisted of himself, and his female counterpart, TA-SENT-NEFERT, , and their son P-neb-taui, ,[2] who is sometimes called "the child," . The third member of this triad wears a disk upon his head, and has a lock of hair at the side of his face like Harpocrates, and he is called the "young sun," and the general titles which are given to Ḥeru-ur and Ta-sent-nefert indicate that in later days they were considered to be identical with Shu and Tefnut.

2. ḤERU-P-KHARṬ, , i.e., "Horus the Younger" (or, the "Child"), the Ἁρποκράτης of the Greeks, so called to

[1] Brugsch, *Religion*, p. 539. [2] See de Morgan, *Kom Ombos*, pp. 156, 181 ff.

ḤERU-PA-KHRAT (HARPOCRATES).

ḤERU KHUTI (HARMACHIS).

distinguish him from Ḥeru-ur, or Horus the Elder. In Egyptian pictures he is represented in the form of a youth wearing a lock of hair, the symbol of youth, on the right side of his head; sometimes he wears the triple crown with feathers and disks, and the like, and sometimes a disk with plumes, , but usually his crown is formed by the united crowns of the South and North, . In one scene he is seated inside a box which rests on the back of a lion.[1] Ḥeru-p-khart̤ was the son of a Horus god by the goddess Rāt-tauit, , who is said to have brought him forth in the temple of Ḥet-ennut̤, , in Hermonthis, in a birth chamber, , in the precincts of the building Qemqem, ; the goddess seems to have been worshipped here under the form of a hippopotamus, . Ḥeru-p-khart̤, or Harpocrates, was a form of the rising sun and represented his earliest rays; the Egyptians distinguished seven forms or aspects of the god, which may be thus enumerated:— 1. Ḥeru-Rā-p-khart̤, , the dweller in Hermonthis. 2. Ḥeru-Shu-p-khart̤ the great, ; his father was Sāaba, , and his mother Ȧnit, . 3. Sma-taui-p-khart̤ [son] of Hathor, . 4. Ḥeru-p-khart̤, the dweller in Busiris, . 5. Ȧḥi, , son of Hathor. 6. Ḥaq-p-khart̤, , the son of Sekhet. 7. Ḥeru-Ḥennu, , i.e., "Horus the Child."[2]

3. Ḥeru-merti, . In this form the god is represented as a man with a hawk's head, above which are the horns of the god Khnemu and the solar disk encircled by a uraeus; in his hand he bears the Utchati, . A passage in a

[1] Lanzone, op. cit., pl. 328.

[2] See Brugsch, *Dict. Géog.*, p. 348.

papyrus quoted by Lanzone [1] calls him "Horus of the Two Eyes," for this is what the name means, "lord of Sheṭennu ( ), Amseti-Åāḥ ( ), in the city of Åpu," i.e., Panopolis, and this seems to show that Ḥeru-merti was a local form of the god Åmsu, or Khem, or Min, as the Moon.

4. Ḥeru-ån-mut-f, , was a local form of Horus which was worshipped at Åteb, , i.e., Edfû, but the exact characteristics of the god here are unknown.

5. Ḥeru-nub, . This was the form of the god which was worshipped at Hierakonpolis, Per-Ḥeru-nubt, , and he was depicted as a hawk seated on the head of an antelope, which, according to Brugsch,[2] commemorates his triumphant victory over Set, the murderer of Osiris.

6. Ḥeru-khenti-Khat, . In this form the god is represented with a human body and the head of a crocodile, on which he wears the horns of Khnemu, and the triple crown and plumes;[3] this form of Horus does not appear to be ancient.

7. Ḥeru-khenti-ån-maati, , i.e., "Horus at the head of sightlessness," or the "Blind Horus;" he appears to represent the god when neither of his eyes was visible.

8. Ḥeru-khuti, , , , i.e., "Horus of the two horizons," or the Harmachis of the Greeks. He was one of the chief forms of the Sun-god Rā, and, speaking generally, represented the sun in his daily course across the skies from the time he left the Mount of Sunrise (Bakhau) to the time when he entered the Mount of Sunset (Manu). Thus he combined in his own person the god Rā and several of his forms, and in the *Book of the Dead* and other funeral works he is joined to Temu, , and to Kheperå, ;[4]

[1] Op. cit. p. 617.

[2] *Religion*, p. 664.

[3] See Lanzone, p. 622, pl. 17; Brugsch, *Religion*, p. 606.

[4] For the passages see my *Vocabulary* to the *Chapters of Coming Forth by Day*, p. 225.

Temu here indicates the god of the setting sun, and Kheperȧ the god of the sun when he is about to rise. When Ḥeru-khuti was identified with the various forms of the Sun-god he was also supposed to possess their particular attributes, and thus it happens that he is said to have produced himself, and it is this fact which supplies the reason why hymns addressed to him are found. In the texts he is called the "lord of heaven," "the great god, lord of Sept-Ḥāt," , a city or district near the First Cataract, "the governor of the Ȧat of Rā," (Heliopolis),

Thothmes IV. making offerings to the Sphinx.

"Ḥeru-khuti-Tem, the lord of the two lands of Ȧnnu," and the "dweller in Beḥuṭet." The chief shrines of the god were, however, situated at Ȧnnu and at Apollinopolis, and the greater of these was Ȧnnu, or Heliopolis, where he was identified with the forms of Rā which were worshipped there. The largest known monument or figure of Ḥeru-khuti is the famous Sphinx, near the Pyramids of Gîzeh, which was his type and symbol. This marvellous object was in existence in the days of Khā-f-Rā, or Khephren, the builder of the Second Pyramid at Gîzeh, and it is probable that it is a very great deal older than his reign, and that it dates from the end of the archaic period. No mention, however, is made of the Sphinx in the inscriptions until the time of Thothmes IV., when we are told in the text inscribed on the stele between the paws of the Sphinx, that the image had become entirely covered over with sand. To this king the god of the Sphinx, Ḥeru-khuti-Rā-Temu-Kheperȧ, appeared one day when he was sleeping his midday sleep, and promised to give him the crown of Egypt if he would clear away the sand from his image, and restore his temple. Thothmes IV. carried out the wishes of the god, and having excavated the Sphinx, and rebuilt the temple between his paws, Thothmes set up an inscribed stele to commemorate his work. Judging by the silence of the ancient monuments about the Sphinx this figure of Ḥeru-khuti cannot have been popular in dynastic times, and if this was so it is possible that it was due to the fact that the Sphinx was thought to be connected in some way with foreigners or with a foreign religion which dated from predynastic times. A recent but fanciful theory makes the Sphinx to be the work of Ȧmenemḥāt, a king of the XIIth Dynasty; its name in Egyptian was Ḥu, . The forms in which Ḥeru-khuti is represented are many, but whether in human form or not, he usually has the head of a hawk; in the examples collected by Signor Lanzone[1] we see him wearing on his head the solar disk encircled with a uraeus or the triple crown, , or the *atef* crown. In one scene he is depicted as a double man with a head having the faces of two hawks, one looking to the right, and the other to the left, and above this two-faced head is an *utchat*, ; in another scene he has the head of a ram, which identifies him with Khnemu, the god of the First Cataract, and in another he is seated on a throne which is carried on poles by two snake- and two beetle-headed gods.

9. Ḥeru-sma-taui, 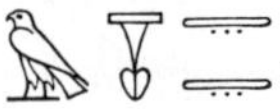, i.e., "Horus, the uniter of the South and North." He is said to be the son of Hathor; his chief places of worship were Ȧat-ḥeḥu, 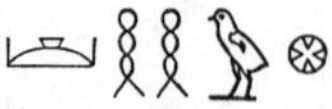, a district near Herakleopolis Magna, and Ȧnt, 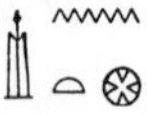, i.e., Denderah, and the city

[1] Op. cit., pll. 229 ff.

HERU – SMA – TAUI.

RĀ-HERU-KHUTI, THE DWELLER IN BEHUTET.

of Khaṭāt, , and the creatures in which he was thought to be incarnate were the hawk and a species of serpent. He is usually depicted with the body of a man with the head of a hawk, or serpent, or man, and he wears as head-dresses, , 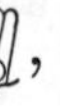, and ; in one scene he is represented as a hawk,[1] and he wears upon his head a disk and plumes, . In this form Horus was believed to spring into existence out of a lotus flower which blossomed in the heavenly abyss of Nu at dawn at the beginning of the year.

10. Ḥeru-ḥekennu, 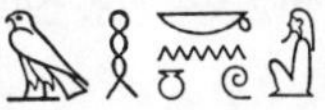. He is said to have been the son of the goddess Bast, and the seats of his worship were the towns of Netert, , and Ḥet-Nefer-Tem; he is usually depicted in the form of a hawk-headed man, with the solar disk encircled by a serpent on his head. The exact attributes of the god are unknown.

11. Ḥeru-Beḥuṭet, . This is one of the greatest and most important of all the forms of Horus, for he represents that form of Ḥeru-khuti which prevailed in the southern heavens at midday, and as such typified the greatest power of the heat of the sun. It was under this form that Horus waged war against Set or Typhon, and the inscriptions are full of allusions to the glorious victory which the god of light gained over the prince of darkness and his fiends.

The principal shrines of the god were at Mesen, , and Qem-baius, , Åat-āb,  (Philae), and Ṭebt, 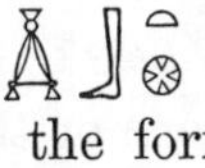 (Tanis); in the last named place he was worshipped under the form of a lion, which wears the triple crown upon its head, and is depicted in the act of trampling upon its enemies, The god is, however, usually depicted with the head of a hawk, and carrying in his hands some weapon which indicates his character as a destroyer. Thus, in one illustration given by Signor Lanzone,[2] we see him holding a weapon like a club or mace

[1] See Lanzone, op. cit., pl. 239.

[2] Op. cit., pll. 242 ff.

in his right hand, and a bow and three arrows in his left [1]; in another he is about to club an ass-headed man in fetters with the club, [2]; in another we see him standing on an oryx or antelope, and holding a long hawk-headed spear in his right hand, and three cords, to each of which is attached a prisoner, . Elsewhere we see him depicted with the head of a lion, which seems to have been the form in which he was worshipped at Tchar, , or Tanis, in the Delta, and in one place he is seated on a throne which rests on the back of a lion. As the god

Horus of Beḥuṭet armed with a bow and arrows and a club.

of generation and reproduction he appears as a hawk with a phallus terminating in the head of a lion, and in a scene of the late period he is represented with the body of a man, and the head and wings of a hawk, kneeling upon two crocodiles; on his head he wears , and in his left hand he holds a scorpion, .

[1] He is here called .

[2] He is here called "smiter of the rebel," .

In an extract from a text inscribed on a wall of the temple of Edfû given by Dr. Brugsch,[1] Ḥeru-beḥuṭet is described as the power which dispels darkness and night, and drives away clouds, rain, and storms, and fills all heaven and the world with his brilliance and light; he rises with golden disk as the holy beetle of gold, and he is declared to be the lord and creator of the gods. He created himself, there is none like unto him, he renews his birth daily, and year by year he performs his appointed course in the heavens, bringing in his train the seasons, and their proper produce. In one of his aspects he is identified with Osiris, and then the goddesses Isis and Nephthys are said to help him to emerge from the abyss of Nu; he made the heavens to be the dwelling-place for his soul, and he created the deep that it might serve as a place wherein to hide his body, which is here called Un-nefer, 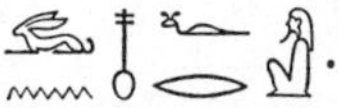. But the forms in which Ḥeru-beḥuṭet appealed most strongly to the mind of the Egyptians were those in which as the god of light he fought against Set, the god of darkness, and as the god of good against the god of evil. We know from a passage in the xviith Chapter of the *Book of the Dead* (line 66) that in very early times a combat took place between Horus and Set, wherein the former destroyed the virility of Set, and the latter cast filth in the face of Horus, and it is this form of the traditional fight between the two "Combatants," or Reḥui, , which is the base of the narrative inscribed on the walls of the great Temple of Edfû. There was, however, one very great difference between the fight of Horus and Set of predynastic times and that described between the Horus and Set known at Edfû; in the former fight the two combatants were unarmed, but in the latter Horus was armed with weapons of iron, and he was

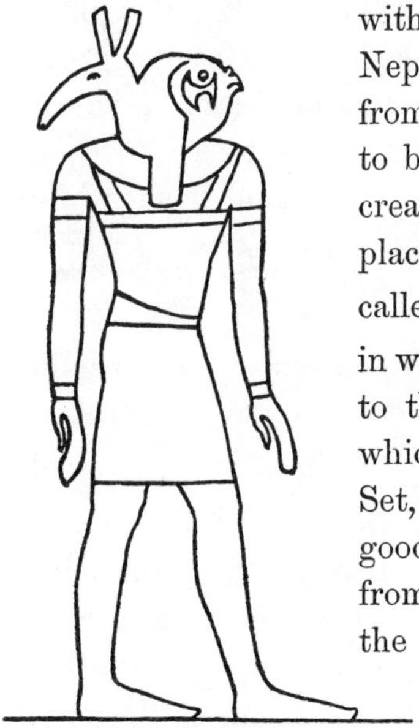

The double god Horus-Set.

[1] *Religion*, p. 548.

accompanied by a number of beings who are called *mesniu*, , or *mesnitu*, .[1] It is pretty certain from ⲃⲁⲥⲛⲉⲧ, the Coptic equivalent of the word *mesneti*, that the *mesniu* were workers in metal, and that this name was first applied to them as blacksmiths, and that at a later period the *mesniu* were men armed with weapons made of metal. The place where metal work was done, i.e., where the ore was smelted and the weapons were forged, was called *mesnet*, , the "foundry," and the worshippers of Horus of Beḥuṭet never tired of describing their god as the "lord of the forge-city," i.e., Edfû, the place where tradition declared he first established himself as the great master blacksmith. And Edfû itself was regarded as the foundry wherein the great disk of the sun was forged, as we see from a passage quoted by Dr. Brugsch, in which it is said "when the "doors of the foundry are opened the Disk riseth up," .[2]

In support of this tradition we find that a certain chamber in the temple of Edfû, which lay just behind the sanctuary, was called *mesnet*, , and it was here that the "blacksmiths" waited in attendance to usher forth the image of the god in his temple. From the representations of the "blacksmiths" given on the walls of the temple of Edfû[3] we see that they were originally men with shaven heads who wore a short tunic and a deep collar, and that in their right hands they carried a spear inverted, , and in their left a metal instrument, . In the same scene in which these occur Horus of Beḥuṭet is represented standing in a boat, dressed like his followers, and driving a long spear into the head of a hippopotamus beneath the boat with his right hand, and holding the monster in restraint by a double chain which he grasps in his left hand. In the bows of the boat kneels Isis, who also holds the hippopotamus by a chain in each hand, and we may note that

[1] Variants are , , .

[2] *Wörterbuch*, p. 703.

[3] See Naville, *Mythe d'Horus*, Geneva, 1870, pl. 7.

ḤERU-NETCH-TEF-F.

ḤERU-NETCH-ḤRĀ-TEF.-F.

the tackle of the boat consists of chains, presumably of iron, and not of ropes. In another place[1] Horus stands on the back of the hippopotamus, the legs of which are tied together by chains, and the lower jaw of which is held fast by a chain. The story of the defeat of Set by Ḥeru-Beḥuṭet is told in the texts on the walls of the temple of Edfû substantially as follows:—In the year 363, , of Rā-Ḥeru-khuti, , the king of the South and North who liveth for ever and ever, his Majesty found himself in the country of Ta-kens (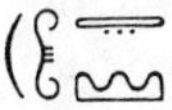, or Nubia), for he had gone to the district of Uauat,[2] because certain folk had conspired against their lord. Having suppressed the rebellion he returned to Edfû, and deputed his son Ḥeru-beḥuṭet to continue the war on his behalf; this god had observed how men had conspired against his father, and he was ready to carry out his behests. Thereupon Ḥeru-beḥuṭet flew up to heaven in the form of a winged disk, , and ever after he was called "great god, lord of heaven."

From the height of heaven he was able to see his father's enemies, and he chased them in the form of a great winged disk; he attacked them with such wrath and vigour, that they lost their senses and could see neither with their eyes nor hear with their ears, 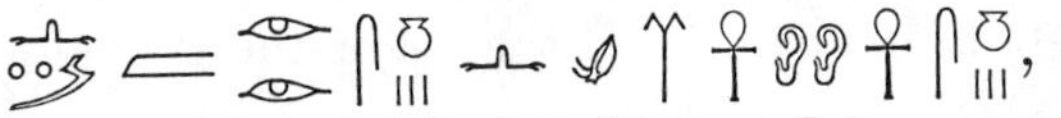, and every man fell upon his neighbour and slew him, and in a moment all were dead. And straightway Horus, with many-coloured shapes and feathers, , returned to his form as a winged disk and took up his position in the boat of Rā. At this juncture Thoth declared that Horus, son of Rā, should be called Ḥeru-Beḥuṭet, and Beḥuṭet (Edfû) should be called the city of Horus; and Rā referred with pleasure to the blood which his son had shed and which he likened to grapes. Then Horus suggested that Rā should come and look upon his dead enemies, and Rā, escorted by

1 Naville, op. cit., pl. 9.

2 Note the pun on the name Uauat, , and the verb "to murmur, conspire," .

Hathor, and followed by the goddess Ästherṭet, , who is described as the "mistress of horses," 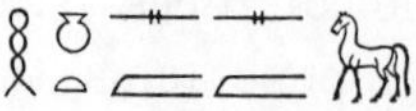, and who in the form of a woman with the head of a lioness is seen standing in a chariot, agrees to his son's proposal. The chariot of the goddess is drawn by four horses, which trample upon the foes of Rā, who lie upon the ground bound with fetters. When Rā saw this he said to Horus, "This is a very pleasant life," , and therefore the temple of Horus was called "Pleasant Life," from that day. Then Thoth observed, "This was the spearing of my foes," and therefore Edfû was called Ṭeb, , from that day; and he further said to Horus, "Thou art a great protector," 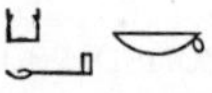, and straightway the boat of Horus was called "Great Protector." After this Rā proposed that they should journey upon the water, and his enemies also went to the water, and as soon as they had entered it they turned into crocodiles, *emsuḥu* , and hippopotamuses, , *tepu*, and when they were near enough to him they opened their mouths intending to swallow up the god. Then Horus came along with his "blacksmiths," 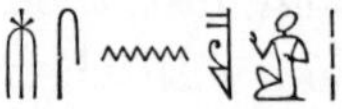, each having a spear made of divine iron, , and a chain, 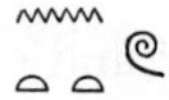, in his hand, and they slew the crocodiles, and the hippopotamuses, and they brought in 651[1] enemies, , immediately. Rā-Ḥeru-khuti next ordered that statues of himself should be set up in the land of the south in the place called Ḥet-ā-nekht, , and Thoth applauded Horus because he had made use of the formulae which were to be found in the Book of the slaughter of the Hippopotamus, ; from that day the blacksmiths of Ḥeru-Beḥuṭet have existed at Edfû.

[1] Naville gives (pl. xiii., l. 8) 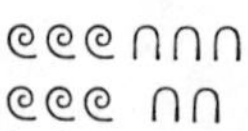, but Brugsch (*Abhandlungen Königlichen Gesellschaft der Wissenschaften zu Göttingen*, Bd. xiv., p. 216) and Wiedemann both give 381, i.e., they read .

And Horus once again took the form of a winged disk, and placed himself in the bows of the boat of Rā, and he took with him the two goddesses Nekhebet, , and Uatchit, , in the form of two serpents, that they might destroy the crocodiles and the hippopotamuses in their dens. As soon as the enemies of Rā perceived that they were being followed they turned round and fled to the south, but they were overtaken by Horus and his blacksmiths, each with his spear and his chain in his hands, and a mighty slaughter took place on a plain which was situated to the south-east of Thebes, , and which on account of the terrible scenes of carnage that were enacted there was called Tcheṭemet, , i.e., "slaughter." This was the second slaughter of the foes of Rā, and after this they retreated northwards, to the region of the Mediterranean Sea, and they were utterly disheartened and in fear of Horus; but this god followed after them in the boat of Rā, and with him were his companions who were provided with spears and chains, Horus himself was provided with a battle spear, , and a chain, , and blacksmiths, , and when he had waited a whole day he saw his foes to the north-east of Dendera, , and having attacked them he made a third great slaughter, *khai*, among them: the name of the place where the enemy was defeated was called "Divine Slaughter," , and it was situated quite close to Dendera. Ḥeru-Beḥuṭet was made the god of the region, and the acacia, , and the sycamore, , were sacred to him.

Once more the enemy fled to the north and was pursued closely by Horus, who was armed as before; for four whole days and nights, , he saw nothing whatsoever of the enemy, for they had changed themselves into crocodiles and hippopotamuses, but when he did see them he attacked them with great vigour and slew them in large numbers. One hundred and forty-two of them he bound in chains and dragged on to the boat of Rā, and he captured also a "male hippopotamus," ; all the fiends he slew, and he gave their entrails to his companions, and their bodies to the gods and goddesses who were in the boat of Rā near the town of Ḥeben, . As a proof of his victory he got up and stood upon the back of the hippopotamus, and as a result he was called "Ḥer-pesṭ," i.e., "He who is on the back." All these things took place on the piece of ground which formed the temple estate of the town of Ḥeben, and which measured 342 *khet*, 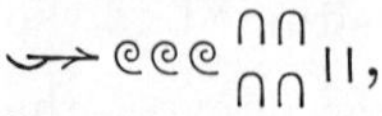, on the South, North, West, and East. The enemy, however, was not wholly defeated, and some fled to the north hoping to reach the "Great Green Sea," ; but the god Horus followed after them and slew many of the rebels, the remainder of whom went to the Sea of Mertet, , and there joined themselves to the fiends of Set, 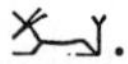. After some difficulty Horus found out where the enemies were, and having come up with them he captured 381 rebels, whom he slew in the bows of the boat of Rā, and he sent one body to each of his companions. When Set saw what had been done to his friends he cried out and uttered awful imprecations and complaints of the terrible destruction which Horus had wrought, and because of his foul words, 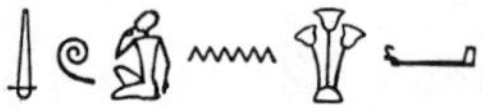, *meṭu-neḥa*, the fiend was ever after called Neḥaḥa, . Horus straightway attacked Set, and hurled his lance at him, and threw him down upon the ground in a place near the city which was always afterwards called Per-Rereḥu, 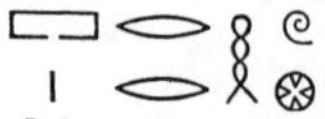; when he came back he brought Set with him, and his spear was in his neck, 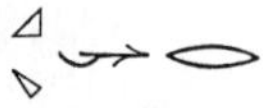 , and the legs of the monster were chained, and his mouth had been closed by a blow from the club of the god. After these exploits Rā ordered that Horus should be called Urui-Ṭenṭen, 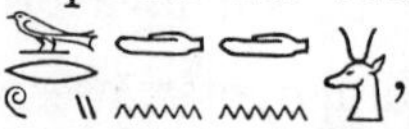, and he further decreed that the enemies of himself and Horus, Set and his confederates, should be handed over to the goddess Isis and her son Horus for them to do with them as they pleased. Thereupon Isis and Horus took up their position near Rā, and the young god drove his weapon, *māb*, into Set, at a place called "She-nu-āḥa," , i.e., "Lake of Battle," or, "She-neter," , i.e., "Lake of God;" he next cut off his head, and the heads of his followers, in the presence of Rā and the great company of the gods, and then dragged his body through the length and breadth of his land with his spear thrust through his head and his back.

Then Rā ordered that Horus, the son of Isis, should drag the body of the monster about, and because of this "dragging" the place was called "Åtḥa," , ever after. At this juncture the divine Isis asked her father Rā that the winged sun-disk, , might be given to her son Horus as a talisman, because he had cut off the heads of the fiend and his companions, and as a result Ḥeru-beḥuṭet and Horus, son of Isis, together pursued the foe Set, and both gods were of the same form and appearance. They had the bodies of men, and the heads of hawks, and they wore the White and Red Crowns, with plumes, and uraei. All these events took place on the seventh day of the month Tybi, , and the place wherein they happened was called Åat-shatet, .

After these things Set changed himself into a serpent which hissed loudly, and he sought out a hole for himself in the ground wherein he hid himself and lived, whereupon Rā said, "the monster "Ba ( ), hath turned himself into a hissing serpent, let "Horus, the son of Isis, set himself above his hole in the form of a "pole on the top of which is the head of Horus, ( ), so that he "may never again come forth therefrom." As the result of this the serpent of that town was called "Hisser" or "Roarer," , Hemhemet, and Horus the son of Isis stood upon him in the form of a pole, or staff, on the top of which was the head of a hawk. When all these things were done the boat of Rā arrived at Per-āḥa, , or "House of Battle"; the fore part of the boat was made of acacia wood, and the after part of sycamore wood, and both kinds of wood were, henceforth, holy.

Meanwhile, however, there still remained some of the enemies of Rā in the land, and this god exhorted his son to set out and to make an end of them, whereupon Horus told his father that if he would allow the boat to go whither he pleased, he would treat the enemy in such a way that it would be pleasing to Rā. When the boat had sailed but a little way on the water of Meḥ, 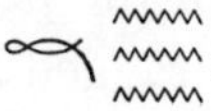, he found one of the friends of Set, and having hurled his spear at him, he caught him, and slaughtered him in the presence of Rā, at a place called Åstâbet, . A truce for six days and six nights then followed, and Horus had rest, while Isis made use of her words of power to keep away Ba, i.e., Set, from the district called "Ån-ruṭ-f." Soon afterwards Horus slew 106 of the enemy, and then made a final attack upon them in the neighbourhood of Ån-ḥat, 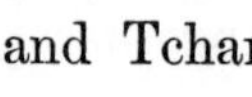, and Tchar, , or Tanis; some made their escape and succeeded in getting away to the mountains, and others threw themselves into the sea. Horus changed himself into the form of a lion, with the head of a man surmounted by the triple crown, and grasping in his hand his keen-edged knife he pursued them, and brought back 142 of the enemy, whom he slew, and he tore out their tongues, and their blood gushed out upon the ridges of the ground, 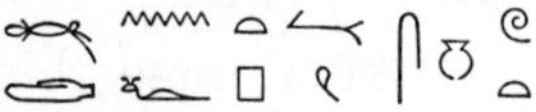
.

When this was done Rā told Horus that he wished to travel further upon the sea, and to smite the remainder of his foes who still lived in the form of crocodiles and hippopotami near Egypt, but Horus told him that it was impossible to sail further on the sea because the one-third of the enemy which still remained were therein.[1] When Thoth heard this he recited certain chapters containing magical formulae, with the view of protecting the Boat and the vessels of the blacksmiths which were with it, and of quieting the sea during the period of storm. It is clear that when these chapters had been recited, Rā and his company set out and went over the whole sea, but as no more enemies were seen they

[1] .

returned to Egypt, travelling by night. Finally, Horus and his companions went back to Nubia, to the town of Shâsḥertet, , where he destroyed the rebels of Uauat, and their ablest soldiers. When this was done Horus changed himself once more into the form of the winged sun-disk with uraei, and took with him the goddesses Nekhebet and Uatchit in the form of two serpents, that they might consume with fire any rebels who still remained. When the gods who were in his boat saw this they said, "Great indeed is that which Horus hath done by means "of his double snake diadem; he hath smitten the enemy who "were afraid of him!" And Horus said, "Henceforward let the "double snake diadem of Ḥeru-Beḥuṭet be called Ur-uatchti "(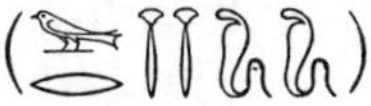);" and it was so. After these things Horus journeyed on in his ship, or boat, and arrived at Apollinopolis Magna (Edfû) , and Thoth decreed that he should be called the "Light-giver, who cometh forth from the horizon "();" hereupon Horus commanded Thoth that the winged sun-disk with uraei, 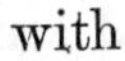, should be brought into every sanctuary wherein he dwelt and in every sanctuary of all the gods of the lands of the South and of the North, and in Àmentet, in order that they might drive away evil from therein. Then Thoth made figures of the winged sun-disk with uraei, and distributed them among the temples, and sanctuaries, and places wherein there were any gods, and this is what is meant by the winged disks with uraei which are seen over the entrances of the courts of the temples of all the gods and goddesses of Egypt. The snake goddess on the right hand side of the disk is Nekhebet, and that on the left is Uatchit.[1]

The above legend is very important for the study of Egyptian mythology, notwithstanding the fact that in its form here described it belongs to a very modern period. The fundamental facts of the story are very old, for they belong to the earliest period of

[1] For the text of the legend summarized above see Naville, *Mythe d'Horus*, pll. xii. ff.; and for a translation, with transliteration of text and commentary, see Brugsch, *Die Sage von der geflügelten Sonnenscheibe* in the *Abhandlungen* of the Royal Society of Sciences in Göttingen (Phys. Classe, Bd. xiv., p. 173 ff.).

Egyptian history, and are derived from the old nature myth of the combat between Light and Darkness. With these, however, we have mingled another element, which is apparently historical, and is also of very great antiquity. In the original fight between Rā and Āpep, or Horus and Set, the Sun-god was accompanied by his followers, whose duties, apparently, consisted in watching the combat, and who were, like Rā himself, unconnected with the earth. But in the fight of Ḥeru-Beḥuṭet with Set, the companions of the gods were beings in the forms of men who were armed with spears and chains for fettering purposes, and they were rewarded by him after the manner of men. The god himself was armed with a very long spear made of "iron of the god" or "divine iron," and with a chain of unusual length, and his method of fighting was to hurl his spear at his foes, and when it had struck home, he fettered them with his chain, and having dragged them to his boat, slaughtered them at leisure. The first great defeat of the enemy took place at Ȧat-Tcheṭemi, , near Thebes; the second took place at Neter-Khaiṭā, , near Dendera, and was followed by the overthrow of small bodies of them in the neighbouring nomes going towards the north; and the last great conquest was effected by the god, who took the form of a lion, at Tchar, , or Tanis, in the east of the Delta, not far from the modern Suez Canal.

All these facts indicate that we are not dealing entirely with mythological events, and it is nearly certain that the triumphant progress ascribed to Ḥeru-Beḥuṭet is based upon the exploits of some victorious invader who established himself at Edfû in very early times, and then made his way with his followers northwards, beating down all opposition as he went. It is pretty clear that he owed his success chiefly to the superiority of the weapons with which he and his men were armed, and to the material of which they were made; given equality of bravery in two bodies of men opposed each to the other, troops armed with weapons of flint would not long oppose successfully those armed with weapons of iron. In other words, the followers of Horus, who are called

HORUS, THE SON OF ISIS, THE SON OF OSIRIS.

*mesniti* in the text, as we have already shown, were actually workers in metal, or, "blacksmiths," and men who knew how to smelt iron ore and to forge the metal into weapons of offence and defence. These men called their workshop or foundry *mesnet* or *mesnit*, and later, when their leader and themselves had become deified, and priests had been appointed to perform the worship of the god, the portion of the temple which was set apart for them was also called *mesnet* or *mesnit*, and when the metal statue of the god of the rising sun, Ḥeru-Beḥuṭet, was brought out by them from their chamber the god was said to issue from the foundry wherein he had been cast, and the *mesnet* was identified with that portion of the sky from which the Sun-god appeared.

It is, of course, impossible to say who were the blacksmiths that swept over Egypt from south to north, or where they came from, but the writer believes that they represent the invaders in predynastic times, who made their way into Egypt, from a country in the East, by way of the Red Sea, and by some road across the eastern desert, e.g., that through the Wâdî Ḥammâmât, or that which touches the Nile a little to the south of Thebes. They brought with them the knowledge of working in metals and of brick-making, and having conquered the indigenous peoples in the south, i.e., those round about Edfû, they made that city the centre of their civilization, and then proceeded to conquer and occupy other sites, and to establish sanctuaries for their god or gods.[1] In later times the indigenous priesthoods merged the legendary history of the deified king of the blacksmiths in that of Horus, the god of heaven in the earliest times, and in that of Rā, which belonged to a later period. The priests of Edfû found many parts of this mixed history very difficult to explain, and they endeavoured to get out of their difficulties by the fabrication of foolish etymologies and puns, whereby they sought to elucidate events and names. These, however, have a certain importance, for they at least prove that parts of the legends were not understood when the puns or plays on words were made, and that the

[1] The historical element in the legend was long ago recognized by Maspero; see *Les Forgerons d'Horus et la Légende de l'Horus d'Edfou* (in *Bib. Egypt.*, tom. ii., pp. 313 ff.).

legends themselves are of great antiquity; another point is also made clear by them, i.e., that the Egyptians themselves were not better informed on such subjects than we are.

12. ḤERU-THEMĀ, , i.e., "Horus the piercer." This form of Horus is that in which the god attacked Set, the murderer of his father Osiris, with his long spear with a sharp-pointed iron head; he is represented in the form of a hawk-headed man in the act of driving his long spear into some unseen foe on or below the ground.

13. ḤERU-ḤEBENU, , i.e., Horus of Ḥebenu, or Ḥebennut, , the metropolis of the sixteenth nome of Upper Egypt.[1] He is mentioned in the myth of Ḥeru-Beḥuṭet, with whom he is often identified, and he is usually depicted in the form of a hawk-headed man standing upon the back of an antelope; this animal was supposed to be connected with Set, and Horus of Ḥebennu mounted upon his back as a symbol of his sovereignty over the god of darkness and all his host.

14. ḤERU-SA-ÅST-SA-ÅSÅR, , i.e., "Horus, son of Isis, son of Osiris," like many other forms of Horus, represented in general the rising sun, and appears to have been to the Egyptians exactly what Apollo was to the Greeks in this respect; the aspects of this god were many, and in consequence his shrines were very numerous both in the South and in the North. In him were at one time or another included all the various Horus gods, beginning with Ḥeru, , the god of the heights of heaven, and Horus the Elder, and ending with the least important Horus, i.e., the god of some provincial town. His principal aspects were, however, two, i.e., he represented the new Sun which was born daily, and which was the successor of Ḥeru-khuti or of Rā, and he was also the offspring of the dead man-god Osiris and his lawful successor. Horus, the son of Isis and of Osiris, was a god whose attributes appealed strongly to the Egyptians from one end of Egypt to the other, because in him

[1] Brugsch, *Dict. Géog.*, p. 490; and Brugsch, *Religion*, pp. 558 ff.

every man and woman saw the type of what he or she wished to possess, that is to say, renewed life, and life as opposed to death, and movement as opposed to inactivity, and intercourse with the living instead of with the dead. In a way Osiris and Horus were complements, each of the other, but the chief difference was that Osiris represented the past, and Horus the present, or, as we have it expressed in the *Book of the Dead* (xvii. 15), "Osiris is Yester-"day, and Rā (i.e., Horus grown up) is to-day,"  . The texts are not always consistent in the matter of the paternity of Horus, for though Isis is invariably regarded as his mother, his father is sometimes said to be Osiris, and sometimes Rā; but this inconsistency is easily accounted for by remembering that Osiris is, under one aspect, a form of the dead Sun-god. Of the circumstances under which Horus was begotten we gain a good idea from a hymn to Osiris in which the sorrow of his mother Isis at the death of her husband is described. The goddess was greatly distressed, but she was equipped with mighty words of power, and she knew how to utter them so that they might have the greatest effect, and she set out in search of the dead body of Osiris and never rested until she had found him. With her hair she made light, and with her wings she stirred the air as she made lamentation for her brother Osiris, and at length she brought his body into a state of activity, and was then united to him; thus she became with child by him, and her son Horus was born in a secret place where she suckled him and reared him.[1]

This spot appears to have been situated among the papyrus swamps in the Delta, and the event is alluded to in many scenes in which the goddess is seen, suckling her child amidst a dense mass of papyrus plants. Soon after the birth of her child she was persecuted by Set, who kept herself and Horus prisoners in a house, but by the help of Thoth she escaped with her child one evening, and set out on her way under the protection of seven scorpions called Tefen, , Befen, , Mestet,

[1] See Chabas, *Revue Archéologique*, 1857, p. 65; Ledrain, *Monuments Égyptiens*, pll. 22 ff.

, Mestetef, , Petet, , Thetet, , and Matet, . These scorpions probably represent the seven stars of the constellation Canis Major, in which the stars of Isis and Sothis were situated. The last three scorpions showed Isis the way and led her to the town of Per-Sui, ,[1] or Crocodilopolis, and then on to the city of Thebti, the city of the Two Sandals-Goddesses, , where the swamp country begins. Whilst Isis was absent one day Horus was stung by a scorpion, and when she came home she found him lying on the ground, and the foam was on his lips, and his heart was still, and there was not a muscle or limb of him which was not rigid ; she had protected him against Set, and against the possibility of attack by any being in the papyrus swamps, but a scorpion had stung the child, and he was dead. Whilst Isis was lamenting his death her sister Nephthys came with Serqet, the scorpion goddess, and advised her to cry out to heaven for help, and she did so, and her cry penetrated to Rā in his "Boat of Millions of Years." The great god stopped his boat, and Thoth came down with words of power, and by means of these her son was once more raised to life and health. Soon after these things had taken place Horus set to work to avenge the death of his father Osiris, and it was under his form of "Horus, the avenger of his father," ,[2] that he appealed so strongly to the imagination of the Egyptians.

According to a notice in the Calendar given in the Fourth Sallier Papyrus (Brit. Mus., No. 10,184), Horus began his fight with Set, which lasted three days, on the 26th day of the month of Thoth, and the two gods fought in the form of two men. Isis was present at the fight and, because she in some way supported Set against Horus, her son turned upon her with the fury of a "panther of the south," and cut off her head. Thoth, however, seeing what had been done, took the head of the goddess, and by

[1] The story is told on the *Metternichstele*, ed. Golénischeff, Leipzig, 1877, pl. iii., ll. 46 ff.

[2] For references to him in the *Book of the Dead* see my *Vocabulary*, p. 225.

ḤERU-NETCH-TEF-RĀ.

THE FOUR CHILDREN OF HORUS, OR THE GODS OF THE CARDINAL POINTS.

HĀPI. MESTHȦ. ṬUAMUTEF. QEBḤSENNUF.

THE DECEASED RISING FROM THE FUNERAL CHEST, WHICH IS THE TYPE OF THE AAT OF ABYDOS WITH THE SYMBOL OF LIFE IN EACH HAND.

means of his words of power transformed it into the head of a cow, and then fixed it upon the body of Isis.[1] According to Plutarch (*De Iside et Osiride*), Isis found that her son Horus had succeeded in fettering Set and in binding him in chains, but not wishing that he should perish she loosed his fetters and set him at liberty; then it was that Horus tore off her head the symbols of sovereignty which were upon it. We have no means of assigning a date to the composition of the above legend, but it must be very old, and it is easy to see that it is only a version of the older legend of the combat between Rā and Āpep, and Ḥeru-ur and Set, and Ḥeru-Beḥuṭet and Set, and it is, of course, one of the sources of all the post-Christian legends of the overthrow of dragons by kings and heroes, e.g., Alexander the Great and Saint George. When Horus had overcome Set he succeeded to the inheritance of his father, and took his seat upon the throne of Osiris, and reigned in his stead; and, in the words addressed to Osiris by the official Hunefer, "Horus "is triumphant in the presence of the whole company of the gods, "the sovereignty over the world hath been given unto him, and his "dominion is in the uttermost parts of the earth. The throne of "the god Seb hath been adjudged unto him, along with the rank "which hath been founded by the god Temu, and which hath been "stablished by decrees in the Chamber of Books, and hath been "inscribed upon an iron tablet according to the command of thy "father Ptaḥ-Tanen, on the great throne. . . . Gods celestial and "gods terrestrial transfer themselves to the service of thy son "Horus, and they follow him into his hall, [where] a decree is "passed that he shall be lord over them, and they perform the "decree straightway."[2]

Now, besides the fight in which he engaged with Set, Horus performed many other filial duties which endeared him to the Egyptians. Thus he took the greatest care that every ceremony which could possibly benefit the deceased was performed on his father's behalf, and every detail of the mummification of the god, and of the method of swathing, and of the placing of amulets, etc., upon the body was watched by him with loving attention, and his

[1] Chabas, *Calendrier*, Paris, 1863, pp. 29 ff.

[2] *Book of the Dead*, Chap. clxxxiii., ll. 12 ff.

filial affection became the pattern which was followed by every pious Egyptian from time immemorial. We find, however, that Horus was believed to help the dead generally, even as he helped Osiris, and all men hoped that he would come to their assistance after death, and act as a mediator between the judge of the Underworld and themselves. In the Judgment Scene in the *Book of the Dead* (Papyrus of Ani, plates 3 and 4), Horus, the son of Isis, leads the deceased, after his heart has been weighed, into the presence of Osiris, and he says to his father, "I have come to thee, "O Un-nefer, and I have brought unto thee Osiris Ani," and then goes on to say that Thoth has weighed Ani's heart in the Balance according to the decree of the gods, and has found it right and true. He also asks Osiris that Ani may be allowed to appear in his presence, and that cakes and ale may be given to him, and that he may be among the followers of Horus for ever. In none of the variants of the Judgment Scene do we find that the place of Horus as introducer of the dead is taken by any other god, and there is no doubt that this duty was assigned to him because it was believed that Osiris would favourably receive those who were led into his presence by the son who had done so much for him. From the Pyramid Texts we learn that, at the time when man believed that it was necessary to have a ladder in order to ascend into heaven from the earth, Horus was regarded as the god of the ladder, and that he was entreated to set up the ladder and to hold it in place whilst the deceased climbed up it. Sometimes Rā held one side of it whilst Horus held the other, and sometimes its supporters were Horus and Set, but even so the deceased seems sometimes to have experienced difficulty in ascending it, for we read that Horus had to give him a push upwards with his two fingers.[1]

More than this, however, was done for the deceased by Horus, for he took the bodies of the dead under his care just as he took the body of his father Osiris into his own hands, and superintended the performance of his funeral rites and ceremonies. In this great work he was assisted by a number of beings called Ḥeru-shemsu,

[1] English renderings of the passages will be found in my *Egyptian Magic*, pp. 52 ff.

, i.e., "Followers of Horus." Now we know from several passages in the *Book of the Dead* that Osiris, Rā, Nefer-Tem, Neb-er-tcher, Meḥi, Hathor, and, in fact, all great gods were ministered to by a number of lesser gods, but none of these are of the importance of the followers of Horus, and none of them are as old. We have already seen that the original Horus-god, , who represented the face of heaven, was supposed to have long hair which hung down from his face, and which probably supported it, and that in the myth of Shu the supports of this god, i.e., the four pillars, , which held up the vast, rectangular, iron plate that formed the floor of heaven were placed in the tresses of Horus. At a later period, when the four followers of Horus, son of Isis, were identified with the followers of the older Horus, these gods were made to dwell near the pillars of Shu and to have dominion over them, and also over the four quarters of heaven, and they took the place of the earlier gods of the cardinal points. In the *Book of the Dead* these four children of Horus play very prominent parts, and the deceased endeavoured to gain their help and protection at all costs, both by offerings and prayers. In the pictures of the funeral procession four men draw along the coffin containing the mummied intestines of the deceased, four animals are taken for sacrifice, and all the instruments used in the ceremony of "opening the mouth," as well as the vases, and boxes of unguents, etc., are in quadruplicate. Even prayers and formulae are said four times over, e.g., in Chapter xl., the deceased in addressing the Eater of the Ass says, "I know thee," four times; and in Chapter cxxiv., he says, "I am pure," four times. Most important of all, however, it was to remember that the four children of Horus shared the protection of the body of the deceased among them, and as far back as the Vth Dynasty we find that they presided over his life in the underworld. The names of the four gods are:—Ḥāp, 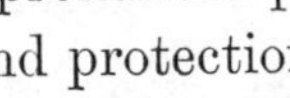, Ṭuamutef, 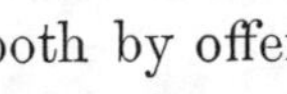, Åmset, 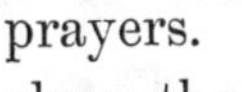, and Qebḥsennuf, 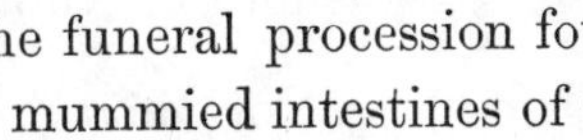; this is the order in which they are mentioned in the Pyramid Texts, but in

later times the order of the names and the spelling vary thus:— Merthà, , Ḥāpi, , Ṭuamutef, , and Qebḥ-sennuf, . The two arms of the deceased were identified with Ḥāpi and Ṭuamutef, and his two legs with Àmset and Qebḥsennuf; and when he went into the Sekhet-Àaru they were his guides and went in with him, two on each side. Ḥāpi represented the north and protected the small viscerae of the body; Ṭuamutef represented the east, and protected the heart and lungs; Àmset represented the south, and protected the stomach and large intestines, and Qebḥsennuf represented the west, and protected the liver and the gall bladder. Associated with the four gods, perhaps as female counterparts, were the goddesses Nephthys, Neith, Isis, and Selqet, or Serqet.

As Horus, son of Isis, was so thoroughly identified with Horus the Elder, and with other forms of the rising sun, it is not surprising to find that the sanctuaries of the god were very numerous, and that they existed in all parts of the country; the names of a great many of these have been collected by Signor Lanzone,[1] and from them we learn that Horus, dweller in the two Egypts, , was lord of Nubti, (Ombos), and lord of Uast, (Thebes), and of Màām, , Kenset, , Ḥet-Ānt, , Re-ur, , Pe, , Behen, , Nekhen, , Per-netchem, , Re-āu, , Ḥurent, , Ka-qem, , Reqetit, , Therer, , Bak, , Àat-āat, , Ḥu, , Tchart, , Àat-āb, , Ḥut, , Ḥet-suten, , Petchatcha, , It, , Rethma , Ḥeben, , Sekhem, , Àbṭu, , Shes-en-meḥ, , Ḥet-neh, , Ḥebt, , Shep, , Khat, , Qāḥ,

[1] Op. cit., p. 569.

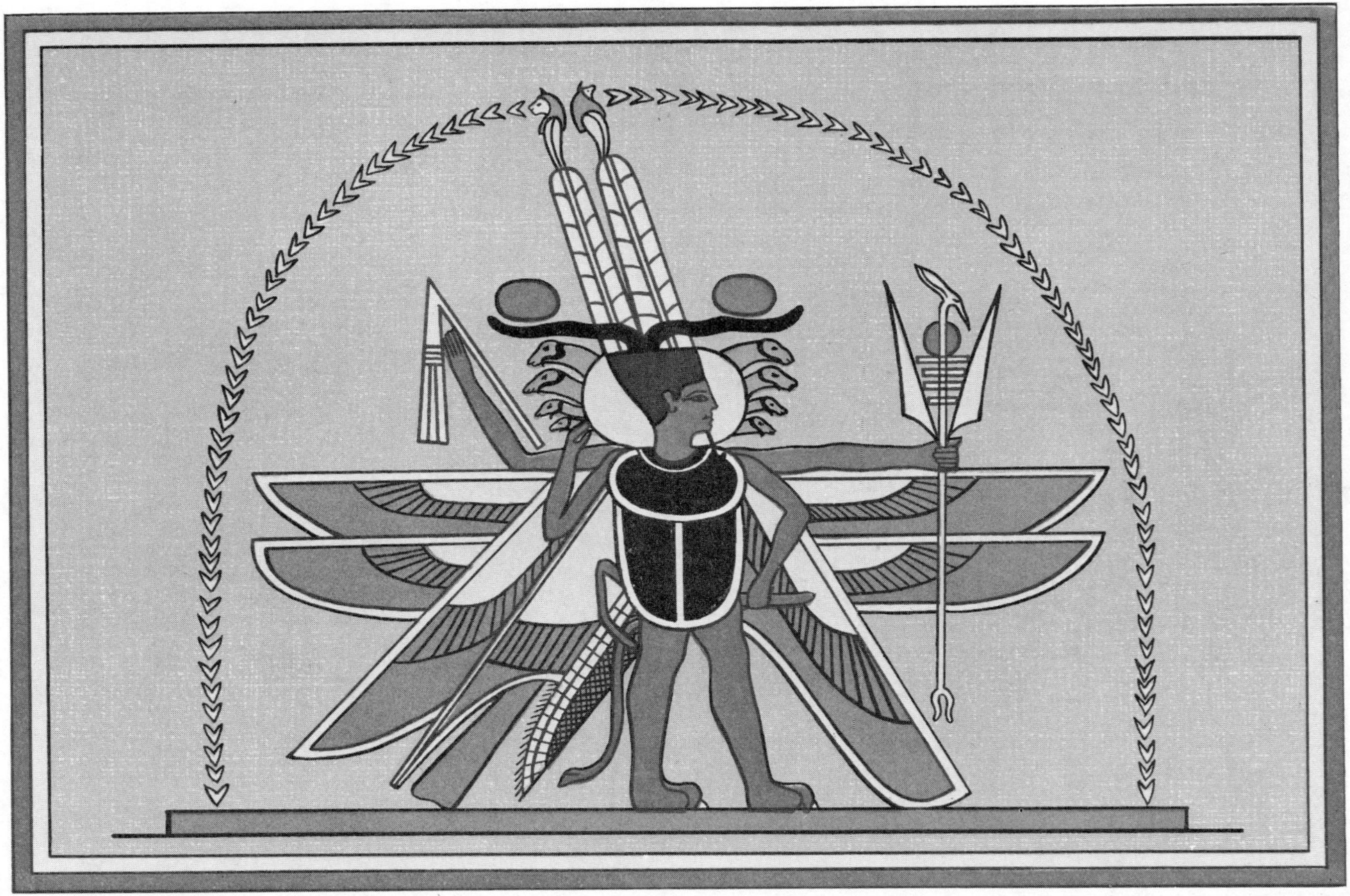

THE GOD COMPREHENDING ALL GODS.

HORUS, THE SON OF ISIS, THE SON OF OSIRIS.

, Ṭenretut, , Ȧnt, , and Baka, , etc.

The forms in which Horus, son of Isis, is depicted are both numerous and interesting, and they show how completely he absorbed the attributes of all the other Horus gods. Thus he is represented as a child seated on a lotus flower, with one of his forefingers touching his lips, and with the lock of hair on the side of his head; he wears the crowns of the South and North, and holds both  and .[1] In another section he stands on the back of a hippopotamus, into the head of which he is driving a spear; in this instance he is clearly identified with Ḥeru-Beḥuṭet. In late dynastic times the god was depicted in a great many fantastic forms, and the various attributes which were ascribed to him are indicated in many curious ways. Thus as guardian of the funeral coffer of Osiris he has the head of a hawk, on which is the triple crown, with the body of a lion, and a tail in the form of a head and neck of some unknown animal. Elsewhere he is represented with seven heads, among which are those of a bull, a ram, a cat, and a crocodile, and with the body of a man, ithyphallic, and the legs and hoofs of a bull, and the wings of a bird; in one hand he holds a knife, and in the other a serpent.

But besides the attributes of the other Horus gods, Horus, son of Isis, was endowed with many of the characteristics of other gods. Thus with the god Ȧnpu or Anubis, he becomes Ḥeru-em-Ȧnpu, i.e., Horus as Anubis, and is said to dwell in the "divine hall," ; he recalls under this name the god "Hermanubis," who is mentioned by Plutarch (*De Iside et Osiride*, § 61) and by Diodorus (lines 18, 87). This dual god is represented in the form of a man with the head of a jackal, and it is impossible to distinguish him by his picture from the two jackal gods Ȧnpu, or Anubis, and Ȧp-uat, who are only two forms of one and the same god. Strictly speaking, Ȧnpu is the "opener of the roads of the South, the power of the two lands," , and Ȧpuat is the "opener of the roads of the North, the power of

[1] See Lanzone, op. cit., pll. 214 ff.

heaven," [1] The two jackal gods are often seen depicted on stelae, where they symbolize the two halves of the year, and the night and the day sky, and the periods of waxing and waning of the powers of nature in summer and winter.

The particular form of Horus which was identified with Horus, son of Isis, was Horus of Ḥebennu, , the Hipponon of the Greeks, where also Anubis was specially venerated. The identification of Horus, son of Isis, with Anubis is easy to explain, for both gods assisted in mummifying the dead body of Osiris, and it is expressly stated in the *Book of the Dead* (xvii. 125 ff.), that it is Anubis who passes through the purification chamber in the *Mesqet* , and that he stood "behind the chest which contained the inner parts of Osiris." According to the same chapter (lines 100-108), it was Anubis who appointed the SEVEN SPIRITS, "the followers of their lord Sepa," , to be the protectors of the dead body of Osiris. One authority quoted in the same chapter stated that the Seven Spirits, , were the Four Children of Horus, already mentioned above, and Maa-àtef-f, , and Kheri-beq-f, , and Ḥeru-khenti-maati, ; but another authority gives the names of the Seven Spirits as follows:—1. Netcheḥ-netcheḥ; 2. Àaqeṭeṭ; 3. Àn-erṭā-nef-bes-f-khenti-heh-f; 4. Āq-ḥer-àmmi-unnut-f; 5. Ṭesher-maati-àmmi-ḥet-Ànes; 6. Ubes-ḥrà-per-em-khetkhet; 7. Maa-em-ḳerḥ-àn-nef-em-hru.[2] In connexion with these must be

[1] *Book of the Dead*, Chap. cxlii., § iv. 24, 25.

[2] 

mentioned the goddess Ḥetep-sekhus, 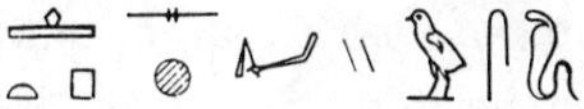, who is identified either with the Eye of Rā or with the flame which follows Osiris to burn up his enemies, and the assessors of that section of the Underworld which is called Ȧn-ȧareretef, , or Ȧn-ȧreṭf, 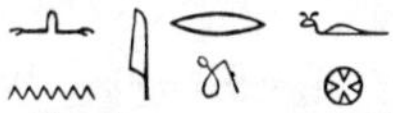, i.e., the "place where nothing grows," the chief of whom was Ḥeru-netch-ḥrȧ-ȧtef-f, , or "Horus, the avenger of his father."

15. Ḥeru-pa-khart, , i.e., "Horus the Child." We have already described Horus the Child, who was the son and successor of Horus the Elder, and brief mention must be made of Horus the Child who was the son and successor of Osiris. The greater number of the attributes which belonged to the old Horus gods were transferred to the son of Isis and Osiris, especially in late dynastic times when the worship of Osiris was dominant in Egypt, and Horus the Child became the type of the new birth, and new life, the first hours of the day, and the first days of the month, and the first months of the year, and in fact of everything which was young and vigorous. Soon, however, the characteristics of the great forms of the Sun-god were added to his own, and his original conception as Horus the Child was somewhat forgotten; at times it is very difficult to distinguish in the texts exactly which Horus is referred to. In all the great sanctuaries of Egypt, from the period of the New Empire onwards, we find that Horus the Child, or Harpocrates, was identified by the priests of the local gods as a form of their principal deities in which the chiefs of the companies or triads of gods had renewed and rejuvenated themselves. The late Dr. Brugsch collected a large number of examples of this fact,[1] and he proved that as Ḥeru-sma-taui-pa-khart he was identified with Tem, and was said to be son of Ḥeru-khuti and Hathor; that joined with Ȧḥi, 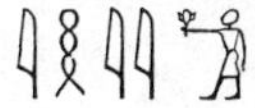, Harpocrates became a form of Rā, and was called "son of Hathor, to whom Isis gave birth," and was regarded as the offspring of Un-nefer, 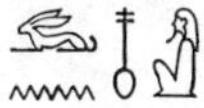,

[1] *Religion und Mythologie*, p. 373.

i.e., of Osiris; and that he was also made to be the renewed form of the gods Shu, Seb, Khensu, and Åmsu, or Min.

In connexion with Horus, son of Isis, in one or other of his forms must be mentioned the interesting legend which is preserved in the cxiith Chapter of the *Book of the Dead*, and which has reference to the district or place called Khat, , of the dweller in Khat, in the city of Ānpet, , in the nome of Ḥā-meḥit, , i.e., the sixteenth nome of Lower Egypt. Strictly speaking, Ānpet was the name of the temple and quarter of the city of Mendes, the local triad of which consisted of Ba-neb-Ṭeṭet, , Ḥā-meḥit, , and Ḥeru-pa-kharṭ. Mendes was full of associations with the worship of the god Osiris, for in the temple there were preserved the phallus and the back-bone of Osiris; the temple was called Ḥet-baiut, , i.e., "House of the Rams," and the place where the relics were found Per-khent, .[1] The rams here referred to recall the legend in which the Ram of Mendes was said to unite within himself the souls of Rā, Osiris, Shu, and Kheperȧ, and he was known as the "Ram with four heads upon one neck," .[2] It is possible that he is also referred to in the text of Pepi I. (line 419) where a god with four faces is mentioned, . In the Chapter above mentioned the deceased is made to ask a number of gods, "Do ye know for what reason the city of Pe hath "been given unto Horus?" and he goes on to say, "I, even I, "know it though ye know it not. Behold, Rā gave the city to him "in return for the injury to his Eye; for which cause Rā said to "Horus, 'Let me see what is coming to pass in thine eye,' and "forthwith he looked thereat. Then Rā said unto Horus, 'Look "at that black pig,' and he looked, and straightway an injury was "done unto his eye, that is to say, a mighty storm [took place

1 .

2 See de Rougé, *Géographie Ancienne*, p. 114.

"therein]. Then said Horus unto Rā, 'Verily, my eye seems as if "it were an eye upon which Suti had inflicted a blow'; and [thus "saying] he ate his heart.[1] Then said Rā to those gods, 'Place ye "him in his chamber, and he shall do well.' Now the black pig "was Suti (Set) who had transformed himself into a black pig, and "he it was who had aimed the blow of fire which struck the eye of "Horus. Then said Rā unto those gods, 'The pig is an abominable "'thing unto Horus; but he shall do well, although the pig is an "'abomination unto him.' Then the company of the gods, who "were among the divine Followers of Horus when he existed in "the form of his own child, said, 'Let sacrifices be made of his "bulls, and of his goats, and of his pigs.' Now the father of "Mesthi, Ḥāpi, Ṭuamutef, and Qebḥ-sennuf is Horus, and their "mother is Isis. Then said Horus to Rā, 'Give me two divine "'brethren in the city of Pe and two divine brethren in the city of "'Nekhen, who [have sprung] from my body and who shall be with "'me in the guise of everlasting judges, and then shall the earth "'blossom and thunder-clouds and rain be done away.' And the "name of Horus became Ḥer-uatch-f, ."

In addition to the forms of Horus mentioned in the above paragraphs the Pyramid Texts make known the following:— 1. Ḥeru-Åāḥ, , i.e., Horus, the Moon-god;[2] 2. Ḥeru-khent-peru, ;[3] 3. Ḥeru-àm-Ḥennu, ;[4] and Ḥeru of Ṭat, .[5] According to the same authorities Horus possessed one white eye and one black, ,[6] which king Unȧs is said to have taken to illumine his face; and two other titles of the god are "Horus of the two blue eyes," ,[7] and "Horus of the two red eyes," .[8] In the Theban Recension of the

[1] I.e., he lost his temper and raged.

[2] , Tetȧ, l. 365.

[3] Unȧs, l. 202. [4] Unȧs, l. 211. [5] Unȧs, l. 218.

[6] Unȧs, l. 37. [7] Unȧs, l. 369. [8] Unȧs, l. 869.

*Book of the Dead* these titles are also mentioned (Chap. clxxvii. 7) as well as the following:—Ḥeru-āa-åbu, , Ḥeru-āḥāi, , Ḥeru-åmi-åbu-ḥer-åb-åmi-khat, , Ḥeru-åmi-åthen, , Ḥeru-em-khebit, , Ḥeru-neb-ureret, , Ḥeru-ḥer-neferu, , Ḥeru-khenṭ-ḥeḥ, , Ḥeru-khenti-ḥeḥ, , Ḥeru-sekhai, , Ḥeru-sheṭ-ḥrå, , etc. Finally, in the text of Unås (line 462 ff.) we meet with the form of Ḥeru-Sepṭ, , who is mentioned in connexion with Rā, Tem, Thoth, and Horus of Ṭat, and the star Nekhekh, . Ḥeru-Sepṭ is a form of Horus, presumably the god of the rising sun, united to the particular form of the same god Sepṭ which was worshipped in the twentieth nome of Lower Egypt, i.e., the nome Sepṭ, . In the examples given by Signor Lanzone of the various forms under which Sepṭ is depicted he is sometimes seen in the form of a man having upon his head either the symbol , or double plumes, , or a disk, ⊙, and sometimes in the form of a mummied hawk, , with plumes on his head, and the symbol in front of him, and the *menåt*, , on his back. The titles which accompany these representations describe him as the "lord of the east," i.e., the eastern part of the Delta and Arabia. On a shrine discovered at Saft al-Henna by M. Naville he appears in the form of the god Bes, , who is represented with outspread arms, hands, and wings, and with feathers on the top of his head. In this form he is called, "Sepṭ, the smiter of the Menti," , i.e., the tribes of the Eastern Desert and Arabia. Sepṭ was clearly a god of battles, , and he was called the "Bull that trampleth on the Menti;" he was the

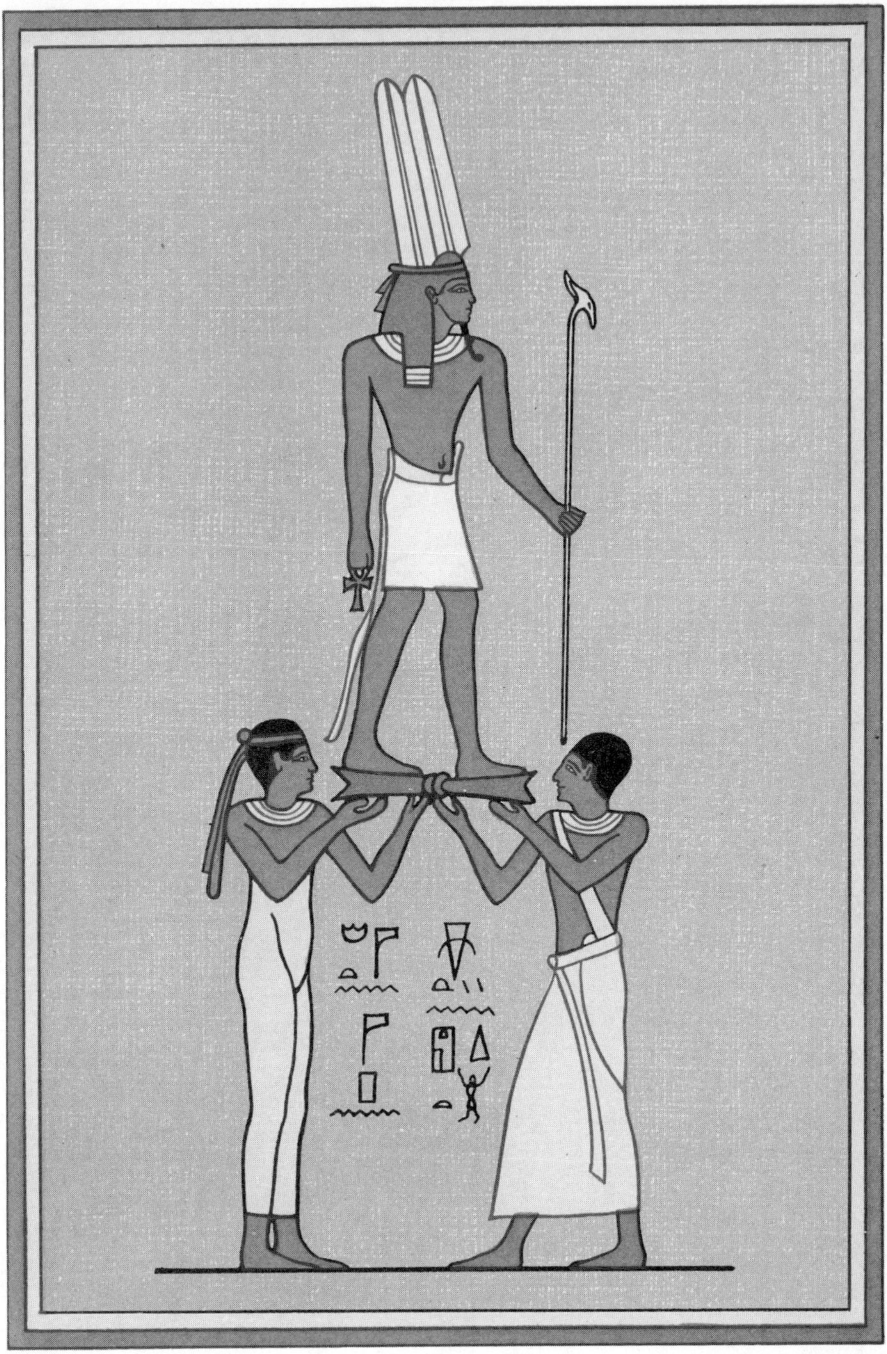

THE GOD SEPT.

PTAH FASHIONING THE EGG OF THE WORLD UPON A POTTER'S WHEEL, WHICH HE WORKS WITH HIS FOOT.

"strengthener of Egypt, and the protector of the temples of the gods."[1]

The principal seat of the worship of the god was in the metropolis of the nome, i.e., at Per-Sepṭ, ; if Ḳesem, , was a distinct city from Per-Sepṭ a temple to the god may have stood there also. The female counterpart of Ḥeru-Sepṭ was a form of the goddess Hathor to whom, in the twentieth nome of Lower Egypt, the name SEPTIT, , was given; his sanctuary contained some fine *nebes*[2] trees, hence its name *ȧst nebes*, , "house of *nebes* trees." As the "lord of battle," , Sepṭ is depicted in the form of a hawk-headed lion with the tails of a lion and a hawk, and in his hands, which are those of a man, he holds a bow and a club; on his head are a disk[3] and plumes. Sepṭ is mentioned even in the *Book of the Dead* with the attributes of a god of war, and in Chapter xvii. (line 30) he is said to "thwart the acts of the foes of Neb-er-tcher." In the xxxiind Chapter the deceased drives away the Crocodile of the South, and says, "I am Sepṭ"; and in the cxxxth Chapter (line 11) we read of the "slaughtering block of the god Sepṭu," . Up to the present no satisfactory explanation has been given of the object which is the symbol of the god Sepṭ, but it appears to have been some kind of a triangle; a figure or model of it was preserved at Ȧmen-kheperutet, , which is described in the Edfû list as , i.e., "the hidden of Khas (?) en-Sepṭ."

[1] De Rougé, *Géographie Ancienne*, p. 141.

[2] The *Cordia Sebestena*, or *Zizyphus Lotos W.*, according to Brugsch, *Religion*, p. 567.

[3] Lanzone, op. cit., p. 1048.

## CHAPTER XVI

# THE GREAT TRIAD OF MEMPHIS, PTAḤ, , SEKHET, , AND I-EM-ḤETEP, .

THE greatest of all the old gods of Memphis was undoubtedly PTAḤ, , or PTAḤ-NEB-ĀNKH, , and his worship, in one form or another, goes back to the earliest part of the dynastic period. He has usually been regarded as a form of the Sun-god, and as the personification of the rising sun, either at the time when it begins to rise above the horizon or immediately after it has risen. The name has often been explained to mean "Opener," and to be derived from a root which was cognate in meaning with the well-known Semitic root *pâthakh*, פָּתַח, in fact Ptaḥ was thought to be the "Opener" of the day just as Tem was considered to be the "Closer" of the day. The chief drawback, however, to the acceptance of this derivation is the fact that Ptaḥ never forms one of the groups of the chief forms of the Sun-god in the texts, and his attributes are entirely different from those of Kheperȧ, Tem, Ḥeru, and Rā. Moreover, although the word *ptaḥ*, , is found in Egyptian it never has the meaning "to open," in the sense of opening a door, and the determinative which follows it,[1] , proves conclusively that although it does mean "to open" it is always in the sense of "to engrave, to carve, to chisel," and the like; compare Heb. פִּתּוּחַ "engraving, sculpture." The meaning proposed for the name "Ptaḥ" by Dr. Brugsch is "sculptor, engraver," and many passages in the texts of all periods make it plain that Ptaḥ was the chief god of all handicraftsmen,

[1] Brugsch, *Wörterbuch*, p. 528.

and of all workers in metal and stone. What the form of the god was originally it is, unfortunately, impossible to say, but from the titles which the dynastic Egyptians gave to him it is clear that his main characteristics did not change from the period of the IInd Dynasty to that of the Ptolemies and Romans. At a very early period he was identified with one of the great primeval gods of Egypt, and he was called "the very great god who came into "being in the earliest time," 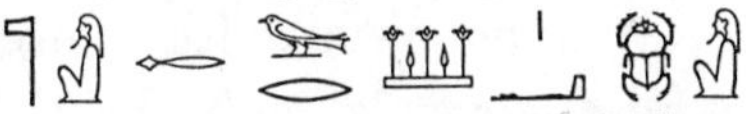; "father "of fathers, Power of powers," ; "father of "beginnings, and creator of the egg[s] of the Sun and Moon," ; "lord of Maāt, king of the two "lands, the god of the Beautiful Face in Thebes, who created his "own image, who fashioned his own body, who hath established Maāt throughout the two lands;"[1] "Ptaḥ, the Disk of heaven, illuminer "of the two lands with the fire of his two eyes."[2] In the text of Tetȧ (lines 87, 97) the "workshop of Ptaḥ," 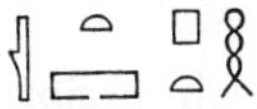, is mentioned, and the general sense of the passages indicates that it was Ptaḥ who was believed to fashion the new bodies in which the souls of the dead were to live in the Underworld. Ptaḥ, as we shall see later from the passages quoted from the *Book of the Dead*, was the great artificer in metals, and he was at once smelter, and caster, and sculptor, as well as the master architect and designer of everything which exists in the world. The Greeks and the Latins rightly identified one form of him with Hephaistos and Vulcan.

Ptaḥ was the fellow-worker with Khnemu in carrying into effect the commands concerning the creation of the universe which were issued by Thoth, and whilst the latter was engaged in fashioning man and animals, the former was employed in the construction of the heavens and the earth. The large rectangular

1 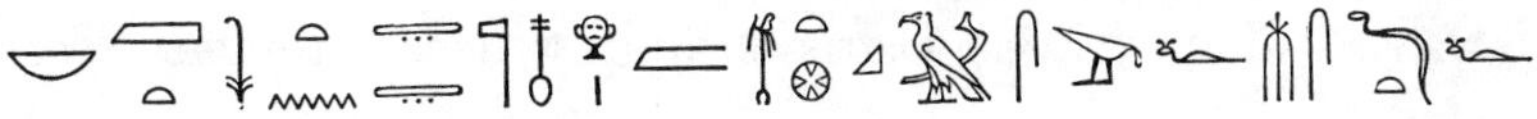 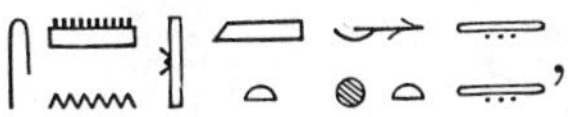, Lanzone, op. cit., p. 240.

2 , *Ibid.*, p. 240.

iron slab which formed the floor of heaven and the roof of the sky was beaten out by Ptaḥ, and he and his assistants made the stays and supports which held it in position. In the character of architect of the universe he partakes of the nature of Thoth, especially in respect of his title "lord of Maāt;" and, as the god who beat out the iron firmament with a hammer and supported it, his attributes resemble those of Shu. In other capacities he was supposed to be endowed with powers which we are wont to associate with other gods, and thus we find enumerated in religious and funeral texts Ptaḥ-Åsår (Ptaḥ-Osiris), Ptaḥ-Ḥāpi, Ptaḥ-Nu, Ptaḥ-Seker, Ptaḥ-Seker-Åsår, Ptaḥ-Seker-Tem, Ptaḥ-Tanen, and the like. The part which Ptaḥ in his various forms plays in the *Book of the Dead* is well illustrated by the following:—In Chapter iv. he is said to come forth from the Great Temple of the Aged One in Ånnu; in Chapter xi. the deceased says, "I shall "stand up like Horus, I shall sit down like Ptaḥ, I shall be mighty "like Thoth, and I shall be strong like Tem." From Chapter xxiii. we learn that Shu or Ptaḥ performed the ceremony of "opening the mouth" of the gods with an iron knife; in Chapter xlii. the feet of the deceased are identified with the feet of Ptaḥ; in Chapter lxiv., line 8, he is said to have covered his sky with crystal; Chapter lxxxii. is a text by the use of which a man transforms himself into Ptaḥ, when his tongue becomes like that of the god; in Chapter cxlv., line 67, the "writings of Ptaḥ" are referred to; in Chapter cli.A Mesthå tells the deceased that he has "stablished his house firmly according to what Ptaḥ hath commanded;" and in Chapter cliii., line 6, the "hook of Ptaḥ" is mentioned; in Chapter clxvi. Ptaḥ is said to overthrow the enemies of the deceased (see also Chapter clxxii. 10). In Chapter cli. the hair of the deceased is compared to that of Ptaḥ-Seker, and in Chapter clxx. this god is said to give him help with his *khakeru*, , weapons from his divine house. In a hymn to Osiris (Chapter xv.) Osiris is addressed as Un-nefer Ḥeru-khuti, and as "Ptaḥ-Seker-Tem, , in Ånnu, the "lord of the hidden place, and the creator of Ḥet-ka-Ptaḥ (i.e., "'the House of the Double of Ptaḥ,' or Memphis);" finally, Ptaḥ-

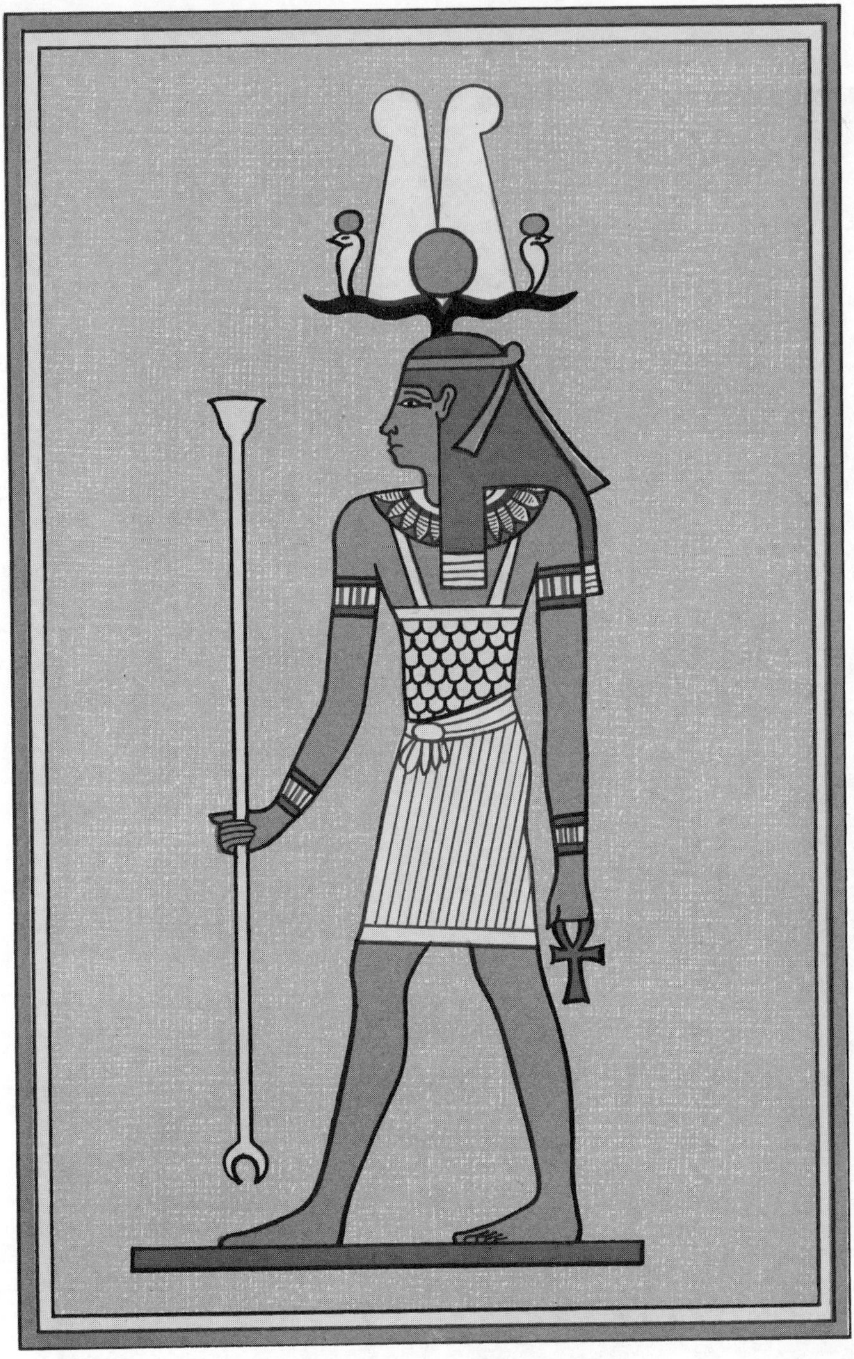

THE GOD PTAḤ-SEKER.

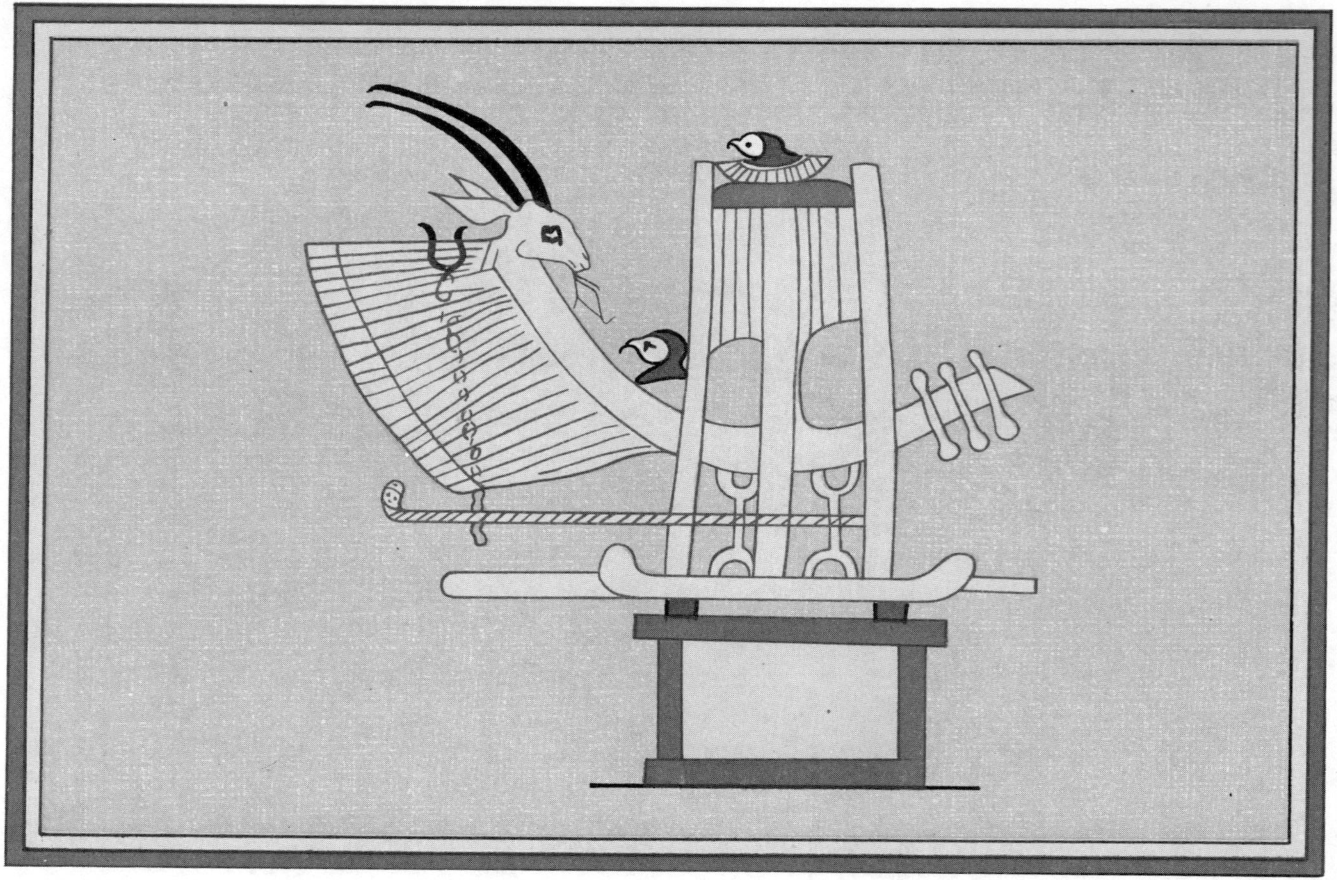

THE ARK OF THE GOD SEKER ON ITS SLEDGE.

Tanen is mentioned in Chapter clxxxiii., line 15, as having caused to be inscribed certain decrees concerning Horus upon an "iron tablet."

The commonest form in which Ptaḥ is represented is that of a bearded man with a bald head who is shrouded in a close-fitting garment, from an opening in the front of which project his two hands; from the back of his neck hangs the *menȧt*, symbol of pleasure and happiness, and in his hands he holds a sceptre, 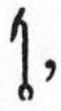, and the emblems of "life," , and "stability," . When standing upright his feet rest upon a pedestal made in the shape of the sign *maāt* , and when seated his throne rests upon a pedestal of similar shape. At the back of standing figures of the god we sometimes see an obelisk, , or the ṭeṭ, , which symbolizes both "stability" and the tree trunk in which the body of Osiris was hidden by Isis. Ptaḥ under his forms of Ptaḥ-Nu, , and Ptaḥ-Ḥāpi, 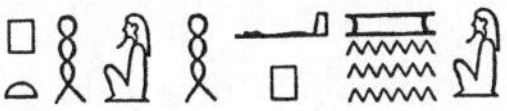, merely represents the union of the great celestial workman and architect with the primeval elements of earth and water, and there are no representations specially set apart for these forms.

On the other hand, his forms of Ptaḥ-Seker, or Ptaḥ-Seker-Ȧsȧr, 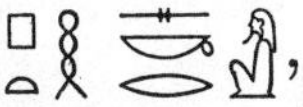, , and Ptaḥ-Tanen, 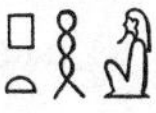
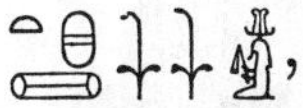, must be specially considered. Ptaḥ-Seker represents a personification of the union of the primeval creative power with a form of the inert powers of darkness, or in other words, Ptaḥ-Seker is a form of Osiris, that is to say, of the night sun, or dead Sun-god. Seker is depicted in the form of a hawk-headed man in mummied form resembling that of Ptaḥ, and his hands project from the front of his close-fitting garment and hold the emblems of sovereignty and dominion, , , 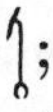; sometimes he has the head of a man and holds in each hand a knife.[1] Seker was originally a power of darkness, or of the night, which in later times was identified with forms of the night sun like Tem. He is

[1] Lanzone, op. cit., pl. 368, No. 4.

Seker-Åsår.

called "the great god, who came into being "in the beginning, he who resteth upon the "darkness," . In the xviith Chapter of the *Book of the Dead* (line 113) occurs a petition in which the deceased begs to be delivered from the "great god who carrieth away "the soul, who eateth hearts, and who "feedeth upon offal, the guardian of the "darkness, the god who is in the Seker "boat, ," and in the explanation of the passage which is given in answer to the question, "Who is this?" the god who is in the Seker boat is said to be either SUTI, , or SMAM-UR, , the soul of Seb. Thus it is clear that Seker was an ancient spirit or god whose attributes were such that he might well be represented by Set, or Suti, the enemy of Rā, or by the soul of the earth-god Seb. In comparatively early dynastic times Seker was exalted to the position of god of that portion of the Underworld which was allotted to the souls of the inhabitants of Memphis and the neighbourhood, and it is tolerably certain that he was regarded as the tutelary deity of the necropolis of Ṣaḳḳâra.

Ptolemy Euergetes and the Ḥennu Boat.

The SEKER BOAT which has been mentioned above is often represented on sepulchral monuments and papyri, and it was certainly made to play a very prominent part in certain solemn, sacred ceremonies. It was not made in the form of an ordinary boat, but one end of it was very much higher than the other, and was made in the shape of the head of some kind of gazelle or oryx; the centre of the boat was occupied by a carefully closed coffer which was surmounted by a hawk with protecting wings stretched out over the top of it. This coffer contained the body of the dead Sun-god AF, or of Osiris, and it rested upon a framework or sledge which was provided with runners. On the great day of the festival of Seker which was celebrated in many places throughout Egypt, the ceremony of placing the Seker boat upon its sledge was performed at sunrise, at the moment when the rays of the sun were beginning to spread themselves over the earth. The whole ceremony was under the direction of the high priest of Memphis, whose official title was "Ur kherp ḥem," 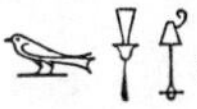, "i.e., great chief of the hammer"; this official was expected to lift the Seker Boat upon its sledge, and to march at the head of the procession of priests which drew the loaded sledge round the sanctuary. By this action the revolution of the sun and other celestial bodies was symbolized, but no texts explaining the symbolism have come down to us. From the inscriptions which are found at Memphis and in the neighbourhood we know that the office of high priest of Ptaḥ was considered to be a most honourable position, and that many men of noble family and of high rank held it as far back as the period of the IInd Dynasty. Now since the priestly office existed in those remote times it is only reasonable to assume that the Seker Boat also existed, and that the ceremonies with which it was used in the later period were also performed in the earlier; the god Seker was, even when the Pyramids were built, an ancient god, and the chief characteristics of his worship must be as old as the god himself.

The name given to the Seker Boat is "Ḥennu," 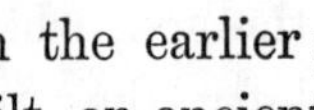, and it is mentioned several times in the *Book of the Dead*, and sometimes in connexion with traditions of great importance.

Thus after the lxivth Chapter we have a rubric which states that the composition was found in the masonry below the shrine of Ḥennu during the reign of Semti (Ḥesepti) a king of the Ist Dynasty; now Ḥennu can only be the god of the Ḥennu boat, and the shrine of Ḥennu must be the place where it was kept. A most valuable proof of the antiquity of this boat is found on an ebony tablet in the British Museum[1] which was made for the royal chancellor Ḥemaka, who flourished during the reign of Semti, whose Horus name was Ṭen. On this we see a representation of the king dancing before Osiris, who is seated within a shrine on the top of a flight of steps, and in the register immediately below it is a figure of the Ḥennu Boat. The Seker or Ḥennu Boat was probably a form of the Sektet Boat, i.e., the boat in which the sun sailed over the sky during the second half of his daily journey, and in which he entered the Underworld in the evening, for Rā the Aged, , is said to be like Horus, and Rā the Babe, , to be like Seker. The sanctuaries of Seker must have been extremely numerous[2] in Lower Egypt in very early dynastic times, but it appears that before the great development of Rā worship took place, the god Seker was already identified with and merged in Ptaḥ, and that these gods were adored together in one temple. The forms in which Ptaḥ-Seker is represented are interesting, for they illustrate the attributes of the double god, and prove that it was Ptaḥ who usurped the characteristics of Seker, and that Seker was the older god. Ptaḥ-Seker is often depicted in the form of a man who wears upon his head a crown composed of disk, plumes, horns, and uraei with disks on their heads, ; a cognate form is perhaps that reproduced by Lanzone[3] in which the god, who in this case is called "Ptaḥ whose double plumes are lofty," has upon his head horns, plumes, and a uraeus, and a uraeus upon his forehead. Another interesting form is that of a mummy with a disk and the two feathers of Maāt, , upon his head.[4] Elsewhere he is found in the usual form of Ptaḥ seated upon

[1] No. 32,650.

[2] See a list given by Lanzone, op. cit., p. 1117.

[3] Op. cit., pl. 94, No. 4.

[4] *Ibid.*, pl. 95.

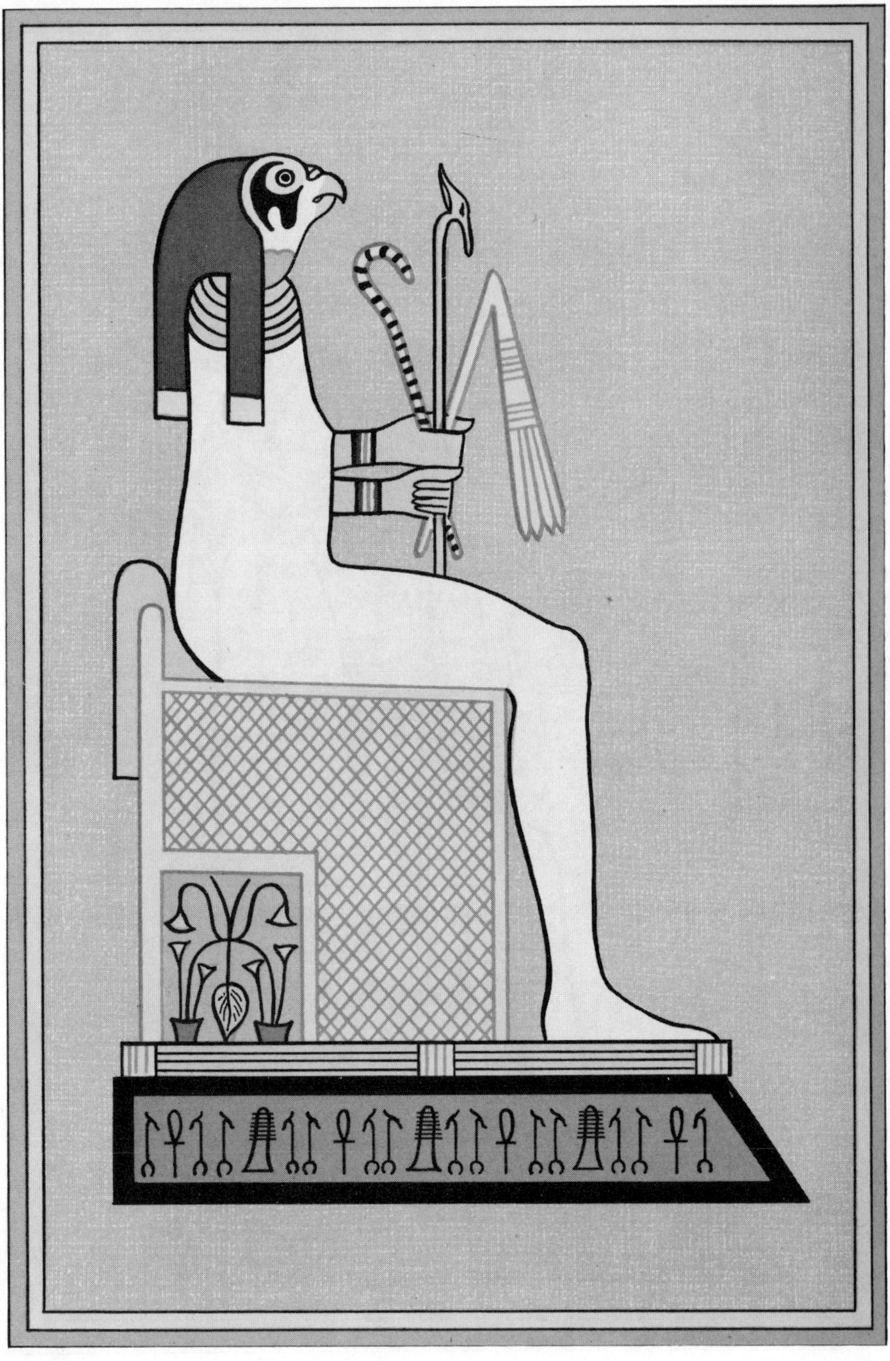

SEKER

TATENEN

a throne behind Osiris and followed by Anubis, Horus, son of Isis, and Hathor.

Under the name of PTAḤ-SEKER-ÅSÅR we find Ptaḥ and Seker united with Osiris to form a remarkable triad, which is depicted in various ways. A common representation of the god is the hawk, with the White Crown and plumes upon his head, standing upon a low pedestal, from the front of which projects a serpent; in this form he is often met with on painted coffins and sepulchral chests. In the Papyrus of Ånhai (Brit. Mus., plate 5) the god is seated within a shrine in human form with the crown, , upon his head; behind him stand Isis and Nephthys. The titles here given to him are, "Dweller in the secret place, great "god, lord of Ta-tchesertet, king of eternity, governor of ever-"lastingness,"  . Before the god is the skin of the pied bull, of which the head has been cut off, with blood dripping from it into a bowl, and perched on the side of the throne is his son Horus in the form of a hawk. The cornice of the shrine in which the god is seated is composed of uraei with disks on their heads, and before it stand the Mer goddess of the South, , wearing a red garment, and the Mer goddess of the North, , wearing a blue garment, and it is quite clear from the general arrangement of the vignette that in the XXIInd Dynasty Ptaḥ-Seker-Åsår was wholly identified with Osiris. A very interesting form of the triune god is that in which he appears as a squat pigmy with a large, bald head, and thick limbs; on the top of his head he usually has a beetle, but occasionally plumes are given to him. An examination of the variants of this form proves that he was supposed to possess all the virile power of Åmsu, or Min, and the creative power of Kheperå, which is symbolized by the beetle, and the youth and vigour of Harpocrates, which is represented by the lock of hair on the right side of his head; and as sometimes he stands upon a crocodile, and holds a serpent in each hand, he must have possessed besides the powers of several of the great solar gods. Ptaḥ-Seker-Åsår is, then, like Osiris, the type and symbol of the resurrection from the dead, and he has been fittingly described as the "triune god of the resurrection"; that he was the outcome of some local Memphite belief, or the result of some compromise between the priests of Osiris and the priests of the old Memphite god is tolerably certain, but there is no evidence to show exactly what belief, or doctrine, or dogma was associated with this mysterious god who united within himself the attributes of Seker, and those of Ptaḥ the architect and builder of the material world, and of Kheperȧ the self-begotten and self-born, and Osiris the giver of everlasting life.

Finally must be mentioned Ptaḥ in his connexion with the primeval god TENEN, , or TA-TU-NEN, , or TA-THUNEN, , or TA-THU-NENET, 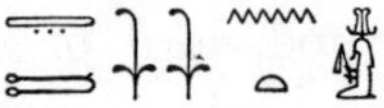. This god is represented in the form of a man, either sitting or standing, who wears on his head the crown, 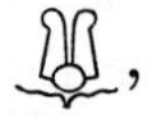, and holds in his hands the symbols of sovereignty and dominion, , , and ; in a figure reproduced by Lanzone[1] we see him seated upon the oval object, . Another figure represents the god seated with a potter's wheel before him, which he works with his foot, and on the upper part of it is the egg of the world which he is fashioning with his hands; elsewhere he is depicted with a scimitar in his right hand, which suggests that in one form he was regarded as a destructive power of nature, or as a warrior-god. Tenen, or Ta-Tenen, must have been one of the earliest gods of Lower Egypt, and have been a personification of a nature power, the exact attributes of which appear to have been unknown even to the Egyptians. In the early part of the dynastic period it was thought that Ptaḥ, the local god of Memphis, might be fittingly identified with Tenen, or Ta-Tenen, and his name was, therefore, joined to that of the older god, just as in later days the name of Ȧmen was joined to that of Rā; later Tenen and Ta-tenen were merely forms and names of Ptaḥ. From a hymn to Ptaḥ-Tenen,[2] which is probably a product of the XXth or XXIst Dynasty, we may gain some

Op. cit., pl. 401, No. 3.

[2] For the hieratic text see Lepsius, *Denkmäler*, vi., pl. 118.

idea of the meaning of the name Ta-tenen, "Ta," , is of course "earth," and "Tenen," , is probably to be connected with the word, , *enen*, or *nen*, which means "inertness, inactivity, rest, motionless," and the like, and if this derivation be correct Ta-Tenen must be the god of the inert but living matter of the earth.

The passage on which this view is based is a very difficult one, and appears to read, "There was given to thee a SEKHEM "(i.e., Power) upon the earth in its things which were in a state "of inactivity, and thou didst gather them together after thou "didst exist in thy form of Ta-Tenen, in thy becoming the 'Uniter "of the two lands,' which thy mouth begot and which thy hands "fashioned."[1] It is, as Dr. Brugsch suggested, quite possible that in this passage the writer was not discussing the derivation of the name Tenen, or Ta-Tenen, seriously, and was only making a play upon the words of similar sound. In the hymn to Ptaḥ-Tenen already mentioned we find the following address to the god and titles:—"Homage to thee, O Ptaḥ-Tenen, thou great god, "whose form is hidden! Thou openest thy soul and thou wakest "up in peace, O father of the fathers of all the gods, thou Disk "of heaven! Thou illuminest it with thy two Eyes, and "thou lightest up the earth with thy brilliant rays in peace."

. In the lines which follow he is called the "begetter of men," , the "maker

1 .

of their lives," the "creator of the gods," "he who passeth through eternity and everlastingness," 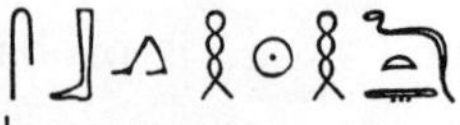, "of multitudinous forms," , "the hearer of prayers which men make to him," 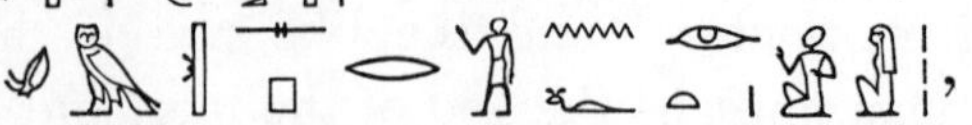, "builder of his own limbs," 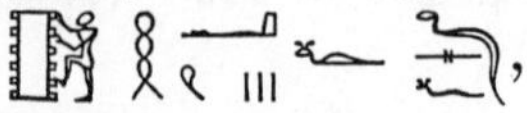, and maker of his body, "when as yet heaven and earth were not created, and when the "waters had not come forth," 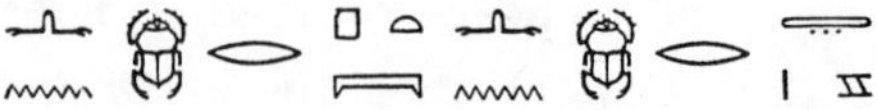 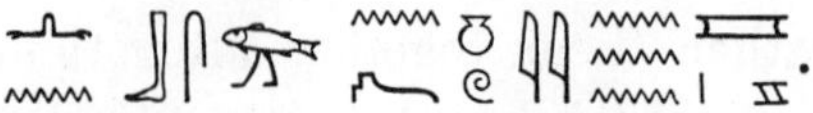. "Thou didst knit together the "earth, thou didst gather together thy members, thou didst "embrace thy limbs, and thou didst find thyself in the condition "of the One who made his seat, and who fashioned (or, moulded) "the two lands.[1] Thou hadst no father to beget thee in thy "person, and thou hadst no mother to give birth unto thee; thou "didst fashion thyself without the help of any other being. Fully "equipped thou didst come forth fully equipped."[2] Next we have an allusion to thy "aged son," , i.e., Rā, and to the dissipation of night and darkness by the sun and moon, which are called the "Eyes" of Ptaḥ-Tenen. The hymn continues, "Thy feet are upon the earth and thy head is in the heights above "in thy form of the dweller in the Ṭuat. Thou bearest up the "work which thou hast made, thou supportest thyself by thine "own strength, and thou holdest up thyself by the vigour of thine "own hands. . . . The upper part of thee is heaven and the lower "part of thee is the Ṭuat." 

1 

2 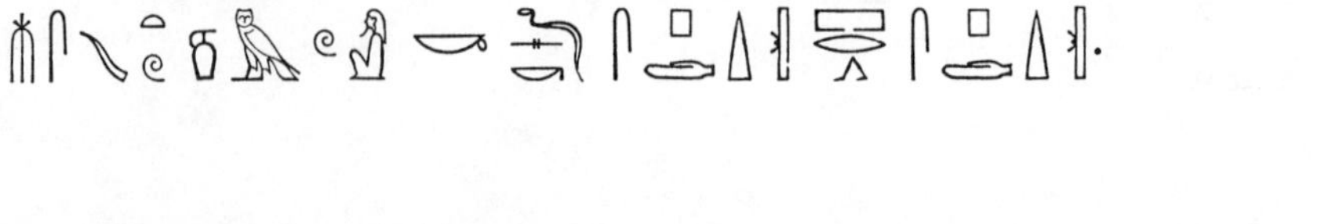

"The winds come forth from thy nostrils, and the celestial water "from thy mouth, and the staff of life (i.e., wheat, barley, etc.), "proceeds from thy back; thou makest the earth to bring forth "fruit, and gods and men have abundance, and they see Meḥ-urit "cattle in thy field. When thou art at rest the darkness cometh, "and when thou openest thy two eyes beams of light are produced. "Thou shinest in thy crystal form according to [the wont of] "thy majesty. . . . . The company of the gods of thy supreme "company praise thee, and they acclaim thee at thy rising and "hymn thee at thy setting in the land of life." A few lines lower down Ptaḥ-Tenen is called the "great god who stretched out the "heavens, who maketh his disk to revolve in the body of Nut and "to enter into the body of Nut in his name of RĀ, Moulder of "gods, and of men, and of everything which is produced, maker of "all lands, and countries, and the Great Green Sea in his name of "KHEPER-TA (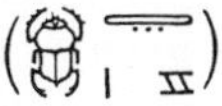), Bringer of Ḥāpi (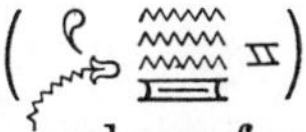) from his "source, making to flourish the staff of life, maker of grain which "cometh forth from him in his name Nu the Aged (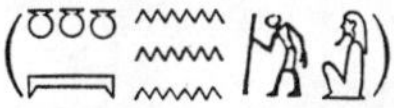), "who maketh fertile the watery mass of heaven, and maketh to "come forth the water on the mountains to give life to men "and women () in his name of ÅRI-ĀNKH "(), Maker of the Ṭuat with all its arrangements, "who driveth away the flame from those who live in their corners "in his name of SUTEN-TAUI (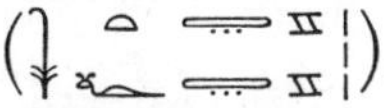), King of eternity "and everlastingness, and lord of life." Among other titles of the god in this hymn we have:—"Babe, born daily,"  ; "Aged one on the borders of eternity," 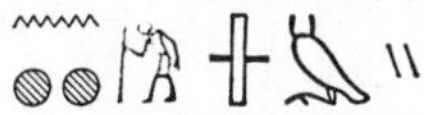 ; "Aged one traversing eternity," 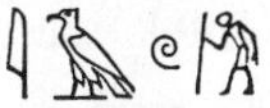 ; "Inert one passing over all his aspects," 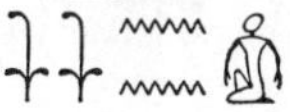 ; "Exalted one without his strength," 

; "Lord of the hidden throne, hidden is he," ; "Hidden one, whose eternal "form is unknown," 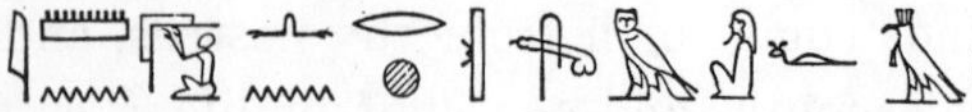; "Lord of years, giver of life at will," 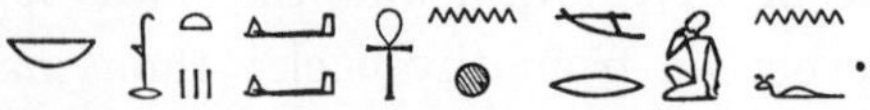.

The above extracts are sufficient to show the importance of the god Ptaḥ-Tenen in the eyes of the Egyptians about B.C. 1100, at which time, if we may judge from palaeographical evidence, the hymn was probably written, and there is no reason for supposing that he was thought less of during any period of Egyptian history. The papyrus upon which the text is inscribed is said to have been found at Thebes, and there is no doubt that the style of writing closely resembles the fine bold hand of the great papyrus of Rameses III., king of Egypt about B.C. 1200, which also was discovered at Thebes; we should not, however, expect to find, in the city of Åmen-Rā, the king of the gods, papyri containing hymns to Ptaḥ-Tenen, the god of Memphis, in which this god is made to possess all the attributes of all the great gods of Egypt, yet such has been, undoubtedly, the case. The fact that the triad of Ptaḥ, Sekhet, and Nefer-Tem was worshipped at Thebes is another proof of the influence which the priests of Heliopolis exerted over the religious views of the Thebans in almost every period of Egyptian history after the VIth Dynasty.

Returning now to the consideration of Ptaḥ in his simplest form, it must be noted that the principal centre of his worship was in the city of Men-nefer, 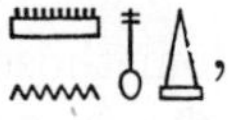, i.e., Memphis, the capital of Åneb-ḥetch, 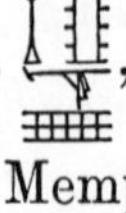, the first nome of Lower Egypt. The commonest names for Memphis in the religious texts are:—1. Ḥā-nefer, 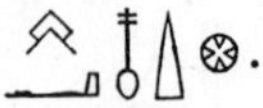. 2. Ḥet-ka-Ptaḥ,[1] 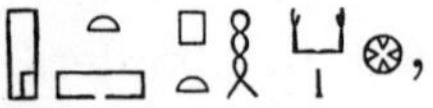, from which the Greek name for Egypt, Ἄιγυπτος, has been commonly derived. 3. Khut-taui, 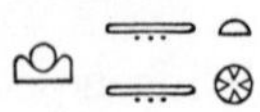, i.e., "horizon of the two lands."

[1] I.e., "House of the Double of Ptaḥ."

4. Ḥet-ka-khnem-neteru,[1] . 5. Ànebu, , i.e., the "city of walls." 6. Makha-taui, , i.e., "the balance of the two lands." In the city of Memphis or its neighbourhood were the temples of Ptaḥ, Sekhet, Bast, Hathor, Osiris, Seker, and I-em-ḥetep, the most important being the Het-àa, , "the house of the Aged One," i.e., Rā. In the temple called Ānkh-taui, , were the sacred persea and acacia trees; in Ḥekennut, , Osiris was worshipped; in Ḥet-utet, , i.e., "house of the begetter," the cult of Khnemu was observed; another sacred place was called the "Path of Anubis," ; and another Ta-ḥet-pa-Àten, , i.e., the "House of the Disk"; and in Tepeḥ-tchat, , was yet another sacred tree.[2]

Àsàr-Ḥāpi (Serapis).

The Serapeum, which was discovered by M. Mariette in 1868, was known by the name of "Neter-ḥet per en Àsàr-Ḥāp," ; a district called Baḥtet, , was the centre of the worship of Seker; the district of Pa-penāt, , was the centre of the worship of Bast; Osiris was adored in the district of Ḥekennut, ; Hathor was adored in the district of Smen-Maāt, ; Khnemu was adored at Uafet, ; and Ptaḥ and Sekhet and their son I-em-ḥetep appear to have possessed temples wherein they were worshipped exclusively. The city of Memphis is often called in the hieroglyphic texts "Àneb," a name which is written ,

[1] I.e., "House of the Double which uniteth the gods."
[2] See de Rougé, *Géographie*, pp. 4 ff.

or , or ,[1] and there is no doubt that the appellation of "Walls" was given to it because of its strong fortifications. Once a year the priests of Ptaḥ-Seker-Åsår formed a solemn procession, and led by the Sem-priest, , and usually accompanied by the king, they marched all round the walls of Memphis; it is probable that the image of this triune god was carried in the procession. The god Ptaḥ himself was worshipped in a temple on the eastern side of the city called "Åneb-åbt," ; the temple of Tenen bore the name of "Åneb Åthi," ; and Ptaḥ-Seker-Åsår was adored in a temple on the south side of the city called "Åneb-rest-f," i.e., "his southern wall," . The whole city was known by the name of "White Wall," , to which reference is made by Herodotus[2] (iii. 91).

The principal female counterpart of Ptaḥ was the goddess Sekhet, , who was at once his sister and wife, and the mother of his son Nefer-Tem, and a sister-form of the goddess Bast. She is generally depicted in the form of a woman with the head of a lioness which is surmounted by the solar disk encircled by an uraeus, , but sometimes the disk is omitted, and a uraeus only is seen upon her head. The name of the goddess appears in the Pyramid Texts (Unås, line 390), where after the statement that Unås hath proceeded from the thighs of the company of the gods, , he is said to have been conceived by Sekhet, , and by Sheskhentet, , and by Sothis, . In comparatively late dynastic times Sekhet and Bast were identified with forms of Hathor, and were regarded as the goddesses of the West and the East respectively, just as Nekhebet and Uatchet were the goddesses of the South and the North respectively. Each goddess had the head of a lioness, but the body of Sekhet is said to have been draped in a red garment whilst that of Bast was arrayed in a green garment. Several special forms of Sekhet are known to have existed, viz., Sekhet, lady of Rekht,

[1] Brugsch, *Dict. Géog.*, p. 55.

[2] ἐν τῷ Λευκῷ Τείχεϊ τῷ ἐν Μέμφι.

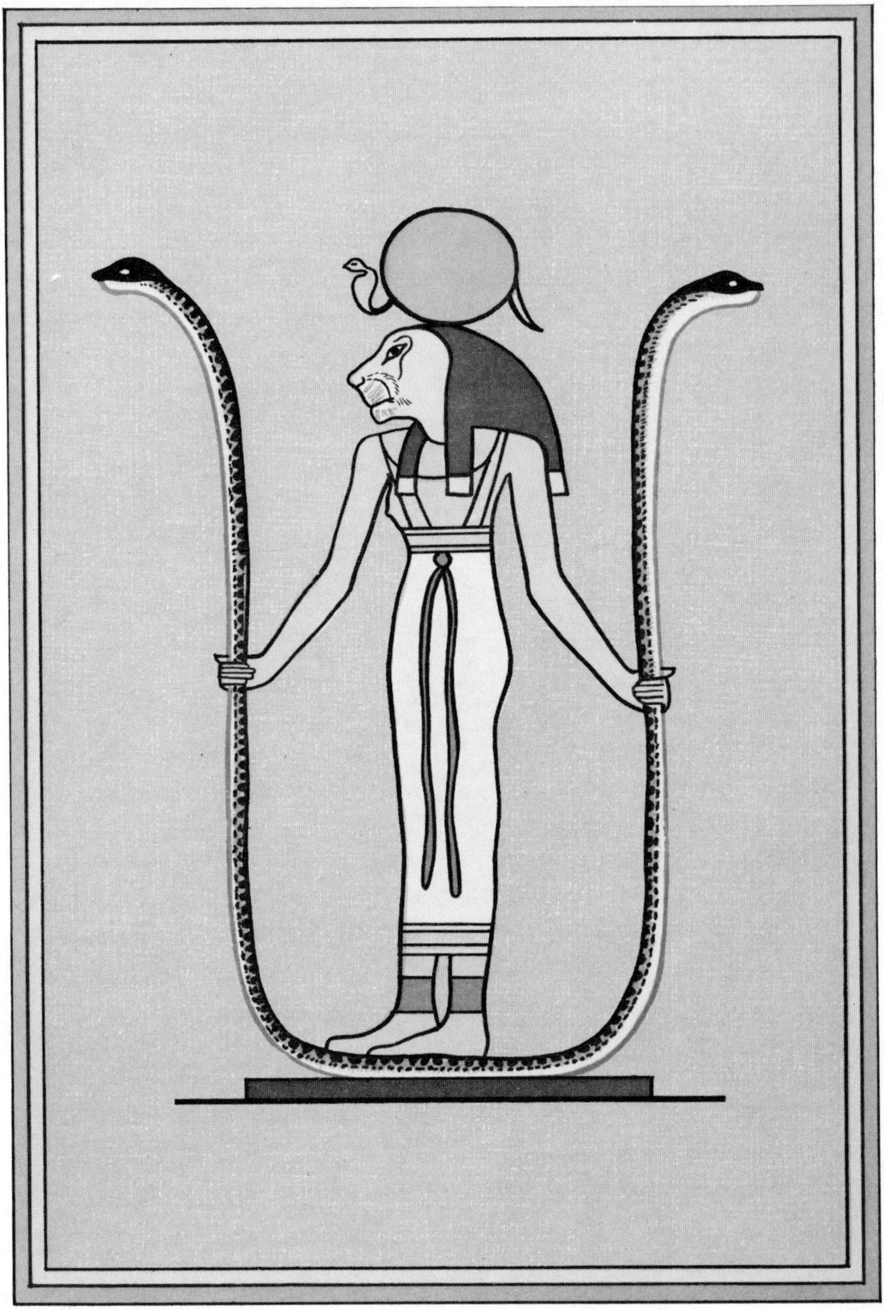

THE GODDESS SEKHET.

, Sekhet, lady of Sa, , Sekhet, lady of Reḥesaui, , Sekhet, the great lady, the queen of Ȧnt, , Sekhet in Bȧshu, , Sekhet in Saḥ, , Sekhet-Nut in Ḥet-khāt, , and Sekhet in Nefer (?)-Shuu, . The principal titles of Sekhet were "Mighty lady, lady of Flame, Tefnut in Senemet," [1]; "greatly beloved one of Ptaḥ, lady of heaven, mistress of the two lands," ; "lady of Ṭep-nef," ; "lady of Tchār, , and of Sehert, "; "chief of the Libyan lands, mistress of Pa-mertet," .

The name "Sekhet" appears to be derived from or connected with the root *sekhem*, , "to be strong, mighty, violent," and the like, and as she was the personification of the fierce, scorching, and destroying heat of the sun's rays, these attributes would be very suitable for her character. In the form of the serpent-goddess Meḥenet, , she took up her position on the head of her father Rā, and poured out from herself the blazing fire which scorched and consumed his enemies who came near, whilst at those who were some distance away she shot forth swift fiery darts which pierced through and through the fiends whom they struck. In a text quoted by Dr. Brugsch [2] she is made to say, "I set the fierce heat of the fire for a distance of millions "of cubits between Osiris and his enemy, and I keep away from "him the evil ones, and remove his foes from his habitation." One of the commonest names of the goddess is "Nesert," i.e., Flame, as a destroying element, and in texts of all periods she plays the part of a power which protects the good and annihilates the wicked.

[1] Var. .

[2] *Religion*, p. 520.

In some aspects she may be compared with Uatchet, of whom a well-known name is "Lady of flame." We have already said that in some respects Sekhet may be regarded as a form of Hathor and Net, and indeed several of the titles of the last named goddesses are bestowed upon her, e.g., "Lady of Åmentet, lady of Manu "(i.e., the mountain of the setting sun), the queen of the Libyan "lands," etc.; these appear to suggest a western or Libyan origin for the goddess.

In connexion with Sekhet and her relationship with Hathor, Net, and Maāt must be mentioned the Seven Wise Ones of the goddess Meḥ-urt, who together with Thoth, , ṬEKH, planned the world; they were born of Meḥ-urt, , at the feet of Nu, 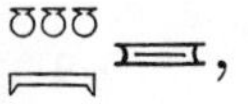, in their home in Nehet-rest, , and they came forth from the water, from the pupil of the Eye of Rā, and they took the form of seven hawks and flew upwards, and together with ÅSṬEN, 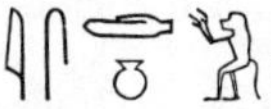, a form of Thoth, they presided over learning and letters. The names of these Seven Wise Ones, , are:—NEFER-ḤĀTI, ĀPER-PEḤUI, NEB-ṬESHERU, KA, BÅK, KHEKH, and SÅN.[1] Ptaḥ, as the master architect and workman who carried out the designs of Thoth and his Seven Wise Ones, partook, in some respects, of the characteristics of them all, and as Sekhet was his female counterpart she appears to have acquired some of their attributes also, because Thoth was in reality only a personification of the intelligence of Ptaḥ. It is in this way that Sekhet becomes identified with the goddess Maāt, for Maāt was the inseparable companion of Thoth, and inasmuch as Thoth was contained in Ptaḥ, Maāt became the female counterpart of Ptaḥ and a sister form of Sekhet. In one of the titles of Sekhet given above, the goddess is identified with Tefnut, the female counterpart of Shu;

[1] 
; see Dümichen, *Tempelinschriften*, pl. 25; Brugsch, *Religion*, p. 522.

The Goddess SEKHET.

The Goddess SEKHET.

this need cause no surprise, because Thoth was only the Hermopolitan form of Shu, and Tefnut was therefore his female counterpart, and as Ptaḥ absorbed Thoth, that is to say, Shu, the female counterpart of Ptaḥ (i.e., Sekhet) absorbed the female counterpart of Thoth, or Shu (i.e., Tefnut). In many texts Sekhet is called the "Eye of Rā," 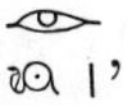, and in a scene reproduced by Lanzone[1] we see the goddess in the form of a woman, with the *Utchat*, , in place of a head, kneeling upon a rectangular throne, whilst a hawk with outstretched wings stands behind her. Her titles in this form are, "Great lady, beloved of Ptaḥ, holy one, powerful one, "dweller in Åt-Tefnut," .

We have already mentioned the small porcelain figures of Ptaḥ-Seker-Åsår, and seen how they were intended to represent the union of the powers of the three great gods whose names are here joined together, and we must now note that on the backs of certain examples we find outlined the form of a goddess, who might be identified with any of the female counterparts of the great gods to whom the head of a lioness was given by Egyptian sculptors and artists. The goddess here found, however, is Bast, 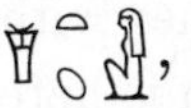, who was for some time confounded by Egyptologists with the goddess Pekheth, 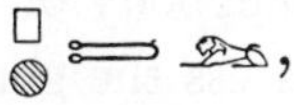, or Pekhet, , or Pekh, , the Cat or Lioness deity of Pekhit, , in honour of whom a temple of Pekheth, , was hewn out of the solid rock in the mountain near the modern village of Beni Hasan in Upper Egypt; this temple is known by the names of "Stabl al-Anṭar," and "Speos Artemidos." The name Pekht, or Pakht, or Pasht means the "tearer," and is, of course, suitable for a goddess who possessed the attributes of the cat or lioness; this goddess was the lady of Ånt, 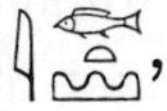, and of Set, , or , the supplementary nome of which the city Pekht, 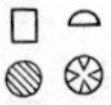, was the capital.[2] Her title was "lady of Sepṭ," , i.e., of the star Sothis, and she was identified with Isis and with a form of

[1] Op. cit., pl. 364, No. 3.

[2] *Dict. Géog.*, pp. 225, 226.

Hathor, and also with a form of Sekhet. In the great inscription of Beni Hasan (line 18) we find the mention of Horus Pakht, , and we may therefore assume that Pakht was in some way connected with one of the forms of Horus, and that she was a local deity of great importance.

It is probable that Bast was a female counterpart of the triune god Ptaḥ-Seker-Åsår, and that she possessed attributes which cannot at present be clearly defined. As a nature power she represented the gentle, fructifying heat of the sun, and its regenerative influence in the most comforting form. In late dynastic times Bast, and Sekhet, and Rā formed a deity whose existence is made known to us by a Chapter in the *Book of the Dead* (clxiv.). In the vignette Sekhet-Bast-Rā is represented as a woman with a man's head, and wings attached to her arms, and the heads of two vultures springing either from her head or neck; she has the phallus of a man and the claws of a lion. One vulture's head is like that of PEKHAT, , and has plumes upon it, and the other is like that of an ordinary vulture, and appears to have plumes upon it also; the man's head has upon it the united crowns of the South and North, and taken together with the phallus they indicate that the body of the woman, who is here called Mut, was supposed to possess the generative and procreative powers of Rā.

The text which forms the chapter is a very interesting one, and reads:—" Homage to thee, O Sekhet-Bast-Rā, thou mistress " of the gods, thou bearer of wings, thou lady of the red apparel " ( *ānes*), queen of the crowns of the South and North, " only One, sovereign of her father, superior to whom the " gods cannot be, thou mighty one of enchantments (or, words " of power) in the Boat of Millions of Years, thou who art pre- " eminent, who risest in the seat of silence, mother of PASHAKASA " (), queen of PAREHAQA-KHEPERU " (), mistress and lady of " the tomb, Mother in the horizon of heaven, gracious one, beloved, " destroyer of rebellion, offerings are in thy grasp, and thou art "standing in the bows of the boat of thy divine father to over- "throw Qeṭu.[1] Thou hast placed Maāt in the bows of his boat. "Thou art the fire goddess Ȧmmi-seshet (), "whose opportunity escapeth her not; thy name is TEKAHARESA- "PUSAREMKAKAREMET (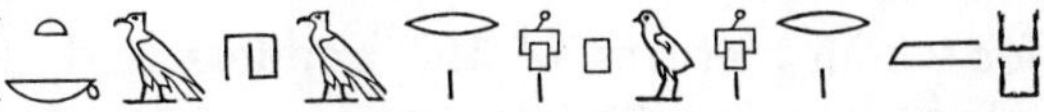 "). Thou art like unto the mighty flame of the "goddess SAQENAQAT (), which is in the "bows of the boat of thy father ḤAREPUKAKASHARESHABAIU "(), "for behold, thus is [his] name in the speech of the Negroes, and "of the Ȧnti, and of the people of Ta-kensetet (Nubia). Praise "be unto thee, O Lady, who art mightier than the gods, words of "adoration rise unto thee from the Eight Gods of Hermopolis. "The living souls who are in their hidden places praise the "mystery of thee, O thou who art their mother, thou source from "which they sprang, who makest for them a place in the hidden "Underworld, who makest sound their bones and preservest them "from terror, who makest them strong in the abode of everlasting- "ness, who preservest them from the evil chamber of the souls "of ḤES-ḤRȦ[2] (), who is among the company "of the gods. Thy name is SEFI-PER-EM-ḤES-ḤRȦ-ḤAPU-TCHET-F "()." On each side of Sekhet-Bast-Rā in the vignette is a dwarf with two faces, one of a hawk and one of a man, and the body of each is fat; each has on his head the disk and plumes, , and each has one hand and arm raised after the manner of Ȧmsu, or Min. The name of one dwarf is ȦTARE-ȦM-TCHER-QEMTU-RENNU-PAR-SHETA,  , and that of the other, PA-NEMMȦ-NEMMȦ. . Finally, the last name given to Sekhet-Bast-Rā is UTCHAT-SEKHET-URT-ḤENT-NETERU, 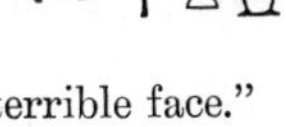

[1] , the name of a fiend. [2] I.e., "god of the terrible face."

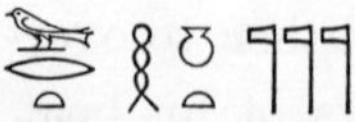, and she is said to be the emanation of Mut, "who "maketh souls to be as gods, who maketh bodies to be sound, and "who delivereth them from the abode of the fiends which is in the "chamber of the evil one." According to the Rubric, the deceased for whom pictures of the goddess and the two dwarfs were made would become like the immortals, and worms would not eat his body, and his soul would never be fettered, and he would drink water at the source of the river, and would have a homestead of his own in Sekhet-Åanre, and he would become a star of heaven, and he would fight and overcome the fiends TAR, , and NEKÅU, .

The third member of the Memphite triad is NEFER-TEM, , or NEFER-TEMU, 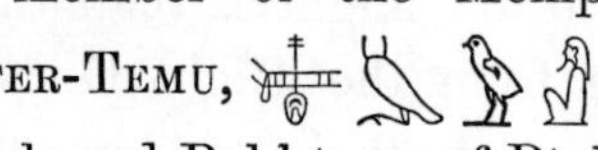, who is the son of Ptaḥ and Sekhet, or of Ptaḥ and Pakht, or of Ptaḥ and Bast. He is usually represented in the form of a man who holds in his hands either the *tchām* sceptre, , and the symbol of life, or the lotus sceptre surmounted by plumes, ; in these forms he is called "NEFER-TEM KHU TAUI," and "NEFER-TEM KHU TAUI ĀNKH REKHIT," , and 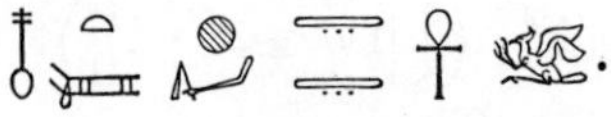. The small blue and green glazed porcelain statues of the god make him to stand upon a lion, and sometimes he appears in religious scenes with the lotus flower, or the lotus flower and plumes upon his head.[1] In some cases Nefer-Tem has the head of a lion, and his body has the form of a mummy, and consistently with this his hands project from a close-fitting garment, and he holds in them the *tchām* sceptre and flail, 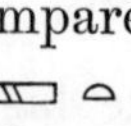. In the earliest times the lotus flower was associated with Nefer-Tem, and in the Pyramid Texts we find allusions to this fact. Thus in the text of Unås (line 392) the dead king is compared to a lotus at the nostrils of the Great Sekhem, 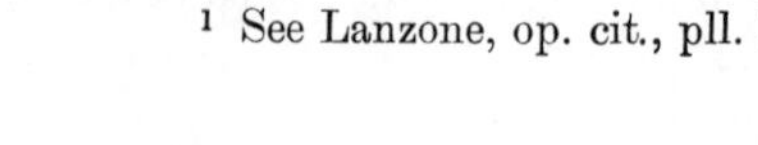, and a line or two further on it is said, "Unås hath risen like Nefer-Tem from the lotus to

[1] See Lanzone, op. cit., pll. 147 and 148.

The God NEFER-TEMU.

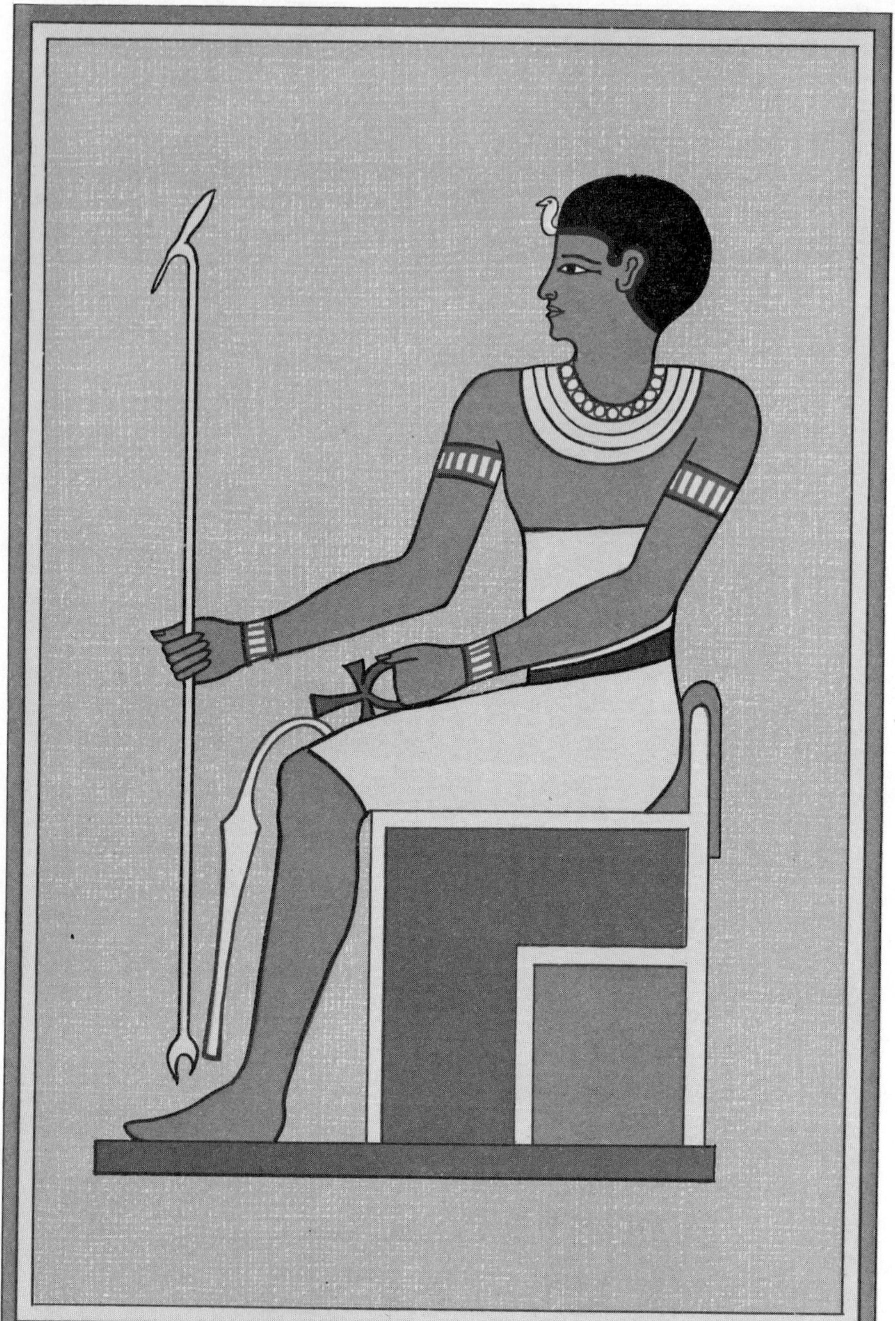

THE GOD I-EM-ḤETEP (IMOUTHIS).

"the nostrils of Rā, and he goeth forth from the horizon on each "day, and the gods are sanctified by the sight of him."[1]

In the Theban Recension of the *Book of the Dead* (xvii. 24) is a passage which appears to show that the attributes of Nefer-Tem were not well defined, and we find him mentioned in connexion with a number of gods in a manner which is hard to explain. The text makes the deceased to beseech Rā to deliver him from the god "whose form is hidden, and whose eyebrows are like unto "the two arms of the Balance on the night of reckoning destruc- "tion," and in answer to the question, "Who then is this?" we have the words, "It is Ȧn-ā-f," i.e., the "god who bringeth his "arm," ,[2] who is usually regarded as a form of Ȧmsu, or Min. The words "night of reckoning destruction" are explained by making them refer to the burning of the damned and the slaughter of the wicked on the block of the god by the "Slaughterer of Souls," , ṬENṬ-BAIU. The opinions of the Egyptian theologians differed greatly as to the identity of this god ṬENṬ-BAIU, for some thought he was NEMU,[3] , the headsman of Osiris, and others thought he might be Āpep, with one head, or Horus with two heads, or Horus the Great of Sekhem, or Thoth, or Nefer-Tem, or Sepṭu, . When we remember that Nefer-Tem is the "young Tem," i.e., a god of the rising sun, and that the Horus gods and Sepṭu were likewise forms of the rising sun, it is evident that Nemu and Āpep must have had some characteristic in common with the son of Pṭaḥ and Sekhet. From Chapters lxxxi., versions A and B, we learn that the deceased had power to transform himself into a lotus; in the first version of the text he says, "I am the pure lotus which springeth up from "the divine splendour that belongeth to the nostrils of Rā," and in the second we read, "Hail, thou Lotus, thou type of the god

1 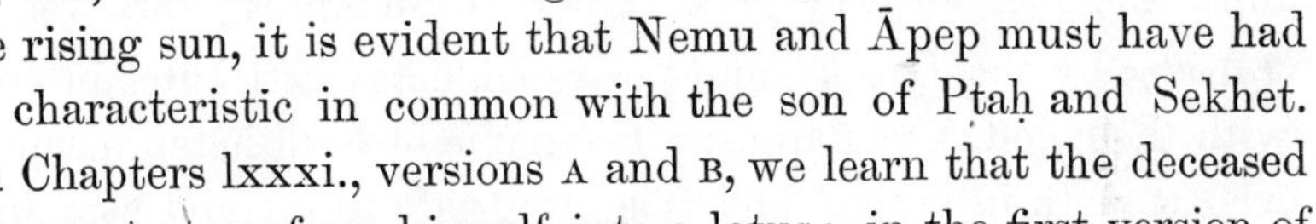

2 He is one of the Forty-two Assessors in the Hall of Maāti.

3 See *Book of the Dead*, cliii.A 8, 31, 32; cliii. 5; clxx. 6.

"Nefer-Tem! I am he who knoweth you, and I know your "names among the gods, the lords of the Underworld, and I am "one of you." The vignette of the first version is a lotus, and that of the second is a lotus plant with a flower and buds growing out of a pool of water, and out of the flower springs a human head, i.e., the head of the deceased.

The idea conveyed by the last vignette seems to have originated in the mind of some early writer who was accustomed to see the sun rise over the flooded lands of the Delta where the lotus grew in abundance. In Chapter clxxiv. 19, the deceased says, "I rise like Nefer-Tem, who is the lotus at the nostrils of "Rā, when he cometh forth from the horizon each day," and in Chapter clxxviii. 36, Nefer-Tem has the same title. We must also note that he is the thirty-fourth Assessor in the Hall of Maāti and that the deceased makes the following address to him:—"Hail, Nefer-Tem, who comest forth from Ḥet-ka-"Ptaḥ (Memphis), I have not acted with deceit, and I have not "worked wickedness." In the late Egyptian texts Nefer-Tem is identified with a number of gods, all of whom are practically forms of Horus and Thoth, and in consequence the mother of each of these gods becomes his mother.

The Egyptian texts prove that besides Nefer-Tem another son of Ptaḥ called I-EM-ḤETEP, 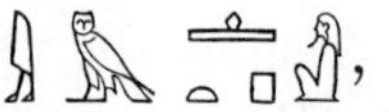, was regarded as the third member of the great triad of Memphis; he was called Ἰμοῦθης by the Greeks, and possessed many attributes in common with their god Aesculapius. The name of I-em-ḥetep means, "He who cometh in peace," and is appropriate to the god who brought the art of healing to mankind. The god is represented like Ptaḥ, with a bald head, and he is depicted in a seated position with a roll of papyrus open upon his knees; he was a god of study and learning in general, but he owed his great power to the knowledge of medicine which he possessed. As a god of learning he partook of some of the attributes of Thoth, and he was supposed to take the place of this god in the performance of funeral ceremonies, and in superintending the embalming of the dead; in later times he absorbed the duties of Thoth as "scribe of the gods," and the authorship of the words of power which protected the dead from enemies of every kind in the Underworld was ascribed to him. In certain aspects the god had a funeral character which somewhat resembled that of Ptaḥ-Seker-Åsår, although he is not mentioned in the Theban Recension of the *Book of the Dead*. In the "Ritual of Embalmment"[1] it is said to the deceased, "Thy soul uniteth "itself to I-em-ḥetep whilst thou art in the funeral valley, and thy "heart rejoiceth because thou dost not go into the dwelling of "Sebek, and because thou art like a son in the house of his father, "and doest what pleaseth thee in the city of Uast (Thebes)." The oldest shrine of the god was situated close to the city of Memphis, and was called "the Temple of I-em-ḥetep, the son of Ptaḥ," 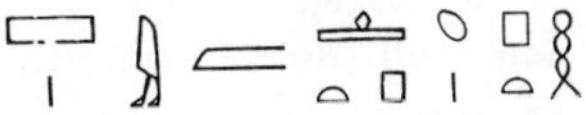, to which the Greeks gave the name, τὸ 'Ασκληπιεῖον;[2] it stood well outside the city, and lay quite near the Serapeum, on the edge of that portion of the desert which formed the necropolis of the city. Under the Ptolemies a small temple was built in honour of I-em-ḥetep on the Island of Philae; the hieroglyphic inscriptions are those of Ptolemy IV., Philopator, but the Greek text over the door was placed there by the command of Ptolemy V., Epiphanes. From one of the former we learn that the god was entitled, "Great one, son of Ptaḥ, the creative god, "made by Thenen, begotten by him and beloved by him, the god "of divine forms in the temples, who giveth life to all men, the "mighty one of wonders, the maker of times (?), who cometh unto "him that calleth upon him wheresoever he may be, who giveth "sons to the childless, the chief *kher-ḥeb* (, i.e., the wisest "and most learned one), the image and likeness of Thoth the "wise."[3]

I-em-ḥetep was the god who sent sleep to those who were suffering and in pain, and those who were afflicted with any kind of disease formed his special charge; he was the good physician both of gods and men, and he healed the bodies of mortals during life, and superintended the arrangements for the preservation of the same after death. If we could trace his history to its

[1] See Maspero, op. cit., p. 80. [2] Brugsch, *Dict. Géog.*, p. 1098.
[3] See Brugsch, *Thesaurus*, p. 783; *Religion*, p. 527; Sethe, *Imhotep*, 1903.

beginning we should find probably that he was originally a very highly skilled "medicine man" who had introduced some elementary knowledge of medicine amongst the Egyptians, and who was connected with the practice of the art of preserving the bodies of the dead by means of drugs, and spices, and linen bandages. He was certainly the god of physicians and of all those who were occupied with the mingled science of medicine and magic, and when we remember that several of the first kings of the Early Empire are declared by Manetho, whose statements have been supported by the evidence of the papyri, to have written, i.e., caused to be edited, works on medicine, it is clear that the adoration of the god of medicine was in Memphis as old as the archaic period. In the songs which were sung in the temple of Ȧntuf, the writer says, "I have heard the words of I-em-ḥetep and of "Ḥeru-ṭāṭā-f, (), which are repeated over and over "again, but where are their places this day? Their walls are "overthrown, their seats (or places) have no longer any being, and "they are as if they had never existed. No man cometh to declare "unto us what manner of beings they were, and none telleth us "of their possessions," etc. Ḥeru-ṭāṭā-f, as we know from later texts, was a very learned man, even though his speech could only with difficulty be understood, and we also know the prominent part which he took as a recognized man of letters in bringing to the court of his father, Khufu, the magician Teṭṭeṭa, and how his name is associated with the "finding" of certain Chapters of the *Book of the Dead*. Of the sage I-em-ḥetep, who is mentioned in connexion with him, it is difficult not to think that he was famous as a skilled physician whose acts and deeds were worthy of being classed with the words of Ḥeru-ṭāṭā-f.

From the manner in which these great and wise men are referred to it is clear that they, who were the chosen representatives of the ablest and most learned among men, had become, even at the time when the Songs of Ȧntuf were composed, mythical beings in whole or in part, and there is no good reason why I-em-ḥetep, the third member of the triad of Memphis, should not be a deified form of a distinguished physician who was attached to the priesthood of Rā, and who flourished before the end of the rule of the kings of the IIIrd Dynasty. The pictures and figures of the god suggest that he was of human and of strictly local origin, but it is not evident how he came to usurp the place of Nefer-Tem at Memphis, especially as he was not the son of Ptaḥ by Sekhet, or Bast, or any form of these goddesses. The worship of I-em-ḥetep was commoner in the Saïte and Ptolemaïc periods than in the Early and Middle Empires, and all the bronze figures of the god belong to a period subsequent to the XXIInd Dynasty. The titles given to him in the inscriptions at Philae may, it is true, represent ancient beliefs, but it is improbable, and as he does not appear in the Theban Recension of the *Book of the Dead* it is tolerably certain that his worship was as popular and fashionable at Memphis immediately before and during the Ptolemaïc period as that of Ȧmen-ḥetep, the son of Ḥāpu, the famous sage who had seen and conversed with the gods, was at Thebes about the same time.

END OF VOL. I.